Meet the *Cooking Light* Foods Staff

On these pages we present the *Cooking Light* Foods Staff (from left in each photograph). They've given character to every recipe in this cookbook with their diligence in testing and editing and their creativity in styling and photographing the food.

Jill Melton, Senior Food Editor; Michele Mann, Editorial Assistant; Matthew Solan, Associate Editor

Doug Crichton, Editor;
Nathalie Dearing, Managing Editor

Becky Pate, Test Kitchens Director; Test Kitchens Staff:
Kathleen Kanen, Leigh Fran Jones

Test Kitchens Staff: Julie Walton, John Kirkpatrick, Kellie Kelley

John Stark, Senior Editor; Ellen Carroll, Senior Editor–Projects

Susan Dendy, Art Director; Lee Puckett, Senior Photographer; Cindy Manning Barr, Photo Stylist

Assistant Food Editors: Cynthia LaGrone, Alyson Moreland; Mary Creel, Food Editor

Cooking Light ®

ANNUAL RECIPES 1997

Oxmoor House ®

Library of Congress Catalog Number: 96-71335
ISBN: 0-8487-1528-4
ISSN: 1091-3645

Manufactured in the United States of America
First printing 1996

Be sure to check with your health-care provider
before making any changes in your diet.

WE'RE HERE FOR YOU!

We at Oxmoor House are dedicated to serving you with reliable
information that expands your imagination and enriches your
life. We welcome your comments and suggestions. Please write
to us at:
Oxmoor House, Inc.
Editor, *Cooking Light® Annual Recipes*
2100 Lakeshore Drive
Birmingham, AL 35209

To order additional copies of this book or any
others, call 1-205-877-6560.

Cover: *Sizzling Steak Fajitas* (page 19)

Back cover: *Lemon Cream Tart* (page 298)

Page 1: *Easy Chocolate-Caramel Brownies* (page 313)

Page 2: *Garlic-Rosemary Roasted Chicken* (page 251),
Bistro Shoestring Potatoes (page 253)

Cooking Light®

Editor: Doug Crichton
Art Director: Susan Waldrip Dendy
Managing Editor: Nathalie Dearing
Senior Food Editor: Jill G. Melton, M.S., R.D.
Senior Editor: John Stark
Senior Editor–Projects: Ellen Templeton Carroll,
    M.S., R.D.
Food Editor: Mary S. Creel, M.S., R.D.
Associate Editor: Matthew Solan
Assistant Food Editors: Cynthia Nicholson LaGrone,
    L. Alyson Moreland
Photo Stylist: Cindy Manning Barr
Senior Photographer: Howard L. Puckett
Test Kitchens Director: Rebecca J. Pate
Test Kitchens Staff: Leigh Fran Jones,
    M. Kathleen Kanen, Kellie Gerber Kelley,
    John Kirkpatrick, Julie Walton, Karen Mitchell Wilcher
Copy Chief: Tim W. Jackson
Copy Editors: Lisa C. Bailey, Ritchey Halphen
Production Coordinators: Hazel R. Eddins,
    Polly Pabor Linthicum
Editorial Coordinator: Carol C. Noe
Editorial Assistants: Michele Mann, Stacey L. Strawn
Editor-at-Large: Graham Kerr

Oxmoor House, Inc.

Editor-in-Chief: Nancy Fitzpatrick Wyatt
Senior Foods Editor: Katherine M. Eakin
Senior Editor, Editorial Services: Olivia Kindig Wells
Art Director: James Boone

Cooking Light® Annual Recipes 1997

Foods Editor: Cathy A. Wesler, R.D.
Assistant Foods Editor: Caroline A. Grant, M.S., R.D.
Copy Editor: Jacqueline B. Giovanelli
Editorial Assistant: Julie A. Cole
Designer: Faith Nance
Production and Distribution Director: Phillip Lee
Associate Production Manager: Theresa L. Beste
Production Assistant: Valerie L. Heard
Indexer: Mary Ann Laurens

CONTENTS

Welcome

You're holding something pretty unusual. Sure, it's the 12th annual *Cooking Light* cookbook. But for the first time, this cookbook is drawn exclusively from the pages of the nation's largest epicurean magazine: *Cooking Light*.

Confused? Let me go back a few years and explain. "Cooking Light" was born in 1983—not as a magazine but as a periodic recipe column in a magazine—our sister publication, *Southern Living*. Readers responded so positively to the column that in 1986 we launched *Cooking Light Cookbook* as an annual book. Again, the response from readers was overwhelming. Demand grew so rapidly that we launched *Cooking Light* as a magazine in 1987.

Because of that unusual sequence, and because at six issues per year the magazine didn't produce enough recipes to fill an annual cookbook, *Cooking Light Cookbook* continued to be produced separately from *Cooking Light* magazine. Until this year, that is, when we increased our frequency to nine issues.

So let me formally welcome you to the first annual cookbook from *Cooking Light* magazine.
SOME EXCITING FEATURES INCLUDE:

◆ **More luscious recipes than ever before— nearly 700 in all**, ranging from creamy cheesecakes to crispy pizzas.

◆ The best ingredients from each season, **in recipes ordered by month.**

◆ **Three indexes** to help you find what you're looking for quickly and easily.

◆ Only the best recipes from **three registered dietitians, four test kitchens professionals, and two chefs** on our staff—in addition to **expert recipe developers from around the world.**

◆ **Recipes that are all tested at least twice** in our Test Kitchens to ensure the greatest taste and ease of preparation.

◆ **Sophisticated computer analysis of each recipe** to make sure it meets our strict nutritional standards.

Readers write almost daily to tell us that they love getting each issue of *Cooking Light* because of our recipes, healthy lifestyles stories, and indepth food-trends coverage. We wanted to make sure you could actually lift this book off the shelf, though, so we've focused on just the recipes.

I hope that you'll enjoy this special cookbook and that you'll let us know how we can make it even better next year. In the meantime, happy cooking!

Best Regards,

Editor

Our Favorite Recipes of the Year

There's not a recipe that goes into *Cooking Light* magazine that we're not proud of. It doesn't matter how nutritious, low in fat, or beautiful a dish is—if it doesn't taste great it will not appear in our pages. Every day our Test Kitchens staff, along with editors and writers from *Cooking Light*, gather in our Test Kitchens to sample our recipes. We made more than 4,000 in 1996!

What do we look for in a Cooking Light recipe? Obviously taste, but there are other important factors, too, such as: **Do-ability** (Can readers find the ingredients? Must they have a certificate from the Cordon Bleu to attempt it?); **broadness of appeal** (Will readers cook it? If several of our taste testers proclaim, "I've got to make this at home!", it's probably a hit); **relevancy** (Does the recipe use ingredients that reflect our times?); and **yum appeal** (Who'd ever believe that sumptuous cheesecake is really light?). Out of all the recipes that we passed in 1996, we've put together a list of our favorite favorites. Here's hoping that they become yours, too.

◆ COUSCOUS-AND-FETA CAKES (page 20): Vegetarian cooking has come a long way from its hippy-dippy image. Though downhome and familiar, these soul-comforting griddle cakes are light and healthy, and made without chicken, seafood, or any other kind of meat.

◆ HERBED MEAT LOAF WITH SUN-DRIED TOMATO GRAVY (page 46): Nothing is more homey, and well-loved, than meat loaf. It was our challenge to bring this American classic into the nineties, which we've done by creating this lightened version. Of the many meat loaves that we featured, this was our favorite.

◆ DOUBLE-CHOCOLATE CHEWS (page 61): These cookies have a soft, brownie-like texture. The full, rich chocolate flavor of the cookie itself is intensified by chocolate chips throughout. Although no one will guess it, they're light. This is good news because no one can eat just one cookie—especially one of these.

◆ CHICKEN POT STICKERS (page 68): Exotic though they may be, these Chinese dumplings are surprisingly easy to make. Ours are baked, then lightly sautéed in oil to keep them light. Fun appetizers for parties, these pot stickers feature a varied combination of lively flavors and different textures.

◆ ANZAC BISCUITS (page 70): This Australian biscuit is really a cookie. It wowed our Test Kitchens with its buttery taste and appearance (derived from using margarine and golden cane syrup) and its crispy, yet chewy texture.

◆ ROASTED CHICKEN-AND-WHITE BEAN PIZZAS (page 139): Taking 17 minutes to prepare and only 8 minutes to cook, these pizzas offer a change from the traditional red sauce—they feature an earthy combination of ingredients: roasted chicken, rosemary, and garlic.

◆ KEY LIME PIE (page 165): With its creamy filling, crisp crust, and sweet and fluffy meringue, this heavenly pie is indeed big news—less than 300 calories, and only 14 percent calories from fat. Seconds are a must.

◆ APRICOT PARIS BREST (page 166): This exquisite dessert is true culinary legerdemain: a light, ring-shaped cream puff! When cooked, apricots become meltingly tender and their unique flavor intensifies, especially in sweets.

◆ RISOTTO WITH SUN-DRIED TOMATOES AND BASIL (page 216): This risotto is the very definition of fine dining. With its creamy sauce and separate, firm grains of rice, its sophisticated flavor is achieved through surprisingly few but select ingredients. Be sure to garnish with fresh basil and shaved parmesan.

◆ CREAMY FOUR-CHEESE MACARONI (page 242): This low-fat mac/cheese is a brilliant interpretation of America's favorite high-fat comfort food. Why settle for merely one cheese when you can have four, all blending in perfect, tangy harmony? Our more flavorful, spirited mac/cheese has half the fat of "mom's" heavy version.

◆ GARLIC-ROSEMARY ROASTED CHICKEN (page 251): Don't let the simplicity of this dish throw you: It tastes, smells, and looks like a million. The inspiration for this whole roasted chicken is the classic French bistro, which is famous for serving earthy, perfectly roasted chickens.

◆ EASY CHOCOLATE-CARAMEL BROWNIES (page 313): Talk about a triple threat: In addition to chocolate batter, the ingredients for these decadent brownies include chocolate chips and caramel candies. Hard to believe that something so rich-tasting could be so light. Or easy to make.

HOW TO USE IT AND WHY Glance at the end of any *Cooking Light* recipe, and you'll see how committed we are to helping you make the best of today's light cooking. With three registered dietitians, four test kitchens professionals, two chefs, and a computer system that analyzes every ingredient we use, *Cooking Light* gives you authoritative dietary detail like no other magazine. We go to such lengths so you can see how our recipes fit into your healthy eating plan. If you're trying to lose weight, the calorie and fat figures will help most. But if you're keeping a close eye on the sodium, cholesterol, and saturated fat in your diet, we provide those numbers, too. Many women don't get enough iron or calcium; we can also help there. Finally, there's a fiber analysis for those of us who don't get enough roughage.

What it means and how we get there: We list calories, protein, fat, fiber, iron, and sodium at the end of each recipe, but there are a few things we abbreviate for space.

- *sat* for saturated fat
- *g* for gram
- *CHOL* for cholesterol
- *mono* for monounsaturated fat
- *CARB* for carbohydrates
- *poly* for polyunsaturated fat
- *mg* for milligram
- *CALC* for calcium

We get numbers for those categories based on a few assumptions: When we give a range for an ingredient, we calculate the lesser amount. Some alcohol calories evaporate during heating; we reflect that. And only the amount of marinade absorbed by the food is calculated.

Your Daily Nutrition Guide			
	WOMEN AGES 25 TO 50	WOMEN OVER 50	MEN OVER 24
Calories	2,000	2,000 or less	2,700
Protein	50g	50g or less	63g
Fat	67g or less	67g or less	90g or less
Saturated Fat	22g or less	22g or less	30g or less
Carbohydrates	299g	299g	405g
Fiber	25g to 35g	25g to 35g	25g to 35g
Cholesterol	300mg or less	300mg or less	300mg or less
Iron	15mg	10mg	10mg
Sodium	2,400mg or less	2,400mg or less	2,400mg or less
Calcium	800mg	800mg	800mg

Calorie requirements vary according to your size, weight, and level of activity. This chart is a good general guide; additional nutrients are needed during some stages of life. For example, kids' calorie and protein needs are based on height and vary greatly as they grow. Compared to adults, teenagers require less protein but more calcium and slightly more iron. Pregnant or breast-feeding women need more protein, calories, and calcium. Also, the need for iron increases during pregnancy but returns to normal after birth.

JANUARY FEBRUARY

Meeting Your Kneads

With a bread machine and our light recipes, you can have your kitchen smelling like a corner bake shop. All it takes is the simple press of a button.

But before you press that button, read the instruction book that comes with your bread machine and the following helpful hints:

• Add ingredients to your bread machine according to the manufacturer's instructions. Different machines necessitate adding ingredients in varying orders, depending on whether the machine features a yeast dispenser.

• Various machines make different amounts of bread, ranging from 1- to 2-pound loaves. Look at the amount of flour called for in your instruction book, and scale these recipe accordingly.

• Since bread flour is a high-protein flour that stands up to lots of kneading, we used it in our recipes. (All-purpose flour may be substituted.)

• Experiment with new flavor combinations, adding herbs and spices and substituting ingredients.

• Always include a sweetener, such as honey or sugar, for tenderness and salt for enhanced flavor.

• Yeast makes the most difference in the final product. Although you can use rapid-rise yeast, we found that bread-machine or dry yeast works best. You can substitute 2¼ teaspoons of bread-machine yeast for one packet of dry yeast.

• Occasionally, bread-machine yeast causes the bread to rise so much that it touches the top of the machine and burns. If this happens, reduce the amount of yeast by 25%, then by one-third, if needed.

ROMANO-OREGANO BREAD

- 3 cups bread flour
- 1 cup water
- ¾ cup (3 ounces) grated fresh Romano cheese
- 3 tablespoons sugar
- 1 tablespoon dried oregano
- 1½ tablespoons olive oil
- 1 teaspoon salt
- 1 package dry yeast

Follow manufacturer's instructions for placing all ingredients into bread pan; select bake cycle, and start bread machine. Yield: 1 (1½-pound) loaf, 12 servings.

CALORIES 181 (21% from fat); PROTEIN 6.6g; FAT 4.2g (sat 1.5g, mono 1.8g, poly 0.5g); CARB 28.7g; FIBER 0.2g; CHOL 7mg; IRON 1.8mg; SODIUM 281mg; CALC 87mg

COUNTRY RYE BREAD

- 2 cups bread flour
- 1¼ cups rye flour
- 1 cup water
- 1 tablespoon caraway seeds
- 3 tablespoons honey
- 2 tablespoons vegetable oil
- 1 teaspoon salt
- 1 package dry yeast

Follow manufacturer's instructions for placing all ingredients into bread pan; select bake cycle, and start bread machine. Yield: 1 (1-pound) loaf, 8 servings.

CALORIES 214 (18% from fat); PROTEIN 5.1g; FAT 4.2g (sat 0.7g, mono 1.2g, poly 2g); CARB 39.2g; FIBER 2.4g; CHOL 0mg; IRON 1.8mg; SODIUM 294mg; CALC 14mg

GOOD-FOR-TOAST WHEAT BREAD

- 1⅔ cups bread flour
- 1½ cups whole-wheat flour
- 1 cup water
- 3 tablespoons sugar
- 1 tablespoon vegetable oil
- 1½ teaspoons dry yeast
- 1¼ teaspoons salt

Follow manufacturer's instructions for placing all ingredients into bread pan; select bake cycle, and start bread machine. Yield: 1 (1½-pound) loaf, 12 servings.

CALORIES 143 (11% from fat); PROTEIN 4.5g; FAT 1.8g (sat 0.3g, mono 0.4g, poly 0.8g); CARB 28g; FIBER 2g; CHOL 0mg; IRON 1.5mg; SODIUM 245mg; CALC 8mg

TENDER YEAST ROLLS

In this recipe, the machine simply mixes the dough and allows it to rise in anticipation of your final shaping and baking.

- 4 cups bread flour
- 1 cup water
- 6 tablespoons sugar
- 3 tablespoons vegetable oil
- 1¼ teaspoons salt
- 1 egg, lightly beaten
- 1 package dry yeast
- Vegetable cooking spray

Follow manufacturer's instructions for placing first 7 ingredients into bread pan; select dough cycle, and start bread machine. Remove dough from machine (do not bake).

Turn dough out onto a lightly floured surface, and knead dough 30 seconds. Cover dough, and let rest 10 minutes.

Punch dough down, and divide into 18 equal portions. Shape each portion into a ball, and place on baking sheets coated with cooking spray. Cover and let rise in a warm place (85°), free from drafts, 20 minutes. Preheat oven to 400°. Uncover rolls, and bake at 400° for 13 minutes or until browned. Remove rolls from pans, and serve warm or at room temperature. Yield: 1½ dozen (serving size: 1 roll).

CALORIES 152 (18% from fat); PROTEIN 4.1g; FAT 3.1g (sat 0.6g, mono 0.8g, poly 1.4g); CARB 26.4g; FIBER 0.1g; CHOL 12mg; IRON 1.5mg; SODIUM 167mg; CALC 6mg

MAMA'S OATMEAL BREAD

This bread tastes delicious toasted and slathered with your favorite jam, jelly, or marmalade. It's also a great substitute for whole wheat bread.

¾ cup boiling water
½ cup quick-cooking oats
¼ cup firmly packed
     brown sugar
3 tablespoons margarine, melted
1 teaspoon salt
3 cups bread flour
¼ cup water
1 egg, lightly beaten
1 package dry yeast

Combine first 5 ingredients in a bowl; stir well. Let cool slightly.

Follow manufacturer's instructions for placing oat mixture and remaining ingredients into bread pan; select bake cycle, and start bread machine. Yield: 1 (1¾-pound) loaf, 14 servings.

CALORIES 160 (20% from fat); PROTEIN 4.6g; FAT 3.5g (sat 0.7g, mono 1.3g, poly 1.1g); CARB 27.3g; FIBER 0.4g; CHOL 15mg; IRON 1.6mg; SODIUM 203mg; CALC 12mg

A DILLY-OF-AN-ONION BREAD

3½ cups bread flour
1 cup water
½ cup chopped onion
3 tablespoons sugar
1 tablespoon dried dill
2 tablespoons vegetable oil
2 teaspoons salt
2 teaspoons paprika
1 package dry yeast

Follow manufacturer's instructions for placing all ingredients into bread pan; select bake cycle, and start machine. Yield: 1 (1¾-pound) loaf, 14 servings.

CALORIES 137 (16% from fat); PROTEIN 3.8g; FAT 2.5g (sat 0.4g, mono 0.6g, poly 1.2g); CARB 24.6g; FIBER 0.3g; CHOL 0mg; IRON 1.6mg; SODIUM 336mg; CALC 11mg

ANADAMA BREAD

This early American yeast bread has very traditional flavors. The yellow cornmeal and molasses are typical ingredients found in breads made in nineteenth-century New England.

1 cup boiling water
½ cup yellow cornmeal
¼ cup molasses
3 tablespoons margarine,
     melted
2 tablespoons sugar
1 egg, lightly beaten
3 cups bread flour
½ teaspoon salt
1 teaspoon dry yeast

Combine boiling water, cornmeal, molasses, melted margarine, and sugar in a medium bowl; stir well to combine. Let mixture cool slightly, and stir in beaten egg.

Follow manufacturer's instructions for placing cornmeal mixture, bread flour, salt, and dry yeast into bread pan; select bake cycle, and start bread machine. Yield: 1 (1¾-pound) loaf, 14 servings.

CALORIES 174 (18% from fat); PROTEIN 4.5g; FAT 3.4g (sat 0.7g, mono 1.3g, poly 1.1g); CARB 31g; FIBER 0.3g; CHOL 16mg; IRON 1.9mg; SODIUM 120mg; CALC 19mg

SPENDING YOUR BREAD

How do you find a bread machine that's right for you?

◆ Make sure the machine will fit on your counter—with the lid open.
◆ Small households may prefer machines that make 1-pound loaves. Bigger families—or ones with hungry bread lovers—may opt for machines that make 1½- or 2-pound loaves, which are the most common sizes.

◆ Check out the time cycles of the many machines available. Some take two hours from start to finish; others have a four-hour cycle.
◆ Machines come in different sizes, with a variety of settings and timers. A simple machine may be purchased for as little as $79, while deluxe models often cost upwards of $400.
◆ You'll find differences in the way machines bake bread—some

brown more; others yield a taller product. It may take a few bakings until you adjust to your machine's personality.
◆ For slicing bread, an electric knife yields the best results. If you don't have one, a serrated knife will do. Or you can buy a bread-slicing stand, available at department and variety stores, for about $35. It comes with an electric knife.

At the Winter Garden

This exciting cast of vegetables takes center stage at your neighborhood market this season. Catch them while you can.

MUSTARD-AND-HERB-MARINATED VEGETABLES

  2   small red potatoes (about 6 ounces)
1½   cups small broccoli florets
1½   cups small cauliflower florets
1½   cups cherry tomatoes, halved
1½   cups small mushrooms, halved
1½   cups cubed zucchini
  ⅔   cup white wine vinegar
  ½   cup water
  ¼   cup minced shallots
  2   tablespoons Dijon mustard
1½   tablespoons olive oil
  1   teaspoon dried basil
  1   teaspoon dried oregano
  1   teaspoon dried rosemary, crushed
  ½   teaspoon salt
  ¼   teaspoon dried crushed red pepper

Arrange potatoes in a steamer basket over boiling water. Cover and steam 15 minutes or until tender. Let cool. Cut each potato into 4 wedges, and cut each wedge in half crosswise.

Combine potatoes and next 5 ingredients in a large glass dish; set aside. Combine vinegar and remaining 9 ingredients in a jar; cover tightly, and shake vigorously. Pour over vegetables, and toss gently to coat. Cover and marinate in refrigerator 8 hours, stirring occasionally. Yield: 8 servings (serving size: 1 cup).

CALORIES 77 (37% from fat); PROTEIN 2.3g; FAT 3.2g (sat 0.4g, mono 2g, poly 0.4g); CARB 10.4g; FIBER 2.2g; CHOL 0mg; IRON 1mg; SODIUM 273mg; CALC 31mg

QUICK 'N' EASY BEET SALAD

  1   cup coarsely chopped no-salt-added canned beets
  ½   cup frozen green peas, thawed
  2   tablespoons sliced green onions
  1   tablespoon chopped fresh parsley
  2   tablespoons fat-free Italian dressing
  2   lettuce leaves
  1   hard-cooked egg, chopped

Combine first 4 ingredients in a medium bowl. Pour dressing over beet mixture; toss gently. Cover and chill 2 hours. Serve on lettuce-lined salad plates; sprinkle with hard-cooked egg. Yield: 2 servings (serving size: 1 cup beet mixture and ½ egg).

CALORIES 109 (26% from fat); PROTEIN 6.6g; FAT 3.2g (sat 0.8g, mono 1g, poly 0.5g); CARB 14.5g; FIBER 3g; CHOL 110mg; IRON 1.9mg; SODIUM 274mg; CALC 44mg

ZESTY ITALIAN ACORN SQUASH

  2   medium acorn squash (about 2 pounds)
  ½   cup thinly sliced onion
  2   teaspoons olive oil
  1   (1½ x ½-inch) strip orange rind
  1   tablespoon coarsely chopped fresh basil
  ½   teaspoon freshly ground pepper
  1   garlic clove, minced
  1   (14½-ounce) can plum tomatoes, undrained and chopped
  ½   cup (2 ounces) shredded part-skim mozzarella cheese
Basil sprigs (optional)

Preheat oven to 400°.

Cut each squash crosswise into 4 (1-inch-thick) rings; discard seeds and end pieces. Set squash aside.

Combine onion, oil, and orange rind in a 13 x 9-inch baking dish; toss well. Bake at 400° for 15 minutes or until onion is golden. Discard orange rind. Arrange squash in dish, slightly overlapping the rings. Combine chopped basil, pepper, garlic, and tomatoes; spoon over squash rings. Cover and bake at 400° for 30 minutes or until squash is tender. Top with cheese; bake, uncovered, an additional 5 minutes or until cheese melts. Garnish with basil sprigs, if desired. Yield: 4 servings (serving size: 2 squash rings and ½ cup sauce).

CALORIES 149 (30% from fat); PROTEIN 5.9g; FAT 4.9g (sat 1.8g, mono 2.4g, poly 0.4g); CARB 23.4g; FIBER 3g; CHOL 8mg; IRON 1.8mg; SODIUM 239mg; CALC 178mg

TWO-APPLE SALAD

  1   small fennel bulb, trimmed and cut into julienne strips
  1   medium Red Delicious apple, quartered and cut into julienne strips
  1   medium Granny Smith apple, quartered and cut into julienne strips
  ¼   cup finely shredded carrot
  ¼   cup sliced green onions
  1   tablespoon water
  1   tablespoon white wine vinegar
  2   teaspoons vegetable oil
  ½   teaspoon sugar
  ¼   teaspoon salt

Combine first 5 ingredients in a medium bowl; toss well, and set aside.

Combine water, vinegar, oil, sugar, and salt in a bowl; stir with a wire whisk until blended. Add to fennel mixture, tossing gently to coat. Divide mixture among 4 salad plates. Yield: 4 servings (serving size: 1 cup).

CALORIES 70 (33% from fat); PROTEIN 1.1g; FAT 2.6g (sat 0.4g, mono 0.6g, poly 1.2g); CARB 11.9g; FIBER 2.3g; CHOL 0mg; IRON 1.1mg; SODIUM 153mg; CALC 43mg

CABBAGE GRATIN

Vegetable cooking spray
4 cups coarsely chopped green cabbage
1 cup coarsely shredded carrot
½ cup sliced green onions
1 cup skim milk
¼ cup (1 ounce) Gruyère cheese
½ teaspoon caraway seeds
¼ teaspoon salt
2 eggs, lightly beaten
1 egg white
2 tablespoons minced fresh parsley
1 tablespoon grated Parmesan cheese

Preheat oven to 375°.
Coat a small saucepan with cooking spray; place over medium heat until hot. Add cabbage, carrot, and green onions; sauté 7 minutes or until tender. Spoon cabbage mixture into a 10 x 6-inch baking dish coated with cooking spray.
Combine milk and next 5 ingredients in a medium bowl; stir well. Pour over cabbage mixture. Combine parsley and Parmesan cheese; sprinkle over cabbage mixture. Bake at 375° for 40 minutes or until a knife inserted in center comes out clean. Let stand 5 minutes before serving. Yield: 6 servings (serving size ½ cup).

CALORIES 91 (38% from fat); PROTEIN 7.4g; FAT 3.8g (sat 2g, mono 1.6g, poly 0.5g); CARB 7.5g; FIBER 2g; CHOL 117mg; IRON 1mg; SODIUM 200mg; CALC 159mg

ZESTY BROCCOLI-CAULIFLOWER GRATIN

⅓ cup dry breadcrumbs
2 tablespoons (½ ounce) finely shredded extra-sharp Cheddar cheese
2 cups small broccoli florets
2 cups small cauliflower florets
Vegetable cooking spray
1 tablespoon reduced-calorie margarine, melted
1 tablespoon coarse-grained mustard
¼ teaspoon white pepper

Preheat oven to 425°.
Combine breadcrumbs and Cheddar cheese; stir breadcrumb mixture well, and set aside.
Arrange broccoli and cauliflower in a steamer basket over boiling water. Cover and steam 4 minutes or until vegetables are crisp-tender. Drain vegetables, and place in a 1½-quart casserole dish coated with cooking spray. Combine margarine, mustard, and white pepper in a small bowl; drizzle over broccoli and cauliflower, and toss well. Sprinkle breadcrumb mixture over vegetables, and bake at 425° for 8 minutes or until thoroughly heated. Yield: 4 servings (serving size: 1 cup).

CALORIES 90 (36% from fat); PROTEIN 4.5g; FAT 3.6g (sat 1.1g, mono 1g, poly 0.9g); CARB 11.3g; FIBER 2.9g; CHOL 4mg; IRON 1mg; SODIUM 174mg; CALC 72mg

FOR TWO

I Dream of Panini

Served with salad or fruit, these hearty Italian sandwiches make an ideal lunch or light dinner. Add a glass of wine, and you're supping alfresco on the Piazza San Marco.

PANINI WITH SAUTÉED SPINACH AND CHICKPEA SPREAD

¾ cup drained canned chickpeas (garbanzo beans)
2 tablespoons lemon juice
1 tablespoon water
2 teaspoons capers
2 teaspoons olive oil
2 garlic cloves, minced
4 cups torn fresh spinach
⅛ teaspoon pepper
2 (2½-ounce) submarine rolls

Place first 4 ingredients in a food processor, and process until smooth, scraping sides of processor bowl occasionally. Set aside.
Heat oil in a large nonstick skillet over medium heat until hot. Add garlic, and sauté 1 minute. Add spinach; sauté 1 minute. Remove skillet from heat, and stir in pepper.
Slice each roll in half horizontally. Spread chickpea mixture over bottom halves of bread. Top with spinach mixture, and cover with top halves of bread. Yield: 2 servings.

CALORIES 366 (18% from fat); PROTEIN 14.9g; FAT 7.4g (sat 1.3g, mono 4.2g, poly 1.3g); CARB 63g; FIBER 12.1g; CHOL 0mg; IRON 6.3mg; SODIUM 999mg; CALC 221mg

PROSCIUTTO-AND-FONTINA PANINI

1 (5.25-ounce) package focaccia (Italian flatbread) or 1 (8-ounce) package Italian cheese-flavored pizza crust (such as Boboli)
8 very thin slices prosciutto (about 2 ounces)
¼ cup (1 ounce) shredded fontina cheese
1 cup trimmed arugula or watercress
2 (⅛-inch-thick) red onion slices, separated into rings
2 teaspoons balsamic vinegar
⅛ teaspoon pepper

Preheat oven to 300°.
Slice each bread round in half horizontally. Divide prosciutto slices between bottom halves of bread, and top prosciutto with fontina cheese, arugula, and red onion slices. Drizzle balsamic vinegar over sandwiches, and sprinkle with pepper; cover with top halves of bread. Wrap sandwiches tightly in aluminum foil, and bake at 300° for 15 minutes. Yield: 2 servings.

CALORIES 330 (31% from fat); PROTEIN 20.2g; FAT 11.5g (sat 5.6g, mono 2.5g, poly 0.6g); CARB 40.3g; FIBER 4.3g; CHOL 33mg; IRON 0.9mg; SODIUM 846mg; CALC 220mg

VEAL-AND-EGGPLANT PANINI WITH SUN-DRIED TOMATO MAYONNAISE

¼ cup boiling water
6 sun-dried tomatoes, packed without oil
2 tablespoons skim milk
3 tablespoons dry breadcrumbs
¼ pound lean veal scaloppine, cut into 2 equal portions
2 (¼-inch-thick) eggplant slices
Vegetable cooking spray
2 (3-inch-thick) slices Italian bread
1 tablespoon reduced-calorie mayonnaise

Combine boiling water and tomatoes in a small bowl; let stand 15 minutes or until softened. Drain tomatoes, reserving 1 teaspoon liquid. Mince tomatoes, and set aside.

Preheat oven to 400°.

Place milk in a bowl. Place breadcrumbs in a shallow dish. Dip veal in milk, and dredge in breadcrumbs. Repeat procedure with eggplant slices. Place veal and eggplant slices in a single layer on a jelly-roll pan coated with cooking spray. Bake at 400° for 12 minutes, turning after 6 minutes.

Cut each bread slice in half horizontally. Combine minced tomatoes, reserved liquid, and mayonnaise in a small bowl; stir well.

Spread mayonnaise mixture over top halves of bread. Divide veal and eggplant between bottom halves of bread; cover with top halves of bread. Yield: 2 servings.

CALORIES 388 (13% from fat); PROTEIN 22.1g; FAT 5.4g (sat 1.2g, mono 1.6g, poly 1.7g); CARB 61.3g; FIBER 3g; CHOL 51mg; IRON 3.1mg; SODIUM 824mg; CALC 79mg

SAUSAGE-AND-SPINACH PANINI

Vegetable cooking spray
1 (4-ounce) Italian-flavored turkey sausage link, cut in half crosswise
4 cups torn fresh spinach
2 (1½-ounce) French bread rolls
1 garlic clove, halved
1 teaspoon olive oil
⅛ teaspoon ground red pepper
Dash of salt

Coat a large nonstick skillet with cooking spray, and place over medium heat until hot. Add sausage, and cook 10 minutes, turning occasionally.

Remove sausage from skillet; carefully slice each piece in half lengthwise, cutting to, but not through, other side. Open the halves, laying sausage flat. Return sausage to skillet, placing cut sides down; cook 2 minutes or until sausage is done. Remove sausage from skillet; set aside, and keep warm. Add spinach to skillet; cover and cook 2 minutes or until wilted. Remove spinach from skillet; set aside, and keep warm.

Slice each French bread roll in half horizontally. Rub cut sides of bread with garlic halves, and brush with olive oil. Coat skillet with cooking spray, and place skillet over medium-high heat until hot. Arrange bread, cut sides down, in skillet, and cook for 1 minute or until toasted.

Place spinach on bottom halves of bread, and sprinkle with pepper and salt. Top each sandwich with sausage, and cover with top halves of bread. Yield: 2 servings.

CALORIES 230 (29% from fat); PROTEIN 13g; FAT 7.5g (sat 1.8g, mono 3.6g, poly 1.7g); CARB 28.1g; FIBER 5.2g; CHOL 23mg; IRON 4.5mg; SODIUM 538mg; CALC 137mg

FAST FOOD

How to Treat a Fajita

Sometime in the early '80s, the fajita rose from culinary obscurity to Reagan-like popularity. Suddenly fajitas were on every menu, and their popularity has never waned. Although most culinariologists believe the fajita has Southwestern roots, no one is sure just who stuffed and folded the first one into being.

A fajita generally consists of marinated flank or skirt steak that's cut into thin strips and wrapped in warm tortillas, accompanied by a variety of garnishes; a popular variation is the chicken fajita. This got us to thinking: Considering that fajitas are a healthy, fun way to eat—not to mention a breeze to prepare—why do people usually eat them only in restaurants? In the following recipes, we offer delicious, creative adaptations that can be easily done at home.

SESAME-PORK FAJITAS

Moo shu shells are similar to flour tortillas, but are made with wheat or rice flour. They can be found in Oriental markets.
Preparation time: 30 minutes
Cooking time: 10 minutes

1 pound pork tenderloin
2 teaspoons dark sesame oil
1 teaspoon peeled, grated gingerroot
¼ teaspoon salt
¼ teaspoon ground red pepper
2 garlic cloves, minced
4 moo shu shells
Vegetable cooking spray
¼ cup hoisin sauce

Trim fat from pork, and cut pork into thin strips. Combine pork and next 5 ingredients in a heavy-duty, zip-top plastic bag; seal bag, and shake well to coat. Marinate in refrigerator 20 minutes.

Heat moo shu shells according to package directions.

Coat a medium nonstick skillet with cooking spray, and place over medium-high heat until hot. Add pork mixture, and stir-fry 4 minutes or until done.

Divide pork mixture evenly among warm moo shu shells. Drizzle hoisin sauce over pork mixture, and roll up. Yield: 4 servings (serving size: 1 fajita).

CALORIES 267 (23% from fat); PROTEIN 26.7g; FAT 6.8g (sat 1.3g, mono 2.9g, poly 2g); CARB 24g; FIBER 0.3g; CHOL 74mg; IRON 1.8mg; SODIUM 553mg; CALC 20mg

SIZZLING STEAK FAJITAS

Here's a fairly traditional version of the fajita: seasoned flank steak cut into thin strips.
Preparation time: 15 minutes
Cooking time: 15 minutes

- ¾ pound lean flank steak
- 2 teaspoons ground cumin
- 2 teaspoons chili powder
- ¼ teaspoon salt
- ⅛ teaspoon garlic powder
- ⅛ teaspoon black pepper
- ⅛ teaspoon ground red pepper
- 4 (8-inch) flour tortillas
- 1 teaspoon vegetable oil
- 2 cups sliced onion
- ⅓ cup green bell pepper strips
- ⅓ cup red bell pepper strips
- ⅓ cup yellow bell pepper strips
- 1 tablespoon lime juice
- ¼ cup nonfat sour cream
- Commercial green salsa (optional)
- Cilantro sprigs (optional)

Trim fat from steak. Slice steak diagonally across grain into thin strips. Combine steak, cumin, chili powder, salt, garlic powder, black pepper, and ground red pepper in a heavy-duty, zip-top plastic bag; seal bag, and shake well to coat.

Heat the tortillas according to package directions.

Heat oil in a large nonstick skillet over medium-high heat until hot. Add steak, onion, and bell peppers; sauté 6 minutes or until steak is done. Remove from heat; stir in lime juice. Divide evenly among warm tortillas, and roll up. Serve with sour cream. Garnish with green salsa and cilantro sprigs, if desired. Yield: 4 servings (serving size: 1 fajita and 1 tablespoon sour cream).

CALORIES 330 (34% from fat); PROTEIN 22.6g; FAT 12.6g (sat 4.2g, mono 4.9g, poly 2.2g); CARB 31g; FIBER 3.3g; CHOL 43mg; IRON 4.3mg; SODIUM 425mg; CALC 81mg

ISLAND FISH FAJITAS

Be sure not to overmarinate the fish, or it will become mushy.
Preparation time: 30 minutes
Cooking time: 15 minutes

- 2 tablespoons fresh lime juice
- ½ teaspoon lemon pepper
- ¼ teaspoon ground cumin
- 1½ pounds snapper fillets, skinned and cut into ½-inch-wide strips
- 4 (10-inch) flour tortillas
- 1 teaspoon vegetable oil
- 1 cup vertically sliced red onion
- ½ cup red bell pepper strips
- ½ cup green bell pepper strips
- Vegetable cooking spray
- Pineapple Salsa

Combine fresh lime juice, lemon pepper, ground cumin, and snapper fillets in a heavy-duty, zip-top plastic bag; seal bag, and shake well to coat. Marinate the snapper strips in refrigerator 20 minutes.

Heat tortillas according to package directions.

Heat oil in a small nonstick skillet over medium-high heat until hot. Add sliced onion and bell pepper strips, and sauté 5 minutes or until crisp-tender. Remove skillet from heat; set aside, and keep warm.

Remove snapper from marinade, and discard marinade. Arrange snapper strips in a single layer on a broiler pan coated with cooking spray. Broil 8 minutes or until fish flakes easily when tested with a fork, turning after 4 minutes. Divide fish and bell pepper mixture evenly among warm tortillas, and roll up. Spoon Pineapple Salsa over fajitas. Yield: 4 servings (serving size: 1 fajita and ¼ cup salsa).

CALORIES 417 (18% from fat); PROTEIN 40.9g; FAT 8.2g (sat 1.4g, mono 2.5g, poly 3.1g); CARB 43.3g; FIBER 3.7g; CHOL 63mg; IRON 3mg; SODIUM 392mg; CALC 143mg

Pineapple Salsa:

- 1 cup finely chopped pineapple
- ¼ cup minced red onion
- 1 tablespoon seeded, minced jalapeño pepper

Combine all ingredients in a small bowl, and stir well. Cover and chill. Yield: 1 cup (serving size: ¼ cup).

CALORIES 24 (1% from fat); PROTEIN 0.3g; FAT 0.2g (sat 0g, mono 0g, poly 0.1g); CARB 5.9g; FIBER 0.8g; CHOL 0mg; IRON 0.2mg; SODIUM 1mg; CALC 5mg

MARINADE MAINSTAYS

◆ One of the easiest ways to marinate food is in a zip-top plastic bag. The bag takes little space in the refrigerator, and it's convenient to flip the bag over to make sure all of the food takes on the flavor.

◆ The safe way to marinate meats, fish, and poultry is in the refrigerator, not on the kitchen counter at room temperature.

◆ Marinades with acidic ingredients such as vinegar, wine, citrus juices, and yogurt provide flavor and help tenderize lean cuts of meat. But don't marinate too long—some red meats can marinate to mush, and poultry and fish can become tough. Be sure to follow each recipe for fork-tender results.

MENU SUGGESTION

LAMB FAJITAS WITH
CUCUMBER-DILL SAUCE

*Chickpea, cherry tomato,
and red onion salad*

*Toss chickpeas, cherry tomatoes, and
red onion with lemon juice, olive oil,
salt, and pepper.

LAMB FAJITAS WITH CUCUMBER-DILL SAUCE

The inspiration for these fajitas is the gyro, the Greek lamb-filled pita sandwich. Make the sauce first so it can chill while the lamb marinates.
Preparation time: 25 minutes
Cooking time: 10 minutes

- ¾ pound lean boneless leg of lamb
- 1 teaspoon olive oil
- ½ teaspoon dried oregano
- ¼ teaspoon salt
- ¼ teaspoon pepper
- 2 garlic cloves, minced
- 4 (8-inch) flour tortillas
- 1 teaspoon olive oil
- ¼ cup thinly sliced fresh mint leaves
  Cucumber-Dill Sauce

Trim fat from lamb, and cut lamb into thin strips. Combine lamb, 1 teaspoon olive oil, oregano, salt, pepper, and minced garlic in a heavy-duty, zip-top plastic bag; seal bag, and shake well to coat. Marinate in refrigerator 20 minutes.

Heat tortillas according to package directions.

Heat 1 teaspoon olive oil in a nonstick skillet over medium-high heat until hot. Add lamb mixture; sauté 6 minutes. Divide lamb mixture evenly among tortillas; sprinkle with mint, and roll up. Serve with Cucumber-Dill Sauce. Yield: 4 servings (serving size: 1 fajita and 6 tablespoons sauce).

CALORIES 324 (27% from fat); PROTEIN 25.3g; FAT 9.6g
(sat 2.3g, mono 4.6g, poly 1.9g); CARB 32.8g; FIBER 1.8g;
CHOL 56mg; IRON 3.5mg; SODIUM 471mg; CALC 193mg

Cucumber-Dill Sauce:

- 1 cup peeled, seeded, and diced cucumber
- ¼ teaspoon dried dillweed
- 1 garlic clove, minced
- 1 (8-ounce) carton plain nonfat yogurt

Combine all ingredients in a small bowl; stir well. Cover and chill. Yield: 1½ cups (serving size: 6 tablespoons).

CALORIES 38 (2% from fat); PROTEIN 3.5g; FAT 0.1g
(sat 0.1g, mono 0g, poly 0g); CARB 5.7g; FIBER 0.2g;
CHOL 1mg; IRON 0.2mg; SODIUM 45mg; CALC 121mg

CABBAGE-AND-JICAMA SLAW

If you can't find jicama, just increase the amount of cabbage from 3 cups to 5.
Preparation time: 10 minutes
Cooking time: 0 minutes

- 3 cups thinly sliced green cabbage
- 2 cups (3 x ¼-inch) julienne-cut peeled jicama
- 1 (11-ounce) can mandarin oranges in light syrup, drained
- 2 tablespoons white vinegar
- ½ teaspoon salt
- ⅛ teaspoon pepper
- 1 (8-ounce) carton plain low-fat yogurt

Combine first 3 ingredients in a large bowl. Combine vinegar, salt, pepper, and yogurt in a small bowl; stir well. Pour yogurt mixture over cabbage mixture; toss gently to coat. Cover and chill. Yield: 4 servings (serving size: 1 cup).

CALORIES 102 (1% from fat); PROTEIN 4.1g; FAT 1g
(sat 0.6g, mono 0.3g, poly 0.1g); CARB 19.9g; FIBER 1.3g;
CHOL 3mg; IRON 0.8mg; SODIUM 347mg; CALC 136mg

INSPIRED VEGETARIAN

My Heart Belongs to Patty

Sizzling with innovative flavors, these patties and croquettes are perfect for today's table.

Patties and croquettes are the essence of comfort food—familiar, inviting, and soul-satisfying. Yet with today's health-conscious society, these favorites have been shown the door. However, with a little creativity and a lot less fat, we've refashioned these little cakes. Try a sampling and see if you're ready to welcome back the patty.

COUSCOUS-AND-FETA CAKES

An electric skillet or griddle works well for this recipe because there's more room for the cakes. Otherwise, use a nonstick skillet, and cook in batches. They're delicious plain or served with marinara sauce.

- 2½ cups water
- 1 cup uncooked couscous
- 1 tablespoon plus 1 teaspoon olive oil, divided
- 1 cup minced red onion
- 1 cup minced red bell pepper
- ½ cup minced green bell pepper
- 2 garlic cloves, minced
- 1 cup (4 ounces) crumbled feta cheese
- ½ cup all-purpose flour
- ½ cup egg substitute
- 2 tablespoons minced fresh parsley
- ¼ teaspoon salt
- ¼ teaspoon white pepper

Bring water to a boil in a small saucepan; stir in couscous. Remove from heat; cover and let stand 10 minutes. Fluff with a fork.

Place 1 teaspoon oil in an electric skillet; heat to 375°. Add onion, bell peppers, and garlic; sauté 5 minutes. Combine couscous, onion mixture, cheese, and remaining ingredients in a large bowl; stir well.

Place ½ teaspoon oil in skillet; heat to 375°. Place 4 one-third cup portions of couscous mixture in skillet, shaping each portion into a 3-inch cake in the skillet. Cook 6 minutes or until golden brown, turning cakes carefully after 3 minutes. Repeat procedure with remaining oil and couscous mixture. Yield: 12 servings (serving size: 2 cakes).

CALORIES 242 (28% from fat); PROTEIN 10g; FAT 7.6g (sat 3.2g, mono 3.2g, poly 0.6g); CARB 34g; FIBER 2.4g; CHOL 16mg; IRON 2.2mg; SODIUM 344mg; CALC 112mg

SUN-DRIED TOMATO-BASIL RICE CAKES

The preparation time may seem long, but some of the steps can be done ahead.

    4   cups peeled, diced eggplant
    ½   teaspoon salt, divided
    ½   teaspoon dried Italian
        seasoning
    2   cups boiling water
    2   ounces sun-dried tomatoes,
        packed without oil (about 24)
    2   cups water
    1   cup uncooked jasmine or
        long-grain rice
    ½   teaspoon olive oil
    ½   cup finely chopped onion
    1   garlic clove, minced
    ½   cup dry breadcrumbs
    ¼   cup chopped fresh basil
    1   tablespoon capers, chopped
    2   eggs, lightly beaten
    2   tablespoons olive oil, divided
Red Pepper Sauce (optional)
        (recipe on page 22)
Basil leaves (optional)

Preheat oven to 375°.

Place eggplant on a foil-lined baking sheet, spreading evenly. Sprinkle ¼ teaspoon salt and Italian seasoning over eggplant. Bake at 375° for 35 minutes or until tender.

Combine 2 cups boiling water and tomatoes in a bowl; let stand 30 minutes or until softened. Drain tomatoes, reserving ¼ cup liquid. Chop tomatoes; set aside.

Bring 2 cups water to a boil in a medium saucepan. Add rice; cover, reduce heat, and simmer 25 minutes or until liquid is absorbed. Remove from heat; fluff with a fork.

Heat ½ teaspoon oil in a large nonstick skillet over medium-high heat until hot. Add onion and garlic; sauté 3 minutes.

Combine onion mixture, rice, tomatoes, reserved ¼ cup liquid, eggplant, remaining ¼ teaspoon salt, breadcrumbs, basil, capers, and eggs in a large bowl. Divide mixture into 16 equal portions, shaping each portion into a 3½-inch cake.

Heat 1½ teaspoons oil in skillet over medium-high heat until hot. Add 4 cakes, and cook 6 minutes or until golden, turning cakes carefully after 3 minutes. Repeat procedure with remaining oil and cakes. Serve with Red Pepper Sauce, if desired, and garnish with basil leaves, if desired. Yield: 8 servings (serving size: 2 cakes).

CALORIES 198 (26% from fat); PROTEIN 5.8g; FAT 5.8g (sat 1.1g, mono 3.4g, poly 0.7g); CARB 31.3g; FIBER 1.4g; CHOL 55mg; IRON 2mg; SODIUM 457mg; CALC 58mg

PATTY PARTICULARS

The culinary terminology—griddlecakes, patties, and croquettes—is somewhat interchangeable. Here's how to distinguish them:

◆ **Griddlecakes** are usually the flattest variety, with the most surface area to brown (our Noodle Pancakes with Shiitake Mushrooms on page 22 are a perfect example).
◆ **Patties,** such as old-fashioned fish cakes, are thicker and moister in the center.
◆ **Croquettes** are typically oval-shaped and bound with béchamel or cream sauce.

BLACK BEAN PATTIES WITH CILANTRO AND LIME

Canned beans simplify the preparation of this Southwestern-style recipe.

    1   tablespoon olive oil
    1   cup chopped onion
    ½   cup chopped green bell pepper
    ½   cup chopped red bell pepper
    1   tablespoon minced jalapeño
        pepper
    1   teaspoon chili powder
    ½   teaspoon dried oregano
    ½   teaspoon ground cumin
    ¼   teaspoon salt
    2   garlic cloves, minced
    1   (15-ounce) can black beans,
        undrained
 1½   cups dry breadcrumbs
    ¼   cup yellow cornmeal
    2   tablespoons minced fresh
        cilantro
    1   tablespoon fresh lime juice
    ¼   cup (1 ounce) shredded
        Monterey Jack cheese
Vegetable cooking spray
    ⅔   cup salsa

Heat oil in a large nonstick skillet over medium-high heat until hot. Add onion and next 8 ingredients; sauté 3 minutes or until onion is tender. Add beans; sauté 1 minute. Combine bean mixture, breadcrumbs, cornmeal, cilantro, and lime juice in a large bowl; stir well.

Place 1 cup bean mixture in a food processor, and process until smooth. Add puréed bean mixture and cheese to remaining bean mixture; stir well. Divide into 10 equal portions, shaping each into a 3-inch patty.

Wipe skillet dry with paper towels. Coat skillet with cooking spray, and place over medium-high heat until hot. Add 5 patties, and cook 3 minutes or until browned, turning patties carefully after 1½ minutes. Repeat procedure with remaining patties. Serve with salsa. Yield: 5 servings (serving size: 2 patties and 2 tablespoons salsa).

CALORIES 311 (21% from fat); PROTEIN 12.5g; FAT 7.2g (sat 1.9g, mono 3.3g, poly 1g); CARB 50.3g; FIBER 8.6g; CHOL 4mg; IRON 5.1mg; SODIUM 525mg; CALC 173mg

HERB 'N' SPINACH CAKES

To get the most water out of the spinach, press the thawed greens between heavy paper towels.

Vegetable cooking spray
1½ cups chopped onion
3 garlic cloves, minced
1 teaspoon dried rosemary, crushed
¼ teaspoon ground nutmeg
2 (10-ounce) packages frozen chopped spinach, thawed, drained, and squeezed dry
2½ cups peeled, cooked, and mashed baking potatoes
¾ cup dry breadcrumbs, divided
¼ cup grated Parmesan cheese
½ teaspoon salt
¼ teaspoon pepper
2 egg whites
1 tablespoon olive oil, divided
Red Pepper Sauce (optional)

Coat a large nonstick skillet with cooking spray, and place over medium-high heat until hot. Add onion and garlic; sauté 5 minutes or until tender. Add rosemary, nutmeg, and spinach; cook 2 minutes. Place spinach mixture in a large bowl; let cool slightly. Add mashed potatoes, ¼ cup breadcrumbs, cheese, salt, pepper, and egg whites; stir well. Divide spinach mixture into 12 equal portions, shaping each into a 3½-inch

cake. Dredge cakes in remaining ½ cup breadcrumbs.

Coat skillet with cooking spray; add 1 teaspoon oil, and place over medium heat until hot. Add 4 cakes, and cook 6 minutes or until lightly browned, turning cakes carefully after 3 minutes. Repeat procedure with remaining olive oil and cakes. Serve immediately with Red Pepper Sauce, if desired. Yield: 6 servings (serving size: 2 cakes).

CALORIES 166 (24% from fat); PROTEIN 8.9g; FAT 4.5g (sat 1.2g, mono 2.2g, poly 0.6g); CARB 24.5g; FIBER 5.4g; CHOL 2.6mg; IRON 4.8mg; SODIUM 461mg; CALC 211mg

RED PEPPER SAUCE

While the 41% fat value in our nutritional analysis sounds high, each tablespoon of sauce contains less than 0.5 grams of fat.

2 medium red bell peppers (about 1 pound)
1 cup tomato juice
1 tablespoon tahini (sesame seed paste)
1 tablespoon tomato paste
1 tablespoon lemon juice
1 teaspoon dried oregano
1 garlic clove, minced

Cut bell peppers in half lengthwise; discard seeds and membranes. Place peppers, skin sides up, on a foil-lined baking sheet; flatten with hand. Broil 10 minutes or until blackened. Place bell peppers in a heavy-duty, zip-top plastic bag, and seal; let stand 15 minutes. Peel peppers.

Place bell peppers and remaining ingredients in a food processor; process until smooth. Yield: 1½ cups (serving size: 3 tablespoons).

CALORIES 24 (41% from fat); PROTEIN 0.8g; FAT 1.1g (sat 0.2g, mono 0.4g, poly 0.5g); CARB 3.5g; FIBER 0.7g; CHOL 0mg; IRON 0.7mg; SODIUM 114mg; CALC 16mg

NOODLE PANCAKES WITH SHIITAKE MUSHROOMS

If you're not sensitive to sodium, you can substitute a 4.23-ounce package of udon (Oriental-style noodles) for the spaghetti. Discard the seasoning packets; you won't need them.

1 cup boiling water
1 (1-ounce) package dried shiitake mushrooms
3 cups water
4 ounces uncooked spaghetti
½ cup fine, dry breadcrumbs
½ cup coarsely shredded carrot
½ cup thinly sliced green onions
½ cup finely chopped water chestnuts
1 tablespoon cornstarch
1 tablespoon low-sodium soy sauce
1 teaspoon peeled, grated gingerroot
½ teaspoon pepper
3 egg whites, lightly beaten
1 garlic clove, minced
1 tablespoon vegetable oil, divided
Asian Black Bean Sauce

Combine 1 cup boiling water and mushrooms in a bowl; cover and let stand 30 minutes or until softened. Drain mushrooms, and finely chop.

Bring 3 cups water to a boil in a large saucepan. Add spaghetti, and cook 20 minutes or until very tender. Drain spaghetti (do not rinse); let cool to room temperature.

Combine spaghetti, mushrooms, breadcrumbs, and next 9 ingredients in a large bowl; stir well. Divide into 8 equal portions, shaping each into a 3½-inch cake.

Heat 1½ teaspoons oil in a nonstick skillet over medium-high heat. Add 4 cakes; cook 6 minutes or until golden, turning carefully after 3 minutes. Repeat procedure with remaining oil and cakes. Serve with Asian Black Bean Sauce. Yield: 4 servings (serving size: 2 pancakes and about ⅓ cup sauce).

CALORIES 408 (12% from fat); PROTEIN 18.4g; FAT 5.5g (sat 1g, mono 1.4g, poly 2.3g); CARB 70.4g; FIBER 7.6g; CHOL 0mg; IRON 4.8mg; SODIUM 652mg; CALC 87mg

Asian Black Bean Sauce:

1 (15-ounce) can black beans, undrained
1 tablespoon low-sodium soy sauce
1 teaspoon peeled, grated gingerroot
½ teaspoon grated orange rind
⅛ teaspoon dried crushed red pepper
1 garlic clove, minced

Combine all the ingredients in a medium saucepan; bring to a boil. Reduce heat, and simmer, uncovered, 20 minutes. Yield: 1⅔ cups (serving size: about ⅓ cup).

CALORIES 113 (5% from fat); PROTEIN 7.6g; FAT 0.6g (sat 0.1g, mono 0g, poly 0.2g); CARB 20.4g; FIBER 8.4g; CHOL 0mg; IRON 1.8mg; SODIUM 309mg; CALC 26mg

FOOD FOR THOUGHT

The Enlightened Chef

For Chef Octavio Becerra, his passion for complex flavors all began with his maternal grandfather and rattlesnake tacos. "My grandfather, besides filling my imagination with stories about politicians, famous outlaws, writers, and even famous Mexican chefs, taught me how to eat and how to keep my mind open to anything."

For Chef Becerra, food has always involved an alchemy of great flavors and healthy ingredients coming together in an unexpected assortment of tastes, textures, and visual combinations. And, the food served at his Los Angeles restaurant, Pinot Bistro, often involves the layering of flavors to achieve the complexity he desires.

SEA BASS WITH VEGETABLE NAGE

1 whole garlic head
½ teaspoon olive oil
2 cups Vegetable Nage, divided
1 teaspoon white wine vinegar
¼ teaspoon pepper
Dash of salt
2 teaspoons olive oil
½ cup sliced onion
½ cup sliced carrot
¼ cup Chardonnay or other dry white wine
1 tablespoon minced shallots
2 thyme sprigs
1 bay leaf
4 (6-ounce) sea bass fillets
1 tablespoon plus 1 teaspoon chopped shallots

Preheat oven to 400°.

Remove white papery skin from garlic head (do not peel or separate cloves). Rub ½ teaspoon olive oil over garlic head, and wrap in aluminum foil. Bake garlic at 400° for 45 minutes; let cool 10 minutes. Separate garlic cloves; peel 4 cloves, and reserve for garnish. Squeeze remaining cloves to extract garlic pulp; discard skins.

Combine garlic pulp, 1 cup Vegetable Nage, vinegar, pepper, and salt in a blender. Cover and process until smooth. With blender on, add 2 teaspoons olive oil, and process until well blended; pour into a small saucepan, and cook over low heat until warm. Set the garlic nage aside, and keep warm.

Combine remaining 1 cup Vegetable Nage, onion, and the next 5 ingredients in a large skillet; bring to a simmer. Add fish; cover, reduce heat, and simmer 4 minutes or until fish is opaque in color.

Place fish in 4 shallow bowls; discard poaching liquid, vegetables, and herbs. Drizzle ¼ cup warm garlic nage over each fillet; sprinkle with 1 teaspoon shallots, and garnish with a peeled garlic clove. Yield: 4 servings.

CALORIES 267 (37% from fat); PROTEIN 33.4g; FAT 11.1g (sat 1.2g, mono 6g, poly 2.3g); CARB 7.1g; FIBER 0.3g; CHOL 116mg; IRON 3.3mg; SODIUM 135mg; CALC 174mg

Vegetable Nage:

A nage is a flavorful French stock made from either vegetables or fish and herbs.

1½ tablespoons olive oil
4 cups sliced leek
2 cups diced onion
1⅓ cups diced fennel bulb
⅓ cup chopped celery
1 whole head garlic, unpeeled and cut in half
2 cups water
15 thyme sprigs
15 parsley sprigs
3 bay leaves
1 (750-milliliter) bottle Chardonnay or other dry white wine

Heat olive oil in a large saucepan over medium heat until hot. Add leek, onion, fennel bulb, celery, and garlic halves; cover, reduce heat to low, and cook 45 minutes, stirring often. Add 2 cups water and remaining ingredients, and bring to a boil. Reduce heat, and simmer, uncovered, 1 hour. Strain mixture through a sieve into a bowl, and discard solids. Yield: 4 cups.

Shortcut: Substitute 1 cup canned vegetable broth and 1 cup Chardonnay or other dry white wine for the Vegetable Nage, if desired.

Note: Refrigerate the remaining Vegetable Nage in an airtight container for up to 1 week, or freeze it for up to 3 months.

S T E P
b y
S T E P

1

*Using a small
knife with a
sharp tip, cut
vanilla beans
in half
lengthwise.*

2

*Scrape seeds
out with knife blade.*

O R

3

*Push seeds
out of
vanilla bean
half with
thumbnail.*

TECHNIQUE

Vanilla—with Personality

If you think vanilla is synonymous with plain or dull, you haven't cooked with vanilla beans. We've got the how-to and the recipes.

Cooking with vanilla beans—as opposed to the commercial extract that you buy in those little glass bottles—adds a profound flavor to many dishes. The difference is well worth the trouble—and that trouble is slight. Extracting the pulp from the pod is simple; just follow our step-by-step instructions. (Most supermarkets carry vanilla beans in the spice section; if yours doesn't, consult our list of mail-order sources on this page.)

VANILLA-BUTTERMILK ICE MILK

1 (6-inch) vanilla bean, split
    lengthwise
2 cups 2% low-fat milk
¾ cup sugar
1 cup low-fat buttermilk
1 (12-ounce) can evaporated
    skimmed milk

Scrape seeds from vanilla bean; place seeds and bean in a medium saucepan. Pour 2% low-fat milk into pan; cook over medium-low heat to 180° or until tiny bubbles form around edge of pan (do not boil). Remove from heat; discard vanilla bean.

Pour vanilla-milk mixture into a large bowl; add sugar, stirring until sugar dissolves. Stir in buttermilk and evaporated milk; cover and chill.

Pour mixture into the freezer can of an ice-cream freezer, and freeze according to manufacturer's instructions. Spoon ice milk into a freezer-safe container; cover and freeze at least

1 hour. Yield: 16 servings (serving size: ½ cup).

CALORIES 76 (11% from fat); PROTEIN 3.2g; FAT 0.9g; (sat 0.6g, mono 0.2g, poly 0g); CARB 14g; FIBER 0g; CHOL 3mg; IRON 0.1mg; SODIUM 48mg; CALC 118mg

VANILLA WAFERS

Vegetable cooking spray
1 tablespoon all-purpose flour
½ cup sugar
¼ cup cornstarch
2 tablespoons margarine, melted
1 egg
1 (6-inch) vanilla bean, split
    lengthwise
¾ cup all-purpose flour
½ teaspoon baking powder
⅛ teaspoon salt

Preheat oven to 350°. Coat 2 large baking sheets with cooking spray, and dust with 1 tablespoon flour; set aside.

Combine sugar and next 3 ingredients in a bowl; stir with a wire whisk. Scrape seeds from vanilla bean. Add seeds to sugar mixture; reserve bean for another use. Add ¾ cup flour, baking powder, and salt; stir until smooth.

Drop dough by teaspoonfuls 2 inches apart onto baking sheets. Bake at 350° for 15 minutes. Remove cookies from baking sheets; let cool on wire racks. Yield: 3 dozen (serving size: 1 cookie).

CALORIES 32 (23% from fat); PROTEIN 0.5g; FAT 0.8g; (sat 0.2g, mono 0.3g, poly 0.2g); CARB 5.6g; FIBER 0.1g; CHOL 6mg; IRON 0.2mg; SODIUM 17mg; CALC 4mg

MAIL-ORDER SOURCES

If you're unable to locate vanilla beans at your local grocery store, try one of these mail-order sources.
• KCJ Vanilla Co., Box 126-CLM, Norwood, PA 19074. Send $1 to receive a catalog and recipes.
• Penzeys Ltd., P.O. Box 1448, Waukesha, WI 53187; 414/574-0277, fax 414/574-0278.
• Vanns Spices, 1238 E. Joppa Road, Baltimore, MD 21286; 410/583-1643, fax 410/583-1783.

OLD-FASHIONED VANILLA BREAD PUDDING WITH WINTER FRUIT

    1   (6-inch) vanilla bean, split
          lengthwise
 1½   cups 2% low-fat milk
    ½   cup boiling water
    ½   cup chopped dried mixed fruit
    ¼   cup raisins
    1   tablespoon margarine, melted
  10   (½-inch-thick) slices Italian
          bread (about 6½ ounces)
Vegetable cooking spray
    1   cup evaporated skimmed milk
    ½   cup sugar
    ⅛   teaspoon salt
    ⅛   teaspoon ground cinnamon
    2   eggs
    2   egg whites

Scrape seeds from vanilla bean; place the seeds and bean in a small heavy saucepan. Pour 2% low-fat milk into pan, and cook over medium-low heat to 180° or until tiny bubbles form around edge of pan (do not boil). Remove from heat; let cool. Discard bean.

Combine boiling water, mixed fruit, and raisins in a small bowl; cover and let stand 30 minutes or until softened (do not drain).

Preheat oven to 350°. Brush margarine over bread slices; place bread on a baking sheet. Bake for 10 minutes or until lightly toasted. Arrange half of bread in an 8-inch square baking dish coated with cooking spray, tearing bread slices to fit dish. Spoon softened fruit and soaking liquid over bread; top with remaining bread.

Combine the vanilla-milk mixture, evaporated milk, and remaining 5 ingredients in a medium bowl; stir well with a wire whisk. Pour over bread, pressing gently with a spoon to moisten.

Cover dish, and place in a 13 x 9-inch baking pan; add hot water to pan to a depth of 1 inch. Bake at 350° for 30 minutes. Uncover and bake an additional 20 minutes or until set. Serve warm. Yield: 8 servings.

CALORIES 237 (15% from fat); PROTEIN 8.8g; FAT 3.9g; (sat 1.3g, mono 1.4g, poly 0.7g); CARB 41.5g; FIBER 0.9g; CHOL 58mg; IRON 1.2mg; SODIUM 278mg; CALC 166mg

---

VANILLA TIPS

◆ Expect to pay $2 to $3 a bean.
◆ Choose beans that are pliable or leathery rather than brittle.
◆ Make vanilla sugar by placing split vanilla beans (anywhere from 2 to 6, depending on how strong you want the vanilla taste), with or without seeds, in about 2 cups of sugar for approximately two weeks.
◆ Vanilla beans freeze well; just pop them into the microwave for 15 to 30 seconds to plump and thaw.
◆ When using vanilla in recipes, you can substitute 1 tablespoon of vanilla extract for 1 (6-inch) vanilla bean.
◆ If you make your own vanilla extract, it will be more fragrant and flavorful than any you can buy. Basically, all you do is store split vanilla beans—about 4 or 5 beans with or without seeds, whole or in pieces—in 2 cups of vodka. The vanilla mixture will get better and better as time goes on. As you use it, continue adding more vodka and bean pieces (with seeds removed) to maintain an even consistency of flavor.

PLUMS POACHED IN SAUTERNES AND VANILLA

    1   (6-inch) vanilla bean, split
          lengthwise
 1½   cups Sauternes or other sweet
          white wine
    4   large plums, halved and pitted
          (about 10 ounces)
    2   tablespoons honey
    1   tablespoon fresh lime juice
    ¼   cup vanilla low-fat yogurt
    4   lime rind strips (optional)

Scrape seeds from vanilla bean into a saucepan; reserve bean for another use. Add Sauternes; stir well. Bring mixture to a boil over medium-high heat. Add plum halves, cut sides up, in a single layer in saucepan; cover, reduce heat, and simmer 15 minutes. Remove

plums from saucepan with a slotted spoon; set aside, and keep warm.

Bring Sauternes mixture to a boil over medium-high heat; cook 4 minutes or until reduced to 1 cup. Remove from heat; stir in honey and lime juice.

Place 2 plum halves into each of 4 dessert compotes; top each with about ¼ cup Sauternes mixture and 1 tablespoon yogurt. Garnish with lime rind, if desired. Yield: 4 servings.

CALORIES 108 (5% from fat); PROTEIN 1.3g; FAT 0.6g (sat 0.2g, mono 0.3g, poly 0.1g); CARB 21.6g; FIBER 1.5g; CHOL 1mg; IRON 0.1mg; SODIUM 154mg; CALC 28mg

---

VANILLA GLAZE

Recipe by vanilla expert Patricia Rain.

    ¾   cup red wine vinegar
    ¼   cup sugar
    1   (6-inch) vanilla bean, split
          lengthwise
 1½   cups fat-free chicken broth
    ¾   cup Madeira
    ¼   cup water
    1   tablespoon cornstarch
    ⅛   teaspoon salt

Combine vinegar and sugar in a saucepan. Bring to a boil; cook 7 minutes. Scrape seeds from bean; place seeds and bean in saucepan. Stir in broth and Madeira; return to a boil. Cook 15 minutes, stirring often.

Combine water, cornstarch, and salt in a small bowl; stir well, and add to pan. Bring mixture to a boil, and cook 1 minute, stirring constantly; discard bean. Yield: 1 cup (serving size: 1 tablespoon).

CALORIES 21 (0% from fat); PROTEIN 0.7g; FAT 0g; CARB 4.4g; FIBER 0g; CHOL 0mg; IRON 0mg; SODIUM 35mg; CALC 1mg

VANILLA CUSTARD SAUCE

¼ cup sugar
1 tablespoon cornstarch
Dash of salt
1 cup 2% low-fat milk
¾ cup evaporated skimmed milk
1 egg, lightly beaten
1 (6-inch) vanilla bean, split
   lengthwise

Combine first 3 ingredients in the top of a double boiler. Gradually add milks and egg, stirring with a wire whisk until smooth. Scrape seeds from vanilla bean; stir seeds into milk mixture, reserving bean for another use. Place pan over simmering water, and cook 12 minutes or until slightly thickened, stirring constantly. Serve warm or at room temperature. Yield: 2 cups (serving size: ¼ cup).

CALORIES 72 (16% from fat); PROTEIN 3.6g; FAT 1.3g (sat 0.6g, mono 0.4g, poly 0.1g); CARB 11.5g; FIBER 0g; CHOL 31mg; IRON 0.2mg; SODIUM 55mg; CALC 110mg

ORCHID ORIGINS

Did you ever wonder where vanilla comes from? Its source is a wrinkled brown bean, the product of a climbing orchid native to southeastern Mexico.

The beans grow 4 to 12 inches in length; after harvest, they go through a fermentation-and-drying process for four to six months. During this time, they turn from light to dark brown as they shrivel into the pencil-thin, brownish-black vanilla beans that we buy encased in glass tubes; they also develop their characteristic sweet aroma.

The prize inside each vanilla bean is a rich, concentrated paste—the pure essence of vanilla. This paste is actually made up of thousands of tiny dotlike seeds.

READER RECIPES

Stand Up and Cheer

For Super Bowl Sunday, our readers have sent us the makings of a substantial, low-fat buffet. No matter which team you're rooting for, make it your winning goal to eat healthy.

SPICY ORANGE HUMMUS

This hummus dip is so flavorful, you'll never miss the olive oil!
—Beth Woodham, Mobile, Alabama

¼ cup parsley leaves
2 tablespoons chopped onion
1 garlic clove
¼ cup unsweetened orange juice
2 tablespoons tahini (sesame seed paste)
2 tablespoons rice vinegar
2 teaspoons low-sodium soy sauce
1 teaspoon Dijon mustard
¼ teaspoon salt
¼ teaspoon ground ginger
¼ teaspoon ground coriander
¼ teaspoon ground turmeric
¼ teaspoon ground cumin
¼ teaspoon paprika
1 (15-ounce) can chickpeas (garbanzo beans), drained

Drop parsley, onion, and garlic through food chute with food processor on, and process until minced. Add orange juice and remaining ingredients, and process until smooth. Serve with pita triangles. Yield: 1¾ cups (serving size: 1 tablespoon).

CALORIES 21 (3% from fat); PROTEIN 0.8g; FAT 0.7g (sat 0.1g, mono 0.2g, poly 0.3g); CARB 3g; FIBER 0.8g; CHOL 0mg; IRON 0.3mg; SODIUM 70mg; CALC 10mg

CREAMY MEXICAN CRAB DIP

You can refrigerate this dip, but it's very good served warm.
—Terry Shannon, Gold Beach, Oregon

1 (8-ounce) package Neufchâtel cheese
1 (8-ounce) block nonfat cream cheese
1 (6-ounce) can lump crabmeat, undrained
½ cup salsa

Place cheeses in a microwave-safe bowl, and cover with wax paper. Microwave at MEDIUM (50% power) 2 to 3 minutes or until softened, stirring with a wire whisk until smooth.

Drain crabmeat through a sieve into a bowl, reserving 1 tablespoon liquid. Add reserved liquid, crabmeat, and salsa to cheese; stir well. Serve warm or at room temperature with baked tortilla chips, raw vegetables, or breadsticks. Yield: 2½ cups (serving size: 1 tablespoon).

CALORIES 24 (49% from fat); PROTEIN 2.3g; FAT 1.3g (sat 0.8g, mono 0g, poly 0g); CARB 0.5g; FIBER 0.1g; CHOL 9mg; IRON 0.1mg; SODIUM 80mg; CALC 25mg

HEALTHY DIPPERS

A little imagination can add new dimensions to dips. Choose a variety of vegetables with different textures and colors to serve as dippers.

Asparagus spears
Broccoli florets
Carrot sticks
Cauliflower florets
Celery sticks
Cucumber slices
Green onions
Green or red bell pepper strips
Jicama strips
Mushrooms
Snow peas
Sugar snap peas
Turnip strips
Yellow squash slices
Zucchini slices

SOUTH-OF-THE-BORDER BAKE

No one can ever guess that this casserole is light. It can be made ahead, but I add the sour cream and toppings right before I put it on the table.

—Mary Agnes Taylor, Fayette, Tennessee

2 cups no-salt-added tomato sauce
1 tablespoon white vinegar
1 to 1½ teaspoons chili powder
¼ teaspoon ground cumin
¼ teaspoon garlic powder
⅛ to ¼ teaspoon ground red pepper
4 cups sliced zucchini
1½ cups frozen whole-kernel corn, thawed
1½ cups (6 ounces) shredded reduced-fat sharp Cheddar cheese, divided
¾ cup crushed baked tortilla chips
1 (4½-ounce) can chopped green chiles, undrained
Vegetable cooking spray
½ cup nonfat sour cream
½ cup chopped green bell pepper
½ cup chopped tomato

Preheat oven to 350°.

Combine first 6 ingredients in a medium saucepan; bring to a simmer over medium heat, stirring often. Reduce heat to low, and cook, uncovered, 12 minutes; set aside.

Combine zucchini, corn, ¾ cup cheese, chips, and green chiles in a bowl; stir well. Spoon zucchini mixture into a 13 x 9-inch baking dish coated with cooking spray. Pour tomato sauce mixture over casserole; bake, uncovered, at 350° for 25 minutes. Sprinkle remaining cheese over casserole, and bake an additional 5 minutes.

Spread sour cream over casserole, and sprinkle with bell pepper and tomato. Yield: 8 servings.

CALORIES 157 (26% from fat); PROTEIN 10.3g; FAT 4.6g (sat 2.4g, mono 1.2g, poly 0.3g); CARB 20.8g; FIBER 2g; CHOL 14mg; IRON 0.8mg; SODIUM 206mg; CALC 202mg

---

MENU SUGGESTION

CHICKEN NOODLE BAKE

Dilled peas and celery

Apple-butterscotch sundaes

*Sauté 8 cups celery sticks in 1 tablespoon oil for 10 minutes. Add 1 cup frozen green peas, ¼ cup white wine vinegar, and 1 tablespoon fresh dillweed; sauté 1 minute.

CHICKEN NOODLE BAKE

I love making my Chicken Noodle Bake for company. It freezes and reheats well, and everyone likes it.

—Tracey Bell, Fort Worth, Texas

1 cup 1% low-fat cottage cheese
½ cup light cream cheese
½ cup nonfat sour cream
½ cup nonfat mayonnaise
½ cup chopped onion
½ cup chopped green bell pepper
¼ cup minced fresh parsley
2 tablespoons margarine
⅓ cup all-purpose flour
½ cup skim milk
1 (10½-ounce) can low-salt chicken broth
½ teaspoon poultry seasoning
¼ teaspoon salt
¼ teaspoon pepper
Dash of garlic powder
6 cooked lasagna noodles
Vegetable cooking spray
3 cups diced cooked chicken breast
½ cup dry breadcrumbs
2 tablespoons chopped fresh parsley
¼ teaspoon paprika

Preheat oven to 375°.

Combine first 4 ingredients in a medium bowl; beat at high speed of an electric mixer until well-blended. Stir in onion, bell pepper, and ¼ cup parsley; set aside.

Melt margarine in a medium saucepan over medium heat. Add flour; cook 1 minute, stirring constantly with a wire whisk. Gradually add milk and broth, stirring constantly. Bring to a boil over medium heat; cook 3 minutes or until thickened, stirring constantly. Stir in poultry seasoning, salt, pepper, and garlic powder. Remove from heat; set sauce aside.

Arrange 3 noodles in bottom of a 13 x 9-inch baking dish coated with cooking spray; top with half of cottage cheese mixture, half of chicken, and half of sauce. Repeat layers, ending with sauce.

Combine breadcrumbs, 2 tablespoons parsley, and paprika; sprinkle over casserole. Bake, uncovered, at 375° for 30 minutes. Serve immediately. Yield: 8 servings.

CALORIES 321 (24% from fat); PROTEIN 26.1g; FAT 8.4g (sat 2.9g, mono 3.1g, poly 1.7g); CARB 33.2g; FIBER 1.4g; CHOL 50mg; IRON 2.6mg; SODIUM 618mg; CALC 91mg

---

CHICKEN COOKERY

Don't have leftover chicken? Try these suggestions when a recipe calls for cooked chicken.

♦ Determine how much chicken is needed by counting on ½ cup chopped chicken per chicken breast half.

♦ Chicken cooks quickly with the help of a microwave oven. To microwave chicken for Chicken Noodle Bake, arrange 6 skinned, boned chicken breast halves in a baking dish. Cover with heavy-duty plastic wrap, turning back one corner to vent. Microwave at HIGH 7 minutes or until done, rotating dish a quarter-turn after 4 minutes.

♦ On the cooktop: Bring 1 cup water to a boil in a large skillet over medium-high heat. Reduce heat to simmer, and add 6 skinned, boned chicken breast halves. Cover skillet, and cook 15 minutes or until done, turning chicken after 8 minutes.

COCOA CAKE

Because we're on the go a lot, we need a good snack food that keeps well. Cocoa Cake is quick and easy to put together, and it keeps very well if stored in an airtight container.
—Amy Wodzenski, Masontown, West Virginia

1¼   cups sugar
⅔   cup boiling water
2   egg whites, lightly beaten
1   (4-ounce) jar prune baby food
1¾   cups sifted cake flour
½   cup unsweetened cocoa
1   teaspoon baking powder
½   teaspoon baking soda
½   teaspoon salt
     Vegetable cooking spray
1   tablespoon powdered sugar

Preheat oven to 350°.
Combine 1¼ cups sugar and boiling water in a small bowl, stirring until sugar dissolves. Let cool. Add egg whites and baby food to cooled sugar mixture; stir until well-blended.
Combine flour and next 4 ingredients in a medium bowl; stir well. Add egg white mixture to flour mixture, stirring just until dry ingredients are moistened.
Pour batter into a 9-inch square baking pan coated with cooking spray. Bake at 350° for 40 minutes or until cake springs back when touched lightly in center. Let cool completely in pan on a wire rack. Sift powdered sugar over top of cake. Yield: 12 servings (serving size: 1 piece).

CALORIES 167 (4% from fat); PROTEIN 2.9g; FAT 0.7g (sat 0.3g, mono 0g, poly 0.1g); CARB 37.4g; FIBER 0.2g; CHOL 0mg; IRON 1.8mg; SODIUM 162mg; CALC 31mg

---

MENU

FRUITED
CORNISH HENS

*Couscous
or rice*

ORANGE-KISSED
BRUSSELS
SPROUTS

BOURBON
BREAD
PUDDING WITH
BUTTERSCOTCH
SAUCE

*525 calories and 7.6
grams fat (13% fat)
per menu serving*

It's All in the Game

Here's a sumptuous feast you can throw together with little time or planning. These Fruited Cornish Hens are guaranteed to impress.

Here's what you do: Arrive home from work, then announce what a hard day it was. After some lamenting—"Gosh, I barely have the energy to cook. Whatever can I find in the cupboard to make?"—you stagger into the kitchen, ever the martyr. An hour later, you emerge with an exotic repast that will have everyone's jaw on the floor.

No, this is not some David Copperfield trick, all smoke and mirrors. There is, however, a method to our magic, so let us pull back the curtains and show you how it's done. First of all, the exotic ingredients that make these Cornish hens so tasty are actually easy to find or substitute. Second, we've carefully chosen a dessert that can cook in the oven with the hens: same time, same temperature. While the entrée and dessert bake away, cook the couscous (or rice, if you prefer) and steam the Brussels sprouts. Later, after the main course is completed and everyone leaps up to clear the table in a display of newfound respect, heat the butterscotch sauce to pour over the dessert.

FRUITED CORNISH HENS

Remember to add the fruit after 50 minutes.

2   (1¼-pound) Cornish hens
2   tablespoons Madras curry powder
     Vegetable cooking spray
½   cup mango chutney
¼   cup fresh lime juice
¾   cup coarsely chopped Rome apple
¾   cup coarsely chopped Anjou pear
¾   cup coarsely peeled, chopped kiwifruit
¾   cup cranberries

Preheat oven to 450°.
Remove and discard giblets from hens. Rinse hens under cold water, and pat dry. Remove skin, and trim excess fat; split hens in half lengthwise using an electric knife. Rub hen halves with curry powder. Place hen halves, meaty sides up, in a shallow roasting pan coated with cooking spray. Bake at 450° for 25 minutes.
Combine chutney and lime juice; stir well.
Reduce oven temperature to 350°, and brush chutney mixture over hen halves. Bake for 25 minutes. Arrange apple, pear, kiwifruit, and cranberries around hen halves in pan; bake an additional 10 minutes or until hen juices run clear.
Place 1 hen half and ¾ cup fruit on each of 4 plates. Yield: 4 servings.
Note: Frozen, thawed cranberries may be substituted for fresh cranberries, if desired.

CALORIES 264 (17% from fat); PROTEIN 17.4g; FAT 5.1g (sat 1.2g, mono 1.8g, poly 1.1g); CARB 39.1g; FIBER 4.1g; CHOL 49mg; IRON 2.3mg; SODIUM 117mg; CALC 51mg

◆ You can substitute one broiler-fryer chicken for two Cornish hens. If you do, though, remember that the cooking times may vary slightly.

◆ If you like, you can substitute steamed broccoli for the Brussels sprouts; the orange rind provides a nice flavor complement to either vegetable.

◆ Madras curry powder, which is hotter than regular curry powder, gives the Cornish hens a big flavor boost. If you can't find Madras, however, regular curry powder is fine.

◆ We call for mango chutney, but any fruit chutney will work.

◆ The fruits that accompany the Cornish hens—kiwifruit, pear, apple, and cranberries—are nice winter pairings with the Brussels sprouts.

◆ You can easily split the Cornish hens with kitchen scissors.

◆ This menu works well as a special meal for company.

ORANGE-KISSED BRUSSELS SPROUTS

When you grate the orange rind, avoid the bitter-tasting white layer, or pith, just beneath the surface.

1 **pound Brussels sprouts, trimmed and halved**
1 **teaspoon grated orange rind**
⅓ **cup fresh orange juice**
¼ **teaspoon salt**
⅛ **teaspoon pepper**

Arrange Brussels sprouts in a steamer basket over boiling water. Cover and steam 15 minutes or until tender. Drain Brussels sprouts, and return to pan. Add orange rind, orange juice, salt, and pepper; cook over medium heat 1 minute, stirring constantly. Yield: 4 servings (serving size: ¾ cup).

CALORIES 53 (1% from fat); PROTEIN 3.6g; FAT 0.3g (sat 0.1g, mono 0g, poly 0.2g); CARB 11.5g; FIBER 4.5g; CHOL 0mg; IRON 1.5mg; SODIUM 172mg; CALC 46mg

BOURBON BREAD PUDDING WITH BUTTERSCOTCH SAUCE

1 **(16-ounce) loaf unsliced French bread**
2 **cups skim milk**
½ **cup firmly packed brown sugar**
¼ **cup bourbon**
1½ **teaspoons vanilla extract**
2 **eggs**
⅔ **cup golden raisins**
Vegetable cooking spray
½ **cup fat-free butterscotch-flavored sundae syrup**

Preheat oven to 350°.

Trim crust from bread, using a serrated knife, and discard crust. Cut bread into 1-inch cubes. Arrange bread cubes in a single layer on a baking sheet. Bake at 350° for 18 minutes or until toasted.

Combine skim milk, brown sugar, bourbon, vanilla extract, and eggs in a large bowl; stir well. Add bread cubes and raisins; toss gently. Cover and chill 45 minutes.

Spoon mixture into a 9-inch square baking dish coated with cooking spray. Cover and bake at 350° for 30 minutes. Uncover and bake an additional 25 minutes or until pudding is set.

Pour syrup into a small microwave-safe bowl. Microwave at HIGH 30 seconds or until warm. Serve syrup with bread pudding. Yield: 9 servings (serving size: 1 piece pudding and 1 tablespoon syrup).

Note: For a dessert that's even easier to prepare, top a commercial light pound cake or angel food cake with fat-free butterscotch-flavored sundae syrup.

CALORIES 208 (10% from fat); PROTEIN 6g; FAT 2.2g (sat 0.6g, mono 0.7g, poly 0.9g); CARB 40.8g; FIBER 0.7g; CHOL 51mg; IRON 1.1mg; SODIUM 223mg; CALC 98mg

2 (1¼-pound) Cornish hens

skim milk

1 (16-ounce) loaf unsliced French bread

eggs

brown sugar

vanilla

2 limes

1 large Rome apple

1 large Anjou pear

2 or 3 kiwifruit

1 (12-ounce) package fresh or frozen cranberries

1 large orange

1 pound Brussels sprouts

fat-free butterscotch-flavored sundae syrup

bourbon

raisins

Madras curry powder

mango chutney

Under the Sea

There's no mystery to cooking fresh oysters, clams, and mussels. Low in fat and high in protein, these underwater treasures make hearty winter dishes.

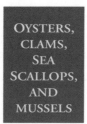

OYSTERS, CLAMS, SEA SCALLOPS, AND MUSSELS

These gifts from the sea (called bivalves because they have two shells that are hinged together) are some of man's oldest, most accessible food sources. If you've yet to cook with bivalves, the time of year to begin is January, when oysters, clams, and mussels are at their most plentiful.

Most of our recipes call for cooking the bivalves in their shells, which makes for a dramatic table presentation—as the shells gently open, like flowers in time-lapse photography, the treasures within infuse other ingredients, such as parsley, tomatoes, and garlic, with their aromatic juices.

How do they fare nutritionally? Oysters contain just 2 grams of fat and 60 calories in a 3-ounce serving. Clams are among the leanest of bivalves, with only 1 gram of fat and 60 calories per 3 ounces of edible meat. A 3-ounce serving of mussels contains 73 calories and 2 grams of fat.

MUSSELS MARINARA

1 tablespoon olive oil
1 cup finely chopped onion
3 garlic cloves, minced
2 cups chopped tomato
½ cup dry white wine
⅓ cup chopped fresh flat-leaf parsley
2 tablespoons chopped fresh basil
½ teaspoon salt
½ teaspoon black pepper
¼ teaspoon crushed red pepper
2 bay leaves
5 pounds fresh mussels, scrubbed and debearded (about 100 mussels)
5 cups hot cooked linguine (10 ounces uncooked pasta)
Basil sprigs (optional)

Heat oil in a large stockpot over medium-high heat until hot. Add onion and garlic; sauté 3 minutes. Add tomato and next 7 ingredients; cook over medium heat 5 minutes.

Add mussels; cover and cook 10 minutes or until mussels open. Discard bay leaves and any unopened shells.

Place 1 cup linguine in each shallow bowl. Remove mussels from tomato mixture, using a slotted spoon. Place mussels over pasta in each bowl. Spoon tomato mixture over each serving. Garnish with basil sprigs, if desired. Yield: 5 servings (serving size: about 1 cup pasta, 20 mussels, and ½ cup sauce).

CALORIES 305 (17% from fat); PROTEIN 16g; FAT 5.6g; (sat 0.9g, mono 2.5g, poly 1.2g); CARB 47.6g; FIBER 4.1g; CHOL 20mg; IRON 5.8mg; SODIUM 451mg; CALC 56mg

PASTA SHELLS WITH SEAFOOD-TOMATO SAUCE

Sea scallops are also bivalves and are available fresh in the winter.

2½ pounds small fresh clams, scrubbed (about 45 clams)
¾ pound fresh mussels, scrubbed and debearded (about 10 mussels)
2 tablespoons cornmeal
Vegetable cooking spray
2 tablespoons olive oil
3 cups chopped onion
2 cups diced green bell pepper
4 garlic cloves, minced
½ cup chopped fresh parsley
½ cup dry red wine
½ teaspoon salt
½ teaspoon pepper
¼ teaspoon dried rosemary, crushed
¼ teaspoon dried thyme
2 (14½-ounce) cans no-salt-added whole tomatoes, undrained and chopped
1 (8-ounce) bottle clam juice
1 (8-ounce) can no-salt-added tomato sauce
1 pound medium-size shrimp, peeled and deveined
1 pound sea scallops
10 cups hot cooked small pasta shells (about 1¼ pounds uncooked pasta)

Place clams and mussels in a large bowl, and cover with cold water. Sprinkle with cornmeal; let stand 30 minutes. Drain and rinse.

Coat a large Dutch oven with cooking spray; add olive oil, and place over medium heat until hot. Add onion, bell pepper, and garlic; sauté 5 minutes.

Add chopped parsley and next 8 ingredients; bring to a boil. Cover, reduce heat, and simmer 1 hour, stirring occasionally.

Add clams, mussels, shrimp, and sea scallops, and stir well. Cover and cook over medium heat 8 minutes or until clam and mussel shells open and shrimp and sea scallops are done. Discard any unopened shells. Serve over pasta. Yield: 10 servings (serving size: 1½ cups seafood mixture and 1 cup pasta).

CALORIES 386 (12% from fat); PROTEIN 27.1g; FAT 5.2g (sat 0.7g, mono 2.3g, poly 1.2g); CARB 56.9g; FIBER 3g; CHOL 75mg; IRON 7.1mg; SODIUM 348mg; CALC 101mg

ITALIAN SEAFOOD SALAD

This salad is best served at room temperature.

1 large red bell pepper
¼ cup dry white wine
16 small fresh clams (about 13 ounces), scrubbed
16 fresh mussels (about 10 ounces), scrubbed and debearded
12 medium-size shrimp (about ¼ pound), peeled and deveined
2 tablespoons chopped fresh flat-leaf parsley
1½ tablespoons fresh lemon juice
1½ teaspoons extra-virgin olive oil
¼ teaspoon salt
⅛ to ¼ teaspoon dried rosemary, crushed
⅛ teaspoon pepper
4 medium pitted ripe olives, halved
4 pitted green olives, halved
1 garlic clove, crushed
4 (1-ounce) slices Italian bread, toasted
Lemon wedges (optional)
Parsley sprigs (optional)

Cut bell pepper in half lengthwise; discard seeds and membranes. Place pepper, skin side up, on a foil-lined baking sheet; flatten with hand. Broil 10 minutes or until blackened. Place bell pepper in a heavy-duty, zip-top plastic bag, and seal; let stand 15 minutes. Peel pepper. Cut bell pepper into julienne strips; set aside.

Bring wine to a boil in a large skillet. Add clams, mussels, and shrimp; cover, reduce heat, and simmer 5 minutes or until clam and mussel shells open. Discard any unopened shells. Remove shellfish with a slotted spoon, and set aside. Reserve 1 tablespoon

cooking liquid; discard remaining liquid. Remove meat from 12 clam and 12 mussel shells; discard shells. Set aside remaining 4 clams and 4 mussels in shells. Cut cooked shrimp in half lengthwise.

Combine shelled clams and mussels, shrimp, reserved cooking liquid, bell pepper, chopped parsley, and next 8 ingredients in a bowl; toss well. Cover and chill at least 2 hours. Let stand at room temperature 20 minutes before serving. Serve with bread slices and remaining clams and mussels in shells. Garnish with lemon wedges and parsley sprigs, if desired. Yield: 4 servings (serving size: ⅓ cup salad, 1 clam, 1 mussel, and 1 slice toast).

CALORIES 164 (21% from fat); PROTEIN 11.6g; FAT 3.9g (sat 0.6g, mono 2.1g, poly 0.7g); CARB 20.5g; FIBER 1.7g; CHOL 47mg; IRON 4.2mg; SODIUM 481mg; CALC 42mg

BUYING, STORING, CLEANING

◆ Bivalves must be alive when you buy them, so it's important that shells are not chipped, cracked, or open. To determine if bivalves that gape are still alive, tap them a few times on a counter. If they close, they're alive.

◆ Store bivalves between 32° and 40°F (keep mussels at the low end and clams at the high end) in net bags, on trays, or in large bowls draped with wet cloths. If kept in closed containers, bivalves suffocate.

◆ Before preparing clams, place them in a sink or bowl full of water, and add a couple of tablespoons of cornmeal. The clams will eat the meal and rid themselves of sand and grit. Afterwards, scrub them thoroughly under cool running water.

◆ Snip the beards from mussels just prior to cooking.

FETTUCCINE WITH MUSSELS AND MUSHROOMS

2 pounds fresh mussels, scrubbed and debearded (about 48 mussels)
2 tablespoons cornmeal
3 cups sliced fresh mushrooms
1½ cups low-salt chicken broth
1 cup red bell pepper rings
½ cup chopped onion
½ cup thinly sliced carrot
½ cup dry white wine
½ teaspoon salt
½ teaspoon dried basil
½ teaspoon dried oregano
¼ teaspoon black pepper
⅛ teaspoon dried crushed red pepper flakes
1 (14½-ounce) can no-salt-added whole tomatoes, undrained and chopped
1 garlic clove, minced
4 cups hot cooked fettuccine (about 8 ounces uncooked pasta)
¼ cup chopped fresh parsley

Place mussels in a large bowl, and cover with cold water. Sprinkle with cornmeal; let stand 30 minutes. Drain and rinse.

Combine mushrooms and next 12 ingredients in a large Dutch oven; bring to a boil. Reduce heat, and simmer, uncovered, 3 minutes. Add mussels; cover and cook over medium-high heat 3 minutes or until mussels open. Discard any unopened shells.

Spoon fettuccine into shallow bowls; top with mushroom sauce and mussels. Sprinkle with parsley. Yield: 4 servings (serving size: 1 cup pasta, 1½ cups mushroom sauce, 12 mussels, and 1 tablespoon parsley).

CALORIES 302 (10% from fat); PROTEIN 16.6g; FAT 3.2g (sat 0.4g, mono 0.9g, poly 1.1g); CARB 52.6g; FIBER 4.3g; CHOL 16mg; IRON 6.5mg; SODIUM 512mg; CALC 85mg

CREOLE OYSTER PO' BOY

New Orleans legend says this sandwich was brought home by mischievous husbands to placate their wives, so it was nicknamed "The Peacemaker."

⅓ cup cornmeal
⅓ cup fine, dry breadcrumbs
½ teaspoon garlic powder
¼ teaspoon salt
¼ teaspoon ground red pepper
¼ teaspoon black pepper
2 tablespoons low-fat buttermilk
1 egg white
2 (10-ounce) containers standard oysters, drained
Vegetable cooking spray
1 (1-pound) loaf French bread (about 16 inches long)
Creole Mayonnaise
2 cups thinly sliced iceberg lettuce
24 thin tomato slices

Combine first 6 ingredients in a bowl. Combine buttermilk and egg white. Dip oysters in buttermilk mixture; dredge in cornmeal mixture.

Coat a large nonstick skillet with cooking spray, and place over medium heat until hot. Add oysters; cook 3 minutes on each side or until browned.

Cut bread loaf in half horizontally, and spread Creole Mayonnaise over cut sides of bread. Arrange lettuce and tomato slices over bottom half of loaf; top with oysters and top half of loaf. Cut loaf into 8 pieces. Serve immediately. Yield: 8 sandwiches.

CALORIES 285 (15% from fat); PROTEIN 11.5g; FAT 4.8g (sat 1.3g, mono 0.8g, poly 2.2g); CARB 46.3g; FIBER 2.6g; CHOL 35mg; IRON 6.1mg; SODIUM 655mg; CALC 74mg

Creole Mayonnaise:

¼ cup reduced-fat mayonnaise
1 tablespoon minced green onions
1 tablespoon minced fresh parsley
2 teaspoons sweet pickle relish
2 teaspoons Creole or other coarse-grained mustard
1 teaspoon capers
½ teaspoon hot sauce

Combine all ingredients in a bowl; stir well, and set aside. Yield: ⅓ cup (serving size: 2 teaspoons).

CALORIES 24 (60% from fat); PROTEIN 0.1g; FAT 1.6g (sat 0.5g, mono 0g, poly 1g); CARB 2.2g; FIBER 0.1g; CHOL 0mg; IRON 0.1mg; SODIUM 136mg; CALC 1mg

MOULES MARINIÈRE

Moules means "mussels" in French, while marinière *refers to a sauce made with onions, white wine, and herbs.*

2 cups dry white wine
1 cup finely chopped onion
⅓ cup chopped fresh flat-leaf parsley
½ teaspoon salt
½ teaspoon freshly ground pepper
4 thyme sprigs
3 garlic cloves, minced
2 bay leaves
5 pounds fresh mussels, scrubbed and debearded (about 100 mussels)
1½ tablespoons all-purpose flour
1½ tablespoons margarine, softened
5 (1-ounce) slices French bread

Combine first 8 ingredients in a large stockpot; stir well. Add mussels; cover and cook over high heat 13 minutes or until mussels open, stirring well after 3 minutes. Discard thyme, bay leaves, and any unopened shells. Remove mussels with a slotted spoon; spoon evenly into 5 individual shallow bowls.

Combine flour and margarine in a small bowl; stir well. Add flour mixture to wine mixture, stirring with a wire whisk until blended. Bring to a boil, and cook 8 minutes or until slightly thickened.

Spoon the white wine mixture over mussels. Serve with French bread slices. Yield: 5 servings (serving size: about 20 mussels, ¾ cup sauce, and 1 slice bread).

CALORIES 200 (24% from fat); PROTEIN 12.1g; FAT 5.3g (sat 1g, mono 1.9g, poly 1.5g); CARB 25.5g; FIBER 1.7g; CHOL 20mg; IRON 4.3mg; SODIUM 654mg; CALC 49mg

WHAT TO LOOK FOR

• **OYSTERS** • Oysters usually take the name of the place where they grow. Regardless of their habitat, oysters are generally one of the following species: The **Atlantic**, or **Eastern**, **oyster** has a salty flavor and slightly fatty texture; The plump, juicy **European oyster** is farmed off the coasts of New England, California, and Washington, and has a mild, rather sweet taste; The **Pacific oyster** tastes mild and sweet, although those from California may taste stronger. When cooking with oysters, keep the fatter ones for frying and baking and the smaller ones for soups and stuffings.

• **CLAMS** • While oysters can be eaten whole regardless of size, the larger the clam, the more likely it is to be chopped up or tenderized before being consumed. Tiny imported **Manila clams**, for example, are simply steamed, whereas the giant, leathery **geoduck** (pronounced "gooey duck") has to be pounded for sautéing. The **surf clam** is by far the most common variety; it's generally minced for chowders or cut into strips for breading. **Soft-shell clams** are usually fried or steamed in the shell. The **soft-shelled steamer** is the pride of New England; the **razor clam** (the shell resembles a straight razor) is its West Coast counterpart. The clams most often sold in markets are the hard-shells. **Littlenecks**, the smallest, are ideal for steaming. The larger **cherrystones** and **topneck clams** can be steamed or baked. **Chowder clams** are chopped up for soups and stews because their meat is rather chewy.

• **MUSSELS** • There are two varieties of mussels generally available in the United States: the **blue** (or **common**) **mussel** and the **New Zealand mussel**. The blue mussel has a shiny black exterior and an iridescent blue interior shell. The New Zealand mussel is also called the **green-shelled mussel** because of its color.

and top with clams. Serve with lemon wedges. Yield: 4 servings (serving size: 2 cups pasta, ½ cup wine sauce, and 9 clams).

CALORIES 429 (9% from fat); PROTEIN 16.4g; FAT 4.4g (sat 0.6g, mono 1.9g, poly 1g); CARB 82.1g; FIBER 4.7g; CHOL 7mg; IRON 7.7mg; SODIUM 321mg; CALC 73mg

LINGUINE
WITH CLAM SAUCE

Leaving the clams in their shells adds visual interest.

36	small fresh clams (about 2 pounds), scrubbed
2	tablespoons cornmeal
2	teaspoons olive oil
3	tablespoons chopped shallots
1½	cups dry white wine
⅓	cup minced fresh flat-leaf parsley
½	teaspoon salt
¼	to ½ teaspoon dried crushed red pepper flakes
¼	teaspoon black pepper
8	garlic cloves, minced
8	cups hot cooked linguine (about 16 ounces uncooked pasta)
4	lemon wedges

Place clams in a large bowl; cover with cold water. Sprinkle with cornmeal; let stand 30 minutes. Drain clams, and rinse well.

Heat oil in a large non-stick skillet over medium-high heat until hot. Add shallots; sauté 2 minutes. Add wine and next 5 ingredients; bring to a boil. Add clams; cover, reduce heat, and simmer 5 minutes or until shells open. Discard any unopened shells. Remove clams with a slotted spoon, and set aside.

Place pasta in each of 4 shallow bowls; spoon wine sauce over pasta,

SPANISH SHELLFISH

This is an impressive, yet easy, first course. It is typical of the kind of dish you might see in tapas bars in Spain.

¼	cup dry sherry
⅛	teaspoon saffron threads, crushed
	Vegetable cooking spray
¾	cup julienne-cut red bell pepper
½	cup chopped onion
¼	cup diced low-sodium 96%-fat-free ham
2	garlic cloves, minced
⅓	cup canned crushed tomatoes
1	tablespoon chopped almonds, toasted
¼	teaspoon salt
¼	teaspoon pepper
12	small fresh clams (about 10 ounces), scrubbed
12	fresh mussels (about ½ pound), scrubbed and debearded
12	medium-size shrimp (about ¼ pound), peeled and deveined
1	tablespoon chopped fresh parsley

Combine sherry and saffron in a small bowl; set aside.

Coat a large skillet with cooking spray; place over medium-high heat until hot. Add bell pepper, onion, ham, and garlic; sauté 4 minutes. Add sherry mixture, tomatoes, almonds, salt, and pepper; bring mixture to a boil. Add clams; cover, reduce heat, and simmer 3 minutes. Add mussels; cover and simmer 3 minutes. Add shrimp; cover and simmer an additional 5 minutes or until clam and mussel shells open. Discard any unopened shells. Sprinkle with

chopped parsley. Yield: 4 servings (serving size: 3 clams, 3 mussels, 3 shrimp, and ¼ cup tomato mixture).

CALORIES 93 (24% from fat); PROTEIN 11.1g; FAT 2.5g (sat 0.3g, mono 0.9g, poly 0.6g); CARB 6.5g; FIBER 1.1g; CHOL 54mg; IRON 2.9mg; SODIUM 329mg; CALC 45mg

Grateful for Soup

On a cold winter's day, there's nothing like a warm bowl of soup to resuscitate your body and soul.

Not only are old-fashioned winter soups fortified by beans and whole grains up-to-date nutritionally, they're also the soul of economy. Soups usually require only the humblest cuts of meat—your neighborhood butcher may even throw in the soupbone for free. And if extra company arrives unexpectedly, soups have a way of "growing" to meet the need—more easily, perhaps, than does the dining-room table.

BEAN-AND-PASTA STEW

By jazzing up a commercial soup mix, we have created a soup that tastes homemade without all the time and effort.

2 cups water
½ cup sliced carrot
1 tablespoon chili powder
2 tablespoons tomato paste
1 (14.5-ounce) can no-salt-added stewed tomatoes
3 (10½-ounce) cans low-salt chicken broth
1 (4.9-ounce) package bean medley with pasta soup mix (such as Kettle Creations)
2 cups torn fresh spinach

Combine first 7 ingredients in a large Dutch oven, and bring to a boil. Reduce heat, and simmer, uncovered, for 25 minutes or until the beans are tender, stirring occasionally. Add spinach, and cook an additional 5 minutes. Yield: 5 servings (serving size: 1½ cups).

CALORIES 171 (15% from fat); PROTEIN 8.7g; FAT 2.8g (sat 0.7g, mono 0.9g, poly 0.5g); CARB 29.6g; FIBER 5.2g; CHOL 0mg; IRON 3.3mg; SODIUM 667mg; CALC 81mg

TURKEY-AND-BLACK BEAN CHILI

This slightly sweet chili is reminiscent of picadillo, a Hispanic dish made with raisins. In this recipe, we use prunes.

1¼ pounds ground raw turkey breast
1 teaspoon vegetable oil
1¼ cups finely chopped onion
3 garlic cloves, finely chopped
1 tablespoon chili powder
2 teaspoons dried oregano
1 teaspoon ground cumin
½ teaspoon salt
¼ teaspoon ground red pepper
2¼ cups water
12 whole pitted prunes (about ¼ pound), chopped
1 (15-ounce) can black beans, undrained

Cook turkey in a large nonstick skillet over medium-high heat until browned, stirring to crumble. Drain in a colander.

Heat oil in skillet over medium heat until hot. Add onion and garlic, and sauté 7 minutes. Add chili powder, oregano, cumin, salt, and red pepper; cook 1 minute.

Return turkey to skillet; stir in 2¼ cups water, prunes, and beans. Bring to a boil; reduce heat, and simmer, uncovered, 5 minutes. Serve Turkey-and-Black Bean Chili over rice, if desired. Yield: 5 servings (serving size: 1 cup).

CALORIES 281 (8% from fat); PROTEIN 32.3g; FAT 2.5g (sat 0.5g, mono 0.6g, poly 0.8g); CARB 33.7g; FIBER 8.4g; CHOL 71mg; IRON 4.4mg; SODIUM 430mg; CALC 73mg

CHUNKY VEGETABLE SOUP

Yielding 12 cups, this soup goes a long way. With our freezing instructions, you can reheat it for future meals.

Vegetable cooking spray
2 teaspoons vegetable oil
1 cup chopped onion
2 garlic cloves, minced
7 cups water
1 tablespoon dried basil
¾ teaspoon salt
½ teaspoon dried marjoram
½ teaspoon pepper
1 pound red potatoes, cut into 1-inch cubes
½ pound small carrots, cut into 1-inch pieces
1 (15½-ounce) can cannellini beans or other white beans, drained
1 (14.5-ounce) can whole tomatoes, undrained and chopped
1 (10-ounce) package frozen large lima beans
½ cup uncooked orzo (rice-shaped pasta)
½ cup shredded part-skim mozzarella cheese

Coat a large Dutch oven with cooking spray; add oil, and place over medium-high heat until hot. Add chopped onion and garlic; sauté 5 minutes or until onion is tender. Add water and next 9 ingredients; bring to a boil. Cover, reduce heat, and simmer 20 minutes.

Add orzo; cook, uncovered, over medium heat an additional 10 minutes. Ladle soup into individual bowls, and sprinkle with cheese. Yield: 8 servings (serving size: 1½ cups soup and 1 tablespoon cheese).

Note: Refrigerate remaining soup in an airtight container for up to 1 week, or freeze it for up to 3 months.

CALORIES 224 (12% from fat); PROTEIN 10.6g; FAT 2.9g (sat 1g, mono 0.7g, poly 0.8g); CARB 40.4g; FIBER 5.2g; CHOL 4mg; IRON 3.3mg; SODIUM 574mg; CALC 127mg

BEAN-AND-BARLEY SOUP

Smoked turkey sausage adds considerable flavor to this healthy, high-fiber soup.

- 1 tablespoon olive oil
- 1 cup chopped onion
- 1 cup chopped carrot
- ½ cup chopped celery
- 2 garlic cloves, minced
- ½ cup uncooked pearl barley
- ¼ pound smoked turkey sausage, cut into ½-inch cubes
- 2 cups frozen baby lima beans
- 1¾ cups water
- ⅛ teaspoon pepper
- 2 (14¼-ounce) cans fat-free chicken broth
- 1 (14.5-ounce) can diced tomatoes, undrained
- ½ teaspoon hot sauce

Heat oil in a large Dutch oven over medium-high heat until hot. Add chopped onion, carrot, celery, and garlic; sauté 5 minutes.

Add barley and sausage; sauté 4 minutes. Add beans, water, pepper, broth, and tomatoes; bring to a boil. Reduce heat, and simmer, uncovered, 45 minutes. Remove from heat; stir in hot sauce. Yield: 6 servings (serving size: 1½ cups).

CALORIES 228 (26% from fat); PROTEIN 13.4g; FAT 6.7g (sat 1.6g, mono 3.3g, poly 1.3g); CARB 29.5g; FIBER 4.9g; CHOL 16mg; IRON 2.4mg; SODIUM 423mg; CALC 78mg

MENU SUGGESTION

VEGETARIAN MINESTRONE

Cantaloupe slices

Crusty bread

*Fat-free chocolate snack cake

*When there's no time to bake from scratch, pick up a fat-free snack cake mix. All you need are the mix, egg whites, water, and 30 minutes.

VEGETARIAN MINESTRONE

This earthy, elegant soup is probably one of our most economical, using ingredients that are commonly on hand.

- 2 teaspoons olive oil
- ¾ cup chopped onion
- 3 cups water
- 2 cups diced zucchini
- 1 cup diced carrot
- 1 cup drained canned cannellini beans or other white beans
- ¾ cup diced celery
- ½ teaspoon dried basil
- ¼ teaspoon salt
- ¼ teaspoon dried oregano
- ⅛ teaspoon coarsely ground pepper
- 1 (14.5-ounce) can diced tomatoes, undrained
- 1 garlic clove, minced
- ¼ cup uncooked ditalini (very short tubular macaroni) or elbow macaroni
- 1 tablespoon plus 1 teaspoon grated Parmesan cheese

Heat oil in a large saucepan over medium-high heat until hot. Add onion; sauté 4 minutes or until lightly browned.

Add water and next 10 ingredients to saucepan; bring to a boil. Cover, reduce heat to medium-low, and cook 25 minutes.

Add pasta; cover and cook an additional 10 minutes. Ladle into individual bowls, and sprinkle with cheese. Yield: 4 servings (serving size: 1½ cups soup and 1 teaspoon cheese).

CALORIES 176 (17% from fat); PROTEIN 8.8g; FAT 3.3g (sat 0.7g, mono 1.9g, poly 0.5g); CARB 30.2g; FIBER 4.4g; CHOL 1mg; IRON 2.9mg; SODIUM 699mg; CALC 112mg

WHITE BEAN SOUP

Originating from a Brazilian recipe, this piquant soup gets its thickness from the puréed beans. This dish requires minimal work, mostly chopping the ham and onion.

- 1 pound Great Northern beans or other white beans
- 1 tablespoon olive oil
- 1 cup minced fresh onion
- ¾ cup diced lean smoked ham
- 2 tablespoons seeded, minced jalapeño pepper
- 1 garlic clove, minced
- 7 cups water
- ¾ teaspoon salt
- ¼ teaspoon pepper
- ¼ cup chopped fresh flat-leaf parsley

Sort and wash beans, and place in a Dutch oven. Cover with water to 2 inches above beans. Bring to a boil; cook 2 minutes. Remove from heat; cover and let stand 1 hour. Drain beans; set aside. Wipe pan with a paper towel.

Heat oil in pan over medium heat until hot. Add onion, ham, jalapeño pepper, and garlic; sauté 7 minutes or until onion is tender. Add beans, water, salt, and pepper; bring to a boil. Partially cover, reduce heat, and simmer 1 hour.

Place 2 cups of bean mixture in a blender or food processor; cover and process until smooth. Return purée to pan; stir in parsley. Yield: 5 servings (serving size: 1½ cups).

CALORIES 381 (12% from fat); PROTEIN 25.2g; FAT 5.1g (sat 1.1g, mono 2.7g, poly 0.8g); CARB 60.7g; FIBER 11.8g; CHOL 12mg; IRON 5.7mg; SODIUM 640mg; CALC 174mg

Chinese Take-In

MENU

ORIENTAL
FLANK STEAK

EGG FRIED
RICE

*Steamed
broccoli*

*Fortune
cookies*

About 577 calories
and 18 grams fat
(28% calories
from fat)

Why order out when you can make Egg Fried Rice and Oriental Flank Steak at home? They're easy and impressive–and there are no little boxes to dispose of.

Should you open your fortune cookie early, don't be surprised if it says, "Great success awaits you." With this foolproof Chinese menu—Oriental Flank Steak complemented by Egg Fried Rice—that forecast is guaranteed. Serve the steak and rice with steamed broccoli, and you have a complete Chinese dinner—one that's probably far lighter and healthier than comparable fare from the local take-out joint. And should you possess the patience to wait until after dinner to open your fortune cookie, don't be surprised if it says, "You have many admirers."

SHOPPING
LIST

bean sprouts
garlic
green onions
broccoli
soy sauce
rice
sesame oil
sesame seeds
fortune cookies
frozen green peas
4 eggs
flank steak

ORIENTAL FLANK STEAK

¼ cup soy sauce
1 teaspoon sugar
2 garlic cloves, minced
1 (1¼-pound) flank steak
1 teaspoon sesame seeds, toasted

Combine soy sauce, sugar, and garlic. Place flank steak on a broiler pan; broil 8 minutes on each side or until desired degree of doneness, basting occasionally with soy sauce mixture. Sprinkle with sesame seeds, and cut diagonally across the grain into thin slices. Yield: 5 servings (serving size: 3 ounces).

CALORIES 180 (53% from fat); PROTEIN 18.1g; FAT 10.5g (sat 4.4g, mono 4.4g, poly 0.5g); CARB 2.4g; FIBER 0g; CHOL 48mg; IRON 2.1mg; SODIUM 720mg; CALC 14mg

EGG FRIED RICE

2 teaspoons dark sesame oil
2 eggs
2 egg whites
1 tablespoon vegetable oil
4 cups cold, cooked rice
1 cup frozen green peas, thawed
¾ teaspoon salt
¼ teaspoon pepper
1 cup bean sprouts
⅓ cup chopped green onions

Combine the sesame oil, eggs, and egg whites in a small bowl; stir well, and set aside.

Heat vegetable oil in a large nonstick skillet or wok over medium-high heat until hot. Add egg mixture, and stir-fry 2 minutes. Add rice; stir-fry 3 minutes. Add green peas, salt, and pepper; stir-fry 5 minutes. Add bean sprouts and green onions; stir-fry 2 minutes. Serve immediately. Yield: 5 servings (serving size: 1 cup).

CALORIES 289 (21% from fat); PROTEIN 9.5g; FAT 6.8g (sat 1.4g, mono 2.3g, poly 2.4g); CARB 45.7g; FIBER 1.2g; CHOL 88mg; IRON 2.5mg; SODIUM 435mg; CALC 42mg

Three Ways to Perfect EGG FRIED RICE

Although the steak requires minimal preparation, the Egg Fried Rice does require a couple of simple tricks. So that it tastes like the real thing and you don't end up with egg on your face, follow these tips.

1. The rice must be cold—that's because cold rice contains less liquid, which allows the oil to coat the grains and keep them from sticking together. You might even want to make the rice the day before.

2. Leave the soy sauce bottle in the pantry. Soy sauce discolors the rice and gives it a soggy, gummy texture.

3. Start with hot oil, in either a large nonstick skillet or a wok. If the temperature is too low, the rice will absorb the oil making the final product taste greasy.

Fruited Cornish Hens, page 28

Romano-Oregano Bread, page 14

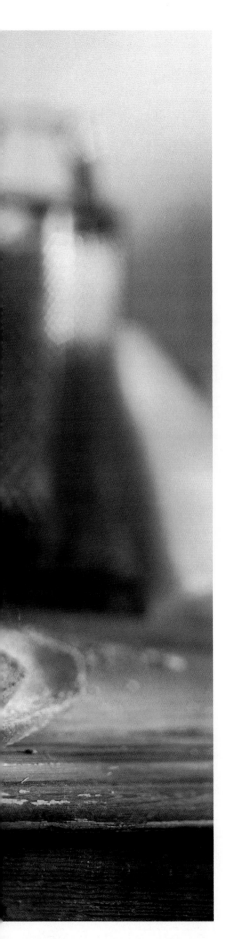

*Mustard-and-Herb-Marinated
Vegetables, page 16*

*Prosciutto-and-Fontina Panini,
page 17*

Chunky Vegetable Soup,
page 34

Mussels Marinara, page 30

Can't Stand the Cold? Get into the Kitchen

And make this New Year your healthiest ever.

This is the classic season for change—this is often when people join a health club, hoping to make good friends who'll keep them there beyond March. It's also the season when folks keep out the cold with cooking comforts. So if you can't stand the cold, get into the kitchen!

When nutrition needs vary in your household, how do you keep from overwhelming yourself in the kitchen? Do you cook two separate meals and then collapse from the effort? Not with my tandemizing concept.

In this column, I'll show you how to satisfy all the folks in your household without preparing two meals at one sitting. This is where the concept of tandemizing comes in: It lets you make delicious, practical meals that suit both a low-fat diet and a more moderate, prevention-focused one.

BRAISED CHICKEN WITH PEPPER SAUCE AND CHEESE POLENTA

Cheese Polenta
Vegetable cooking spray
¼ teaspoon salt
⅛ teaspoon pepper
4 small chicken leg quarters (about 2 pounds), skinned
1 teaspoon olive oil
1 cup chopped onion
3 garlic cloves, chopped
1 cup diced red bell pepper
1 cup low-salt chicken broth
½ cup dry white wine or nonalcoholic wine
2 teaspoons chopped fresh rosemary
2 bay leaves
2 tablespoons no-salt-added tomato paste
4 canned anchovy fillets, finely chopped or 2 teaspoons anchovy paste
1 tablespoon cornstarch
2 tablespoons water
1 teaspoon grated lemon rind

Prepare Cheese Polenta, and spread in bottom of a 9-inch square baking pan coated with cooking spray. Press plastic wrap over surface of polenta, and chill 2 hours or until firm.

Preheat oven to 350°.

Sprinkle salt and pepper over chicken. Coat a large oven-proof Dutch oven with cooking spray; add oil, and place over medium-high heat until hot. Add chicken, and cook 3 minutes on each side or until browned. Remove chicken from pan; set aside. Add onion and garlic, and sauté 2 minutes. Add bell pepper, broth, wine, rosemary, and bay leaves; stir to deglaze pan. Stir in tomato paste and anchovies.

Return chicken to pan; bring to a boil. Bake chicken mixture at 350° for 45 minutes or until done.

Remove chicken from pan with a slotted spoon; set aside, and keep warm. Combine cornstarch and water in a small bowl; stir well. Add cornstarch mixture and lemon rind to pan; bring mixture to a boil, and cook 1 minute or until thickened, stirring constantly. Discard bay leaves. Return chicken to pan, and cook an additional 4 minutes or until thoroughly heated.

Cut polenta into 4 (4½-inch) squares. Cut each square diagonally into 2 triangles. Place polenta triangles on a broiler pan coated with cooking spray, and broil 3 minutes on each side or until lightly browned.

Arrange 1 chicken leg quarter and 2 polenta triangles on each of 4 plates; spoon ½ cup sauce over each serving. Yield: 4 servings.

CALORIES 475 (28% from fat); PROTEIN 44.4g; FAT 15g (sat 6.8g, mono 4.6g, poly 2.8g); CARB 40.3g; FIBER 5.7g; CHOL 155mg; IRON 4.5mg; SODIUM 1,065mg; CALC 73mg

Cheese Polenta:

1¼ cups cornmeal
½ teaspoon salt
4 cups water
½ cup (2 ounces) crumbled Gorgonzola cheese or blue cheese

Place cornmeal and salt in a large saucepan. Gradually add water, stirring constantly with a wire whisk. Bring to a boil, and reduce heat to medium. Cook, uncovered, 15 minutes, stirring often. Remove from heat; stir in cheese. Yield: 4 servings.

CALORIES 185 (26% from fat); PROTEIN 6.1g; FAT 5.3g (sat 2.7g, mono 1.5g, poly 0.7g); CARB 29.4g; FIBER 4.2g; CHOL 14mg; IRON 1.4mg; SODIUM 396mg; CALC 29mg

Lower-Fat Version:

• Omit Gorgonzola cheese from the polenta, and add ¼ teaspoon salt.
• Substitute 4 (6-ounce) skinned chicken breast halves for the leg quarters. Bake per recipe.

CALORIES 334 (14% from fat); PROTEIN 31.9g; FAT 5.1g (sat 0.8g, mono 1.6g, poly 1.2g); CARB 40.2g; FIBER 5.7g; CHOL 66mg; IRON 3.3mg; SODIUM 1,044mg; CALC 38mg

Star Light, Star Bright

Meet the Hollywood chefs who create healthy meals for today's fit celebrities. So that you too can feel like a star, try their delicious recipes at home.

Sharing their favorite low-fat recipes are five Los Angeles-based chefs who, for over a decade, have been counting calories for a list of stellar clients. Even though these chefs are on the cutting edge, preparing food in restaurants and bistros with long waiting lists, their glamorous recipes are easy to make at home. Most are main-course dinner dishes with easy-to-find ingredients. You've seen the stars—now meet their chefs, celebrities in their own field.

BARBECUED SCALLOPS WITH SAFFRON COUSCOUS

—Chef Peter Roelant

¼ cup ketchup
¼ cup plum sauce
2 tablespoons fresh lime juice
1 tablespoon prepared horseradish
⅛ teaspoon pepper
16 large sea scallops (about 1½ pounds)
1¼ cups water
1 cup chopped tomato
⅓ cup diced carrot
⅓ cup chopped onion
¼ cup chopped celery
¼ teaspoon salt
¼ teaspoon saffron threads, crushed
⅛ teaspoon pepper
1 cup uncooked couscous
2 teaspoons extra-virgin olive oil

Combine first 5 ingredients in a bowl; stir well. Arrange scallops in a single layer in a 1½-quart casserole; spoon about 6 tablespoons ketchup mixture over scallops. Cover and chill 30 minutes.

Combine water and next 7 ingredients in a medium saucepan, and bring to a boil; gradually stir in couscous. Remove from heat; cover and let stand 5 minutes. Add oil, and fluff couscous with a fork.

Uncover scallops, and broil 6 minutes on each side or until done.

Spoon couscous mixture onto individual plates; top with scallops, and drizzle remaining ketchup mixture over scallops. Garnish with fresh fruit slices and parsley sprigs, if desired. Yield: 4 servings (serving size: 1 cup couscous, 4 scallops, and 1 tablespoon sauce).

CALORIES 380 (10% from fat); PROTEIN 35g; FAT 4.2g (sat 0.5g, mono 1.8g, poly 0.8g); CARB 50.3g; FIBER 3.2g; CHOL 56mg; IRON 1.9mg; SODIUM 935mg; CALC 67mg

SHRIMP COUSCOUS WITH SEAFOOD BROTH

—Chef Serge Falesitch

1½ pounds unpeeled rock shrimp or medium-sized shrimp
1 teaspoon unsalted butter
1⅓ cups chopped onion
½ cup chopped celery
⅓ cup chopped carrot
1 teaspoon chopped fresh or ¼ teaspoon dried thyme
4 garlic cloves, chopped
6 cups coarsely chopped tomato
4 cups water
1 cup dry white wine
1 tablespoon tomato paste
1 teaspoon unsalted butter
½ teaspoon salt
⅛ teaspoon pepper
1 cup uncooked couscous
1 tablespoon olive oil
1 cup diced red bell pepper
1 cup diced yellow bell pepper
½ cup diced yellow squash
½ cup diced zucchini

Peel shrimp, reserving shells, and devein. Set shrimp aside.

Melt 1 teaspoon butter in a large Dutch oven over medium heat. Add reserved shrimp shells, onion, celery, carrot, thyme, and garlic; sauté 3 minutes. Add tomato, water, wine, and tomato paste; bring to a boil. Reduce heat, and simmer, uncovered, 35 minutes. Place half of seafood broth in a blender, and process until smooth. Strain puréed seafood broth through a sieve into a bowl; discard solids. Repeat entire process with remaining seafood broth.

Combine 1 cup seafood broth, 1 teaspoon butter, salt, and pepper in a medium saucepan, and bring to a boil; gradually stir in couscous. Remove from heat; cover and let stand 5 minutes. Fluff with a fork.

Heat oil in a nonstick skillet over medium-high heat until hot. Add shrimp; sauté 1 minute. Add bell peppers, squash, and zucchini; sauté 3 minutes. Stir in couscous and an additional 1½ cups seafood broth; cook 1 minute. Yield: 6 servings (serving size: 1 cup).

Note: Store remaining seafood broth in an airtight container in refrigerator for up to 1 week, or freeze for up to 3 months.

CALORIES 276 (21% from fat); PROTEIN 27.8g; FAT 6.3g (sat 1.6g, mono 2.4g, poly 1.3g); CARB 27.7g; FIBER 3.2g; CHOL 176mg; IRON 4.7mg; SODIUM 381mg; CALC 79mg

BARLEY RISOTTO WITH JULIENNE CHICKEN AND PARMESAN

—Chef Joachim Splichal

1 tablespoon olive oil
¾ cup diced carrot
1 thyme sprig
¾ cup diced celery
¾ cup thinly sliced leek
½ cup finely chopped onion
½ teaspoon salt
¼ teaspoon pepper
6 (4-ounce) skinned, boned chicken breast halves, cut into ¼-inch strips
1¾ cups uncooked pearl barley (about 12 ounces)
6 cups fat-free chicken broth
1 cup water
⅓ cup chopped fresh flat-leaf parsley
¼ cup freshly grated Parmesan cheese

Heat oil in a Dutch oven over medium-high heat until hot. Add carrot and thyme; sauté 1 minute. Add celery, leek, and onion; sauté 1 minute. Add salt, pepper, and chicken; sauté 5 minutes. Add barley; sauté 1 minute.

Add broth and water; bring to a boil. Cover, reduce heat, and simmer 40 minutes. Remove from heat; discard thyme. Stir in parsley and cheese. Yield: 9 servings (serving size: 1 cup).

CALORIES 281 (12% from fat); PROTEIN 27.6g; FAT 3.8g (sat 1.1g, mono 1.7g, poly 0.6g); CARB 33.9g; FIBER 6.9g; CHOL 46mg; IRON 2mg; SODIUM 362mg; CALC 74mg

TURKEY LOAF

—Chef Yvonne Doone

2 teaspoons vegetable oil
1 cup finely chopped onion
¾ cup finely chopped carrot
½ cup finely chopped green onions
½ cup finely chopped celery
½ cup finely chopped red bell pepper
2 garlic cloves, minced
2½ pounds ground raw turkey breast
1 cup dry breadcrumbs
⅓ cup ketchup
1 teaspoon salt
1 teaspoon pepper
¼ teaspoon ground nutmeg
¼ teaspoon ground cumin
¼ teaspoon ground coriander
4 egg whites, lightly beaten
Vegetable cooking spray
½ cup ketchup
3 tablespoons brown sugar

Preheat oven to 350°.

Heat oil in a large nonstick skillet over medium heat until hot. Add onion and next 5 ingredients; sauté 5 minutes or until tender. Combine onion mixture, ground turkey, and next 8 ingredients in a large bowl; stir well (mixture will be wet).

Shape meat mixture into a 9 x 5-inch loaf on a broiler pan coated with cooking spray. Bake at 350° for 30 minutes. Combine ½ cup ketchup and brown sugar; brush over turkey loaf. Bake an additional 30 minutes or until done; let stand 10 minutes before slicing. Yield: 12 servings (serving size: 1 slice).

CALORIES 186 (10% from fat); PROTEIN 24.4g; FAT 2g (sat 0.4g, mono 0.9g, poly 0.4g); CARB 16.7g; FIBER 1.5g; CHOL 59mg; IRON 2.2mg; SODIUM 533mg; CALC 48mg

HOLLYWOOD CHEFS SHINE BRIGHT

★ PETER ROELANT

In a town generously populated with weight-conscious celebrities, Peter Roelant, chef-proprietor of Four Oaks Restaurant, has gained the devotion of many Oscar-, Emmy-, and Grammy-winning clients. His inventive "haute-healthy" cuisine possesses just the right elements—a fusion of intense and interesting flavors that are fat- and calorie-conscious by nature.

★ SERGE FALESITCH

To win over some of Hollywood's most health-conscious regulars, Serge Falesitch opened a restaurant called Eclipse, specializing in the ultimate low-fat food—fish. He prepares the freshest fish obtainable in a variety of imaginative ways, including hearth-roasted whole fish, as well as broiled, grilled, boiled, steamed, sautéed, and braised dishes.

★ JOACHIM SPLICHAL

At Chef Joachim Splichal's Patina Restaurant you'll find what most everyone in the film business is after: low-fat, reduced-calorie dishes that not only taste delicious but look nothing like diet food.

★ YVONNE DOONE

Yvonne Doone is known for her homey, hearty dishes. She reveals that most of the calories in her recipes come from vegetables, grains, beans, some lean proteins, and little dairy.

★ AKASHA KHALSA

For more than a decade, Akasha Khalsa has created an enlightened vegetarian cuisine that even includes a luscious array of fat-free muffins, cakes, and cookies.

PINEAPPLE UPSIDE-DOWN CAKES

—Chef Akasha Khalsa

Vegetable cooking spray
¼   cup plus 2 tablespoons brown sugar
6   drained canned unsweetened pineapple slices
1¾ cups all-purpose flour
1   teaspoon baking powder
½   teaspoon baking soda
¼   teaspoon salt
¾   cup low-fat buttermilk
¾   cup maple syrup
¼   cup vegetable oil
2   tablespoons vanilla extract
1   tablespoon lemon juice

Preheat oven to 350°.

Coat each cup of a minibundtlette pan with cooking spray. Place 1 tablespoon brown sugar and 1 pineapple slice in the bottom of each cup; set aside.

Combine flour, baking powder, baking soda, and salt in a bowl; make a well in center of mixture. Combine buttermilk, syrup, oil, vanilla, and lemon juice; stir well. Add to flour mixture, stirring just until moistened.

Divide cake batter evenly among prepared minibundtlette cups. Bake at 350° for 30 minutes or until a wooden pick inserted in center of cakes comes out clean. Invert cakes onto a wire rack. Serve warm or at room temperature. Yield: 6 cakes (serving size: 1 cake).

CALORIES 417 (22% from fat); PROTEIN 4.9g; FAT 10.1g (sat 2g, mono 2.7g, poly 4.5g); CARB 75.1g; FIBER 1g; CHOL 0mg; IRON 2.6mg; SODIUM 232mg; CALC 123mg

LIGHTEN UP

Manicotti from Heaven

We've lightened this Italian comfort food, making it delicious without all the fat and calories.
Presenting our low-fat spinach-stuffed manicotti, which tastes just as good as it smells when it's baking in the oven.

FOUR-CHEESE MANICOTTI

If you don't have individual casserole dishes, use a 13 x 9-inch baking dish to prepare this entrée.

12   uncooked manicotti shells
Vegetable cooking spray
½   cup finely chopped onion
3   garlic cloves, minced
1   cup (4 ounces) shredded part-skim mozzarella cheese, divided
½   cup freshly grated Parmesan cheese, divided
1   teaspoon dried Italian seasoning
½   teaspoon pepper
1   (15-ounce) carton nonfat ricotta cheese
1   (6-ounce) package garden vegetable-flavored light cream cheese, softened
4   ounces block nonfat cream cheese, softened
½   (10-ounce) package frozen chopped spinach, thawed, drained, and squeezed dry
1   (27½-ounce) jar reduced-fat, reduced-sodium tomato-and-herb pasta sauce
Oregano sprigs (optional)

Preheat oven to 350°.

Cook pasta according to package directions, omitting salt and fat; set aside.

Coat a small nonstick skillet with cooking spray, and place skillet over medium-high heat until hot. Add onion and garlic; sauté 3 minutes. Remove from heat; set aside.

Combine ½ cup mozzarella cheese, ¼ cup Parmesan cheese, and next 5 ingredients in a bowl; beat at medium speed of an electric mixer until smooth. Stir in onion mixture and spinach.

Spoon mozzarella cheese mixture into cooked manicotti (about ⅓ cup per shell).

Divide 1 cup sauce evenly between 6 individual casserole dishes coated with cooking spray. Arrange 2 stuffed manicotti in each dish. Pour remaining sauce over each serving. Place dishes on a baking sheet. Cover each dish with foil, and bake at 350° for 25 minutes. Sprinkle with remaining mozzarella and Parmesan cheeses; bake, uncovered, an additional 5 minutes. Garnish with oregano, if desired. Yield: 6 servings (serving size: 2 manicotti).

CALORIES 386 (27% from fat); PROTEIN 30g; FAT 11.7g (sat 6.9g, mono 3.1g, poly 0.7g); CARB 41.5g; FIBER 4.3g; CHOL 49mg; IRON 0.9mg; SODIUM 1,012mg; CALC 495mg

BEFORE & AFTER	
SERVING SIZE	
2 manicotti	2 manicotti
CALORIES PER SERVING	
581	386
FAT	
39.3g	11.7g
PERCENT OF TOTAL CALORIES	
61%	27%
CHOLESTEROL	
130mg	49mg
SODIUM	
1,412mg	1,012mg

HOW WE DID IT

• For the cheese filling, we used a nonfat ricotta cheese and a combination of nonfat and light cream cheeses. For added flavor, we used Fleur de Lait, a garden vegetable-flavored light cream cheese.

• We cut the mozzarella and Parmesan cheese by about half.

$\mathcal{M}$ARCH

Always a Comfort

*Meat loaf is back, this time with flair.
We've got seven exciting recipes that take
the dish to new heights.*

Why is meat loaf back in business? Obviously, the comfort factor plays a major role. After a stressful day at work, a ratatouille just doesn't say, "there, there." "The tougher things get, the more we want to be comforted and not feel deprived," says Dr. Joyce Brothers, who is a meat loaf aficionada.

Served with potatoes and a vegetable, nothing's more comforting or American than a meat loaf dinner. But because meat loaf traditionally has a lot of fat and cholesterol, it was our challenge to lighten it significantly. And we've succeeded—these are meat loaves for the millennium, meat loaves that take up where mom's left off.

But no offense to mom: We've included a classic, ketchup-topped meat loaf, too, the kind you remember so fondly from childhood. We've also included a recipe for roasted mashed potatoes, as well as sandwich suggestions for the leftovers.

HERBED MEAT LOAF WITH SUN-DRIED TOMATO GRAVY

Don't bake this meat loaf on a broiler rack or the pan drippings you'll need for the gravy will evaporate.

1 cup sun-dried tomatoes, packed without oil (about 24)
3 cups boiling water
Vegetable cooking spray
1 cup finely chopped onion
1 cup finely chopped green bell pepper
2 garlic cloves, crushed
1 (1-ounce) slice whole wheat bread, torn into small pieces
2 tablespoons 1% low-fat milk
½ cup (2 ounces) shredded sharp provolone cheese
2 teaspoons dried basil
1 teaspoon dried oregano
1 teaspoon pepper
½ teaspoon salt
½ teaspoon dried thyme
2 egg whites
1¾ pounds ultra-lean ground beef
Sun-Dried Tomato Gravy

Combine tomatoes and boiling water in a bowl; cover and let stand 15 minutes or until softened. Drain well, and finely chop; set aside.

Preheat oven to 350°.

Coat a medium nonstick skillet with cooking spray, and place over medium-high heat until hot. Add onion, bell pepper, and garlic; sauté 5 minutes or until tender. Set aside.

Place bread in a large bowl. Drizzle milk over bread; toss well to moisten bread. Add tomatoes, onion mixture, cheese, and next 6 ingredients, stirring well. Crumble beef over tomato mixture, and stir just until mixture is blended.

Pack meat mixture into a 9 x 5-inch loaf pan coated with cooking spray. Bake at 350° for 55 minutes or until meat loaf reaches 170°. Let meat loaf stand in pan 10 minutes.

Remove meat loaf from pan, and reserve drippings for Sun-dried Tomato Gravy, if desired. Cut loaf into 16 slices. Serve with Sun-Dried Tomato Gravy. Yield: 8 servings (serving size: 2 slices and 3 tablespoons gravy).

Sandwich suggestion: Serve leftover meat loaf slices open-faced on toasted sandwich bread; top with gravy.

CALORIES 230 (36% from fat); PROTEIN 24.8g; FAT 9.1g (sat 4g, mono 3.5g, poly 0.5g); CARB 15.1g; FIBER 1.1g; CHOL 71mg; IRON 2mg; SODIUM 752mg; CALC 138mg

Sun-Dried Tomato Gravy:

¼ cup sun-dried tomatoes, packed without oil (about 6)
1 cup boiling water
2½ tablespoons all-purpose flour
1¼ cups 1% low-fat milk
¼ cup meat loaf pan drippings or beef broth
1 tablespoon finely chopped green onions
¼ teaspoon salt
¼ teaspoon dried basil
⅛ teaspoon pepper

Combine tomatoes and boiling water in a bowl; cover and let stand 15 minutes or until softened. Drain well, and finely chop; set aside.

Place flour in a small saucepan; gradually add milk, stirring with a wire whisk until blended. Stir in tomatoes, pan drippings, and remaining ingredients. Cook over medium heat, stirring constantly with a wire whisk, 10 minutes or until mixture is thickened. Yield: 1½ cups (serving size: 3 tablespoons).

ROASTED MASHED POTATOES

4   medium baking potatoes
     (about 2 pounds)
1   cup 2% low-fat milk
2   tablespoons margarine
¾   teaspoon salt
¼   teaspoon pepper

Preheat oven to 400°. Wrap each potato in foil, and bake at 400° for 1½ hours. Cut potatoes into chunks.

Combine milk, margarine, salt, and pepper in a large saucepan, and cook over medium-low heat until warm. Remove from heat; add potatoes to pan, and beat at medium speed of an electric mixer until smooth. Yield: 8 servings (serving size: ½ cup).

CALORIES 133 (24% from fat); PROTEIN 3.8g; FAT 3.5g (sat 1g, mono 1.4g, poly 1g); CARB 22.3g; FIBER 2g; CHOL 2mg; IRON 1.5mg; SODIUM 277mg; CALC 55mg

PORCINI MUSHROOM-AND-VEAL MEAT LOAF

1   cup finely chopped onion
1   cup water
½   cup dried porcini mushrooms
      (about ½ ounce), chopped
¼   cup dry red wine
1½   tablespoons soy sauce
¼   teaspoon sugar
⅛   teaspoon dried rosemary,
      crushed
1   large garlic clove, minced
1½   tablespoons Dijon mustard
½   teaspoon pepper
¾   cup fresh whole wheat
      breadcrumbs
1½   pounds lean ground veal
Vegetable cooking spray

Preheat oven to 375°. Combine first 8 ingredients in a small saucepan; bring to a boil. Cook 8 minutes or until reduced to 1 cup. Combine mushroom mixture, mustard, and pepper in a large bowl; stir well. Stir in breadcrumbs; let cool slightly.

Crumble veal over mushroom mixture; stir just until blended. Pack veal mixture into an 8 x 4-inch loaf pan

coated with cooking spray. Bake at 375° for 50 minutes or until meat loaf reaches 160°. Let meat loaf stand in pan 10 minutes.

Remove meat loaf from pan; cut loaf into 12 slices. Yield: 6 servings (serving size: 2 slices).

Note: Ground turkey or chicken can be substituted for ground veal.

Sandwich suggestion: Serve leftover meat loaf slices on kaiser rolls with herbed mayonnaise and lettuce.

CALORIES 232 (25% from fat); PROTEIN 29.4g; FAT 6.5g (sat 1.7g, mono 2.1g, poly 0.7g); CARB 12.2g; FIBER 1.4g; CHOL 101mg; IRON 1.6mg; SODIUM 471mg; CALC 44mg

TIPS FROM THE TEST KITCHENS

◆ Place all ingredients except the ground meat in your mixing bowl, then crumble the meat over the mixture. Don't be afraid to use your hands to knead the seasonings into the meat.

◆ An instant-read thermometer, which quickly registers the temperature of the center of the loaf, is a fail-safe way to check for doneness. Sometimes the loaf pulls away from the sides of the pan before it is fully cooked.

◆ Let the meat loaf stand at room temperature 10 minutes before cutting so the slices won't fall apart.

◆ Because our meat loaves are lower in fat than traditional recipes, there are very little fat drippings. But if you desire, you can use a draining meat loaf pan. This two-piece pan consists of one pan with holes in the bottom that fits into a slightly larger pan, allowing fat to drain from the meat loaf into the larger pan.

LAMB-AND-EGGPLANT LOAF

This Lebanese-inspired meat loaf recipe uses eggplant, feta cheese, mint, and—instead of breadcrumbs—bulgur, which is found with rice and other grains in supermarkets.

1   medium eggplant (about
      1 pound)
1   cup chopped onion
2   large garlic cloves, minced
½   cup crumbled feta cheese
⅓   cup uncooked bulgur
2   tablespoons minced fresh
      parsley
2   tablespoons lemon juice
2   teaspoons minced fresh mint
½   teaspoon salt
¼   teaspoon ground coriander
¼   teaspoon ground cumin
¼   teaspoon pepper
2   egg whites
1   pound lean ground lamb
Vegetable cooking spray

Preheat oven to 350°. Pierce eggplant with a fork; place on a baking sheet. Bake at 350° for 45 minutes or until tender. Let cool; peel and finely chop.

Place a small nonstick skillet over medium-high heat until hot. Add onion and garlic, and sauté 3 minutes or until tender.

Combine eggplant, onion mixture, cheese, and next 9 ingredients in a large bowl; stir well. Crumble lamb over eggplant mixture, and stir just until ingredients are blended.

Pack mixture into an 8 x 4-inch loaf pan coated with cooking spray. Bake at 350° for 1 hour and 10 minutes or until meat loaf reaches 160°. Let meat loaf stand in pan 10 minutes.

Remove meat loaf from pan; cut loaf into 12 slices. Yield: 6 servings (serving size: 2 slices).

Sandwich suggestion: Serve leftover meat loaf slices in pita bread halves with cucumber slices and plain low-fat yogurt.

CALORIES 208 (30% from fat); PROTEIN 20.8g; FAT 6.9g (sat 3.1g, mono 2.3g, poly 1.3g); CARB 15.7g; FIBER 2.2g; CHOL 58mg; IRON 2.6mg; SODIUM 376mg; CALC 100mg

SZECHWAN CHICKEN MEAT LOAF

This Asian-inspired meat loaf packs a flavor punch. Don't bake this meat loaf on a broiler pan, or you'll lose the flavor in the drippings that drain into the bottom of the pan. Cook the rice in advance to reduce the prep time.

1   teaspoon dark sesame oil
2   tablespoons finely chopped green onions
2   tablespoons finely chopped carrot
2   tablespoons finely chopped celery
½   teaspoon peeled, minced gingerroot or ⅛ teaspoon ground ginger
2   garlic cloves, minced
1   cup cooked long-grain rice
¼   cup chopped water chestnuts
2   tablespoons soy sauce
2   tablespoons all-purpose Szechwan hot and spicy sauce
1   pound ground chicken or ground turkey
    Vegetable cooking spray
2   tablespoons sesame seeds, toasted

Preheat oven to 350°.

Heat oil in a small nonstick skillet over medium-high heat until hot. Add green onions, carrot, celery, gingerroot, and garlic; sauté 2 minutes or until tender.

Combine green onion mixture, rice, water chestnuts, soy sauce, and Szechwan sauce in a large bowl; stir well. Crumble chicken over green onion mixture, and stir just until blended.

Pack mixture into an 8 x 4-inch loaf pan coated with cooking spray; sprinkle sesame seeds over top of loaf. Bake at 350° for 50 minutes or until meat loaf reaches 160°. Let loaf stand in pan 10 minutes.

Remove meat loaf from pan; cut into 12 slices. Serve with Chinese hot mustard and sweet-and-sour sauce, if desired. Yield: 6 servings (serving size: 2 slices).

Sandwich suggestion: Serve leftover meat loaf slices on sandwich bread with Chinese hot mustard and very thinly sliced green cabbage.

CALORIES 163 (27% from fat); PROTEIN 18.1g; FAT 4.8g (sat 0.9g, mono 1.5g, poly 1.5g); CARB 11.1g; FIBER 0.5g; CHOL 53mg; IRON 1.4mg; SODIUM 404mg; CALC 22mg

---

MENU SUGGESTION

RIO GRANDE MEAT LOAF

Mexicorn

**Avocado, orange, and olive salad*

*Combine ¼ cup white wine vinegar, ¼ cup orange juice, 1 tablespoon olive oil, and ¼ teaspoon chili powder; drizzle over salads.

RIO GRANDE MEAT LOAF

With the popularity of Mexican food, why not a south-of-the-border meat loaf? This one uses black beans, jalapeño pepper, and, in place of breadcrumbs, crushed taco shells.

½   cup chopped onion
½   cup chopped green bell pepper
⅓   cup chopped fresh cilantro
2   tablespoons seeded, minced jalapeño pepper
1   teaspoon salt
2   teaspoons ground cumin
2   teaspoons chili powder
½   teaspoon pepper
4   taco shells, finely crushed (about 1½ ounces)
2   egg whites
3   large garlic cloves, minced
1   (15-ounce) can black beans, rinsed and drained
2   pounds ground round
    Vegetable cooking spray

Preheat oven to 375°. Combine first 12 ingredients in a large bowl, and stir well. Crumble beef over vegetable mixture, and stir just until blended.

Pack mixture into a 9 x 5-inch loaf pan coated with cooking spray. Bake at 375° for 1 hour or until meat loaf reaches 160°. Let meat loaf stand in pan 10 minutes.

Remove meat loaf from pan; cut loaf into 16 slices. Serve with commercial salsa, if desired. Yield: 8 servings (serving size: 2 slices).

Sandwich suggestion: Serve leftover meat loaf slices in taco shells; top with shredded lettuce, chopped tomato, and shredded cheese.

CALORIES 234 (29% from fat); PROTEIN 28.9g; FAT 7.5g (sat 2.3g, mono 3.2g, poly 0.9g); CARB 11.6g; FIBER 1.9g; CHOL 66mg; IRON 4.1mg; SODIUM 483mg; CALC 31mg

---

NORMANDY-STYLE MEAT LOAF

In the region of France known as Normandy, meat is often paired with fruit—in this meat loaf, it's pork and prunes. Because there's no guarantee that packaged ground pork comes from a lean cut, you might want to ask your butcher to grind a piece from the loin.

    Vegetable cooking spray
½   teaspoon anise seeds
1   cup finely chopped onion
½   cup port or other sweet red wine
½   cup pitted, chopped prunes
1   tablespoon Dijon mustard
¾   teaspoon salt
¼   teaspoon pepper
2   (1-ounce) slices pumpernickel bread, torn into small pieces
1½ pounds lean ground pork

Preheat oven to 375°.

Coat a small saucepan with cooking spray, and place over medium heat until hot. Add anise seeds; sauté 1 minute. Add onion; sauté 3 minutes or until tender. Add wine and prunes; bring to a boil. Cook 3 minutes, stirring occasionally.

Combine prune mixture, mustard, salt, pepper, and bread in a large bowl; toss well to moisten bread. Let mixture cool slightly.

Crumble pork over prune mixture, and stir just until blended. Pack pork mixture into a 9 x 4-inch loaf pan coated with cooking spray. Bake at 375° for 1 hour or until meat loaf reaches 160°. Let meat loaf stand in pan 10 minutes.

Remove meat loaf from pan; cut loaf into 16 slices. Yield: 8 servings (serving size: 2 slices).

Sandwich suggestion: Serve leftover meat loaf slices on pumpernickel bread with herbed mayonnaise and lettuce.

CALORIES 183 (31% from fat); PROTEIN 19.7g; FAT 6.4g (sat 2.1g, mono 2.8g, poly 0.7g); CARB 6.9g; FIBER 0.8g; CHOL 54mg; IRON 1.1mg; SODIUM 376mg; CALC 18mg

MAMA'S MEAT LOAF

- 1 cup chopped onion
- 1 cup chopped green bell pepper
- 3 tablespoons minced fresh parsley
- 1 teaspoon pepper
- ¾ teaspoon salt
- 2 garlic cloves, minced
- 1 egg, lightly beaten
- 1 (1-ounce) slice white bread, torn into small pieces
- 1½ pounds ground round
- Vegetable cooking spray
- ⅓ cup ketchup

Preheat oven to 350°.

Combine onion, green bell pepper, parsley, pepper, salt, garlic, egg, and bread in a large bowl, tossing to moisten bread. Crumble meat over onion mixture, and stir just until blended.

Pack mixture into a 9 x 5-inch loaf pan coated with cooking spray. Spread ketchup over top of meat loaf. Bake at 350° for 1 hour or until meat loaf reaches 160°. Let meat loaf stand in pan 10 minutes.

Remove meat loaf from pan; cut loaf into 6 slices. Yield: 6 servings (serving size: 1 slice).

Sandwich suggestion: Serve leftover slices on whole wheat bread with mayonnaise, lettuce, and Cheddar cheese.

CALORIES 220 (28% from fat); PROTEIN 27.4g; FAT 6.9g (sat 2.4g, mono 2.9g, poly 0.5g); CARB 10.8g; FIBER 1.4g; CHOL 101mg; IRON 3.4mg; SODIUM 552mg; CALC 29mg

First Class Sections

Because citrus fruits usually hail from warm, sunny climes, they nearly always satisfy that longing for sunshine. The other advantage for the cook is the amazing versatility of citrus fruits—they can be prepared raw or cooked, and complement most any kind of food without surrendering their tart, heady flavors. Here's the latest on how to use these fruits to their best advantage. So let the sunshine into your kitchen.

CHICKEN IN CITRUS SAUCE

Based on a classic French recipe, the citrus sauce is also delicious with pork chops, game hens, and turkey thighs.

- ½ cup water
- 2 tablespoons (½-inch) julienne-cut orange rind
- 1 tablespoon (½-inch) julienne-cut grapefruit rind
- 2 teaspoons (½-inch) julienne-cut lemon rind
- 1 teaspoon (½-inch) julienne-cut lime rind
- ¾ cup fresh orange juice
- 2 tablespoons fresh grapefruit juice
- 2 teaspoons fresh lemon juice
- 2 teaspoons fresh lime juice
- ¾ cup low-salt chicken broth
- ¼ cup dry red wine
- 1 teaspoon sugar
- ¼ teaspoon salt
- ¼ teaspoon pepper
- 8 chicken thighs (about 3 pounds), skinned
- 1 teaspoon margarine
- 1 tablespoon white wine vinegar
- ½ teaspoon cornstarch

Combine first 5 ingredients in a saucepan; bring to a boil. Cover, reduce

heat, and simmer 10 minutes. Drain, reserving citrus rind. Combine citrus rind, citrus juices, broth, wine, and sugar in a bowl; stir well. Set aside.

Sprinkle salt and pepper over chicken. Heat margarine in a large nonstick skillet over medium-high heat until hot. Add chicken; cook 3 minutes on each side. Add juice mixture; cover, reduce heat, and simmer 35 minutes. Remove chicken from skillet with tongs or a slotted spoon; set aside, and keep warm.

Combine vinegar and cornstarch; stir well. Add cornstarch mixture to juice mixture in skillet; simmer, uncovered, 10 minutes or until thickened and slightly reduced, stirring constantly. Spoon sauce over chicken. Yield: 4 servings (serving size: 2 chicken thighs and ¼ cup sauce).

CALORIES 198 (29% from fat); PROTEIN 26g; FAT 6.3g (sat 1.5g, mono 2g, poly 1.6g); CARB 9.8g; FIBER 0.2g; CHOL 106mg; IRON 1.9mg; SODIUM 284mg; CALC 29mg

EARL GREY SORBET

This grown-up, not-too-sweet sorbet is wonderful served as a palate cleanser between courses, or as a dessert after a rich meal.

- 2 cups boiling water
- ⅔ cup sugar
- ¼ cup loose Earl Grey tea
- ½ cup fresh lemon juice

Combine first 3 ingredients in a medium bowl; stir well. Cover and steep 5 minutes.

Strain tea mixture through a fine sieve into a bowl; discard tea leaves. Stir lemon juice into tea; cover and chill.

Pour tea into the freezer can of an ice-cream freezer, and freeze according to manufacturer's instructions. Spoon sorbet into a freezer-safe container; cover and freeze sorbet at least 3 hours or overnight. Yield: 10 servings (serving size: ½ cup).

CALORIES 57 (0% from fat); PROTEIN 0.1g; FAT 0g; CARB 14.9g; FIBER 0g; CHOL 0mg; IRON 0mg; SODIUM 1mg; CALC 1mg

PEELING

Use a hand-held grater to get finely grated rind. Avoid the white pith beneath the skin—it's bitter.

To remove orange rind easily, use a vegetable peeler.

To julienne, cut a piece of rind (obtained by using a vegetable peeler) lengthwise into long, thin slices.

SECTIONING

Cut off ends of fruit. Stand fruit on end; cut skin off from top to bottom.

Slice between membranes with a sharp paring knife to remove sections.

JUICING

Gently roll the fruit on a flat surface, using the palm of your hand, to soften the pulp inside.

Cut the fruit in half crosswise; then use a hand-held reamer, a citrus juicer, or an electric juicer.

GARNISHING

For curls, use a channel knife to remove long, thin strips of lemon rind.

To obtain the zest, remove only the colored part of the skin with a citrus zester.

CITRUS-SEAFOOD SALAD

Add some crusty rolls and a glass of crisp white wine, and you have an elegant light meal.

- 1 pound large shrimp
- 1 cup water
- ½ cup dry white wine
- ¼ teaspoon dried thyme
- ¼ teaspoon dried marjoram
- ¾ pound bay scallops
- ½ cup thinly sliced red onion, separated into rings
- ¼ teaspoon grated orange rind
- ¼ cup fresh orange juice
- 1 tablespoon fresh lemon juice
- 1 tablespoon olive oil
- 1 tablespoon Dijon mustard
- ¾ teaspoon sugar
- ¼ teaspoon pepper
- ⅛ teaspoon salt
- 6 cups small spinach leaves
- 2 cups orange sections
- 1 medium peeled cucumber, halved lengthwise and sliced

Peel and devein shrimp.

Combine water and next 3 ingredients in a large skillet; bring to a boil. Add shrimp and scallops; cover, reduce heat, and simmer 4 minutes or until shrimp turn pink and scallops are done. Drain.

Combine shrimp, scallops, and onion in a large bowl. Combine orange rind and next 7 ingredients in a small bowl; stir well. Pour ¼ cup orange juice mixture over shrimp mixture; toss well, cover, and chill 30 minutes. Cover and chill remaining orange juice mixture.

Add spinach, orange sections, and cucumber to shrimp mixture; pour remaining orange juice mixture over salad, and toss well. Yield: 6 servings (serving size: 2 cups).

CALORIES 206 (20% from fat); PROTEIN 27.3g; FAT 4.5g (sat 0.7g, mono 2g, poly 1g); CARB 14.3g; FIBER 5.1g; CHOL 134mg; IRON 3.8mg; SODIUM 373mg; CALC 139mg

CARROT-AND-ONION AGRODOLCE

Agrodolce is Italian for "sour-sweet." Italians cook many vegetables this way, serving them as part of an antipasto or as a side dish. Try this version, either hot or cold, with roasted meats and poultry.

  1 tablespoon olive oil
  2 cups trimmed, peeled baby
       carrots
  2 medium peeled onions, each
       cut into 8 wedges
 ⅓ cup apple juice
  2 tablespoons raisins
  1 tablespoon brown sugar
  2 tablespoons fresh lemon juice
 ½ teaspoon salt
 ¼ teaspoon rubbed sage
  1 lemon, thinly sliced

Heat oil in a large nonstick skillet over medium-high heat until hot. Add carrots and onions; reduce heat to medium, and cook 25 minutes or until golden, stirring frequently. Stir in apple juice and remaining ingredients; cover, reduce heat, and simmer 15 minutes or until carrots are tender, stirring occasionally. Yield: 4 servings (serving size: ¾ cup).

Note: True baby carrots are usually sold in a bundle with their green tops intact. They are sweeter than the smaller carrots sold in a bag.

CALORIES 124 (27% from fat); PROTEIN 1.9g; FAT 3.7g (sat 0.5g, mono 2.5g, poly 0.4g); CARB 24.6g; FIBER 3.5g; CHOL 0mg; IRON 0.9mg; SODIUM 318mg; CALC 53mg

CITRUS COMPOTE

  4 small navel oranges
  2 large red grapefruit
 ¾ cup water
 ¼ cup sugar
  2 tablespoons triple sec or other
       orange-flavored liqueur
  1 tablespoon grenadine

Remove rind from 2 oranges using a vegetable peeler (avoid the white pith of the rind). Cut the orange rind into 1-inch-long strips to equal 3 tablespoons. Repeat procedure with 1 grapefruit.

Peel and section all oranges and grapefruit over a large bowl; squeeze membranes to extract juice, reserving ¼ cup juice. Set orange and grapefruit sections aside, and discard membranes.

Combine rind strips, water, and sugar in a small saucepan, and bring to a boil. Cover, reduce heat, and simmer 2 minutes. Stir in reserved citrus juice, and simmer, uncovered, 10 minutes or until slightly thickened. Remove from heat; stir in liqueur and grenadine. Pour syrup mixture into a small bowl; cover and chill 30 minutes.

Arrange ¾ cup orange and grapefruit sections on each of 4 salad plates, and spoon ¼ cup juice mixture over each serving. Yield: 4 servings.

CALORIES 164 (2% from fat); PROTEIN 1.7g; FAT 0.3g (sat 0g, mono 0g, poly 0.1g); CARB 37.6g; FIBER 4g; CHOL 0mg; IRON 0.2mg; SODIUM 1mg; CALC 48mg

FOR TWO

Good Things Come in Threes

Soup, salad, and a sandwich: Put them together using innovative ingredients, and you have an exciting meal of substance.

We've done some tinkering in the kitchen and come up with two light-and healthy soup, salad, and sandwich menus. Besides being innovatively delicious, these hearty combos are easy to prepare. They're perfect meals for after work, when you're hungry and tired.

> **MENU**
>
> HOT PEPPERED PINTO
> SOUP WITH GARLIC
>
> ROAST BEEF-AND-BLUE
> CHEESE SANDWICH
>
> CREAMY SHREDDED
> CABBAGE SALAD

HOT PEPPERED PINTO SOUP WITH GARLIC

      Vegetable cooking spray
 ⅓ cup chopped onion
 ⅓ cup chopped green bell pepper
  3 garlic cloves, minced
  1 tablespoon chili powder
  2 tablespoons fresh lime juice
 ½ teaspoon dried oregano
 ½ teaspoon ground cumin
 ¼ teaspoon ground red pepper
 ¼ teaspoon hot sauce
 ⅛ teaspoon salt
 ⅛ teaspoon black pepper
  1 (10½-ounce) can low-salt
       chicken broth
  1 (16-ounce) can pinto beans,
       drained

Coat a medium saucepan with cooking spray, and place skillet over medium-high heat until hot. Add onion, bell pepper, and garlic; sauté 3 minutes. Add chili powder and next 8 ingredients; bring to a boil. Stir in half of beans; cover, reduce heat, and simmer 10 minutes.

Place soup in a food processor or blender, and process until smooth. Return to pan; stir in remaining beans. Cook until thoroughly heated. Yield: 2 servings (serving size: 1¼ cups).

CALORIES 269 (10% from fat); PROTEIN 15g; FAT 2.9g (sat 0.6g, mono 0.7g, poly 0.9g); CARB 48.8g; FIBER 8.2g; CHOL 0mg; IRON 5.9mg; SODIUM 642mg; CALC 111mg

ROAST BEEF-AND-BLUE CHEESE SANDWICH

2 tablespoons nonfat mayonnaise
1 tablespoon Dijon mustard
¼ teaspoon pepper
2 (2-ounce) onion sandwich buns, sliced
2 romaine lettuce leaves
4 tomato slices
4 green bell pepper rings
4 red onion slices
4 ounces thinly sliced lean deli roast beef
2 tablespoons crumbled blue cheese

Combine mayonnaise, mustard, and pepper, and stir well; spread on cut sides of sandwich buns.

Line the bottom half of each sandwich bun with a lettuce leaf; top with tomato, bell pepper, onion, roast beef, cheese, and top halves of buns. Yield: 2 servings.

CALORIES 309 (31% from fat); PROTEIN 18.6g; FAT 10.7g (sat 4.5g, mono 2.7g, poly 1.4g); CARB 35.1g; FIBER 2.5g; CHOL 5mg; IRON 2mg; SODIUM 1,133mg; CALC 53mg

CREAMY SHREDDED CABBAGE SALAD

3 cups very thinly presliced green cabbage
¼ cup chopped onion
1 tablespoon sugar
3 tablespoons nonfat mayonnaise
1 tablespoon cider vinegar
¼ teaspoon salt
Dash of pepper

Combine cabbage and onion in a bowl. Combine sugar and next 4 ingredients in a small bowl; stir well with a wire whisk.

Pour dressing mixture over cabbage mixture, and toss well. Cover and chill 1 hour. Yield: 2 servings (serving size: 1 cup).

CALORIES 77 (2% from fat); PROTEIN 1.5g; FAT 0.2g (sat 0g, mono 0g, poly 0.1g); CARB 18.6g; FIBER 2.9g; CHOL 0mg; IRON 0.7mg; SODIUM 598mg; CALC 54mg

---

MENU

BAKED POTATO SOUP WITH BACON

ROASTED VEGETABLE PITAS WITH SOUR CREAM DRESSING

TABBOULEH WITH FRESH MINT-YOGURT DRESSING

BAKED POTATO SOUP WITH BACON

1 pound baking potatoes, cubed
2 cups 2% low-fat milk
2 teaspoons reduced-calorie margarine
½ teaspoon salt
¼ teaspoon pepper
¼ cup sliced green onions
1 tablespoon plus 1 teaspoon bottled real bacon bits

Place potato cubes in a medium saucepan; add water to cover, and bring to a boil. Cook 15 minutes or until very tender; drain. Return potatoes to pan, and mash to desired consistency. Add milk, margarine, salt, and pepper; stir well. Cook over medium heat until thoroughly heated, stirring frequently.

Ladle soup into individual bowls; top with green onions and bacon bits. Yield: 2 servings (serving size: 2 cups soup, 2 tablespoons green onions, and 2 teaspoons bacon bits).

CALORIES 364 (21% from fat); PROTEIN 14.6g; FAT 8.4g (sat 3.4g, mono 2.5g, poly 1g); CARB 58.4g; FIBER 3.8g; CHOL 23mg; IRON 1.1mg; SODIUM 922mg; CALC 320mg

---

ROASTED VEGETABLE PITAS WITH SOUR CREAM DRESSING

You can also use eggplant, yellow squash, and red bell pepper in this sandwich. Feel free to experiment.

2 tablespoons crumbled feta cheese
2 tablespoons nonfat sour cream
2 tablespoons skim milk
½ teaspoon prepared horseradish
Dash of pepper
1 cup sliced zucchini
1 cup (1-inch) pieces green bell pepper
½ teaspoon dried oregano
1½ teaspoons olive oil
¼ teaspoon salt
2 garlic cloves, minced
1 large tomato (about 8 ounces), cut into 8 wedges
1 medium onion (about 8 ounces), cut into 8 wedges
Vegetable cooking spray
1 (7-inch) pita bread round, halved

Combine first 5 ingredients in a small bowl; stir well, and set aside.

Combine zucchini and next 7 ingredients in a bowl; toss gently. Spoon vegetable mixture onto rack of a broiler pan coated with cooking spray. Broil 10 minutes or until tender and lightly browned, stirring occasionally.

Divide vegetable mixture evenly between pita halves. Drizzle 2 tablespoons dressing over vegetable mixture in each pita half. Yield: 2 servings.

CALORIES 208 (30% from fat); PROTEIN 7.7g; FAT 6.9g (sat 1.9g, mono 3.2g, poly 1g); CARB 30.8g; FIBER 4.2g; CHOL 7mg; IRON 2.4mg; SODIUM 532mg; CALC 115mg

TABBOULEH WITH FRESH MINT-YOGURT DRESSING

¾ cup water
¼ cup uncooked bulgur
2 tablespoons peeled, seeded, and diced cucumber
2 tablespoons frozen green peas, thawed
1 tablespoon diced onion
¼ cup plain low-fat yogurt
2 tablespoons minced fresh parsley
1 tablespoon minced fresh mint
1 tablespoon minced green onions
1½ teaspoons skim milk
¾ teaspoon fresh lemon juice
¾ teaspoon vegetable oil
⅛ teaspoon salt
1 small garlic clove, crushed
2 medium tomatoes (about ¾ pound)
⅛ teaspoon salt

Bring water to a boil in a small saucepan; stir in bulgur. Remove from heat; cover and let stand 15 minutes or until bulgur is tender. Drain well, and let cool.

Combine bulgur, diced cucumber, green peas, and diced onion in a bowl, and toss gently. Combine yogurt and next 8 ingredients in a bowl, and stir well. Pour yogurt mixture over bulgur mixture, and toss gently.

Core tomatoes, and cut each into 6 wedges, cutting to, but not through, base of tomato. Spread tomato wedges slightly apart, and place on serving plates. Sprinkle ⅛ teaspoon salt evenly over tomatoes, and spoon ½ cup bulgur mixture into each tomato. Yield: 2 servings.

CALORIES 54 (18% from fat); PROTEIN 2.3g; FAT 1.1g (sat 0.3g, mono 0.3g, poly 0.5g); CARB 10g; FIBER 2.5g; CHOL 0.5mg; IRON 0.7mg; SODIUM 118mg; CALC 31mg

Robert Redford's
Messenger of Light

When Chef Don Heidel arrived at Sundance Resort in Utah, he took hold of the kitchen's reins with a healthy new cuisine inspired by Native American flavors.

But first he had to meet the expectations of Sundance founder Robert Redford. "Bob was away on a project. I called and told him the menu he'd been using was old, and that I wanted to change it," says Heidel, 33. "He was a bit hesitant, so I said, 'Why don't you fly in, and we'll spend a day in the kitchen cooking?' He was taken aback; nobody had ever asked him to do that before. So we did, and when we were finished, he told me, 'You do anything you want—just do the best you possibly can.'"

The Native Americans inspire Heidel, who sees them as early environmentalists. "Everything they did was out of respect for the land. I try to borrow what I can from that, like burning herbs to ash (which the Native Americans originally did for medicinal purposes) before adding them to dishes."

HOPI INDIAN STEW WITH POZOLE

1 tablespoon olive oil
1 cup peeled, diced sweet potato
½ cup peeled, diced turnip
1½ cups diced green bell pepper
1½ cups diced red bell pepper
1 cup diced zucchini
1 cup diced yellow squash
1⅓ cups sliced oyster mushroom caps (about 3½ ounces)
5 cups Corn Stock (page 54) or 3 (14½-ounce) cans vegetable broth
1½ cups Grilled Corn Kernels (page 54)
½ cup canned white hominy (pozole blanco), drained
1 teaspoon minced fresh thyme
1 teaspoon rubbed sage
1 teaspoon coriander seeds, toasted
⅛ teaspoon pepper
¼ cup water
1 tablespoon cornstarch

Heat oil in a large Dutch oven over medium heat until hot. Add sweet potato and turnip; sauté 5 minutes or until lightly browned. Add bell peppers, zucchini, and squash; sauté 3 minutes. Add mushrooms, and sauté 1 minute. Add Corn Stock, Grilled Corn Kernels, hominy, thyme, sage, coriander seeds, and ⅛ teaspoon pepper.

Combine water and cornstarch in a small bowl, stirring until well-blended; add to stew. Bring to a boil; reduce heat, and simmer 5 minutes or until slightly thickened, stirring constantly. Yield: 10 servings (serving size: 1 cup).

CALORIES 92 (27% from fat); PROTEIN 2.4g; FAT 2.8g (sat 0.5g, mono 1.4g, poly 0.6g); CARB 16.4g; FIBER 2.8g; CHOL 0mg; IRON 1.2mg; SODIUM 754mg; CALC 17mg

TORTILLA SOUP

"There are two varieties (of tortilla soup)—one with a tomato base and the other with a Cuban-influenced, clear base. I combined the two for a heartier, brothlike soup with a completely different flavor."

Vegetable cooking spray
- 3 (6-ounce) skinned chicken breast halves
- 5 cups Corn Stock or 3 (14½-ounce) cans vegetable broth
- ¼ cup chopped fresh cilantro
- 2 teaspoons cumin seeds
- 2 teaspoons coriander seeds
- 1 jalapeño pepper, halved and seeded
- 1 small unpeeled onion, sliced
- 1 tablespoon olive oil
- 1½ cups Grilled Corn Kernels
- 1½ cups diced red onion
- ¼ cup chopped fresh cilantro
- 2 garlic cloves, minced
- 4 cups diced tomato
- 1 tablespoon seeded, minced jalapeño pepper
- ¼ teaspoon salt
- ¼ teaspoon ground cumin
- 4 (6-inch) corn tortillas, cut into (3 x ¼-inch) strips
- ⅛ teaspoon pepper
- 1½ cups peeled, sliced avocado

Coat grill rack with cooking spray; place on grill over medium-hot coals (350° to 400°). Place chicken on rack; grill, covered, about 45 minutes or until chicken is done, turning frequently. Let cool slightly. Remove chicken from bones, reserving bones. Cut chicken into bite-size pieces; set aside.

Combine chicken bones, Corn Stock, and next 5 ingredients in a large Dutch oven. Bring to a boil; reduce heat, and simmer, uncovered, 1 hour. Remove from heat. Strain mixture through a sieve into a large bowl; discard solids. Set stock aside.

Heat olive oil in pan over medium-high heat until hot. Add Grilled Corn Kernels, red onion, ¼ cup cilantro, and garlic; sauté 3 minutes. Add chicken, stock, tomato, and next 5 ingredients.

Cook until thoroughly heated. Ladle soup into individual bowls, and top with avocado. Yield: 12 servings (serving size: 1 cup soup and about 3 slices avocado).

CALORIES 176 (34% from fat); PROTEIN 12.8g; FAT 6.7g (sat 1.2g, mono 3.6g, poly 1.2g); CARB 18.3g; FIBER 3.3g; CHOL 27mg; IRON 1.6mg; SODIUM 707mg; CALC 45mg

CORN STOCK

Vegetable cooking spray
- 1 small unpeeled onion, sliced
- 2 garlic cloves, minced
- 3 scraped corn cobs (reserved from Grilled Corn Kernels)
- 8 (14½-ounce) cans vegetable broth

Coat a large Dutch oven with cooking spray, and place over medium-high heat until hot. Add onion and garlic; sauté 5 minutes. Add corn cobs and broth; bring to a boil. Reduce heat, and simmer, uncovered, 1 hour. Remove from heat; cover and let stand 30 minutes. Strain mixture through a large sieve into a large bowl; discard solids. Yield: 10 cups.

Shortcut: Substitute the 3 (14½-ounce) cans vegetable broth for the 5 cups Corn Stock in Hopi Indian Stew with Posole and in Tortilla Soup.

GRILLED CORN KERNELS

Vegetable cooking spray
- 3 ears fresh corn, shucked

Coat grill rack with cooking spray; place on grill over medium-hot coals (350° to 400°). Place corn on rack; grill, covered, 20 minutes or until corn is lightly browned, turning frequently. Let cool. Cut corn kernels from cobs. Reserve corn cobs for Corn Stock, if desired. Yield: 1½ cups corn kernels.

SPANISH FORK CHICKEN STEW

"This stew was created with ingredients from our (the resort's) garden. The name was taken from Spanish Fork, a canyon here in Utah."

- 1 dried ancho chile (about ½ ounce)
- ¼ cup boiling water
- 3 cups peeled, cubed butternut squash (about 1 pound)
- 2 tablespoons olive oil, divided
- ½ teaspoon salt, divided
- ½ teaspoon pepper, divided
Vegetable cooking spray
- 1 pound skinned boned chicken breasts, diced
- 3 cups quartered mushrooms (about 8 ounces)
- 1 cup chopped onion
- ½ cup chopped yellow bell pepper
- ½ cup chopped red bell pepper
- 5 garlic cloves, minced
- 6 cups chopped tomato
- 2 cups sliced zucchini
- 1 teaspoon ground cinnamon
- 1 teaspoon ground cumin
- 1 (15½-ounce) can white hominy (pozole blanco), drained
- 1 tablespoon plain nonfat yogurt
- 5 teaspoons chopped fresh cilantro

Remove stem and seeds from chile. Combine chile and boiling water in a small bowl; cover and let stand 1 hour. Place chile and water in a food processor, and process until mixture is smooth. Spoon chile purée into a small bowl, and set aside.

Preheat oven to 400°.

Combine squash, 2 teaspoons oil, ⅛ teaspoon salt, and ⅛ teaspoon pepper in a 13 x 9-inch baking dish coated with cooking spray; toss well. Cover and bake at 400° for 5 minutes.

Sprinkle ¼ teaspoon salt and ¼ teaspoon pepper over chicken. Heat 2 teaspoons oil in a large Dutch oven over medium heat until hot. Add chicken and mushrooms; sauté 5 minutes. Remove chicken mixture from pan, and set aside.

Heat remaining 2 teaspoons oil in pan over medium-high heat until hot. Add onion, bell peppers, and garlic; sauté 3 minutes. Add 1 tablespoon chile purée, squash, chicken mixture, and next 6 ingredients; cover, reduce heat, and simmer 25 minutes, stirring often. Remove from heat; stir in yogurt. Ladle stew into individual bowls; sprinkle with cilantro. Serve with additional chile purée, if desired. Yield: 5 servings (serving size: 2 cups stew and 1 teaspoon cilantro).

Note: Chef Heidel prefers to serve this stew in a small, hollowed-out sourdough bread round.

CALORIES 330 (24% from fat); PROTEIN 27.5g; FAT 8.8g (sat 1.3g, mono 4.6g, poly 1.5g); CARB 39.6g; FIBER 8.3g; CHOL 53mg; IRON 4.6mg; SODIUM 454mg; CALC 112mg

VEGETABLE PAELLA

- 1 cup dried cannellini beans or other white beans
- 1 cup dried lima beans
- 2 tablespoons olive oil
- 1⅔ cups chopped tomato
- 1 cup chopped red bell pepper
- 1 cup chopped yellow bell pepper
- ¾ cup chopped onion
- ¾ cup diced zucchini
- ¾ cup diced yellow squash
- 1 tablespoon chopped fresh rosemary or 1 teaspoon dried rosemary
- 2 garlic cloves, minced
- ⅔ cup water
- ⅓ cup kalamata olives, pitted and sliced
- 1¼ teaspoons saffron threads, crushed
- 1 teaspoon paprika
- ½ teaspoon salt
- ¼ teaspoon pepper
- 3 (14½-ounce) cans vegetable broth
- 3 cups cooked wild rice (cooked without salt and fat)

Sort and wash beans; place in a large Dutch oven. Cover with water to 2 inches above beans; bring to a boil, and cook 2 minutes. Remove from

heat; cover and let stand 1 hour. Drain beans in a colander, and set aside.

Heat oil in Dutch oven over medium heat until hot. Add tomato and next 7 ingredients; sauté 5 minutes or until tender. Add beans, water, and next 6 ingredients; cover, reduce heat, and simmer 1 hour or until beans are tender. Stir in rice, and simmer an additional 3 minutes. Yield: 8 servings (serving size: 1 cup).

CALORIES 267 (21% from fat); PROTEIN 11.6g; FAT 6.3g (sat 1.1g, mono 3.7g, poly 1.2g); CARB 44.1g; FIBER 6.9g; CHOL 0mg; IRON 4.4mg; SODIUM 926mg; CALC 82mg

---

MENU SUGGESTION

VEGETABLE CHILI WITH HARVEST BEANS

Cornsticks

Fresh fruit

*Add shredded Cheddar cheese, chopped green chiles, or whole-kernel corn to basic cornstick batter for extra flavor.

VEGETABLE CHILI WITH HARVEST BEANS

- 1 cup dried black beans
- 1 cup dried calypso or pinto beans
- 1 cup dried snowcap, Appaloosa, or pinto beans
- 2 tablespoons olive oil
- 1¾ cups diced onion
- ¾ cup diced red bell pepper
- ¾ cup diced green bell pepper
- ¾ cup diced yellow bell pepper
- ½ cup seeded, minced jalapeño pepper (about 4 large)
- 3 garlic cloves, minced
- 2½ tablespoons chili powder
- 2 tablespoons ground cumin
- 1 teaspoon ground red pepper
- ½ teaspoon salt
- ⅛ teaspoon black pepper
- ½ cup masa harina or cornmeal
- 2 tablespoons unsweetened cocoa
- 5 (14½-ounce) cans vegetable broth

Sort and wash beans; place in a large Dutch oven. Cover with water to 2 inches above beans, and bring to a boil; cook 2 minutes. Remove from heat; cover and let stand 1 hour. Drain beans in a colander, and set aside.

Heat oil in pan over medium-high heat until hot. Add onion and next 5 ingredients; sauté for 10 minutes or until tender. Add chili powder and next 4 ingredients; sauté 1 minute. Stir in harina and cocoa. Add beans and broth; stir well. Bring to a boil; reduce heat, and simmer, uncovered, 2 hours or until beans are tender, stirring occasionally. Yield: 13 servings (serving size: 1 cup).

CALORIES 231 (16% from fat); PROTEIN 11.4g; FAT 4.1g (sat 0.8g, mono 2.1g, poly 0.8g); CARB 39.5g; FIBER 7.4g; CHOL 0mg; IRON 4.2mg; SODIUM 810mg; CALC 77mg

NAVAJO PEACH-APPLE CRISP

- 2⅓ cups peeled, sliced fresh or thawed frozen peaches
- 1¾ cups peeled, sliced Granny Smith apple
- ¼ cup honey
- 1 tablespoon peach brandy
- ½ teaspoon vanilla extract
- ¼ teaspoon ground cinnamon
- Vegetable cooking spray
- ½ cup all-purpose flour
- ¼ cup firmly packed brown sugar
- ⅛ teaspoon salt
- 3 tablespoons chilled reduced-calorie margarine, cut into small pieces
- 2 tablespoons pine nuts

Preheat oven to 375°.

Combine first 6 ingredients in a 2-quart casserole coated with cooking spray; toss well. Combine flour, sugar, and salt in a bowl; cut in margarine with a pastry blender until the mixture resembles coarse meal. Stir in pine nuts. Sprinkle flour mixture over peach mixture. Bake at 375° for 30 minutes or until lightly browned and bubbly. Yield: 6 servings (serving size: ½ cup).

CALORIES 226 (27% from fat); PROTEIN 2.2g; FAT 6.9g (sat 1.2g, mono 2.7g, poly 2.4g); CARB 41.6g; FIBER 2.4g; CHOL 0mg; IRON 1.0mg; SODIUM 110mg; CALC 16mg

Waiting for Gâteau

Years ago, back in 1970, my wife, Treena, and I ate a very rich dessert at the Frogmill Inn in Hampshire, England. Then riddled with clotted cream and crème de cacao, it's now a rolled sponge cake with a low-fat cocoa sauce, almonds, and an elegant coating of meringue. I've named it Jolynn's Meringue Gâteau after Jolynn Lambert—the first Cooking Light reader to report back on my tandemizing idea (January/February, page 41).

JOLYNN'S MERINGUE GÂTEAU

Vegetable cooking spray
1 cup sifted cake flour
1 tablespoon cornstarch
½ cup sugar
1 teaspoon olive oil
3 egg yolks
2 egg whites
1 teaspoon vanilla extract
4 egg whites
½ teaspoon cream of tartar
1 tablespoon sugar
Chocolate Syrup
Pastry Cream
4 egg whites
½ teaspoon cream of tartar
½ cup sifted powdered sugar
¼ teaspoon almond extract
1 tablespoon sliced almonds, toasted

Preheat oven to 450°.

Coat a 15 x 10-inch jelly-roll pan with cooking spray; line bottom of pan with wax paper. Coat wax paper with cooking spray, and set pan aside.

Combine flour and cornstarch in a small bowl; stir well, and set aside. Combine ½ cup sugar, oil, 3 egg yolks, and 2 egg whites in a large bowl; beat at high speed of an electric mixer until thick and pale (about 5 minutes). Add vanilla; beat until blended. Add flour mixture to egg mixture, beating at low speed until blended; set aside.

Beat 4 egg whites and ½ teaspoon cream of tartar at high speed until foamy. Add 1 tablespoon sugar; beat until stiff peaks form. Gently fold egg white mixture into batter; pour batter into prepared pan, spreading evenly. Bake at 450° for 6 minutes. Remove cake from oven. Turn oven off.

Loosen cake from sides of pan, and turn out onto a dishtowel; carefully peel off wax paper, and let cake cool 1 minute. Starting at narrow end, roll up cake and towel together. Place, seam side down, on a wire rack, and let cool completely (about 1 hour).

Unroll cake carefully; remove towel. Brush Chocolate Syrup over cake, leaving a ½-inch margin around outside edges. Spread Pastry Cream over syrup, leaving a 2-inch margin around outside edges. Reroll cake; place, seam side down, on an ovenproof serving platter.

Preheat oven to 325°. Beat 4 egg whites and ½ teaspoon cream of tartar at high speed of mixer until foamy. Add powdered sugar, 1 tablespoon at a time, beating until stiff peaks form. Add almond extract, and beat until

blended. Spread meringue over cake roll (cake should be completely covered with meringue), and sprinkle almonds over meringue. Bake at 325° for 25 minutes. Cover loosely, and chill at least 1 hour. Yield: 10 servings (serving size: 1 slice).

CALORIES 289 (22% from fat); PROTEIN 9.5g; FAT 7.1g (sat 3.3g, mono 2.5g, poly 0.5g); CARB 47.3g; FIBER 0.2g; CHOL 69mg; IRON 1.5mg; SODIUM 89mg; CALC 117mg

Chocolate Syrup:

½ cup semisweet chocolate morsels
2 tablespoons sugar
2 tablespoons Dutch process cocoa
2 tablespoons water
¼ teaspoon vanilla extract

TALE OF THE TAPE			
	Calories per Serving	Fat Grams per Serving	% Calories from Fat per Serving
Jolynn's Meringue Gâteau	289	7.1	22
Lighter-Than-Light Version	232	2.7	10

Combine first 4 ingredients in a small saucepan, and stir well. Cook over medium heat until smooth. Remove from heat, and stir in vanilla. Let cool. Yield: ½ cup.

Pastry Cream:

1 (32-ounce) carton vanilla
    low-fat yogurt
¼ cup sifted powdered sugar
3 tablespoons maple syrup
¼ teaspoon almond extract

Place a colander in a 2-quart glass measure or medium bowl. Line colander with 4 layers of cheesecloth, allowing cheesecloth to extend over edges of colander. Spoon yogurt into colander; cover loosely with plastic wrap, and refrigerate 12 hours. Spoon yogurt cheese into a bowl; discard liquid. Add remaining ingredients to yogurt cheese, and stir well. Yield: 2 cups.

LIGHTER THAN LIGHT

Here's how you can lower the fat in Jolynn's Meringue Gâteau even further without sacrificing the taste.

◆ Omit the chocolate morsels in the Chocolate Syrup, and increase the water to 3 tablespoons.

◆ Use 1 (32-ounce) carton plain nonfat yogurt in the Pastry Cream, and use ⅛ teaspoon vanilla extract in addition to the almond extract. Increase the sugar to ⅓ cup.

CALORIES 232 (10% from fat); PROTEIN 9.2g; FAT 2.7g (sat 0.7g, mono 1.1g, poly 0.4g); CARB 41.6g; FIBER 0.1g; CHOL 65mg; IRON 1.3mg; SODIUM 89mg; CALC 130mg

---

Culinary Chameleon

Creamy-textured tofu takes on the flavor of whatever is cooked with it.

Things have changed with tofu. In the '60s it gained popularity as a counter-culture cuisine and had a reputation for tasting like earth shoes. But now we know that if you prepare tofu properly, it's quite delicious. And it's so good for you—tofu is cholesterol-free and the fat it contains is unsaturated. Tofu is also high in protein, iron, and calcium.

Before you add it to a dish, tofu has almost no flavor of its own. In a sense, it's a culinary chameleon, absorbing the essence of whatever is cooked with it—strongly.

Perhaps the most important thing about trying tofu for the first time is that you keep an open mind. If you see any hesitant facial expressions around the dinner table, just tell everybody, "Hey, dudes, get with it. These are the '90s!"

TOFU OR NOT TOFU

We found reduced-fat tofu to be just as delicious and versatile in these recipes as regular tofu (these recipes call for both). To lower the fat content even further in the recipes that call for the regular, substitute the reduced-fat variety. Regular tofu gets 57% of its calories from fat, while reduced-fat tofu gets 26% of its calories from fat.

TOFU PICCATA

2 (10.5-ounce) packages extra-
    firm tofu, drained and cut
    into 1-inch cubes
1 tablespoon lemon juice
⅓ cup cornstarch
¼ cup grated Parmesan cheese
¼ cup dry breadcrumbs
1 tablespoon minced fresh
    parsley
1 teaspoon dried Italian
    seasoning
3 egg whites
Vegetable cooking spray
4 cups hot cooked linguine
    (about 8 ounces uncooked
    pasta)
2 cups marinara sauce
1 tablespoon drained capers
Lemon wedges (optional)

Place tofu cubes and lemon juice in a large heavy-duty, zip-top plastic bag; seal bag, and shake gently to coat. Add cornstarch to bag; seal bag, and shake gently to coat. Let stand 1 hour.

Combine Parmesan cheese, breadcrumbs, parsley, and Italian seasoning in another large heavy-duty, zip-top plastic bag; seal bag, and shake well. Place egg whites in a shallow bowl; stir well. Dip tofu cubes into egg whites using a slotted spoon, and add to cheese mixture in bag; seal bag, and shake gently to coat.

Coat a large nonstick skillet with cooking spray, and place over medium heat until hot. Add tofu cubes, and cook 8 minutes or until browned, turning occasionally.

Spoon pasta onto individual plates, and top with tofu cubes. Spoon marinara sauce over tofu and pasta; sprinkle with capers. Serve with lemon wedges, if desired. Yield: 4 servings (serving size: 1 cup pasta, 1 cup tofu, ½ cup marinara sauce, and ¾ teaspoon capers).

CALORIES 495 (27% from fat); PROTEIN 26.1g; FAT 14.6g (sat 2.9g, mono 4.6g, poly 5.8g); CARB 69.2g; FIBER 5.2g; CHOL 4mg; IRON 11.9mg; SODIUM 1,229mg; CALC 287mg

Tofu (or soybean curd, as it's also called) is sold in several varieties: firm, extra-firm, and silken. It is available in most supermarket produce sections or at Asian groceries. Recently it has become available in a light version, which contains at least a third less fat. Firm and extra-firm styles may be cut into cubes or sticks and stir-fried, baked, grilled, or broiled.

Before preparing tofu, rinse it in cold water. To store it, keep it in water in the refrigerator, and change the water every two days. Tofu will last this way for a week. It may also be kept frozen for up to three months, but freezing makes the texture chewier.

THAI-SEARED TOFU

½ cup chopped fresh basil
½ cup chopped fresh cilantro
½ cup low-sodium soy sauce
½ cup fresh lime juice
¼ cup chopped fresh mint
1 tablespoon peeled, minced gingerroot
2 tablespoons molasses
1 tablespoon vegetable oil
2 teaspoons curry powder
½ teaspoon dried crushed red pepper
4 garlic cloves, minced
2 (10.5-ounce) packages reduced-fat firm tofu, drained
Vegetable cooking spray
6 cups hot cooked vermicelli (about 12 ounces uncooked pasta)
Flowering basil (optional)

Combine first 11 ingredients in a medium bowl, and stir with a wire whisk until blended. Cut each tofu cake crosswise into 4 slices. Place tofu slices in soy sauce mixture, and marinate in refrigerator at least 2 hours.

Coat a large nonstick skillet with cooking spray, and place skillet over medium-high heat until hot. Remove tofu slices from marinade, reserving marinade. Add tofu slices to skillet, and cook 2 minutes on each side or until browned. Remove from skillet; set aside, and keep warm.

Add reserved marinade to skillet, and bring to a simmer over medium-high heat. Spoon pasta onto individual plates, and top with tofu slices. Drizzle warm marinade over tofu and pasta. Garnish with flowering basil, if desired. Yield: 4 servings (serving size: 1½ cups pasta, 2 tofu slices, and ½ cup sauce).

CALORIES 428 (15% from fat); PROTEIN 18.8g; FAT 6.9g (sat 1.1g, mono 1.6g, poly 3.2g); CARB 69.3g; FIBER 3.9g; CHOL 0mg; IRON 4.1mg; SODIUM 914mg; CALC 61mg

TOFU-AND-SHIITAKE MUSHROOM PILAF

2 teaspoons olive oil
1 cup uncooked basmati rice
¾ cup chopped onion
1 (14½-ounce) can vegetable broth
1 cup sliced shiitake mushroom caps (about 3 ounces)
½ cup chopped carrot
½ cup chopped celery
1 teaspoon peeled, grated gingerroot
2 garlic cloves, minced
1 cup cubed firm tofu (about 6 ounces)
½ teaspoon salt
¼ teaspoon pepper
Vegetable cooking spray
2 tablespoons minced fresh cilantro

Preheat oven to 350°.

Heat oil in a large saucepan over medium-high heat until hot. Add rice and onion; sauté 2 minutes. Add broth; bring to a boil. Add mushrooms, carrot, celery, gingerroot, and garlic; cover, reduce heat, and simmer 20 minutes or until rice is tender and liquid is absorbed.

Combine rice mixture, tofu cubes, salt, and pepper in a 2-quart casserole coated with cooking spray; toss gently. Cover and bake at 350° for 20 minutes or until thoroughly heated. Sprinkle cilantro over pilaf. Yield: 5 servings (serving size: 1 cup).

CALORIES 206 (19% from fat); PROTEIN 6.5g; FAT 4.3g (sat 0.6g, mono 1.8g, poly 1.2g); CARB 35.9g; FIBER 2.1g; CHOL 0mg; IRON 3.9mg; SODIUM 605mg; CALC 65mg

BRAISED FIVE-SPICE TOFU

1 cup tomato juice
½ cup ketchup
¼ cup low-sodium soy sauce
1 tablespoon grated orange rind
1 tablespoon peeled, grated gingerroot
2 tablespoons hoisin sauce
2 tablespoons molasses
1 tablespoon rice vinegar
2 teaspoons Chinese five-spice powder
½ teaspoon dried crushed red pepper
3 garlic cloves, minced
3 star anise
1 tablespoon dark sesame oil
1 pound firm or extra-firm tofu, drained and cut into 1-inch cubes
2 cups (1-inch) sliced green onions
1 cup chopped onion
1 cup diagonally sliced carrot
1 cup diced green bell pepper
1 cup chopped tomato

Combine first 12 ingredients in a bowl; stir well, and set aside.

Heat oil in a large nonstick skillet over medium heat until hot. Add tofu, and cook 6 minutes or until browned, turning occasionally. Add tomato juice mixture, green onions, and remaining ingredients; bring to a boil. Cover, reduce heat, and simmer 15 minutes or until vegetables are crisp-tender. Discard star anise. Serve over rice. Yield: 4 servings (serving size: 1½ cups tofu mixture).

CALORIES 291 (30% from fat); PROTEIN 13.5g; FAT 9.8g (sat 1.4g, mono 2.7g, poly 4.9g); CARB 41.9g; FIBER 6.9g; CHOL 0mg; IRON 9.2mg; SODIUM 1,174mg; CALC 224mg

GRIDDLED TOFU WITH GARLIC-SESAME BOK CHOY

1 cup water
¼ cup low-sodium soy sauce
1 tablespoon sesame seeds
1 tablespoon brown sugar
1 tablespoon rice vinegar
2 teaspoons peeled, minced gingerroot
1 teaspoon dried crushed red pepper
2 teaspoons dark sesame oil
3 garlic cloves
2 (10.5 ounce) packages reduced-fat firm tofu, drained
Vegetable cooking spray
1 teaspoon vegetable oil
1 teaspoon dark sesame oil
12 cups thinly sliced bok choy
1 teaspoon peeled, minced gingerroot
2 garlic cloves, minced
2½ cups diagonally sliced green onions
1 tablespoon low-sodium soy sauce

Combine first 9 ingredients in a blender; cover and process until smooth. Pour puréed sesame seed mixture into a bowl. Cut each tofu cake crosswise into 4 slices. Place slices in sesame seed mixture, and marinate in refrigerator at least 2 hours.

Coat a large nonstick skillet with cooking spray; place over medium-high heat until hot. Remove tofu from marinade; discard marinade. Add tofu to skillet; cook 2 minutes on each side or until browned. Remove from skillet; keep warm.

Heat vegetable oil and 1 teaspoon sesame oil in skillet over medium-high heat until hot. Add bok choy, 1 teaspoon gingerroot, and garlic; sauté 2 minutes. Add green onions and 1 tablespoon soy sauce; sauté 2 minutes.

Spoon bok choy mixture onto individual plates, and top with tofu slices. Yield: 4 servings (serving size: 2 cups bok choy mixture and 2 tofu slices).

CALORIES 187 (40% from fat); PROTEIN 13.9g; FAT 8.2g (sat 1.2g, mono 2.5g, poly 3.7g); CARB 15g; FIBER 3.9g; CHOL 0mg; IRON 2.9mg; SODIUM 761mg; CALC 278mg

Smart Cookies

Next time you get caught with your hand in the cookie jar, don't worry. These homemade, low-fat treats are far more delicious than the store-bought varieties—and much better for you.

APRICOT PINWHEELS

1 cup apricot preserves
¾ cup minced dried apricots (about 3 ounces whole apricots)
2½ tablespoons orange juice
2¾ cups all-purpose flour
¾ teaspoon baking powder
¼ teaspoon baking soda
¼ teaspoon salt
¼ cup stick margarine, softened
1 cup granulated sugar
½ cup firmly packed brown sugar
2½ tablespoons vegetable oil
½ teaspoon vanilla extract
3 egg whites
Vegetable cooking spray

Combine first 3 ingredients in a small saucepan; bring to a boil. Reduce heat to medium-low, and cook 10 minutes, stirring occasionally. Remove from heat; cover and let cool completely.

Combine flour, baking powder, baking soda, and salt in a large bowl; stir well, and set aside.

Place margarine in a large mixing bowl; beat at medium speed of an electric mixer until light and fluffy. Gradually add sugars, beating at medium speed until well-blended. Add oil, vanilla, and egg whites; beat well. Add flour mixture, and beat until well-blended.

Divide dough in half. Working with one half at a time (cover remaining half to keep from drying), gently press dough into a 4-inch square on heavy-duty plastic wrap, and cover with additional plastic wrap. Roll each half of dough, still covered, into a 12-inch square. Chill 30 minutes.

Remove top sheet of plastic wrap, and divide apricot mixture evenly between dough squares. Roll up each square jelly-roll fashion, peeling plastic wrap from bottom of dough while rolling. (Dough may be soft.) Wrap each roll individually in plastic wrap, and freeze 8 hours.

Preheat oven to 350°. Cut each roll into 24 (½-inch-thick) slices, and place 1 inch apart on baking sheets coated with cooking spray. Bake at 350° for 10 minutes. Remove from baking sheets; let cool on wire racks. Yield: 4 dozen (serving size: 1 cookie).

CALORIES 89 (18% from fat); PROTEIN 1.1g; FAT 1.8g (sat 0.3g, mono 0.6g, poly 0.7g); CARB 17.7g; FIBER 0.3g; CHOL 0mg; IRON 0.5mg; SODIUM 39mg; CALC 10mg

LEMON SNAPS

2 cups all-purpose flour
2 teaspoons baking powder
¼ teaspoon baking soda
1 cup sugar
1 tablespoon grated lemon rind, divided
½ teaspoon ground ginger
¼ cup plus 2½ tablespoons stick margarine, softened
2 teaspoons light-colored corn syrup
2 teaspoons vanilla extract
1 egg
3 tablespoons sugar
Vegetable cooking spray

Combine first 3 ingredients in a bowl; stir well, and set aside.

Place 1 cup sugar, 2 teaspoons lemon rind, and ginger in a food processor; process 1 minute or until the sugar mixture is lemon-colored, scraping the sides of the processor bowl once.

Spoon sugar mixture into a large bowl; add margarine to the sugar mixture, and beat at medium speed of an electric mixer until light and fluffy. Add corn syrup, vanilla extract, and egg; beat well. Stir in flour mixture (dough will be stiff).

Combine remaining 1 teaspoon lemon rind and 3 tablespoons sugar in a small bowl; stir well. Set lemon-sugar aside.

Preheat oven to 375°. Coat hands lightly with cooking spray, and shape dough into 60 (1-inch) balls. Roll balls in lemon-sugar, and place 2 inches apart on baking sheets coated with cooking spray. Flatten the balls with the bottom of a glass.

Bake at 375° for 7 minutes, and let cool 5 minutes. Remove the cookies from baking sheets, and let cool on wire racks. Yield: 5 dozen (serving size: 1 cookie).

CALORIES 44 (29% from fat); PROTEIN 0.6g; FAT 1.4g (sat 0.3g, mono 0.6g, poly 0.4g); CARB 7.4g; FIBER 0.1g; CHOL 4mg; IRON 0.2mg; SODIUM 21mg; CALC 11mg

---

THE ROAD TO A LIGHT COOKIE

Making light cookies is a lot like conducting a science experiment—the right balance of ingredients is crucial. Here are our tips for making great cookies.

◆ If the batter seems dry and you're tempted to add more liquid, don't. This makes for a cakelike cookie that spreads too much.
◆ Don't forget the corn syrup—it makes the cookies crisp yet keeps them from drying out. Too much corn syrup, however, will make them soggy.
◆ Always use stick margarine instead of the kind in a tub. Also, be careful not to use low-fat margarine or anything that's labeled "spread."
◆ To measure flour, lightly spoon it into the measuring cup, then level with a knife.

EASY PEANUT BUTTER COOKIES

1⅔ cups all-purpose flour
1½ tablespoons cornstarch
1¾ teaspoons baking powder
½ teaspoon baking soda
¾ cup firmly packed brown sugar
¼ cup vegetable oil
¼ cup sugar
¼ cup creamy peanut butter
1½ tablespoons light-colored corn syrup
2½ teaspoons vanilla extract
1 egg
Vegetable cooking spray
3 tablespoons granulated sugar

Combine first 4 ingredients in a bowl; stir well, and set aside. Combine brown sugar and next 3 ingredients in a large bowl; beat at medium speed of an electric mixer until well-blended. Add corn syrup, vanilla, and egg; beat well. Stir in flour mixture.

Preheat oven to 375°. Coat hands lightly with cooking spray, and shape

---

dough into 48 (1-inch) balls. Roll balls in 3 tablespoons granulated sugar, and place 2 inches apart on baking sheets coated with cooking spray. Flatten balls with the bottom of a glass.

Bake at 375° for 7 minutes or until lightly browned. Remove cookies from baking sheets, and let cool on wire racks. Yield: 4 dozen (serving size: 1 cookie).

CALORIES 59 (31% from fat); PROTEIN 1g; FAT 2g (sat 0.4g, mono 0.7g, poly 0.8g); CARB 9.5g; FIBER 0.2g; CHOL 5mg; IRON 0.3mg; SODIUM 23mg; CALC 14mg

---

OATMEAL-RAISIN HERMITS

Make sure the raisins you use are fresh and soft. Dry raisins will absorb the moisture from the cookie dough, making the cookies dry.

1½ cups all-purpose flour
¾ teaspoon baking powder
¾ teaspoon baking soda
½ teaspoon ground cinnamon
¼ teaspoon salt
⅛ teaspoon ground nutmeg
1¼ cups firmly packed brown sugar
¼ cup plus 2 tablespoons stick margarine, melted
2 tablespoons light-colored corn syrup
1 tablespoon vanilla extract
1 tablespoon water
3 egg whites
1⅔ cups regular oats
1⅔ cups raisins
⅓ cup chopped pecans, toasted
Vegetable cooking spray

Preheat oven to 350°.

Combine first 6 ingredients in a bowl; stir well, and set aside. Combine brown sugar and next 5 ingredients in a large bowl; beat at medium speed of an electric mixer until well-blended. Stir in oats, raisins, and pecans; let stand 5 minutes. Stir in flour mixture.

Drop dough by level tablespoons 2 inches apart onto baking sheets coated with cooking spray. Bake at 350° for 12 minutes or until almost set. Let cool 2 minutes or until firm. Remove cookies from baking sheets; let cool on wire racks. Yield: 3½ dozen (serving size: 1 cookie).

CALORIES 97 (24% from fat); PROTEIN 1.5g; FAT 2.6g (sat 0.4g, mono 1.2g, poly 0.8g); CARB 17.5g; FIBER 0.8g; CHOL 0mg; IRON 0.6mg; SODIUM 64mg; CALC 17mg

MOLASSES CRACKLES

2⅔ cups all-purpose flour
1¼ teaspoons baking powder
1 teaspoon ground ginger
¼ teaspoon baking soda
2¼ teaspoons ground cinnamon
¾ teaspoon ground cloves
⅛ teaspoon salt
½ cup dark molasses
¼ cup plus 3 tablespoons vegetable oil
2½ tablespoons dark corn syrup
¼ teaspoon grated orange rind
1⅓ cups sifted powdered sugar, divided
1 egg
Vegetable cooking spray

Combine first 7 ingredients in a bowl; stir well, and set aside. Combine molasses and next 3 ingredients in a large bowl; beat at medium speed of an electric mixer until blended. Add 1 cup powdered sugar and egg; beat until well-blended. Stir in flour mixture. Cover and freeze 1 hour.

Preheat oven to 375°. Coat hands lightly with cooking spray, and shape dough into 48 (1-inch) balls. Roll balls in remaining powdered sugar, and place 2 inches apart on baking sheets coated with cooking spray. Bake at 375° for 8 minutes. Let cool 2 minutes or until firm. Remove cookies from baking sheets, and let cool on wire racks. Yield: 4 dozen (serving size: 1 cookie).

CALORIES 69 (29% from fat); PROTEIN 0.9g; FAT 2.2g (sat 0.4g, mono 0.6g, poly 1g); CARB 11.7g; FIBER 0.2g; CHOL 5mg; IRON 1mg; SODIUM 17mg; CALC 40mg

DOUBLE-CHOCOLATE CHEWS

1¾ cups all-purpose flour
⅔ cup sifted powdered sugar
⅓ cup unsweetened cocoa
2¼ teaspoons baking powder
⅛ teaspoon salt
1 cup semisweet chocolate mini-morsels, divided
3 tablespoons vegetable oil
1 cup firmly packed brown sugar
2½ tablespoons light-colored corn syrup
1 tablespoon water
2½ teaspoons vanilla extract
3 egg whites
Vegetable cooking spray

Preheat oven to 350°.
Combine first 5 ingredients in a bowl; stir well, and set aside.
Combine ¾ cup chocolate morsels and oil in a small saucepan; cook over low heat until chocolate melts, stirring constantly. Pour melted chocolate mixture into a large bowl, and let cool 5 minutes. Add brown sugar and next 4 ingredients to chocolate mixture; stir well. Stir in flour mixture and remaining chocolate morsels.

Drop dough by level tablespoons 2 inches apart onto baking sheets coated with cooking spray. Bake at 350° for 8 minutes. Let cool 2 minutes or until firm. Remove cookies from baking sheets; let cool on wire racks. Yield: 4 dozen (serving size: 1 cookie).

CALORIES 64 (23% from fat); PROTEIN 0.9g; FAT 1.6g (sat 0.6g, mono 0.5g, poly 0.5g); CARB 11.8g; FIBER 0.1g; CHOL 0mg; IRON 0.5mg; SODIUM 13mg; CALC 19mg

RASPBERRY THUMBPRINTS

1½ cups all-purpose flour
¼ cup cornstarch
½ teaspoon baking powder
¼ teaspoon baking soda
¼ teaspoon salt
¼ cup plus 3 tablespoons stick margarine, softened
½ cup sugar
2 tablespoons light-colored corn syrup
2½ teaspoons vanilla extract
½ teaspoon grated lemon rind
⅛ teaspoon almond extract
1 egg
Vegetable cooking spray
¼ cup seedless raspberry jam

Combine first 5 ingredients in a bowl; stir well, and set aside. Combine margarine and the next 6 ingredients in a large bowl; beat at medium speed of an electric mixer until well-blended. Stir in flour mixture; cover and freeze 30 minutes or until firm.

Preheat oven to 375°. Shape dough into 36 (1-inch) balls. Place balls 1 inch apart on baking sheets coated with cooking spray. Press thumb into the center of each cookie, leaving an indentation. Spoon about ¼ teaspoon jam into center of each cookie. Bake at 375° for 10 minutes; let cool 2 minutes or until firm. Remove cookies from baking sheets, and let cool on wire racks. Yield: 3 dozen (serving size: 1 cookie).

CALORIES 65 (33% from fat); PROTEIN 0.8g; FAT 2.4g (sat 0.5g, mono 1g, poly 0.7g); CARB 10g; FIBER 0.2g; CHOL 6mg; IRON 0.3mg; SODIUM 55mg; CALC 6mg

BAKING THE BEST BATCH

◆ Unless otherwise specified, always preheat the oven at least 10 minutes before baking.
◆ Use shiny baking sheets for baking. Dark ones absorb more heat and cause cookies to overbrown.

◆ Let cookies cool completely before storing.
◆ To keep cookies fresh, store soft ones in an airtight container, and crisp cookies in a jar with a loose-fitting lid.

Healthy Hawaiian Cuisine

"It was like one big Club Med," says Chef Amy Ferguson-Ota, recalling her first impression of Hawaii in 1985. Although she was already one of America's top executive chefs, she could not resist the call of the trade winds. As executive chef at the Ritz-Carlton Mauna Lani, on the "Big Island" of Hawaii, she's developed a menu entitled "Healthy Hawaii Cuisine" featuring an array of colorful, highly flavorful, low-fat and fat-free dishes. "Healthy Hawaii Cuisine was created to offer a feast of honest island flavors without adding any butter, cream, or oil," she says. Her light, exotic dishes include *Ulu* Vichyssoise (breadfruit soup), and fish and pasta dishes baked in natural *ti*-leaf packages.

Thanks to chefs like Ferguson-Ota, paradise just keeps getting better.

STEAMED FISH WITH BANANA-CURRY SAUCE

The Hawaiian technique for preparing this dish would be to steam the fish in banana leaves. We used parchment paper because it's easier to find.

- ¼ cup low-fat coconut milk
- 3 tablespoons chopped fresh cilantro
- 2 tablespoons minced fresh lemon grass or 1 teaspoon grated lemon rind
- 2 tablespoons minced shallot
- 2 tablespoons chopped fresh or freeze-dried chives
- 2 tablespoons fresh lime juice
- 1 teaspoon seeded, minced red jalapeño pepper
- 1 teaspoon fish sauce
- Dash of salt
- 1 garlic clove, minced
- 4 (6-ounce) halibut fillets
- Banana-Curry Sauce

Combine first 10 ingredients in a large heavy-duty, zip-top plastic bag. Add fillets; seal bag, and marinate in refrigerator 8 hours, turning bag occasionally. Remove fillets from bag; discard marinade.

Cut 4 (12-inch) squares of parchment paper. Place each fillet on a square of parchment paper, and wrap tightly. Place fillets in a vegetable steamer. Steam, covered, 15 minutes

or until fish flakes easily when tested with a fork. Unwrap fillets; serve with Banana-Curry Sauce. Serve with rice. Yield: 4 servings (serving size: 1 fillet and ¼ cup sauce).

CALORIES 261 (20% from fat); PROTEIN 36.8g; FAT 5.9g (sat 1.5g, mono 1.7g, poly 1.6g); CARB 14.2g; FIBER 1.6g; CHOL 80mg; IRON 2.4mg; SODIUM 260mg; CALC 104mg

Banana-Curry Sauce:

- ½ teaspoon olive oil
- ¼ cup chopped Vidalia or other sweet onion
- 2 small ripe bananas, quartered
- 1 shallot, quartered
- 1 garlic clove, halved
- 1¾ teaspoons curry powder
- ¾ cup canned low-sodium chicken broth, undiluted
- 1 tablespoon rice vinegar
- 1½ teaspoons honey
- Dash of salt

Heat oil in a medium nonstick skillet over medium-high heat until hot. Add onion and next 3 ingredients; sauté 2 minutes. Add curry powder, and sauté 30 seconds. Add chicken broth, and simmer 5 minutes, stirring occasionally.

Place onion mixture, vinegar, honey, and salt in a blender; cover and process until smooth. Yield: 1 cup (serving size: ¼ cup).

CALORIES 56 (18% from fat); PROTEIN 1.1g; FAT 1.1g (sat 0.2g, mono 0.6g, poly 0.1g); CARB 11.5g; FIBER 1.4g; CHOL 0mg; IRON 0.6mg; SODIUM 24mg; CALC 10mg

The Package Deal

By combining prepackaged doughs with convenience foods, you can have fancy breads on the table with little effort.

When sitting down to eat, it's the little things that impress: cloth napkins instead of paper, separate plates for the salad course, and soft music instead of TV. But if you truly want to knock people's socks off (in a humble, understated way, of course), accompany meals, teatimes, coffee gatherings, and the like with tasty homemade breads. Problem is, such breads often rank least in importance when you're in a rush to get food to the table. Quoth the raven, "Nevermore."

By combining prepackaged bread doughs with ready-made foods, you can create an array of sweet and savory breads that take less-than-expected time or effort to pull off. And these breads not only impress the tastebuds, but they're healthy, too. On that you can quoth us.

LEMON-GLAZED CRANBERRY ROLLS

Try these sweet rolls with a cup of tea at brunch or as an afternoon snack.
Preparation time: 10 minutes
Cooking time: 15 minutes

- 1 (10-ounce) can refrigerated pizza crust dough
- ½ cup orange marmalade
- ⅔ cup dried cranberries
- Vegetable cooking spray
- ½ cup sifted powdered sugar
- 1½ teaspoons lemon juice
- 1 teaspoon hot water

Preheat oven to 375°.

Unroll pizza dough, and pat into a 12 x 9-inch rectangle. Spread marmalade over dough, leaving a ½-inch border. Sprinkle dried cranberries over marmalade, pressing gently into dough. Beginning with a long side, roll up dough jelly-roll fashion; pinch seam to seal (do not seal ends of roll). Cut roll into 12 (1-inch) slices. Place slices, cut sides up, into muffin cups coated with cooking spray. Bake at 375° for 15 minutes or until golden. Remove rolls from pan, and place on a wire rack.

Combine powdered sugar, lemon juice, and hot water in a small bowl, stirring until smooth. Drizzle icing over warm rolls. Yield: 12 rolls (serving size: 1 roll).

Note: Substitute ⅓ cup apple jelly for the orange marmalade and ⅔ cup raisins for the cranberries, if desired.

CALORIES 155 (6% from fat); PROTEIN 2.9g; FAT 1g (sat 0.3g, mono 0g, poly 0g); CARB 34.7g; FIBER 3g; CHOL 0mg; IRON 0.3mg; SODIUM 229mg; CALC 15mg

SAVING YOUR DOUGH

To slice the roll of dough without squishing the slices, slide a long piece of string or dental floss under the roll of dough. Cross ends of string over top of roll, and slowly pull ends to cut through the roll.

MENU SUGGESTION
DATE-AND-WALNUT SAMBOUSEKS
Vanilla yogurt and mueslix

Strawberries

*Make and freeze the sambouseks. For breakfast on the run, simply thaw and reheat.

DATE-AND-WALNUT SAMBOUSEKS

Enjoy these Arabic "little turnovers" as a breakfast pastry or a light dessert.
Preparation time: 15 minutes
Cooking time: 25 minutes

1   cup pitted, chopped dates
½   cup orange juice
2   tablespoons finely chopped walnuts
1   teaspoon vanilla extract
½   teaspoon ground cinnamon
1   (7.5-ounce) can refrigerated biscuit dough (10 biscuits)
Vegetable cooking spray
1   egg, lightly beaten
1   tablespoon sesame seeds

Preheat oven to 350°.

Combine chopped dates and orange juice in a medium saucepan; cover and cook over low heat for 15 minutes or until the liquid is absorbed. Remove pan from heat, and mash dates with a fork until smooth. Stir in chopped walnuts, vanilla, and cinnamon.

Divide the dough into 10 biscuits. Working with 1 biscuit at a time, pat each biscuit into a 4-inch circle. Spoon about 1 tablespoon of date mixture onto half of each circle. Fold dough over filling, and press the edges together with a fork to seal. Place the filled pastries about 2 inches apart on a baking sheet coated with cooking spray. Brush beaten egg over pastries, and sprinkle with sesame seeds.

Bake the pastries at 350° for 25 minutes or until lightly browned. Remove from pan, and let cool on a wire rack. Yield: 10 pastries (serving size: 1 pastry).

CALORIES 163 (20% from fat); PROTEIN 3.9g; FAT 3.6g (sat 0.7g, mono 1.5g, poly 1.1g); CARB 29.8g; FIBER 1.8g; CHOL 22mg; IRON 1mg; SODIUM 147mg; CALC 31mg

CRISP-AND-SPICY CHEESE TWISTS

Use a pizza cutter to cut strips more easily.
Preparation time: 8 minutes
Cooking time: 8 minutes

¼   cup grated Parmesan cheese
1   teaspoon paprika
⅛   teaspoon ground red pepper
1   (10-ounce) can refrigerated pizza crust dough
Butter-flavored vegetable cooking spray

Preheat oven to 425°.

Combine Parmesan cheese, paprika, and red pepper in a small bowl; stir well, and set aside.

Unroll pizza dough, and roll into an 8 x 12-inch rectangle. Lightly coat surface of dough with cooking spray, and sprinkle with 2 tablespoons cheese mixture. Fold the dough in half to form a 6 x 8-inch rectangle. Roll dough into a 12 x 8-inch rectangle. Lightly coat surface of dough with cooking spray, and sprinkle with remaining cheese mixture. Using fingertips, press cheese mixture into dough.

Cut the dough into 16 (8-inch-long) strips. Gently pick up both ends of each strip, and twist dough. Place the twisted strips of dough ½ inch apart on a large baking sheet coated with cooking spray.

Bake at 425° for 8 minutes or until lightly browned. Remove from baking sheet, and let cool on wire racks. Yield: 16 breadsticks (serving size: 1 breadstick).

CALORIES 68 (15% from fat); PROTEIN 2.7g; FAT 1.1g (sat 0.5g, mono 0.1g, poly 0g); CARB 11.9g; FIBER 0.6g; CHOL 1mg; IRON 0.3mg; SODIUM 189mg; CALC 25mg

MEXICAN SALSA BREAD

Preparation time: 7 minutes
Cooking time: 15 minutes

- 1 cup (4 ounces) shredded reduced-fat Monterey Jack cheese, divided
- ¾ cup picante sauce
- ⅓ cup chopped fresh cilantro
- 1 (1-pound) Italian cheese-flavored pizza crust (like Boboli)

Preheat oven to 350°. Combine ½ cup cheese, picante sauce, and cilantro in a small bowl; stir well. Spread over pizza crust, and sprinkle with remaining cheese. Place on a baking sheet, and bake at 350° for 15 minutes or until cheese melts. Cut into wedges. Yield: 8 servings (serving size: 1 wedge).

CALORIES 143 (31% from fat); PROTEIN 8.9g; FAT 4.9g (sat 2.2g, mono 1g, poly 0.1g); CARB 16.3g; FIBER 0.1g; CHOL 13mg; IRON 0.4mg; SODIUM 520mg; CALC 122mg

ROSEMARY-AND-GARLIC BREADSTICKS

These savory breadsticks could accompany almost any soup or stew.
Preparation time: 12 minutes
Cooking time: 20 minutes

- 1 tablespoon olive oil
- 1 tablespoon chopped fresh or 1 teaspoon dried rosemary
- ¼ teaspoon pepper
- 2 garlic cloves, minced
- 1 (11-ounce) can refrigerated soft breadstick dough
- Olive oil-flavored vegetable cooking spray

Preheat oven to 350°.
Heat olive oil in a small nonstick skillet over medium heat until hot. Add rosemary, pepper, and garlic; sauté for 1 minute. Remove from heat, and set aside.
Unroll breadstick dough (do not separate dough into breadsticks). Beginning in the center of dough, spread rosemary mixture to one short end of dough. Fold other half of dough over rosemary mixture, pinching ends together to seal.
Cut dough along perforations to form 8 breadsticks. Twist each folded breadstick, and place on a baking sheet coated with cooking spray. Bake breadsticks at 350° for 15 minutes or until golden. Yield: 8 breadsticks (serving size: 1 breadstick).

CALORIES 127 (30% from fat); PROTEIN 3.1g; FAT 4.3g (sat 0.7g, mono 2.2g, poly 1.1g); CARB 18.4g; FIBER 1.1g; CHOL 0mg; IRON 0.1mg; SODIUM 290mg; CALC 3mg

OLIVE-AND-CHEESE PINWHEELS

Preparation time: 10 minutes
Cooking time: 20 minutes

- 1 tablespoon olive oil
- 1 teaspoon dried oregano
- 4 ounces block nonfat cream cheese, softened
- ⅓ cup chopped pimento-stuffed green olives
- 1 (11-ounce) can refrigerated soft breadstick dough
- Vegetable cooking spray

Preheat oven to 400°.
Combine first 3 ingredients in a medium bowl; beat at medium speed of an electric mixer until smooth. Stir in olives.
Unroll breadstick dough (do not separate the dough into breadsticks). Spread cheese mixture evenly over dough. Beginning with a short side, roll up dough tightly, jelly-roll fashion; pinch the seam to seal (do not seal ends of roll). Cut the dough along perforations into 8 slices. Place slices, cut sides up, into muffin cups coated with cooking spray. Bake at 400° for 20 minutes. Yield: 8 rolls (serving size: 1 roll).

CALORIES 143 (30% from fat); PROTEIN 5.1g; FAT 4.7g (sat 0.8g, mono 2.5g, poly 1.1g); CARB 18.9g; FIBER 1.2g; CHOL 3mg; IRON 0.3mg; SODIUM 426mg; CALC 48mg

SWEET ONION-AND-POPPY SEED FLATBREAD

Preparation time: 25 minutes
Cooking time: 25 minutes

- 1 pound Vidalia or other sweet onions
- Vegetable cooking spray
- 2 tablespoons chopped parsley
- 1 teaspoon poppy seeds
- ¼ teaspoon salt
- ⅛ teaspoon pepper
- 1 (11-ounce) can refrigerated French bread dough

Preheat oven to 350°.
Peel onions, and cut in half lengthwise. Cut each half crosswise into thin slices.
Coat a large nonstick skillet with cooking spray, and place over medium-high heat until hot. Add onions; sauté 8 minutes or until golden. Remove from heat; stir in parsley, poppy seeds, salt, and pepper.
Unroll bread dough, and place on a baking sheet coated with cooking spray; pat into a 16 x 7-inch rectangle. Spread onion mixture over dough, leaving a ½-inch border. Bake at 350° for 25 minutes or until golden brown. Remove from pan; let cool 5 minutes on a wire rack. Yield: 8 servings (serving size: 1 [4 x 3½-inch] piece).

CALORIES 140 (10% from fat); PROTEIN 5.5g; FAT 1.5g (sat 0.3g, mono 0.5g, poly 0.5g); CARB 26.4g; FIBER 1.1g; CHOL 0mg; IRON 1.6mg; SODIUM 344mg; CALC 28mg

Banquets of Imagination

For the average cook, preparing a dim sum feast at home may appear daunting—but that need not be the case. Our recipes are actually riddles in simplicity, with step-by-step instructions. You can, of course, prepare this entire feast or just one or two dishes, if you'd rather. As for locating ingredients, won ton wrappers and gyoza skins are available at Oriental food stores.

STEAMED PEARL BALLS

Lining the bamboo steamer with steamed green cabbage leaves keeps the balls from sticking.

½   cup uncooked long-grain rice
½   pound ground chicken or turkey
½   cup finely chopped mushrooms
½   cup minced green onions
1   tablespoon low-sodium soy sauce
2   teaspoons cornstarch
1   teaspoon peeled, minced gingerroot
½   teaspoon sugar
½   teaspoon dark sesame oil
Steamed green cabbage leaves

Place ½ cup rice in a small bowl; cover with water to 1 inch above rice, and let stand 1 hour. Drain rice well; place rice in a shallow dish, and set aside.

Combine chicken and next 7 ingredients in a medium bowl; stir well. Drop mixture by rounded tablespoons into rice, rolling to form rice-coated balls.

Line a bamboo or vegetable steamer with steamed cabbage leaves. Place balls ½ inch apart in steamer; cover with steamer lid. Add water to a large skillet to a depth of 1 inch; bring to a boil.

Place steamer in skillet, and steam balls 20 minutes or until rice is tender. Remove balls from steamer. Yield: 14 appetizers (serving size: 1 ball).

CALORIES 55 (25% from fat); PROTEIN 3.8g; FAT 1.5g (sat 0.4g, mono 0.6g, poly 0.4g); CARB 6.3g; FIBER 0.2g; CHOL 12mg; IRON 0.5mg; SODIUM 46mg; CALC 6mg

HOT MUSTARD SAUCE

3   tablespoons dry mustard
3   tablespoons water
1½   teaspoons rice vinegar
¼   teaspoon salt

Combine all ingredients in a small bowl, and stir with a wire whisk until blended. Let stand 10 minutes. Yield: ¼ cup (serving size: 1 tablespoon).

CALORIES 20 (63% from fat); PROTEIN 1.1g; FAT 1.4g (sat 0.1g, mono 1g, poly 0.3g); CARB 0.6g; FIBER 0.1g; CHOL 0mg; IRON 0.3mg; SODIUM 147mg; CALC 11mg

LEMON-SOY DIPPING SAUCE

⅓   cup low-sodium soy sauce
2   tablespoons fresh lemon juice
1   tablespoon water

Combine all ingredients in a small bowl, and stir well. Yield: ½ cup (serving size: 1 tablespoon).

CALORIES 6 (0% from fat); PROTEIN 0.5g; FAT 0g; CARB 1.2g; FIBER 0g; CHOL 0mg; IRON 0.2mg; SODIUM 322mg; CALC 2mg

FRAGRANT GINGER-HOT PEPPER SAUCE

1   tablespoon vegetable oil
¼   cup peeled, minced gingerroot
2   teaspoons crushed red pepper
½   teaspoon salt
2   large garlic cloves, minced
¼   cup chopped fresh cilantro
¼   cup minced green onions
2½   tablespoons water

Heat vegetable oil in a small skillet over medium heat until hot. Add minced gingerroot and next 3 ingredients; sauté 2 minutes.

Remove mixture from heat; spoon into a small bowl, and stir in fresh cilantro, green onions, and water. Yield: ½ cup (serving size: 1 tablespoon).

CALORIES 22 (74% from fat); PROTEIN 0.3g; FAT 1.8g (sat 0.3g, mono 0.5g, poly 0.8g); CARB 1.3g; FIBER 0.3g; CHOL 0mg; IRON 0.2mg; SODIUM 150mg; CALC 9mg

---

DELIGHTFUL DIM SUM

In America, most cities that have Chinatowns also have dim sum parlors. Cantonese for "heart's delight" or "a bit of heart" (depending on the translation), dim sum includes a variety of small, mouthwatering snacks. Carts loaded with a variety of dishes, hot and steaming from the kitchen, are wheeled around to the tables periodically. To order, customers need only point to the foods they can't resist.

PORK-AND-SHRIMP DUMPLINGS

- ½ pound lean ground pork
- ¼ pound medium-size shrimp, peeled and minced
- ½ cup finely chopped canned water chestnuts
- ¼ cup minced green onions
- ¼ cup low-salt chicken broth
- 1 tablespoon cornstarch
- 1 tablespoon dry sherry
- ½ teaspoon salt
- 1½ teaspoons peeled, minced gingerroot
- 32 won ton wrappers
- 2 teaspoons cornstarch
- Steamed green cabbage leaves

Combine first 9 ingredients in a medium bowl; stir well, and set aside.

Working with 1 won ton wrapper at a time (cover the remaining wrappers to keep them from drying out), spoon about 1 tablespoon pork mixture into center of each wrapper. Moisten edges of dough with water, and bring 2 opposite corners to center, pinching points to seal. Bring remaining 2 corners to center, pinching points to seal. Pinch 4 edges together to seal. Place dumplings on a large baking sheet sprinkled with 2 teaspoons cornstarch, and cover loosely with a towel to keep from drying out.

Line a bamboo steamer with steamed cabbage leaves. Place dumplings ½ inch apart in steamer; cover with steamer lid. Add water to a large skillet to a depth of 1 inch; bring water to a boil. Place steamer in skillet; steam dumplings for 10 minutes. Remove dumplings from steamer. Yield: 32 appetizers (serving size: 1 dumpling).

CALORIES 37 (15% from fat); PROTEIN 2.7g; FAT 0.6g (sat 0.2g, mono 0.2g, poly 0.1g); CARB 4.6g; FIBER 0g; CHOL 9mg; IRON 0.4mg; SODIUM 83mg; CALC 6mg

---

DIM SUM TIPS

- ◆ For our dim sum steamed dishes, we used a bamboo steamer because it's large enough to cook several dumplings at once. You can also use a less expensive vegetable steamer, although it won't hold as many dumplings and it may take several batches to cook them all. Be sure to cover the first few batches of dumplings so they don't dry out after they've been steamed.
- ◆ Some of our recipes call for lining the steamer with steamed cabbage leaves. The number of leaves needed will vary according to the size of the leaves. The leaves can be blanched in boiling water, steamed in a vegetable steamer, or steamed in the bamboo steamer before adding the appetizers to the rack. You can discard the steamed leaves afterward.
- ◆ All of the fillings and dipping sauces can be made ahead of time. You can assemble the dumplings up to 30 minutes before cooking (assembled too far in advance, the ends of the wrappers will dry out); cover tightly, and refrigerate. The exception is the Curried Chicken Buns because the yeast dough has a specific rising time.

PORK-AND-PEANUT DUMPLINGS

The pork-and-peanut filling is typical of fun kor, *which are traditionally wrapped in a dough that is made with wheat and tapioca starches.*

- 1 cup boiling water
- ½ ounce dried shiitake mushrooms
- ½ pound lean ground pork
- 1 tablespoon peeled, minced gingerroot
- 1 garlic clove, minced
- 1 tablespoon cornstarch
- ¼ cup chopped fresh cilantro
- 3 tablespoons chopped unsalted dry-roasted peanuts
- 3 tablespoons sliced green onions
- 2 tablespoons low-sodium soy sauce
- ½ teaspoon sugar
- 30 (3-inch) gyoza skins
- Steamed green cabbage leaves

Combine boiling water and dried mushrooms in a small bowl; cover and let stand 30 minutes. Drain mushrooms, reserving ¼ cup mushroom liquid, and let cool completely. Discard mushroom stems, and finely chop caps; set aside.

Cook pork, gingerroot, and garlic in a large nonstick skillet over medium heat until browned, stirring to crumble. Drain well, and return pork mixture to skillet.

Combine reserved mushroom liquid and cornstarch; stir well. Add to skillet; cook over medium heat 30 seconds or until thickened, stirring constantly. Remove from heat; stir in chopped mushroom caps, cilantro, and next 4 ingredients.

Working with 1 gyoza skin at a time (cover remaining skins to keep them from drying out), spoon about 2 teaspoons pork mixture into center of each skin. Moisten edges of skin with water. Fold in half, pinching edges together to seal. Place dumplings, seam sides up, on a baking sheet; cover with a towel to keep from drying out.

Line a bamboo steamer with steamed green cabbage leaves. Place dumplings ½ inch apart in steamer, and cover with steamer lid. Add water to a large skillet to a depth of 1 inch, and bring to a boil. Place steamer in skillet, and steam dumplings 10 minutes. Remove dumplings from steamer. Yield: 30 appetizers (serving size: 1 dumpling).

CALORIES 41 (29% from fat); PROTEIN 2.5g; FAT 1.3g (sat 0.4g, mono 0.6g, poly 0.3g); CARB 4.5g; FIBER 0.2g; CHOL 6mg; IRON 0.4mg; SODIUM 71mg; CALC 6mg

SEAFOOD-STUFFED BELL PEPPERS

- ½ cup low-salt chicken broth
- 1 tablespoon dry sherry
- 1 tablespoon low-sodium soy sauce
- 1 teaspoon cornstarch
- ½ teaspoon sugar
- ½ teaspoon rice vinegar
- ½ teaspoon dark sesame oil
- ¼ teaspoon salt
- ¼ pound medium-sized shrimp, peeled
- ¼ pound flounder fillet, chopped
- 1 tablespoon dry sherry
- 1 teaspoon cornstarch
- 1 teaspoon peeled, coarsely chopped gingerroot
- ½ teaspoon salt
- 2 green onions, cut into 1-inch pieces
- 1 egg white
- 2 small green bell peppers
- ½ teaspoon cornstarch
- 1 tablespoon vegetable oil
- ½ cup low-salt chicken broth

Combine first 8 ingredients in a small bowl; stir well, and set cornstarch mixture aside.

Peel and devein shrimp. Place shrimp and next 7 ingredients in a food processor, and pulse until mixture is coarsely ground.

Cut each bell pepper lengthwise into quarters; discard seeds and membranes. Cut each quarter in half crosswise. Place pepper pieces, cut sides up, on a large baking sheet. Sprinkle ½ teaspoon cornstarch over the insides of pepper pieces. Spoon about 1 tablespoon of shrimp mixture into the cavity of each pepper piece.

Heat 1 tablespoon vegetable oil in a large nonstick skillet over medium-high heat until hot. Place stuffed pepper pieces, filling sides down, in skillet; cook 2 minutes or until filling is golden. Turn pepper pieces over, and add ½ cup chicken broth to skillet. Bring to a boil, and cook 3 minutes or until liquid evaporates. Add cornstarch mixture; bring to a boil, and cook 1 minute or until thickened, stirring constantly. To serve, spoon sauce over stuffed pepper pieces. Yield: 16 appetizers (serving size: 1 pepper piece).

CALORIES 33 (35% from fat); PROTEIN 3.3g; FAT 1.3g (sat 0.2g, mono 0.3g, poly 0.6g); CARB 1.3g; FIBER 0.1g; CHOL 14mg; IRON 0.4mg; SODIUM 165mg; CALC 8mg

FOUR-FLAVOR DUMPLINGS

Gyoza (ghe-O-za) skins are round wrappers available at Oriental food stores. You can substitute won ton wrappers cut into circles instead.

- 1 cup boiling water
- ½ ounce dried shiitake mushrooms
- ¼ pound ground chicken or turkey
- ¼ cup thawed, drained, and squeezed dry frozen chopped spinach
- ¼ cup minced green onions
- 1½ teaspoons cornstarch
- 1½ teaspoons dry sherry
- 1½ teaspoons oyster sauce
- ½ teaspoon dark sesame oil
- ⅛ teaspoon salt
- 32 (3-inch) gyoza skins
- ⅓ cup frozen tiny green peas, thawed
- ¼ cup finely diced carrot
- 8 medium shrimp, peeled and quartered
- 2 teaspoons cornstarch
- Steamed green cabbage leaves

Combine boiling water and mushrooms in a bowl; cover and let stand 30 minutes. Drain; discard mushroom stems, and mince caps.

Combine chicken and next 7 ingredients in a bowl; add 3 tablespoons minced mushrooms (set remaining mushrooms aside), and stir well. Set chicken mixture aside.

Working with 1 gyoza skin at a time (cover remaining skins to keep them from drying out), moisten 4 equally spaced points around edge of skin with water. Spoon about 1 teaspoon chicken mixture into center of skin. Bring 4 moistened points over filling to center, pressing together with fingers.

Push fingers toward center of circle to form 4 pockets (if pockets do not open enough for chicken mixture to be visible, use the tip of a knife to separate the dough and open pockets). For each dumpling, fill first pocket with mushrooms, second pocket with peas, third pocket with carrot, and fourth pocket with 1 piece of shrimp. Place filled dumplings on a large baking sheet sprinkled with 2 teaspoons cornstarch; cover loosely with a towel to keep from drying out.

Line a bamboo steamer with steamed cabbage leaves. Place filled dumplings ½ inch apart in steamer, and cover with steamer lid. Add water to a large skillet to a depth of 1 inch; bring to a boil. Place steamer in skillet, and steam dumplings 10 minutes; remove dumplings from steamer. Serve dumplings with dipping sauces. Yield: 32 appetizers (serving size: 1 dumpling).

CALORIES 31 (12% from fat); PROTEIN 2.2g; FAT 0.4g (sat 0.1g, mono 0.1g, poly 0.1g); CARB 4.5g; FIBER 0.2g; CHOL 8mg; IRON 0.4mg; SODIUM 63mg; CALC 10mg

HOW TO SHAPE FOUR-FLAVOR DUMPLINGS

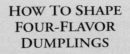

1. Moisten 4 equally spaced points around edge of gyoza skin. Bring 4 moistened points together, pressing with fingers.

2. Push fingers toward center of gyoza skin to form 4 pockets.

CHICKEN POT STICKERS

2 teaspoons vegetable oil
2 cups finely chopped green cabbage
½ cup water
½ pound ground chicken or turkey
⅓ cup minced green onions
1 tablespoon peeled, minced gingerroot
½ teaspoon salt
½ teaspoon dark sesame oil
1 egg white
1 garlic clove, crushed
30 won ton wrappers
2 teaspoons cornstarch
1 tablespoon plus 1 teaspoon vegetable oil, divided
1 cup water, divided

Heat 2 teaspoons vegetable oil in a large nonstick skillet over medium-high heat until hot. Add cabbage; cook 9 minutes or until lightly browned, stirring frequently. While cabbage cooks, add ½ cup water, 1 tablespoon at a time, to keep cabbage from sticking to pan. Spoon cabbage into a medium bowl; let cool completely. Add chicken and next 6 ingredients to bowl; stir well.

Working with 1 won ton wrapper at a time (cover remaining won ton wrappers to keep them from drying out), spoon about 1 tablespoon chicken mixture into the center of each wrapper.

Moisten edges of wrapper with water, and bring 2 opposite corners to center, pinching points to seal. Bring the remaining 2 corners to center, pinching points to seal. Pinch 4 edges together to seal. Place pot stickers on a large baking sheet sprinkled with cornstarch; cover loosely with a towel to keep them from drying out.

Heat 2 teaspoons vegetable oil in a large nonstick skillet over medium heat until hot. Place half of pot stickers in bottom of skillet; cook 3 minutes or until bottoms are lightly browned. Add ½ cup water to skillet; cover and cook 3 minutes or until liquid is absorbed. Place pot stickers on a platter; set aside, and keep warm.

Wipe skillet with a paper towel. Repeat procedure with remaining vegetable oil, remaining pot stickers, and remaining water. Yield: 30 appetizers (serving size: 1 pot sticker).

CALORIES 40 (32% from fat); PROTEIN 2.3g; FAT 1.4g (sat 0.3g, mono 0.4g, poly 0.6g); CARB 4.4g; FIBER 0.1g; CHOL 7mg; IRON 0.3mg; SODIUM 86mg; CALC 7mg

Pot Stickers, Spinach Variation:

1 cup boiling water
1 (⅞-ounce) package dried shiitake mushrooms
½ cup cooked long-grain rice
⅓ cup finely chopped canned water chestnuts
⅓ cup minced green onions
1 tablespoon cornstarch
1 tablespoon peeled, minced gingerroot
1 teaspoon dark sesame oil
1 (10-ounce) package frozen chopped spinach, thawed, drained, and squeezed dry
1 egg white
1 garlic clove, minced
30 won ton wrappers

Combine boiling water and mushrooms in a bowl; cover and let stand 30 minutes. Drain; discard mushroom stems, and mince caps.

Combine mushroom caps, rice, and next 8 ingredients, and stir well. Fill won ton wrappers with spinach mixture, preparing wrappers and cooking per previous directions. Yield: 30 appetizers (serving size: 1 pot sticker).

CALORIES 39 (21% from fat); PROTEIN 1.2g; FAT 0.9g (sat 0.2g, mono 0.3g, poly 0.4g); CARB 6.4g; FIBER 0.5g; CHOL 1mg; IRON 0.5mg; SODIUM 47mg; CALCIUM 15mg

CURRIED CHICKEN BUNS

1 package dry yeast
1 tablespoon sugar
⅔ cup warm water (105° to 115°)
2 cups all-purpose flour
½ teaspoon salt
2 teaspoons vegetable oil
1 teaspoon baking powder
Vegetable cooking spray
½ cup dry sherry
½ cup water
1 pound chicken thighs, skinned
1 tablespoon cornstarch
2 teaspoons vegetable oil
½ cup finely chopped onion
2 teaspoons curry powder
2 teaspoons peeled, minced gingerroot
1 garlic clove, crushed
½ teaspoon salt
Steamed green cabbage leaves

Dissolve yeast and sugar in ⅔ cup warm water in a small bowl; let stand 5 minutes.

Place flour and ½ teaspoon salt in a food processor; pulse 2 times or until blended. With processor on, slowly add yeast mixture and 2 teaspoons oil through chute; process until dough leaves sides of bowl and forms a ball.

Turn the dough out onto a lightly floured surface. Sprinkle baking powder over surface of dough, and knead lightly (about 2 minutes).

Place dough in a large bowl coated with cooking spray, turning to coat top. Cover and let rise in a warm place (85°), free from drafts, 1 hour or until doubled in bulk.

Combine sherry, ½ cup water, and chicken in a medium saucepan; bring to a boil. Cover, reduce heat, and simmer 25 minutes or until chicken is done. Remove chicken from cooking liquid, and let cool. Set aside ½ cup cooking liquid, and let cool completely. Discard remaining cooking liquid. Remove chicken from bones, and shred chicken.

Combine ½ cup cooking liquid and cornstarch; stir well, and set mixture aside.

Heat 2 teaspoons oil in a medium nonstick skillet over medium heat until hot. Add onion; sauté 3 minutes or until tender. Stir in curry powder, gingerroot, and garlic; cook 30 seconds. Add cornstarch mixture; bring to a boil, and cook for 1 minute, stirring constantly. Remove from heat; stir in shredded chicken and ½ teaspoon salt. Set aside.

Punch dough down, and turn out onto a lightly floured surface. Divide dough into 14 equal portions. Working with 1 portion at a time (cover remaining portions to keep dough from drying out), roll each portion into a 4-inch circle. Spoon about 1½ tablespoons of chicken mixture onto center of each circle. Bring edges of dough to center, pinching edges together to seal and form a bundle. Cover and let rise 45 minutes or until puffy (dough will not double in size).

Line a bamboo steamer with steamed cabbage leaves. Place buns, seam sides down, ½ inch apart in steamer; cover with steamer lid. Add water to a large skillet to a depth of 1 inch; bring to a boil. Place steamer in skillet, and steam buns 15 minutes. Remove buns from steamer. Yield: 14 appetizers (serving size: 1 bun).

Note: To bake buns, preheat oven to 350°. Place buns, seam sides down, on a baking sheet coated with cooking spray. Combine 1 egg and 1 tablespoon water; brush over buns. Bake at 350° for 18 minutes. Baking will give the buns a crustier texture; steaming makes the dough moister and a little sticky.

CALORIES 100 (19% from fat); PROTEIN 4.8g; FAT 2.1g (sat 0.4g, mono 0.6g, poly 0.8g); CARB 15.2g; FIBER 0.8g; CHOL 12mg; IRON 1.1mg; SODIUM 181mg; CALC 21mg

In Due Course

Using some of our readers' best recipes, we've put together a divine dinner menu.

BARBECUED ORIENTAL FLANK STEAK

This steak is a frequent request for family dinners. It is so delicious one of my sons forgoes his vegetarian diet whenever I prepare it. One important thing to remember when making this recipe is to cook the steak just until it's pink in the middle; if it cooks too long, it gets tough.

—Terry Shannon, Gold Beach, Oregon

1   (1-pound) lean flank steak
¼   cup sherry
¼   cup low-sodium soy sauce
¼   cup honey
2   tablespoons white vinegar
1   tablespoon peeled, minced gingerroot
1   teaspoon dark sesame oil
2   garlic cloves, crushed
Vegetable cooking spray

Trim fat from steak. Combine steak and next 7 ingredients in a large heavy-duty, zip-top plastic bag; seal bag. Marinate in refrigerator 8 hours, turning bag occasionally.

Remove steak from bag; reserve marinade. Coat grill rack with cooking spray; place on grill over medium-hot coals (350° to 400°). Place steak on rack; grill, covered, 8 minutes on each side or until desired degree of doneness, basting frequently with reserved marinade. Place remaining marinade in a saucepan; cook over medium heat 1 minute.

Cut steak diagonally across the grain into thin slices. Serve with warm marinade. Yield: 4 servings (serving size: 3 ounces).

CALORIES 310 (41% from fat); PROTEIN 21.8g; FAT 14.1g (sat 5.6g, mono 5.8g, poly 0.9g); CARB 19g; FIBER 0g; CHOL 60mg; IRON 2.4mg; SODIUM 462mg; CALC 11mg

GRILLED VEGETABLE PACKETS

These packets are an easy and unique side dish. Just seal the vegetables in foil, and place them on the grill. I have found that it's best to put the carrots on top of the other vegetables so they will not burn.

—Ruth Bouldin, Murfreesboro, Tennessee

4   small baking potatoes, quartered
4   onion slices
4   green bell pepper rings
4   plum tomatoes, quartered
1   cup thinly sliced carrot
4   tablespoons reduced-calorie margarine
¼   teaspoon salt
¼   teaspoon pepper

Fold 4 (16 x 12-inch) sheets of heavy-duty aluminum foil in half lengthwise to make a crease. Open the foil, and layer 4 potato pieces, 1 onion slice, 1 bell pepper ring, 4 tomato pieces, ¼ cup carrot, and 1 tablespoon margarine on half of each foil sheet; sprinkle each serving with salt and pepper. Fold foil over vegetables, and tightly seal the edges.

Place vegetable packets on grill rack over medium-hot coals (350° to 400°), and grill 15 minutes; turn packets, and cook an 10 additional minutes or until potato pieces are tender. Yield: 4 servings.

CALORIES 189 (28% from fat); PROTEIN 4.2g; FAT 5.9g (sat 1g, mono 2.1g, poly 2.5g); CARB 31.3g; FIBER 4g; CHOL 0mg; IRON 2.3mg; SODIUM 308mg; CALC 36mg

SPINACH SALAD

When you're preparing a special dinner and want something more than the usual iceberg and bottled dressing, this salad is perfect. If you're in a rush, don't worry. Just combine all the ingredients for the dressing in a jar, shake it up, toss with the spinach, onions, and mushrooms, and you have a beautiful beginning to your meal.

—Joan Gusweiler, Cincinnati, Ohio

1 (10-ounce) package fresh
   spinach
½ cup thinly sliced red onion,
   separated into rings
1 (8-ounce) package presliced
   fresh mushrooms
2 tablespoons sesame seeds
3 tablespoons cider vinegar
2 tablespoons water
2 tablespoons honey
1 tablespoon Dijon mustard
1 tablespoon vegetable oil
½ teaspoon pepper
1 garlic clove, minced

Tear spinach into bite-size pieces, and place in a large bowl. Add onion and mushrooms; set aside. Combine sesame seeds and next 7 ingredients in a jar. Cover tightly, and shake vigorously. Pour over spinach mixture; toss well. Yield: 5 servings (serving size: 2 cups).

CALORIES 106 (44% from fat); PROTEIN 3.4g; FAT 5.2g (sat 0.8g, mono 1.6g, poly 2.2g); CARB 14g; FIBER 3.2g; CHOL 0mg; IRON 2.8mg; SODIUM 138mg; CALC 98mg

ANZAC BISCUITS

Having recently arrived in the United States from Australia, I'm having a trial-and-error period as I adapt my recipes using American ingredients. But I had instant success with this Australian favorite, and I hope your readers enjoy them, too.

—Sandy Bennett, Waldport, Oregon

1 cup regular oats
1 cup all-purpose flour
1 cup firmly packed brown sugar
½ cup shredded sweetened
   coconut
½ teaspoon baking soda
¼ cup stick margarine, melted
3 tablespoons water
2 tablespoons golden cane syrup
   or light-colored corn syrup
Vegetable cooking spray

Preheat oven to 325°.

Combine first 5 ingredients in a bowl; stir well. Add margarine, water, and syrup; stir well. Drop by level tablespoons 2 inches apart onto baking sheets coated with cooking spray. Bake at 325° for 12 minutes or until almost set. Remove from oven; let stand 2 to 3 minutes or until firm. Remove cookies from baking sheets; place on wire racks, and let cool completely. Yield: 2 dozen (serving size: 1 cookie).

Note: We found these cookies were much better when made with golden cane syrup. Cane syrup is thicker and sweeter than corn syrup and can be found in supermarkets, in cans, next to the jellies and syrups or in stores specializing in Caribbean and Creole cookery.

CALORIES 98 (27% from fat); PROTEIN 1.2g; FAT 2.9g (sat 1g, mono 0.9g, poly 0.7g); CARB 17.3g; FIBER 0.6g; CHOL 0mg; IRON 0.6mg; SODIUM 59mg; CALC 11mg

Dinner Is Brewing

Beer's malty flavor adds depth and roundness to food.

You don't think of beer as belonging on the spice rack, somewhere between the basil and the cinnamon. But beer is indeed a flavor enhancer, as the following recipes demonstrate. No need to put a "not-for-minors" label on these dishes: Most of the beer's alcohol evaporates during cooking, leaving behind only its unmistakable aroma and the flavor imparted by hops, which are dried flowers.

In our recipes you can use typical American lagers, like Coors, Budweiser, and Miller (light beers also work well). So what are you waiting for? Get out those six-packs, and start seasoning.

BEER-BATTER BAKED FISH

1 tablespoon all-purpose flour
¼ teaspoon salt
4 (6-ounce) orange roughy or
   other lean white fish fillets
Vegetable cooking spray
½ cup all-purpose flour
¼ teaspoon pepper
½ cup beer
1 tablespoon extra-virgin olive
   oil
1 egg yolk
2 egg whites

Preheat oven to 500°.

Sprinkle 1 tablespoon flour and salt over 1 side of fillets. Place fillets, flour sides up, in a 13 x 9-inch baking dish coated with cooking spray.

Combine ½ cup flour and pepper in a medium bowl. Gradually add beer, oil, and egg yolk, stirring with a wire whisk until blended.

Beat egg whites at high speed of an electric mixer until stiff peaks form. Gently fold egg whites into the beer mixture, and spread evenly over fillets. Bake at 500° for 10 minutes. Yield: 4 servings (serving size: 1 fillet).

CALORIES 248 (22% from fat); PROTEIN 29.3g; FAT 6.2g (sat 0.9g, mono 3.8g, poly 0.6g); CARB 14.7g; FIBER 0.5g; CHOL 88mg; IRON 1.3mg; SODIUM 430mg; CALC 13mg

BEER-STEAMED SHRIMP WITH ANGEL HAIR PASTA

1   pound medium-size shrimp
1   (12-ounce) bottle beer
1   cup vertically sliced onion
1½   teaspoons grated lemon rind
½   teaspoon salt
¼   teaspoon black pepper
Dash of dried crushed red pepper
1   garlic clove, minced
2   tablespoons extra-virgin olive oil
2   tablespoons lemon juice
4   cups hot cooked angel hair (about 8 ounces uncooked pasta)
Minced fresh parsley

Peel and devein shrimp.

Bring beer to a boil in a Dutch oven over high heat. Add shrimp; cover and cook 2 minutes. Remove shrimp with a slotted spoon; set shrimp aside, and keep warm.

Add onion and the next 5 ingredients to pan; bring to a boil. Cook, uncovered, 4 minutes. Remove from heat; gradually add oil and lemon juice, stirring constantly with a wire whisk. Add pasta; toss well.

Divide pasta mixture among indi-vidual serving plates; top with shrimp, and sprinkle with parsley. Yield: 4 servings (serving size: 1 cup pasta and 3 ounces shrimp).

CALORIES 391 (22% from fat); PROTEIN 30g; FAT 9.7g (sat 1.4g, mono 5.4g, poly 1.7g); CARB 44.7g; FIBER 2.7g; CHOL 172mg; IRON 4.8mg; SODIUM 470mg; CALC 85mg

BEER-AND-ALLSPICE BROILED DRUMSTICKS

1   cup dark beer
2   tablespoons cider vinegar
1½   tablespoons seeded, minced serrano chile
2   teaspoons ground allspice
¾   teaspoon salt
¼   teaspoon pepper
2   garlic cloves, minced
8   chicken drumsticks, skinned
Vegetable cooking spray

Combine first 8 ingredients in a large heavy-duty, zip-top plastic bag. Seal bag, and marinate chicken in refrigerator at least 1 hour, turning bag occasionally.

Remove chicken from bag; reserve marinade. Bring marinade to a boil in a small saucepan.

Place chicken on broiler pan coated with cooking spray, and broil 20 minutes, turning occasionally and basting with reserved marinade. Yield: 4 servings (serving size: 2 drumsticks).

CALORIES 164 (28% from fat); PROTEIN 24.5g; FAT 5.1g (sat 1.3g, mono 1.6g, poly 1.2g); CARB 4.2g; FIBER 0.3g; CHOL 79mg; IRON 1.2mg; SODIUM 526mg; CALC 27mg

BEER-AND-SOY BRAISED BEEF

Star anise is a dark-brown pod with a distinctive licorice flavor similar to that of regular aniseeds.

1   pound lean beef stew meat
¼   teaspoon white pepper
1   teaspoon vegetable oil
3   tablespoons low-sodium soy sauce
1   (12-ounce) bottle dark beer
2   thin gingerroot slices
2   green onions
1   (3-inch) cinnamon stick
2   star anise pods (optional)
2   cups sliced carrot
2   cups sliced leek (about 2 medium)
6   cups hot cooked couscous

Trim fat from meat; cut meat into ¾-inch cubes, and sprinkle with pepper. Heat oil in a Dutch oven over medium-high heat until hot. Add meat; cook 3 minutes or until browned, stirring often. Add soy sauce and next 4 ingredients; stir in star anise, if desired. Bring to a boil; cover, reduce heat, and simmer 1 hour.

Add carrot and leek; cook, uncovered, an additional 30 minutes or until vegetables are tender. Discard gingerroot, green onions, cinnamon, and star anise. Serve over couscous. Yield: 6 servings (serving size: ⅔ cup meat mixture and 1 cup couscous).

CALORIES 453 (13% from fat); PROTEIN 30.9g; FAT 6.3g (sat 1.5g, mono 1.8g, poly 1.8g); CARB 70.9g; FIBER 4.5g; CHOL 44mg; IRON 5.1mg; SODIUM 370mg; CALC 57mg

BEER-CHEESE BREAD

¾ cup beer
¼ cup margarine
3½ cups bread flour, divided
1 tablespoon sugar
½ teaspoon salt
½ teaspoon dry mustard
¼ teaspoon ground red pepper
1 package active dry yeast
1 egg, lightly beaten
1 cup shredded reduced-fat sharp Cheddar cheese
Vegetable cooking spray

Combine beer and margarine in a small saucepan; place over medium-low heat until very warm (120° to 130°).

Combine 1½ cups flour and next 5 ingredients in a large bowl. Add beer mixture and egg; beat at medium speed of an electric mixer 2 minutes or until smooth. Stir in cheese and 1½ cups flour to form a soft dough.

Turn dough out onto a lightly floured surface. Knead dough until smooth and elastic (about 8 minutes); add enough of remaining ½ cup flour, 1 tablespoon at a time, to prevent dough from sticking to hands. Place dough in a large bowl coated with cooking spray, turning to coat top. Cover and let rise in a warm place (85°), free from drafts, 1 hour or until doubled in bulk.

Punch dough down; cover and let rest 10 minutes. Place dough in a 1-quart soufflé dish coated with cooking spray. Cover and let rise 40 minutes or until doubled in bulk.

Preheat oven to 375°. Bake loaf at 375° for 20 minutes. Cover loosely with foil; bake an additional 20 minutes or until loaf sounds hollow when tapped. Remove loaf from dish; let cool on a wire rack. Yield: 16 servings (serving size: 1 slice).

CALORIES 150 (29% from fat); PROTEIN 5.3g; FAT 4.8g (sat 1.5g, mono 1.8g, poly 1.1g); CARB 20.9g; FIBER 0.8g; CHOL 18mg; IRON 1.3mg; SODIUM 163mg; CALC 70mg

BEER-BAKED SCALLOPED POTATOES

Vegetable cooking spray
1 teaspoon vegetable oil
1½ cups vertically sliced onion
1 cup beer
2 pounds medium-size red potatoes, peeled and cut into ⅛-inch-thick slices
½ teaspoon salt, divided
¼ teaspoon pepper, divided
2 tablespoons all-purpose flour
½ cup skim milk
½ cup (2 ounces) grated Swiss cheese

Preheat oven to 350°.

Coat a large skillet with cooking spray; add oil, and place over medium heat until hot. Add onion, and sauté 5 minutes. Add beer; cook 12 minutes or until liquid evaporates, stirring occasionally. Remove onion mixture from heat, and set aside.

Cook potato slices in boiling water to cover 8 minutes or until potato slices are crisp-tender; drain. Rinse under cold water, and drain well.

Place one-third of potato slices in an 11 x 7-inch baking dish coated with cooking spray, and sprinkle with half of salt and half of pepper. Spread half of onion mixture over potato slices. Repeat procedure with half of remaining potato slices, and remaining salt, pepper, and onion mixture. Top with remaining potato slices.

Place flour in a small bowl. Gradually add milk, stirring with a wire whisk until blended. Pour milk mixture evenly over potato slices. Cover with aluminum foil, and cut 3 (1-inch) slits in foil.

Bake at 350° for 45 minutes. Uncover; sprinkle with cheese, and bake an additional 10 minutes or until cheese melts. Yield: 6 servings (serving size: 1 cup).

CALORIES 201 (17% from fat); PROTEIN 7.4g; FAT 3.7g (sat 1.9g, mono 0.9g, poly 0.6g); CARB 35.4g; FIBER 3.3g; CHOL 9mg; IRON 1.4mg; SODIUM 244mg; CALC 139mg

BUTTERNUT SQUASH SOUP

1 tablespoon olive oil
2 cups chopped onion
½ teaspoon ground cumin
2 garlic cloves, sliced
4 cups peeled, cubed butternut squash (about 1½ pounds)
1½ cups one-third-less sodium chicken broth
1 cup dark beer
1 teaspoon salt
¼ cup plain nonfat yogurt

Heat oil in a large saucepan over medium heat until hot. Add chopped onion, cumin, and garlic; sauté 6 minutes or until tender. Add squash cubes, and cook 2 minutes, stirring frequently. Add broth, beer, and salt; bring to a boil. Cover, reduce heat, and simmer 30 minutes or until squash is tender.

Place squash mixture in a blender; cover and process until mixture is smooth. Return squash mixture to pan, and cook until thoroughly heated. Ladle soup into individual bowls, and top with yogurt. Yield: 4 servings (serving size: 1 cup soup and 1 tablespoon yogurt).

CALORIES 145 (22% from fat); PROTEIN 3.5g; FAT 3.7g (sat 0.5g, mono 2.6g, poly 0.4g); CARB 27.5g; FIBER 3.4g; CHOL 0mg; IRON 1.2mg; SODIUM 609mg; CALC 124mg

Thai-Seared Tofu, page 58

Herbed Meat Loaf with Sun-Dried Tomato Gravy, page 46

Double-Chocolate Chews, page 61

Easy Peanut Butter Cookies, page 60

Crisp-and-Spicy Cheese Twists,
page 63

Mexican Salsa Bread, page 64

Lemon-Glazed Cranberry Rolls, page 62

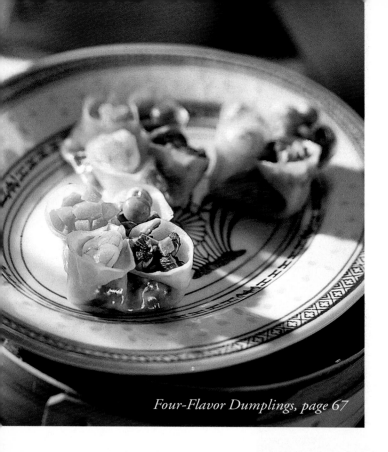
Four-Flavor Dumplings, page 67

Beer-and-Soy Braised Beef, page 71

Collards with Smoked Pork, page 77

The Greening of America

Used to be that greens were boiled with a hunk of pork, then doused with hot sauce and vinegar. Tasty though that is, the fat and sodium can hit alarm-bell levels—even more so if you add traditional corn bread. So we've come to the rescue with healthy and delicious recipes for collards, mustard greens, dandelion greens, and kale.

Greens come loaded with beta carotene, vitamin C, calcium, and iron. Know, though, that their dark outer leaves may contain as much as 50% more beta carotene than the inner leaves and several times as much vitamin C and calcium. And be careful about overcooking because that'll cost you some of those nutrients.

The bitter greens of winter used to be associated almost solely with the South, but nowadays they're the rage in restaurants and markets nationwide. So wherever you live, you should have no problem finding them. Of course, you can't eat greens without corn bread, so we've provided a recipe for a healthy jalapeño variety made with low-fat buttermilk.

ASIAN-STYLE DANDELION GREENS

2   pounds dandelion greens (about 4 small bunches) or fresh spinach
4   quarts water
Vegetable cooking spray
¼   cup minced green onions
1   tablespoon low-sodium soy sauce
1   tablespoon rice vinegar
1   teaspoon dark sesame oil
¼   teaspoon salt
1   tablespoon sesame seeds, toasted

Remove tough ends from stems of dandelion greens, and wash leaves thoroughly. Bring 4 quarts water to a boil in an 8-quart Dutch oven or stockpot. Add greens, and cook 5 minutes; drain well. Place greens on paper towels, and squeeze until barely moist; set aside.

Coat pan with cooking spray, and place over medium heat until hot. Add green onions, and sauté 3 minutes or until tender. Add dandelion greens, soy sauce, vinegar, oil, and salt; sauté until thoroughly heated. Spoon into a serving bowl, and sprinkle with sesame seeds. Yield: 4 servings (serving size: 1 cup).

CALORIES 70 (37% from fat); PROTEIN 6g; FAT 2.9g (sat 0.4g, mono 0.9g, poly 1.2g); CARB 8g; FIBER 5.1g; CHOL 0mg; IRON 6.9mg; SODIUM 395mg; CALC 272mg

MUSTARD GREENS WITH LENTILS

This recipe is ideal as a meatless main dish.

2   pounds mustard greens
2   quarts water
1   cup dried lentils
3   garlic cloves, halved
1   bay leaf
¼   cup balsamic vinegar
2   tablespoons minced shallots
3   tablespoons water
2   tablespoons olive oil
½   teaspoon salt
¼   teaspoon pepper
½   cup crumbled feta cheese

Remove stems from mustard greens. Wash leaves thoroughly, and pat dry. Coarsely chop leaves to equal 16 cups.

Bring 2 quarts water to a boil in an 8-quart Dutch oven or stockpot. Add chopped mustard greens; cover and cook 7 minutes. Drain greens, reserving cooking liquid. Rinse greens under cold water; drain greens, and pat dry. Set greens aside.

Return cooking liquid to pan. Add lentils, garlic, and bay leaf; bring to a boil. Cover, reduce heat, and simmer 25 minutes or until lentils are tender. Drain; discard cooking liquid, garlic, and bay leaf.

Combine mustard greens and lentils in a bowl. Combine vinegar and next 5 ingredients in a small bowl, and stir well with a wire whisk. Pour dressing over greens mixture, tossing gently to coat. Sprinkle with cheese. Yield: 4 servings (serving size: 1 cup).

CALORIES 324 (29% from fat); PROTEIN 21.6g; FAT 10.7g (sat 3.1g, mono 5.9g, poly 1g); CARB 40.4g; FIBER 6.9g; CHOL 13mg; IRON 7.8mg; SODIUM 513mg; CALC 328mg

COLLARDS WITH SMOKED PORK

Instead of bacon fat, cook your collards in this pork-flavored broth until they're tender.

3   pounds collards
4   cups water
1   cup chopped onion
¼   teaspoon salt
¼   teaspoon pepper
3   garlic cloves, chopped
2   (16-ounce) cans one-third-less-sodium chicken broth
2   smoked ham hocks (about 1¼ pounds)
Hot pepper sauce (optional)

Remove stems from collards. Wash leaves thoroughly, and pat dry. Coarsely chop leaves to equal 10 cups.

Combine water, onion, salt, pepper, garlic, chicken broth, and ham hocks in an 8-quart Dutch oven or stockpot; bring to a boil. Add collards; cover, reduce heat, and simmer 1 hour or until collards are tender, stirring occasionally. Remove from heat.

Remove ham hocks from pan; let cool. Remove ham from bones, and finely chop; discard bones, skin, and fat. Add chopped ham to collard mixture; stir well. Cook over medium heat until thoroughly heated. Serve with hot pepper sauce, if desired. Yield: 6 servings (serving size: 1 cup).

CALORIES 77 (36% from fat); PROTEIN 4.8g; FAT 3.1g (sat 0.9g, mono 1.3g, poly 0.5g); CARB 8.8g; FIBER 0.6g; CHOL 6mg; IRON 1.1mg; SODIUM 310mg; CALC 27mg

TYPES OF GREENS

♦ **COLLARDS** Full-bodied in flavor, collards have white-veined, wide green leaves with a leathery texture. Choose bunches with leaves as small as you can find and stems that aren't too thick.

♦ **DANDELION GREENS** The slender, saw-toothed leaves of dandelion greens have a slightly bitter taste.

♦ **KALE** The curly-edged leaves of kale are greenish blue or grayish green and hold their texture well when cooked.

♦ **MUSTARD GREENS** They have a light, almost lime-green color and a pungent, mustardlike flavor. The leaves are softer and more delicately ruffled than kale. Turnip greens can be substituted for mustard greens or collards.

KALE WITH FUSILLI AND ROASTED GARLIC

Roasting garlic mellows its intense flavor, so there's no need to be timid about biting into whole roasted cloves.

1 whole garlic head
1 pound kale
3 quarts water
1 (10¼-ounce) can low-salt chicken broth
3 cups uncooked fusilli (twisted spaghetti)
1 tablespoon extra-virgin olive oil
¼ teaspoon salt
¼ teaspoon dried crushed red pepper
½ cup grated fresh Parmesan cheese

Preheat oven to 350°.

Remove white papery skin from garlic head, and separate cloves. Peel cloves, and wrap in foil; bake at 350° for 30 minutes or until tender. Set garlic aside.

Remove stems from kale, and wash leaves thoroughly. Pat leaves dry, and coarsely chop to equal 3 cups.

Combine water and broth in a large Dutch oven; bring to a boil. Add kale; cook 5 minutes or until tender. Drain kale, reserving cooking liquid. Return cooking liquid to pan; bring to a boil. Add pasta; cook 8 minutes or until tender. Drain pasta, reserving 3 tablespoons cooking liquid.

Combine pasta, reserved cooking liquid, kale, roasted garlic cloves, oil, salt, and pepper in a bowl; toss well. Spoon pasta mixture onto individual plates, and sprinkle with cheese. Yield: 8 servings (serving size: ¾ cup and 1 tablespoon cheese).

CALORIES 230 (18% from fat); PROTEIN 9.7g; FAT 4.7g (sat 1.5g, mono 1.9g, poly 0.6g); CARB 37.6g; FIBER 1.5g; CHOL 5mg; IRON 2.5mg; SODIUM 214mg; CALC 140mg

JALAPEÑO WHOLE-KERNEL CORN BREAD

Butter-flavored vegetable cooking spray
2 teaspoons vegetable oil
1 cup yellow cornmeal
¾ cup all-purpose flour
1 tablespoon sugar
2 teaspoons baking powder
1 teaspoon salt
1 cup frozen whole-kernel corn, thawed and drained
1 cup low-fat buttermilk
⅓ cup nonfat sour cream
¼ cup chopped fresh cilantro
1 tablespoon seeded, chopped jalapeño pepper
1 tablespoon vegetable oil
2 eggs, lightly beaten

Preheat oven to 400°.

Coat a 9-inch cast iron skillet with cooking spray; add 2 teaspoons oil. Place skillet in oven for 8 minutes.

Combine cornmeal, flour, sugar, baking powder, and salt in a large bowl. Combine corn and next 6 ingredients in a bowl; stir well with a wire whisk. Add to cornmeal mixture, stirring until dry ingredients are moistened. Spoon into preheated skillet. Bake at 400° for 25 minutes or until a wooden pick inserted in center comes out clean. Yield: 9 servings (serving size: 1 wedge).

CALORIES 174 (24% from fat); PROTEIN 6g; FAT 4.6g (sat 1.2g, mono 1.3g, poly 1.5g); CARB 27.5g; FIBER 1.6g; CHOL 49mg; IRON 1.6mg; SODIUM 297mg; CALC 105mg

BUYING GREENS

When you're buying greens, keep in mind that a pound of raw greens will yield about 2 cups of cooked greens.

GOOD IDEAS

Winter Survival Kit

These elegant one-course dinners will take the chill off those chilly winter nights.

A pot of well-seasoned broth, stocked with vegetables, meats, or seafood, is an ideal antidote for this blustery time of year. These international favorites can be a stylish and unexpected way to feed guests. To make the most of your soup dinner, here are some tips.

• A stockpot with a capacity of at least 10 quarts is essential.

• A skimmer, a colander, and a very fine strainer are helpful. A big, sturdy strainer can double as a colander and be turned into a fine strainer by lining it with cheesecloth or a linen napkin.

• For generous servings, shallow, wide soup bowls are best.

• Along with a soup spoon, each guest should have a fork—as well as a knife, for that good crusty bread on the side.

CHINESE HOT POT OF BEEF

Browning the spice-coated meat intensifies this soup's flavor and color.

2½ pounds beef short ribs
 1 tablespoon low-sodium soy sauce
 2 teaspoons five-spice powder
12½ cups water, divided
 ½ teaspoon black peppercorns
 3 medium onions, quartered
 3 green onions
 2 medium carrots, cut into 2-inch pieces
2½ cups sliced mushrooms
1½ cups cubed firm tofu (about ½ pound)
 3 tablespoons low-sodium soy sauce
 1 teaspoon salt
 4 cups hot cooked Chinese-style noodles (about 8 ounces uncooked)
 ¼ cup thinly sliced green onions
 ¼ cup chopped fresh cilantro

Preheat oven to 400°.

Combine beef ribs, 1 tablespoon soy sauce, and five-spice powder in a 13 x 9-inch baking pan; toss to coat. Bake for 30 minutes. Remove ribs from pan, and set aside. Add ½ cup water to pan, and stir to deglaze pan.

Combine the pan drippings, ribs, remaining 12 cups water, peppercorns, onions, 3 green onions, and carrots in a large Dutch oven or stockpot; bring to a boil. Reduce heat, and simmer, uncovered, 2 hours.

Remove ribs from broth, and let cool completely. Remove meat from bones; discard bones, fat, and gristle. Place meat in a bowl; cover and chill. Strain broth through a sieve into a large bowl; discard solids. Cover broth, and chill 12 hours.

Skim solidified fat from surface of broth, and discard. Combine broth, meat, mushrooms, tofu, 3 tablespoons soy sauce, and salt in Dutch oven; bring to a simmer. Cover and cook 10 minutes. Spoon noodles into individual soup bowls. Ladle soup into each bowl, and sprinkle with sliced green onions and cilantro. Yield: 8 servings (serving size: 2 cups soup, ½ cup noodles, 1½ teaspoons sliced green onions, and 1½ teaspoons cilantro).

CALORIES 232 (31% from fat); PROTEIN 19.5g; FAT 8.1g (sat 2.9g, mono 3.1g, poly 1.2g); CARB 22.3g; FIBER 1.9g; CHOL 30mg; IRON 3.1mg; SODIUM 581mg; CALC 43mg

POT-AU-FEU WITH GREEN SAUCE

 2 large onions (about 1 pound)
 1 (2-pound) beef brisket
 3 quarts water
 ½ teaspoon pepper
 ¼ teaspoon salt
 8 large carrots, cut into 2-inch pieces
 5 garlic cloves, halved
 4 celery stalks, cut into 2-inch pieces
 4 bay leaves
 4 large parsley sprigs
 3 medium leeks (about 1¾ pounds), trimmed and cut in half lengthwise
 2 medium turnips (about ½ pound), peeled and quartered
Green Sauce

Peel onions, leaving roots intact; cut each onion into 4 wedges. Trim fat from brisket; discard fat. Thinly slice brisket. Combine brisket, onions, water, and next 9 ingredients in a large Dutch oven or stockpot; bring to a boil. Reduce heat, and simmer, uncovered, 2 hours or until brisket is tender. Cover and simmer 1 hour.

Strain mixture through a cheesecloth-lined colander into a large bowl; discard garlic, bay leaves, parsley, and leeks. Cover broth, and chill at least 24 hours. Place brisket, onions, carrots, celery, and turnips in a bowl; cover and chill.

Skim solidified fat from surface of broth, and discard. Combine broth and brisket mixture in Dutch oven, and cook over medium heat until thoroughly heated.

Ladle soup into large shallow bowls, and top with Green Sauce. Serve with parslied potatoes. Yield: 8 servings (serving size: 1¼ cups broth, 2 ounces meat, one-eighth of vegetables, and 2 tablespoons Green Sauce).

CALORIES 222 (35% from fat); PROTEIN 20.1g; FAT 8.6g (sat 2.9g, mono 3.9g, poly 0.4g); CARB 16.7g; FIBER 4.7g; CHOL 56mg; IRON 3mg; SODIUM 473mg; CALC 67mg

Green Sauce:

 1 cup fresh flat-leaf parsley leaves
 ⅓ cup fresh lemon juice
 2 tablespoons capers
 1 tablespoon water
 ¼ teaspoon pepper
 8 pitted green olives
 6 green onions, cut into 2-inch pieces
 1 canned anchovy fillet or 1 teaspoon anchovy paste
 1 garlic clove, minced

Combine all ingredients in a food processor; process until smooth. Yield: 1 cup (serving size: 2 tablespoons).

CALORIES 17 (32% from fat); PROTEIN 0.8g; FAT 0.6g (sat 0.1g, mono 0.4g, poly 0.1g); CARB 2.8g; FIBER 0.7g; CHOL 0mg; IRON 0.8mg; SODIUM 294mg; CALC 24mg

GREEK LAMB-AND-ARTICHOKE SOUP

Part of the broth is combined with the eggs before they're added to the soup. This technique, known as tempering, keeps the eggs from curdling.

2½ quarts water
  3 medium leeks, trimmed and halved
  2 bay leaves
  1 medium onion, peeled and halved
  1 fennel bulb, quartered
1½ pounds lean ground lamb
  1 cup fresh breadcrumbs
  ½ cup tomato juice
  2 teaspoons dried dillweed
  ½ teaspoon salt
  ½ teaspoon ground oregano
  ½ teaspoon pepper
  2 garlic cloves, minced
  2 cups cooked rice
  ⅓ cup fresh lemon juice
  2 (15-ounce) cans cannellini beans or other white beans, drained
  2 (14-ounce) cans quartered artichoke hearts, drained
  2 eggs

Combine first 5 ingredients in a large Dutch oven or stockpot; bring to a boil. Partially cover, reduce heat, and simmer 45 minutes. Remove from heat, and set aside.

Combine lamb and next 7 ingredients in a bowl, and stir well. Shape mixture into 24 (1¼-inch) meatballs. Place a large nonstick skillet over medium-high heat until hot. Add meatballs, and cook 10 minutes or until browned, stirring frequently. Remove from skillet, and pat dry with paper towels; set aside, and keep warm.

Strain stock through a colander into a large bowl; discard solids. Reserve 2 cups stock; set aside. Return remaining stock to pan, and bring to a boil; add meatballs, rice, lemon juice, beans, and artichokes. Return to a boil; reduce heat to low.

Place eggs in a small bowl; stir well. Gradually add reserved 2 cups stock, stirring constantly with a wire whisk. Slowly drizzle egg mixture into soup, stirring constantly. Yield: 7 servings (serving size: 2 cups).

Note: Reheat the soup over medium-low heat (do not boil) so the egg does not curdle.

CALORIES 404 (20% from fat); PROTEIN 34.1g; FAT 9.2g (sat 3.2g, mono 3.8g, poly 0.9g); CARB 46.4g; FIBER 3.4g; CHOL 130mg; IRON 5.3mg; SODIUM 774mg; CALC109mg

BOUILLABAISSE

  ¼ cup nonfat mayonnaise
  2 teaspoons tomato paste
  ⅛ teaspoon ground red pepper
  1 small garlic clove, crushed
  1 tablespoon olive oil
  3 cups thinly sliced fennel bulb (about 1 large bulb)
  1 cup chopped onion
  1 tablespoon fresh or 1 teaspoon dried thyme
  2 garlic cloves, crushed
  1 cup water
  ¼ teaspoon salt
  ¼ teaspoon saffron threads (optional)
  ¼ teaspoon black pepper
  ¾ pound small red potatoes, quartered
  2 (8-ounce) bottles clam juice
  1 (10¾-ounce) can tomato purée
  1 pound skinned halibut fillets, cut into 2-inch pieces
  ½ pound bay scallops
  ½ pound large shrimp, peeled and deveined
Minced fresh parsley (optional)
  6 (½-inch-thick) slices French bread, toasted

Combine first 4 ingredients in a bowl; stir well. Cover and chill.

Heat olive oil in a large Dutch oven over medium-high heat until hot. Add sliced fennel, onion, thyme, and 2 garlic cloves, and sauté until tender.

Add water and the next 6 ingredients to fennel mixture; bring to a boil. Cook for 15 minutes or until potatoes are crisp-tender. Add the halibut, scallops, and shrimp; cover, reduce heat, and simmer for 5 minutes or until seafood is done.

Ladle soup into individual bowls, and garnish with parsley, if desired. Serve with toast topped with tomato-mayonnaise mixture. Yield: 6 servings (serving size: 1½ cups soup, 1 toast slice, and about 1 tablespoon tomato-mayonnaise).

CALORIES 323 (16% from fat); PROTEIN 35.4g; FAT 5.8g (sat 0.9g, mono 2.4g, poly 1.4g); CARB 32.6g; FIBER 3.3g; CHOL 106mg; IRON 4.7mg; SODIUM 853mg; CALC 153mg

CHICKEN IN A POT WITH CORNMEAL-HERB DUMPLINGS

The onions are left unpeeled as the broth simmers to give it a more golden color.

  2 large onions (about 1 pound)
  3 quarts water
  4 chicken thighs (about 2 pounds), skinned
  3 chicken breast halves (about 1½ pounds), skinned
  3 chicken drumsticks (about ¾ pound), skinned
  8 large carrots, cut into 2-inch pieces
  4 large celery stalks, cut into 2-inch pieces
  ¾ teaspoon salt
  ½ teaspoon pepper
  ⅛ teaspoon dried dillweed
  4 large parsley sprigs
  4 garlic cloves, crushed
Cornmeal-Herb Dumplings
Minced fresh parsley (optional)
Minced fresh chives (optional)

Cut each onion into 4 wedges, leaving roots and skin intact. Combine the onion wedges and the next 11 ingredients in a large Dutch oven or stockpot, and bring to a boil. Reduce heat, and simmer, uncovered, for 1½ hours or until chicken is done and vegetables are tender. Strain the mixture through a cheesecloth-lined colander into a large bowl; discard the parsley sprigs and garlic.

Remove chicken from bones, and discard bones. Peel the onions; discard peel. Place chicken-vegetable mixture in a bowl; cover and chill. Cover broth, and chill at least 24 hours.

Skim the solidified fat from surface of broth, and discard. Prepare Cornmeal-Herb Dumplings. Combine broth and chicken-vegetable mixture in Dutch oven, and cook over medium heat until thoroughly heated. Ladle soup into large shallow bowls; top with Cornmeal-Herb Dumplings. Garnish soup with minced parsley and minced chives, if desired. Yield: 8 servings (serving size: 1¾ cups soup and 4 dumplings).

CALORIES 346 (24% from fat); PROTEIN 27.7g; FAT 9.2g (sat 2.2g, mono 3.8g, poly 1.9g); CARB 37.9g; FIBER 5.9g; CHOL 121mg; IRON 3.3mg; SODIUM 644mg; CALC137mg

Cornmeal-Herb Dumplings:

The dough can be prepared, covered, and chilled about a half-hour ahead of time.

    1   cup yellow cornmeal
    1   cup all-purpose flour
    2   teaspoons baking powder
    2   teaspoons dried dillweed
    1   teaspoon salt
    ¼   teaspoon pepper
    ¼   cup water
    1   tablespoon olive oil
    2   eggs

Combine first 6 ingredients in a medium bowl. Combine water, olive oil, and eggs, and stir well. Add to dry ingredients, stirring until well-blended. With moistened hands, shape dough into 32 (1-inch) balls, and set aside.

Bring 2 quarts of water to a simmer in a large saucepan, and add half of dumplings. Cover and cook for 10 minutes or until done (do not let boil). Remove dumplings with a slotted spoon; set aside, and keep warm. Repeat procedure with remaining dumplings. Yield: 8 servings (serving size: 4 dumplings).

CALORIES 148 (23% from fat); PROTEIN 4.5g; FAT 3.7g (sat 0.7g, mono 1.9g, poly 0.6g); CARB 24.3g; FIBER 2.1g; CHOL 55mg; IRON 1.7mg; SODIUM 316mg; CALC 82mg

LIGHTEN UP

Don't Give Up the Shrimp

We heard your distress call for a low-fat shrimp scampi.

Ahoy, shrimp lovers, we've got news from the galley. Here's a quick, easy recipe for Shrimp Scampi that cuts the calories by one-fifth and reduces the fat by nearly two-thirds. The only thing we didn't curtail is the rich, buttery taste. Our version is served with angel hair pasta, and you know that biting into the warm shrimp and pasta together is one of those rare earthy pleasures in life.

As for presentation: The key to making Shrimp Scampi that looks like the work of a professional chef is butterflying the shrimp. This simple technique involves cutting the shrimp down the back (almost but not all the way through) so that they open up, or butterfly. And in case you're wondering, scampi is the Italian name for the tail portion of several varieties of lobsterettes. Because shrimp and scampi are pretty much the same thing, the phrase Shrimp Scampi is a redundancy—but who cares about grammar when you're hungry?

HOW WE DID IT

◆ Changed butter to margarine and decreased the amount.
◆ Omitted the oil.
◆ Added chopped red bell pepper to boost carbohydrates and add color.
◆ Increased the white wine to make more of a sauce.
◆ Served shrimp with angel hair pasta to increase carbohydrates.

BEFORE & AFTER	
SERVING SIZE	
8 shrimp	
1 cup pasta	
CALORIES PER SERVING	
472	383
FAT	
21.2g	8.7g
PERCENT OF TOTAL CALORIES	
40%	20%

SHRIMP SCAMPI

    2   pounds large unpeeled shrimp (48 shrimp)
    3   tablespoons margarine
    1   cup chopped red bell pepper
    8   garlic cloves, crushed
    ½   cup dry white wine
    ¼   cup minced fresh parsley
    ¼   cup fresh lemon juice
    ½   teaspoon salt
    ¼   teaspoon pepper
        Paprika
    6   cups hot cooked angel hair (about ¾ pound uncooked pasta)

Peel shrimp, leaving tails intact. Starting at tail end, cut each shrimp down the back, cutting to, but not through, underside of shrimp. Arrange 8 shrimp, cut sides down, in each of 6 gratin dishes; set aside.

Melt margarine in a small skillet over medium heat. Add bell pepper and garlic; sauté 2 minutes. Remove from heat; stir in wine, parsley, lemon juice, salt, and ¼ teaspoon pepper. Spoon wine mixture evenly over shrimp; sprinkle paprika over shrimp, and broil 6 minutes or until shrimp is done. Serve with angel hair pasta. Yield: 6 servings (serving size: 8 shrimp and 1 cup pasta).

CALORIES 383 (20% from fat); PROTEIN 29.9g; FAT 8.7g (sat 1.6g, mono 2.9g, poly 3g); CARB 41.8g; FIBER 2.7g; CHOL 172mg; IRON 5.2mg; SODIUM 435mg; CALC 87mg

Ham It Up

Let the March winds blow—before you know it, you'll have a hearty ham casserole bubbling in the oven.

> **MENU**
>
> **HAM-AND-LIMA BEAN CASSEROLE**
>
> **TRICOLOR SLAW**
>
> *Apple wedges and fat-free caramel syrup*
>
> About 577 calories and 10 grams fat (15% calories from fat)

HAM-AND-LIMA BEAN CASSEROLE

1½ cups water
1½ cups frozen baby lima beans, thawed
¾ cup finely chopped green bell pepper
⅓ cup chopped onion
1¼ cups chopped extra-lean ham (about 6 ounces)
1 cup (4 ounces) shredded reduced-fat sharp Cheddar cheese
1 teaspoon Worcestershire sauce
1 (14¾-ounce) can no-salt-added cream-style corn
Vegetable cooking spray
¼ cup plus 2 tablespoons skim milk
2 tablespoons chopped green onions
¾ cup low-fat biscuit and baking mix

Preheat oven to 400°.

Bring water to a boil in a medium saucepan. Add lima beans, bell pepper, and onion; cover and cook 5 minutes. Drain.

Combine lima bean mixture, ham, cheese, Worcestershire sauce, and corn in a bowl; stir well. Spoon into a 2-quart casserole coated with cooking spray. Cover and bake at 400° for 20 minutes.

Combine milk and green onions in a bowl, and stir in baking mix. Drop batter by spoonfuls onto ham mixture to form 6 biscuits. Bake, uncovered, 20 minutes or until biscuits are golden. Yield: 6 servings (serving size: about ¾ cup casserole and 1 biscuit).

Note: You can also assemble the casserole ahead of time, except for the biscuit topping; cover and chill overnight in refrigerator or freeze up to 1 month (thaw the frozen casserole overnight in refrigerator). Let the casserole stand at room temperature 30 minutes; add the biscuit topping, and bake as directed.

CALORIES 317 (18% from fat); PROTEIN 19.8g; FAT 6.2g (sat 2.7g, mono 1.8g, poly 0.5g); CARB 70.7g; FIBER 2.2g; CHOL 28mg; IRON 2.8mg; SODIUM 846mg; CALC 220mg

TRICOLOR SLAW

⅓ cup reduced-fat mayonnaise
⅓ cup plain nonfat yogurt
1½ tablespoons Dijon mustard
1 tablespoon cider vinegar
1½ teaspoons sugar
1 (16-ounce) package cabbage-and-carrot coleslaw

Combine mayonnaise, yogurt, Dijon mustard, cider vinegar, and sugar in a large bowl; stir well. Add coleslaw; toss well to coat. Yield: 6 servings (serving size: 1 cup).

CALORIES 76 (34% from fat); PROTEIN 2.4g; FAT 2.9g (sat 0.9g, mono 0g, poly 1.8g); CARB 14.1g; FIBER 3.3g; CHOL 0mg; IRON 0mg; SODIUM 146mg; CALC 25mg

> **SHOPPING LIST**
>
> 1 (16-ounce) package cabbage-and-carrot coleslaw
> 1 green bell pepper
> 1 onion
> green onions
> Red Delicious apples
> reduced-fat mayonnaise
> Dijon mustard
> Worcestershire sauce
> cider vinegar
> 1 (14¾-ounce) can no-salt-added cream-style corn
> sugar
> low-fat biscuit and baking mix
> fat-free caramel-flavored sundae syrup
> frozen baby lima beans
> plain nonfat yogurt
> skim milk
> reduced-fat sharp Cheddar cheese
> extra-lean ham

Spring Forward

Celebrate the change of seasons with two
menus that pay homage to the light.

With April comes daylight saving time, which means resetting your clocks, and your attitudes. In honor of longer days, balmy weather, and feeling good, we've created two menus that have the bright look and tastes of the season. Our colorful, easy-to-make menus trumpet the year's new crop of vegetables and fruits. And after months of dried and canned ingredients, what says renewal more than fresh herbs? We've topped our baked chicken breasts with a creamy buttermilk sauce infused with fresh thyme. Finally, because daylight savings mean light at the end of the driveway when you get home from work, you can rechristen the outdoor grill with our peppered salmon steaks and marinated vegetables.

MENU

CHILLED BEET-AND-
FENNEL SOUP

GRILLED SALMON
PEPPER STEAKS

GRILLED MARINATED
VEGETABLES

DAIQUIRI ICE WITH
KIWIFRUIT

About 704 calories (28% from fat)

CHILLED BEET-AND-FENNEL SOUP

    1   pound small beets
    2   teaspoons fennel seeds
   ¼   cup water
    1   tablespoon olive oil
  1¾   cups chopped fresh fennel bulb
    1   cup chopped onion
  1½   cups low-fat buttermilk
   ½   teaspoon salt
   ¼   teaspoon pepper

Leave root and 1 inch of stem on beets; scrub with a brush. Place beets and fennel seeds in a medium saucepan; cover with water, and bring to a boil. Cover, reduce heat, and simmer 35 minutes or until tender. Pour beets through a fine sieve into a bowl, reserving fennel seeds and 3 cups cooking liquid. Rinse beets under cold water; drain. Peel beets; cut into ½-inch cubes, reserving ¾ cup for garnish. Combine remaining beets, reserved cooking liquid, and fennel seeds in a bowl; set aside.

Combine ¼ cup water and olive oil in a medium nonstick skillet; place over medium-high heat until hot. Add fennel bulb and onion; bring to a boil. Cover, reduce heat, and simmer 20 minutes or until tender.

Combine fennel bulb mixture, beet mixture, buttermilk, salt, and pepper in a food processor or blender; cover and process until smooth. Pour soup into a bowl; cover and chill thoroughly. Ladle ¾ cup soup into each individual bowl, and top each with 2 tablespoons reserved beets. Yield: 6 servings.

CALORIES 103 (31% from fat); PROTEIN 4.6g; FAT 3.6g (sat 1g, mono 1.8g, poly 0.3g); CARB 14.4g; FIBER 1.4g; CHOL 0mg; IRON 1.5mg; SODIUM 289mg; CALC 128mg

GRILLED SALMON PEPPER STEAKS

    2   tablespoons cracked pepper
    6   (6-ounce) salmon steaks
   ⅔   cup rice vinegar
    2   tablespoons fresh lemon juice
    2   tablespoons Dijon mustard
    1   tablespoon dark sesame oil
   ¼   teaspoon salt
   ⅛   teaspoon pepper
    4   garlic cloves, minced
  Vegetable cooking spray
   ¼   teaspoon cornstarch

Sprinkle cracked pepper evenly over both sides of each salmon steak, and place steaks in a 13 x 9-inch baking dish. Combine vinegar and next 6 ingredients in a small bowl; stir well. Pour vinegar mixture over steaks; cover and marinate in refrigerator 1 hour, turning steaks occasionally.

Coat grill rack with cooking spray; place on grill over medium hot coals (350° to 400°). Remove steaks from dish, reserving marinade. Bring marinade to a boil in a small saucepan. Place steaks on rack, and grill, covered, 5 minutes on each side or until fish flakes easily when tested with a fork, basting often with half of reserved marinade.

Combine remaining half of marinade and cornstarch in a small saucepan; bring to a boil, and cook 1 minute or until thickened, stirring constantly with a wire whisk. Spoon about 1 tablespoon sauce over each steak. Yield: 6 servings.

CALORIES 280 (48% from fat); PROTEIN 30.6g; FAT 14.9g (sat 2.5g, mono 6.9g, poly 3.7g); CARB 3.8g; FIBER 0.6g; CHOL 96mg; IRON 1.3mg; SODIUM 321mg; CALC 21mg

GRILLED MARINATED VEGETABLES

1½ pounds small red potatoes, halved
2 cups sliced yellow squash
2 cups sliced zucchini
12 green onions, trimmed
2 large red bell peppers, cut into ½-inch-wide strips
⅔ cup rice vinegar
2 tablespoons fresh lemon juice
2 tablespoons Dijon mustard
1 tablespoon dark sesame oil
¼ teaspoon salt
¼ teaspoon pepper
4 garlic cloves, minced
Vegetable cooking spray

Place potatoes in a medium saucepan; cover with water, and bring to a boil. Reduce heat, and simmer 10 minutes or until tender; drain.

Combine potatoes and next 11 ingredients in a large heavy-duty, zip-top plastic bag. Seal bag, and marinate 30 minutes, turning bag occasionally.

Remove vegetables from bag; reserve marinade. Place vegetables in a wire grilling basket coated with cooking spray. Place grill rack on grill over medium-hot coals (350° to 400°). Place grilling basket on rack; grill 7½ minutes on each side or until tender. Place reserved marinade in a small saucepan; cook over medium heat 3 minutes, and pour over vegetables. Yield: 6 servings (serving size: 1 cup).

CALORIES 153 (19% from fat); PROTEIN 4.5g; FAT 3.2g (sat 0.4g, mono 1.1g, poly 1.2g); CARB 28.5g; FIBER 4.4g; CHOL 0mg; IRON 2.8mg; SODIUM 263mg; CALC 58mg

DAIQUIRI ICE WITH KIWIFRUIT

2¼ cups water
¾ cup sugar
½ cup light rum
½ cup fresh lime juice
1 tablespoon grated lime rind
3 kiwifruit, peeled and thinly sliced
Mint sprigs (optional)
Lime slices (optional)

Combine water and sugar in a saucepan; cook over low heat 2 minutes or until sugar dissolves. Remove from heat; stir in rum, lime juice, and rind.

Pour mixture into the freezer can of a ½-gallon hand-turned or electric ice-cream freezer. Freeze according to manufacturer's instructions. Arrange kiwifruit and scoops of daiquiri ice on plates; garnish with mint and lime, if desired. Yield: 6 servings (serving size: ½ cup ice and ½ kiwifruit).

CALORIES 168 (2% from fat); PROTEIN 0.6g; FAT 0.3g (sat 0g, mono 0.1g, poly 0g); CARB 31.4g; FIBER 1.3g; CHOL 0mg; IRON 0.2mg; SODIUM 1mg; CALC 13mg

---

MENU

CHICKEN WITH CREAMY HERB SAUCE

ASPARAGUS-AND-TOMATO PASTA SALAD

COCONUT PAVLOVAS WITH TROPICAL FRUITS AND ICE CREAM

GINGER BEER COCKTAIL

About 688 calories (18% from fat)

CHICKEN WITH CREAMY HERB SAUCE

6 (4-ounce) skinned, boned chicken breast halves
⅓ cup balsamic vinegar
1 teaspoon dried oregano
½ teaspoon salt
½ teaspoon pepper
3 garlic cloves, unpeeled
¼ cup low-fat buttermilk
2 tablespoons minced fresh parsley
3 tablespoons reduced-calorie mayonnaise
1 tablespoon water
1½ teaspoons minced fresh or ½ teaspoon dried thyme
⅛ teaspoon salt
⅛ teaspoon pepper

Preheat oven to 375°. Arrange chicken in a 13 x 9-inch baking dish.

Pour vinegar over chicken; sprinkle with oregano, ½ teaspoon salt, and ½ teaspoon pepper. Place garlic in dish. Bake at 375° for 25 minutes or until chicken is done, basting with pan drippings.

Remove garlic from dish; peel. Place garlic in a bowl; mash into a paste. Add buttermilk and next 6 ingredients; stir with a wire whisk until blended.

Cut breasts diagonally across the grain into thin slices. Arrange 1 sliced breast half on each plate; spoon 1½ tablespoons sauce over each. Yield: 6 servings.

CALORIES 156 (21% from fat); PROTEIN 26.8g; FAT 3.6g (sat 0.8g, mono 0.9g, poly 1.4g); CARB 2.4g; FIBER 0.2g; CHOL 68mg; IRON 1.1mg; SODIUM 380mg; CALC 35mg

ASPARAGUS-AND-TOMATO PASTA SALAD

2 cups diagonally sliced asparagus (about 1 pound)
⅓ cup orange juice
3 tablespoons white wine vinegar
2 tablespoons water
1 tablespoon olive oil
2 teaspoons Dijon mustard
¼ teaspoon freshly ground pepper
⅛ teaspoon salt
2 cups cooked small seashell macaroni (about 1 cup uncooked pasta)
1½ cups quartered cherry tomatoes
1 cup diced yellow bell pepper
½ cup thinly sliced fresh basil leaves
⅓ cup pitted, chopped kalamata olives
¼ cup thinly sliced green onions
2 tablespoons capers

Arrange asparagus in a steamer basket over boiling water. Cover and steam 2 minutes or until crisp-tender; drain and set aside.

Combine orange juice and next 6 ingredients in a bowl; stir with a wire whisk. Add asparagus, pasta, and remaining ingredients; toss well. Yield: 6 servings (serving size: 1 cup).

CALORIES 138 (30% from fat); PROTEIN 4.3g; FAT 4.6g (sat 0.7g, mono 2.9g, poly 0.8g); CARB 21.3g; FIBER 3.2g; CHOL 0mg; IRON 2.1mg; SODIUM 453mg; CALC 39mg

COCONUT PAVLOVAS WITH TROPICAL FRUITS AND ICE CREAM

Named after ballerina Anna Pavlova, this famous dessert consists of a meringue base with a fruit sauce and creamy topping.

2 cups (1-inch) cubed fresh pineapple
1 cup fresh orange sections
1 cup peeled, cubed mango
⅓ cup dried sweet cherries
2 tablespoons sugar
2 tablespoons white rum
⅛ teaspoon ground cinnamon
3 egg whites
¼ teaspoon cream of tartar
¼ teaspoon almond extract
⅔ cup sugar
½ cup flaked sweetened coconut, toasted
1½ cups vanilla low-fat ice cream
Mint sprigs (optional)

Preheat oven to 250°.
Combine first 7 ingredients in a bowl; stir well, and set aside.
Line a large baking sheet with parchment paper. Draw 6 (4-inch) circles on paper; turn paper over.
Beat egg whites and cream of tartar at high speed of an electric mixer until foamy. Add extract; beat well. Gradually add ⅔ cup sugar, 1 tablespoon at a time, beating until stiff peaks form. Fold coconut into egg white mixture.
Spoon egg white mixture onto circles on parchment paper. Using the back of spoon, shape meringues into nests with 1-inch sides.
Bake meringue nests at 250° for 1 hour or until dry. Turn oven off, and let meringue nests cool in closed oven at least 4 hours. Carefully remove meringue nests from paper.
Spoon ¼ cup vanilla ice cream into each meringue nest, and top each with about ⅔ cup fruit mixture. Garnish with mint sprigs, if desired. Yield: 6 servings.

CALORIES 295 (16% from fat); PROTEIN 4.3g; FAT 5.1g (sat 3.8g, mono 0.2g, poly 0.1g); CARB 68.8g; FIBER 3.4g; CHOL 13mg; IRON 0.7mg; SODIUM 66mg; CALC 43mg

GINGER BEER COCKTAIL

Ginger beer is a carbonated beverage that tastes like a stronger version of ginger ale. It is made both with and without alcohol.

¾ cup orange juice
4 (11.5-ounce) bottles ginger beer
1 medium cucumber, cut lengthwise into thin strips
1 medium Red Delicious apple, cut into thin wedges
1 medium orange, cut into thin wedges

Combine all ingredients in a large pitcher; stir well. Serve over ice. Yield: 2 quarts (serving size: 1 cup).

CALORIES 99 (1% from fat); PROTEIN 1g; FAT 0.1g (sat 0g, mono 0g, poly 0g); CARB 13.9g; FIBER 1.9g; CHOL 0mg; IRON 0.2mg; SODIUM 9mg; CALC 22mg

TECHNIQUE

Pure Fluff

Bring a warm, golden-crusted soufflé to the table, and watch everyone sit up as if you'd concocted it from air. Is it any wonder that the French named this baked dish after the verb *souffler*, meaning "to breathe, blow, puff, or whisper"?

What may look as if it takes an act of culinary genius to prepare couldn't be easier, but it's important to keep some key instructions in mind. Soufflés are delicate things that can rise as quickly as expectant hopes and be deflated even faster. They must therefore be eaten immediately, so plan your mealtimes appropriately.

Soufflés take patience, timing, and a firm-but-gentle hand—remember who's the boss and stay in control, especially when folding in the egg whites. Our Soufflé Strategy tells you how.

ASPARAGUS-DILL SOUFFLÉ

A quality Swiss cheese can substitute for Gruyère.

Vegetable cooking spray
¾ pound fresh asparagus
3 tablespoons all-purpose flour
1½ cups 2% low-fat milk
1 (4-ounce) carton egg substitute
¾ cup (3 ounces) grated Gruyère cheese
1 cup mashed potatoes, cooked without salt or fat
2 teaspoons chopped fresh or ½ teaspoon dried dillweed
¼ teaspoon salt
¼ teaspoon ground red pepper
5 egg whites
½ teaspoon cream of tartar

Preheat oven to 400°.
Cut a piece of aluminum foil long enough to fit around a 1½-quart soufflé dish, allowing a 1-inch overlap; fold foil lengthwise into thirds. Lightly coat one side of foil and bottom of dish with cooking spray. Wrap foil around outside of dish, coated side against dish, allowing it to extend 4 inches above rim to form a collar; secure with string or masking tape.
Snap off tough ends of asparagus; remove scales with a knife or vegetable peeler, if desired. Arrange asparagus in a steamer basket over boiling water. Cover and steam 3 minutes or until crisp-tender; drain. Thinly slice asparagus spears to equal ½ cup; set aside. Cut remaining asparagus spears in half; set aside.
Place flour in a medium saucepan. Gradually add milk, stirring with a wire whisk until well-blended. Bring to a boil over medium heat; cook 3 minutes, stirring constantly, or until thickened.
Place egg substitute in a large bowl. Gradually stir one-fourth of hot milk mixture into egg substitute; add to remaining hot mixture, stirring constantly with a wire whisk. Remove from heat; add cheese, stirring until cheese melts.
Place milk mixture, halved asparagus spears, mashed potatoes, and next

3 ingredients in a blender; cover and process until smooth. Transfer to a large bowl; stir in sliced asparagus.

Beat egg whites and cream of tartar at high speed of an electric mixer until stiff peaks form. Gently stir one-fourth of the egg white mixture into the milk mixture. Gently fold in remaining egg white mixture.

Pour egg white mixture into prepared soufflé dish. Bake at 400° for 10 minutes. Reduce oven temperature to 350°, and bake an additional 45 minutes or until puffed and golden. Remove foil collar, and serve immediately. Yield: 6 servings.

CALORIES 187 (33% from fat); PROTEIN 13.2g; FAT 6.8g (sat 3.4g, mono 2.5g, poly 0.8g); CARB 15.2g; FIBER 1.3g; CHOL 26mg; IRON 1.3mg; SODIUM 369mg; CALC 259mg

STEP
by
STEP

Cut a piece of aluminum foil long enough to fit around your soufflé dish, including a 1-inch overlap. Fold the foil lengthwise into thirds. Lightly coat one side of the foil with vegetable cooking spray. Wrap the foil around the outside of the soufflé dish, coated side against dish, allowing it to extend 4 inches above rim. Secure the foil in place with string, masking tape, or a metal straight pin.

SOUFFLÉ STRATEGY

Is it done yet? Here's how to know: Leave the soufflé undisturbed during baking. Even if you're tempted to open the oven door and watch it rise, DON'T! You may be watching it fall instead. First, look through your oven window. When the top appears browned, crusty, and dry, it's time to test the soufflé for doneness. Do so by inserting a knife blade into the center. If it comes out moist and clean, the soufflé should be ready. Otherwise, slide it back into the oven, and bake it 10 additional minutes. Repeat the checking procedure.

And here's what not to do ...

◆ Don't overbeat the egg whites; if whipped for too long, they will separate, turn grainy, and be difficult to fold in.

◆ Don't be in a hurry when removing the collar. Hasty action can cause the soufflé to fall prematurely.

◆ Don't stir the soufflé mixture too roughly; instead, gently fold.

◆ Don't have the base sauce too hot when egg whites are folded into it.

◆ Don't open and close the oven door too aggressively.

WHITE BEAN SOUFFLÉ WITH THYME AND GARLIC

This soufflé would make a great accompaniment to our recipe for Rack of Lamb on page 89.

Vegetable cooking spray
1 teaspoon olive oil
1 cup chopped onion
6 garlic cloves, chopped
1 teaspoon minced fresh or
   ¼ teaspoon dried thyme
¼ teaspoon salt
⅛ teaspoon pepper
1 (15.8-ounce) can Great
   Northern beans, drained
1 (4-ounce) carton egg substitute
½ cup (2 ounces) grated Asiago
   cheese
5 egg whites
½ teaspoon cream of tartar

Preheat oven to 375°.

Cut a piece of aluminum foil long enough to fit around a 1-quart soufflé dish, allowing a 1-inch overlap; fold foil lengthwise into thirds. Lightly coat one side of foil and bottom of dish with cooking spray. Wrap foil around outside of dish, coated side against dish, allowing the foil to extend 4 inches above rim to form a collar; secure the collar with string or masking tape.

Heat oil in a small skillet over medium-high heat until hot. Add onion and garlic; sauté 2 minutes or until tender.

Combine onion mixture, thyme, and next 4 ingredients in a blender or food processor; cover and process until smooth. Spoon bean mixture into a large bowl. Stir in cheese; set aside.

Beat egg whites and cream of tartar at high speed of an electric mixer until stiff peaks form. Gently stir one-fourth of the egg white mixture into the bean mixture. Gently fold in remaining egg white mixture.

Pour egg white mixture into prepared soufflé dish. Bake at 375° for 1 hour or until puffed and golden. Carefully remove foil collar, and serve immediately. Yield: 6 servings.

CALORIES 138 (27% from fat); PROTEIN 11.8g; FAT 4.1g (sat 2g, mono 1.5g, poly 0.3g); CARB 13.8g; FIBER 2.2g; CHOL 10mg; IRON 1.5mg; SODIUM 325mg; CALC 145mg

SANTA FE CORN SOUFFLÉ

Roasted red peppers and corn pair up in this colorful Southwestern-inspired soufflé.

Vegetable cooking spray
  1   cup coarsely shredded carrot
  ¼   cup finely chopped onion
  1   (10-ounce) package frozen cream-style corn
  2   tablespoons all-purpose flour
  1   tablespoon yellow cornmeal
  1   cup skim milk
  1   (4-ounce) carton egg substitute
  2   tablespoons chopped bottled roasted red bell pepper
  1   teaspoon minced fresh or ¼ teaspoon dried cilantro
  ½   teaspoon salt
  ¼   teaspoon chili powder
  ¼   teaspoon pepper
  4   egg whites
  ½   teaspoon cream of tartar

Preheat oven to 400°.

Cut a piece of aluminum foil long enough to fit around a 2-quart soufflé dish, allowing a 1-inch overlap; fold foil lengthwise into thirds. Lightly coat one side of foil and bottom of dish with cooking spray. Wrap foil around outside of dish, coated side against dish, allowing it to extend 4 inches above rim to form a collar; secure with string or masking tape.

Arrange carrot and onion in a steamer basket over boiling water. Cover and steam 3 minutes; drain and set aside. Cook corn according to package directions; set aside.

Combine flour and cornmeal in a medium saucepan. Gradually add milk, stirring with a wire whisk until well-blended. Stir in corn. Bring milk mixture to a boil over medium heat, and cook 1 minute or until thickened, stirring constantly.

Place egg substitute in a large bowl. Gradually add hot milk mixture to egg substitute, stirring constantly with a wire whisk. Stir in carrot mixture, bell pepper, cilantro, salt, chili powder, and pepper; set aside.

Beat egg whites and cream of tartar at high speed of an electric mixer

until stiff peaks form. Gently stir one-fourth of egg white mixture into milk mixture. Gently fold in the remaining egg white mixture.

Pour egg white mixture into prepared soufflé dish. Bake at 400° for 10 minutes. Reduce oven temperature to 350°, and bake an additional 45 minutes or until puffed and golden. Carefully remove foil collar, and serve immediately. Yield: 6 servings.

CALORIES 110 (6% from fat); PROTEIN 7.2g; FAT 0.7g (sat 0.1g, mono 0g, poly 0.1g); CARB 18.4g; FIBER 1.8g; CHOL 1mg; IRON 0.9mg; SODIUM 427mg; CALC 66mg

---

MENU SUGGESTION

ARTICHOKE-CRAB SOUFFLÉ

Fennel-orange salad

Sesame rolls

New York Cheesecake (page 99)

*Combine thinly sliced fennel bulb and orange sections; toss with champagne vinaigrette.

ARTICHOKE-CRAB SOUFFLÉ

Vegetable cooking spray
  2   bacon slices
  ¼   cup finely chopped onion
  2   tablespoons all-purpose flour
  1½   cups 2% low-fat milk
  ¼   cup egg substitute
  ¼   cup (1 ounce) grated fresh Parmesan cheese
  ¼   teaspoon salt
  ⅛   teaspoon white pepper
  ⅛   teaspoon ground red pepper
  1   (14-ounce) can artichoke hearts, drained and finely chopped
  ½   pound lump crabmeat, shell pieces removed
  4   egg whites
  ½   teaspoon cream of tartar

Preheat oven to 400°.

Cut a piece of aluminum foil long enough to fit around a 2-quart soufflé dish, allowing a 1-inch overlap; fold foil lengthwise into thirds. Lightly coat one side of foil and bottom of dish with cooking spray. Wrap foil around outside of dish, coated side against dish, allowing it to extend 4 inches above rim to form a collar; secure with string or masking tape.

Cook bacon in a large nonstick skillet over medium-high heat until crisp. Remove bacon from skillet. Drain, reserving 1 tablespoon bacon fat in skillet. Crumble bacon, and set aside. Add onion to bacon fat in skillet, and sauté 2 minutes or until tender. Add flour, and cook 1 minute, stirring constantly with a wire whisk. Gradually add milk, stirring constantly. Bring to a boil over medium heat, and cook 1 minute or until thickened, stirring constantly.

Place egg substitute in a large bowl. Gradually add hot milk mixture to egg substitute, stirring constantly with a wire whisk. Stir in bacon, cheese, salt, peppers, artichokes, and crabmeat; set aside.

Beat egg whites and cream of tartar at high speed of an electric mixer, until stiff peaks form. Gently stir one-fourth of the egg white mixture into the milk mixture. Gently fold in remaining egg white mixture.

Pour egg white mixture into prepared soufflé dish. Bake at 400° for 10 minutes. Reduce oven temperature to 350°, and bake an additional 45 minutes or until puffed and golden. Carefully remove foil collar, and serve immediately. Yield: 6 servings.

Note: To make individual soufflés, prepare 6 (8-ounce) ramekins as directed above. Divide soufflé mixture evenly among ramekins, and place on a large baking sheet. Bake as directed above.

CALORIES 151 (26% from fat); PROTEIN 17.2g; FAT 4.4g (sat 2g, mono 1.3g, poly 0.5g); CARB 10.8g; FIBER 0.2g; CHOL 48mg; IRON 1.3mg; SODIUM 453mg; CALC 194mg

SOUTHERN BRUNCH SOUFFLÉ WITH CHIVES

The "Southern" part of this recipe is the grits. With the addition of turkey sausage, the soufflé makes a filling breakfast or brunch dish.

Vegetable cooking spray
½ pound turkey breakfast sausage
2 (14½-ounce) cans no-salt-added chicken broth
1 cup quick-cooking grits, uncooked
2 teaspoons Dijon mustard
½ teaspoon salt
¼ teaspoon pepper
3 ounces light cream cheese with garlic and spices
1 (4-ounce) carton egg substitute
½ cup chopped fresh or freeze-dried chives
5 egg whites
½ teaspoon cream of tartar

Preheat oven to 400°.

Cut a piece of aluminum foil long enough to fit around a 2-quart soufflé dish, allowing a 1-inch overlap; fold foil lengthwise into thirds. Lightly coat one side of foil and bottom of dish with cooking spray. Wrap foil around outside of dish, coated side against dish, allowing it to extend 4 inches above rim to form a collar; secure with string or masking tape.

Remove casings from sausage. Cook sausage in a large saucepan over medium heat until browned, stirring to crumble. Drain sausage in a colander, and pat dry with paper towels. Wipe sausage drippings from pan with a paper towel.

Bring broth to a boil in pan, and gradually stir in grits. Cover, reduce heat, and simmer 5 minutes, stirring occasionally. Remove from heat; add sausage, mustard, salt, pepper, and cheese, stirring until the cheese melts.

Place egg substitute in a large bowl. Gradually add hot broth mixture to egg substitute, stirring constantly with a wire whisk. Stir in chives; set aside.

Beat egg whites and cream of tartar in a medium bowl at high speed of an electric mixer until stiff peaks form.

Gently stir one-fourth of egg white mixture into broth mixture. Gently fold in remaining egg white mixture.

Pour egg white mixture into prepared soufflé dish. Bake at 400° for 10 minutes. Reduce oven temperature to 375°, and bake an additional 55 minutes or until puffed and golden. Carefully remove foil collar, and serve immediately. Yield: 6 servings.

CALORIES 210 (31% from fat); PROTEIN 12.4g; FAT 7.3g (sat 2.9g, mono 1.9g, poly 1.1g); CARB 22g; FIBER 1.9g; CHOL 10mg; IRON 1.7mg; SODIUM 598mg; CALC 31mg

CLASSICS

Rack of Lamb

There aren't many entrées that beat rack of lamb, especially when it's seasoned with fresh garlic and rosemary and served warm from the oven. Our rack of lamb calls for a bread coating—one made not only with garlic and rosemary, but with mustard, honey, and black pepper, too. To complement the lamb, and give a nod to Spring, serve it with asparagus, roasted new potatoes, and roasted garlic.

ROSEMARY-CRUSTED RACK OF LAMB WITH HERBED JELLY

1 (1½-pound, 8-rib) lean rack of lamb
2 tablespoons Dijon mustard
1 tablespoon honey
2 garlic cloves, crushed
1 cup fresh whole wheat breadcrumbs
2 teaspoons finely chopped fresh or ¾ teaspoon dried rosemary
¼ teaspoon salt
¼ teaspoon cracked pepper
Herbed Jelly
Rosemary sprigs (optional)

Preheat oven to 425°. Trim the fat from lamb, and place, meat side up, on rack of a broiler pan. Insert meat thermometer into the thickest part of lamb, making sure thermometer does not touch bone. Set aside.

Combine mustard, honey, and garlic; stir well. Spread mustard mixture over lamb. Combine breadcrumbs and next 3 ingredients; stir well. Pat breadcrumb mixture into mustard mixture on lamb.

Bake lamb at 425° for 40 minutes or until thermometer registers 150° (medium-rare) to 160° (medium). Slice into 8 chops; serve with Herbed Jelly, and garnish with rosemary sprigs, if desired. Yield: 4 servings (serving size: 2 lamb chops and 3 tablespoons Herbed Jelly).

CALORIES 328 (24% from fat); PROTEIN 18.8g; FAT 8.9g (sat 2.9g, mono 3.4g, poly 1.1g); CARB 44g; FIBER 1.1g; CHOL 53mg; IRON 2mg; SODIUM 564mg; CALC 44mg

Herbed Jelly:

½ cup apple jelly
2 tablespoons white wine vinegar
2 tablespoons water
1 rosemary sprig

Combine all ingredients in a saucepan; bring to a boil. Remove from heat; stir well. Let stand 15 minutes; discard rosemary sprig. Serve warm or at room temperature. Yield: ¾ cup (serving size: 3 tablespoons).

CALORIES 102 (0% from fat); PROTEIN 0.2g; FAT 0g; CARB 26.6g; FIBER 0.1g; CHOL 0mg; IRON 0mg; SODIUM 14mg; CALC 4mg

From Bags to Riches

By using prepackaged salad and vegetable mixes, we've increased your options for creative, easy-to-prepare entrées and sides.

Just when you think there aren't any good ideas left in the world, along come these handy timesavers: prepackaged salad and vegetable mixes. These see-through bags contain various combinations or, in some cases, one particular green (such as romaine or cabbage). If you haven't tried these garden mixes, then step right up: They're sliced, diced, prewashed, and ready to toss.

Of course, one great idea begets another: By combining bagged salads and vegetables with other ingredients, such as chicken, ham, sun-dried tomatoes, chiles, or bacon, a new world of healthy, innovative entrées and side dishes emerges. So don't delay—act now for a quick, delicious meal.

SUN-DRIED TOMATO-VEGETABLE PASTA

Preparation time: 18 minutes
Cooking time: 12 minutes

- 1 (3-ounce) package sun-dried tomatoes, packed without oil
- 2 garlic cloves, peeled
- ½ cup fresh basil leaves
- 3 tablespoons grated Romano cheese
- ¼ teaspoon pepper
- 1½ teaspoons olive oil
- 1 (12-ounce) package ready-to-eat broccoli, carrots, and cauliflower, coarsely chopped
- Vegetable cooking spray
- 2 tablespoons chopped shallots
- ½ cup low-salt chicken broth
- 1 (14.5-ounce) can whole tomatoes, undrained and chopped
- 4 cups hot cooked angel hair (about 8 ounces uncooked pasta)
- 1 tablespoon plus 1 teaspoon pine nuts, toasted

Chop sun-dried tomatoes; set aside.
Drop garlic cloves through food chute with food processor on, and process until minced. Add basil leaves, and process until minced. Add Romano cheese and pepper, and process until blended. With the food processor on, slowly pour olive oil through food chute, and process until well-blended. Set pesto aside.

Arrange mixed vegetables in a steamer basket over boiling water. Cover and steam vegetables 4 minutes or until crisp-tender. Set steamed vegetables aside.

Coat a large nonstick skillet with cooking spray, and place over medium heat until hot. Add chopped sun-dried tomatoes and shallots; sauté 3 minutes. Stir in broth and canned tomatoes; bring to a boil. Reduce heat, and simmer, uncovered, 5 minutes. Remove from heat; stir in pesto and steamed vegetables.

Spoon pasta evenly onto 4 individual plates, and top with vegetable mixture; sprinkle with toasted pine nuts. Yield: 4 servings (serving size: 1 cup pasta, 1 cup vegetable mixture, and 1 teaspoon pine nuts).

CALORIES 378 (17% from fat); PROTEIN 15.4g; FAT 7g (sat 1.7g, mono 2.6g, poly 1.6g); CARB 66.2g; FIBER 2.3g; CHOL 6mg; IRON 3.4mg; SODIUM 879mg; CALC 131mg

GRILLED CHICKEN CAESAR

Preparation time: 18 minutes
Cooking time: 10 minutes

- 1 tablespoon chili powder
- 2 tablespoons Worcestershire sauce
- 1 teaspoon ground cumin
- ¼ teaspoon pepper
- 1 garlic clove, crushed
- 1 pound skinned, boned chicken breasts, cut into 1-inch-wide strips
- Vegetable cooking spray
- ¾ cup low-fat buttermilk
- 3 tablespoons grated Romano cheese
- 1 tablespoon lemon juice
- 1 teaspoon anchovy paste
- ½ teaspoon dry mustard
- ¼ teaspoon pepper
- 1 garlic clove, minced
- 1 (10-ounce) package ready-to-eat romaine salad
- 2 cups halved cherry tomatoes
- ¾ cup plain croutons

Combine first 6 ingredients in a medium bowl; stir well, and set aside.

Coat grill rack with cooking spray; place grill rack on grill over medium-hot coals (350° to 400°). Place chicken strips on grill rack, and grill, covered, 5 minutes on each side or until chicken strips are done.

Combine buttermilk and next 6 ingredients in a large bowl; stir well. Add romaine salad, tomatoes, and croutons; toss gently to coat. Spoon salad mixture onto each of 4 plates, and top with chicken strips. Yield: 4 servings (serving size: 2½ cups salad mixture and 3 ounces chicken).

Note: Substitute 12 cups sliced romaine lettuce for 1 (10-ounce) package ready-to-eat romaine salad, if desired.

CALORIES 289 (26% from fat); PROTEIN 33.8g; FAT 8.3g (sat 2.8g, mono 2.5g, poly 1.3g); CARB19g; FIBER 3.2g; CHOL 78mg; IRON 2.9mg; SODIUM 429mg; CALC 186mg

SPICY ASIAN SLAW

Preparation time: 5 minutes

- ¼ cup rice vinegar
- 2 tablespoons low-sodium soy sauce
- 2 teaspoons dark sesame oil
- ¼ teaspoon dried crushed red pepper
- ¼ cup sliced green onions
- 1 (16-ounce) package ready-to-eat coleslaw
- 1 tablespoon chopped fresh parsley
- 2 teaspoons sesame seeds, toasted

Combine first 4 ingredients in a bowl; stir well. Add green onions and coleslaw; toss gently. Sprinkle with parsley and sesame seeds; serve immediately. Yield: 4 servings (serving size: 1 cup).

CALORIES 74 (36% from fat); PROTEIN 1.7g; FAT 3g (sat 0.4g, mono 1.2g, poly 1.3g); CARB 10.5g; FIBER 2.8g; CHOL 0mg; IRON 0.4mg; SODIUM 235mg; CALC 21mg

HOT BACON SLAW

Preparation time: 5 minutes
Cooking time: 7 minutes

- 2 bacon slices
- 1 (16-ounce) package ready-to-eat coleslaw
- ¼ cup balsamic vinegar
- 1½ tablespoons brown sugar
- 3 tablespoons water
- ½ teaspoon seasoned salt
- ¼ teaspoon ground red pepper

Cook bacon in a large nonstick skillet over medium-high heat until crisp; remove bacon from skillet, reserving drippings in skillet. Set bacon aside.

Add coleslaw to drippings; sauté over medium-high heat 3 minutes. Add vinegar and next 4 ingredients; cook 1 minute, stirring constantly. Remove from heat; crumble bacon, and stir into coleslaw. Serve warm. Yield: 3 servings (serving size: 1 cup).

CALORIES 94 (22% from fat); PROTEIN 3.4g; FAT 2.3g (sat 0.8g, mono 1.1g, poly 0.3g); CARB 16.4g; FIBER 6.7g; CHOL 5mg; IRON 0.3mg; SODIUM 172mg; CALC 5mg

ITALIAN ANTIPASTO SALAD

The Mediterranean-style salad we used contains romaine, radicchio, and endive.
Preparation time: 20 minutes

- 1 (10-ounce) package ready-to-eat Mediterranean-style salad
- 1 cup drained canned no-salt-added chickpeas (garbanzo beans)
- ⅔ cup thinly sliced lean deli ham, cut into ½-inch-wide strips (about ¼ pound)
- 1 (14-ounce) can quartered artichoke hearts, drained
- 1 large red bell pepper, cut into rings
- ¼ cup balsamic vinegar
- 2 tablespoons water
- 1 tablespoon olive oil
- 1 teaspoon dried oregano
- 2 teaspoons Dijon mustard
- ¼ teaspoon pepper
- 1 tablespoon grated nonfat Parmesan cheese
- Chopped fresh parsley (optional)

Arrange salad on a serving platter, and top with chickpeas, ham, artichokes, and bell pepper rings. Combine vinegar and next 5 ingredients; stir well, and drizzle over salad. Sprinkle cheese over salad, and garnish with chopped parsley, if desired. Yield: 4 servings (serving size: 3 cups).

CALORIES 127 (30% from fat); PROTEIN 8.3g; FAT 4.2g (sat 0.7g, mono 2.3g, poly 0.8g); CARB 15.1g; FIBER 1.8g; CHOL 12mg; IRON 1.9mg; SODIUM 466mg; CALC 38mg

---

MENU SUGGESTION

CHICKEN TACO SALAD

*Gazpacho

Low-fat banana milk shake

*Add 1½ cups chopped cucumber, ½ cup chopped bell pepper, ¼ cup sliced green onions, 1 tablespoon lemon juice, and ½ teaspoon hot sauce to 4 cups vegetable juice.

CHICKEN TACO SALAD

Preparation time: 15 minutes

- 1 cup diced tomato
- ¾ cup low-fat sour cream
- ½ cup diced red onion
- 3 tablespoons chopped fresh cilantro
- ½ teaspoon ground cumin
- ¼ teaspoon salt
- 1 (½-pound) package ready-to-eat roasted chicken breasts, shredded
- 1 (16-ounce) package ready-to-eat garden salad
- 1 (4.5-ounce) can chopped green chiles, undrained
- 1 (13.5-ounce) bag baked tortilla chips (about 16 cups)

Combine first 9 ingredients in a large bowl, and toss well. Divide tortilla chips evenly among 8 plates; top each serving with 1 cup salad mixture. Yield: 8 servings.

CALORIES 279 (16% from fat); PROTEIN 13.4g; FAT 5.1g (sat 2.3g, mono 1.9g, poly 0.4g); CARB 47.6g; FIBER 4.8g; CHOL 9mg; IRON 0.4mg; SODIUM 480mg; CALC 32mg

Reinventing the Chicken

Sometimes you have to go back to the drawing board, and that's what we've done with these classic recipes. We've adapted them for today's tastes without compromising their flavors.

Because chicken can be the leanest of meats—most of the fat is contained in the skin, which can be removed—we decided to lighten up some chicken favorites that are usually considered too heavy for the health-conscious diner. Now that we've gone back to the culinary drawing board, you can go back to enjoying your favorite chicken recipes. These are classics just waiting to happen again.

SOUTHWESTERN "FRIED" CHICKEN

Chili powder and ground cumin lend a south-of-the-border spark to this oven-fried chicken.

- 1 tablespoon garlic powder
- 1 tablespoon onion powder
- 1 tablespoon paprika
- 1 tablespoon chili powder
- 1 teaspoon ground cumin
- ½ teaspoon salt
- ½ teaspoon pepper
- 8 (6-ounce) skinned chicken breast halves
- 1½ cups low-fat buttermilk
- ½ cup fine, dry breadcrumbs
- ½ cup yellow cornmeal
- Vegetable cooking spray

Combine first 7 ingredients in a small bowl; stir well. Rub chicken with 3 tablespoons spice mixture. Set remaining spice mixture aside.

Place chicken in a 13 x 9-inch baking dish; let stand 10 minutes. Pour buttermilk over chicken, turning to coat. Cover and marinate in refrigerator 2 hours, turning chicken occasionally. Remove chicken from dish; discard buttermilk.

Preheat oven to 400°.

Combine remaining spice mixture, breadcrumbs, and cornmeal in a dish; stir well. Dredge chicken in breadcrumb mixture; place on a baking sheet coated with cooking spray. Bake at 400° for 20 minutes. Lightly coat chicken with cooking spray, and bake an additional 20 minutes or until chicken is done (do not turn). Yield: 8 servings (serving size: 1 breast half).

CALORIES 250 (18% from fat); PROTEIN 34.4g; FAT 5g (sat 1.4g, mono 1.6g, poly 1.3g); CARB 15g; FIBER 1.4g; CHOL 87mg; IRON 2.4mg; SODIUM 299mg; CALC 61mg

CHICKEN NORMANDY

Because Normandy is France's apple country, it's no wonder that chicken and apples make a classic combination. We've updated this duo with a sour cream sauce.

- ¼ cup all-purpose flour
- ¼ teaspoon salt
- ¼ teaspoon pepper
- 2 chicken breast halves (about 1 pound), skinned
- 2 chicken thighs (about ½ pound), skinned
- 2 chicken drumsticks (about ½ pound), skinned
- 1 tablespoon plus 1 teaspoon vegetable oil, divided
- 2 teaspoons all-purpose flour
- 1¼ cups apple juice
- ¼ cup Calvados* or brandy
- 1 cup chopped Granny Smith apple
- ½ cup chopped shallots
- 1 bay leaf
- ½ cup nonfat sour cream
- 1 tablespoon margarine
- 2 tablespoons sugar
- 2 Granny Smith apples (about 1 pound), cored and each cut crosswise into 8 rings

Combine first 3 ingredients in a large heavy-duty, zip-top plastic bag. Add chicken; seal bag, and shake well to coat chicken. Heat 1 tablespoon oil in a large nonstick skillet over medium heat until hot. Add chicken, and cook 5 minutes on each side or until browned. Remove chicken from skillet; set aside.

Place 2 teaspoons flour in a small bowl. Gradually add apple juice and apple brandy, stirring with a wire whisk until blended. Set apple juice mixture aside.

Heat remaining 1 teaspoon oil in skillet over medium heat. Add chopped apple and shallots; sauté 5 minutes or until tender. Return chicken to skillet. Add apple juice mixture and bay leaf, and bring to a boil. Cover, reduce heat, and simmer 35 minutes or until chicken is done, stirring occasionally. Discard bay leaf.

Remove from heat; stir in sour cream. Remove chicken mixture from skillet, and place on a serving platter; set aside, and keep warm. Wipe skillet dry with paper towels.

Melt margarine in skillet over medium heat. Add sugar and apple rings; sauté 5 minutes or until lightly browned. Serve with chicken mixture. Yield: 4 servings (serving size: 1 breast or 1 thigh and 1 drumstick, ½ cup sauce, and 4 apple rings).

Calvados is a dry apple brandy made in the Calvados region of Normandy, France.

CALORIES 476 (25% from fat); PROTEIN 40.4g; FAT 13.3g (sat 2.9g, mono 4.4g, poly 4.5g); CARB 47.8g; FIBER 4.7g; CHOL 120mg; IRON 2.7mg; SODIUM 322mg; CALC 44mg

SESAME CHICKEN NUGGETS

This fast-food favorite goes Oriental with the addition of sesame seeds and lime juice; to reduce the fat, it's baked instead of fried. For color contrast, use a mixture of black sesame seeds (available at many Asian markets) and the lighter variety.

⅓ cup coarse-grained mustard
⅓ cup honey
2 tablespoons lime juice
¼ teaspoon salt
⅛ teaspoon pepper
1 pound skinned, boned chicken breasts, cut into 1-inch pieces
2 egg whites
½ cup sesame seeds, toasted
½ cup fine, dry breadcrumbs
Vegetable cooking spray

Preheat oven to 350°.
Combine first 3 ingredients in a shallow bowl; stir well, and set aside.
Sprinkle the salt and pepper over chicken, and set aside. Place egg whites in a bowl, and stir well. Combine toasted sesame seeds and breadcrumbs in a shallow dish, and stir well. Dip chicken in egg whites; dredge in sesame seed mixture.
Arrange chicken in a single layer on a baking sheet coated with cooking

spray. Bake at 350° for 15 minutes, turning once. Serve chicken with mustard mixture. Yield: 4 servings (serving size: about 3 ounces chicken and 3 tablespoons mustard mixture).

CALORIES 409 (30% from fat); PROTEIN 34g; FAT 13.8g (sat 2.3g, mono 5.4g, poly 5g); CARB 39.3g; FIBER 1.6g; CHOL 72mg; IRON 4.9mg; SODIUM 613mg; CALC 240mg

CHICKEN SALAD WITH NORTH AFRICAN SPICES

Chicken salad is not just an American favorite. This enlivened variation features a fragrant mix of spices based on a traditional Tunisian blend. (For convenience's sake, we call for ground spices, but you can also use whole spices that you've roasted and ground yourself.) This salad is equally delicious chilled or served immediately.

1 cup plain nonfat yogurt
2 tablespoons lemon juice
1 teaspoon caraway seeds, crushed
½ teaspoon ground cumin
½ teaspoon ground coriander
¼ teaspoon salt
¼ teaspoon dried crushed red pepper
¼ teaspoon black pepper
3 cups chopped cooked chicken breast (about 1½ pounds, skinned and boned)
1 cup drained canned chickpeas (garbanzo beans)
½ cup julienne-cut red bell pepper
½ cup julienne-cut green bell pepper
½ cup chopped red onion
¼ cup chopped fresh parsley
1 (2¼-ounce) can sliced ripe olives, drained

Combine first 8 ingredients in a medium bowl; stir well. Add chicken and remaining ingredients; toss well. Yield: 5 servings (serving size: 1 cup).

CALORIES 233 (17% from fat); PROTEIN 29.4g; FAT 4.3g (sat 1g, mono 1.7g, poly 1g); CARB 18.5g; FIBER 4.2g; CHOL 66mg; IRON 2.5mg; SODIUM 414mg; CALC 139mg

PEKING CHICKEN

Peking duck is simplified and made healthier by using chicken. We've also substituted flour tortillas for the customary Mandarin pancakes.

1 cup hoisin sauce
¼ cup low-sodium soy sauce
¼ cup rice vinegar
¼ cup honey
1 tablespoon peeled, grated gingerroot
4 garlic cloves, minced
2 pounds skinned, boned chicken breast halves
Vegetable cooking spray
1 tablespoon dark sesame oil, divided
8 (8-inch) flour tortillas
1 cup sliced green onions

Combine first 6 ingredients in a medium bowl; stir well. Reserve 1 cup hoisin sauce mixture; set aside. Cut chicken diagonally across the grain into thin slices. Add chicken to the remaining sauce mixture in bowl, and stir well. Cover and marinate in refrigerator up to 8 hours, stirring occasionally. Remove chicken from bowl; discard marinade.
Coat a large nonstick skillet with cooking spray; add 1½ teaspoons oil, and place over medium-high heat until hot. Add half of chicken; cook 5 minutes or until done. Remove chicken from skillet, and set aside. Repeat procedure with remaining oil and chicken.
Warm tortillas according to package directions. Spread 2 tablespoons reserved hoisin sauce mixture down the center of each tortilla. Arrange one-eighth of chicken slices and 2 tablespoons green onions down the center of each tortilla; roll up tortillas. Yield: 8 servings.

CALORIES 393 (15% from fat); PROTEIN 31.8g; FAT 6.6g (sat 1.1g, mono 2.4g, poly 2.4g); CARB 49.7g; FIBER 2.2g; CHOL 66mg; IRON 3mg; SODIUM 920mg; CALC 95mg

STUFFED CHICKEN PARMESAN

In this update, an Italian-American favorite is stuffed with sun-dried tomatoes and cheese.

    1   cup boiling water
    8   sun-dried tomatoes, packed
          without oil
    1   tablespoon water
    2   egg whites
    ⅔   cup dry Italian-seasoned
          breadcrumbs
    ⅓   cup all-purpose flour
    ¼   cup (1 ounce) grated fresh
          Parmesan cheese
    ¼   teaspoon pepper
    4   (4-ounce) skinned, boned
          chicken breast halves
    4   very thin slices fresh Parmesan
          cheese (about ½ ounce)
    2   teaspoons capers
 Vegetable cooking spray
    2   cups hot cooked angel hair
          (about 8 ounces uncooked
          pasta)
 Chunky Tomato Sauce

Combine boiling water and sun-dried tomatoes in a bowl; let stand 30 minutes or until softened. Drain tomatoes, and set aside.

Preheat oven to 400°.

Combine 1 tablespoon water and egg whites in a shallow bowl; stir well, and set aside. Combine breadcrumbs, flour, grated Parmesan cheese, and pepper in a shallow dish; stir well, and set aside.

Cut a horizontal slit through thickest portion of each chicken breast half to form a pocket. Stuff 2 sun-dried tomatoes, 1 slice of cheese, and ½ teaspoon capers into each pocket, and close opening with a wooden pick. Dip each breast half in egg white mixture; dredge in breadcrumb mixture.

Place chicken on a baking sheet coated with cooking spray. Lightly coat chicken with cooking spray, and bake at 400° for 15 minutes. Turn chicken over, and lightly coat with cooking spray. Bake an additional 10 minutes or until done. Discard wooden picks.

Place ½ cup pasta on each of 4 plates, and top with stuffed chicken. Spoon ¾ cup Chunky Tomato Sauce over each serving. Yield: 4 servings.

CALORIES 496 (18% from fat); PROTEIN 42.3g; FAT 9.8g (sat 3.5g; mono 4.6g; poly 1.7g); CARB 59.5g; FIBER 5g; CHOL 73mg; IRON 4.4mg; SODIUM 1,116mg; CALC 196mg

Chunky Tomato Sauce:

    1   tablespoon olive oil
    1   cup chopped onion
    2   garlic cloves, minced
    6   cups coarsely chopped tomato
          (about 3 pounds)
    ⅓   cup tomato paste
    2   tablespoons balsamic
          vinegar
    1   teaspoon sugar
    ¼   teaspoon salt
    ¼   teaspoon black pepper
    ¼   teaspoon dried crushed red
          pepper
    ¼   cup chopped fresh basil

Heat oil in a large nonstick skillet over medium heat until hot. Add onion and garlic; sauté 5 minutes or until tender. Add tomato and next 6 ingredients; stir well. Reduce heat, and simmer, uncovered, 15 minutes. Remove from heat; stir in basil. Yield: 5 cups (serving size: 1¼ cups).

Note: Substitute 3 (14.5-ounce) cans diced tomatoes, undrained, for 6 cups chopped tomato, if desired. Omit salt when using canned tomatoes.

CALORIES 130 (32% from fat); PROTEIN 3.8g; FAT 4.6g (sat 0.6g; mono 2.7g; poly 0.8g); CARB 22.4g; FIBER 5.3g; CHOL 0mg; IRON 2.1mg; SODIUM 186mg; CALC 38mg

THE ENLIGHTENED CHEF

Food for Thought

How do film and TV industry folk keep their figures camera-ready? Many call on Diet Designs, a daily meal-planning, preparation, and delivery service in Culver City, California, founded by nutritionist-chef Carrie Latt Wiatt.

GRILLED CHICKEN WITH MARSALA-CURRANT CREAM SAUCE

The only fat in this recipe is in the chicken—there's none at all in the cream sauce.

    1½ cups dry Marsala wine, divided
    1   cup sliced shiitake mushroom
          caps
    ¼   cup dried currants
    4¼ cups fat-free chicken broth,
          divided
    2   cups thinly sliced leek
    ½   cup chopped shallots
    ¼   cup evaporated skimmed milk
    2   teaspoons cornstarch
    ½   teaspoon lemon juice
    ⅛   teaspoon salt
    6   (4-ounce) skinned, boned
          chicken breast halves
 Vegetable cooking spray

Combine ¼ cup wine, mushrooms, and currants in a small saucepan; bring to a boil. Reduce heat, and simmer, uncovered, 3 minutes. Remove from heat, and set aside.

Heat ¼ cup broth in a medium nonstick skillet over medium-high heat until hot. Add leek and shallots, and sauté 10 minutes. Add remaining wine and remaining broth; bring to a boil. Reduce heat, and simmer, uncovered, 20 minutes.

Combine milk and cornstarch in a small bowl; stir until blended. Add milk mixture and mushroom mixture to skillet; bring to a boil, and cook 1 minute, stirring constantly. Remove from heat, and stir in lemon juice and salt; set aside, and keep warm.

Coat grill rack with cooking spray; place on grill over medium-hot coals (350° to 400°). Place chicken on grill rack, and grill, covered, 6 minutes on each side or until chicken is done. Spoon cream sauce over chicken. Yield: 6 servings (serving size: 1 chicken breast half and ½ cup sauce).

CALORIES 237 (13% from fat); PROTEIN 33.6g; FAT 3.5g (sat 0.9g, mono 1.1g, poly 0.8g); CARB 16.3g; FIBER 0.7g; CHOL 73mg; IRON 2.2mg; SODIUM 261mg; CALC 80mg

INSPIRED VEGETARIAN

Go with the Grain

As grains and other vegetarian dishes move to the center of the American plate, the demand for healthy, alternative dishes keeps growing. The recipes that follow were created with those needs in mind, using six different grains that will soon be household staples. And like rice, these new grains couldn't be simpler to cook—just boil water.

MENU SUGGESTION

ZUCCHINI BOATS WITH BULGUR

Lamb kebabs

Hummus and pita bread

*Place 2 (15-ounce) cans drained chickpeas, ⅓ cup tahini, ⅓ cup lemon juice, ⅓ cup water, and 3 garlic cloves in a food processor; process until smooth. Serve with pita bread.

ZUCCHINI BOATS WITH BULGUR

¾ cup uncooked bulgur
¾ cup boiling water
6 small zucchini (about 1½ pounds)
2 teaspoons olive oil
1 cup chopped onion
¼ teaspoon ground cumin
2 garlic cloves, minced
¾ cup finely crumbled feta cheese
¼ cup dried currants
2 tablespoons minced fresh mint
2 tablespoons minced fresh parsley
2 tablespoons fresh lemon juice
¼ teaspoon salt
¼ teaspoon pepper

Combine bulgur and boiling water in a bowl; stir well. Cover and let stand 30 minutes.

Preheat oven to 375°.

Cut each zucchini in half lengthwise; scoop out pulp, leaving a ¼-inch-thick shell, and set shells aside. Chop pulp to measure 1½ cups; reserve remaining pulp for another use.

Heat oil in a large nonstick skillet over medium heat until hot. Add 1½ cups zucchini pulp, onion, cumin, and garlic; sauté 1 minute. Add bulgur, feta cheese, and next 6 ingredients; stir well.

Spoon ⅓ cup bulgur mixture into each zucchini shell, and place in a 13 x 9-inch baking dish. Cover and bake at 375° for 25 minutes. Yield: 4 servings (serving size: 3 stuffed shells).

Note: To make Zucchini-Bulgur Bake, replace zucchini pulp with 1½ cups peeled, chopped zucchini. Spoon bulgur mixture into a 1-quart casserole instead of shells. Cover and bake at 375° for 25 minutes.

CALORIES 237 (29% from fat); PROTEIN 9.2g; FAT 7.7g (sat 3.6g, mono 2.7g, poly 0.6g); CARB 36.9g; FIBER 6.7g; CHOL 19mg; IRON 2.1mg; SODIUM 400mg; CALC 164mg

---

AMARANTH-MAPLE CORNBREAD

A little wedge of this rich, dense cornbread goes a long way. The amaranth gives it a wonderful, crunchy texture.

Vegetable cooking spray
1 teaspoon vegetable oil
2 cups yellow cornmeal
1½ cups all-purpose flour
1 cup uncooked whole-grain amaranth
1 tablespoon baking powder
½ teaspoon baking soda
½ teaspoon salt
1 cup low-fat buttermilk
⅔ cup maple syrup
2 tablespoons vegetable oil
2 eggs
2 tablespoons chopped pecans

Preheat oven to 400°.

Coat a 9-inch cast-iron skillet with cooking spray; add 1 teaspoon oil. Place in a 400° oven for 7 minutes.

Combine cornmeal and next 5 ingredients in a large bowl. Combine buttermilk, syrup, 2 tablespoons oil, and eggs in a small bowl; stir well with a wire whisk. Add to cornmeal mixture, stirring until dry ingredients are moistened.

Pour batter into the preheated skillet; sprinkle pecans over batter. Bake at 400° for 25 minutes or until a wooden pick inserted in center comes out clean. Yield: 16 servings (serving size: 1 wedge).

CALORIES 224 (18% from fat); PROTEIN 5.4g; FAT 4.5g (sat 0.9g, mono 1.3g, poly 1.0g); CARB 39.6g; FIBER 2.0g; CHOL 28mg; IRON 1.6mg; SODIUM 131mg; CALC 85mg

GRAINS GLOSSARY

• AMARANTH • One of the smallest seeds harvested, amaranth has a crunchy texture. Most amaranth is ground into flour and baked in breads and cereal. High in protein, it has an earthy, sweet, cornlike flavor. We use it in our Amaranth-Maple Cornbread.

• BULGUR • Often confused with but not the same as cracked wheat, bulgur is wheat kernels that have been steamed, dried, and crushed. Bulgur, which has a tender, chewy texture, works best in salads and pilafs; it cooks in only 30 minutes. We use it in our Zucchini Boats with Bulgur.

• PEARL BARLEY • Used in soups and stews, pearl barley has had the bran removed. Steamed and polished, it cooks in 20 to 30 minutes. (Most of the barley grown in the United States is used to feed livestock or malted to make beer and whiskey.) We use it in our Mushroom-Grain Chowder.

• QUINOA • The "supergrain of the future," quinoa (pronounced keenwah) contains more protein than any other grain. The seeds are small, round, and cream-colored, although some varieties are black. Unlike some other whole grains, quinoa becomes soft when cooked—almost resembling caviar in texture. We use it in our Pumpkinseed-Quinoa Pilaf and in Mushroom-Grain Chowder.

• WHEAT BERRIES • These whole, unprocessed wheat kernels are best in pilafs and casseroles, and they make an excellent crouton alternative for salad toppings. High in protein and fiber, they must be soaked for eight hours, then cooked for one hour (they're chewy when cooked). We use them in our Southwestern Wheat Berry Pilaf.

PUMPKINSEED-QUINOA PILAF

Pumpkinseed kernels can be found in specialty and health-food stores.

1½ cups water
¾ cup uncooked quinoa
2 teaspoons olive oil
1 cup peeled, diced jicama
1 cup chopped red onion
1 cup frozen whole-kernel corn, thawed
½ cup chopped red bell pepper
½ cup chopped green bell pepper
2 teaspoons seeded, minced jalapeño pepper
1 cup chopped tomato
½ cup sliced green onions
⅓ cup unsalted pumpkinseed kernels, toasted
2 tablespoons chopped fresh cilantro
3 tablespoons fresh lime juice
½ teaspoon salt
1 small jalapeño (optional)

Combine water and quinoa in a medium saucepan; bring to a boil. Cover, reduce heat, and simmer 20 minutes or until quinoa is tender and liquid is absorbed. Remove from heat, and fluff with a fork; set aside.

Heat oil in a large nonstick skillet over medium heat until hot. Add jicama and next 5 ingredient; sauté 5 minutes or until vegetables are tender. Add quinoa, tomato, and next 5 ingredients; sauté 1 minute or until thoroughly heated. Garnish with small jalapeño, if desired. Yield: 5 servings (serving size: 1 cup).

CALORIES 228 (31% from fat); PROTEIN 8.7g; FAT 7.9g (sat 2.2g, mono 2.8g, poly 2.9g); CARB 33.3g; FIBER 4.3g; CHOL 0mg; IRON 5.1mg; SODIUM 249mg; CALC 57mg

SOUTHWESTERN WHEAT BERRY PILAF

To save time, soak the wheat berries the night before making the pilaf.

¾ cup uncooked wheat berries
2 (6-inch) Anaheim chiles
1 cup diced red bell pepper
1 cup peeled, diced jicama
¾ cup minced red onion
⅓ cup minced fresh cilantro
3 tablespoons fresh lime juice
1½ tablespoons olive oil
½ teaspoon salt
2 garlic cloves, minced
1 (15-ounce) can black beans, rinsed and drained
Cilantro sprigs (optional)

Place wheat berries in a medium bowl; cover with water to 2 inches above wheat berries. Cover and let stand 8 hours. Drain.

Place wheat berries in a medium saucepan; cover with water to 2 inches above wheat berries. Bring to a boil; reduce heat, and cook, uncovered, 1 hour or until tender. Drain and set aside.

Cut chiles in half lengthwise; discard seeds and membranes. Place chile halves, skin sides up, on a foil-lined baking sheet; flatten with palm of hand. Broil chiles 8 minutes or until blackened. Place chiles in a heavy-duty, zip-top plastic bag, and seal; let stand 10 minutes. Peel and discard skins; chop chiles.

Combine chiles, wheat berries, bell pepper, and next 8 ingredients in a large bowl; stir well. Serve chilled or at room temperature. Garnish with cilantro sprigs, if desired. Yield: 6 servings (serving size: 1 cup).

CALORIES 190 (21% from fat); PROTEIN 7.4g; FAT 4.4g (sat 0.6g, mono 2.5g, poly 0.5g); CARB 33g; FIBER 6.2g; CHOL 0mg; IRON 1.6mg; SODIUM 309mg; CALC 27mg

MUSHROOM-GRAIN CHOWDER

½ cup boiling water
1 (⅞-ounce) package dried shiitake mushrooms
1 tablespoon olive oil
1 cup chopped onion
1 cup chopped celery
1 cup chopped carrot
¾ cup chopped fennel bulb
½ cup uncooked pearl barley
⅓ cup uncooked quinoa
½ cup dried lentils
4 thyme sprigs
3 bay leaves
4 cups water
3 (14½-ounce) cans vegetable broth
2 cups sliced fresh mushrooms
¾ teaspoon salt
½ teaspoon pepper

Combine ½ cup boiling water and shiitake mushrooms in a bowl; cover and let stand 30 minutes. Drain mushrooms, reserving liquid. Discard mushroom stems; slice mushroom caps, and set aside.

Heat olive oil in a large Dutch oven over medium-high heat until hot. Add onion and next 8 ingredients; sauté 3 minutes. Add 4 cups water and vegetable broth; bring to a boil. Cover, reduce heat, and simmer 35 minutes, stirring occasionally.

Add shiitake mushrooms, fresh mushrooms, salt, and pepper; cover and simmer an additional 10 minutes. Yield: 8 servings (serving size: 1½ cups).

CALORIES 171 (17% from fat); PROTEIN 7.4g; FAT 3.2g (sat 0.3g, mono 1.4g, poly 0.5g); CARB 29.6g; FIBER 5.6g; CHOL 0mg; IRON 2.7mg; SODIUM 617mg; CALC 42mg

The Ancient Line Between Land & Sea

A trip to the Chesapeake would be incomplete without a bowl of oyster chowder. But you don't have to wait for a trip to the Eastern shore to enjoy it. Most of the ingredients in this creamy chowder are probably already in your kitchen. Just pick up some fresh oysters from the local seafood market, add them to the other ingredients, then savor the flavor of chowder—wherever you are.

OYSTER-AND-CORN CHOWDER

2 (12-ounce) containers standard oysters, undrained
¼ cup all-purpose flour
1 tablespoon margarine
½ cup chopped onion
⅓ cup chopped celery
⅓ cup chopped carrot
4 cups 2% low-fat milk
2 cups diced red potato
1 (16-ounce) package frozen whole-kernel corn
1 teaspoon salt
½ teaspoon hot sauce
⅛ teaspoon pepper
¼ cup plus 2 tablespoons chopped green onions

Drain oysters, reserving juice, and set oysters aside. Place flour in a small bowl. Gradually add oyster juice, stirring with a wire whisk until blended; set aside.

Melt margarine in a Dutch oven over medium heat. Add ½ cup onion, celery, and carrot; sauté 5 minutes. Add milk and diced potato; bring to a simmer. Cover and cook 10 minutes. Add corn; cover and cook 5 minutes. Add oysters, oyster juice mixture, salt, hot sauce, and pepper; cook, uncovered, 6 minutes or until edges of oysters curl. Ladle into soup bowls, and top with green onions. Yield: 7 servings (serving size: 1½ cups).

CALORIES 244 (23% from fat); PROTEIN 13.1g; FAT 6.2g (sat 2.5g, mono 1.7g, poly 1.2g); CARB 36.1g; FIBER 3.1g; CHOL 49mg; IRON 5.6mg; SODIUM 517mg; CALC 218mg

A Cheesecake Triumph

We've taken cheesecakes to new heights in taste and texture, with less than half the fat. And they're easy to do at home.

Here's to our cheesecake triumphs: We've created recipes that match traditional cheesecakes in richness and texture while cutting the fat. We've simplified our recipes, too: The cream cheese mixtures are done in a bowl—no egg whites to beat separately and fold in. Additional ingredients are either folded in, mixed in the crusts, or placed on top.

How can you tell when a cheesecake is done or "almost set"? Gently shake the pan; if the outside top edges are firm and the very center moves slightly, the cheesecake is done.

BROWNIE CHEESECAKE

- 1 (10.25-ounce) package fudge brownie mix
- 1 tablespoon water
- 1 teaspoon vegetable oil
- 1 (2½-ounce) jar prune baby food
- 1 egg white
- Vegetable cooking spray
- 1 cup nonfat cottage cheese
- 2 (8-ounce) blocks Neufchâtel cheese, softened
- 1 (8-ounce) block nonfat cream cheese, softened
- 1½ cups sugar
- 1 tablespoon vanilla extract
- ¼ teaspoon salt
- 3 eggs
- ¼ cup semisweet chocolate mini-morsels

Preheat oven to 350°.
Combine first 5 ingredients in a bowl; stir well. Spread into bottom of a 9-inch square baking pan coated with cooking spray. Bake at 350° for 25 minutes; let cool on a wire rack.

Tear brownies into small pieces. Press half of pieces into bottom of a 9-inch springform pan coated with cooking spray. Set aside pan and remaining brownie pieces.

Preheat oven to 300°. Place cottage cheese in a large bowl; beat at medium-high speed of an electric mixer until almost smooth. Add cheeses; beat until smooth. Add sugar, vanilla, and salt; beat well. Add eggs, 1 at a time, beating well after each addition. Stir in chocolate.

Pour half of cheese mixture into prepared pan; top with remaining brownie pieces. Pour remaining cheese mixture over brownie pieces.

Bake at 300° for 40 minutes or until almost set. Turn oven off, and let cheesecake stand 40 minutes in oven with door closed. Remove cheesecake from oven, and let cool to room temperature. Cover and chill at least 8 hours. Yield: 16 servings (serving size: 1 wedge).

CALORIES 271 (30% from fat); PROTEIN 9.6g; FAT 9.1g (sat 5.3g, mono 0.6g, poly 0.3g); CARB 37.7g; FIBER 0.8g; CHOL 65mg; IRON 0.2mg; SODIUM 373mg; CALC 69mg

TROPICAL CHEESECAKE

- ¼ cup sugar
- 1 tablespoon stick margarine, softened
- 1 tablespoon egg white
- 1⅔ cups vanilla wafer crumbs (about 36 cookies)
- Vegetable cooking spray
- 1¾ cups nonfat cottage cheese
- 1 (8-ounce) block Neufchâtel cheese, softened
- 1 cup low-fat sour cream
- ½ cup sugar
- ½ cup cream of coconut
- ¼ cup all-purpose flour
- 1 teaspoon coconut extract
- 3 eggs
- ¾ cup pineapple-orange-banana juice concentrate, undiluted
- ½ cup water
- 1 teaspoon unflavored gelatin
- ½ cup peeled, cubed mango
- 3 kiwifruit, peeled and thinly sliced
- 6 strawberries, halved
- Mint sprigs (optional)

Preheat oven to 350°.
Place first 3 ingredients in a bowl; beat at medium speed of an electric mixer until smooth. Add crumbs; stir well. Press crumb mixture into bottom and 1½ inches up sides of a 9-inch springform pan coated with cooking spray. Bake at 350° for 12 minutes; let cool on a wire rack.

Preheat oven to 300°. Place cheeses in a food processor, and process 2 minutes or until cheese is smooth, scraping sides of processor bowl once. Add sour cream and next 5 ingredients; process 20 seconds, scraping sides of processor bowl once.

Pour cheese mixture into prepared pan; bake at 300° for 1½ hours or until almost set. Turn oven off, and let cheesecake stand 1 hour in oven with door closed. Remove cheesecake from oven; cover and chill 1 hour.

Combine juice concentrate and ½ cup water in a small saucepan. Sprinkle gelatin over concentrate mixture; let stand 1 minute. Cook over low heat, stirring until gelatin dissolves. Place pan in a large ice-filled bowl; stir gelatin mixture 10 minutes or until cooled to room temperature. Pour gelatin mixture over cheesecake, spreading evenly. Cover and chill at least 8 hours. Serve with fresh fruit. Garnish with mint sprigs, if desired. Yield: 12 servings (serving size: 1 wedge and fresh fruit garnish).

CALORIES 316 (35% from fat); PROTEIN 10.4g; FAT 12.4g (sat 6.5g, mono 2.2g, poly 0.6g); CARB 42.3g; FIBER 1g; CHOL 77mg; IRON 0.6mg; SODIUM 285mg; CALC 69mg

NEW YORK CHEESECAKE

²/₃ cup all-purpose flour
2 tablespoons sugar
2 tablespoons chilled stick margarine, cut into small pieces
1 tablespoon ice water
Vegetable cooking spray
3 (8-ounce) blocks nonfat cream cheese, softened
2 (8-ounce) blocks Neufchâtel cheese, softened
1³/₄ cups sugar
3 tablespoons all-purpose flour
1 tablespoon vanilla extract
1¹/₂ teaspoons grated orange rind
1 teaspoon grated lemon rind
¹/₄ teaspoon salt
5 eggs
Lemon zest (optional)
Orange slices (optional)
Lemon slices (optional)

Preheat oven to 400°.
Place ²/₃ cup flour and 2 tablespoons sugar in a food processor, and pulse 2 times or until combined. Add chilled margarine; pulse 6 times or until mixture resembles coarse meal. With processor on, slowly pour ice water through food chute, processing just until blended (do not allow dough to form a ball). Firmly press dough mixture into bottom of a 9-inch springform pan coated with cooking spray. Bake at 400° for 10 minutes; let cool on a wire rack.
Preheat oven to 525° or to highest oven setting.
Combine cream cheese and Neufchâtel cheese in a large bowl; beat at high speed of an electric mixer until

smooth. Add 1³/₄ cups sugar and next 5 ingredients; beat well. Add eggs, 1 at a time, beating well after each addition.
Pour cheese mixture into prepared pan; bake at 525° for 7 minutes. Reduce oven temperature to 200°, and bake 45 minutes or until almost set. Remove cheesecake from oven, and let cool to room temperature. Cover and chill at least 8 hours. Garnish with lemon zest, orange slices, and lemon slices, if desired. Yield: 16 servings (serving size: 1 wedge).

CALORIES 261 (32% from fat); PROTEIN 11.7g; FAT 9.2g (sat 4.8g, mono 1.3g, poly 0.7g); CARB 31.4g; FIBER 0.2g; CHOL 97mg; IRON 0.6mg; SODIUM 449mg; CALC 147mg

CARAMEL SWIRL-AND-APPLE CHEESECAKE

So that the yogurt has ample time to drain and become yogurt cheese, start this cheesecake a day ahead.

1 (32-ounce) carton vanilla low-fat yogurt
¹/₄ cup sugar
1 tablespoon stick margarine, softened
1 egg white
1¹/₄ cups graham cracker crumbs (about 40 crackers)
1 teaspoon ground cinnamon
Vegetable cooking spray
¹/₄ cup firmly packed brown sugar
¹/₄ cup orange juice
3 cups peeled, cubed Golden Delicious apple (about 1¹/₄ pounds)
¹/₂ cup sugar
3 tablespoons cornstarch
1 tablespoon vanilla extract
¹/₄ teaspoon salt
1 (8-ounce) block Neufchâtel cheese, softened
1 (8-ounce) block nonfat cream cheese, softened
2 eggs
¹/₃ cup fat-free caramel-flavored sundae syrup
2 tablespoons fat-free caramel-flavored sundae syrup
Cinnamon sticks (optional)

Place colander in a 2-quart glass measure or bowl. Line colander with 4 layers of cheesecloth, allowing cheesecloth to extend over edge of bowl. Spoon yogurt into colander. Cover colander loosely with plastic wrap; refrigerate 12 hours. Spoon yogurt cheese into a bowl; discard liquid. Cover and refrigerate.
Preheat oven to 350°. Combine ¹/₄ cup sugar, margarine, and egg white in a bowl; beat at medium speed of an electric mixer until blended. Add crumbs and ground cinnamon; stir well. Firmly press crumb mixture into bottom and 1¹/₂ inches up sides of a 9-inch springform pan coated with cooking spray. Bake at 350° for 10 minutes; let cool on a wire rack.
Preheat oven to 300°. Combine brown sugar and orange juice in a large nonstick skillet; bring to a boil. Add apple; cook 8 minutes or until apple is tender and liquid evaporates, stirring occasionally. Set aside.
Combine yogurt cheese, ¹/₂ cup sugar, and next 5 ingredients in a bowl; beat at medium speed of mixer until smooth. Add eggs, 1 at a time, beating well after each addition.
Spoon apple mixture into prepared pan. Pour cheese mixture over apples; top with ¹/₃ cup sundae syrup, and swirl with a knife to create a marbled effect. Bake at 300° for 1 hour until almost set. Turn oven off; loosen cake from sides of pan using a narrow metal spatula or knife. Let cheesecake stand 40 minutes in oven with door closed.
Remove cheesecake from oven, and let cool to room temperature. Cover and chill at least 8 hours. Drizzle 2 tablespoons sundae syrup over top; garnish with cinnamon sticks, if desired. Yield: 12 servings (serving size: 1 wedge).

CALORIES 286 (25% from fat); PROTEIN 10.4g; FAT 8g (sat 3.7g, mono 1.3g, poly 0.5g); CARB 44.2g; FIBER 0.9g; CHOL 55mg; IRON 0.7mg; SODIUM 384mg; CALC 160mg

TRIPLE-CHOCOLATE CHEESECAKE

This cheesecake tastes like a creamy frozen fudge pop.

    ¼ cup sugar
    1 tablespoon stick margarine
    1 tablespoon egg white
 1⅓ cups chocolate graham cracker
       crumbs (about 16 crackers)
       Vegetable cooking spray
    3 tablespoons dark rum
    3 (1-ounce) squares semisweet
       chocolate
    ¼ cup chocolate syrup
    1 (8-ounce) block nonfat cream
       cheese, softened
    1 (8-ounce) block Neufchâtel
       cheese, softened
    1 cup sugar
    2 tablespoons unsweetened
       cocoa
    1 teaspoon vanilla extract
    ¼ teaspoon salt
    2 eggs
    ½ cup low-fat sour cream
    1 tablespoon sugar
    2 teaspoons unsweetened cocoa
       Chocolate curls (optional)

Preheat oven to 350°.

Place first 3 ingredients in a bowl; beat at medium speed of an electric mixer until blended. Add crumbs; stir well. Firmly press crumb mixture into bottom and 1 inch up sides of an 8-inch springform pan coated with cooking spray. Bake at 350° for 10 minutes; let cool on a wire rack.

Combine rum and chocolate squares in the top of a double boiler. Cook over simmering water 2 minutes or until chocolate melts, stirring often. Remove from heat; add chocolate syrup, stirring until smooth.

Preheat oven to 300°. Place cheeses in a large bowl; beat at medium speed of mixer until smooth. Add 1 cup sugar, 2 tablespoons cocoa, vanilla, and salt; beat until smooth. Add rum mixture; beat at low speed until well-blended. Add eggs, 1 at a time, beating well after each addition.

Pour cheese mixture into prepared pan; bake at 300° for 40 minutes or

until almost set. Combine sour cream, 1 tablespoon sugar, and 2 teaspoons cocoa; stir well. Turn oven off, and spread sour cream mixture over cheesecake. Let cheesecake stand 45 minutes in oven with door closed. Remove cheesecake from oven, and let cool to room temperature. Cover and chill at least 8 hours. Garnish with chocolate curls, if desired. Yield: 12 servings (serving size: 1 wedge).

CALORIES 260 (35% from fat); PROTEIN 7.5g; FAT 10.1g (sat 5.5g, mono 2g, poly 0.5g); CARB 35.9g; FIBER 0.1g; CHOL 57mg; IRON 0.7mg; SODIUM 205mg; CALC 85mg

FOR TWO

Just a Little Oven

When there are only two of you, why fire up the stove? You can make all kinds of dishes in a toaster oven.

SIMPLE CHICKEN FAJITAS

    2 tablespoons balsamic vinegar
    1 tablespoon lemon juice
    2 teaspoons olive oil
    ½ teaspoon dried oregano
    2 (4-ounce) skinned, boned
       chicken breast halves
    2 curly leaf lettuce leaves
    2 tablespoons salsa
    2 (6-inch) flour tortillas
       Red onion rings (optional)
       Fresh oregano (optional)

Combine first 4 ingredients in a shallow dish. Add chicken, turning to coat. Cover and marinate in refrigerator 1 to 8 hours, turning chicken occasionally.

Place drip tray on toaster oven pan. Remove chicken from dish, and discard marinade. Place chicken on drip tray, and broil 10 minutes on each side or until chicken is done. Divide

chicken, lettuce, and salsa evenly between tortillas; roll up. Garnish with onion rings and fresh oregano, if desired. Yield: 2 servings.

CALORIES 276 (22% from fat); PROTEIN 29.8g; FAT 6.7g (sat 1.4g, mono 2.9g, poly 1.8g); CARB 21.1g; FIBER 1.6g; CHOL 72mg; IRON 2.3mg; SODIUM 304mg; CALC 69mg

FRUIT CRISP

Virtually any kind of berries will work in this dessert. You might also try pineapple tidbits in place of the mandarin oranges, and cherries in place of strawberries.

    ½ cup sliced strawberries
    ½ cup frozen blueberries,
       thawed
    2 teaspoons lemon juice
    1 (11-ounce) can mandarin
       oranges in light syrup,
       drained
    3 tablespoons all-purpose flour
    2 tablespoons brown sugar
    2 tablespoons quick-cooking
       oats
    ¼ teaspoon ground cinnamon
    ⅛ teaspoon ground nutmeg
    2 tablespoons chilled reduced-
       calorie stick margarine, cut
       into small pieces

Preheat toaster oven to 350°.

Combine first 4 ingredients in a small bowl; toss gently. Divide fruit mixture evenly between 2 (10-ounce) custard cups; set aside.

Combine flour and next 4 ingredients in a small bowl; stir well. Cut in margarine with a pastry blender or 2 knives until mixture resembles coarse meal. Sprinkle flour mixture evenly over fruit. Cover and bake at 350° for 20 minutes. Uncover and bake an additional 5 minutes or until crisp. Yield: 2 servings.

Note: To bake in a conventional oven, place custard cups on a baking sheet. Bake at 350° for 30 minutes or until crisp (do not cover).

CALORIES 250 (29% from fat); PROTEIN 2.5g; FAT 8.1g (sat 1.6g, mono 3.4g, poly 2.6g); CARB 44.4g; FIBER 3.5g; CHOL 0mg; IRON 1.5mg; SODIUM 122mg; CALC 24mg

GREEK TOMATOES

Any variety of feta cheese can be used in this recipe.

- 3 small plum tomatoes (about 6 ounces), cut in half
- Vegetable cooking spray
- 1 tablespoon fine, dry breadcrumbs
- 2 tablespoons crumbled feta cheese with basil and tomato
- ¼ teaspoon dried oregano
- ⅛ teaspoon pepper

Preheat toaster oven to 350°.

Place tomato halves on toaster oven pan coated with cooking spray. Sprinkle breadcrumbs over each tomato half, and top with cheese. Sprinkle with oregano and pepper. Bake at 350° for 20 minutes. Serve warm. Yield: 2 servings (serving size: 3 tomato halves).

Note: To bake in a conventional oven, place tomato halves on a baking sheet. Bake at 350° for 25 minutes or until thoroughly heated.

CALORIES 54 (38% from fat); PROTEIN 2.2g; FAT 2.3g (sat 1.1g, mono 0.4g, poly 0.2g); CARB 6.9g; FIBER 1.3g; CHOL 6mg; IRON 0.8mg; SODIUM 116mg; CALC 50mg

CINNAMON BAGEL CHIPS

These crispy snacks put a fun new spin on cinnamon toast. Kids will love them.

- 2 (2-ounce) frozen unsplit plain bagels, thawed
- 1 tablespoon reduced-calorie stick margarine
- Butter-flavored vegetable cooking spray
- 1 teaspoon sugar
- ½ teaspoon ground cinnamon

Preheat toaster oven to 350°.

Cut each bagel horizontally into 4 slices, using a serrated knife. Place margarine in a small microwave-safe bowl; microwave at HIGH 15 seconds or until margarine melts. Lightly coat bagel slices with cooking spray, and brush with margarine.

Arrange bagel slices in a single layer on toaster oven pan. Combine sugar and cinnamon; stir well, and sprinkle over bagel slices. Bake at 350° for 12 minutes or until crisp. Remove from pan, and let cool completely on a wire rack. Store bagel chips in an airtight container. Yield: 8 chips (serving size: 4 chips).

Note: Substitute cinnamon-raisin bagels for plain bagels, if desired. To bake bagel chips in a conventional oven, place bagel slices on a baking sheet. Bake at 350° for 15 minutes or until crisp.

CALORIES 199 (22% from fat); PROTEIN 6g; FAT 4.9g (sat 0.9g, mono 1.7g, poly 1.6g); CARB 32.8g; FIBER 1.3g; CHOL 0mg; IRON 2.2mg; SODIUM 358mg; CALC 49mg

LIGHTEN UP

Carbon Copy

Say 'Ciao' to fat and calories with our Pasta Carbonara.

A traditional Pasta Carbonara doesn't call for many ingredients—primarily pasta, eggs, Parmesan cheese, olive oil, and a slab or two of bacon. But how do you lighten a dish so sinfully rich that it necessitates a nap afterwards? More importantly, how do you make it taste like the real thing? We gave it a try, and by the time we finished, we had reduced the fat by a whopping 64% and cut the cholesterol by an amazing 78%.

Of course, none of this would mean a thing if our Pasta Carbonara didn't taste every bit as decadent as it sounds—and it does. Imagine: Pasta Carbonara that is light, healthy, and a breeze to prepare. And after you enjoy it, there's no need to lie down.

PASTA CARBONARA

- 6 ounces turkey bacon, chopped
- 2 garlic cloves, minced
- 6 cups hot cooked thin spaghetti (about 12 ounces uncooked pasta)
- ¼ cup grated Parmesan cheese
- 2 tablespoons minced fresh parsley
- ¼ teaspoon freshly ground pepper
- 1 cup 2% low-fat milk
- ¼ cup plus 2 tablespoons egg substitute

Cook bacon in a large nonstick skillet over medium-high heat until crisp. Add garlic, and sauté 1 minute or until tender. Reduce heat to low; stir in pasta, cheese, parsley, and pepper.

Combine milk and egg substitute; stir well. Pour milk mixture over spaghetti mixture, and cook 3 minutes or until sauce thickens, stirring constantly. Serve immediately. Yield: 6 servings (serving size: 1 cup).

CALORIES 284 (19% from fat); PROTEIN 14.4g; FAT 6.1g (sat 2.1g, mono 2.3g, poly 1.3g); CARB 44.1g; FIBER 2.3g; CHOL 23mg; IRON 2.4mg; SODIUM 441mg; CALC 114mg

BEFORE & AFTER	
SERVING SIZE	
1 cup	1 cup
CALORIES PER SERVING	
400	284
FAT	
17g	6.1g
PERCENT OF TOTAL CALORIES	
38%	19%
CHOLESTEROL	
109mg	23mg
SODIUM	
590mg	441mg

HOW WE DID IT

- ◆ Substituted the same amount of turkey bacon for regular bacon.
- ◆ Omitted the olive oil.
- ◆ Tossed the pasta with a mixture of egg substitute and low-fat milk instead of 3 whole eggs.

Seasonable Stroganoff

Spring into action with this low-fat stroganoff that's made in a skillet. Fresh green beans sautéed with a few sliced almonds round out a light menu.

SKILLET STROGANOFF

To keep the sour cream from curdling, remove the pan from the heat before stirring it in.

½ pound ground raw turkey breast
½ pound lean ground pork
1 cup fresh rye breadcrumbs
1 tablespoon dried parsley flakes
½ teaspoon dried tarragon
½ teaspoon onion powder
2 egg whites
Vegetable cooking spray
2 cups water
1 tablespoon beef-flavored bouillon granules
1 (4-ounce) can mushroom stems and pieces, drained
2½ cups uncooked medium egg noodles
½ cup low-fat sour cream
½ cup sliced green onions

Combine first 7 ingredients in a bowl, and stir well. Shape mixture into 24 (1-inch) meatballs. Coat a large nonstick skillet with cooking spray, and place over medium-high heat until hot. Add meatballs, and cook 6 minutes, or until browned on all sides. Drain well. Wipe drippings from skillet with a paper towel.

Return meatballs to skillet. Add water, bouillon granules, and mushrooms; bring to a boil. Stir in noodles; cover, reduce heat, and simmer 10 minutes or until noodles are tender, stirring occasionally. Remove from heat; stir in sour cream. Sprinkle with green onions. Yield: 6 servings (serving size: 1 cup).

CALORIES 273 (29% from fat); PROTEIN 22.5g; FAT 8.9g (sat 3.5g, mono 2.9g, poly 1.2g); CARB 24.5g; FIBER 1.5g; CHOL 75mg; IRON 2.4mg; SODIUM 596mg; CALC 54mg

STRAWBERRIES AND CREAM

6 cups sliced strawberries
¼ cup plus 2 tablespoons low-fat sour cream
3 tablespoons brown sugar

Spoon strawberries into individual dessert dishes; top with sour cream, and sprinkle with sugar. Yield: 6 servings (serving size: 1 cup strawberries, 1 tablespoon sour cream, and 1½ teaspoons brown sugar).

CALORIES 82 (26% from fat); PROTEIN 1.4g; FAT 2.4g (sat 1.2g, mono 0.6g, poly 0.4g); CARB 15.5g; FIBER 3.9g; CHOL 6mg; IRON 0.7mg; SODIUM 9mg; CALC 40mg

SHOPPING LIST

green beans

green onions

strawberries

beef-flavored bouillon granules

onion powder

parsley flakes

tarragon

brown sugar

almonds

1 (4-ounce) can mushroom stems and pieces

egg noodles

rye bread

2 eggs

low-fat sour cream

½ pound lean ground pork

½ pound ground raw turkey breast

COOKING WITH KERR

Julia and Me

When Julia Child ticks, I usually tock. We've known of each other for more than 30 years—the last two years personally—and our approaches to food have been decidedly disparate. But the beauty of our newfound friendship is that we're both working toward the same end: great taste, aroma, color, and texture that make eating an enjoyable, memorable experience.

At a recent Public Broadcasting Service event in Seattle, Julia and I convened to explore "A Day in Our Lives: All Meals Considered." What an experience it turned out to be! At breakfast with Seattle's press corps, we shared fresh orange juice and Julia's soft-scrambled eggs, in which she holds back one egg of three and adds it just before serving (along with the cream, of course), with crisp bacon on the side.

I ate it—I mean, that was only proper, wasn't it? It was delicious. And Julia, notwithstanding her ban on "health food," did nibble at my English muffin slathered with fresh yogurt cheese and Seville marmalade. "It's really not bad," she said, actually smiling.

It went on like that all day in a sea of Julia's sweetbreads and my roast ostrich tenderloin. In the midst of all that, I made a simple roasted-vegetable sandwich that went over very well.

Never did it seem to be a competition for attention or approval, but always a creative search for enjoyable food.

TRY THESE OTHER USES FOR THE ROASTED VEGETABLES:

◆ Toss with pasta, such as penne or rigatoni.
◆ Sprinkle with feta cheese, and spoon over couscous for a meatless main dish.
◆ Serve as a vegetable side dish. Even though the recipe calls for ½ garlic head, you can roast the entire head, then mix the extra pulp with olive oil and serve with the reserved bread from the hollowed-out French bread loaf.

ROASTED-VEGETABLE SANDWICH

½   garlic head
2   cups sliced portobello mushrooms
1¼ cups diagonally sliced zucchini
1   cup seeded, chopped Anaheim chile
1   cup thinly peeled, sliced acorn squash
½   cup thinly sliced red onion
2   plum tomatoes, halved lengthwise and seeded
Vegetable cooking spray
¼   teaspoon salt
¼   teaspoon dried thyme
¼   teaspoon pepper
4   rosemary sprigs
1   (8-ounce) carton plain nonfat yogurt
2   tablespoons Dijon mustard
¼   teaspoon balsamic vinegar
1   (1-pound) loaf French bread, cut in half lengthwise

Preheat oven to 350°.
Remove white papery skin from garlic head (do not peel or separate the cloves). Wrap head in foil; set aside.
Arrange mushrooms and next 5 ingredients on a jelly-roll pan coated with cooking spray. Sprinkle salt, thyme, and pepper over vegetables;

toss well. Nestle rosemary sprigs into vegetables. Bake garlic and vegetables at 350° for 45 minutes, stirring vegetables every 15 minutes. Discard rosemary sprigs. Separate garlic cloves, and squeeze to extract garlic pulp; discard skins. Set garlic pulp aside.

Spoon yogurt onto several layers of heavy-duty paper towels; spread to ½-inch thickness. Cover with additional paper towels; let stand 10 minutes. Scrape yogurt into a bowl, using a rubber spatula. Stir in garlic pulp, mustard, and vinegar; set aside.

Hollow out top and bottom halves of bread, leaving a 1-inch-thick shell; reserve torn bread for another use. Spread yogurt mixture over top and bottom halves of loaf. Arrange vegetables on bottom half of loaf; replace top half. Wrap loaf in foil; bake at 350° for 15 minutes. Cut into 6 equal portions. Yield: 6 servings.

CALORIES 261 (7% from fat); PROTEIN 10.4g; FAT 2g (sat 0.5g, mono 0.6g, poly 0.8g); CARB 47.8g; FIBER 3g; CHOL 2mg; IRON 2mg; SODIUM 679mg; CALC 148mg

ROASTED-VEGETABLE SANDWICH WITH HAM AND CHEESE

Add 2 ounces thinly sliced lean deli ham, 1 tablespoon grated fresh Parmesan cheese, and 1 tablespoon sliced ripe olives per serving.

CALORIES 368 (18% from fat); PROTEIN 23.6g; FAT 7.2g (sat 2.5g, mono 3.1g, poly 1.4g); CARB 49.1g; FIBER 3.3g; CHOL 32mg; IRON 3.1mg; SODIUM 1,656mg; CALC 229mg

Good to Grow

Whether you're a beginning gardener or a seasoned expert, you'll enjoy the harvest of your labors in this chunky tomato sauce. Try making this recipe after you've picked your long-awaited first tomatoes off the vine.

CHUNKY GARDEN-TOMATO SAUCE

1	tablespoon olive oil
1	cup chopped onion
4	garlic cloves, minced
5½	cups seeded, chopped tomato
¼	cup chopped fresh basil
2	tablespoons chopped fresh oregano
1	teaspoon sugar
½	teaspoon salt
¼	teaspoon pepper

Heat oil in a large nonstick skillet over medium heat until hot. Add onion and garlic, and sauté 3 minutes. Add tomato and remaining ingredients, and bring to a boil, stirring occasionally. Reduce heat, and simmer, uncovered, 10 minutes, stirring occasionally. Serve over pasta or polenta, or on toasted French baguette slices. Yield: 3½ cups (serving size: ½ cup).

CALORIES 63 (36% from fat); PROTEIN 1.7g; FAT 2.5g (sat 0.3g, mono 1.5g, poly 0.4g); CARB 10.2g; FIBER 2.4g; CHOL 0mg; IRON 0.9mg; SODIUM 181mg; CALC 25mg

Dinner Theater

For Greeks, eating is entertainment. Grab a seat to find out why: The show is about to start.

The Greek passion for quality has fueled Western civilization for millennia. And it doesn't need much to be ignited: just friends and family—and food, which is at the center of all Greek entertaining. At a *mezes* (appetizer) party, for example, guests choose from an array of dishes prepared by people who take great pride in their specialties. The buffet we've provided features an assortment of festive appetizers and main dishes. They're simple to make, and most can be done in advance. So the next time you're having people over, do as the Greeks do. All you need is a large table for food—and room for dancing (after all, when Greeks entertain, passion is hard to contain).

STUFFED GRAPE LEAVES
Dolmades

1	cup plain low-fat yogurt
3	tablespoons chopped fresh or 1 tablespoon dried mint, divided
1	teaspoon grated lemon rind
1	teaspoon honey
30	large bottled grape leaves
2	tablespoons olive oil
1¾	cups finely chopped onion
1	garlic clove, minced
¼	cup fresh lemon juice, divided
2	cups hot cooked rice (cooked without salt or fat)
½	cup dried currants
⅓	cup pine nuts, toasted
1	tablespoon chopped fresh or 1 teaspoon dried dillweed
½	teaspoon salt
¼	teaspoon pepper
1	(15-ounce) can chickpeas (garbanzo beans), rinsed and drained
	Vegetable cooking spray

Combine yogurt, 2 tablespoons mint, lemon rind, and honey in a bowl, and stir well. Cover and chill.

Rinse grape leaves under cold water; drain well, and pat dry with paper towels. Remove stems, and discard.

Heat oil in a nonstick skillet over medium heat until hot. Add onion; sauté 10 minutes. Add garlic; sauté 1 minute. Remove from heat; stir in remaining mint, 2 tablespoons lemon juice, rice, and next 6 ingredients.

Preheat oven to 350°. Spoon 1 rounded tablespoon of rice mixture onto center of each grape leaf. Bring 2 opposite points of a leaf to center, and fold over filling. Beginning at 1 short side, roll up leaf tightly, jelly-roll fashion. Repeat procedure with remaining grape leaves.

Place stuffed grape leaves, seam sides down, in a 13 x 9-inch baking dish coated with cooking spray. Drizzle remaining lemon juice over leaves. Cover and bake at 350° for 30 minutes or until thoroughly heated. Serve grape leaves warm or chilled with yogurt mixture. Yield: 30 dolmades (serving size: 1 dolma and 1½ teaspoons yogurt mixture).

CALORIES 60 (32% from fat); PROTEIN 1.9g; FAT 2.1g (sat 0.4g, mono 1g, poly 0.5g); CARB 9.2g; FIBER 1g; CHOL 0mg; IRON 0.6mg; SODIUM 119mg; CALC 32mg

LAMB ON A SKEWER
Arni Souvlakia

2 pounds lean boneless leg of
    lamb
⅓ cup low-salt chicken broth
⅓ cup fresh lemon juice
⅓ cup white wine
1 tablespoon chopped fresh or
    1 teaspoon dried thyme
1 tablespoon chopped fresh or
    1 teaspoon dried rosemary
1 tablespoon minced fresh or
    1 teaspoon dried oregano
1 tablespoon olive oil
¼ teaspoon salt
¼ teaspoon pepper
5 garlic cloves, minced
Vegetable cooking spray
3 (6-inch) pita bread rounds,
    cut in half
1½ cups thinly sliced lettuce
1½ cups seeded, chopped plum
    tomato
¼ cup plus 2 tablespoons
    chopped onion
Yogurt-Mint Sauce

Trim fat from lamb; cut lamb into 36 (1-inch) cubes. Combine lamb and next 10 ingredients in a large heavy-duty, zip-top plastic bag; seal bag, and marinate in refrigerator at least 8 hours.

Remove lamb from bag, reserving marinade. Bring marinade to a boil in a small saucepan.

Thread 6 lamb cubes onto each of 6 (10-inch) skewers. Place skewers on rack of a broiler pan coated with cooking spray, and broil 10 minutes, turning occasionally, and basting with reserved marinade.

Fill each pita half with 6 lamb cubes, ¼ cup lettuce, ¼ cup tomato, 1 tablespoon onion, and 2 tablespoons Yogurt-Mint Sauce. Yield: 6 servings (serving size: 1 stuffed pita half).

CALORIES 322 (31% from fat); PROTEIN 32.7g; FAT 11.2g (sat 3.3g, mono 5.3g, poly 1g); CARB 19.5g; FIBER 1.6g; CHOL 89mg; IRON 4.2mg; SODIUM 352mg; CALC 84mg

Yogurt-Mint Sauce:

⅓ cup plain nonfat yogurt
⅓ cup nonfat sour cream
1½ tablespoons fresh lemon juice
2¼ teaspoons minced fresh mint
⅛ teaspoon salt
2 garlic cloves, minced

Combine all ingredients; cover and chill. Yield: ¾ cup (serving size: 2 tablespoons).

CALORIES 18 (0% from fat); PROTEIN 1.6g; FAT 0g; CARB 2.5g; FIBER 0g; CHOL 0mg; IRON 0mg; SODIUM 67mg; CALC 27mg

---

MENU SUGGESTION

BAKED PENNE WITH VEAL

Broccoli with lemon

*Pears with honey, Parmesan, and raspberries

*Peel, halve, and core pears. Score halves; place on baking pan. Top with honey and shaved Parmesan. Broil until cheese melts. Top with raspberries.

BAKED PENNE WITH VEAL
Pastitsio

1 pound ground veal
Vegetable cooking spray
4 cups chopped onion
1 teaspoon salt
1 teaspoon ground cinnamon
½ teaspoon sugar
½ teaspoon pepper
¼ teaspoon ground cloves
4 garlic cloves, minced
3 (14.5-ounce) cans diced
    tomatoes, undrained
2 tablespoons margarine
2 tablespoons all-purpose flour
3 cups 1% low-fat milk
1½ cups egg substitute
½ teaspoon salt
⅛ teaspoon pepper
6 cups hot cooked penne (about
    12 ounces uncooked pasta)
½ cup (2 ounces) grated fresh
    Romano cheese
¼ teaspoon ground cinnamon

Cook veal in a large nonstick skillet over medium heat until browned, stirring to crumble. Drain in a colander; set aside.

Coat skillet with cooking spray, and place over medium-high heat until hot. Add onion; sauté 10 minutes. Add 1 teaspoon salt and next 6 ingredients; bring to a boil. Reduce heat, and simmer, uncovered, 20 minutes, stirring occasionally. Return veal to skillet; simmer an additional 10 minutes. Set veal mixture aside.

Melt margarine in a medium saucepan over medium heat. Add flour, stirring constantly with a wire whisk until blended. Gradually add milk, stirring constantly. Bring to a boil; reduce heat, and simmer 10 minutes or until slightly thickened, stirring constantly. Remove from heat, and set aside.

Place egg substitute in a medium bowl; beat at high speed of an electric mixer until doubled in volume. Gradually add hot milk mixture to egg substitute, stirring constantly with a wire whisk. Stir in ½ teaspoon salt and ⅛ teaspoon pepper.

Preheat oven to 350°.

Combine veal mixture and pasta in a large bowl; stir well. Spoon veal mixture evenly into 2 (11 x 7-inch) baking dishes coated with cooking spray. Pour sauce evenly over each dish of veal mixture (poke with a fork in several places to allow the sauce to run to the bottom of the dish). Combine cheese and ¼ teaspoon cinnamon, stirring well; sprinkle evenly over each dish of veal mixture. Cover and bake at 350° for 30 minutes. Uncover and bake an additional 15 minutes. Let stand 15 minutes before serving. Yield: 12 servings (6 servings per baking dish).

CALORIES 276 (36% from fat); PROTEIN 18.9g; FAT 10.9g (sat 2.9g, mono 3.3g, poly 1.1g); CARB 33.7g; FIBER 2.7g; CHOL 38mg; IRON 2.7mg; SODIUM 615mg; CALC 196mg

GREEK RED SNAPPER
Psari Plaki

1 tablespoon olive oil
2 cups chopped onion
2½ cups seeded, chopped tomato
½ cup minced fresh parsley
½ cup dry white wine
⅛ teaspoon pepper
4 bay leaves
2 large garlic cloves, minced
8 (6-ounce) snapper or grouper
  fillets
Vegetable cooking spray
1½ tablespoons fresh lemon juice
½ teaspoon salt
4 medium peeled baking
  potatoes (about 1¾ pounds),
  each cut lengthwise into 12
  wedges
1 tablespoon olive oil
¼ teaspoon salt
8 (½-inch-thick) slices tomato
8 (¼-inch-thick) rings green bell
  pepper

Preheat oven to 350°.

Heat 1 tablespoon oil in a large nonstick skillet over medium heat until hot. Add onion; sauté 7 minutes or until tender. Add chopped tomato and next 5 ingredients; reduce heat, and simmer, uncovered, 15 minutes or until liquid evaporates, stirring occasionally. Set aside.

Arrange fillets in a 13 x 9-inch baking dish coated with cooking spray. Sprinkle lemon juice and ½ teaspoon salt over fillets, and top with onion mixture. Place potato wedges over onion mixture, and drizzle with 1 tablespoon oil and ¼ teaspoon salt. Top with tomato slices and bell pepper rings. Bake, uncovered, at 350° for 1 hour and 20 minutes or until potatoes are tender.

Place 1 fillet and 6 potato wedges on each of 8 plates. Spoon onion mixture evenly over each serving, and top each serving with 1 tomato slice and 1 bell pepper ring. Yield: 8 servings.

CALORIES 296 (19% from fat); PROTEIN 38.8g; FAT 6.2g (sat 1g, mono 3g, poly 1.2g); CARB 20.8g; FIBER 3.8g; CHOL 63mg; IRON 4.4mg; SODIUM 350mg; CALC 106mg

---

MENU SUGGESTION
GREEK-STYLE SCAMPI
GREEK SALAD WITH FETA AND OLIVES

Parslied orzo

*Cook orzo in chicken broth according to package directions. Transfer to a serving bowl; fluff with fork. Add chopped fresh parsley.

GREEK-STYLE SCAMPI

1 teaspoon olive oil
5 garlic cloves, minced
3 (28-ounce) cans whole
  tomatoes, drained and
  coarsely chopped
½ cup chopped fresh parsley,
  divided
1¼ pounds large shrimp, peeled
  and deveined
1 cup crumbled feta cheese
2 tablespoons fresh lemon juice
¼ teaspoon freshly ground
  pepper

Preheat oven to 400°.

Heat oil in a large Dutch oven over medium heat until hot. Add garlic; sauté 30 seconds. Add tomatoes and ¼ cup parsley; reduce heat, and simmer, uncovered, 10 minutes. Add shrimp, and cook 5 minutes. Pour mixture into a 13 x 9-inch baking dish; sprinkle with cheese. Bake at 400° for 10 minutes. Sprinkle with remaining parsley, juice, and pepper. Yield: 6 servings.

CALORIES 191 (31% from fat); PROTEIN 19.9g; FAT 6.5g (sat 3.2g, mono 1.7g, poly 1g); CARB 14.4g; FIBER 2.1g; CHOL 125mg; IRON 3.8mg; SODIUM 752mg; CALC 211mg

---

GREEK SALAD WITH FETA AND OLIVES
Salata me Feta ke Elies

8 cups torn romaine lettuce
4 cups torn escarole
1½ cups thinly sliced red onion,
  separated into rings
1½ cups thinly sliced green bell
  pepper rings
1½ cups thinly sliced red bell
  pepper rings
½ cup thinly sliced radishes
¼ cup pitted, sliced kalamata
  olives
2 medium tomatoes, each cut
  into 8 wedges
Oregano Vinaigrette
½ cup crumbled feta cheese

Combine first 8 ingredients in a large bowl. Pour vinaigrette over salad; toss well. Sprinkle cheese over salad. Yield: 10 servings (serving size: about 1⅔ cups).

CALORIES 61 (49% from fat); PROTEIN 2.6g; FAT 3.3g (sat 1.3g, mono 1.6g, poly 0.4g); CARB 7.7g; FIBER 2.2g; CHOL 5mg; IRON 1.5mg; SODIUM 165mg; CALC 71mg

Oregano Vinaigrette:

¼ cup dry white wine
¼ cup fresh lemon juice
1 tablespoon extra-virgin olive oil
1 tablespoon chopped fresh or
  1 teaspoon dried oregano
¼ teaspoon salt
¼ teaspoon pepper
4 garlic cloves, minced

Combine all ingredients in a jar; cover tightly, and shake vigorously. Yield: about ⅔ cup (serving size: 1 tablespoon).

CALORIES 20 (62% from fat); PROTEIN 0.1g; FAT 1.4g (sat 0.2g, mono 1.0g, poly 0.1g); CARB 10.9g; FIBER 0.5g; CHOL 0mg; IRON 1.4mg; SODIUM 591mg; CALC 6mg

April Flours

It isn't just spring that's in the air. From across the country comes the smell of freshly baked breads.

At 82, I guess you could say I've had quite a history with food. In fact, I'm writing a cookbook entitled Cooking My Way Through Life. *The book re-lives experiences I've had, from work-ing as a vegetarian chef to baking in a gambling club. I started cooking light about a year ago, after I was diag-nosed with a heart condition. I've had a lot of success revamping old recipes, and this one was a favorite with the entire family.*

—Lucille A. MacDonald, Reno, Nevada

GRAM'S POTATO ROLLS

1½ cups regular oats, uncooked
2 cups peeled, cubed baking potato
1 package active dry yeast
1 teaspoon sugar
⅓ cup warm water (105° to 115°)
1 cup water
¾ cup instant nonfat dry milk powder
¼ cup sugar
2 tablespoons vegetable oil
2 teaspoons salt
7 cups all-purpose flour, divided
Vegetable cooking spray
2 egg whites, lightly beaten
1 tablespoon sesame or poppy seeds

Place oats in a food processor, and process until ground. Spoon ground oats into a bowl; set aside.

Place potato in a medium saucepan; cover with water, and bring to a boil. Cook for 10 minutes or until potato is tender. Place potato and cooking liq-uid in food processor, and process un-til smooth; set aside.

Dissolve yeast and 1 teaspoon sugar in ⅓ cup warm water in a large bowl; let stand 5 minutes. Stir in puréed potato mixture, 1 cup water, milk powder, ¼ cup sugar, oil, and salt. Add ground oats and 3 cups flour; beat at medium speed of an electric mixer until smooth. Stir in 3½ cups flour to form a soft dough. Turn dough out onto a lightly floured sur-face. Knead dough until smooth and elastic (about 10 minutes); add enough of the remaining flour, 1 ta-blespoon at a time, to keep dough from sticking to hands.

Place dough in a large bowl coated with cooking spray, turning to coat top. Cover and let rise in a warm place (85°), free from drafts, 45 minutes or until doubled in bulk. Punch dough down, and turn out onto a lightly floured sur-face. Divide dough in half; cover one half tightly with plastic wrap, and refrig-erate. Divide other half into 24 equal portions. Divide each portion into 3 equal pieces, and shape each piece into a ball. Place 3 balls into each of 24 muffin cups coated with cooking spray. Brush egg white over rolls, and sprinkle with half of seeds. Cover and let rise 45 min-utes or until doubled in bulk.

Preheat oven to 350°. Uncover the rolls; bake at 350° for 12 minutes or until golden. Remove remaining half of dough from refrigerator; uncover and let stand 15 minutes or until room temperature. Divide dough into 24 equal portions, and proceed as above. Yield: 4 dozen (serving size: 1 roll).

Note: To make 2 (9-inch) loaves, di-vide dough in half. Roll each half into a 14 x 8-inch rectangle. Starting at short side, roll up each rectangle, pressing firmly to eliminate air pock-ets; pinch seam and ends to seal. Place loaves, seam sides down, in 2 (9 x 5-inch) loaf pans coated with cooking spray. Brush egg white over loaves, and sprinkle with seeds. Cover and let rise 45 minutes or until doubled in bulk. Uncover and bake at 350° for 40 min-utes, shielding tops of loaves with foil after 25 minutes, if necessary.

CALORIES 99 (9% from fat); PROTEIN 3.3g; FAT 1g (sat 0.2g, mono 0.3g, poly 0.5g); CARB 18.9g; FIBER 0.9g; CHOL 0mg; IRON 1.1mg; SODIUM 111mg; CALC 30mg

I served this bread—and my grand-mother's original recipe—at a light cooking class I taught at my church. The class tasted both recipes, and they all liked the lighter version much better.
—Kelly McPherson, Pleasant Grove, Utah

ZUCCHINI BREAD

2 cups coarsely shredded zucchini
3 cups all-purpose flour
1¾ cups sugar
1 teaspoon baking soda
1 teaspoon salt
1 teaspoon ground cinnamon
¼ teaspoon baking powder
¾ cup applesauce
½ cup egg substitute
⅓ cup vegetable oil
1 tablespoon vanilla extract
Vegetable cooking spray

Preheat oven to 350°.

Place zucchini on several layers of paper towels, and cover with addi-tional paper towels. Let stand 5 min-utes, pressing down occasionally. Set zucchini aside.

Combine flour and next 5 ingredi-ents in a large bowl, and stir well; make a well in center of mixture. Combine zucchini, applesauce, egg substitute, oil, and vanilla; add to dry ingredients, stirring just until dry in-gredients are moistened.

Spoon batter evenly into 2 (7½ x 3-inch) loaf pans coated with cooking spray. Bake at 350° for 1 hour and 15 minutes or until a wooden pick in-serted in center comes out clean. Let cool in pans 10 minutes on a wire rack; remove from pans, and let cool completely on wire rack. Yield: 2 loaves, 28 servings (serving size: 1 slice).

CALORIES 128 (20% from fat); PROTEIN 1.9g; FAT 2.8g (sat 0.5g, mono 0.8g, poly 1.3g); CARB 23.9g; FIBER 0.5g; CHOL 0mg; IRON 0.8mg; SODIUM 136mg; CALC 9mg

I concocted this recipe to satisfy my craving for real New England maple syrup, without the mess, calories, and fat of pancakes or waffles. These muffins are my husband's favorite!
—Laura Larsen, Wethersfield, Connecticut

MAPLE-WALNUT MUFFINS

2¼ cups all-purpose flour
1 cup sugar
1 teaspoon baking powder
½ teaspoon baking soda
¼ teaspoon salt
½ cup chilled reduced-calorie stick margarine, cut into small pieces
2 tablespoons maple syrup
1 teaspoon imitation maple flavoring
3 egg whites, lightly beaten
1 (8-ounce) carton plain nonfat yogurt
Vegetable cooking spray
¼ cup chopped walnuts

Preheat oven to 350°.

Combine first 5 ingredients in a large bowl; cut in margarine with a pastry blender or 2 knives until mixture resembles coarse meal. Combine maple syrup, maple flavoring, egg whites, and yogurt; add to dry ingredients, stirring just until dry ingredients are moistened.

Spoon batter evenly into 18 muffin cups coated with cooking spray; sprinkle walnuts evenly over batter. Bake at 350° for 25 minutes or until muffins spring back when touched lightly in center. Remove from pans immediately; let cool on a wire rack. Yield: 1½ dozen (serving size: 1 muffin).

CALORIES 148 (27% from fat); PROTEIN 3g; FAT 4.4g (sat 0.8g, mono 1.6g, poly 1.6g); CARB 24.9g; FIBER 0.5g; CHOL 0mg; IRON 0.8mg; SODIUM 124mg; CALC 40mg

After receiving a recipe for chocolate bread from a coworker, I began experimenting to create this recipe. I am allergic to chocolate, so I substituted cocoa.
—Gloria Wiech, Frontenac, Minnesota

CHOCOLATE CINNAMON ROLLS

1 package active dry yeast
2 tablespoons sugar
1¼ cups warm skim milk (105° to 115°)
¼ cup stick margarine, melted
½ teaspoon vanilla extract
1 egg, lightly beaten
4 cups bread flour, divided
⅓ cup unsweetened cocoa
½ teaspoon salt
Vegetable cooking spray
1 egg white, lightly beaten
¼ cup sugar
1 teaspoon ground cinnamon
1 cup sifted powdered sugar
2 tablespoons skim milk
1 teaspoon vanilla extract

Dissolve yeast and 2 tablespoons sugar in 1¼ cups warm milk in a large bowl; let stand 5 minutes. Add melted margarine, ½ teaspoon vanilla, and egg; stir well. Stir in 3½ cups flour, cocoa, and salt to form a soft dough. Turn dough out onto a lightly floured surface, and knead until smooth and elastic (about 10 minutes); add enough of the remaining flour, 1 tablespoon at a time, to keep dough from sticking to hands.

Place dough in a large bowl coated with cooking spray, turning to coat top. Cover and let rise in a warm place (85°), free from drafts, 45 minutes or until doubled in bulk.

Punch dough down. Turn out onto a lightly floured surface; roll into a 16 x 8-inch rectangle. Brush egg white over entire surface of dough. Combine ¼ cup sugar and ground cinnamon; sprinkle evenly over dough. Starting at long side, roll up dough tightly, jelly-roll fashion; pinch seam to seal (do not seal ends of roll). Cut roll into 16 (1-inch-thick) slices, using string or dental floss. Arrange slices, cut sides up, in

a 13 x 9-inch baking pan coated with cooking spray. Cover and let rise 30 minutes or until doubled in bulk.

Preheat oven to 350°; bake rolls at 350° for 20 minutes. Combine powdered sugar, 2 tablespoons milk, and 1 teaspoon vanilla; stir well. Drizzle glaze over rolls. Yield: 16 servings (serving size: 1 roll).

CALORIES 221 (17% from fat); PROTEIN 6.2g; FAT 4.1g (sat 0.9g, mono 1.5g, poly 1.2g); CARB 39.3g; FIBER 0.2g; CHOL 14mg; IRON 2mg; SODIUM 126mg; CALC 39mg

THE RISE ON YEAST

Yeast comes in granular form in individual packages labeled **active dry yeast** or **rapid-rise yeast** or in cake form as moist **compressed yeast.** One package of dry yeast contains 2½ teaspoons and can be interchanged with one 0.6-ounce cake.

If you want to substitute rapid-rise yeast in a recipe calling for active dry yeast, a slight change in the procedure will ensure success and your dough will rise up to 50% faster. Add rapid-rise yeast directly to a small portion of the dry ingredients before you add hot liquid (120° to 130°). This procedure will hasten rising by increasing the dough's temperature. Because the dry ingredients protect the yeast, warmer liquids can be added.

Caramel Swirl-and-Apple Cheesecake, page 99

Grilled Salmon Pepper Steaks, page 84

Grilled Marinated Vegetables, page 85

Asparagus-Dill Soufflé, page 86

Thai Noodle Salad with Vegetables and Spicy Peanut Sauce, page 122

*Peppered Flank Steak Sandwich
with Onion Marmalade, page 119*

Greek-Style Scampi, page 106

Beef and Broccoli with Oyster Sauce, page 130

Curry-Almond Chicken, page 131

Asian Flank Steak, page 120

Grape-and-Currant Tart with Fontina Cheese, page 128

Daiquiri Ice with Kiwifruit, page 85

Curry Flank Steak with Tropical Fruit Salsa, page 119

Roasted-Vegetable Chiles Rellenos, page 125

$\mathcal{M}$AY

The World's Most Versatile Steak

For too long people didn't know what to do with flank steak, a less-tender, though leaner, cut of beef. So they ignored it. But once people realized that all it needed was some tenderizing, it quickly came into its own, proving to be one of the meat counter's most versatile choices. You can skewer, score, stack, stuff, and roll this cut of beef distinguished by its long, flat shape and fibers running the length of the cut.

To make flank steak more tender, we've marinated it in different liquids, such as lime juice, wine, and vinegar. When serving, just be sure to slice the steak properly, which is across the grain with a very sharp knife. So never mind that flank steak used to get the brush. In today's lighter world, it's a lean and versatile star.

GREEK STUFFED STEAK

⅓ cup finely chopped red onion
⅓ cup chopped pickled pepperoncini peppers
2 tablespoons fine, dry breadcrumbs
¼ teaspoon salt
¼ teaspoon garlic powder
1 (10-ounce) package frozen chopped spinach, thawed, drained, and squeezed dry
1 (1½-pound) lean flank steak
Vegetable cooking spray
½ cup water
½ cup dry red wine
½ teaspoon dried oregano
Feta Mashed Potatoes

Combine first 6 ingredients in a bowl; stir well, and set aside.

Trim fat from steak. Using a sharp knife, cut horizontally through center of steak, cutting to, but not through, other side; open flat as you would a book. Place steak between 2 sheets of heavy-duty plastic wrap, and flatten to an even thickness, using a meat mallet or rolling pin. Spread spinach mixture over steak, leaving a 1-inch margin around outside edges. Roll up steak, jelly-roll fashion, starting with short side. Secure at 2-inch intervals with heavy string.

Coat a large Dutch oven with cooking spray, and place over medium-high heat until hot. Add steak, browning well on all sides. Add water, wine, and oregano to pan; bring to a boil. Cover, reduce heat, and simmer 1 hour or until tender. Remove string, and cut steak into 16 slices. Serve with cooking liquid and Feta Mashed Potatoes. Yield: 8 servings (serving size: 2 steak slices, 2 tablespoons cooking liquid, and ½ cup Feta Mashed Potatoes).

CALORIES 271 (29% from fat); PROTEIN 20.6g; FAT 8.6g (sat 3.7g, mono 3.2g, poly 0.5g); CARB 28g; FIBER 3.2g; CHOL 43mg; IRON 3mg; SODIUM 448mg; CALC 95mg

Feta Mashed Potatoes:

2 pounds baking potatoes, peeled and cubed
¼ cup skim milk
3 tablespoons crumbled feta cheese
2 tablespoons nonfat sour cream
½ teaspoon salt
½ teaspoon dried oregano
¼ teaspoon pepper

Place potatoes in a medium saucepan; cover with water, and bring to a boil. Cover, reduce heat, and simmer 20 minutes or until potatoes are very tender.

Drain potatoes well, and return to pan; beat at high speed of an electric mixer until smooth. Add skim milk, feta cheese, sour cream, salt, oregano, and pepper; beat well. Yield: 8 servings (serving size: ½ cup).

CALORIES 111 (6% from fat); PROTEIN 3g; FAT 0.7g (sat 0.4g, mono 0.1g, poly 0.1g); CARB 23.6g; FIBER 1.7g; CHOL 3mg; IRON 0.4mg; SODIUM 187mg; CALC 30mg

BRACIOLA WITH NOODLES

Braciola is the Italian term for a thin, rolled, stuffed piece of meat that is braised in stock or wine.

½ cup fresh breadcrumbs
½ cup minced fresh parsley
⅓ cup freshly grated Parmesan cheese
3 tablespoons capers
2 tablespoons pine nuts, toasted
2 tablespoons fresh lemon juice
1 teaspoon olive oil
4 garlic cloves, minced
1 (1½-pound) lean flank steak
Vegetable cooking spray
1½ cups low-fat spaghetti sauce
½ cup dry red wine
8 cups hot cooked fettuccine (about 16 ounces uncooked pasta)

Combine first 8 ingredients in a bowl; stir well, and set aside.

Trim fat from steak. Using a sharp knife, cut horizontally through center of steak, cutting to, but not through, other side; open flat as you would a book. Place steak between 2 sheets of heavy-duty plastic wrap, and flatten to an even thickness using a meat mallet or rolling pin. Spread breadcrumb mixture over steak, leaving a ½-inch margin around outside edges. Roll up steak, jelly-roll fashion, starting with short side. Secure at 2-inch intervals with heavy string.

Coat a large Dutch oven with cooking spray, and place over medium-high heat until hot. Add steak, browning well on all sides. Remove steak from pan; set aside, and keep warm.

Add spaghetti sauce and wine to pan, scraping bottom of pan with a wooden spoon to loosen particles that cling to pan. Bring to a boil; return steak to pan. Cover, reduce heat, and simmer 1 hour or until steak is tender. Remove string; cut steak into 16 slices. Spoon 1 cup pasta onto each of 8 individual plates; top with 2 steak slices and ⅓ cup sauce. Yield: 8 servings.

CALORIES 410 (31% from fat); PROTEIN 24.9g; FAT 14.2g (sat 5.2g, mono 5.6g, poly 1.6g); CARB 44g; FIBER 2.5g; CHOL 46mg; IRON 3.9mg; SODIUM 531mg; CALC 80mg

CURRY FLANK STEAK WITH TROPICAL FRUIT SALSA

After this spicy entrée, serve a cooling pineapple sorbet for dessert. The Tropical Fruit Salsa is delicious as an accompaniment to grilled chicken breasts and grilled tuna or swordfish.

1 (1-pound) lean flank steak
¼ cup dry sherry
¼ cup orange juice
2 teaspoons curry powder
1 teaspoon ground ginger
½ teaspoon ground cumin
¼ teaspoon pepper
Vegetable cooking spray
Tropical Fruit Salsa

Trim fat from steak. Combine steak and next 6 ingredients in a large heavy-duty, zip-top plastic bag. Seal bag, and marinate in refrigerator 8 to 12 hours, turning bag occasionally. Remove steak from bag; discard marinade.

Prepare grill or broiler. Place steak on grill rack or broiler pan coated with cooking spray, and cook 7 minutes on each side or until steak is desired degree of doneness. Cut steak diagonally across the grain into thin slices. Serve steak with Tropical Fruit Salsa. Yield: 4 servings (serving size: 3 ounces steak and ½ cup salsa).

CALORIES 270 (43% from fat); PROTEIN 21.6g; FAT 12.8g (sat 5.3g, mono 5.2g, poly 0.5g); CARB 15.4g; FIBER 2.6g; CHOL 57mg; IRON 2.9mg; SODIUM 72mg; CALC 33mg

Tropical Fruit Salsa:

½ cup diced fresh pineapple
½ cup diced orange sections
½ cup diced peeled papaya
½ cup diced Granny Smith apple
¼ cup diced red bell pepper
¼ cup thinly sliced green onions
1 tablespoon sugar
2 tablespoons orange juice
1 tablespoon minced fresh cilantro
¼ teaspoon dried crushed red pepper
⅛ teaspoon ground cumin

Combine all ingredients in a bowl; stir well. Cover and chill at least 2 hours. Yield: 2 cups (serving size: ½ cup).

CALORIES 55 (0% from fat); PROTEIN 0.7g; FAT 0.3g (sat 0g, mono 0g, poly 0.1g); CARB 13.7g; FIBER 2.3g; CHOL 0mg; IRON 0.5mg; SODIUM 3mg; CALC 23mg

THE SLICE IS RIGHT

When serving flank steak, use a very sharp knife, and cut diagonally (at an angle) across the grain. Flank steak tends to toughen as it stands, so you'll want to slice the entire steak immediately after cooking.

Two of our recipes (the Braciola with Noodles and the Greek Stuffed Steak) call for you to butterfly the flank steak. It's not difficult once you get the hang of it, but you need to use a very sharp knife. Cut horizontally through center of steak, cutting to, but not through, other side; open flat as you would a book.

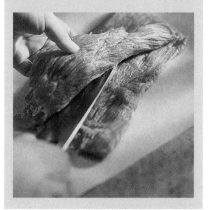

PEPPERED FLANK STEAK SANDWICHES WITH ONION MARMALADE

The ground pepper adds a depth of flavor and cuts the slight sweetness of the onion marmalade.

Vegetable cooking spray
1 teaspoon vegetable oil
⅓ cup sugar
3 cups chopped onion
¼ teaspoon salt
¼ cup orange juice
1 tablespoon bourbon (optional)
1 (1½-pound) lean flank steak
2 teaspoons Dijon mustard
¼ teaspoon salt
5 garlic cloves, crushed
1 to 2 tablespoons coarsely ground pepper
8 (1½-ounce) whole wheat hamburger buns, split and toasted

Coat a large nonstick skillet with cooking spray; add oil, and place over medium heat until hot. Add sugar; cook until sugar dissolves, stirring constantly. Cook an additional 2 minutes or until golden, stirring constantly. Add onion and ¼ teaspoon salt. (Caramelized sugar will harden and stick to spoon, but will melt again.) Cook 20 minutes or until onion is golden, stirring occasionally. Add orange juice and bourbon; cook 5 minutes or until liquid evaporates. Remove from heat. Set aside; keep warm.

Trim fat from steak. Combine mustard, ¼ teaspoon salt, and garlic; stir well. Rub mixture over sides of steak. Press pepper into mixture on steak.

Coat grill rack with cooking spray; place on grill over medium-hot coals (350° to 400°). Place steak on rack; grill 8 minutes on each side or until desired degree of doneness. Cut diagonally across the grain into thin slices.

Spoon steak evenly over bottom halves of buns; top each with 1½ tablespoons onion mixture and top half of bun. Yield: 8 servings.

CALORIES 331 (34% from fat); PROTEIN 20g; FAT 12.7g (sat 4.8g, mono 5g, poly 1.2g); CARB 33.9g; FIBER 2.7g; CHOL 56mg; IRON 2.8mg; SODIUM 461mg; CALC 48mg

ASIAN FLANK STEAK

This Thai-inspired dish is best served over jasmine rice, although regular white rice will do fine.

1 (1½-pound) lean flank steak
⅓ cup fresh lime juice
¼ cup minced fresh mint
¼ cup low-sodium soy sauce
2 tablespoons peeled, minced gingerroot
2 tablespoons seeded, minced jalapeño pepper
3 garlic cloves, minced
Vegetable cooking spray
1½ pounds green beans, trimmed
1 cup halved cherry tomatoes

Trim fat from steak. Combine steak and next 6 ingredients in a large heavy-duty, zip-top plastic bag. Seal bag, and marinate in refrigerator 8 to 12 hours, turning bag occasionally. Remove steak from bag, reserving marinade.

Coat grill rack with cooking spray; place on grill over medium-hot coals (350° to 400°). Place steak on rack; grill 8 minutes on each side or until desired degree of doneness. Cut steak diagonally across the grain into thin slices; thread steak slices on skewers, if desired. Set aside, and keep warm.

Pour reserved marinade through a sieve into a large microwave-safe bowl. Microwave at HIGH 1 minute or until marinade boils. Arrange beans in a steamer basket over boiling water. Cover and steam 3 minutes or until crisp-tender. Add green beans and tomatoes to hot marinade; toss gently to coat. Serve with steak. Yield: 6 servings (serving size: 3 ounces steak and 1 cup green bean mixture).

CALORIES 252 (45% from fat); PROTEIN 23.3g; FAT 12.6g (sat 5.3g, mono 5.2g, poly 0.5g); CARB 11.5g; FIBER 2.8g; CHOL 57mg; IRON 3.4mg; SODIUM 338mg; CALC 53mg

TANGY FLANK STEAK WITH HORSERADISH CREAM

The diamond scoring pattern on the steak allows more surface area for the marinade. To bring out the flavor of the steak even further, don't forget to serve it with the Horseradish Cream.

1 (1-pound) lean flank steak
½ cup cider vinegar
½ cup thawed apple juice concentrate, undiluted
1 tablespoon chopped fresh or 1 teaspoon dried rosemary
3 tablespoons prepared horseradish
1 tablespoon Worcestershire sauce
Vegetable cooking spray
Horseradish Cream

Trim fat from flank steak. Score a diamond pattern on both sides of steak. Combine flank steak, cider vinegar, apple juice concentrate, rosemary, horseradish, and Worcestershire sauce in a large heavy-duty, zip-top plastic bag. Seal bag, and marinate flank steak in refrigerator 8 to 12 hours, turning bag occasionally. Remove flank steak from bag, and discard marinade.

Prepare grill or broiler. Place flank steak on grill rack or broiler pan coated with cooking spray, and cook 7 minutes on each side or until flank steak is desired degree of doneness. Cut flank steak diagonally across the grain into thin slices. Serve flank steak with Horseradish Cream. Yield: 4 servings (serving size: 3 ounces steak and 2½ tablespoons Horseradish Cream).

CALORIES 258 (44% from fat); PROTEIN 23g; FAT 12.5g (sat 5.2g, mono 5.1g, poly 0.4g); CARB 11.8g; FIBER 0.2 g; CHOL 57mg; IRON 2.5mg; SODIUM 120mg; CALC 23mg

Horseradish Cream:

½ cup nonfat sour cream
2 tablespoons chopped green onions
1 tablespoon prepared horseradish

Combine all ingredients in a small bowl, and stir well. Cover and chill. Yield: 4 servings (serving size: 2½ tablespoons).

CALORIES 22 (0% from fat); PROTEIN 2.1g; FAT 0g; CARB 2.6g; FIBER 0.1g; CHOL 0mg; IRON 0.1mg; SODIUM 24mg; CALC 5mg

GARLICKY BROWN RICE

2 tablespoons olive oil
2 cups uncooked short-grain brown rice
6 garlic cloves, minced
1½ cups water
2 (13¾-ounce) cans no-salt-added chicken broth
½ teaspoon salt
4 tablespoons thinly sliced green onions

Heat oil in a large skillet over medium-high heat until hot. Add rice, and sauté for 1 minute. Add garlic; sauté for 2 minutes. Stir in water, broth, and salt; bring to a boil. Cover, reduce heat, and cook over medium-low heat 45 minutes or until liquid is absorbed. Spoon into a bowl; fluff with a fork. Top with green onions. Yield: 6 servings (serving size: 1 cup).

CALORIES 291 (23% from fat); PROTEIN 6.2g; FAT 7.4g (sat 1g, mono 4g, poly 1g); CARB 48.9g; FIBER 2.3g; CHOL 0mg; IRON 1mg; SODIUM 274mg; CALC 23mg

A STEAK IN YOUR HEALTH

You may have heard that you can't eat steak on a low-fat diet. But you can enjoy beef by eating small portions of lean cuts like flank steak, round steak, and sirloin. Just remember that 3 ounces of meat—about the size of a deck of cards—is the American Heart Association's recommendation for one serving. And that amount provides a good start toward the recommended daily iron requirements for women: 15mg for women ages 25 to 50 and 10mg for women over 50.

Gold Shines in New York

When Rozanne Gold was deciding on a profession, it was a tossup between psychology (for which she earned a degree from Tufts University), advertising, or her real passion: food and cooking. It was her first "big-time" job in the late '70s—as chef to then-New York City Mayor Ed Koch—that made her realize that all of her talents would be necessary for her future in cooking.

Gold spends much of her time as culinary counselor to Windows on the World in New York's World Trade Center. The restaurant offers a selection of her low-fat gourmet dishes.

PAN-SEARED SALMON WITH WATERCRESS PURÉE

Spinach can be substituted for watercress in this recipe from Rozanne Gold.

  2   quarts water
1½   cups peeled, cubed red potato
  8   cups trimmed watercress or torn fresh spinach (about 1 pound)
  1   tablespoon butter
  ½   teaspoon salt, divided
  2   tablespoons water
  ¾   cup diced yellow bell pepper
  ¾   cup diced red bell pepper
  6   (6-ounce) skinned salmon fillets (about 1 inch thick)
Vegetable cooking spray

Bring 2 quarts water to a boil in a large Dutch oven. Add cubed potato, and cook 15 minutes. Add watercress, and cook an additional 10 minutes. Drain well.

Place watercress-potato mixture, butter, and ¼ teaspoon salt in a food processor, and process until smooth; set aside, and keep warm.

Heat 2 tablespoons water in a large nonstick skillet over low heat. Add bell peppers; cover and cook 10 minutes or until tender, stirring occasionally. Spoon bell pepper mixture into a bowl; set aside, and keep warm.

Sprinkle remaining ¼ teaspoon salt over fish; set aside. Coat skillet with cooking spray, and place over medium-high heat until hot. Add fish, and cook 4 minutes on each side or until fish flakes easily when tested with a fork.

Spoon ⅓ cup puréed watercress mixture onto each of 6 plates; arrange 1 fillet on each plate, and top each with 2 tablespoons bell pepper mixture. Yield: 6 servings.

CALORIES 349 (43% from fat); PROTEIN 38.4g; FAT 16.8g (sat 3.8g, mono 7.6g, poly 3.4g); CARB 9.3g; FIBER 2.2g; CHOL 121mg; IRON 1.6mg; SODIUM 324mg; CALC 69mg

A Treat Among the Greens

Salads have really grown up, achieving entrée status on the menus of many creative restaurants. These salads offer a vivid contrast of flavors and textures and are served with great-tasting low-fat or no-fat dressings—such as Lime-Cilantro Vinaigrette and Spicy Peanut Sauce.

These recipes span the globe with ethnic flavors and diverse tastes. When you serve Thai Noodle Salad, watch as guests eat crisp raw sweet potato for the first time. (Don't be surprised if the peanut sauce served over it becomes one of your favorite condiments.) Also, Mexican Cobb Salad makes an excellent sandwich filling, whether stuffed in a pita or rolled up in a tortilla.

Next time you're served a traditional salad at a friend's house or in a restaurant, just smile and think how much better it would be with a treat among the greens.

ENLIGHTENED CAESAR SALAD WITH TOFU CROUTONS

  1   tablespoon cornmeal
  1   teaspoon dried oregano
  1   pound extra-firm light tofu, drained and cut into ½-inch cubes
  1   tablespoon tamari
Vegetable cooking spray
16   cups sliced romaine lettuce
Caesar Dressing

Combine cornmeal and oregano; stir well. Combine tofu and tamari; toss gently to coat. Sprinkle cornmeal mixture over tofu; toss gently to coat.

Coat a large nonstick skillet with cooking spray, and place over medium heat until hot. Add tofu; cook 3 minutes or until lightly browned, turning occasionally. Remove tofu from skillet; set aside.

Place lettuce in a bowl. Drizzle ¾ cup Caesar Dressing over lettuce; toss well. Spoon 2 cups salad into each bowl; top each with ½ cup tofu croutons. Serve immediately. Yield: 5 servings.

Note: Store remaining dressing in an airtight container in refrigerator for up to 1 week. Serve with salad greens.

CALORIES 104 (25% from fat); PROTEIN 10.7g; FAT 2.9g (sat 0.7g, mono 0.4g, poly 0.4g); CARB 7.8g; FIBER 3.2g; CHOL 3mg; IRON 2.2mg; SODIUM 230mg; CALC 149mg

Caesar Dressing:

  1   cup plain nonfat yogurt
  ½   cup grated Parmesan cheese
  ½   cup low-fat buttermilk
  2   tablespoons 1% low-fat milk
  1   tablespoon reduced-calorie mayonnaise
  1   tablespoon Dijon mustard
  ¼   teaspoon salt
  ¼   teaspoon pepper
  2   garlic cloves, minced

Combine all ingredients in a small bowl, and stir well with a wire whisk. Yield: 2 cups (serving size: 2 tablespoons).

CALORIES 28 (40% from fat); PROTEIN 2.2g; FAT 1.2g (sat 0.6g, mono 0.3g, poly 0.2g); CARB 1.9g; FIBER 0g; CHOL 3mg; IRON 0.1mg; SODIUM 134mg; CALC 75mg

THAI NOODLE SALAD WITH VEGETABLES AND SPICY PEANUT SAUCE

Udon noodles often come with a seasoning packet. Simply discard it for this recipe.

½ pound udon noodles (thick, round fresh Japanese wheat noodles) or spaghetti
6 cups thinly sliced romaine lettuce
4 cups thinly sliced green cabbage
2 cups peeled, coarsely shredded uncooked sweet potato
12 thinly sliced red bell pepper rings
12 thinly sliced green bell pepper rings
1 cup peeled, coarsely shredded daikon or carrot
1 cup bean sprouts
Spicy Peanut Sauce
Fresh basil leaves, cilantro sprigs, and mint sprigs (optional)

Cook noodles in boiling water for 3 minutes (omit seasoning packet, if included). Drain; rinse under cold water, and set aside.

Combine lettuce and cabbage in a large bowl; toss well. Place lettuce mixture on a large platter. Place noodles in center of platter on top of lettuce mixture. Arrange sweet potato, red bell pepper, green bell pepper, daikon, and bean sprouts around noodles in individual mounds over lettuce mixture.

Drizzle Spicy Peanut Sauce over salad. Garnish with basil, cilantro, and mint, if desired. Yield: 6 servings.

CALORIES 220 (22% from fat); PROTEIN 7.5g; FAT 5.4g (sat 0.9g, mono 2.1g, poly 1.6g); CARB 37.7g; FIBER 5.5g; CHOL 0.5mg; IRON 2.5mg; SODIUM 329mg; CALC 72mg

Spicy Peanut Sauce:

⅓ cup fresh lime juice
1½ tablespoons peeled, minced gingerroot
3 tablespoons water
3 tablespoons low-sodium soy sauce
3 tablespoons creamy peanut butter
1½ tablespoons honey
2 teaspoons chile paste
3 garlic cloves, minced

Combine all ingredients in a small bowl; stir well with a wire whisk. Yield: ¾ cup (serving size: 2 tablespoons).

CALORIES 84 (50% from fat); PROTEIN 2.6g; FAT 4.7g (sat 0.8g, mono 2g, poly 1.2g); CARB 8.9g; FIBER 0.7g; CHOL 1mg; IRON 0.2mg; SODIUM 304mg; CALC 7mg

STEVE'S HOUSE MIXED GREENS

This combination of greens has just the right balance of peppery, bitter, and mellow flavors. However, you can use any combination of salad greens you like. Invite friends because the recipe makes a whopping 30 cups.

8 cups sliced romaine lettuce (about 1 head)
8 cups torn escarole (about 1 head)
4 cups torn red leaf lettuce (about 1 large head)
4 cups torn curly endive (about ½ head)
4 cups torn radicchio (about 2 heads)
2 cups trimmed arugula (about 4 bunches)

Combine all ingredients in a large bowl, and toss well. Store mixed greens in perforated zip-top plastic vegetable bags. Yield: 30 cups.

MEXICAN COBB SALAD

When preparing this salad for company, arrange it on one large platter, and let guests serve themselves.

8 cups Steve's House Mixed Greens
1 cup diced tomato
1 cup diced red onion
1 cup peeled, diced jicama or carrot
1 cup diced green bell pepper
1 cup fresh corn kernels (about 2 large ears)
1 cup peeled, diced avocado
1 (16-ounce) can black beans, rinsed and drained
1 cup (4 ounces) shredded reduced-fat Monterey Jack cheese
1 cup baked tortilla chips, coarsely crushed
Lime-Cilantro Vinaigrette

Place 2 cups mixed salad greens on each of 4 individual plates. Arrange ¼ cup tomato, ¼ cup onion, ¼ cup jicama, ¼ cup bell pepper, ¼ cup corn, ¼ cup avocado, and one-fourth of beans in individual rows over the salad greens on each plate. Sprinkle ¼ cup Monterey Jack cheese and ¼ cup crushed chips over each salad. Drizzle ¼ cup Lime-Cilantro Vinaigrette over each salad. Yield: 4 servings.

CALORIES 373 (32% from fat); PROTEIN 21g; FAT 13.1g (sat 4.4g, mono 5.9g, poly 1.7g); CARB 49.6g; FIBER 9.8g; CHOL 19mg; IRON 5.1mg; SODIUM 741mg; CALC 328mg

Lime-Cilantro Vinaigrette:

- ¾ cup tomato juice
- ½ cup cilantro sprigs
- ¼ cup fresh lime juice
- ½ teaspoon dried oregano
- ¼ teaspoon salt
- ¼ teaspoon ground cumin
- 1 small jalapeño pepper, seeded and halved

Place all ingredients in a food processor or blender; cover and process until smooth. Pour into a bowl; set aside. Yield: 1 cup (serving size: ¼ cup).

CALORIES 16 (6% from fat); PROTEIN 0.7g; FAT 0.1g (sat 0g, mono 0.1g, poly 0g); CARB 4.1g; FIBER 0.6g; CHOL 0mg; IRON 0.9mg; SODIUM 316mg; CALC 20mg

---

MENU SUGGESTION

BISTRO PASTA SALAD

Italian vegetable soup

*Nectarines in wine syrup

*Boil 1 cup dry red wine, ⅓ cup sugar, 2 strips of orange rind, ⅓ cup orange juice, and 1 cinnamon stick until thick and syrupy. Let cool. Add 4 sliced peeled nectarines; chill 4 hours.

BISTRO PASTA SALAD

- 4 cups torn fresh spinach
- 4 cups cooked orecchiette or small seashell macaroni (about 8 ounces uncooked)
- 1 cup chopped tomato
- ½ cup vertically sliced red onion
- 1 (6-ounce) jar marinated artichoke hearts, drained and chopped
- 12 oil-cured ripe olives
- Sun-Dried Tomato Vinaigrette
- ¾ cup crumbled feta cheese

Combine first 6 ingredients in a large bowl. Pour 1 cup Sun-dried Tomato Vinaigrette over spinach mixture, and toss well. Sprinkle crumbled feta cheese over salad. Yield: 4 servings (serving size: 2 cups).

Note: Store remaining vinaigrette in an airtight container in refrigerator for up to 1 week. Serve with hot pasta.

CALORIES 307 (29% from fat); PROTEIN 12.4g; FAT 10g (sat 4g, mono 4.2g, poly 1.2g); CARB 44.8g; FIBER 5.3g; CHOL 19mg; IRON 4.2mg; SODIUM 613mg; CALC 204mg

Sun-Dried Tomato Vinaigrette:

- 1 cup sun-dried tomatoes, packed without oil (about 2 ounces)
- 2 cups boiling water
- ¾ cup water
- ¾ cup no-salt-added tomato juice
- 2 tablespoons olive oil
- 2 tablespoons balsamic vinegar
- 1 tablespoon tomato paste
- ½ teaspoon pepper
- ¼ teaspoon salt
- 1 garlic clove, peeled

Combine sun-dried tomatoes and 2 cups boiling water in a bowl; let stand 20 minutes. Drain.

Place sun-dried tomatoes, ¾ cup water, and remaining ingredients in a food processor or blender; cover and process until smooth. Yield: 1¾ cups (serving size: 2 tablespoons).

CALORIES 32 (59% from fat); PROTEIN 0.8g; FAT 2.1g (sat 0.3g, mono 1.4g, poly 0.2g); CARB 3.3g; FIBER 0.1g; CHOL 0mg; IRON 0.1mg; SODIUM 129mg; CALC 6mg

---

EXOTIC MUSHROOM SALAD

Marinating the mushrooms for 8 hours gives them a lot more flavor, though as little as 1 hour will do.

Balsamic Dressing
- 6 cups sliced mushrooms (about 1 pound)
- 4 medium portobello mushrooms, sliced
Vegetable cooking spray
- 2 (15-ounce) cans cannellini beans or other white beans, drained
- 8 cups Steve's House Mixed Greens
- 4 teaspoons pine nuts, toasted

Combine Balsamic Dressing and sliced mushrooms in a large heavy-duty,

---

zip-top plastic bag. Seal bag, and marinate mushroom mixture in refrigerator 1 to 8 hours. Remove mushrooms from bag, reserving Balsamic Dressing.

Place mushrooms on broiler pan coated with cooking spray, and broil 7 minutes or until browned. Combine mushrooms, reserved dressing, and beans in a bowl; toss gently.

Place 2 cups salad greens on each of 4 individual plates. Spoon 1½ cups mushroom mixture over each salad, and top each with 1 teaspoon toasted pine nuts. Yield: 4 servings.

CALORIES 253 (32% from fat); PROTEIN 12.8g; FAT 8.9g (sat 1.1g, mono 4.7g, poly 1.6g); CARB 32g; FIBER 4.2g; CHOL 0mg; IRON 6.1mg; SODIUM 241mg; CALC 87mg

Balsamic Dressing:

- ¼ cup balsamic vinegar
- ¼ cup minced green onions
- 2 tablespoons minced fresh parsley or 2 teaspoons dried parsley flakes
- 1 tablespoon minced fresh or 1 teaspoon dried tarragon
- 2 tablespoons Dijon mustard
- 1½ tablespoons olive oil
- 1 tablespoon water
- ⅛ teaspoon pepper
- 3 garlic cloves, minced

Combine all ingredients in a bowl, and stir well. Yield: ¾ cup (serving size: 3 tablespoons).

CALORIES 61 (82% from fat); PROTEIN 0.3g; FAT 5.6g (sat 0.7g, mono 4g, poly 0.5g); CARB 2.1g; FIBER 0.3g; CHOL 0mg; IRON 0.4mg; SODIUM 226mg; CALC 13mg

Mexico's Golden Light

If you think all Mexican food is heavy, then discover the real thing: comida familiar.

The original Mexican *cocina* (cuisine) was light and healthful. The Aztec diet was primarily vegetarian, based on indigenous crops of chiles, corn, beans, squash, and tomatoes.

Both the nutritional profiles and cooking methods of these ingredients mark the Mexican larder for a modern diet. Wrapping foods in cornhusks, banana leaves, spinach, or chiles provides a cozy cocoon for concentrating essences. Steaming and grilling techniques underscore different components without requiring additional fat for flavor. Herbs, spices, nuts, and seeds are toasted before blending into a sauce, and tomatoes, chiles, garlic, and onions are roasted; both toasting and roasting intensify flavors. The varying spice mixes build on the simplicity of cooking styles, contributing a deep complexity to the food. Stirred into simmering broths or rubbed directly onto seafood, poultry, or meat, their exotic perfumes beguile. Most of these spices, as well as other Mexican foodstuffs, can be purchased at the supermarket or at a grocery store that features Latin-American products.

In addition to being fairly easy to get, Mexican products are similarly easy to prepare. This is simple home cooking known as *comida familiar* (family food).

PAPAYA-PINEAPPLE KEBABS WITH GOLDEN CARAMEL SAUCE

Cooked under a broiler or grilled, this dessert adds a sprightly taste to either brunch or dinner.

3 cups peeled, cubed papaya, divided
¼ cup fresh lime juice
2 tablespoons dark rum
2 teaspoons vanilla extract
1 cup water
¾ cup grated piloncillo or firmly packed brown sugar
3 whole cloves
1 (4-inch) cinnamon stick
3 cups cubed pineapple
Vegetable cooking spray

Place ¾ cup papaya, lime juice, rum, and vanilla in a food processor, and process until smooth; set aside.

Combine water, piloncillo, cloves, and cinnamon in a medium saucepan; cook over medium heat 13 minutes. Increase heat to medium-high, and cook an additional 10 minutes or until the consistency of thin syrup (do not stir). Remove from heat; let stand 1 minute. Discard cloves and cinnamon stick. Carefully stir in puréed papaya mixture. Pour sauce into a bowl; set aside.

Thread remaining papaya cubes and pineapple cubes alternately onto each of 6 (10-inch) skewers. Place skewers on rack of a broiler pan coated with cooking spray; broil 8 minutes or until lightly browned, basting occasionally with caramel sauce. Serve kebabs with remaining sauce. Yield: 6 servings (serving size: 1 kebab and 3 tablespoons sauce).

CALORIES 177 (3% from fat); PROTEIN 0.8g; FAT 0.6g (sat 0.1g, mono 0.1g, poly 0.1g); CARB 44.4g; FIBER 2.4g; CHOL 0mg; IRON 0.9mg; SODIUM 14mg; CALC 48mg

MEXICO'S GOLDEN SWEETNESS

Piloncillo is an unrefined pure cane sugar produced in Mexico and in the U.S. that can be found in some grocery stores, Latin-American markets, and through Melissa's/World Variety Produce (800/588-0151). The cone-shaped blocks are rock-hard and a bit of a chore to chop by hand. But they can be easily grated with the coarse shredder blade of a food processor. If you can't find piloncillo, brown sugar is a good substitute.

STEAMED FISH IN SPINACH WITH PICKLED PEPPERS AND ONIONS

If red snapper isn't available, use perch, trout, sea bass, or any white fish fillets your fishmonger recommends. If you can't find the achiote (annatto) seeds, omit them; the vegetables and juices will still be a zesty garnish. Store any leftovers in the refrigerator for sandwiches, salads, or tortilla toppings.

1 cup yellow bell pepper rings, halved
1 cup grapefruit juice
1 tablespoon piloncillo or brown sugar
½ teaspoon ground achiote seeds or annatto (optional)
½ teaspoon seeded, sliced habanero chile or 1 tablespoon seeded, sliced jalapeño pepper
1 small red onion, halved lengthwise and thinly sliced (about 1 cup)
1 bay leaf
½ teaspoon salt, divided
⅛ teaspoon pepper
4 (6-ounce) skinned red snapper fillets
5 cups torn fresh spinach

Combine first 7 ingredients in a medium saucepan, and stir well. Bring to a boil, and cook 2 minutes, stirring occasionally. Remove from heat; discard bay leaf, and stir in ⅛ teaspoon salt. Pour into a bowl; let stand 2 hours.

Sprinkle remaining salt and pepper over fish. Arrange 2½ cups spinach in a steamer basket over boiling water, and top with fish. Arrange remaining spinach over fish. Cover and steam 9 minutes or until fish flakes easily when tested with a fork.

Place spinach and fish evenly on 4 individual plates, and top with pickled vegetables and juice mixture. Yield: 4 servings.

CALORIES 231 (11% from fat); PROTEIN 37.6g; FAT 2.7g (sat 0.6g, mono 0.5g, poly 1g); CARB 13.3g; FIBER 3.6g; CHOL 62mg; IRON 3.9mg; SODIUM 427mg; CALC 136mg

ROASTED-VEGETABLE CHILES RELLENOS

Chiles rellenos are stuffed with everything from cheese in the north of Mexico to crab or seafood along the Gulf Coast. Though chiles rellenos are usually fried, they are baked in this vegetarian version. Bell peppers can be substituted for the poblano chiles.

  4 large poblano chiles (about 1 pound)
  2 pounds tomatoes
  2 medium onions, peeled and quartered
  6 garlic cloves, unpeeled
  1 drained canned chipotle chile in adobo sauce
  1 cup water
  4 oregano sprigs
  1 bay leaf
  ¼ teaspoon salt
Dash of pepper
1¼ cups frozen or fresh corn kernels (about 2 ears)
  1 cup diced chayote or zucchini
  ⅔ cup fine, dry breadcrumbs
  ¼ cup thinly sliced green onions
  2 tablespoons minced fresh cilantro
  ¼ teaspoon salt
Dash of pepper
Fresh chives (optional)
Fresh cilantro sprigs (optional)

Preheat oven to 500°.

Remove stem ends of poblano chiles, leaving chiles whole; discard seeds and membranes. Set aside.

Place tomatoes, onions, and garlic on a foil-lined jelly-roll pan. Bake at 500° for 30 minutes (garlic should be lightly browned; remove before 30 minutes, if necessary). Let vegetables cool 10 minutes. Peel tomatoes and garlic; discard skins. Remove cores from tomatoes. Place tomatoes, garlic, onion, and chipotle chile in a food processor, and process until smooth. Strain through a sieve into a large saucepan; discard solids. Add water, oregano, and bay leaf to pan; bring to a boil. Reduce heat, and simmer, uncovered, 40 minutes or until reduced to 2 cups. Remove from heat; discard oregano and bay leaf. Add ¼ teaspoon salt and dash of pepper to tomato mixture; set sauce aside, and keep warm.

Combine corn and next 6 ingredients in a bowl; stir well. Pack ¾ cup corn mixture into each poblano chile. Place stuffed chiles on foil-lined jelly-roll pan. Bake at 500° for 20 minutes or until chiles are blackened, turning after 10 minutes; peel chiles.

Spoon ½ cup tomato sauce onto each of 4 plates; top with chiles. Garnish with chives and cilantro, if desired. Yield: 4 servings.

CALORIES 255 (10% from fat); PROTEIN 10g; FAT 2.7g (sat 0.5g, mono 0.7g, poly 1.1g); CARB 54.7g; FIBER 9.5g; CHOL 0mg; IRON 4.7mg; SODIUM 514mg; CALC 115mg

---

TIPS FROM OUR HOT LINE

Although the general rule is the smaller the chile, the hotter it is, chiles can be unpredictable. **Poblanos** are usually mild and are the traditional choice for chiles rellenos. **Jalapeño** and **habanero chiles** are hotter and more unpredictable. It's easier to core the chiles and shake out the seeds before roasting them. Remember to handle chiles with care; wear rubber gloves while working with chiles, wash your hands thoroughly afterward, and avoid touching your face and eyes.

VEAL STEW WITH CILANTRO-CHILE SAUCE

This type of stew is typical of Mexico's rustic comfort food. Although veal is rare in Mexico, it's used here because it balances the fresh citrus so well. This dish goes well with tortillas and rice.

  1 (2-pound) boneless veal leg roast
3½ cups low-salt chicken broth
  1 cup sliced carrot
  ¾ cup sliced celery
  ½ cup thinly sliced green onions
  ⅓ cup seeded, thinly sliced jalapeño pepper
  ⅓ cup fresh cilantro leaves
  6 garlic cloves
  1 bay leaf
  ½ cup orange juice
  ¼ cup fresh lemon juice
  ½ teaspoon salt
  ¼ cup thinly sliced green onions
  2 tablespoons minced fresh cilantro

Preheat oven to 325°.

Trim fat from roast. Combine roast, broth, and next 7 ingredients in a large Dutch oven; bring to a boil. Remove from heat; cover and bake at 325° for 1 hour and 15 minutes or until roast is tender. Remove roast from pan, reserving cooking liquid and vegetables. Let roast stand 10 minutes. Separate roast into bite-size pieces, and shred with 2 forks; set aside.

Remove bay leaf from cooking liquid, and discard. Place cooking liquid and vegetables in a blender. Cover and process until smooth. Return vegetable purée to pan. Add fruit juices; bring to a boil, and cook 18 minutes or until vegetable purée is reduced to 2 cups. Return shredded roast to pan; stir in salt. Cook over medium heat until thoroughly heated. Ladle stew into individual bowls, and top with ¼ cup green onions and minced cilantro. Serve with flour tortillas. Yield: 4 servings (serving size: 1 cup stew, 1 tablespoon green onions, and 1½ teaspoons minced cilantro).

CALORIES 323 (16% from fat); PROTEIN 52.1g; FAT 5.6g (sat 1.3g, mono 1.3g, poly 0.5g); CARB 14.8g; FIBER 2.3g; CHOL 177mg; IRON 4mg; SODIUM 544mg; CALC 67mg

SCALLOPS MARGARITA

This recipe depends on the components of a margarita to give zing to the pickled vegetables. In keeping with the margarita theme, coarse salt can be substituted for table salt.

1½   cups fresh lime juice
¼   cup plus 2 tablespoons tequila
¼   cup plus 2 tablespoons triple sec or other orange-flavored liqueur
½   teaspoon salt
⅓   cup fresh cilantro leaves
4   small poblano chiles (about ¾ pound)
2   medium zucchini, halved lengthwise
4   cups cauliflower florets
1   cup diced carrot
¾   cup frozen or fresh corn kernels (about 1½ ears)
¾   cup (½-inch) sliced green beans
⅓   cup thinly sliced red onion, separated into rings
1½   pounds sea scallops
    Vegetable cooking spray
¼   teaspoon salt
    Cilantro sprigs (optional)

Combine first 4 ingredients in a large bowl, and stir well. Remove ½ cup lime juice mixture from bowl, and place in a blender; set remaining lime juice mixture aside. Add cilantro leaves to blender; cover and process until smooth; set cilantro mixture aside.

Cut chiles in half lengthwise; discard seeds and membranes. Flatten chile halves with palm of hand; set aside. Place zucchini halves, skin sides up, on a foil-lined baking sheet; broil 4 minutes. Turn zucchini over, and add chiles to pan, placing chiles skin sides up. Broil an additional 6 minutes or until chiles are blackened. Set zucchini aside. Place chiles in a heavy-duty, zip-top plastic bag, and seal; let stand 15 minutes. Peel chiles; discard skin. Cut chiles and zucchini into ½-inch pieces; set aside.

Place cauliflower into a large Dutch oven of boiling water; cook 3 minutes. Add carrot, corn, and green beans;

cook an additional 5 minutes or until vegetables are crisp-tender. Drain vegetables well. Add cauliflower mixture, chile pieces, zucchini pieces, and onion rings to lime juice mixture in bowl; toss well.

Place scallops on rack of a broiler pan coated with cooking spray; sprinkle ¼ teaspoon salt over scallops. Broil scallops 4 minutes on each side or until done.

Spoon vegetables onto 4 individual plates, and top with scallops. Drizzle cilantro mixture over scallops. Garnish with cilantro sprigs, if desired. Yield: 4 servings (serving size: 2 cups vegetables, 5 ounces scallops, and 2 tablespoons sauce).

CALORIES 411 (5% from fat); PROTEIN 35.1g; FAT 2.5g (sat 0.3g, mono 0.2g, poly 0.9g); CARB 44.1g; FIBER 6.8g; CHOL 56mg; IRON 3.1mg; SODIUM 755mg; CALC 129mg

PORK WITH PAPAYA SALSA AND PINEAPPLE-CHILE SAUCE

In Puebla, Oaxaca, and Guerrero, fruit and meat—such as pineapple, papaya, and raisins with pork—make a popular combination. The salsa (admittedly more Tex-Mex than Mex) cools the heat of the chile sauce.

½   teaspoon whole cloves
½   teaspoon coriander seeds
¼   teaspoon whole allspice
¼   teaspoon black peppercorns
1   (1-inch) piece cinnamon stick
1   (1-pound) pork tenderloin
1   pound Anaheim chiles
2   cups cubed pineapple
2   tablespoons fresh lime juice
¼   teaspoon salt
2   tablespoons minced fresh mint
4   cups peeled, cubed ripe papaya
¼   cup raisins
2   tablespoons thinly sliced green onions
2   tablespoons fresh lime juice
    Vegetable cooking spray
2   tablespoons grated piloncillo or brown sugar
¼   teaspoon salt
    Fresh mint sprigs (optional)

Combine first 5 ingredients in a small skillet. Place over medium heat until hot, and cook 3½ minutes or until toasted, stirring constantly. Place spice mixture in a spice or coffee grinder, and process until finely ground. Rub spice mixture over pork; cover and refrigerate 2 hours.

Cut chiles in half lengthwise; discard seeds and membranes. Place chile halves, skin sides up, on a foil-lined baking sheet. Broil 10 minutes or until blackened. Place chiles in a heavy-duty, zip-top plastic bag, and seal; let stand 10 minutes. Peel chiles; discard skin. Chop chiles; set aside.

Place pineapple in a blender; cover and process until smooth. Remove ½ cup pineapple purée from blender, and place in a large bowl; set aside. Add chopped chiles, 2 tablespoons lime juice, and ¼ teaspoon salt to pineapple purée in blender; cover and process until smooth. Pour into a small nonaluminum skillet; stir in 2 tablespoons minced mint.

Add papaya, raisins, green onions, and 2 tablespoons lime juice to ½ cup pineapple purée in bowl; stir well. Cover salsa, and chill.

Preheat oven to 400°. Place pork on rack of a broiler pan coated with cooking spray; sprinkle piloncillo sugar and ¼ teaspoon salt over pork. Bake at 400° for 30 minutes or until a meat thermometer registers 160°. Cut pork diagonally across the grain into thin slices; set aside, and keep warm.

Cook pineapple-chile purée mixture over medium heat until thoroughly heated, stirring occasionally; spoon purée onto 4 individual plates. Arrange pork slices over purée, and spoon papaya salsa over pork. Garnish with fresh mint sprigs, if desired. Yield: 4 servings (serving size: 3 ounces pork, 1 cup salsa, and ¼ cup sauce).

CALORIES 340 (14% from fat); PROTEIN 29.7g; FAT 5.4g (sat 1.6g, mono 2.1g, poly 0.8g); CARB 47.7g; FIBER 6.4g; CHOL 83mg; IRON 3.6mg; SODIUM 370mg; CALC 86mg

Lost in Tuscany

Classic Tuscan ingredients—olive oil (when Tuscans call for *oil*, they always mean extra-virgin—nothing else will do), tomatoes, garlic, capers, and fresh herbs like tarragon, parsley, and mint—perch on top of crusty bread slices to create a true taste of Tuscany. This crostini recipe, courtesy of Paola de Mari's cooking school in Poggio San Polo, Italy, is an appetizing beginning to any Italian meal.

The Fruits of Your Labor

Life does have its perfect matches. But few combinations satisfy like fresh fruit and cheese, especially with a glass of good wine. To improve upon perfection, to develop fruit-and-cheese dessert recipes that brilliantly marry flavors and textures has been our daunting task. In other words, to take fruit and cheese to a whole other realm of gastronomic pleasure. All of our fruit-and-cheese dishes are daring, exciting, and offer a good bit of surprise. This may not be a perfect world, but with these recipes, it's getting there.

CROSTINI EMPOLI

Wait until you're ready to assemble the crostini to combine the tomato and parsley mixtures.

  2 cups seeded, chopped tomato
 ¼ teaspoon salt
 ⅛ teaspoon pepper
  1 tablespoon chopped fresh parsley
  1 tablespoon capers
  1 teaspoon chopped fresh tarragon
  1 teaspoon olive oil
 ½ teaspoon chopped fresh mint
  1 hard-cooked egg, chopped
  1 garlic clove, halved
 16 (½-inch-thick) slices diagonally cut French bread baguette (about 8 ounces), toasted
  1 tablespoon olive oil

Combine first 3 ingredients in a bowl. Cover and chill 1 hour.

Combine parsley and next 5 ingredients in a bowl. Cover and chill 1 hour.

Rub cut sides of garlic over 1 side of each bread slice. Combine tomato mixture and parsley mixture; spoon 2 tablespoons mixture onto each bread slice. Drizzle with 1 tablespoon oil. Serve immediately. Yield: 16 appetizers (serving size: 1 crostino).

CALORIES 68 (26% from fat); PROTEIN 2.1g; FAT 2g (sat 0.4g, mono 1.1g, poly 0.3g); CARB 10.3g; FIBER 0.6g; CHOL 14mg; IRON 0.5mg; SODIUM 180mg; CALC 11mg

COEUR À LA CRÈME WITH GOAT CHEESE

Serve with an extra-dry French Champagne, which actually tastes slightly sweet.

 1⅓ cups nonfat block cream cheese
  1 cup nonfat ricotta cheese
  1 cup nonfat sour cream
 ½ cup sifted powdered sugar
  2 ounces chèvre (goat cheese)
  1 teaspoon unflavored gelatin
 ¼ cup cold water
  5 cups berries (such as raspberries, blueberries, or sliced strawberries)
 20 gingersnaps

Line a 4-cup coeur à la crème mold with a double layer of damp cheesecloth; allow cheesecloth to extend over edge of mold.

Position knife blade in food processor bowl. Add first 5 ingredients to bowl; process until smooth. Sprinkle gelatin over cold water in a saucepan; let stand 1 minute. Cook over low heat, stirring until gelatin dissolves, about 2 minutes. Remove from heat; let cool slightly. Add ¼ cup cheese mixture to gelatin mixture, stirring with a wire whisk; add to remaining cheese mixture in processor, and process 1 minute. Spoon cheese mixture into prepared mold. Fold cheesecloth over top of cheese mixture; place mold in a shallow dish, and chill at least 12 hours.

To serve, unfold cheesecloth, and invert cheese mixture onto a serving plate; remove cheesecloth. Serve with berries and gingersnaps. Yield: 10 servings (serving size: ⅓ cup crème, ½ cup berries, and 2 gingersnaps).

CALORIES 200 (19% from fat); PROTEIN 12.2g; FAT 4.1g (sat 1.5g, mono 1.4g, poly 0.9g); CARB 28.4g; FIBER 3.3g; CHOL 19mg; IRON 1.1mg; SODIUM 318mg; CALC 201mg

GRAPE-AND-CURRANT TART WITH FONTINA CHEESE

Serve with a late-harvest Sémillon (a sweet dessert wine) from Washington State.

½   cup boiling water
¼   cup dried currants
6   (¾-ounce) slices white bread
Vegetable cooking spray
1½ cups skim milk, divided
1¼ cups (5 ounces) diced fontina
      cheese
1¼ cups seedless red grapes, halved
2   tablespoons all-purpose flour
⅓   cup sugar
2   tablespoons yellow cornmeal
1   teaspoon grated lemon rind
3   egg whites, lightly beaten
1   egg, lightly beaten
1   teaspoon extra-virgin olive oil
1   tablespoon sugar
2   teaspoons chopped fresh
      rosemary

Preheat oven to 350°.
Combine boiling water and currants; let stand 15 minutes. Drain and set aside.
Trim crusts from bread; discard crusts. Cut each slice into 4 triangles; arrange triangles in a single layer in a 10-inch quiche dish coated with cooking spray. Pour ½ cup milk over bread; let stand 5 minutes. Top with currants, cheese, and grapes.
Place flour in a bowl, and gradually add remaining 1 cup milk, stirring with a wire whisk until blended. Stir in ⅓ cup sugar, cornmeal, lemon rind, egg whites, and egg; pour over tart. Drizzle oil over tart, and sprinkle with 1 tablespoon sugar and rosemary. Bake at 350° for 45 minutes or until set; let cool on a wire rack. Yield: 8 servings.

CALORIES 219 (31% from fat); PROTEIN 9.8g; FAT 7.6g (sat 3.9g, mono 2.4g, poly 0.6g); CARB 28.6g; FIBER 0.8g; CHOL 49mg; IRON 0.8mg; SODIUM 108mg; CALC 174mg

CREAM CHEESE BRÛLÉE WITH RASPBERRIES

Serve with a late-harvest California Riesling.

⅓   cup firmly packed light brown
      sugar
2   tablespoons cornstarch
3   egg whites, lightly beaten
1   egg, lightly beaten
1   (12-ounce) can evaporated
      skimmed milk
1   teaspoon vanilla extract
1   (8-ounce) tub reduced-fat
      cream cheese
1½ cups fresh raspberries
2   tablespoons plus 2 teaspoons
      light brown sugar

Combine first 5 ingredients in the top of a double boiler; stir well. Cook over simmering water 4 minutes or until thickened, stirring constantly with a wire whisk. Remove from heat; add vanilla and cream cheese, stirring until smooth. Gently fold in raspberries.
Spoon ½ cup cheese mixture into each of 8 (6-ounce) ramekins or custard cups. Cover and chill at least 4 hours.
Sprinkle each serving with 1 teaspoon brown sugar. Place ramekins on a baking sheet; broil 1 minute or until sugar melts. Serve immediately. Yield: 8 servings.

CALORIES 177 (28% from fat); PROTEIN 8.4g; FAT 5.6g (sat 3.1g, mono 2g, poly 0.3g); CARB 23.4g; FIBER 1.7g; CHOL 46mg; IRON 0.6mg; SODIUM 242mg; CALC 181mg

FRESH PEAR CAKE WITH BLUE CHEESE

Serve with a light ruby port from Portugal.

⅔   cup sugar
1   cup crumbled blue cheese,
      divided
2   tablespoons stick margarine,
      softened
⅓   cup skim milk
2   egg whites
1   teaspoon vanilla extract
1⅓ cups all-purpose flour
2   teaspoons baking powder
Vegetable cooking spray
2   cups peeled, thinly sliced pear
      (about 3 medium)
¼   cup all-purpose flour
3   tablespoons sugar

Preheat oven to 350°.
Combine ⅔ cup sugar, ½ cup blue cheese, and margarine in a bowl; beat at high speed of an electric mixer until smooth. Add milk, egg whites, and vanilla; beat well.
Combine 1⅓ cups flour and baking powder. Add to cheese mixture, stirring just until moistened. Spread batter into a 9-inch square baking pan coated with cooking spray. Arrange pear slices in a single layer in 3 rows on top of batter, pressing pear slices gently into batter.
Combine ¼ cup flour and 3 tablespoons sugar in a bowl; cut in remaining cheese with a pastry blender or 2 knives until mixture resembles coarse meal. Sprinkle over pears. Bake at 350° for 45 minutes or until browned. Serve warm. Yield: 9 servings.

CALORIES 252 (24% from fat); PROTEIN 6.2g; FAT 6.6g (sat 2.9g, mono 2.2g, poly 1g); CARB 42.6g; FIBER 1.5g; CHOL 10mg; IRON 1.3mg; SODIUM 222mg; CALC 147mg

PINEAPPLE-AND-CHEESE UPSIDE-DOWN CAKE

Serve with a sweet Marsala.

    1   (20-ounce) can unsweetened
          pineapple slices, undrained
    ½   cup firmly packed brown sugar
    2   tablespoons stick margarine
        Vegetable cooking spray
    ¾   cup sugar
    ¼   cup reduced-fat cream cheese,
          softened
    2   tablespoons stick margarine,
          softened
    2   egg whites
    1   egg
    ¾   cup all-purpose flour
    1   teaspoon baking powder
    ¼   teaspoon salt
    ¾   cup (3 ounces) finely shredded
          sharp Cheddar cheese
    ½   teaspoon vanilla extract

Preheat oven to 350°.

Drain pineapple, reserving ¼ cup juice. Place reserved juice and 3 pineapple slices in a blender; cover and process until smooth; set aside.

Combine brown sugar and 2 tablespoons margarine in a saucepan; cook over medium-low heat until melted. Remove from heat; add ¼ cup puréed pineapple, stirring until blended. Pour brown sugar mixture into a 9-inch round cake pan coated with cooking spray.

Cut remaining pineapple slices in half crosswise, and arrange in a single layer over brown sugar mixture; set aside.

Combine ¾ cup sugar, cream cheese, and 2 tablespoons margarine in a large bowl; beat at medium speed of an electric mixer until blended. Add 2 egg whites and egg, 1 at a time, beating after each addition. Combine flour, baking powder, and salt; add to cream cheese mixture, beating until blended. Stir in the remaining puréed pineapple, Cheddar cheese, and vanilla.

Pour batter evenly over pineapple slices. Bake at 350° for 45 minutes or until a wooden pick inserted in the center comes out clean. Let cool in pan 10 minutes; invert cake onto a serving plate. Serve warm. Yield: 12 servings.

CALORIES 212 (32% from fat); PROTEIN 4.2g; FAT 7.5g (sat 2.9g, mono 2.8g, poly 1.4g); CARB 32.5g; FIBER 0.2g; CHOL 29mg; IRON 0.8mg; SODIUM 185mg; CALC 91mg

BRIE STRATA WITH APRICOT-PAPAYA SALSA

Serve with a sweet Sauternes from France.

    1   cup apricot nectar
    ¾   cup dried apricots, quartered
    2   cups peeled, diced papaya
    1   tablespoon honey
    1   tablespoon fresh lime juice
    1   (15-ounce) round Brie
    8   cups (1-inch) cubes French bread
        Vegetable cooking spray
    2   tablespoons brown sugar
    1   (12-ounce) can evaporated
          skimmed milk
    ¼   teaspoon salt
    3   egg whites, lightly beaten
    2   eggs, lightly beaten

Combine nectar and apricots in a microwave-safe bowl. Microwave at HIGH 2 minutes or until mixture boils; cover and let stand 30 minutes or until apricots soften. Drain apricots, reserving 2 tablespoons nectar; discard remaining nectar. Combine apricots, reserved nectar, papaya, honey, and lime juice; stir gently, and set aside.

Remove rind from Brie, and discard. Cut Brie into small pieces.

Arrange half of bread cubes in the bottom of a 9-inch square baking dish coated with cooking spray. Top with half of Brie, and sprinkle with half of brown sugar. Repeat procedure with remaining bread, Brie, and brown sugar.

Combine milk, salt, egg whites, and eggs; stir well. Pour over bread; press firmly with back of spoon to moisten all bread cubes. Cover and chill 30 minutes.

Preheat oven to 350°.

Bake strata at 350° for 35 minutes or until a knife inserted near center comes out clean. Serve warm with salsa. Yield: 9 servings (serving size: 1 strata square and ⅓ cup salsa).

CALORIES 297 (32% from fat); PROTEIN 15.1g; FAT 10.4g (sat 5.6g, mono 3.1g, poly 0.8g); CARB 35.9g; FIBER 1.5g; CHOL 80mg; IRON 1.4mg; SODIUM 534mg; CALC 197mg

PAIRING FRUIT & CHEESE

Here are some other cheese-and-fruit pairings that make hassle-free desserts.

• **CHEDDAR** • Serve a mild-flavored cheddar and other semisoft cheeses with firm, tangy fruits like apples and pears.

• **GOAT CHEESE** • Fresh-tasting goat cheese, with its characteristic sour undertones, goes best with the sweetness of dates, figs, and persimmons.

• **BRIE and CAMEMBERT** • These soft-rind, voluptuous French cheeses pair well with the sweet-sour taste of grapes, kiwifruit, and pomegranates.

• **GORGONZOLA** • The pronounced aroma and creamy, bittersweet character of Gorgonzola demand firm but very ripe pears and some walnuts. This blue cheese also pairs well with very sweet blood oranges.

• **CREAM CHEESE** • The softness, mildness, and smoothness of cream cheese go beautifully with intensely sweet tropical fruits like guavas, papayas, and mangoes.

• **PARMESAN** • The nutlike, salty sweetness of Parmesan is exquisite with the delicacy of peaches, passion-fruit, and quinces.

• **STILTON** • Strong, blue-veined, and very rich, Stilton gains immensely from such dried fruits as cherries and currants, along with a glass of port and a few walnuts.

• **GOUDA and EDAM** • These mild cheeses have a buttery flavor that is enhanced by ripe, juicy fruits like plums and peaches.

Home-Oriented

*Next time you crave Chinese food,
make it at home. These easy-to-do recipes
feature everyone's favorites.*

We've taken some Chinese take-out favorites and adapted them for easy preparation at home. All call for stir-frying, which is one of the healthiest, quickest, and simplest ways to cook. Using a wok or skillet and minimal oil, meat and vegetables are stirred constantly over high heat. The result: crisp, tender, naturally light food bursting with flavor and nutrients. And stir-frying is fun, particularly when done in the presence of hungry friends or family members.

BEEF AND BROCCOLI WITH OYSTER SAUCE

- 3 tablespoons oyster sauce
- 1 tablespoon low-sodium soy sauce
- 1 tablespoon dry sherry
- 1 tablespoon water
- 2 teaspoons sugar
- 1 teaspoon cornstarch
- 1 pound lean flank steak
- 1 tablespoon cornstarch
- 2 tablespoons water
- 1 tablespoon low-sodium soy sauce
- 2 teaspoons sugar
- 1 tablespoon vegetable oil, divided
- 1/3 cup (1/2-inch) diagonally sliced green onions
- 1 tablespoon peeled, minced gingerroot
- 6 cups broccoli florets (about 1 pound)
- 1/4 cup water
- 6 cups hot cooked rice (cooked without salt or fat)

Combine first 6 ingredients; stir until well blended, and set aside.

Trim fat from steak. Cut steak diagonally across the grain into 1-inch-thick slices. Cut slices into thin strips. Combine steak, 1 tablespoon cornstarch, 2 tablespoons water, 1 tablespoon soy sauce, and 2 teaspoons sugar in a medium bowl; stir until well-blended. Cover and marinate in refrigerator 15 minutes.

Heat 2 teaspoons oil in a wok or large nonstick skillet over high heat until hot. Add steak mixture; stir-fry 2 minutes. Remove steak from pan; set aside. Add remaining 1 teaspoon oil, green onions, and gingerroot; stir-fry over medium-high heat 30 seconds. Add broccoli and 1/4 cup water; cover and cook 3 minutes. Return steak to pan, and add oyster sauce mixture; stir-fry 2 minutes or until thick and bubbly. Serve over rice. Yield: 6 servings (serving size: 1 cup beef mixture and 1 cup rice).

CALORIES 424 (21% from fat); PROTEIN 22.2g; FAT 9.9g (sat 3.5g, mono 3.5g, poly 1.5g); CARB 60.4g; FIBER 3.9g; CHOL 38mg; IRON 4.4mg; SODIUM 505mg; CALC 73mg

STEAK-AND-PEPPER STIR-FRY

- 1 pound lean flank steak
- 1/4 cup low-sodium soy sauce
- 1 tablespoon cornstarch
- 1 tablespoon dry sherry
- 1 teaspoon sugar
- 2 tablespoons dark sesame oil, divided
- 1 cup julienne-cut green bell pepper
- 1 cup julienne-cut red bell pepper
- 1 cup vertically sliced onion
- 1/4 teaspoon salt
- 1/4 teaspoon dried crushed red pepper
- 1 tablespoon peeled, grated gingerroot
- 1/4 cup water
- 6 cups hot cooked lo mein noodles (about 16 ounces uncooked)

Trim fat from steak. Cut steak diagonally with the grain into 2-inch-thick slices. Cut slices diagonally across the grain into thin strips. Combine steak, soy sauce, cornstarch, sherry, and sugar in a bowl; stir until well-blended. Cover and marinate in refrigerator 15 minutes.

Heat 1 tablespoon oil in a wok or large nonstick skillet over high heat until hot. Add bell peppers, onion, salt, and crushed red pepper; stir-fry 1 minute. Remove bell pepper mixture from pan; set aside. Add remaining oil, steak mixture, and gingerroot to pan; stir-fry 2 minutes. Return bell pepper mixture to pan, and stir in water; stir-fry 1 minute. Serve with lo mein noodles. Yield: 6 servings (serving size: 1 cup steak mixture and 1 cup noodles).

CALORIES 394 (29% from fat); PROTEIN 22.2g; FAT 12.8g (sat 3.9g, mono 4.8g, poly 2.7g); CARB 45.3g; FIBER 3.2g; CHOL 38mg; IRON 4mg; SODIUM 416mg; CALC 20mg

KUNG PAO PORK

Dried whole red chiles are often packaged in small jars and sold in the spice section of the supermarket.

- 1 tablespoon sugar
- 3 tablespoons water
- 3 tablespoons low-sodium soy sauce
- 2 tablespoons dry sherry
- 1 tablespoon white vinegar
- 1 teaspoon cornstarch
- 1½ teaspoons dark sesame oil
- ¼ teaspoon salt
- 1 pound pork tenderloin
- 1 tablespoon cornstarch
- 1 tablespoon low-sodium soy sauce
- 1 tablespoon vegetable oil, divided
- 8 dried whole red chiles
- 2 cups coarsely chopped green bell pepper
- ¾ cup vertically sliced onion
- 1 teaspoon peeled, minced gingerroot
- ½ cup unsalted dry roasted peanuts
- 6 cups hot cooked rice (cooked without salt or fat)

Combine first 8 ingredients in a small bowl; stir until well-blended. Set aside.

Trim fat from pork. Cut pork into 1-inch cubes. Combine pork, 1 tablespoon cornstarch, and 1 tablespoon soy sauce in a bowl; stir well. Cover and marinate in refrigerator 15 minutes.

Heat 1 teaspoon vegetable oil in a wok or large nonstick skillet over high heat until hot. Add chiles; stir-fry 1 minute or until blackened. Remove from pan with a slotted spoon; set aside. Add remaining oil and pork mixture to pan; stir-fry 2 minutes. Add bell pepper, onion, and gingerroot; stir-fry 1 minute or until vegetables are crisp-tender. Add sherry mixture; stir-fry 1 minute or until thick and bubbly. Remove from heat; stir in chiles and peanuts. Serve over rice. Yield: 6 servings (serving size: ¾ cup pork mixture and 1 cup rice).

CALORIES 449 (23% from fat); PROTEIN 23.8g; FAT 11.7g (sat 2.1g, mono 4.9g, poly 3.8g); CARB 60.4g; FIBER 3.3g; CHOL 49mg; IRON 3.7mg; SODIUM 398mg; CALC 45mg

CURRY-ALMOND CHICKEN

- 3 tablespoons low-sodium soy sauce, divided
- 1½ teaspoons cornstarch, divided
- ¼ teaspoon salt
- 1 pound skinned, boned chicken breasts, cut into bite-size pieces
- ¼ cup dry sherry
- 2 tablespoons rice vinegar
- 1 tablespoon curry powder
- 1 teaspoon sugar
- 1 teaspoon dark sesame oil
- 1 tablespoon vegetable oil
- 1 cup coarsely chopped yellow bell pepper
- ½ cup coarsely chopped onion
- 1 teaspoon peeled, minced gingerroot
- 3 garlic cloves, minced
- 1 (8-ounce) can sliced bamboo shoots, drained
- 4 cups hot cooked rice (cooked without salt or fat)
- ¼ cup sliced green onions
- ¼ cup slivered almonds, toasted

Combine 1 tablespoon soy sauce, ½ teaspoon cornstarch, salt, and chicken in a bowl; stir well. Cover and marinate in refrigerator 30 minutes. Combine remaining soy sauce, remaining cornstarch, sherry, vinegar, curry powder, sugar, and sesame oil in a small bowl; stir well, and set aside.

Heat vegetable oil in a wok or large nonstick skillet over medium-high heat until hot. Add bell pepper, chopped onion, gingerroot, and garlic; stir-fry 3 minutes. Add chicken mixture; stir-fry 5 minutes or until chicken is done. Add sherry mixture and bamboo shoots; stir-fry 1 minute or until thick and bubbly. Serve over rice; sprinkle green onions and almonds over each serving. Yield: 4 servings (serving size: 1 cup chicken mixture, 1 cup rice, 1 tablespoon green onions, and 1 tablespoon almonds).

CALORIES 500 (20% from fat); PROTEIN 34g; FAT 10.9g (sat 1.6g, mono 4.7g, poly 3.5g); CARB 61.3g; FIBER 3.8g; CHOL 66mg; IRON 4.4mg; SODIUM 591mg; CALC 85mg

SWEET-AND-SOUR SHRIMP

- 1 tablespoon cornstarch
- ¼ teaspoon salt
- 1 egg white
- 1 pound large shrimp, peeled and deveined
- 1 (15¼-ounce) can unsweetened pineapple chunks, undrained
- ⅓ cup water
- 3 tablespoons sugar
- 3 tablespoons ketchup
- 3 tablespoons cider vinegar
- 1 tablespoon dry sherry
- 2 teaspoons cornstarch
- 1 teaspoon dark sesame oil
- ¼ teaspoon salt
- 1 tablespoon dark sesame oil
- ½ cup diced onion
- ⅓ cup diced fresh mushrooms
- ⅓ cup frozen green peas
- 4 cups hot cooked rice (cooked without salt or fat)

Combine first 3 ingredients in a medium bowl; stir well with a wire whisk. Add shrimp; stir well. Cover and marinate in refrigerator 15 minutes.

Drain pineapple, reserving 2 tablespoons juice. Combine reserved pineapple juice, water, and next 7 ingredients; stir until well-blended. Set aside.

Remove shrimp from marinade; discard marinade. Heat 1 tablespoon oil in a wok or large nonstick skillet over medium-high heat until hot. Add shrimp; stir-fry 1 minute. Add onion and mushrooms; stir-fry 2 minutes. Add ketchup mixture and peas; stir-fry 1 minute or until thick and bubbly. Remove from heat; stir in pineapple. Serve over rice. Yield: 4 servings (serving size: 1 cup shrimp mixture and 1 cup rice).

CALORIES 508 (11% from fat); PROTEIN 23.5g; FAT 6.4g (sat 1g, mono 2g, poly 2.5g); CARB 87.2g; FIBER 2.2g; CHOL 129mg; IRON 4.7mg; SODIUM 582mg; CALC 88mg

SNOW PEA-AND-CHINESE MUSHROOM STIR-FRY

1 cup boiling water
1 (.75-ounce) package dried black mushrooms
2 teaspoons dark sesame oil
1 (8-ounce) can sliced bamboo shoots, drained
5 cups snow peas (about 1 pound), trimmed
¼ teaspoon salt
¼ teaspoon sugar

Combine 1 cup boiling water and mushrooms in a bowl; cover and let stand 15 minutes. Drain mushrooms, reserving 2 tablespoons soaking liquid. Discard mushroom stems; thinly slice mushroom caps, and set aside.

Heat oil in a wok or large nonstick skillet over medium-high heat until hot. Add mushrooms and bamboo shoots; stir-fry 2 minutes. Add reserved soaking liquid, snow peas, salt, and sugar; stir-fry 2 minutes. Yield: 6 servings (serving size: 1 cup).

CALORIES 82 (20% from fat); PROTEIN 4g; FAT 1.8g (sat 0.3g, mono 0.6g, poly 0.8g); CARB 12.4g; FIBER 3.7g; CHOL 0mg; IRON 2.6mg; SODIUM 104mg; CALC 55mg

STIR-FRIED ASIAN VEGETABLES

¾ cup low-salt chicken broth
1 tablespoon cornstarch
2 tablespoons low-sodium soy sauce
½ teaspoon sugar
⅛ teaspoon pepper
1 tablespoon vegetable oil
1 cup diagonally sliced carrot
1 cup diagonally sliced celery
½ cup chopped onion
1½ cups snow peas, trimmed
1 (15-ounce) can whole baby corn, drained
1 (15-ounce) can whole straw mushrooms, drained

Combine first 5 ingredients in a small bowl; stir with a wire whisk until well blended. Set aside.

Heat oil in a wok or large nonstick skillet over high heat until hot. Add carrot, celery, and onion; stir-fry 2 minutes. Add snow peas, corn, and mushrooms; stir-fry 2 minutes. Add broth mixture; stir-fry 1 minute or until thick and bubbly. Yield: 6 servings (serving size: 1 cup).

CALORIES 119 (23% from fat); PROTEIN 3.8g; FAT 3g (sat 0.5g, mono 0.8g, poly 1.4g); CARB 21.6g; FIBER 2.4g; CHOL 0mg; IRON 1.5mg; SODIUM 435mg; CALC 31mg

QUICK & EASY WEEKNIGHTS

Making the Cut

Crushed peppercorns and roasted garlic give these lamb chops an earthy, pungent kick. Add potatoes, asparagus, and a rum-raisin bread pudding, and you've got an easy-to-do meal that could be served at the finest bistro.

LAMB CHOPS WITH GARLIC-PEPPERCORN CRUST

Although the blend of black, green, pink, and white peppercorns (available at most grocery stores) creates a more interesting flavor, black will work.

4 (6-ounce, 2-rib) French-cut lean lamb rib chops
2 tablespoons mixed peppercorns, crushed
3 tablespoons bottled minced roasted garlic
2 tablespoons coarse-grained mustard
½ teaspoon salt
Vegetable cooking spray
Rosemary sprigs (optional)

Preheat oven to 375°.

Trim fat from lamb chops. Combine peppercorns, garlic, mustard, and salt in a small bowl; stir well. Spread peppercorn mixture over chops. Place chops in an 11 x 7-inch baking dish coated with cooking spray.

Bake at 375° for 25 minutes or until desired degree of doneness. Garnish with rosemary, if desired. Serve with asparagus and new potatoes. Yield: 4 servings (serving size: 1 chop).

CALORIES 170 (42% from fat); PROTEIN 16.7g; FAT 8g (sat 2.7g, mono 3.2g, poly 0.8g); CARB 6.8g; FIBER 0.6g; CHOL 51mg; IRON 2mg; SODIUM 567mg; CALC 45mg

RUM-RAISIN BREAD PUDDING

⅓ cup raisins
3 tablespoons light rum
1⅓ cups 1% low-fat milk
¼ cup sugar
½ teaspoon ground cinnamon
⅛ teaspoon salt
2 eggs, lightly beaten
1⅔ cups (½-inch) cubed French bread
Vegetable cooking spray

Preheat oven to 325°.

Combine raisins and rum in a small bowl; set aside. Combine milk and next 4 ingredients in a medium bowl; stir with a wire whisk until well blended. Add raisin mixture and bread cubes, stirring until moistened.

Spoon bread mixture evenly into 4 (6-ounce) custard cups coated with cooking spray. Bake at 325° for 40 minutes or until a knife inserted in center comes out clean. Yield: 4 servings.

CALORIES 200 (18% from fat); PROTEIN 7.6g; FAT 4g (sat 1.5g, mono 1.4g, poly 0.5g); CARB 34.7g; FIBER 1g; CHOL 114mg; IRON 1.1mg; SODIUM 228mg; CALC 128mg

SHOPPING LIST

1 pound fresh asparagus
1 lemon
12 round red potatoes
fresh parsley
fresh rosemary
bottled roasted garlic
coarse-grained mustard
raisins
sugar
cinnamon
mixed peppercorns
1 loaf French bread
rock salt
4 lamb rib chops
2 eggs
1% low-fat milk
rum

TIPS TO HELP GET DINNER ON THE TABLE

• **PEPPERCORNS** • Place them in a zip-top plastic bag and pound with a rolling pin or meat mallet to coarsely crush.

• **SALT-ROASTED POTATOES** • Pour 1 cup rock salt in a baking pan. Peel a strip around the middle of each potato and coat the whole potato with cooking spray. Arrange potatoes in a single layer over rock salt. Bake at 375° for 1 hour. Toss with parsley.

• **LEMON ASPARAGUS** • Hold each asparagus spear between your fingers and snap the spear where it naturally breaks. Steam the asparagus, then toss them with 2 tablespoons fresh lemon juice and 1 teaspoon lemon zest.

TECHNIQUE

Simmertime

Poaching is a classic method of cooking that gives flavor but virtually no fat.

One of the gentlest, easiest, healthiest, and tastiest cooking methods is poaching: Food is immersed in liquids such as wine or stock, then simmered until done. It can be applied to all kinds of dishes beyond the predictable eggs and salmon. And because poaching preserves the shape and texture of food, dishes prepared this way can be visually stunning, particularly those using fruit.

Poaching isn't difficult—just have all of your ingredients ready before you start. Remember, too, that cooked food must be removed immediately from its liquid, or it will continue to cook. Although poaching is usually done on the stovetop, we've also included an example that's done in the oven. All you really need is a skillet or Dutch oven, plus a slotted spoon or spatula. So what could be simpler?

OVEN-POACHED HALIBUT PROVENÇALE

This recipe uses a moderate oven temperature to accomplish the same results as stovetop poaching.

Vegetable cooking spray
1 cup dry white wine
6 (6-ounce) halibut steaks
6 cups diced tomato
2 cups finely chopped onion
¼ cup chopped fresh or
    1 tablespoon plus 1 teaspoon
    dried basil
¼ cup chopped fresh parsley or
    1 tablespoon plus 1 teaspoon
    dried parsley flakes
2 tablespoons pitted, minced
    kalamata olives
1 tablespoon olive oil
½ teaspoon salt
½ teaspoon anchovy paste
⅛ teaspoon pepper
2 garlic cloves, minced
¼ cup fine, dry breadcrumbs
1 tablespoon grated Parmesan
    cheese
1 teaspoon olive oil

Preheat oven to 350°.

Coat a 13 x 9-inch baking dish with cooking spray. Add wine, and arrange halibut steaks in dish. Combine tomato and next 9 ingredients in a bowl; stir well, and spoon over steaks. Bake at 350° for 35 minutes or until fish flakes easily when tested with a fork.

Combine breadcrumbs, cheese, and 1 teaspoon oil in a bowl; stir well. Sprinkle over tomato mixture, and broil until crumbs are golden. Serve immediately. Yield: 6 servings (serving size: 5 ounces fish and 1 cup tomato mixture).

CALORIES 305 (22% from fat); PROTEIN 38.9g; FAT 8.6g (sat 1.3g, mono 3.8g, poly 2.1g); CARB 17.9g; FIBER 3.8g; CHOL 81mg; IRON 3.1mg; SODIUM 446mg; CALC 139mg

FLOUNDER WITH THAI SCALLION SAUCE

- 3 cups boiling water
- 2 tablespoons peeled, minced gingerroot
- ½ teaspoon coriander seeds
- 3 regular-size oolong tea bags
- 1 (3-inch) strip lemon rind
- 4 (6-ounce) skinned flounder fillets
- 1 cup (2-inch-long) sliced green onions
- 1 cup (¼-inch-long) diagonally sliced carrot
- ¼ cup minced shallots
- Thai Scallion Sauce

Combine first 5 ingredients in a large bowl; let stand 1 hour.

Roll up flounder fillets jelly-roll fashion, and place in a large skillet. Add green onions, carrot, and shallots. Pour tea mixture through a wire-mesh strainer into skillet, and bring mixture to a boil.

Reduce heat to medium-low; simmer, uncovered, 8 minutes or until fish flakes easily when tested with a fork. Transfer fish, green onions, and carrots to a serving platter using a slotted spoon. Serve with Thai Scallion Sauce. Yield: 4 servings (serving size: 1 fish fillet, about ¼ cup vegetables, and 2 teaspoons Thai Scallion Sauce).

CALORIES 191 (11% from fat); PROTEIN 33.1g; FAT 2.4g (sat 0.5g, mono 0.5g, poly 0.7g); CARB 7.4g; FIBER 1.6g; CHOL 82mg; IRON 1.3mg; SODIUM 628mg; CALC 64mg

Thai Scallion Sauce:

- ½ cup low-sodium soy sauce
- ¼ cup fish sauce
- 2 tablespoons thinly sliced green onions
- 1 tablespoon chopped fresh cilantro
- 2 tablespoons rice vinegar
- 2 teaspoons sugar
- 1 teaspoon chopped fresh mint
- 1 teaspoon dark sesame oil
- ½ teaspoon peeled, minced gingerroot
- ¼ teaspoon chili-and-garlic paste
- 1 garlic clove, minced

Combine all ingredients in a medium bowl; stir well. Yield: 1 cup (serving size: 2 teaspoons).

CALORIES 6 (30% from fat); PROTEIN 0g; FAT 0.2g (sat 0g, mono 0.1g, poly 0.1g); CARB 0.4g; FIBER 0g; CHOL 0mg; IRON 0mg; SODIUM 475mg; CALC 1mg

BOMBAY CURRIED SHRIMP

Fresh basil and light coconut milk give this easy-to-prepare shrimp an updated and aromatic appeal.

- 1½ pounds large shrimp, peeled and deveined
- 1 tablespoon all-purpose flour
- 2 teaspoons vegetable oil
- ½ cup minced shallots
- 1 tablespoon curry powder
- 1 cup diced red bell pepper
- 1½ cups diced tomato
- ½ cup light coconut milk
- ¼ cup chopped fresh or 1 tablespoon plus 1 teaspoon dried basil
- 1 tablespoon fresh lemon juice
- 1 teaspoon sugar
- ½ teaspoon salt
- 1 (10½-ounce) can low-salt chicken broth
- 6 cups hot cooked rice (cooked without salt or fat)
- 3 tablespoons flaked sweetened coconut, toasted

Combine shrimp and flour in a bowl; toss well, and set aside.

Heat oil in a large skillet over medium-high heat until hot. Add shallots and curry powder, and sauté 1 minute. Add bell pepper, and sauté 1 minute. Add tomato, coconut milk, basil, lemon juice, sugar, salt, and broth; bring to a simmer, and cook 2 minutes. Add shrimp mixture; simmer 4 minutes or until shrimp turn pink, stirring occasionally. Spoon shrimp mixture over rice, and sprinkle with toasted coconut. Yield: 6 servings (serving size: 1 cup shrimp mixture, 1 cup rice, and 1½ teaspoons coconut).

CALORIES 397 (14% from fat); PROTEIN 23.2g; FAT 6g (sat 2.1g, mono 0.9g, poly 1.5g); CARB 61.2g; FIBER 2.6g; CHOL 129mg; IRON 5.2mg; SODIUM 361mg; CALC 83mg

CHICKEN BREAST ROULADES WITH HERBS AND BABY VEGETABLES

Roulade is the French term for a slice of meat rolled around a filling. You can serve the leftover poaching broth as a light soup.

- 2 teaspoons olive oil
- 4 cups torn fresh spinach
- 2 garlic cloves, minced
- 4 (4-ounce) skinned, boned chicken breast halves
- ½ teaspoon pepper
- ¼ teaspoon salt
- 4 (3 x 1-inch) strips bottled roasted red bell pepper
- 3 cups low-salt chicken broth
- 1 cup dry white wine
- ¼ teaspoon salt
- ¼ teaspoon black peppercorns
- 3 bay leaves
- 3 basil sprigs
- 3 thyme sprigs
- 2 tarragon sprigs
- 20 baby carrots, scraped
- 12 trimmed Brussels sprouts
- 8 small boiling onions
- 4 small red potatoes, each cut into 4 slices
- ½ cup chopped fresh flat-leaf parsley

Heat oil in a large Dutch oven over medium heat until hot. Add spinach and garlic; sauté 1 minute or until spinach begins to wilt. Remove from heat; set aside.

Place chicken between 2 sheets of heavy-duty plastic wrap and flatten to ¼-inch thickness using a meat mallet or rolling pin. Sprinkle ½ teaspoon pepper and ¼ teaspoon salt over chicken. Spoon spinach mixture evenly down center of each breast half, leaving a ½-inch border. Arrange bell pepper strips crosswise over spinach, and roll up jelly-roll fashion. Tuck in ends of chicken, and secure each roll with wooden picks; set aside.

Combine broth and next 7 ingredients in pan; bring to a simmer, and cook 5 minutes. Add chicken rolls, carrots, Brussels sprouts, onions, and potatoes; simmer 20 minutes or until chicken is done and vegetables are tender. Discard peppercorns, bay leaves, and herb sprigs.

Remove wooden picks from chicken rolls, and thinly slice each roll. Arrange 1 sliced chicken roll, 5 carrots, 3 Brussels sprouts, 2 onions, and 4 potato slices in each of 4 large shallow bowls. Ladle ½ cup cooking liquid into each bowl, and sprinkle each with 2 tablespoons parsley. Yield: 4 servings.

CALORIES 407 (13% from fat); PROTEIN 37.3g; FAT 5.8g (sat 1.1g, mono 2.5g, poly 1g); CARB 55.2g; FIBER 12.5g; CHOL 66mg; IRON 7.7mg; SODIUM 554mg; CALC 188mg

POACHED PEARS WITH VANILLA-HONEY YOGURT SAUCE

The poaching liquid stains the pears, so turn and baste them frequently to ensure an even color.

1¾ cups water
½ cup honey
2 (3-inch) cinnamon sticks
4 medium Anjou pears, peeled, cored, and cut in half lengthwise
Vanilla-Honey Yogurt Sauce

Combine water and honey in a large nonstick skillet; stir with a wire whisk until blended. Add cinnamon sticks. Arrange pear halves, cut sides down, in a single layer in skillet; bring to a simmer over medium-low heat. Cook 30 minutes or until pears are tender, turning and basting every 10 minutes. Remove pears from skillet with a slotted spoon, and place 2 pear halves in each of 4 individual dessert dishes; set aside, and keep warm.

Bring cooking liquid to a boil over high heat, and cook 7 minutes or until reduced to ½ cup. Discard cinnamon sticks. Spoon 2 tablespoons cooking liquid over each serving; top each with 2 tablespoons Vanilla-Honey Yogurt Sauce. Yield: 4 servings.

CALORIES 264 (6% from fat); PROTEIN 2.3g; FAT 1.5g (sat 0.5g, mono 0.4g, poly 0.2g); CARB 66.1g; FIBER 4.3g; CHOL 3mg; IRON 0.7mg; SODIUM 22mg; CALC 74mg

Vanilla-Honey Yogurt Sauce:

1 (8-ounce) carton vanilla low-fat yogurt
2 tablespoons low-fat sour cream
1 tablespoon honey
½ teaspoon vanilla extract

Combine all ingredients in a bowl; stir well. Cover and chill. Yield: 1 cup (serving size: 2 tablespoons).

CALORIES 38 (19% from fat); PROTEIN 1.5g; FAT 0.8g (sat 0.5g, mono 0.2g, poly 0g); CARB 6.3g; FIBER 0g; CHOL 3mg; IRON 0mg; SODIUM 20mg; CALC 53mg

NEW ENGLAND-STYLE BANANAS FOSTER

Don't overcook the banana mixture, or it will turn dark.

⅓ cup maple syrup
⅓ cup dark rum
3½ cups diagonally sliced firm ripe banana
⅓ cup chopped walnuts, toasted
3 cups vanilla nonfat frozen yogurt

Combine syrup and rum in a large nonstick skillet; bring to a simmer over medium-low heat. Add banana; cook 3 minutes, stirring occasionally. Add walnuts; cook 1 minute. Serve immediately over frozen yogurt. Yield: 6 servings (serving size: ½ cup banana mixture and ½ cup frozen yogurt).

CALORIES 296 (13% from fat); PROTEIN 6.2g; FAT 4.4g (sat 0.4g, mono 0.9g, poly 2.7g); CARB 51.9g; FIBER 3g; CHOL 0mg; IRON 0.7mg; SODIUM 65mg; CALC 156mg

Taking the Worry Out of Curry

"She's coming in now and she's behind time, so make it brief, okay?" The security man was huffing with self-importance.

I straightened my tie and stirred the Kare Poaka (curried pork) one more time, leaving the lid tipped to allow the fragrances of spiced coconut, caramel pork, and Kumera to fill the air.

Suddenly, she was there. She smiled with her eyes just like she did in her photos. Then she caught the aroma. "What is that?" she asked, her head turned slightly. "Kare Poaka, your Majesty," I croaked.

The Queen Mother then moved over to the stove and sniffed appreciatively. "It smells wonderful," she said. But since royalty can never stop for a taste, she smiled warmly and moved on.

The original recipe owed its sniff appeal, in part, to two pounds of pork shoulder, one cup of coconut cream, and liberal use of a mild curry powder for just four servings. The fat grams per serving were 58—43 of them saturated fat.

For my first pass at lightening the recipe, I reduced the meat to 12 ounces (three ounces per person instead of eight) and used yogurt cheese rather than cream. This cut the fat percentage from 65% to 21% and the fat grams to 12.

For the second version, I changed the recipe again to take it down to 14% calories from fat. First, the pork had to come down to about one ounce; then all trace of the saturated coconut fat had to go. Because the other flavors are so robust, the taste so well-developed, I thought of tofu. I added the tofu after everything else was ready for the oven. That way it wouldn't break down when stirred for 40 minutes to absorb all the flavor and color.

CURRIED PORK-AND-SWEET POTATO STEW

The list of ingredients is long, but many are spices that are quick to measure and add. Also, this is a meal in itself so you won't need a side dish.

1½ cups plain low-fat yogurt
1 teaspoon maple syrup
¼ teaspoon coconut extract
2 teaspoons olive oil, divided
¾ pound lean, boneless pork loin, cut into ¾-inch cubes
½ teaspoon dark sesame oil
4 cups (1-inch) peeled, cubed sweet potato
1 cup diced onion
1 cup diced red bell pepper
1 cup diced green bell pepper
1 garlic clove, crushed
1 tablespoon curry powder
1½ cups low-salt canned chicken broth
¼ cup no-salt-added tomato sauce
1 bay leaf
1 tablespoon cornstarch
2 tablespoons water
1 tablespoon fresh lemon juice
1 teaspoon garam masala
¼ teaspoon salt
¼ teaspoon ground red pepper
¼ teaspoon coconut extract
2 cups hot cooked rice (cooked without salt or fat)
1 tablespoon chopped fresh parsley

Place a colander in a 2-quart glass measure or medium bowl. Line colander with 4 layers of cheesecloth, allowing cheesecloth to extend over outside edges. Spoon yogurt into colander. Cover yogurt loosely with plastic wrap; refrigerate 12 hours. Spoon yogurt cheese into a bowl; discard liquid. Add maple syrup and ¼ teaspoon coconut extract to yogurt cheese; stir well, and set aside.

Preheat oven to 350°.

Heat 1 teaspoon olive oil in a large ovenproof Dutch oven over medium-high heat until hot. Add pork, browning well on all sides. Remove pork from pan, and set aside.

Heat the remaining 1 teaspoon olive oil and the sesame oil in pan over medium-high heat until hot. Add sweet potato and next 4 ingredients; sauté 2 minutes. Add curry powder; sauté 3 minutes. Return pork to pan, and stir in broth, tomato sauce, and bay leaf. Bring to a boil; remove from heat, and cover. Bake at 350° for 40 minutes.

Strain pork mixture through a colander into a bowl. Discard bay leaf. Return broth mixture to pan; set pork mixture aside.

Combine cornstarch and water in a bowl; stir well. Add cornstarch mixture, lemon juice, garam masala, salt, and ground red pepper to pan; bring to a boil, and cook 1 minute, stirring constantly.

Add one-fourth of broth mixture to yogurt cheese mixture; stir constantly with a whisk. Add yogurt cheese mixture to pan. Return pork mixture to pan; cook over medium heat until heated (do not boil). Remove from heat; stir in ¼ teaspoon coconut extract. Serve over rice; sprinkle with parsley. Yield: 4 servings (serving size: 1¼ cups stew and ½ cup rice).

CALORIES 516 (21% from fat); PROTEIN 27.9g; FAT 12g (sat 3.6g, mono 5.4g, poly 1.6g); CARB 73.4g; FIBER 7.2g; CHOL 53mg; IRON 4.6mg; SODIUM 280mg; CALC 155mg

CURRIED PORK-AND-SWEET POTATO STEW WITH TOFU:

- Reduce olive oil to ½ teaspoon; use to brown pork.
- Reduce pork to ¼ pound.
- Add 1 (10.5-ounce) package light tofu, cut into 32 cubes. Add tofu at the same time browned pork is returned to pan.

CALORIES 443 (14% from fat); PROTEIN 20.6g; FAT 6.9g (sat 1.9g, mono 2.2g, poly 1g); CARB 74.2g; FIBER 6.7g; CHOL 19mg; IRON 4.1mg; SODIUM 305mg; CALC 151mg

KITCHEN TIPS

Choose a pure coconut extract such as one from John Wagner & Sons (800/832-9017). If you use an artificial flavor, your dish might smell like suntan lotion.

- Read the label carefully when selecting tofu. We used firm Lite Silken Tofu from Mori-Nu. A 3-ounce portion contains 1 gram of fat, compared to 7 grams in regular firm tofu.
- Garam masala is a blend of Indian ground spices which can include black pepper, cinnamon, cloves, coriander, cumin, cardamom, dried chiles, and other spices. It can be found in Indian markets or the gourmet section of many supermarkets.
- Remember that the yogurt has to drain 12 hours. You can make a batch of this yogurt cheese ahead of time and store it in an airtight container so it's ready to use whenever you need it.

TALE OF THE TAPE

	Calories per Serving	Fat Grams per Serving	% Calories from Fat per Serving
Curried Pork-and-Sweet Potato Stew	516	12g	21%
Lighter-Than-Light Version (with Tofu)	443	6.9g	14%

Is There a Pizza in the House?

There can be. All it takes is store-bought crusts and our innovative toppings.

Although the first U.S. pizzeria opened in New York in 1895, it wasn't until after World War II that pizza started sweeping the nation. American servicemen returning from Italy began raving about this great Italian dish. Its popularity increased rapidly, and today Americans eat 100 acres of pizza a day, with most of it delivered to their front doors or served in fast food restaurants.

Pizza is actually simple to prepare—except for the yeast-dough crust. Well, we've eliminated that crust procedure, so you can have a pizza in the oven in a matter of minutes.

HAMBURGER-MUSHROOM PIZZA

Preparation time: 15 minutes
Cooking time: 9 minutes

1 (16-ounce) loaf unsliced Italian bread
½ cup traditional bottled pizza sauce
8 (⅛-inch-thick) slices onion, separated into rings
1 cup presliced fresh mushrooms
6 ounces ultra-lean ground beef
1 teaspoon dried Italian seasoning
½ teaspoon garlic powder
¼ teaspoon dried crushed red pepper
1½ cups (6 ounces) preshredded pizza double-cheese (a blend of part-skim mozzarella and Cheddar cheese)

Preheat oven to 500°.

Cut bread in half horizontally. Place both halves of bread, cut side up, on a large baking sheet. Spread ¼ cup pizza sauce over each half of bread. Place onion rings and mushrooms evenly over bread halves. Crumble beef into ½-inch pieces, and spoon beef evenly over bread halves. Sprinkle Italian seasoning, garlic powder, and red pepper evenly over each pizza, and top each with ¾ cup cheese.

Bake at 500° for 9 minutes or until beef is done and cheese melts. Cut each half into 3 equal pieces. Yield: 6 servings (serving size: 1 piece).

CALORIES 301 (29% from fat); PROTEIN 15.1g; FAT 9.7g (sat 2.7g, mono 2.1g, poly 0.8g); CARB 35.4g; FIBER 2g; CHOL 31mg; IRON 2mg; SODIUM 542mg; CALC 155mg

PESTO-PLUM TOMATO PIZZA

Be sure to purchase a good quality pesto-basil sauce. Although it may cost more, the difference will be noticeable.
Preparation time: 15 minutes
Cooking time: 8 minutes

1 (14.5-ounce) package focaccia or 1 (1-pound) Italian cheese-flavored thin pizza crust (such as Boboli)
2 tablespoons pesto-basil sauce (such as Pesto Sanremo)
¾ pound plum tomatoes, sliced
2 large garlic cloves, thinly sliced
½ cup (2 ounces) preshredded part-skim mozzarella cheese
⅓ cup preshredded fresh Parmesan cheese
½ teaspoon coarsely ground pepper
2 tablespoons thinly sliced fresh basil leaves

Preheat oven to 450°.

Place crust on a large baking sheet. Spread pesto sauce over crust; top with tomato, garlic, and cheeses. Sprinkle with pepper. Bake at 450° for 8 minutes or until cheese melts. Remove from oven; sprinkle with basil. Cut into 8 slices. Yield: 4 servings (serving size: 2 slices).

CALORIES 388 (29% from fat); PROTEIN 17.9g; FAT 12.4g (sat 5.3g, mono 4.7g, poly 1.8g); CARB 56.5g; FIBER 5.6g; CHOL 14mg; IRON 1.5mg; SODIUM 794mg; CALC 253mg

---

MENU SUGGESTION

CANADIAN BACON-AND-PINEAPPLE PIZZAS

Sesame salad

*Combine ½ cup rice vinegar, 2 tablespoons soy sauce, 2 tablespoons sesame oil, 1½ teaspoons sugar, and 1 garlic clove; serve over lettuce. Top with a cherry tomato, and sprinkle with toasted sesame seeds.

CANADIAN BACON-AND-PINEAPPLE PIZZAS

Preparation time: 10 minutes
Cooking time: 11 minutes

6 English muffins, split
½ cup tub cream cheese with pineapple
6 (¾-ounce) slices sandwich-style Canadian bacon, coarsely chopped
¼ cup sliced green onions
1 (8-ounce) can unsweetened pineapple tidbits, drained
1½ cups (6 ounces) preshredded nonfat pizza cheese (a blend of nonfat mozzarella and nonfat Cheddar cheeses)

Place muffin halves, cut sides up, on a large baking sheet. Broil 3 minutes or until lightly toasted.

Preheat oven to 425°.

Spread about 2 teaspoons cream cheese over each muffin half. Place Canadian bacon, green onions, and pineapple tidbits evenly over muffin halves; sprinkle each with 2 tablespoons pizza cheese. Bake at 425° for 8 minutes or until cheese melts. Yield: 6 servings (serving size: 2 muffin halves).

CALORIES 373 (21% from fat); PROTEIN 17.3g; FAT 8.9g (sat 4.7g, mono 2.7g, poly 1.1g); CARB 39.9g; FIBER 0.2g; CHOL 36mg; IRON 2.4mg; SODIUM 901mg; CALC 330mg

SOUTH-OF-THE-BORDER PIZZA

For spicier pizzas, serve with salsa and pickled jalapeño slices.
Preparation time: 10 minutes
Cooking time: 16 minutes

6 (7-inch) pita bread rounds, unsplit
Vegetable cooking spray
1 (16-ounce) can fat-free refried beans
1 (4.5-ounce) can chopped green chiles, drained
½ cup diced tomato
¼ cup sliced ripe olives
¾ cup (3 ounces) preshredded Mexican 4-cheese blend (a blend of Monterey Jack, Cheddar, queso quesadilla, and asadero cheeses)
1½ cups thinly sliced iceberg lettuce
¼ cup plus 2 tablespoons nonfat sour cream

Preheat oven to 400°.
Place pita rounds on a large baking sheet coated with cooking spray, overlapping slightly. Bake pita rounds at 400° for 8 minutes or until crisp, turning after 4 minutes. Let cool slightly on a wire rack.
Combine beans and chiles in a bowl; stir well. Spread about ⅓ cup bean mixture over each pita round. (Support the underneath side of the pita with your hand so it does not crack.) Sprinkle tomato, olives, and cheese evenly over pizzas. Place pizzas on baking sheet.
Bake at 400° for 8 minutes or until bean mixture is hot and cheese melts. Remove from oven; top each pizza with ¼ cup lettuce and 1 tablespoon sour cream. Yield: 6 servings.

CALORIES 293 (22% from fat); PROTEIN 14.1g; FAT 7.1g (sat 3.5g, mono 1g, poly 0.7g); CARB 43.4g; FIBER 5g; CHOL 14mg; IRON 3.2mg; SODIUM 736mg; CALC 98mg

ROASTED-VEGETABLE PIZZA

Roasting the vegetables adds a robust flavor.
Preparation time: 10 minutes
Cooking time: 34 minutes

1 (10-ounce) can refrigerated pizza crust dough
Vegetable cooking spray
1 tablespoon fresh or 1 teaspoon dried thyme leaves
2 tablespoons balsamic vinegar
1 teaspoon olive oil
¼ teaspoon salt
4 small round red potatoes, each cut into 8 wedges
4 garlic cloves, thinly sliced
1 small yellow squash, cut into ¼-inch-thick slices
1 small red bell pepper, cut into 2-inch-thick pieces
1 small sweet onion, cut into 12 wedges
1¼ cups (5 ounces) shredded sharp provolone cheese

Preheat oven to 425°.
Unroll pizza dough onto a large baking sheet coated with cooking spray; fold under edges of dough to form an 11-inch circle. Bake at 425° for 7 minutes; set aside.
Preheat oven to 500°.
Combine thyme and next 8 ingredients in a bowl; toss well. Place vegetable mixture in a 13 x 9-inch baking dish. Bake at 500° for 15 minutes, stirring halfway through cooking time.
Reduce oven temperature to 425°. Sprinkle half of cheese over prepared pizza crust. Arrange roasted vegetables over cheese, and top with remaining half of cheese. Bake at 425° for 12 minutes or until crust is lightly browned. Yield: 6 servings (serving size: 1 slice).

CALORIES 293 (27% from fat); PROTEIN 10g; FAT 8.8g (sat 4.2g, mono 2.3g, poly 0.4g); CARB 40.2g; FIBER 2.8g; CHOL 16mg; IRON 2mg; SODIUM 539mg; CALC 208mg

SPINACH-MUSHROOM PIZZA

To save time, thaw and drain the frozen spinach in advance.
Preparation time: 9 minutes
Cooking time: 15 minutes

Vegetable cooking spray
2 tablespoons cornmeal
1 (10-ounce) can refrigerated pizza crust dough
1 (10-ounce) package frozen chopped spinach, thawed, drained, and squeezed dry
¾ cup (3 ounces) preshredded part-skim mozzarella cheese
2 teaspoons bottled minced garlic
1 teaspoon dried Italian seasoning
¼ teaspoon pepper
1 (4.5-ounce) jar sliced mushrooms, drained
2 (14½-ounce) cans pasta-style tomatoes, drained
½ cup crumbled feta cheese

Preheat oven to 425°.
Coat a 15 x 10-inch jelly-roll pan with cooking spray, and sprinkle with cornmeal. Unroll pizza dough, and press dough into pan. Bake at 425° for 6 minutes or just until crust begins to brown.
Combine spinach, mozzarella cheese, garlic, Italian seasoning, and pepper in a bowl; stir well. Spread spinach mixture over crust, leaving a ½-inch border. Top with mushrooms and tomatoes; sprinkle with feta cheese. Bake at 425° for 9 minutes or until crust is lightly browned. (Feta cheese will not melt.) Cut into 6 equal pieces. Yield: 6 servings.

CALORIES 263 (21% from fat); PROTEIN 9.4g; FAT 6g (sat 3.4g, mono 1.6g, poly 0.6g); CARB 33.1g; FIBER 4.3g; CHOL 17mg; IRON 1.6mg; SODIUM 1,154mg; CALC 202mg

ROASTED CHICKEN-AND-WHITE BEAN PIZZAS

The pizza crusts used in this recipe are usually found on a free-standing display in front of the dairy section.
Preparation time: 17 minutes
Cooking time: 8 minutes

1   (15.8-ounce) can Great Northern beans, drained
1   teaspoon lemon juice
⅛   teaspoon garlic powder
⅛   teaspoon pepper
1   (½-pound) package ready-to-eat roasted boneless, skinless chicken breast halves, chopped
¼   teaspoon dried rosemary, crushed
1   (12-ounce) package of 3 (7-inch) pizza crusts (such as Mama Mary's)
1   cup thinly sliced fresh spinach
¾   cup (3 ounces) shredded sharp provolone cheese

Preheat oven to 450°.
Place first 4 ingredients in a blender or food processor; cover and process until smooth. Set aside.
Combine chicken and rosemary in a large bowl, and toss well. Spread ⅓ cup bean mixture evenly over each crust, leaving a ¼-inch border. Top each crust with ½ cup chicken, ⅓ cup spinach, and ¼ cup cheese.
Place pizzas directly on oven rack, and bake at 450° for 8 minutes or until crusts are golden. Yield: 6 servings (serving size: ½ pizza).

CALORIES 338 (25% from fat); PROTEIN 19.4g; FAT 9.6g (sat 3.5g, mono 2.2g, poly 3.1g); CARB 42.6g; FIBER 5g; CHOL 33mg; IRON 2.5mg; SODIUM 584mg; CALC 179mg

---

IN SEASON

Do the Ripe Thing

Few gardening tasks are as pleasant as harvesting the season's first strawberries. No color, shape, texture, or perfume better says that winter is over. And what sunny, delicious times lie ahead—just imagine sliced strawberries cascading off a heavenly angel food cake, floating in a custard sauce, or splashed with liqueur. If you don't have your own strawberry patch, don't fret. Do your picking at your local market, where trucks are now unloading the season's first and freshest supply of bright-red strawberries.

MARINATED STRAWBERRIES IN ORANGE LIQUEUR

This recipe combines the sweet flavor of the strawberry and the tangy taste of orange.

3   cups quartered strawberries
1   tablespoon sugar
2   tablespoons Grand Marnier or other orange-flavored liqueur, divided
¾   cup vanilla low-fat frozen yogurt, softened
1   cup frozen reduced-calorie whipped topping, thawed
1   teaspoon lemon juice

Combine strawberries, sugar, and 1 tablespoon liqueur in a bowl; toss gently. Cover and chill.
Place frozen yogurt in a bowl, and stir until smooth; fold in whipped topping. Add remaining liqueur and lemon juice; stir well.
Spoon ½ cup strawberry mixture into each of 6 dessert dishes; top with ¼ cup yogurt mixture. Yield: 6 servings.

CALORIES 93 (21% from fat); PROTEIN 1.5g; FAT 2.2g (sat 1.3g, mono 0g, poly 0.7g); CARB 15.4g; FIBER 1.9g; CHOL 2mg; IRON 0.3mg; SODIUM 16mg; CALC 41mg

---

STRAWBERRY-BANANA SHORTCAKE

Vegetable cooking spray
1   egg
½   cup sugar
¾   cup low-fat buttermilk
¼   cup margarine, melted
1   teaspoon vanilla extract
2⅓   cups sifted cake flour
2   teaspoons baking powder
¼   teaspoon baking soda
¼   teaspoon salt
1   cup vanilla low-fat yogurt
¼   cup firmly packed brown sugar
1¼   cups thinly sliced strawberries
1¼   cups sliced ripe banana
2   teaspoons lemon juice
1   tablespoon powdered sugar

Preheat oven to 350°.
Coat a 9-inch round cake pan with cooking spray, and line bottom with wax paper. Coat wax paper with cooking spray; set aside.
Beat egg at medium speed of an electric mixer until foamy; gradually add ½ cup sugar, beating well. Combine buttermilk, margarine, and vanilla; set aside. Combine flour and next 3 ingredients. Beating at low speed, add flour mixture to egg mixture alternately with buttermilk mixture, beginning and ending with flour mixture. Pour batter into prepared pan. Bake at 350° for 28 minutes or until a wooden pick inserted in center comes out clean. Let cool in pan 10 minutes on a wire rack; remove from pan. Let cool completely on wire rack.
Combine yogurt and brown sugar; stir well. Using a serrated knife, cut cake in half horizontally; place bottom layer, cut side up, on a serving plate. Spread with half of yogurt mixture; top with strawberries. Combine banana and lemon juice; toss gently. Drain banana, and discard juice. Arrange banana over strawberries; drizzle with remaining yogurt mixture. Top with remaining layer. Sift powdered sugar over top of cake. Yield: 8 servings (serving size: 1 wedge).

CALORIES 282 (21% from fat); PROTEIN 5.4g; FAT 6.5g (sat 1.5g, mono 2.6g, poly 1.8g); CARB 51.4g; FIBER 1.2g; CHOL 26mg; IRON 2.5mg; SODIUM 208mg; CALC 146mg

STRAWBERRY-MERINGUE TORTE

1 (32-ounce) carton vanilla
    low-fat yogurt
6 egg whites
½ teaspoon cream of tartar
½ teaspoon imitation black
    walnut extract
¼ cup plus 2 tablespoons
    granulated sugar
8 whole strawberries with caps
¼ cup red currant jelly, melted
1 cup nonfat sour cream
½ cup sifted powdered sugar
½ teaspoon vanilla extract
2 cups quartered strawberries
2 teaspoons powdered sugar

Place colander in a 2-quart glass measure or medium bowl. Line colander with 4 layers of cheesecloth, allowing cheesecloth to extend over edge. Spoon yogurt into colander. Cover loosely with plastic wrap; refrigerate 12 hours. Spoon yogurt cheese into a bowl; discard liquid. Cover and chill.

Place parchment paper over a large baking sheet. Draw 3 (8-inch) circles on paper. Turn paper over, and secure with masking tape.

Preheat oven to 200°.

Beat egg whites and cream of tartar at high speed of an electric mixer until foamy; add black walnut extract. Gradually add granulated sugar, 2 tablespoons at a time, beating until stiff peaks form (do not underbeat).

Spoon egg white mixture evenly inside circles of prepared baking sheet; using the back of a spoon, spread egg white mixture to fill the circles.

Bake at 200° for 2½ hours or until dry. Turn oven off, and let meringues cool in closed oven at least 12 hours. Carefully remove meringues from paper; set aside.

Combine 8 whole strawberries and jelly in a small bowl; toss gently to coat. Drain strawberries, and discard remaining jelly. Place glazed strawberries on wax paper; set aside.

Add sour cream, ½ cup powdered sugar, and vanilla to yogurt cheese; stir well. Gently fold in quartered strawberries.

To serve, place 1 meringue circle on a serving platter, and gently spread with half of yogurt cheese-strawberry mixture. Top with another meringue circle; gently spread with remaining yogurt cheese-strawberry mixture. Top with remaining meringue circle; sift 2 teaspoons powdered sugar over top of torte, and garnish with glazed strawberries. Yield: 8 servings (serving size: 1 wedge).

CALORIES 197 (10% from fat); PROTEIN 9.6g; FAT 2.1g (sat 0.9g, mono 0.4g, poly 0.1g); CARB 33.9g; FIBER 1.4g; CHOL 3mg; IRON 0.2mg; SODIUM 104mg; CALC 137mg

STRAWBERRIES AND RASPBERRIES IN CUSTARD SAUCE

1½ cups skim milk
¼ cup sugar
1 tablespoon all-purpose flour
4 egg yolks
¾ teaspoon vanilla extract
1½ cups halved strawberries
1½ cups raspberries
Mint sprigs (optional)

Combine first 4 ingredients in the top of a double boiler. Cook over simmering water 38 minutes or until mixture thickens and coats back of a metal spoon, stirring constantly. Pour custard into a bowl, and stir in vanilla. Let custard sauce cool to room temperature. Cover and chill.

Spoon about ⅓ cup custard sauce into each of 6 stemmed glasses; top each with ¼ cup strawberries and ¼ cup raspberries. Garnish with mint, if desired. Yield: 6 servings.

CALORIES 127 (28% from fat); PROTEIN 4.6g; FAT 3.9g (sat 1.2g, mono 1.4g, poly 0.7g); CARB 18.8g; FIBER 3.3g; CHOL 146mg; IRON 0.8mg; SODIUM 37mg; CALC 103mg

STRAWBERRY-RHUBARB TOPPING

3½ cups coarsely chopped rhubarb
½ cup sugar
⅓ cup water
1 tablespoon water
2½ teaspoons cornstarch
3 cups sliced strawberries
½ teaspoon vanilla extract

Combine first three ingredients in a medium saucepan; bring to a boil. Reduce heat, and simmer, uncovered, 5 minutes or until rhubarb is tender. Combine 1 tablespoon water and cornstarch; stir well, and add to rhubarb mixture. Bring to a boil, and cook 1 minute or until thickened, stirring constantly.

Remove from heat; stir in strawberries and vanilla. Serve warm or chilled over angel food cake, sponge cake, or vanilla low-fat ice cream. Yield: 3⅓ cups (serving size: ⅓ cup).

CALORIES 64 (4% from fat); PROTEIN 0.6g; FAT 0.3g (sat 0g, mono 0g, poly 0.1g); CARB 15.7g; FIBER 1.4g; CHOL 0mg; IRON 0.3mg; SODIUM 2mg; CALC 43mg

FOR TWO

Ring Them Bells

At last! Stuffed-pepper recipes that satisfy today's tastes and make a meal in themselves. From vegetarian to Southwestern, these dressed-up peppers—including poblanos—go beyond the old standard of meat-and-rice fillings.

ITALIAN WHITE BEAN-AND-SPINACH CUPS

Sun-dried tomato sprinkles can be found in the canned-tomato section of the supermarket.

    2 large red bell peppers (about 1
         pound)
    1 teaspoon olive oil
    ½ cup sliced green onions
    1 garlic clove, minced
    1 cup thinly sliced spinach leaves
    ⅓ cup low-salt chicken broth
    1 (19-ounce) can cannellini beans
         or other white beans, drained
         and divided
    ½ cup crumbled feta cheese with
         basil and tomato
    2 tablespoons sun-dried tomato
         sprinkles
    2 tablespoons sliced ripe olives
    1 tablespoon balsamic vinegar
    ½ teaspoon dried Italian seasoning
    2 teaspoons Italian-seasoned
         breadcrumbs
    1 teaspoon grated Parmesan cheese

Preheat oven to 350°.

Cut tops off bell peppers; discard tops, seeds, and membranes. Cook peppers in boiling water 5 minutes; drain and set aside.

Heat oil in a large nonstick skillet over medium-high heat until hot. Add green onions and garlic; sauté 2 minutes. Stir in spinach; cook 1 minute or until spinach wilts. Remove from heat, and set aside.

Place broth and ½ cup beans in a food processor or blender; cover and process until smooth. Stir bean purée into spinach mixture. Add remaining beans, feta cheese, tomato sprinkles, olives, vinegar, and Italian seasoning; stir well.

Divide bean mixture evenly between peppers. Combine breadcrumbs and Parmesan cheese; sprinkle evenly over bean mixture. Place stuffed peppers in an 8-inch square baking dish; bake at 350° for 25 minutes. Yield: 2 servings.

CALORIES 369 (29% from fat); PROTEIN 18g; FAT 11.9g; (sat 5.2g, mono 3.8g, poly 1.2g); CARB 49.6g; FIBER 5.8g; CHOL 26mg; IRON 8mg; SODIUM 986mg; CALC 275mg

SONORAN-STYLE POBLANO CHILES

    2 large poblano chiles (about
         8 ounces)
    2 large tomatillos
       Vegetable cooking spray
    ⅓ cup chopped red bell pepper
    ¼ cup chopped green onions
    1 garlic clove, crushed
    2 tablespoons chopped fresh
         cilantro
    ½ teaspoon chili powder
    ¼ teaspoon ground cumin
    ¼ teaspoon pepper
    1 cup drained canned black beans,
         divided
    1 cup shredded cooked chicken
         breast
    ⅓ cup frozen whole-kernel corn,
         thawed
    ¼ cup nonfat sour cream
    ¼ cup (1 ounce) shredded
         reduced-fat Monterey Jack
         cheese, divided

Preheat oven to 400°.

Cut chiles in half lengthwise; discard seeds and membranes. Set aside.

Remove husks from tomatillos, and chop. Coat a medium nonstick skillet with cooking spray, and place over medium-high heat until hot; add tomatillos, bell pepper, green onions, and garlic; sauté 3 minutes. Remove from heat; stir in cilantro, chili powder, cumin, and pepper. Set aside.

Place ½ cup beans in a bowl; mash. Stir in remaining ½ cup beans, bell pepper mixture, chicken, corn, sour cream, and 2 tablespoons cheese.

Divide bean mixture evenly among chile halves. Place stuffed chiles in an 8-inch square baking dish. Sprinkle remaining 2 tablespoons cheese over stuffed chiles; bake at 400° for 20 minutes. Serve with flour tortillas and salsa. Yield: 2 servings (serving size: 2 stuffed chile halves).

Note: You can also substitute ¼ cup chopped drained canned tomatillos or ¼ cup chopped green tomato for fresh tomatillos, if desired.

CALORIES 387 (16% from fat); PROTEIN 38.3g; FAT 6.9g; (sat 2.3g, mono 2g, poly 0.9g); CARB 46.8g; FIBER 5.5g; CHOL 64mg; IRON 6.1mg; SODIUM 363mg; CALC 213mg

┌─────────────────────────────────┐
│ MENU SUGGESTION   │
│   │
│ SANTA FE STUFFED   │
│ CHILES   │
│   │
│ *Mango slaw*   │
│   │
│ *Jalapeño rice*   │
│   │
│ *For slaw, combine cabbage,   │
│ mango, tomato, serrano chile,   │
│ and green onions. Toss with   │
│ lime juice and olive oil.   │
│ *Cook rice with minced jalapeño │
│ to taste.   │
└─────────────────────────────────┘

SANTA FE STUFFED CHILES

Smaller than bell peppers, poblano chiles are usually dark green and have a rich flavor that runs from mild to slightly hot.

    3 medium poblano chiles (about
         9 ounces)
    ⅓ cup grated Parmesan cheese
    ½ cup fresh corn kernels
    ½ cup finely chopped red onion
    ⅓ cup finely chopped plum
         tomato
    ¼ cup fine, dry breadcrumbs
    ¼ cup chopped fresh cilantro
    2 tablespoons plain nonfat
         yogurt
    2 tablespoons reduced-fat
         mayonnaise
    1 teaspoon chili powder
    ½ teaspoon pepper
       Vegetable cooking spray
    6 teaspoons plain nonfat yogurt

Preheat oven to 375°.

Cut chiles in half lengthwise; discard seeds and membranes.

Combine cheese and next 9 ingredients in a bowl; stir well. Divide vegetable mixture evenly among chile halves. Place stuffed chiles on a baking sheet coated with cooking spray. Bake at 375° for 20 minutes. Spoon 1 teaspoon yogurt onto each chile half. Yield: 2 servings (serving size: 3 stuffed chile halves).

CALORIES 310 (30% from fat); PROTEIN 16.2g; FAT 11.2g (sat 5.2g, mono 2.3g, poly 2.9g); CARB 39.7g; FIBER 5.8g; CHOL 16mg; IRON 3.5mg; SODIUM 705mg; CALC 408mg

PIZZERIA PEPPERS

2 large green bell peppers (about 1 pound)
½ pound Italian-flavored turkey sausage
½ cup chopped onion
2 garlic cloves, minced
½ cup sliced mushrooms
1 tablespoon grated Parmesan cheese
2 tablespoons sliced green olives
½ teaspoon dried Italian seasoning
⅛ teaspoon salt
1 (8-ounce) can no-salt-added tomato sauce
¼ cup (1 ounce) shredded part-skim mozzarella cheese
2 (1-ounce) slices Italian bread, toasted

Preheat oven to 350°.

Cut tops off bell peppers; discard tops, seeds, and membranes. Cook peppers in boiling water 5 minutes; drain and set aside.

Remove casings from sausage, and discard casings. Cook sausage, onion, and garlic in a large nonstick skillet over medium heat until browned, stirring to crumble sausage. Add mushrooms; sauté 2 minutes or until tender. Stir in Parmesan cheese, olives, Italian seasoning, salt, and tomato sauce; cook 4 minutes, stirring often.

Divide sausage mixture evenly between peppers, and top with mozzarella cheese. Place stuffed peppers in an 8-inch square baking dish; bake at 350° for 15 minutes. Serve with toasted bread. (Serving size: 1 stuffed pepper and 1 bread slice). Yield: 2 servings.

CALORIES 370 (30% from fat); PROTEIN 23.1g; FAT 12.5g (sat 4.1g, mono 3.8g, poly 2.3g); CARB 44g; FIBER 5.8g; CHOL 55mg; IRON 5.5mg; SODIUM 920mg; CALC 189mg

MOROCCAN COUSCOUS PEPPERS

2 large red bell peppers (about 1 pound)
Olive oil-flavored vegetable cooking spray
½ cup chopped onion
¼ cup sliced mushrooms
¼ cup sliced celery
¼ cup peeled, chopped Rome apple
1 garlic clove, minced
¾ cup low-salt chicken broth
¼ teaspoon salt
¼ teaspoon ground cumin
¼ teaspoon pepper
⅛ teaspoon ground turmeric (optional)
½ cup uncooked couscous
1 teaspoon olive oil
2 tablespoons raisins
1 tablespoon pine nuts, toasted
1 tablespoon chopped fresh parsley

Preheat oven to 350°.

Cut tops off bell peppers; discard tops, seeds, and membranes. Cook peppers in boiling water 5 minutes; drain and set aside.

Coat a large nonstick skillet with cooking spray, and place skillet over medium-high heat until hot. Add onion, mushrooms, celery, apple, and garlic; sauté 3 minutes. Remove from heat; set aside.

Combine broth, salt, cumin, pepper, and turmeric in a medium saucepan. Bring to a boil; stir in couscous and oil. Remove from heat; cover and let stand 5 minutes. Fluff with a fork. Add onion mixture, raisins, pine nuts, and parsley; stir well. Divide couscous mixture evenly between peppers. Place stuffed peppers in an 8-inch square baking dish; bake at 350° for 15 minutes. Yield: 2 servings.

CALORIES 287 (29% from fat); PROTEIN 8.3g; FAT 9.2g (sat 1.8g, mono 3.4g, poly 2.6g); CARB 49.1g; FIBER 7.1g; CHOL 0mg; IRON 4.8mg; SODIUM 355mg; CALC 43mg

HOPPIN' JOHN PEPPERS WITH SPICY CHIPS

2 large green bell peppers (about 1 pound)
Vegetable cooking spray
½ cup chopped 33%-less-sodium cooked ham
¼ cup chopped onion
¼ cup thinly sliced celery
1 garlic clove, minced
1 cup drained canned black-eyed peas
⅔ cup cooked long-grain rice
⅓ cup diced tomato
1 teaspoon Worcestershire sauce
¼ teaspoon dried thyme
¼ teaspoon hot sauce
Dash of ground red pepper
2 tablespoons nonfat sour cream
2 tablespoons (½ ounce) finely shredded reduced-fat sharp Cheddar cheese
Spicy Chips

Preheat oven to 350°.

Cut tops off bell peppers; discard seeds and membranes. Chop tops to measure ⅓ cup; set chopped bell pepper aside.

Cook bell peppers in boiling water 5 minutes; drain and set aside.

Coat a medium saucepan with cooking spray, and place skillet over medium-high heat until hot. Add ⅓ cup chopped bell pepper, ham, onion, celery, and garlic; sauté 8 minutes or until tender.

Remove ham mixture from heat; stir in the black-eyed peas and long-grain rice, diced tomato, Worcestershire sauce, thyme, hot sauce, and ground red pepper. Divide the ham mixture evenly between bell peppers. Place the stuffed bell peppers in an 8-inch square baking dish; cover and bake at 350° for 20 minutes.

Spoon 1 tablespoon sour cream and 1 tablespoon cheese on top of each stuffed pepper. Serve with Spicy Chips. Yield: 2 servings (serving size: 1 stuffed pepper and 4 chips).

CALORIES 395 (17% from fat); PROTEIN 23.1g; FAT 7.6g (sat 2.1g, mono 2.2g, poly 1.7g); CARB 60.9g; FIBER 6.8g; CHOL 26mg; IRON 5.5mg; SODIUM 547mg; CALC 154mg

Spicy Chips:

- 1 (8-inch) flour tortilla
- Butter-flavored vegetable cooking spray
- ⅛ teaspoon garlic powder
- ⅛ teaspoon ground cumin
- ⅛ teaspoon chili powder

Preheat oven to 350°.

Cut tortilla into 8 wedges, and place on a baking sheet. Lightly coat wedges with cooking spray. Combine garlic powder, cumin, and chili powder; sprinkle evenly over wedges. Bake at 350° for 12 minutes or until crisp. Yield: 2 servings (serving size: 4 wedges).

CALORIES 73 (23% from fat); PROTEIN 1.9g; FAT 1.9g (sat 0.2g, mono 0.6g, poly 0.6g); CARB 11.9g; FIBER 0.7g; CHOL 0mg; IRON 0.8mg; SODIUM 102mg; CALC 28mg

LIGHTEN UP

Strawberry Shortcut

Without Strawberry Shortcake, the month of May wouldn't be nearly as merry. We've done our part, lightening this classic seasonal dessert.

STRAWBERRY SHORTCAKE

- 4 cups sliced fresh strawberries
- ¼ cup sugar
- Vegetable cooking spray
- 1 teaspoon all-purpose flour
- ⅓ cup margarine, softened
- ½ cup sugar
- 1¾ cups all-purpose flour
- 1½ teaspoons baking powder
- ¼ teaspoon salt
- ¾ cup skim milk
- ¼ teaspoon almond extract
- 2 egg whites
- ⅛ teaspoon cream of tartar
- 2 tablespoons sugar
- 1 tablespoon turbinado sugar
- 2 cups frozen reduced-calorie whipped topping, thawed and divided
- Mint sprig (optional)

Combine sliced strawberries and ¼ cup sugar in a bowl; stir well. Cover and chill 2 hours.

Preheat oven to 375°.

Line a 9-inch round cake pan with wax paper. Coat pan with cooking spray, and dust with 1 teaspoon flour; set aside.

Beat margarine at medium speed of an electric mixer until creamy; gradually add ½ cup sugar, beating until light and fluffy (about 5 minutes).

Combine 1¾ cups flour, baking powder, and salt; stir well. Add flour mixture to margarine mixture alternately with milk, beginning and ending with flour mixture. Stir in almond extract.

Beat egg whites and cream of tartar at high speed of mixer until foamy. Gradually add 2 tablespoons sugar, 1 tablespoon at a time, beating until stiff peaks form. Gently stir about one-fourth of egg white mixture into batter. Gently fold in remaining egg white mixture.

Pour batter into prepared pan. Sprinkle turbinado sugar over batter. Bake at 375° for 25 minutes or until a wooden pick inserted in center comes out clean. Let cool in pan 10 minutes on a wire rack; remove from pan, and let cool completely on wire rack.

Slice shortcake in half horizontally. Place bottom half of shortcake, cut side up, on a serving plate. Drain strawberries, reserving juice; drizzle half of juice over bottom cake layer. Spread 1 cup whipped topping over cake layer, and arrange half of strawberries over whipped topping. Top with remaining cake layer, cut side down, and drizzle with remaining reserved juice. Spread remaining 1 cup whipped topping over top cake layer, and arrange remaining half of strawberries over whipped topping. Garnish with a mint sprig, if desired. Yield: 10 servings.

CALORIES 258 (29% from fat); PROTEIN 4.2g; FAT 8.2g (sat 2.4g, mono 2.7g, poly 2.6g); CARB 42.7g; FIBER 2.1g; CHOL 1mg; IRON 1.3mg; SODIUM 160mg; CALC 73mg

BEFORE & AFTER	
SERVING SIZE	
1 piece	1 piece
CALORIES	
384	258
FAT	
19.9g	8.2g
PERCENT OF TOTAL CALORIES	
49%	29%
CHOLESTEROL	
103mg	1mg
SODIUM	
148mg	160mg

HOW WE DID IT

- In the shortcake, used 2 egg whites instead of 2 whole eggs and margarine in place of butter.
- For the filling and topping, substituted frozen reduced-calorie whipped topping for heavy whipping cream. This also saves you from having to whip the cream.
- Sprinkled turbinado sugar over top of cake before baking. Turbinado sugar crystals are blond-colored and coarser than granulated sugar, which adds a more interesting texture to the crust. If you don't have any, use granulated sugar.
- To keep the cake from sticking to the pan, lined the bottom with wax paper and coated with cooking spray and a little flour.

Bed and Breakfast

Give a special treat on Mother's Day: Let Mom sleep in while you cook breakfast with easy recipes.

You've just entered the Mother's Day Zone. Submitted for your approval: One day of the year when Mom gets to sleep as late as she wants while her family makes breakfast for her—and serves it to her in bed. Although Mom is indeed worthy of a 10-course, Babette-like feast on this special holiday, the following easy-to-do breakfast recipes by our readers will certainly wow her. Now, if you want to impress her even more, don't stop with breakfast—check out our other recipes for all kinds of lunch and dinner ideas. She'll think she's in another dimension.

APPLE PANCAKES

—Clay Livingston, Front Royal, Virginia

1 cup whole wheat flour
1 cup all-purpose flour
2 teaspoons baking soda
2 teaspoons baking powder
1 teaspoon ground cinnamon
½ teaspoon salt
Dash of ground nutmeg
2 cups low-fat buttermilk
1 tablespoon honey
1 tablespoon molasses
1 tablespoon margarine, melted
2 teaspoons lemon juice
2 eggs
2 cups finely chopped Granny Smith apple
Vegetable cooking spray

Combine first 7 ingredients in a large bowl; stir well. Combine buttermilk and next 5 ingredients in a small bowl; stir well. Add to flour mixture, stirring until smooth. Fold in apple. Let stand 5 minutes.

Spoon about ¼ cup batter for each pancake onto a hot nonstick griddle or nonstick skillet coated with cooking spray. Turn pancakes when tops are covered with bubbles and edges look cooked. Yield: 14 pancakes (serving size: 2 pancakes).

CALORIES 232 (19% from fat); PROTEIN 8.7g; FAT 5g (sat 1.7g, mono 1.4g, poly 1g); CARB 39.7g; FIBER 3.7g; CHOL 63mg; IRON 2.2mg; SODIUM 604mg; CALC 192mg

GERMAN PANCAKES

—Cynthia McMahan, Matthews, North Carolina

½ cup all-purpose flour
1 tablespoon sugar
⅛ teaspoon salt
¾ cup skim milk
1 egg
Vegetable cooking spray
6 tablespoons apricot preserves
Orange slices (optional)
Raspberries (optional)
1½ teaspoons powdered sugar (optional)

Combine first 3 ingredients in a medium bowl; stir well. Combine milk and egg in a small bowl; stir well. Add to flour mixture, stirring well with a wire whisk.

Coat a 10-inch nonstick skillet with cooking spray, and place over medium-high heat until hot. Remove pan from heat, and pour a scant ¼ cup batter into pan; quickly tilt pan in all directions so batter covers pan with a thin film. Cook about 1 minute.

Lift edge of pancake carefully with a spatula to test for doneness (pancake is ready to turn when it can be shaken loose from pan and the underside is lightly browned). Turn pancake over, and cook an additional 30 seconds.

Place pancake on a towel; let cool. Repeat procedure with remaining batter. Stack pancakes between single layers of wax paper or paper towels to prevent sticking. Spread 1 tablespoon preserves over each pancake, and roll up. Garnish with orange slices and raspberries, if desired. Sprinkle with powdered sugar, if desired. Yield: 3 servings (serving size: 2 pancakes).

CALORIES 238 (9% from fat); PROTEIN 6.7g; FAT 2.3g (sat 0.7g, mono 0.8g, poly 0.3g); CARB 49g; FIBER 1g; CHOL 75mg; IRON 1.4mg; SODIUM 164mg; CALC 95mg

BLUEBERRY WAFFLES

—Linda Moskovics, San Diego, California

1¾ cups all-purpose flour
1 tablespoon baking powder
Dash of salt
1¾ cups skim milk
3 tablespoons vegetable oil
2 egg whites, lightly beaten
1 egg, lightly beaten
Vegetable cooking spray
1 cup fresh or frozen blueberries
Additional blueberries (optional)

Combine all-purpose flour, baking powder, and salt in a medium bowl; stir well. Combine milk, oil, egg whites, and egg in a small bowl; stir well. Add milk mixture to flour mixture, stirring until mixtures are well-blended.

Coat a waffle iron with cooking spray, and preheat. Spoon about ⅓ cup of batter per waffle onto hot waffle iron, spreading batter to edges. Spoon 2 tablespoons blueberries per waffle evenly over batter. Cook 6 to 7 minutes or until steaming stops; repeat procedure with remaining batter and blueberries. (Serve with syrup, if desired.) Garnish with additional blueberries, if desired. Yield: 8 (4-inch) waffles (serving size: 1 waffle).

Note: If you are using frozen blueberries, do not thaw them before adding to batter.

CALORIES 189 (30% from fat); PROTEIN 6.4g; FAT 6.3g (sat 1.2g, mono 1.8g, poly 2.7g); CARB 26.7g; FIBER 1.6g; CHOL 29mg; IRON 1.6mg; SODIUM 86mg; CALC 176mg

MENU SUGGESTION

SAUSAGE-AND-EGG CASEROLE

Tomato-topped asparagus

*Tea-steeped fruit compote

*Place 1 pound dried fruit, 1 cup water, 3 tablespoons honey, and 1 tablespoon lemon juice in a pan; bring to a boil. Remove from heat; add 3 jasmine tea bags, and let steep 5 minutes.

SAUSAGE-AND-EGG CASEROLE

—Lynette M. Rohde, Beavercreek, Ohio

1   pound bulk turkey breakfast
    sausage
3   cups (½-inch) cubed white
    bread (about 6 [1-ounce]
    slices)
2   cups skim milk
1½ cups egg substitute
½   cup (2 ounces) shredded
    reduced-fat sharp Cheddar
    cheese
1   teaspoon dry mustard
Vegetable cooking spray

Preheat oven to 350°.
Cook sausage in a nonstick skillet over medium-high heat until browned, stirring to crumble. Drain well.

Combine sausage and next 5 ingredients in a 13 x 9-inch baking dish coated with cooking spray; stir well. Bake at 350° for 45 minutes or until a wooden pick inserted in center comes out clean. Yield: 9 servings.

Note: Look for this sausage product in the fresh-meat or freezer section of the grocery store.

CALORIES 157 (27% from fat); PROTEIN 14.4g; FAT 4.7g (sat 1.7g, mono 1.7g, poly 0.9g); CARB 13.1g; FIBER 0.4g; CHOL 23mg; IRON 1.2mg; SODIUM 471mg; CALC 150mg

QUICK-AND-EASY QUICHE

—Marilou Robinson, Portland, Oregon

1   cup egg substitute
1   cup water
½   cup low-fat buttermilk biscuit
    and baking mix
½   cup instant nonfat dry milk
    powder
½   cup plain nonfat yogurt
2   tablespoons grated fresh
    Parmesan cheese
½   teaspoon dry mustard
¼   teaspoon hot sauce
1   cup (4 ounces) shredded
    reduced-fat sharp Cheddar
    cheese
¾   cup diced low-salt, reduced-fat
    ham
½   cup chopped green onions
Vegetable cooking spray
Green onion slices (optional)
Cherry tomatoes (optional)

Preheat oven to 350°.
Position knife blade in food processor bowl. Add first 8 ingredients to bowl, and process 1 minute or until mixture is smooth. Combine egg substitute mixture, Cheddar cheese, ham, and chopped green onions in a medium bowl; stir well.

Pour egg substitute mixture into a 9-inch pie plate coated with cooking spray. Bake at 350° for 40 minutes or until set. Let stand 5 minutes before serving. Garnish with green onion slices and cherry tomatoes, if desired.

Yield: 6 servings (serving size: 1 wedge).

CALORIES 159 (30% from fat); PROTEIN 18.3g; FAT 5.3g (sat 2.9g, mono 1.6g, poly 0.2g); CARB 9.2g; FIBER 0.2g; CHOL 25mg; IRON 1mg; SODIUM 437mg; CALC 378mg

RISE-AND-SHINE MUFFINS

—Jill Victorn, Wilmette, Illinois

2   teaspoons reduced-calorie
    margarine, divided
4   (1-ounce) slices turkey ham
1   cup egg substitute
4   (¾-ounce) slices reduced-fat
    American cheese
4   whole wheat English muffins,
    split and toasted

Melt 1 teaspoon margarine in a large nonstick skillet over medium heat. Add turkey ham, and cook 1 minute on each side or until lightly browned. Remove from skillet; set aside, and keep warm.

Melt remaining 1 teaspoon margarine in skillet over medium heat. Add egg substitute; cook 45 seconds or until set, stirring occasionally. Place 1 cheese slice on each of 4 muffin halves. Spoon egg substitute mixture evenly over cheese; top with turkey ham and remaining muffin halves. Serve immediately. Yield: 4 servings.

CALORIES 300 (21% from fat); PROTEIN 21.5g; FAT 7g (sat 2.9g, mono 1.5g, poly 1.1g); CARB 38.2g; FIBER 0g; CHOL 10mg; IRON 3.2mg; SODIUM 864mg; CALC 128mg

SWEET KUGEL

–Judith Cadel, Newton Centre, Massachusetts

    1 cup 1% low-fat cottage cheese
    4 (8-ounce) cartons egg substitute
    1 (8-ounce) carton low-fat sour
         cream
    ¾ cup raisins
    ½ cup sugar
    2 tablespoons reduced-calorie
         stick margarine, melted
    1 teaspoon ground cinnamon
    ¼ teaspoon salt
    1 (16-ounce) can sliced peaches
         in juice, drained and coarsely
         chopped
    8 cups cooked egg noodles (about
         12 ounces uncooked)
Vegetable cooking spray
    ⅓ cup coarsely crushed cornflakes

Preheat oven to 350°.

Combine first 9 ingredients in a large bowl; stir well. Add noodles; toss gently to coat. Spoon mixture into a 13 x 9-inch baking dish coated with cooking spray.

Sprinkle crushed cornflakes over noodle mixture; cover and bake for 30 minutes. Uncover and bake an additional 10 minutes. Yield: 12 servings.

CALORIES 270 (13% from fat); PROTEIN 13.3g; FAT 4g (sat 1.8g, mono 1.3g, poly 0.5g); CARB 42.9g; FIBER 2.1g; CHOL 8mg; IRON 1.9mg; SODIUM 312mg; CALC 64mg

---

MENU SUGGESTION

CRUMB-TOPPED FRENCH TOAST

*Broiled Grapefruit

RUSSIAN TEA

*Sprinkle each grapefruit half with 1 teaspoon brown sugar and 1 teaspoon cherry brandy. Broil for 6 minutes or until sugar melts and grapefruit is thoroughly heated.

CRUMB-TOPPED FRENCH TOAST

–Scott Graham, Cedar Park, Texas

    ½ cup skim milk
    ½ teaspoon vanilla extract
    ¼ teaspoon salt
    2 eggs
    1 cup cornflake crumbs
    8 (1-ounce) diagonally-cut slices
         French bread (about 1 inch
         thick)
    ¼ cup margarine, melted

Preheat oven to 450°.

Combine first 4 ingredients in a medium bowl; stir well with a wire whisk. Place cornflake crumbs in a shallow dish.

Dip bread slices into milk mixture, and dredge in cornflake crumbs. Place bread slices on a baking sheet, and drizzle with margarine. Bake at 450° for 15 minutes or until golden brown. Yield: 8 servings (serving size: 1 bread slice).

CALORIES 212 (32% from fat); PROTEIN 5.8g; FAT 7.6g (sat 1.7g, mono 3.3g, poly 2.3g); CARB 29g; FIBER 0.8g; CHOL 56mg; IRON 1.7mg; SODIUM 468mg; CALC 40mg

---

RUSSIAN TEA

–Terry Shannon, Gold Beach, Oregon

    ¾ cup boiling water
    1 regular-sized English breakfast
         tea bag
    ¼ cup orange juice
    ¼ teaspoon ground cinnamon
    ⅛ teaspoon ground cloves

Combine boiling water and tea bag in a large mug; let stand 5 minutes. Discard tea bag. Add remaining ingredients to mug; stir well. Serve with sugar, if desired. Yield: 1 serving.

CALORIES 31 (3% from fat); PROTEIN 0.5g; FAT 0.1g (sat 0g, mono 0g, poly 0g); CARB 7.4g; FIBER 0.3g; CHOL 0mg; IRON 0.3mg; SODIUM 1mg; CALC 14mg

JUNE

A New Dish for the Old World

A low-fat twist on carbonara salutes a country so devoted to spaghetti that it's honored in a museum.

In this month's column, I'm revisiting spaghetti carbonara, a well-loved dish from Rome. Very simply, it's a combination of finely chopped pancetta (bacon), shallow-fried in olive oil, with beaten whole eggs and pecorino, Parmesan, or Romano cheese added. It's served with freshly cooked spaghetti, some cracked black pepper, and perhaps a little chopped flat-leaf parsley. In essence, the dish is eggs-and-bacon spaghetti with cheese.

To be true to the name carbonara, a reduced-fat makeover must retain the ingredients of oil, bacon, eggs, and cheese. But no matter how much you tweak the numbers, if you use these exact ingredients you'll wind up with 10 to 12 grams of fat and about 20% to 25% of calories from fat.

To lighten the traditional recipe, I dropped the oil and used low-salt chicken broth, replaced the bacon with finely chopped sun-dried tomatoes, added some chipotle sauce (spicy smoked peppers) for depth and feel, and used egg substitute instead of whole eggs.

SPAGHETTI LIGURIA

Be sure the pasta-and-tomato mixture is very hot so the egg substitute will cook when it is added.

- 1 cup low-salt chicken broth
- ¾ cup chopped sun-dried tomatoes, packed without oil (about 24)
- 1 teaspoon water
- ½ teaspoon cornstarch
- ½ teaspoon chipotle sauce or hot sauce
- 4 cups hot cooked spaghetti (about 8 ounces uncooked pasta)
- 2 teaspoons olive oil
- ½ cup egg substitute
- 1 tablespoon freshly grated Parmesan cheese
- ¼ cup chopped fresh chives
- 2 tablespoons chopped fresh parsley
- 1 teaspoon pine nuts, toasted
- ½ teaspoon salt
- Green onions (optional)

Combine broth and sun-dried tomatoes in a small saucepan; bring to a boil, and cook 4 minutes or until reduced to ½ cup.

Combine water and cornstarch, stirring until smooth; add to tomato mixture. Stir in chipotle sauce; bring to a boil, and cook 1 minute, stirring constantly. Remove from heat, and set aside.

Combine spaghetti and oil in a medium bowl, and toss well. Add tomato mixture, egg substitute, and next 5 ingredients; toss well. Garnish with green onions, if desired. Serve immediately. Yield: 4 servings (serving size: 1 cup).

CALORIES 329 (14% from fat); PROTEIN 15.2g; FAT 5.3g (sat 0.9g, mono 2.3g, poly 1.1g); CARB 57.2g; FIBER 1.6g; CHOL 1mg; IRON 3.3mg; SODIUM 882mg; CALC 73mg

SPAGHETTI LIGURIA WITH BACON

For those who don't have to eat such a low percentage of fat, you can go up on the amounts of pine nuts and cheese and add some Canadian bacon to the basic recipe. These amounts are for an entire recipe, but they can be adjusted easily based on the needs of your family members.

- ◆ Add ¾ cup (4 ounces) chopped lean Canadian bacon sautéed in 1 teaspoon oil.
- ◆ Increase pine nuts to 1 tablespoon.
- ◆ Increase Parmesan cheese to ¼ cup.

CALORIES 386 (25% from fat); PROTEIN 21.9g; FAT 10.6g (sat 2.7g, mono 4.7g, poly 1.7g); CARB 51.8g; FIBER 1.7g; CHOL 19mg; IRON 3.7mg; SODIUM 1131mg; CALC 126mg

TALE OF THE TAPE	Calories per Serving	Fat Grams per Serving	% Calories from fat per Serving
Spaghetti Liguria	329	5.3	14%
Spaghetti Liguria with Bacon	386	10.6	25%

Roasted Vidalias, page 180

Spaghetti Liguria with Bacon, page 148

Basil Roasted Vegetables over Couscous, page 155

Crab Purses, page 160

Key Lime Pie, page 165

Fresh Tomato-Herb Pizzas, page 154

Getting Back to Basil
and Other Familiar Herbs

Come spring and summer, fresh herbs are readily available, perhaps in your own backyard or on your windowsill. After months of cooking with dried ones, nothing rejuvenates the spirit more than fresh herbs, which give food a whole new zing and dimension. The recipes we offer feature such classic pairings as rosemary with chicken. But don't think of these familiar herbs as mere recipe-enhancers. They just happen to have other mystical and endearing qualities, as our recipes point out.

CHICKEN WITH POTATOES AND ROSEMARY

Vegetable cooking spray
3   (6-ounce) skinned chicken
      breast halves
3   chicken thighs (about 9
      ounces), skinned
3   chicken drumsticks (about 9
      ounces), skinned
1   medium onion, halved
      lengthwise and thinly sliced
      (about 1 cup)
2   garlic cloves, minced
1   (10½-ounce) can low-salt
      chicken broth
1½ tablespoons chopped fresh
      rosemary
¾   teaspoon salt
⅛   teaspoon pepper
2   bay leaves
1½ pounds baking potato, cut into
      ¼-inch slices
1   cup water
2   teaspoons cornstarch

Coat a large Dutch oven with cooking spray; place over medium-high heat until hot. Add half of chicken pieces, browning on all sides. Remove chicken from pan; set aside. Repeat with remaining chicken.

Add onion and garlic; sauté 3 minutes. Add broth, rosemary, salt, pepper, and bay leaves; stir well. Return chicken to pan; top with potatoes. Cover and cook 30 minutes or until done, stirring occasionally.

Remove chicken and vegetables from pan with a slotted spoon; set aside, and keep warm. Discard bay leaves.

Combine water and cornstarch in a small bowl; stir well. Add cornstarch mixture to broth mixture in pan; cook 1 minute or until thick and bubbly, stirring constantly with a wooden spoon to loosen browned bits. Spoon broth mixture over chicken and vegetables. Yield: 6 servings (serving size: 1 chicken breast or 1 thigh and 1 drumstick, ⅔ cup vegetables, and about 3 tablespoons sauce).

CALORIES 267 (22% from fat); PROTEIN 28.3g; FAT 6.4g (sat 1.7g, mono 2.2g, poly 1.4g); CARB 23.1g; FIBER 2.4g; CHOL 75mg; IRON 2.8mg; SODIUM 390mg; CALC 39mg

FRAGRANT WITH POSSIBILITY

• BASIL • This popular herb comes in many different varieties, from lemon basil (popular in Thai cooking) to opal basil, which is a stunning purple. Fresh basil leaves are large and easy to use in cooking. They are a key ingredient in pesto (and in Mediterranean cooking in general) and enhance many tomato dishes.

• DILLWEED • It's made up of feathery green leaves. Dill should not be confused with dill seed, which is the common ingredient used in the brine for making dill pickles. Because dill is sensitive to heat, it's best used in cold or uncooked dishes, especially appetizers and salads.

• MINT • This herb's leaves resemble basil in appearance, but are not as smooth or as big. Fresh mint can be very strong, so use it sparingly. It provides a refreshing zip to drinks, soups, desserts, and salads.

• OREGANO • A common ingredient in Greek and Italian cooking, oregano is fairly strong. It contains small leaves on long, soft stems and goes particularly well with tomato-based dishes, especially pizza.

• ROSEMARY • It contains long, slender, almost prickly leaves on tough stalks. Pulling the leaves opposite the direction in which they are growing releases them from the stems, which are too tough to use. Rosemary is very aromatic and particularly good with chicken, pork, beef, and potatoes.

• TARRAGON • A key ingredient in French cooking (especially béarnaise sauce), tarragon is made up of narrow, pointed, dark-green leaves. Tarragon has an aniselike or licorice flavor and works best in chicken and fish dishes. Use sparingly, as it is quite assertive.

• THYME • In contrast to basil, thyme is composed of tiny leaves. If the stem is thin, it can be chopped up and used along with the leaves. A versatile herb commonly found in French cuisine, thyme goes well with many dishes and ingredients, particularly chicken, fish, and soups.

GRILLED TUNA WITH HERBED MAYONNAISE

If you believe folklore, this low-fat mayonnaise has all kinds of healthy benefits. The oregano supposedly helps end toothaches, baldness, and aching muscles, while the tarragon allegedly prevents fatigue.

- ¼ cup fat-free mayonnaise
- ¼ cup plain fat-free yogurt
- 1 teaspoon chopped fresh oregano
- 1 teaspoon chopped fresh tarragon
- 1 teaspoon lemon juice
- ¼ teaspoon salt
- ¼ teaspoon pepper
- 4 (6-ounce) tuna steaks (about 1 inch thick)
- Vegetable cooking spray

Combine first 5 ingredients in a small bowl; stir well, and set aside. Sprinkle salt and pepper over tuna; set aside.

Prepare grill. Place tuna on a grill rack coated with cooking spray; grill 3 minutes on each side or until tuna is medium-rare or to desired degree of doneness. Serve with mayonnaise mixture. Yield: 4 servings (serving size: 1 tuna steak and 2 tablespoons mayonnaise mixture).

CALORIES 267 (29% from fat); PROTEIN 40.5g; FAT 8.5g (sat 2.2g, mono 2.7g, poly 2.5g); CARB 4.6g; FIBER 0.1g; CHOL 65mg; IRON 1.9mg; SODIUM 414mg; CALC 33mg

THYME-AND-GARLIC ROASTED TURKEY BREAST

Thyme was once said to be an antidote for shyness and nightmares.

- 2 teaspoons minced fresh thyme
- 1 teaspoon grated lemon rind
- ¼ teaspoon coarsely ground pepper
- ⅛ teaspoon salt
- 2 garlic cloves, crushed
- 1 (2¼-pound) turkey breast half
- Vegetable cooking spray
- Thyme sprigs (optional)

Preheat oven to 400°.

Combine first 5 ingredients in a small bowl. Loosen skin from turkey by inserting one hand, palm side down. Gently push hand beneath the skin and against the meat to loosen skin. Rub thyme mixture over turkey under skin. Press skin to secure.

Place breast half, skin side up, on a broiler pan coated with cooking spray. Insert meat thermometer into meaty part of breast, making sure not to touch bone. Bake at 400° for 1½ hours or until meat thermometer registers 180°. Let stand 10 minutes. Remove skin, and discard. Cut breast into thin slices; garnish with thyme sprigs, if desired. Yield: 6 servings (serving size: 3 ounces).

CALORIES 118 (6% from fat); PROTEIN 25.6g; FAT 0.8g (sat 0.2g, mono 0.1g, poly 0.2g); CARB 0.5g; FIBER 0.1g; CHOL 71mg; IRON 1.4mg; SODIUM 91mg; CALC 14mg

FRESH TOMATO-HERB PIZZAS

According to legend, rosemary is good for improving the memory.

- 1 tablespoon honey
- 1 package dry yeast
- 1 cup warm water (105° to 115°)
- 2½ cups all-purpose flour
- ½ cup yellow cornmeal
- 1 tablespoon chopped fresh thyme
- 1½ teaspoons chopped fresh rosemary
- ¼ teaspoon salt
- 1 tablespoon plus 1 teaspoon olive oil, divided
- Vegetable cooking spray
- 2 tablespoons yellow cornmeal
- ¾ cup chopped onion
- 2 garlic cloves, minced
- 4½ cups chopped plum tomato (about 2 pounds)
- ½ teaspoon salt
- ¼ teaspoon freshly ground pepper
- 2 cups chopped yellow tomato
- 2 cups (6 ounces) finely grated Asiago cheese
- 2 tablespoons chopped fresh basil
- 2 tablespoons chopped fresh oregano

Dissolve honey and yeast in 1 cup warm water in a small bowl; let stand 5 minutes.

Place flour and next 4 ingredients in a food processor; pulse 2 times or until blended. With processor on, slowly add yeast mixture and 1 teaspoon oil through food chute; process until dough leaves sides of bowl and forms a ball. Process an additional minute.

Turn dough out onto a lightly floured surface, and knead 2 minutes. Place dough in a large bowl coated with cooking spray, turning to coat top. Cover dough, and let rise in a warm place (85°), free from drafts, 1 hour or until doubled in bulk.

Preheat oven to 450°.

Punch dough down; divide in half. Roll each half of dough into a 12-inch

---

FRESH HERB TIPS

- ◆ Lots of fresh herbs are interchangeable, so try experimenting with different combinations in our recipes.
- ◆ Try using scissors to "chop" your herbs. Place them in a custard cup or small bowl, and quickly snip back and forth.
- ◆ For an attractive way to store your herbs, place them stem-down in a glass of water.
- ◆ Fresh herbs are not as strong or concentrated as their dried counterparts. The standard substitute of dried herbs for fresh is 1 to 3 (1 part dried to 3 parts fresh). This translates into 1 teaspoon dried for 1 tablespoon fresh.
- ◆ To keep herbs fresh for up to 1 week, trim about ¼ inch from the stem, rinse with cold water, loosely wrap in paper towels, and place in a zip-top bag in the refrigerator.

circle on a lightly floured surface. Place dough on two 12-inch pizza pans or baking sheets that are each coated with cooking spray and sprinkled with 1 tablespoon cornmeal. Crimp edges of dough with fingers to form a rim.

Heat remaining 1 tablespoon oil in a large skillet over medium heat until hot. Add onion and garlic; sauté 3 minutes or until tender. Remove from heat; stir in plum tomato, ½ teaspoon salt, and pepper.

Spread plum tomato mixture over prepared crusts, leaving a ½-inch border. Divide yellow tomato evenly between pizzas; sprinkle each pizza with 1 cup cheese. Bake at 450° for 15 minutes. Remove pizzas to cutting boards; let stand 5 minutes. Sprinkle 1 tablespoon basil and 1 tablespoon oregano over each pizza. Cut each pizza into 8 slices. Yield: 2 pizzas, 4 servings per pizza (serving size: 2 slices).

CALORIES 336 (24% from fat); PROTEIN 14.4g; FAT 9g (sat 4g, mono 3.4g, poly 0.8g); CARB 50.2g; FIBER 4.2g; CHOL 14mg; IRON 3.7mg; SODIUM 576mg; CALC 281mg

MINTED PEAS AND CARROTS

3 cups water
2 cups shelled fresh green peas (about 1¾ pounds)
¾ cup diced carrot
2 teaspoons margarine
1½ cups sliced fresh mushrooms
¼ cup chopped green onions
1 tablespoon minced fresh mint
¼ teaspoon salt

Bring 3 cups water to a boil in a medium saucepan. Add peas and carrot; cook 10 minutes or until tender. Drain; set aside.

Melt margarine in pan over medium heat. Add mushrooms and green onions; sauté 2 minutes. Add pea mixture, mint, and salt; sauté 2 minutes. Yield: 3 servings (serving size: 1 cup).

CALORIES 125 (22% from fat); PROTEIN 6.4g; FAT 3.1g (sat 0.6g, mono 1.2g, poly 1.1g); CARB 19.1g; FIBER 4.8g; CHOL 0mg; IRON 2.1mg; SODIUM 242mg; CALC 41mg

BASIL ROASTED VEGETABLES OVER COUSCOUS

According to folklore, basil is a harbinger of romance. Should a man give a sprig to a woman, she will fall in love with him and never, ever leave him. In Italy, if a woman puts a pot of basil on her windowsill, it means she is ready to receive her suitor. She might have many suitors if she serves this recipe, too.

2 tablespoons minced fresh basil
2 tablespoons balsamic vinegar
1 tablespoon extra-virgin olive oil
¼ teaspoon salt
2 garlic cloves, crushed
2 medium zucchini, cut into 1-inch slices
1 medium red bell pepper, cut into 1-inch pieces
1 medium yellow bell pepper, cut into 1-inch pieces
1 medium red onion, cut into 8 wedges
1 (8-ounce) package mushrooms
3 cups hot cooked couscous
1 (3-ounce) package basil-flavored chèvre (goat cheese), crumbled
⅛ teaspoon pepper
Fresh basil sprigs (optional)

Preheat oven to 425°.
Combine first 5 ingredients in a large bowl. Add zucchini, bell peppers, onion, and mushrooms; toss well to coat. Arrange vegetables in a single layer in a shallow roasting pan. Bake at 425° for 35 minutes or until tender and browned, stirring occasionally.

Spoon roasted vegetables over couscous, and top with cheese. Sprinkle with pepper. Garnish with fresh basil sprigs, if desired. Yield: 4 servings (serving size: 1 cup vegetables, ¾ cup couscous, and 1½ tablespoons cheese).

Note: Substitute feta cheese or plain chèvre for the basil-flavored chèvre, if desired.

CALORIES 285 (28% from fat); PROTEIN 11g; FAT 8.9g (sat 3.7g, mono 3.5g, poly 0.7g); CARB 41.4g; FIBER 3.9g; CHOL 19mg; IRON 2.7mg; SODIUM 439mg; CALC 140mg

MINTY PEACH SORBET

To release the mint's fragrant oils, gently press or crush it with a spoon.

4 cups peeled, chopped peaches (about 2 pounds) or 4 cups frozen sliced peaches
1 cup water
½ cup sugar
2 tablespoons fresh lime juice
2 (4-inch) mint sprigs, crushed

Combine all ingredients in a large saucepan; bring to a boil. Reduce heat, and simmer 7 minutes. Discard mint.

Place mixture in a blender or food processor; cover and process until smooth. Pour into a bowl; cover and chill.

Pour chilled mixture into the freezer can of an ice cream freezer; freeze according to manufacturer's instructions. Yield: 8 servings (serving size: ½ cup).

CALORIES 71 (1% from fat); PROTEIN 0.5g; FAT 0.1g; CARB 18.5g; FIBER 1.2g; CHOL 0mg; IRON 0.1mg; SODIUM 0mg; CALC 4mg

DILLED BLOODY MARY

⅓ cup chopped celery
¼ cup fresh lemon juice
2 tablespoons thinly sliced green onions
1 tablespoon minced fresh dillweed
1 teaspoon brown sugar
1 teaspoon Worcestershire sauce
½ teaspoon hot sauce
¼ teaspoon salt
¼ teaspoon celery seeds
6 (5.5-ounce) cans no-salt-added vegetable juice cocktail, chilled
Fresh dillweed sprigs (optional)

Place first 10 ingredients in a blender; cover and process until smooth. Pour over ice; garnish with dillweed sprigs, if desired. Yield: 6 servings (serving size: ¾ cup).

CALORIES 39 (5% from fat); PROTEIN 1.8g; FAT 0.2g; CARB 8.3g; FIBER 0.2g; CHOL 0mg; IRON 1.3mg; SODIUM 146mg; CALC 33mg

Apple Mint Julep

In Greek mythology, Persephone was so jealous of Hades' falling in love with a nymph named Minthe that the goddess turned her into a lowly plant. Hades was able to soften the spell so that the more Minthe was trod upon, the sweeter she smelled. This fragrant herb is rumored to cure hiccups and soothe sea serpent stings. In this recipe, the fresh mint flavor is infused into the apple juice through a cheesecloth. You can also make it into a granita by freezing the juice mixture.

2 cups chopped fresh mint
8 cups apple juice
½ cup fresh lime juice
Additional mint sprigs (optional)

Place 2 cups chopped mint on a double layer of cheesecloth. Gather edges of cheesecloth together, and tie securely.

Place cheesecloth bag and apple juice in a large saucepan; bring to a boil. Remove from heat; cover and let cool. Pour into a large pitcher; cover and chill. Discard cheesecloth bag; stir in lime juice.

Pour apple juice mixture over ice cubes. Garnish with additional mint sprigs, if desired. Yield: 8 servings (serving size: 1 cup).

Note: To make **Apple Julep Granita,** pour apple juice mixture into a 13 x 9-inch baking dish. Cover and freeze until firm. Remove mixture from freezer; scrape entire mixture with the tines of a fork until fluffy.

For an extra-special beverage, you can make apple julep ice cubes. Pour some of the apple juice mixture into ice cube trays, place a mint sprig in each and freeze. Serve ice cubes with apple juice mixture or with sparkling water.

CALORIES 81 (2% from fat); PROTEIN 0.2g; FAT 0.2g (sat 0g, mono 0g, poly 0.1g); CARB 20.3g; FIBER 0.3g; CHOL 0mg; IRON 0.7mg; SODIUM 5mg; CALC 15mg

---

MENU

ZUCCHINI PICKLE RIBBONS

BEAN DIP WITH BROWNED GARLIC

KALE AND QUINOA PILAF

SPICY MUSHROOMS

BERRY SLAW

Beer or wine

Zucchini Pickle Ribbons

1 cup cider vinegar
1 cup water
¼ cup sugar
2 teaspoons salt
1 teaspoon mustard seeds
1 teaspoon turmeric
½ teaspoon dried crushed red pepper
8 fresh dillweed sprigs
3 garlic cloves, peeled
3 medium zucchini (about 1½ pounds), thinly sliced lengthwise
1 cup thinly sliced onion

Combine first 9 ingredients in a saucepan; bring to a boil. Reduce heat, and simmer, uncovered, 15 minutes.

Combine zucchini and onion in a large bowl; pour hot vinegar mixture over vegetables. Cover and let stand at room temperature 3 hours. Chill at least 8 hours before serving. Yield: 21 servings.

Note: Store, covered, in refrigerator up to 1 month.

CALORIES 18 (5% from fat); PROTEIN 0.4g; FAT 0.1g; CARB 4.5g; FIBER 0.3g; CHOL 0mg; IRON 0.2mg; SODIUM 111mg; CALC 8mg

---

Dining Out

After indulging yourself with this picnic menu, you may never return to civilization.

There is something surreal about escaping your normal surroundings and quietly absorbing the sounds of nature. Being outdoors and removed from the daily routine allows you to focus on the plate at hand. And certainly with these recipes, the picnic never ends.

Bean Dip with Browned Garlic

Overcooking the garlic makes it taste bitter.

1 tablespoon olive oil
4 garlic cloves, minced
2 tablespoons fresh lemon juice
1 tablespoon tahini (sesame seed paste)
1 tablespoon water
1 teaspoon minced fresh rosemary
¼ teaspoon salt
¼ teaspoon pepper
1 (19-ounce) can cannellini beans or other white beans, drained

Heat oil in a small nonstick skillet over medium heat until hot. Add minced garlic, and sauté 1 minute or until lightly browned.

Place garlic mixture, lemon juice, and remaining ingredients in a blender; cover and process until smooth. Serve with toasted pita wedges or carrot sticks. Yield: 1½ cups (serving size: 1 tablespoon).

CALORIES 27 (33% from fat); PROTEIN 1.3g; FAT 1g (sat 0.1g, mono 0.5g, poly 0.2g); CARB 3.6g; FIBER 0.6g; CHOL 0mg; IRON 0.5mg; SODIUM 26mg; CALC 8mg

KALE AND QUINOA PILAF

You can substitute 1 teaspoon of crushed red pepper flakes for the chili paste.

    2 teaspoons vegetable oil
    ½ cup chopped onion
    ½ cup thinly sliced carrot
    ½ cup chopped red bell pepper
    2 garlic cloves, minced
    2 teaspoons curry powder
    1 teaspoon chili paste with garlic
    ½ teaspoon peeled, grated fresh
       gingerroot
    6 cups torn kale
    2 cups cooked brown rice
    1 cup cooked quinoa
    2 tablespoons minced fresh
       cilantro
    1 tablespoon soy sauce
    1 (15-ounce) can chickpeas
       (garbanzo beans), drained

Heat oil in a large nonstick skillet over medium heat until hot. Add onion, carrot, bell pepper, and garlic; sauté 2 minutes. Add curry, chili paste, and gingerroot; sauté 1 minute. Add kale and remaining ingredients; cook 3 minutes or until thoroughly heated, stirring occasionally. Serve at room temperature. Yield: 6 servings (serving size: 1 cup).

CALORIES 256 (15% from fat); PROTEIN 9g; FAT 4.2g (sat 0.6g, mono 1.1g, poly 1.8g); CARB 48g; FIBER 8.2g; CHOL 0mg; IRON 4mg; SODIUM 422mg; CALC 137mg

---

QUINOA QUIPS

When cooked, quinoa is similar to mild brown rice. You'll find that this high-protein seed is soft with a delicate crunch. Look for it in the grains section of your grocery store.

SPICY MUSHROOMS

    1 (3½-ounce) package shiitake
       mushrooms
    2 teaspoons dark sesame oil
    1 tablespoon peeled, minced
       gingerroot
    1 teaspoon chili paste with
       garlic
    2 garlic cloves, minced
    1 (8-ounce) package button
       mushrooms, sliced
    1 (6-ounce) package presliced
       portobello mushrooms
    1 tablespoon hoisin sauce
    1 tablespoon rice vinegar
    1 tablespoon low-sodium soy
       sauce
    2 teaspoons molasses

Remove stems from shiitake mushrooms; discard. Slice shiitake mushroom caps; set aside.

Heat oil in a large nonstick skillet over medium heat until hot. Add gingerroot, chili paste, and garlic; sauté 1 minute. Add shiitake mushroom caps, button mushrooms, and portobello mushrooms; sauté 3 minutes. Add hoisin sauce, rice vinegar, soy sauce, and molasses; cook 1 minute or until sauce thickens. Serve warm, at room temperature, or chilled. Yield: 6 servings (serving size: ½ cup).

CALORIES 52 (33% from fat); PROTEIN 2.1g; FAT 1.9g (sat 0.3g, mono 0.6g, poly 0.8g); CARB 7.9g; FIBER 1.2g; CHOL 0mg; IRON 1.2mg; SODIUM 160mg; CALC 12mg

---

BERRY SLAW

The longer this slaw chills, the juicier and more condensed it becomes. If you serve it immediately, you will actually get double the amount (8 cups).

    6 cups thinly sliced green
       cabbage
    1½ cups sliced strawberries
    ½ cup dried cranberries
    ¼ cup raspberry-flavored
       vinegar
    ¼ cup cranberry juice cocktail
    ½ teaspoon salt
    ½ teaspoon white pepper

Combine all ingredients in a medium bowl; stir well. Cover and chill 8 hours, stirring occasionally. Yield: 4 servings (serving size: 1 cup).

CALORIES 109 (4% from fat); PROTEIN 2.2g; FAT 0.5g (sat 0.1g, mono 0.1g, poly 0.2g); CARB 26.5g; FIBER 4.9g; CHOL 0mg; IRON 1.2mg; SODIUM 317mg; CALC 68mg

---

FAST FOOD

Rub It In

No matter what the main course, these dry rubs are sure to spice it up. The advantage of these spice mixtures is that they replace marinating; simply rub them on the meat, and it's ready to be grilled, baked, or broiled.

GINGER-AND-SPICE CHICKEN THIGHS

Preparation time: 5 minutes
Cooking time: 9 minutes

    2 teaspoons ground ginger
    ¾ teaspoon salt
    ½ teaspoon pepper
    ¼ teaspoon ground nutmeg
    ¼ teaspoon ground cinnamon
    ¼ teaspoon ground allspice
    1 pound skinned, boned chicken
       thighs
       Vegetable cooking spray
    ¼ cup dry white wine

Combine first 6 ingredients in a small bowl; stir well. Rub spice mixture over chicken; let stand 5 minutes.

Coat a large nonstick skillet with cooking spray; place over medium-high heat until hot. Add chicken; cook 2 minutes on each side or until browned. Add wine to skillet; cover, reduce heat to medium-low, and cook 5 minutes or until done. Spoon pan drippings over chicken. Yield: 4 servings (serving size: 3 ounces chicken).

CALORIES 143 (30% from fat); PROTEIN 22.4g; FAT 4.7g (sat 1.2g, mono 1.4g, poly 1.1g); CARB 1.3g; FIBER 0.2g; CHOL 94mg; IRON 1.5mg; SODIUM 539mg; CALC 18mg

MOROCCAN LAMB CHOPS

To intensify the flavors of Moroccan Lamb Chops, apply the dry rub mixture 30 minutes before cooking. A green salad would round out this meal.
Preparation time: 18 minutes
Cooking time: 25 minutes

1 teaspoon ground cumin
1 teaspoon Hungarian sweet paprika
1 teaspoon ground coriander
½ teaspoon salt
¼ teaspoon ground cloves
¼ teaspoon ground red pepper
2 (1½-pound) French-cut lean racks of lamb, 8 ribs each
Vegetable cooking spray
4 cups cooked couscous (cooked without salt or fat)

Preheat oven to 425°.

Combine first 6 ingredients in a small bowl, and stir well. Rub spice mixture evenly over lamb, and let stand 5 minutes.

Place lamb on a broiler pan coated with cooking spray. Bake at 425° for 25 minutes or until desired degree of doneness. Let lamb stand 10 minutes before slicing. Serve with couscous. Yield: 8 servings (serving size: 2 rib chops and ½ cup couscous).

CALORIES 267 (33% from fat); PROTEIN 23.4g; FAT 9.8g (sat 3.3g, mono 3.8g, poly 0.9g); CARB 20.5g; FIBER 1.1g; CHOL 65mg; IRON 2.4mg; SODIUM 211mg; CALC 16mg

CURRIED PORK TENDERLOIN

Preparation time: 8 minutes
Cooking time: 25 minutes

1 pound pork tenderloin
1 tablespoon brown sugar
2 teaspoons curry powder
1 teaspoon dry mustard
½ teaspoon salt
½ teaspoon Hungarian sweet paprika
½ teaspoon pepper
Vegetable cooking spray
½ cup mango chutney

Preheat oven to 425°.

Trim fat from pork. Combine brown sugar and next 5 ingredients in a small bowl; stir well. Rub spice mixture evenly over pork.

Place pork on a broiler pan coated with cooking spray; insert a meat thermometer into thickest portion of tenderloin. Bake at 425° for 25 minutes or until thermometer registers 160° (slightly pink). Let pork stand 5 minutes before slicing. Serve with chutney. Yield: 4 servings (serving size: 3 ounces pork and 2 tablespoons chutney).

CALORIES 240 (17% from fat); PROTEIN 25.2g; FAT 4.6g (sat 1.4g, mono 1.9g, poly 0.5g); CARB 24.2g; FIBER 0.5g; CHOL 79mg; IRON 2.2mg; SODIUM 420mg; CALC 28mg

BEEF WITH PEPPERCORN RUB

Place peppercorns in a zip-top bag, and crush with a meat mallet.
Preparation time: 5 minutes
Cooking time: 8 minutes

1 tablespoon drained brine-packed green peppercorns, crushed
2 teaspoons ground coriander
1½ teaspoons Hungarian sweet paprika
½ teaspoon dried thyme
½ teaspoon pepper
¼ teaspoon salt
4 (4-ounce) beef tenderloin steaks (¾ inch thick)
2 teaspoons olive oil
Vegetable cooking spray
¼ cup cognac
¼ cup water

Combine first 6 ingredients in a small bowl; stir well. Rub steaks with spice mixture; let stand 5 minutes.

Heat oil in a nonstick skillet coated with cooking spray over medium heat until hot. Add steaks; cook 4 minutes on each side or until desired degree of doneness. Remove steaks from skillet; set aside. Add cognac and water to skillet, scraping skillet to loosen browned bits. Cook over medium-high heat 15 seconds or until reduced to ¼ cup, stirring constantly. Spoon cognac mixture over steaks. Yield: 4 servings (serving size: 1 steak and 1 tablespoon sauce).

Note: This dish is higher than our recommended 30% calories from fat. But if you add healthy sides, the meal will be well within our fat guidelines.

CALORIES 197 (46% from fat); PROTEIN 23.9g; FAT 10g (sat 3.3g, mono 4.5g, poly 0.6g); CARB 2.5g; FIBER 0.5g; CHOL 70mg; IRON 4.1mg; SODIUM 210mg; CALC 22mg

ITALIAN-STYLE SHRIMP WITH LEMON AND GARLIC

Preparation time: 25 minutes
Cooking time: 5 minutes

2 teaspoons dried Italian seasoning
2 teaspoons Hungarian sweet paprika
2 teaspoons grated lemon rind
½ teaspoon salt
½ teaspoon freshly ground pepper
3 garlic cloves, minced
1 pound large shrimp, peeled and deveined
Vegetable cooking spray
4 cups hot cooked angel hair (about 8 ounces uncooked pasta)
2 tablespoons fresh lemon juice
1 tablespoon chopped fresh parsley
Lemon zest (optional)

Combine first 6 ingredients in a medium bowl; stir well. Add shrimp; toss well to coat. Thread shrimp evenly onto each of 4 (8-inch) skewers.

Place kebabs on broiler pan coated with cooking spray; broil 2 minutes on each side. Remove shrimp from skewers; arrange over pasta. Drizzle with juice; sprinkle with parsley. Garnish with zest, if desired. Yield: 4 servings (serving size: 3 ounces shrimp and 1 cup pasta).

CALORIES 302 (8% from fat); PROTEIN 24.5g; FAT 2.8g (sat 0.5g, mono 0.4g, poly 1.1g); CARB 43.6g; FIBER 2.8g; CHOL 129mg; IRON 5.3mg; SODIUM 422mg; CALC 86mg

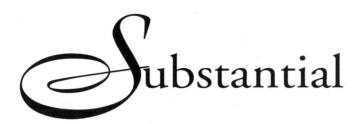

Substantial

Big, bold, and chockablock with meats, vegetables, and cheeses, sub sandwiches are perfect for casual dining and entertaining.

GRILLED-VEGETABLE SANDWICH

¼ cup balsamic vinegar
2 tablespoons olive oil
1 tablespoon fresh or 1 teaspoon dried basil
2 teaspoons molasses
1½ teaspoons fresh or ½ teaspoon dried thyme
¼ teaspoon salt
¼ teaspoon pepper
3 medium zucchini, cut lengthwise into ¼-inch-thick oblong slices
1 medium yellow bell pepper, cut into 6 wedges
2 medium red bell peppers, each cut into 6 wedges
1 large onion, cut into ½-inch slices
1 (16-ounce) loaf French bread
Vegetable cooking spray
¾ cup crumbled feta cheese
2 tablespoons fat-free mayonnaise
¼ cup (1 ounce) freshly grated Parmesan cheese

Combine first 7 ingredients in a large heavy-duty, zip-top plastic bag.

Add zucchini, bell peppers, and onion; seal bag, and marinate in refrigerator 2 hours, turning bag occasionally. Remove vegetables from bag, reserving marinade. Set vegetables aside.

Cut French bread loaf in half horizontally, and brush 3 tablespoons reserved marinade over cut sides of bread; set bread halves and remaining marinade aside.

Place vegetables in a wire grilling basket coated with cooking spray. Place grilling basket on grill rack over medium-hot coals (350° to 400°); grill 5 minutes, basting occasionally with remaining marinade. Turn basket over; grill 2 minutes, basting occasionally. Place bread, cut sides down, on grill rack, and grill an additional 3 minutes or until vegetables are tender and bread is toasted.

Combine feta cheese and mayonnaise in a bowl; stir well. Spread mayonnaise mixture evenly over cut sides of toasted bread; place grilled vegetables on bottom half of bread. Sprinkle Parmesan cheese over the vegetables; top with top half of bread. Cut loaf into 8 pieces. Yield: 8 servings.

CALORIES 294 (27% from fat); PROTEIN 9.8g; FAT 8.8g (sat 3.1g, mono 3.9g, poly 1.1g); CARB 44g; FIBER 2.1g; CHOL 14mg; IRON 2.4mg; SODIUM 682mg; CALC 144mg

STUFFED ITALIAN MEATBALL SUB

1 pound ground chuck
¼ cup fine, dry Italian-seasoned breadcrumbs
¼ cup minced fresh onion
¼ teaspoon salt
¼ teaspoon pepper
1 egg white
1 tablespoon olive oil
1 cup chopped onion
3 garlic cloves, minced
2 tablespoons tomato paste
1 teaspoon sugar
1 teaspoon dried rosemary
¼ teaspoon salt
1 (14.5-ounce) can no-salt-added whole tomatoes, undrained and chopped
¼ cup coarsely chopped fresh basil or 4 teaspoons dried basil
1 (16-ounce) loaf French bread
½ cup (2 ounces) shredded part-skim mozzarella cheese

Preheat oven to 375°.

Combine the first 6 ingredients in a bowl; stir well. Shape mixture into 30 (1-inch) meatballs; place on a broiler pan. Bake meatballs at 375° for 20 minutes or until done.

Heat oil in a large saucepan over medium-high heat until hot. Add 1 cup onion and garlic; sauté 3 minutes or until tender. Add tomato paste, sugar, rosemary, ¼ teaspoon salt, and tomatoes; bring to a boil. Reduce heat, and simmer 15 minutes. Remove from heat; stir in meatballs and basil.

Cut bread loaf in half horizontally. Scoop out bread from bottom half of loaf, leaving a 1-inch-thick bread shell; reserve bread for another use. Spoon meatballs and sauce into bread shell; sprinkle with cheese. Top with top half of bread. Cut loaf into 8 pieces. Yield: 8 sandwiches.

CALORIES 347 (29% from fat); PROTEIN 19g; FAT 11.3g (sat 4.1g, mono 5g, poly 0.5g); CARB 41.2g; FIBER 2.3g; CHOL 38mg; IRON 2.8mg; SODIUM 652mg; CALC 91mg

TURKEY-HAVARTI GRINDER

⅓ cup mango chutney
2 tablespoons chopped unsalted, dry-roasted peanuts
2 tablespoons reduced-calorie mayonnaise
Dash of ground red pepper
1 (16-ounce) loaf French bread
1 pound very thinly sliced deli turkey breast
6 curly leaf lettuce leaves
2 ounces thinly sliced reduced-fat Havarti cheese
6 sandwich-cut bread-and-butter pickles
1 medium Red Delicious apple, cored and sliced into rings

Combine first 4 ingredients in a bowl; stir well. Cut bread loaf in half horizontally, and spread chutney mixture over bottom half of bread; top with turkey, lettuce, cheese, pickles, apple, and top half of bread. Cut loaf into 8 pieces. Yield: 8 servings.

CALORIES 321 (17% from fat); PROTEIN 19.1g; FAT 5.9g (sat 1.3g, mono 1.1g, poly 1g); CARB 45g; FIBER 2.3g; CHOL 8mg; IRON 1.8mg; SODIUM 951mg; CALC 94mg

TECHNIQUE

Changing Your Won Ton Ways

Although primarily used in Chinese cooking, won ton wrappers can be used to make all kinds of non-Oriental dishes such as ravioli and fruit tarts. Available at most supermarkets, won ton wrappers are sheets of prerolled, precut pasta squares, minus the egg.

TIPS FOR HANDLING WON TON WRAPPERS

◆ Because won ton wrappers dry out very easily, keep them covered with a damp towel while you're working.
◆ The wrappers come in a variety of shapes and sizes: square, circular, thin, medium, and thick. We used a medium thickness to test our recipes, but don't be afraid to experiment.
◆ Using egg whites to seal the won ton wrappers ensures that they don't open during cooking.
◆ Egg roll wrappers also work well for these recipes.
◆ Stuffed won tons can be frozen before cooking. Freeze stuffed won tons on a baking sheet, then place in a zip-top plastic bag. (If you don't freeze them first, they'll stick together.) When ready, thaw and proceed with cooking instructions.

CRAB PURSES

These elegant appetizers can be steamed up to an hour ahead, then resteamed to heat them just before serving.

24 green onion tops, cut into 3-inch julienne strips
6 ounces lump crabmeat, shell pieces removed
1 (4-ounce) block fat-free cream cheese
¼ cup minced green onions
2 teaspoons fresh lemon juice
½ teaspoon hot sauce
¼ teaspoon salt
⅛ teaspoon pepper
24 won ton wrappers
1 egg white, lightly beaten
Vegetable cooking spray
2 tablespoons low-sodium soy sauce
1 tablespoon water
1 tablespoon fresh lemon juice

Drop green onion strips in boiling water, and cook 10 seconds or until limp. Drain onion strips; set aside.

Combine crabmeat and next 6 ingredients in a bowl; stir well.

Working with 1 won ton wrapper at a time (cover remaining wrappers with a damp towel to keep them from drying out), spoon 2 teaspoons crabmeat mixture into center of wrapper. Moisten edges of wrapper with egg white; gather 4 corners of wrapper, and crimp to seal, forming a purse. Tie 1 green onion strip around crimped top of purse. Repeat procedure with remaining won ton wrappers, crabmeat mixture, egg white, and green onion strips.

Arrange half of won ton purses in a single layer in a vegetable steamer coated with cooking spray. Steam purses, covered, 8 minutes or until tender. Carefully remove purses from steamer; set aside, and keep warm. Repeat procedure with remaining half of purses.

Combine soy sauce, water, and 1 tablespoon lemon juice in a small bowl; stir well. Serve with purses. Yield: 2 dozen appetizers (serving size: 1 purse and ½ teaspoon sauce).

CALORIES 126 (7% from fat); PROTEIN 10g; FAT 0.9g (sat 0g, mono 0g, poly 0.3g); CARB 18.4g; FIBER 1.2g; CHOL 26mg; IRON 1.7mg; SODIUM 566mg; CALC 109mg

SHRIMP-AND-PORK POT STICKERS

It's said that pot stickers were invented when a very old chef in the royal court forgot about a pan of dumplings that he was boiling. When he heard them sizzling after the water had evaporated, he found that he had created delicate dumplings with crunchy, crisp bottoms.

- ¼ cup sliced green onions
- ¼ cup chopped fresh cilantro
- 2 tablespoons water
- 2 teaspoons peeled, minced gingerroot
- ½ teaspoon salt
- ½ teaspoon dark sesame oil
- ½ pound medium shrimp, peeled and deveined
- ½ pound lean ground pork
- 1 garlic clove, halved
- 1 egg white
- 1 tablespoon all-purpose flour
- 36 won ton wrappers
- 1 egg white, lightly beaten
- 1 tablespoon plus 1 teaspoon vegetable oil, divided
- 1 cup water, divided
- Sesame-Orange Dipping Sauce

Place first 10 ingredients in a food processor; process until mixture is coarsely ground.

Sprinkle 1 tablespoon flour over a large baking sheet; set aside. Working with 1 won ton wrapper at a time (cover remaining wrappers with a damp towel to keep them from drying out), spoon about 1 tablespoon shrimp mixture into center of wrapper. Moisten edges of wrapper with beaten egg white, and bring 2 opposite corners together. Pinch edges together to seal, forming a triangle. Hold each triangle by top point, and tap on counter to flatten bottom of pot sticker. Place pot sticker, flat side down, on prepared baking sheet; cover loosely with a towel. Repeat procedure with remaining won ton wrappers, shrimp mixture, and egg white.

Heat 2 teaspoons vegetable oil in a large nonstick skillet over medium-high heat until hot. Arrange half of pot stickers, flat side down, in a single layer in bottom of skillet; cook 2 minutes or until bottoms are lightly browned. Add ½ cup water; cover and cook 2 minutes or until liquid is absorbed. Uncover and cook an additional 1 minute. Remove from skillet; set aside, and keep warm. Repeat procedure with remaining 2 teaspoons oil, remaining half of pot stickers, and remaining ½ cup water. Serve with Sesame-Orange Dipping Sauce. Yield: 6 servings (serving size: 6 pot stickers and 2 tablespoons Sesame-Orange Dipping Sauce).

CALORIES 303 (29% from fat); PROTEIN 20.1g; FAT 9.9g (sat 2.4g, mono 3.5g, poly 3g); CARB 31.7g; FIBER 0.4g; CHOL 74mg; IRON 3mg; SODIUM 623mg; CALC 53mg

Sesame-Orange Dipping Sauce:

- ⅓ cup thinly sliced green onions
- ⅓ cup low-salt chicken broth
- ¼ cup orange juice
- 1 tablespoon rice vinegar
- 1 tablespoon low-sodium soy sauce
- 2 teaspoons peeled, grated fresh gingerroot
- 1 teaspoon dark sesame oil

Combine all ingredients in a small bowl; stir well. Yield: ¾ cup (serving size: 2 tablespoons).

CALORIES 17 (5% from fat); PROTEIN 0.3g; FAT 0.9g (sat 0.1g, mono 0.3g, poly 0.3g); CARB 1.9g; FIBER 0.2g; CHOL 0mg; IRON 0.2mg; SODIUM 70mg; CALC 5mg

SHRIMP WON TON SOUP

- ¼ cup sliced green onions
- 1 tablespoon water
- 2 teaspoons cornstarch
- 2 teaspoons lemon juice
- 1½ teaspoons dark sesame oil
- 1 teaspoon peeled, grated fresh gingerroot
- ¼ teaspoon sugar
- 1 pound medium shrimp, peeled and deveined
- 1 (8-ounce) can sliced water chestnuts, drained
- 36 won ton wrappers
- 1 egg white, lightly beaten
- 3 cups water
- 2 (14½-ounce) cans Oriental broth (such as Swanson's)
- ¼ cup (½-inch) diagonally sliced green onions

Place first 9 ingredients in a food processor; pulse 6 times or until coarsely chopped.

Working with 1 won ton wrapper at a time (cover remaining wrappers with a damp towel to keep them from drying out), spoon about 1 tablespoon shrimp mixture into center of wrapper. Moisten edges of wrapper with egg white, and bring 2 opposite corners together. Pinch edges together to seal, forming a triangle. Moisten 2 bottom points of triangle with egg white, and bring points together, overlapping about ½-inch; pinch together to seal. Repeat procedure with remaining won ton wrappers, shrimp mixture, and egg white.

Combine 3 cups water and broth in a large Dutch oven; bring to a boil. Stir broth mixture while adding won tons; cook 1½ minutes or until won tons are tender.

Ladle soup into bowls, and sprinkle with diagonally sliced green onions. Yield: 6 servings (serving size: 1 cup broth mixture, 6 won tons, and 2 teaspoons green onions).

Note: Oriental broth can typically be found next to the canned chicken broth in the supermarket.

CALORIES 241 (11% from fat); PROTEIN 17.8g; FAT 2.9g (sat 0.5g, mono 0.7g, poly 1.2g); CARB 34.8g; FIBER 0.3g; CHOL 91mg; IRON 3.3mg; SODIUM 1,083mg; CALC 60mg

MUSHROOM-FILLED WON TONS WITH SHERRY TOMATO SAUCE

Once assembled, the won tons only take five minutes to steam.

    1 pound mushrooms
    2 teaspoons olive oil
    ⅓ cup minced fresh onion
    ½ teaspoon dried thyme
    1 garlic clove, crushed
    1 tablespoon all-purpose flour
    2 teaspoons lemon juice
    ¾ teaspoon salt
    1 tablespoon all-purpose flour
   18 won ton wrappers
    1 egg white, lightly beaten
       Vegetable cooking spray
       Sherry Tomato Sauce
       Thyme sprigs (optional)

Place half of mushrooms in a food processor, and pulse 8 times or until finely chopped; spoon into a bowl. Repeat procedure with remaining mushrooms; set aside.

Heat oil in a large nonstick skillet over medium heat until hot. Add onion, dried thyme, and garlic; sauté 3 minutes. Add mushrooms; cook over high heat 7 minutes or until most of moisture evaporates, stirring occasionally. Remove from heat. Add 1 tablespoon flour, lemon juice, and salt; stir well. Let cool completely.

Sprinkle 1 tablespoon flour over a large baking sheet; set aside. Working with 1 won ton wrapper at a time (cover remaining wrappers with a damp towel to keep them from drying out), spoon about 1 tablespoon mushroom mixture into center of wrapper. Moisten edges of wrapper with egg white; bring 2 opposite corners to center, pinching points to seal. Bring remaining 2 corners to center, pinching points to seal. Pinch 4 edges together to seal; gently twist center point to form a pouch shape. Place pouch on prepared baking sheet; cover loosely with a towel. Repeat procedure with remaining won ton wrappers, mushroom mixture, and egg white.

Arrange 9 mushroom pouches in a single layer in a steamer basket coated with cooking spray. Steam pouches, covered, 5 minutes or until tender. Carefully remove pouches from steamer; set aside, and keep warm. Repeat procedure with remaining 9 pouches.

Spoon 2 tablespoons Sherry Tomato Sauce onto each of 6 small plates; arrange 3 pouches on each plate. Garnish with thyme sprigs, if desired. Yield: 6 appetizer servings.

CALORIES 146 (19% from fat); PROTEIN 6.2g; FAT 3.1g (sat 0.7g, mono 1.3g, poly 0.5g); CARB 23.7g; FIBER 1.4g; CHOL 5mg; IRON 2.2mg; SODIUM 509mg; CALC 61mg

Sherry Tomato Sauce:

       Vegetable cooking spray
    1 tablespoon minced fresh onion
    1 garlic clove, crushed
    ¾ cup 2% low-fat milk
    1 tablespoon tomato paste
    2 teaspoons all-purpose flour
    ⅛ teaspoon salt
       Dash of pepper
    1 tablespoon dry sherry

Coat a small saucepan with cooking spray; place over medium heat until hot. Add onion and garlic; sauté 1 minute. Combine milk and next 4 ingredients in a small bowl; stir with a whisk until well-blended. Add milk mixture to pan; cook over medium heat 5 minutes or until mixture is thick and bubbly, stirring constantly with a whisk. Remove from heat; stir in sherry. Serve warm. Yield: ¾ cup (serving size: 2 tablespoons).

CALORIES 26 (24% from fat); PROTEIN 1.3g; FAT 0.7g (sat 0.4g, mono 0.2g, poly 0g); CARB 3g; FIBER 0.2g; CHOL 2mg; IRON 0.2mg; SODIUM 66mg; CALC 40mg

SPINACH-AND-CHEESE RAVIOLI

If pressed for time, you can substitute commercial marinara for our Tomato Sauce.

    3 cups Tomato Sauce
    1 teaspoon olive oil
    1 garlic clove, minced
    1 cup (4 ounces) shredded part-skim mozzarella cheese
    ½ cup (2 ounces) shredded Asiago cheese
    ½ cup 1% low-fat cottage cheese
    ¼ cup 1% low-fat milk
    ½ teaspoon dried oregano
    ¼ teaspoon ground nutmeg
    ⅛ teaspoon pepper
    1 (10-ounce) package frozen chopped spinach, thawed, drained, and squeezed dry
   36 won ton wrappers
    1 egg white, lightly beaten
    4 quarts water

Prepare Tomato Sauce; set aside, and keep warm.

Heat oil in a small skillet over medium-high heat until hot. Add garlic, and sauté 1 minute. Place garlic, mozzarella cheese, and next 7 ingredients in a food processor; pulse until well-blended.

Working with 1 won ton wrapper at a time (cover remaining wrappers with a damp towel to keep them from drying out), spoon about 1 tablespoon spinach mixture into center of wrapper. Moisten edges of wrapper with egg white, and bring 2 opposite corners together. Press edges together with a fork to seal, forming a triangle. Repeat procedure with remaining won ton wrappers, spinach mixture, and egg white.

Bring 4 quarts water to a boil in a large Dutch oven. Add 12 ravioli (cover remaining ravioli with a damp towel to keep them from drying out); cook 2 minutes, stirring once. Remove ravioli from water with a slotted spoon; set aside, and keep warm. Repeat procedure with remaining ravioli. Place ravioli in shallow bowls, and top with Tomato Sauce. Yield: 6 servings (serving size: 6 ravioli and ½ cup Tomato Sauce).

CALORIES 306 (25% from fat); PROTEIN 1.9g; FAT 8.6g (sat 4.1g, mono 3.1g, poly 0.7g); CARB 39.2g; FIBER 2.2g; CHOL 23mg; IRON 3.6mg; SODIUM 728mg; CALC 385mg

Tomato Sauce:

- 2 teaspoons olive oil
- 1 cup finely chopped onion
- 1 teaspoon dried oregano
- 1 teaspoon dried basil
- ½ teaspoon dried crushed red pepper
- 2 bay leaves
- 1 garlic clove, minced
- ½ cup water
- ½ cup dry white wine
- ¼ teaspoon salt
- ¼ teaspoon black pepper
- 2 (14.5-ounce) cans no-salt-added whole tomatoes, undrained and chopped

Heat oil in a medium saucepan over medium-high heat until hot. Add onion; sauté 4 minutes. Add oregano, basil, red pepper, bay leaves, and garlic; sauté 1 minute. Stir in water and remaining ingredients; bring to a boil. Reduce heat, and simmer 20 minutes. Yield: 4 cups (serving size: ½ cup).

Note: You can refrigerate the remaining sauce in an airtight container for up to 1 week and use it again.

CALORIES 41 (26% from fat); PROTEIN 1.2g; FAT 1.2g (sat 0.2g, mono 0.8g, poly 0.1g); CARB 7.3g; FIBER 0.6g; CHOL 0mg; IRON 0.8mg; SODIUM 89mg; CALC 48mg

---

SECOND TIME AROUND

Leftover Tomato Sauce (or commercial pasta sauce) is too good to toss out. Instead, cover and refrigerate it to enjoy for another meal.

◆ Serve it over hot cooked spaghetti or noodles.
◆ Spoon it over a pizza crust.
◆ Spoon it over a baked potato as a topping.
◆ Serve it over baked or broiled chicken or fish.

STRAWBERRY WON TON TARTLETTES

Fresh raspberries or blueberries can be used in place of strawberries.

- Vegetable cooking spray
- 12 won ton wrappers
- 1 teaspoon sugar
- 1 egg
- 1½ cups 1% low-fat milk
- ¼ cup sugar
- 2 tablespoons cornstarch
- 1 teaspoon vanilla extract
- ¼ teaspoon almond extract
- 24 small strawberries, halved
- 1 tablespoon powdered sugar

Preheat oven to 400°.

Coat 12 muffin cups with cooking spray. Gently press 1 won ton wrapper into each muffin cup, allowing ends of wrappers to extend above edge of cups. Lightly coat won ton wrappers with cooking spray; sprinkle with 1 teaspoon sugar. Bake at 400° for 5 minutes or until lightly browned. Let cool completely in pan on a wire rack.

Place egg in a medium bowl, and stir well with a whisk; set aside. Combine milk, ¼ cup sugar, and cornstarch in a medium saucepan; stir with a whisk until well-blended. Bring to a boil over medium heat; cook 1 minute, stirring constantly. Gradually add hot milk mixture to egg, stirring constantly with a whisk. Return milk mixture to pan; cook over medium heat 1 minute or until thick and bubbly, stirring constantly. Remove from heat; stir in extracts. Pour the custard into a bowl; cover surface of custard with heavy-duty plastic wrap, and chill.

Remove won ton cups from pan; place cups on individual plates. Spoon chilled custard evenly into won ton cups; top with strawberries, and sprinkle with powdered sugar. Yield: 1 dozen (serving size: 1 tartlette).

CALORIES 77 (16% from fat); PROTEIN 2.4g; FAT 1.4g (sat 0.5g, mono 0.6g, poly 0.9g); CARB 13.6g; FIBER 0.4g; CHOL 20mg; IRON 0.4mg; SODIUM 67mg; CALC 46mg

---

Summer Gathering

Whether for weekend picnics, family reunions, or graduation parties, these recipes will fit almost any get-together.

EASY CORN CASSEROLE

As soon as everybody tastes this casserole, they ask me for the recipe. My family likes it best when served with chili or a spicy Mexican dish.
—Peg Tantillo, Overland Park, Kansas

- ¼ cup egg substitute
- ¼ cup reduced-calorie stick margarine, melted
- 1 (8¾-ounce) can no-salt-added whole-kernel corn, drained
- 1 (8¾-ounce) can no-salt-added cream-style corn
- 1 (8½-ounce) package corn muffin mix
- 1 (8-ounce) carton plain fat-free yogurt
- Vegetable cooking spray

Preheat oven to 350°.

Combine first 6 ingredients in a medium bowl; stir well. Pour into an 8-inch square baking dish coated with cooking spray. Bake at 350° for 45 minutes or until set. Yield: 8 servings.

CALORIES 220 (31% from fat); PROTEIN 5.4g; FAT 7.5g (sat2.5g, mono 2.7g, poly 1.5g); CARB 34.6g; FIBER 0.6g; CHOL 1mg; IRON 0.9mg; SODIUM 287mg; CALC 152mg

DO-AHEAD RATATOUILLE

I call this recipe a "do-ahead" because I can make it the afternoon of a dinner party. Cornbread or baked tortilla chips are two of my favorite accompaniments.

—Marilou Robinson, Portland, Oregon

Olive oil-flavored vegetable
   cooking spray
1 cup sliced onion
1 cup red bell pepper strips
1 cup yellow bell pepper strips
10 garlic cloves, minced
½ cup grated Parmesan cheese
¼ cup chopped fresh or
   4 teaspoons dried basil
¼ cup chopped fresh or
   4 teaspoons dried oregano
¼ teaspoon salt
¼ teaspoon pepper
2 cups sliced zucchini
3 medium tomatoes (about 1½
   pounds), cut into ¼-inch slices
1 small eggplant (about 1
   pound), peeled and cut into
   ¼-inch slices

Preheat oven to 350°.

Coat a large nonstick skillet with cooking spray, and place over medium heat until hot. Add onion, bell peppers, and garlic; sauté 4 minutes. Remove from heat; set aside.

Combine cheese and next 4 ingredients; set aside. Arrange half each of zucchini, tomato, and eggplant slices in a 13 x 9-inch baking dish coated with cooking spray; top with half of onion mixture, and sprinkle with half

of cheese mixture. Repeat layers with remaining ingredients.

Cover and bake for 40 minutes. Uncover; bake 10 additional minutes. Serve warm or at room temperature. Yield: 8 cups (serving size: 1 cup).

CALORIES 67 (28% from fat); PROTEIN 3.9g; FAT 2.1g (sat 1g, mono 0.5g, poly 0.3g); CARB 9.7g; FIBER 2.2g; CHOL 4mg; IRON 1.4mg; SODIUM 175mg; CALC 110mg

FRESH BLUEBERRY COBBLER

I was preparing for a family barbecue, and because I'd started trying to lose weight, I was desperate for a recipe that everyone, including myself, could enjoy. I threw this recipe together, and everyone loved it.

—Barbara A. Abel, Lebanon, Connecticut

4 cups blueberries
1 teaspoon lemon juice
Vegetable cooking spray
1 cup all-purpose flour
½ cup sugar
1 teaspoon baking powder
⅛ teaspoon ground nutmeg
Dash of salt
1 tablespoon vegetable oil
½ teaspoon vanilla extract
2 egg whites, lightly beaten
3 tablespoons sugar
½ teaspoon ground cinnamon

Preheat oven to 350°.

Combine blueberries and lemon juice in a 9-inch square baking dish coated with cooking spray; set aside.

Combine flour and next 4 ingredients in a bowl; make a well in center of mixture. Combine oil, vanilla, and egg whites; stir well with a whisk. Add to flour mixture, stirring just until moist. Drop dough by spoonfuls onto blueberry mixture to form 8 dumplings. Combine 3 tablespoons sugar and cinnamon; sprinkle over dumplings.

Bake at 350° for 35 minutes or until filling is bubbly and dumplings are lightly browned. Yield: 8 servings.

CALORIES 186 (11% from fat); PROTEIN 3g; FAT 2.2g (sat 0.4g, mono 0.6g, poly 1g); CARB 39.8g; FIBER 3.7g; CHOL 0mg; IRON 1mg; SODIUM 22mg; CALC 43mg

FIG BAR BREAD PUDDING WITH AMARETTO SAUCE

Every Thursday night we have clean-out-the-refrigerator time, and I use some of my creative cooking skills to develop a new recipe. One Thursday night I discovered Fig Newtons and amaretto nondairy creamer. I combined them and added a few other ingredients to create this dessert.

—Shirl Brainard, Rio Rancho, New Mexico

7 cups cubed day-old French
   bread
8 fat-free fig fruit chewy cookies,
   crumbled
Vegetable cooking spray
1½ cups skim milk
½ cup sugar
½ cup firmly packed brown sugar
1 tablespoon vanilla extract
½ teaspoon ground cinnamon
1 (12-ounce) can evaporated
   skim milk
1 (8-ounce) carton egg substitute
Amaretto Sauce

Combine bread and crumbled cookies in a 13 x 9-inch baking dish coated with cooking spray.

Combine skim milk and next 6 ingredients in a bowl; stir well. Pour over bread mixture; cover and chill 2 hours.

Preheat oven to 350°.

Uncover bread mixture and bake at 350° for 45 minutes or until a knife inserted in center comes out clean. Serve with Amaretto Sauce. Yield: 10 servings (serving size: 1 piece of pudding and about 3 tablespoons sauce).

CALORIES 323 (6% from fat); PROTEIN 9.3g; FAT 2.3g (sat 0.3g, mono 1.9g, poly 0.2g); CARB 64.6g; FIBER 1.3g; CHOL 3mg; IRON 1.3mg; SODIUM 283mg; CALC 202mg

Amaretto Sauce:

½ cup sugar
½ cup amaretto-flavored liquid
   nondairy creamer
1 cup skim milk
2 tablespoons cornstarch

Combine sugar and nondairy creamer in a 2-quart glass measure or bowl. Microwave at HIGH 2 minutes or until sugar dissolves, stirring every 30 seconds. Combine milk and cornstarch; stir well. Add cornstarch mixture to creamer mixture; stir well. Microwave at HIGH 2 minutes or until thick and bubbly, stirring after 1 minute. Serve warm. Yield: 2 cups (serving size: about 3 tablespoons).

CALORIES 85 (17% from fat); PROTEIN 1g; FAT 1.6g (sat 0g, mono 1.6g, poly 0g); CARB 16.6g; FIBER 0g; CHOL 0mg; IRON 0mg; SODIUM 17mg; CALC 30mg

LIGHTEN UP

The Key To Success

From the southernmost part of the United States comes Key Lime Pie, a creamy-tart dessert that has given culinary immortality to the Florida Keys. That's where small, yellowish Key limes are grown. Of course, you don't have to live there to make Key Lime Pie or even use actual Key limes. Though some stores around the country do carry them, we used regular limes, which work quite nicely.

While retaining the pie's spirited taste and texture, we've trimmed the calories by a third and cut the fat by an even more impressive three-fourths. So go ahead and have an extra slice—as if you could resist.

HOW WE DID IT

- Decreased the number of egg yolks in the filling and used gelatin for thickening
- Switched to fat-free sweetened condensed milk
- Decreased the margarine in the crust and added an egg white to help hold the crumb mixture together

KEY POINTS

- Use a nonaluminum saucepan to cook the filling. If you use an aluminum pan, the acid in the lime juice may interact with the aluminum, giving the filling an off-flavor and grayish color.
- Try to avoid making this pie on a rainy or muggy day. Egg whites won't beat up as high or full when the air is humid.
- You can substitute bottled Key lime juice for fresh juice.
- When making the Graham Cracker Crust, don't melt the margarine.

KEY LIME PIE

1 teaspoon unflavored gelatin
2 tablespoons cold water
½ cup fresh lime juice
2 egg yolks
1 (14-ounce) can fat-free sweetened condensed milk
Graham Cracker Crust
3 egg whites
¼ teaspoon cream of tartar
⅛ teaspoon salt
⅓ cup sugar
Lime slices (optional)

Preheat oven to 325°.
Sprinkle gelatin over cold water in a small bowl; set aside. Combine lime juice and egg yolks in a small heavy saucepan; cook over medium-low heat 10 minutes or until slightly thick and very hot (180°), stirring constantly (do not boil). Add softened gelatin to lime juice mixture; cook 1 minute, stirring until gelatin dissolves. Place pan in a large ice-filled bowl; stir gelatin mixture 3 minutes or until mixture reaches room temperature (do not allow gelatin mixture to set). Strain gelatin mixture into a medium bowl; discard any solids. Gradually add milk, stirring with a whisk until blended (mixture will be very thick);

spoon mixture into Graham Cracker Crust, and spread evenly.
Beat egg whites, cream of tartar, and salt at high speed of an electric mixer until foamy. Gradually add sugar, 1 tablespoon at a time, beating until stiff peaks form. Spread evenly over filling, sealing to edge of crust.
Bake at 325° for 25 minutes; let cool 1 hour on a wire rack. Chill 3 hours or until set. Cut with a sharp knife dipped in hot water. Garnish with lime slices, if desired. Yield: 8 servings (serving size: 1 wedge).

CALORIES 290 (14% from fat); PROTEIN 7.5g; FAT 4.4g (sat 1.1g, mono 1.7g, poly 1.1g); CARB 65.1g; FIBER 0.1g; CHOL 61mg; IRON 0.9mg; SODIUM 230mg; CALC 118mg

Graham Cracker Crust:

2 tablespoons sugar
1 tablespoon chilled stick margarine
1 egg white
1¼ cups graham cracker crumbs
1 teaspoon ground cinnamon
Vegetable cooking spray

Preheat oven to 325°.
Combine first 3 ingredients in a bowl; beat at medium speed of an electric mixer until blended. Add crumbs and cinnamon; toss with a fork until moistened. Press crumb mixture into a 9-inch pie plate coated with cooking spray. Bake at 325° for 20 minutes or until lightly browned; let cool on a wire rack. Yield: 1 (9-inch) crust.

BEFORE & AFTER	
SERVING SIZE	
1 slice	1 slice
CALORIES	
466	290
FAT	
18.5g	4.4g
PERCENT OF TOTAL CALORIES	
36%	14%
CHOLESTEROL	
151mg	61mg
SODIUM	
305mg	230mg

The Here-Today, Gone-Tomorrow

Apricot

For a brief period, fresh apricots flood the market. Here's how you can extend their flavor beyond the season.

The apricot's name derives from the Latin word for "precocious," and no description seems more accurate. Of all the stone fruits, the apricot is the first to appear in markets and, sadly, the first to leave.

The apricot is indeed sensitive: Because the tree blossoms so early, in February, it's susceptible to frost and spring winds. Call them prima donnas, but apricots must be handpicked. Their fruit-bearing season is so short—from late May through July—that you can't put an apricot off until tomorrow unless it's been canned or dried. Highly perishable, a ripe apricot can become mushy if kept on the kitchen counter for even a day.

Despite their sensitive nature, cooking brings about an unexpected graciousness: They become meltingly tender, and their flavor intensifies, as do their perfume and color. Yet such boldness doesn't overpower other ingredients. And unlike most other fruits, you don't have to peel them. Best of all, cooking allows you to preserve the apricot's here-today, gone-tomorrow flavorful freshness.

APRICOT PARIS BREST

Because the filling needs to chill and the pastry must cool completely, this dessert lends itself to advance preparation. Make the filling and pastry a day ahead, and assemble the brest just before serving it.

- 2 cups diced apricots (about ¾ pound)
- 2 tablespoons sugar
- 1 teaspoon grated lemon rind
- 1 tablespoon fresh lemon juice
- ½ cup sugar
- 3 tablespoons cornstarch
- ¼ teaspoon salt
- 1 egg
- 1 cup 1% low-fat milk
- ¼ cup stick margarine, divided
- 1 teaspoon vanilla extract
- 1 cup frozen reduced-calorie whipped topping, thawed
- 1 cup 1% low-fat milk
- 2 teaspoons sugar
- ¼ teaspoon salt
- 1 cup all-purpose flour
- 2 eggs
- 2 egg whites
- Vegetable cooking spray
- 1 tablespoon powdered sugar

Combine first 4 ingredients in a large heavy saucepan; stir well. Cook over high heat 5 minutes or until apri-cots are tender and liquid is slightly thickened, stirring constantly. Spoon into a bowl; let cool completely.

Combine ½ cup sugar and next 3 ingredients in a bowl; stir well. Heat 1 cup milk over medium-high heat in a large heavy saucepan to 180° or until tiny bubbles form around edge (do not boil). Gradually add hot milk to egg mixture, stirring constantly with a whisk. Return milk mixture to pan; add 1 tablespoon margarine. Bring to a boil over medium heat, and cook 1 minute, stirring constantly. Reduce heat to low, and cook an additional minute, stirring constantly. Remove from heat; place pan in a large bowl filled with ice. Let stand until milk mixture is completely chilled (about 10 minutes), stirring frequently and scraping sides of pan. Remove pan from ice; stir in apricot mixture and vanilla. Fold in whipped topping. Spoon into a bowl; cover and chill 2½ hours or until thoroughly chilled.

Preheat oven to 425°.

Combine remaining 3 tablespoons margarine, 1 cup milk, 2 teaspoons sugar, and ¼ teaspoon salt in a large heavy saucepan; bring to a boil over medium-high heat. Remove from heat; add flour, stirring vigorously until mixture leaves sides of pan and forms a ball. Cook over high heat 30 seconds, stirring constantly. Remove from heat. Add 2 eggs and 2 egg whites, one at a time, beating well at medium speed of an electric mixer after each addition (dough will be smooth).

Coat a large baking sheet with cooking spray. Using a spoon, drop dough onto baking sheet in equal mounds to form a 9-inch ring. Using the back of a spoon, spread the mounds of dough to form a 1¼-inch-wide smooth ring. Bake at 425° for 15 minutes. Reduce oven temperature to 350°, and bake an additional 30 minutes or until puffy and browned. Remove from baking sheet; let cool 5 minutes on a wire rack. Cut ring in half horizontally, using a serrated knife; discard soft dough inside. Let ring cool completely.

Place bottom half of cream puff ring on a serving platter. Spoon chilled apricot mixture into bottom half of ring; cover with top half of ring. Chill up to 1 hour. Sift powdered sugar over ring just before serving. Slice with a serrated knife. Yield: 8 servings.

Note: Try this technique to form a cream puff ring: Coat baking sheet with cooking spray; draw a 9-inch circle in cooking spray using the tip of a finger. Drop dough into mounds around traced circle to form a 9-inch ring.

CALORIES 285 (31% from fat); PROTEIN 5.2g; FAT 6.5g (sat 1.9g, mono 2.4g, poly 1.7g); CARB 28g; FIBER 0.8g; CHOL 57mg; IRON 0.9mg; SODIUM 192mg; CALC 68mg

GINGERED APRICOT CRUMBLE

Crystallized or candied ginger (found labeled both ways) is usually sold in small jars in the spice section.

⅔ cup all-purpose flour
½ cup firmly packed brown sugar
1 teaspoon ground cinnamon
¼ teaspoon ground nutmeg
¼ cup chilled stick margarine, cut into small pieces
2 pounds apricots, halved and pitted (about 12 large)
¾ cup firmly packed brown sugar
1 tablespoon chopped crystallized ginger
1 teaspoon vanilla extract
Vegetable cooking spray
2¼ cups vanilla low-fat ice cream

Preheat oven to 375°.
Combine first 4 ingredients in a medium bowl; cut in margarine with a pastry blender or 2 knives until mixture resembles coarse meal. Set aside.
Combine apricots, ¾ cup brown sugar, ginger, and vanilla in a 9-inch square baking dish coated with cooking spray; toss well. Sprinkle flour mixture evenly over apricots. Bake at 375° for 45 minutes or until apricot mixture is bubbly and topping is browned. Serve with ice cream. Yield: 9 servings (serving size: ½ cup crumble and ¼ cup ice cream).

CALORIES 293 (22% from fat); PROTEIN 3.5g; FAT 7g (sat 1.9g, mono 2.7g, poly 1.8g); CARB 56.3g; FIBER 2.4g; CHOL 5mg; IRON 1.8mg; SODIUM 101mg; CALC 94mg

APRICOT-ALMOND TART

This procedure for making piecrust may seem unusual, but the dough is much easier to handle and roll out because it contains less fat than a traditional recipe.

1⅓ cups all-purpose flour, divided
¼ cup plus 1 tablespoon ice water
1 tablespoon sugar
¼ teaspoon salt
¼ cup vegetable shortening
Vegetable cooking spray
⅓ cup sliced almonds, divided
3 tablespoons all-purpose flour
2 pounds apricots, halved and pitted (about 12 large)
¾ cup sugar
½ teaspoon pumpkin pie spice
2 teaspoons water

Preheat oven to 400°.
Combine ⅓ cup flour and ice water, stirring with a whisk until well-blended; set aside. Combine remaining 1 cup flour, 1 tablespoon sugar, and salt in a bowl; cut in shortening with a pastry blender or 2 knives until mixture resembles coarse meal. Add ice water mixture, and mix with a fork until dry ingredients are moist. Roll dough into a 14-inch circle on a lightly floured surface. Place dough on a large baking sheet coated with cooking spray.
Combine 3 tablespoons almonds and 3 tablespoons flour in a food processor; process 30 seconds or until almonds are finely chopped. Sprinkle almond-flour mixture over dough. Arrange apricot halves, cut sides down, over dough, leaving a 2-inch border.
Combine ¾ cup sugar and pie spice in a bowl; stir well. Reserve 1 tablespoon sugar-spice mixture; set aside. Sprinkle remaining sugar-spice mixture over apricots, and top with remaining 2½ tablespoons almonds. Fold 2-inch border of dough over apricots, pressing gently to seal (it will only partially cover apricots). Brush border of dough with 2 teaspoons water, and sprinkle with reserved sugar-spice mixture. Bake at 400° for 45

minutes or until lightly browned. Let cool on baking sheet 5 minutes. Carefully slide tart onto a serving platter using a spatula. Cut into 8 wedges; serve warm. Yield: 8 servings.

CALORIES 284 (26% from fat); PROTEIN 4.6g; FAT 8.1g (sat 1.8g, mono 3.1g, poly 2.6g); CARB 50.4g; FIBER 3.4g; CHOL 4mg; IRON 1.8mg; SODIUM 76mg; CALC 31mg

PIT STOP

Although you don't have to peel apricots in these recipes, you will need to remove the pits. Slice around the "seam," and gently twist the fruit in half. The pit should lift out easily. Place each half, flesh side up, on a cutting board, and chop or slice as directed in the recipe.

APRICOT SORBET

When cooked with sugar, the apricots' flavor becomes even more intense.

3 cups water
1¾ cups sugar
1½ pounds apricots, halved and pitted (about 9 large)
2 teaspoons vanilla extract

Combine water and sugar in a large saucepan, and bring to a boil over medium-high heat, stirring occasionally. Add apricots; bring to a boil. Cover, reduce heat, and simmer 10 minutes or until apricots are tender. Place apricot mixture and vanilla in a blender; cover and process until smooth. Chill.
Pour mixture into the freezer can of an ice cream freezer, and freeze according to manufacturer's instructions. Spoon apricot mixture into a freezer-safe container; cover and freeze 2 hours. Yield: 16 servings (serving size: ½ cup).

CALORIES 107 (2% from fat); PROTEIN 0.5g; FAT 0.2g; CARB 26.6g; FIBER 0.9g; CHOL 0mg; IRON 0.2mg; SODIUM 1mg; CALC 6mg

FRESH APRICOT JAM

If you don't make your own jams and jellies because you're intimidated by canning, this easy recipe will help put homemade in your kitchen.

  6 cups coarsely chopped apricots
     (about 2 pounds)
  3 cups sugar
  2 tablespoons fresh lemon juice

Combine all ingredients in a large bowl; stir well. Cover and let stand at room temperature 24 hours.

Spoon apricot mixture into a large saucepan; bring to a boil over medium heat, stirring frequently. Reduce heat to low, and cook 25 minutes or until a candy thermometer registers 205°.

Pour jam into decorative jars or air-tight containers. Store in refrigerator up to 3 weeks. Yield: 4 cups (serving size: 1 tablespoon).

CALORIES 43 (2% from fat); PROTEIN 0.2g; FAT 0.1g (sat 0g, mono 0g, poly 0g); CARB 11g; FIBER 0.3g; CHOL 0mg; IRON 0.1mg; SODIUM 0mg; CALC 2mg

APRICOT-AND-WINE LIQUEUR

This liqueur can be served as an after-dinner drink, poured over low-fat vanilla ice cream, or mixed with sparkling water. The reserved marinated apricots can be used as a fat-free topping for low-fat ice cream or spooned into a dish with the liqueur drizzled over them.

  2 cups sugar
  1 (750-milliliter) bottle
     Sauvignon Blanc or other dry
     white wine
  2 pounds apricots, quartered and
     pitted (about 12 large)
  1 (3-inch) cinnamon stick
  1 (6-inch) vanilla bean, split
     lengthwise
  2 cups vodka

Combine sugar and wine in a large nonaluminum Dutch oven or stockpot; stir well. Cook wine mixture over medium-high heat 2 minutes or until sugar dissolves, stirring constantly (do not boil). Add apricots, cinnamon stick, and vanilla bean; bring to a boil, and cook 30 seconds, stirring gently after 15 seconds. Remove mixture from heat; gently stir in vodka. Let cool completely. Spoon mixture into a large bowl; cover loosely with cheesecloth or a towel, and refrigerate 4 days.

Drain apricot mixture through a fine sieve, reserving liqueur and marinated apricots. Discard cinnamon stick and vanilla bean. Pour liqueur into decorative bottles, and store in the refrigerator. Spoon the marinated apricots into a bowl; cover and chill. Yield: 6 cups liqueur (serving size: 2 tablespoons).

Note: Apricot liqueur will keep in the refrigerator for several months. Use the marinated apricots within 3 days.

CALORIES 74 (1% from fat); PROTEIN 0.2g; FAT 0.1g; CARB 10.5g; FIBER 0.4g; CHOL 0mg; IRON 0.2mg; SODIUM 1mg; CALC 4mg

THE ENLIGHTENED CHEF

A Taste of New York

According to Executive Chef John Halligan of New York City's Rihga Royal Hotel, there are two types of customers: "Those who want it light and those who don't. It's running about 60% for the lighter dishes right now," he says.

To provide the hotel's daily menus with an ever-changing array of lighter selections, Halligan has incorporated his own creative version of the USDA Food Guide Pyramid. Anywhere pyramid symbols appear on his menus, customers know he has reduced the fat, balanced the ingredients, and counted the calories for them.

GRILLED VEAL SCALOPPINE WITH LEMON MASHED POTATOES AND PORT-WINE SAUCE

Chef Halligan pours the Port-Wine Sauce into a squeeze bottle and squirts small dollops around the entrée.

  1 teaspoon olive oil
  1 pound veal scaloppine
  ¼ teaspoon salt
  ¼ teaspoon pepper
     Vegetable cooking spray
     Lemon Mashed Potatoes
     Port-Wine Sauce
     Thinly sliced green onions

Brush oil over veal, and sprinkle with salt and pepper. Prepare grill or broiler. Place veal on grill rack or broiler pan coated with cooking spray, and cook 1½ minutes on each side or until veal is done. Arrange veal on top of Lemon Mashed Potatoes; serve with Port-Wine Sauce, and garnish with green onions. Yield: 4 servings (serving size: 3 ounces veal, 1 cup Lemon Mashed Potatoes, and 2 tablespoons Port-Wine Sauce).

CALORIES 450 (16% from fat); PROTEIN 34.1g; FAT 7.8g (sat 2.1g, mono 3.1g, poly 0.7g); CARB 56.2g; FIBER 3.1g; CHOL 107mg; IRON 2.9mg; SODIUM 650mg; CALC 98mg

Lemon Mashed Potatoes:

  5 cups peeled, cubed baking
     potato
  ½ cup plain low-fat yogurt
  1 tablespoon fresh lemon juice
  2 teaspoons sugar
  ½ teaspoon salt
  ¼ teaspoon pepper

Place potato in a large saucepan; cover with water, and bring to a boil. Reduce heat; simmer 15 minutes or until tender. Drain potato, and return to pan. Add yogurt, lemon juice, sugar, salt, and pepper; beat at medium speed of an electric mixer until smooth. Yield: 4 servings (serving size: 1 cup).

CALORIES 175 (3% from fat); PROTEIN 5.3g; FAT 0.6g (sat 0.3g, mono 0.1g, poly 0.1g); CARB 38.2g; FIBER 3g; CHOL 2mg; IRON 1.5mg; SODIUM 324mg; CALC 66mg

Port-Wine Sauce:

> 2 **cups port or other sweet red wine**
> ¼ **cup sugar**
> ¼ **cup sherry vinegar**

Combine all ingredients in a medium saucepan. Bring wine mixture to a boil, and cook 35 minutes or until reduced to ½ cup. Yield: ½ cup (serving size: 2 tablespoons).

CALORIES 88 (0% from fat); PROTEIN 0.3g; FAT 0g; CARB 18g; FIBER 0g; CHOL 0mg; IRON 0.3mg; SODIUM 99mg; CALC 10mg

QUICK & EASY WEEKNIGHTS

Simply Salmon

If it feels like you're swimming upstream when it comes to finding good dinner ideas, try this fresh salmon salad in a tangy lime vinaigrette.

MENU

POTATO SALMON SALAD

Garlic Green Beans

Crusty French bread

About 531 calories and 17 grams of fat
(29% calories from fat)

SHOPPING LIST

mixed salad greens

fresh cilantro

1 red bell pepper

1 jalapeño pepper

1 pound green beans

1 lime

garlic

2 onions

1 pound small red potatoes

white wine vinegar

dried oregano

French bread

white wine

1½ pound salmon fillet

POTATO SALMON SALAD

> 8 **small red potatoes (about 1 pound), quartered**
> ½ **teaspoon salt**
> ½ **teaspoon pepper**
> 1½ **pound salmon fillet (1 inch thick)**
> **Vegetable cooking spray**
> 1 **cup (½-inch-thick) slices onion**
> 1 **cup julienne-cut red bell pepper**
> ¼ **cup chopped fresh cilantro**
> 2 **teaspoons seeded, minced jalapeño pepper**
> ¼ **cup white wine vinegar**
> ½ **teaspoon grated lime rind**
> 2 **tablespoons fresh lime juice**
> 1 **teaspoon dried oregano**
> ½ **teaspoon pepper**
> 4 **cups mixed salad greens**

Place potatoes in a saucepan; cover with water, and bring to a boil. Reduce heat; simmer 15 minutes or until potatoes are tender. Drain; set aside.

Sprinkle salt and ½ teaspoon pepper over salmon fillet. Coat a large nonstick skillet with cooking spray; place over medium-high heat until hot. Add fillet; cook 5 minutes. Turn fillet over; add onion, and cook 5 minutes. Remove fillet from skillet; set aside. Cook onion an additional 3 minutes or until golden. Remove onion from skillet; set aside. Add potatoes to skillet; sauté over high heat 3 minutes or until browned. Remove from heat; set aside.

Flake salmon into bite-size pieces. Combine salmon, onion, potatoes, bell pepper, cilantro, and jalapeño pepper in a bowl. Combine vinegar and next 4 ingredients in a small bowl; stir well. Drizzle vinegar mixture over salmon mixture; toss gently to coat. Serve on a bed of mixed greens. Yield: 4 servings (serving size: 2 cups).

Note: Delicate mixed salad greens in a bag labeled mesclun mix or Mediterranean mix are best in this recipe.

CALORIES 404 (34% from fat); PROTEIN 40.2g; FAT 15.2g (sat 2.6g, mono 7.1g, poly 3.4g); CARB 25.6g; FIBER 3.7g; CHOL 115mg; IRON 3.3mg; SODIUM 397mg; CALC 46mg

GARLIC GREEN BEANS

For easy one-skillet green beans, cook beans in a small amount of water in a large skillet until crisp-tender. Drain; add 1 teaspoon oil and 1 clove crushed garlic to beans. Sauté for 2 minutes.

A Cuisine that Knows No Boundaries

When Southern European, North African, and Mideastern flavors blend, it's a whole new adventure in eating.

Most people usually think of Italian, French, and Spanish cuisines as Mediterranean cooking. But standards such as tapas, bouillabaisse, and pasta are making room for more alluring fare from other Mediterranean countries, mostly North Africa and the Levant, a term that encompasses Greece, Turkey, Syria, Lebanon, Israel, and Egypt. Combine dishes from these regions with the more familiar tastes of Spain, France, and Italy, and you get what is being called Med-rim cooking.

Reliant on olives, grains, legumes, fragrant spices, and fresh fruits and vegetables, Med-rim cuisine offers healthful dishes based loosely on foods of the Bible. Known as the "seven spices," they include wheat, barley, wine, figs, pomegranates, olives, and honey. Although all of this fusion may sound complicated, the following recipes are surprisingly easy to make.

THE MED-RIM PANTRY

Have the following ingredients on hand to infuse your food with Med-rim flavor:

• **BULGUR**• dried cracked wheat made from whole wheat berries that are steamed, dried, and crushed.

• **CORIANDER**• dried seeds and the fresh leaves, which are also called cilantro.

• **CUMIN SEED**• native to the Mediterranean area, these aromatic seeds are used whole or ground in many Middle Eastern dishes.

• **GROUND SUMAC** (SOO-mak)• is a deep purple-red powder. A decorative bush that grows wild in the Middle East and Italy, sumac bears clusters of red berries that impart a strong salty-citrus flavor to salads and cooked foods. You can substitute a slightly smaller amount of grated lemon rind for the sumac.

• **ZAHTAR**• a spice blend made from ground sumac, ground dried thyme, and sesame seeds. Alex Mims of Ali Baba Restaurant in Birmingham, Alabama, will ship zahtar (or other hard-to-find ingredients) to you. Call him at 205/823-2222.

• **OTHER ESSENTIALS** • *Garlic, honey, olive oil*

MENU SUGGESTION

SPICY OKRA-AND-CHICKPEA SALAD

Grilled Lebanese garlic chicken

Pita bread

*Marinate chicken in a mixture of lemon juice, olive oil, sweet paprika, minced garlic, salt, and pepper. Grill.

SPICY OKRA-AND-CHICKPEA SALAD

Often thought of as a Southern vegetable, okra is also a Middle East favorite.

    1   tablespoon olive oil
 1½   cups finely chopped onion
 1¼   pounds okra (about 6 cups)
    1   (15-ounce) can chickpeas
         (garbanzo beans), drained
 1½   cups canned tomato purée
    1   tablespoon ground cumin
    2   tablespoons red wine vinegar
   ½   teaspoon sugar
   ¼   teaspoon salt
   ¼   teaspoon crushed red pepper
    1   large garlic clove, crushed

Heat oil in a saucepan over medium-high heat until hot. Add onion; sauté 3 minutes. Add okra; sauté 5 minutes. Add chickpeas and remaining ingredients; bring to a boil. Cover, reduce heat, and simmer 15 minutes. Spoon into a bowl; cover and chill. Yield: 6 servings (serving size: 1 cup).

CALORIES 175 (17% from fat); PROTEIN 6.6g; FAT 3.4g (sat 0.5g, mono 2g, poly 0.6g); CARB 31.9g; FIBER 7.1g; CHOL 0mg; IRON 2.9mg; SODIUM 537mg; CALC 124mg

ZAHTAR PITA

A walk through Jerusalem helps you understand the importance of zahtar to the area's cuisine. This fragrant spice is sold in shops all over the ancient city. Zahtar is sprinkled on freshly baked bread called "bagele." We've substituted pita bread.

4	(7-inch) pita bread rounds
1	egg white, lightly beaten
2	tablespoons zahtar
1	teaspoon olive oil

Preheat oven to 350°.

Place pita bread on a baking sheet; brush egg white over each pita, and sprinkle with zahtar.

Drizzle ¼ teaspoon olive oil over each pita bread round, and bake at 350° for 8 minutes or until edges of bread begin to brown. Cut each pita into 4 wedges. Yield: 8 servings (serving size: 2 wedges).

CALORIES 66 (19% from fat); PROTEIN 2.3g; FAT 1.4g (sat 0.3g, mono 0.7g, poly 0.4g); CARB 10.8g; FIBER 0.4g; CHOL 1mg; IRON 0.6mg; SODIUM 114mg; CALC 19mg

INSIDE-OUT TOMATO SALAD

This is an all-purpose tomato salad or salsa that can be served with meat, fish, chicken, pasta, or on its own.

4	cups peeled, coarsely chopped tomato (about 2¼ pounds)
⅓	cup thinly sliced green onions
¼	cup coarsely chopped fresh cilantro
1½	tablespoons fresh lemon juice
1	tablespoon extra-virgin olive oil
1	tablespoon balsamic vinegar
¾	teaspoon ground sumac or ½ teaspoon grated lemon rind
¼	teaspoon ground cumin
⅛	teaspoon salt
⅛	teaspoon dried crushed red pepper
	Dash of sugar

Combine all ingredients in a bowl; toss well. Yield: 8 servings (serving size: ½ cup).

CALORIES 37 (49% from fat); PROTEIN 0.9g; FAT 2g (sat 0.3g, mono 1.3g, poly 0.3g); CARB 5g; FIBER 1.4g; CHOL 0mg; IRON 0.6mg; SODIUM 47mg; CALC 11mg

ISRAELI VEGETABLE SALAD WITH CREAMY FETA DRESSING

Cubed vegetables are the hallmark of a true Israeli salad. A feta-cheese dressing replaces the traditional olive oil and fresh lemon.

1¼	cups seeded, diced tomato
1	cup peeled, seeded, and diced cucumber
1	cup diced green bell pepper
½	cup diced red bell pepper
½	cup diced radishes
⅓	cup finely chopped fresh parsley
¼	cup finely chopped green onions
	Dash of ground red pepper
½	cup crumbled feta cheese
2	tablespoons boiling water
¾	teaspoon white wine vinegar
2	tablespoons plain fat-free yogurt

Combine first 8 ingredients in a large bowl; set aside.

Place cheese, boiling water, and vinegar in a food processor; process until smooth. Add yogurt; process until blended. Pour cheese mixture over vegetable mixture; toss well. Serve immediately. Yield: 4 servings (serving size: 1 cup).

CALORIES 79 (41% from fat); PROTEIN 3.9g; FAT 3.6g (sat 2.2g, mono 0.7g, poly 0.3g); CARB 9.1g; FIBER 2.3g; CHOL 13mg; IRON 1.6mg; SODIUM 180mg; CALC 110mg

MED-RIM TABBOULEH

Tabbouleh is the signature cracked-wheat salad of many Arabic countries. Here it's highlighted with almonds. The pomegranate molasses adds a unique taste to the dish.

1½	cups uncooked bulgur or cracked wheat
1½	cups boiling water
1	teaspoon olive oil
1½	cups diced onion
¾	cup finely chopped fresh parsley
⅓	cup finely chopped fresh cilantro
¼	cup slivered almonds, toasted
1	tablespoon ground cumin
3	tablespoons fresh lemon juice
2	teaspoons olive oil
1	tablespoon pomegranate molasses
1½	teaspoons dried oregano
½	teaspoon salt
⅛	teaspoon ground allspice

Combine bulgur and boiling water in a large bowl; stir well. Let stand 30 minutes or until water is absorbed.

Heat 1 teaspoon oil in a skillet over medium heat until hot. Add onion; sauté 5 minutes or until tender. Add onion, parsley, and remaining ingredients to bulgur. Cover and chill. Yield: 4 servings (serving size: 1 cup).

CALORIES 285 (25% from fat); PROTEIN 9.2g; FAT 7.8g (sat 1g, mono 4.9g, poly 1.4g); CARB 49.6g; FIBER 12.4g; CHOL 0mg; IRON 3.9mg; SODIUM 316mg; CALC 93mg

---

A NEW GEM OF AN INGREDIENT

Pomegranate molasses is a thick, piquant liquid or concentrate made from reduced pomegranate juice, sugar, and lemon. Except for its vivid ruby color and sweet-tart taste, it resembles traditional molasses. You can find it at Middle Eastern markets or order from Dean & DeLuca Inc. at 800/221-7714.

GRILLED TUNA-AND-PEARL BARLEY NIÇOISE

Barley is an important part of Med-rim cooking. Ancient Eastern civilizations recognized this grain as a versatile food source.

½ cup fresh lemon juice
1 tablespoon thinly sliced fresh basil
2 tablespoons extra-virgin olive oil
2 tablespoons anchovy paste
2 teaspoons herbes de Provence
¼ teaspoon pepper
4 garlic cloves, minced
4 cups water
1 cup uncooked pearl barley
3 cups (1-inch) sliced green beans (about ½ pound)
2 hard-cooked eggs
1 cup finely chopped fennel bulb
½ cup thinly sliced red onion
2 large tomatoes, cut into ¼-inch-thick wedges (about ¾ pound)
2 tablespoons cracked pepper
6 (6-ounce) tuna steaks (about ¾ inch thick)
Vegetable cooking spray
18 niçoise olives

Combine first 7 ingredients in a small bowl; stir well with a whisk. Set aside.

Bring 4 cups water to a boil in a large saucepan. Add barley; cover, reduce heat, and simmer 45 minutes. Remove from heat; let stand, covered, 5 minutes. Spoon barley into a large bowl; set aside.

Drop green beans into a large saucepan of boiling water; cook 2 minutes. Drain and rinse under cold water. Add beans to barley; set aside.

Cut eggs in half lengthwise; remove yolks. Reserve yolks for another use. Slice egg whites. Add sliced egg white, lemon juice mixture, fennel, onion, and tomatoes to barley mixture; toss gently. Set aside.

Firmly press cracked pepper over tuna steaks. Place tuna on grill rack coated with cooking spray; grill 3 minutes on each side until tuna is medium-rare or to desired degree of doneness.

Place 1½ cups barley mixture, 1 tuna steak, and 3 olives on each of 6 plates. Yield: 6 servings.

CALORIES 476 (29% from fat); PROTEIN 47.6g; FAT 15.6g (sat 3.1g, mono 7.1g, poly 3.3g); CARB 37.1g; FIBER 7.7g; CHOL 65mg; IRON 4.9mg; SODIUM 884mg; CALC 83mg

SLOW-BAKED TOMATOES WITH LAMB AND MINTED RICE

Colorful stuffed vegetables—served hot or at room temperature—are a healthy part of many Mediterranean meals. The lamb and rice filling is delicious stuffed in grape leaves, bell peppers, eggplant, or zucchini.

1½ pounds lean ground lamb
2 cups chopped onion
2 tablespoons dried mint flakes
2 teaspoons dried thyme
1 teaspoon ground cumin
½ teaspoon ground cinnamon
Minted Rice
1 (28-ounce) can tomato purée
2 garlic cloves, crushed
⅓ cup minced fresh parsley
½ teaspoon salt
¼ teaspoon pepper
12 large tomatoes

Preheat oven to 375°.

Combine lamb, onion, mint, and thyme in a Dutch oven; cook over medium heat until lamb is brown, stirring to crumble. Drain in a colander; return lamb mixture to pan.

Add cumin, cinnamon, Minted Rice, tomato purée, and garlic cloves to lamb mixture; stir well. Bring to a boil; cover, reduce heat, and simmer 10 minutes (mixture will be thick). Remove from heat; stir in parsley, salt, and pepper.

Cut tops off tomatoes, and set aside tops. Carefully scoop out tomato pulp, leaving shells intact; reserve tomato pulp for another use. Divide lamb mixture evenly among tomato shells; replace tomato tops. Place tomatoes in a 13 x 9-inch baking dish.

Bake, uncovered, at 375° for 20 minutes. Yield: 12 servings.

CALORIES 234 (24% from fat); PROTEIN 16.5g; FAT 6.2g (sat 1.7g, mono 2.8g, poly 0.7g); CARB 29.6g; FIBER 3.8g; CHOL 37mg; IRON 4.1mg; SODIUM 290mg; CALC 59mg

Minted Rice:

1 tablespoon olive oil
1 cup chopped onion
2½ tablespoons dried mint flakes
1 cup uncooked long-grain rice
2 cups low-salt chicken broth
⅛ teaspoon pepper

Heat oil in a medium saucepan over medium heat until hot. Add onion and mint; sauté until onion is tender. Stir in rice. Add chicken broth, and bring to a boil. Cover, reduce heat, and simmer 20 minutes or until liquid is absorbed. Remove from heat; stir in pepper. Yield: 3½ cups (serving size: ½ cup).

CALORIES 133 (18% from fat); PROTEIN 3g; FAT 2.6g (sat 0.4g, mono 1.7g, poly 0.3g); CARB 24.1g; FIBER 0.8g; CHOL 0mg; IRON 1.8mg; SODIUM 26mg; CALC 13mg

CUMIN-YOGURT CHICKEN

Considered more flavorful and juicy, the dark meat of the chicken is preferred over the white in the Med-rim region. These tender thighs are marinated in yogurt and garlic and spiced with cumin and cilantro.

1 cup sliced onion, separated into rings
½ cup chopped fresh cilantro
½ cup plain fat-free yogurt
2 tablespoons ground cumin
¼ teaspoon salt
¼ teaspoon ground red pepper
2 garlic cloves, crushed
8 chicken thighs, skinned (about 3 pounds)
Vegetable cooking spray
2 teaspoons ground sumac or 1 teaspoon grated lemon rind

Combine first 7 ingredients in a large bowl; stir well. Add chicken, stirring to coat with yogurt mixture.

Cover and marinate in refrigerator 3 hours, stirring occasionally.

Preheat oven to 350°.

Place chicken and marinade in a 13 x 9-inch baking dish coated with cooking spray. Sprinkle sumac over chicken mixture. Bake at 350° for 35 minutes. Turn chicken over, and bake an additional 35 minutes or until done. Serve over couscous. Yield: 4 servings (serving size: 2 chicken thighs).

CALORIES 301 (28% from fat); PROTEIN 45.1g; FAT 9.4g (sat 2.3g, mono 3.1g, poly 2.2g); CARB 7.2g; FIBER 1.2g; CHOL 179mg; IRON 4.8mg; SODIUM 364mg; CALC 126mg

MED-RIM FRUIT SOUP

This fruit dessert combines two ingredients found in the Bible: honey and wine.

    2   cups diced plums
    2   cups peeled, diced peaches
    2   cups diced cantaloupe
    2   cups apricot nectar
  ¾   cup Moscato d'Asti or other
        sweet sparkling wine
  ¼   cup water
    2   tablespoons honey
    1   (3-inch) cinnamon stick
    1   bay leaf
Pomegranate seeds (optional)

Combine first 3 ingredients in a large bowl; set aside. Combine nectar and next 5 ingredients in a medium saucepan; bring to a boil. Reduce heat; simmer 10 minutes. Discard cinnamon and bay leaf. Pour nectar mixture over fruit; cover and chill. Garnish with pomegranate seeds, if desired. Yield: 7 servings (serving size: 1 cup).

CALORIES 124 (4% from fat); PROTEIN 1.5g; FAT 0.5g (sat 0.1g, mono 0.3g, poly 0.1g); CARB 31.2g; FIBER 2.8g; CHOL 0mg; IRON 0.6mg; SODIUM 9mg; CALC 17mg

ORANGE, DATE, AND OLIVE OIL CAKE

Oranges, dates, and olive oil are highly valued in Med-rim regions—here they coexist in a cake. Cardamom and orange-flower water add an intense perfume; the flower water, however, can easily be omitted.

    1   cup all-purpose flour
    1   teaspoon ground cardamom
    1   teaspoon baking powder
  ¼   teaspoon baking soda
  ⅛   teaspoon salt
  ½   cup sugar
  ⅓   cup olive oil
  ½   teaspoon vanilla extract
    1   egg
    1   egg white
  ⅓   cup plain fat-free yogurt
    2   tablespoons grated orange rind
Vegetable cooking spray
    8   whole pitted dates, cut in half
        lengthwise
1½ tablespoons sugar
    3   tablespoons fresh
        orange juice
  ¼   teaspoon orange-flower water
        (optional)
Orange rind (optional)
Cinnamon sticks (optional)

Preheat oven to 350°.

Combine first 5 ingredients in a bowl; stir well, and set aside. Combine ½ cup sugar and oil in a large bowl; beat at high speed of an electric mixer 2 minutes. Add vanilla, egg, and egg white; beat 1 minute. Add flour mixture, yogurt, and grated orange rind; beat until well-blended.

Pour batter into a 9-inch springform pan coated with cooking spray; arrange date halves over batter. Bake at 350° for 30 minutes. Combine 1½ tablespoons sugar and orange juice; stir in flower water, if desired. Spoon juice mixture over warm cake. Let cool completely on a wire rack. Garnish with orange rind and cinnamon sticks, if desired. Yield: 8 servings (serving size: 1 slice).

CALORIES 216 (32% from fat); PROTEIN 3.6g; FAT 7.6g (sat 1.5g, mono 4.9g, poly 0.9g); CARB 34.4g; FIBER 1.1g; CHOL 28mg; IRON 1.1mg; SODIUM 97mg; CALC 65mg

FOR TWO

Shish Fulfillment

Probably no dish is more fun to put together than shish kebabs. And we have kebabs to fit every schedule: Some can be prepared in the morning, be put in the refrigerator to marinate, and be ready to go when you walk in the door. Others can be made in an hour or less. Either way, be sure that you don't overcook a kebab, or the meat will lose its juiciness.

LEMON-BASIL VEGETABLE KEBABS

    1   small eggplant
    1   cup sliced yellow squash
    3   tablespoons chopped fresh or
        1 tablespoon dried basil
    2   tablespoons fresh lemon
        juice
    1   teaspoon olive oil
  ¼   teaspoon salt
  ¼   teaspoon pepper
    1   medium red bell pepper, cut
        into 1½-inch pieces
    1   small onion, cut into 4 wedges
Vegetable cooking spray

Peel eggplant; cut in half lengthwise. Cut each half crosswise into ½-inch-thick slices. Combine eggplant, squash, and next 7 ingredients in a large zip-top plastic bag; seal and marinate at room temperature 45 minutes, turning bag occasionally. Remove vegetables from bag, reserving marinade.

Thread vegetables alternately onto 2 (10-inch) skewers. Prepare grill or broiler. Place kebabs on grill rack or broiler pan coated with cooking spray; cook 6 minutes on each side or until done, basting occasionally with reserved marinade. Yield: 2 servings.

CALORIES 88 (32% from fat); PROTEIN 2.6g; FAT 3.1g (sat 0.4g, mono 1.7g, poly 0.4g); CARB 15.2g; FIBER 3.8g; CHOL 0mg; IRON 1.4mg; SODIUM 301mg; CALC 63mg

CHILI-LIME SHRIMP KEBABS

20 large shrimp (about 12 ounces)
2 tablespoons minced fresh cilantro
1 tablespoon seeded, minced jalapeño pepper
2 tablespoons fresh lime juice
1 teaspoon dried oregano
1 teaspoon chili powder
1 teaspoon olive oil
½ teaspoon salt
½ teaspoon pepper
1 garlic clove, minced
8 cherry tomatoes
Vegetable cooking spray
2 cups cooked rice (cooked without salt or fat)

Peel shrimp, leaving tails intact.

Combine cilantro and next 8 ingredients in a bowl; stir well. Add shrimp and tomatoes; toss to coat. Cover and marinate in refrigerator 1 hour; stir occasionally.

Remove shrimp and tomatoes from marinade, reserving marinade. Bring marinade to a boil in a small saucepan.

Thread shrimp and tomatoes alternately onto 4 (10-inch) skewers.

Prepare grill or broiler. Place kebabs on grill rack or broiler pan coated with cooking spray; cook 3 minutes on each side or until done, basting often with reserved marinade. Serve kebabs with rice. Yield: 2 servings (serving size: 2 kebabs and 1 cup rice).

CALORIES 455 (12% from fat); PROTEIN 39.8g; FAT 6.3g (sat 1g, mono 2.2g, poly 1.6g); CARB 57.8g; FIBER 2.7g; CHOL 259mg; IRON 7.1mg; SODIUM 859mg; CALC 140mg

YOGURT-MARINATED LAMB KEBABS

½ pound lean boned leg of lamb
¼ cup plain fat-free yogurt
1 tablespoon finely chopped onion
2 teaspoons olive oil
1½ teaspoons ground cumin
½ teaspoon dried rosemary
½ teaspoon pepper
¼ teaspoon salt
1 garlic clove, minced
2 cups (1-inch) sliced zucchini
6 large cherry tomatoes
1 small onion, cut into 4 wedges
Vegetable cooking spray
2 cups cooked couscous (cooked without salt or fat)

Trim fat from lamb. Cut lamb into 1-inch pieces; set aside.

Combine yogurt and next 7 ingredients in a large zip-top plastic bag. Add lamb, zucchini, tomatoes, and onion wedges; seal bag, and marinate in refrigerator 8 hours, turning bag occasionally. Remove lamb and vegetables from bag, reserving marinade. Bring marinade to a boil in a small saucepan.

Thread lamb onto 2 (10-inch) skewers. Thread zucchini, tomatoes, and onion wedges onto 2 (10-inch) skewers.

Prepare grill or broiler. Place kebabs on grill rack or broiler pan coated with cooking spray; cook 7 minutes on each side or until done, basting occasionally with reserved marinade. Serve kebabs with couscous. Yield: 2 servings (serving size: 1 lamb kebab, 1 vegetable kebab, and 1 cup couscous).

CALORIES 464 (25% from fat); PROTEIN 35.4g; FAT 12.8g (sat 3.1g, mono 6.5g, poly 1g); CARB 53.1g; FIBER 4.3g; CHOL 76mg; IRON 5mg; SODIUM 390mg; CALC 116mg

PORK-AND-PINEAPPLE KEBABS WITH PEANUT SAUCE

1 tablespoon thinly sliced green onions
2 tablespoons reduced-fat peanut butter
2 tablespoons lemon juice
1 tablespoon soy sauce
1 tablespoon water
¼ teaspoon hot sauce
¾ teaspoon curry powder
½ pound lean boned pork loin, cut into 1-inch pieces
½ cup fresh or canned 1½-inch pineapple chunks
1 small red bell pepper, cut into 1-inch pieces
Vegetable cooking spray
1 cup cooked basmati rice (cooked without salt or fat)

Combine first 6 ingredients in a small bowl; stir well with a whisk. Reserve ¼ cup peanut butter mixture; cover and chill. Add curry powder and pork to remaining mixture in bowl; stir well. Cover and marinate in refrigerator 1 to 8 hours.

Let reserved ¼ cup peanut butter mixture stand at room temperature 30 minutes.

Thread pork, pineapple, and bell pepper alternately onto 4 (10-inch) skewers.

Prepare grill or broiler. Place kebabs on grill rack or broiler pan coated with cooking spray; cook 4 minutes on each side or until done. Serve with reserved sauce and rice. Yield: 2 servings (serving size: 2 kebabs, 2 tablespoons sauce, and ½ cup rice).

CALORIES 460 (35% from fat); PROTEIN 29.5g; FAT 17.9g (sat 5.1g, mono 8g, poly 3.1g); CARB 44.1g; FIBER 2.2g; CHOL 77mg; IRON 2.7mg; SODIUM 555mg; CALC 33mg

CARIBBEAN CHICKEN-AND-PAPAYA KEBABS

Black beans and yellow rice pair well with the sunny flavors of this dish.

2 tablespoons low-sodium soy sauce
2 tablespoons molasses
1 tablespoon red wine vinegar
1 tablespoon habanero pepper sauce
½ teaspoon ground allspice
⅛ teaspoon salt
½ pound skinned boned chicken breasts, cut into 1-inch pieces
1 papaya, peeled and cut into 1-inch pieces
Vegetable cooking spray

Combine first 7 ingredients in a bowl; stir well. Cover and marinate in refrigerator 1 to 8 hours. Remove chicken from bowl, reserving marinade. Bring marinade to a boil in a small saucepan.

Thread chicken and papaya alternately onto 2 (10-inch) skewers.

Prepare grill or broiler. Place kebabs on grill rack or broiler pan coated with cooking spray; cook 7 minutes on each side or until done, basting occasionally with reserved marinade. Yield: 2 servings.

CALORIES 250 (13% from fat); PROTEIN 27.2g; FAT 3.6g (sat 0.9g, mono 1.1g, poly 0.7g); CARB 25.5g; FIBER 2.1g; CHOL 72mg; IRON 1.9mg; SODIUM 655mg; CALC 85mg

SKEWERING POINTERS

If you haven't skewered in a while, remember that in terms of taste, efficiency, and appearance, there is no difference between metal and wooden skewers. Metal is good if you skewer often, but avoid round skewers (the meat will turn and twist). Wooden skewers are inexpensive and disposable, but must be soaked in water for 10 minutes before using.

MEDITERRANEAN MEATBALLS

2 tablespoons minced fresh mint
3 tablespoons white wine vinegar
1½ tablespoons water
1 tablespoon olive oil
½ teaspoon sugar
1 large garlic clove, minced
½ pound ultra-lean ground beef
3 tablespoons regular oats
1½ tablespoons finely chopped onion
1 tablespoon skim milk
½ teaspoon ground coriander
½ teaspoon pepper
¼ teaspoon salt
⅛ teaspoon ground cinnamon
8 large mushrooms
1 small onion, cut into 4 wedges
Vegetable cooking spray
1½ cups cooked orzo (about 1 cup uncooked rice-shaped pasta)

Combine first 6 ingredients in a bowl; stir well with a whisk.

Combine beef and next 7 ingredients in a bowl; stir well. Shape into 8 (2-inch) meatballs. Thread meatballs onto 2 (10-inch) skewers. Thread mushrooms and onion alternately onto 2 (10-inch) skewers.

Prepare grill or broiler. Place kebabs on grill rack or broiler pan coated with cooking spray; cook 7 minutes on each side or until done, basting occasionally with mint sauce. Serve with orzo. Yield: 2 servings (serving size: 1 meatball kebab, 1 vegetable kebab, and ¾ cup orzo).

CALORIES 505 (29% from fat); PROTEIN 32.4g; FAT 16 g (sat 4g, mono 8.4g, poly 1.6g); CARB 60.1g; FIBER 4.5g; CHOL 72mg; IRON 4.2mg; SODIUM 548mg; CALC 47mg

FRUIT KEBABS WITH ALMOND SYRUP AND AMARETTI CRUMBS

If pineapple isn't available at your favorite grocery store, you can substitute fresh freestone peaches, cut into wedges.

1 cup (1-inch) cubed fresh pineapple
2 tablespoons brown sugar
½ teaspoon almond extract
1 medium plum or peach, cut into 4 wedges
Vegetable cooking spray
2 tablespoons amaretti cookie crumbs (about 16 small cookies)

Combine first 4 ingredients in a bowl; stir well. Let stand 15 minutes. Remove fruit from bowl, reserving syrup.

Thread pineapple cubes and plum wedges alternately onto 2 (6-inch) skewers.

Prepare grill. Place kebabs on grill rack coated with cooking spray; grill 4 minutes on each side or until thoroughly heated. Drizzle reserved syrup over kebabs; sprinkle with cookie crumbs. Serve with vanilla low-fat ice cream, if desired. Yield: 2 servings.

CALORIES 113 (10% from fat); PROTEIN 0.8g; FAT 1.3g (sat 0g, mono 0.2g, poly 0.2g); CARB 25.8g; FIBER 1.8g; CHOL 0mg; IRON 0.5mg; SODIUM 7mg; CALC 14mg

Children Know Best

They do this Father's Day. Because Dad knew what was best for them, these "kids" are returning the love with new spins on his favorite recipes.

CAESAR SALAD WITH BAGEL CROUTONS

The keys to lightening this salad are in the croutons and the dressing. The croutons are made from baked bagel cubes, and the dressing uses fat-free yogurt as its base.

—Lisa Donoughe

  4 cups (½-inch) cubed bagel
     (about 2 bagels)
Olive oil-flavored vegetable
     cooking spray
  8 cups sliced romaine lettuce
  2 tablespoons freshly grated
     Parmesan cheese
Creamy Caesar Dressing

Preheat oven to 300°.

Place bagel cubes on a baking sheet coated with cooking spray. Bake at 300° for 15 minutes or until toasted.

Combine lettuce, cheese, and croutons in a large bowl. Drizzle Creamy Caesar Dressing over salad; toss well. Serve immediately. Yield: 8 servings (serving size: 1 cup).

CALORIES 82 (30% from fat); PROTEIN 3.8g; FAT 2.7g (sat 0.6g, mono 1.4g, poly 0.3g); CARB 10.6g; FIBER 1.3g; CHOL 2mg; IRON 1.2mg; SODIUM 233mg; CALC 73mg

Creamy Caesar Dressing:

  ⅓ cup plain fat-free yogurt
  2 tablespoons fresh lemon
     juice
  1 tablespoon olive oil
  2 teaspoons red wine vinegar
  2 teaspoons Worcestershire
     sauce
  1 teaspoon anchovy paste
  1 teaspoon Dijon mustard
  ½ teaspoon freshly ground
     pepper
  1 garlic clove, minced

Combine all ingredients in a small bowl, and stir well with a whisk. Yield: ½ cup (serving size: 1 tablespoon).

CALORIES 26 (62% from fat); PROTEIN 0.8g; FAT 1.8g (sat 0.2g, mono 1.3g, poly 0.2g); CARB 1.6g; FIBER 0g; CHOL 0mg; IRON 0.1mg; SODIUM 124mg; CALC 22mg

PLANTAIN HASH

Plantains, very popular in Latin American cuisine, are large and firm and referred to as "cooking bananas." You can substitute green bananas for the plantains.

—Dana Gasby, age 10

  1 tablespoon margarine
  1 cup chopped red bell pepper
  1 cup chopped green onions
  2 cups sliced plantains
  ¼ teaspoon salt
  ¼ teaspoon pepper

Melt 1 tablespoon margarine in a large nonstick skillet over medium-high heat. Add bell pepper and green onions; sauté 2 minutes. Add sliced plantains, salt, and pepper; sauté 10 minutes or until plantains are soft. Serve with grilled fish. Yield: 4 servings (serving size: ½ cup).

CALORIES 203 (16% from fat); PROTEIN 2.5g; FAT 3.5g (sat 0.6g, mono 1.3g, poly 1g); CARB 45.9g; FIBER 1.9g; CHOL 0mg; IRON 1.7mg; SODIUM 190mg; CALC 26mg

CHINESE FONDUE

Beef tenderloin, shrimp, and fresh vegetables turn succulent and tender when dipped in boiling chicken broth instead of oil in this rendition of fondue.

—Andrew Lee

  1 cup small broccoli florets
  1 cup small cauliflower
     florets
  1 cup (2-inch) pieces napa
     (Chinese) cabbage
  ½ cup diagonally sliced carrot
  ½ cup sliced mushrooms
  1 pound beef tenderloin, cut in
     half lengthwise and cut
     crosswise into ¼-inch slices
  ½ pound large shrimp, peeled
     and deveined
  2 cups water
  2 (10½-ounce) cans low-salt
     chicken broth
Chinese Barbecue Sauce
Rémoulade Sauce

Arrange first 7 ingredients on serving platters.

Bring water and chicken broth to a gentle boil in a fondue pot.

Pierce shrimp with skewers, and cook in broth mixture until shrimp turn pink.

Pierce vegetables and beef with skewers, and cook in broth mixture until beef and vegetables are desired degree of doneness. Serve with Chinese Barbecue Sauce and Rémoulade Sauce. Yield: 6 servings.

CALORIES 241 (34% from fat); PROTEIN 25.8g; FAT 9.1g (sat 2.8g, mono 3g, poly 2g); CARB 14.1g; FIBER 1.8g; CHOL 94mg; IRON 4.1mg; SODIUM 784mg; CALC 93mg

Chinese Barbecue Sauce:

½ cup Chinese barbecue sauce
  (char siu sauce)
¼ cup low-sodium soy sauce
1 teaspoon sugar

Combine all ingredients in a small bowl; stir well. Yield: ¾ cup.

Rémoulade Sauce:

¼ cup reduced-calorie mayonnaise
½ cup fat-free plain yogurt
2 tablespoons finely chopped
  green onions
1 tablespoon finely chopped
  fresh parsley
1 garlic clove, crushed

Combine all ingredients in a bowl; stir well. Yield: ¾ cup plus 2 tablespoons.

STEAMED MUSSELS WITH CHARMOULA

Charmoula is a classic Moroccan seasoning blend similar in consistency to Italian pesto.

—Peter Hoffman

Vegetable cooking spray
½ cup chopped onion
¼ cup dry white wine
1 pound small mussels, scrubbed
  and debearded (about 28
  mussels)
Charmoula
½ cup drained canned navy beans
¼ teaspoon salt

Coat a nonstick skillet with cooking spray; place over medium-high heat. Add onion; sauté 3 minutes. Add wine and mussels; cover and cook over high heat 4 minutes or until shells open. Discard any unopened shells. Stir in Charmoula, beans, and salt; cook until thoroughly heated. Yield: 2 servings (serving size: about 14 mussels).

CALORIES 237 (36% from fat); PROTEIN 17g; FAT 9.6g (sat 1.4g, mono 5.5g, poly 1.3g); CARB 10.8g; FIBER 3.5g; CHOL 28mg; IRON 6.8mg; SODIUM 591mg; CALC 97mg

Charmoula:

¼ cup parsley sprigs
¼ cup cilantro sprigs
1 tablespoon fresh lemon juice
1 tablespoon olive oil
½ teaspoon ground cumin
¼ teaspoon peeled, grated fresh
  gingerroot
⅛ teaspoon paprika
Dash of ground red pepper
1 small garlic clove

Place all ingredients in a food processor or blender; cover and process until smooth, and set aside. Yield: ¼ cup.

CALORIES 71 (89% from fat); PROTEIN 0.6g; FAT 7g (sat 1g, mono 5.1g, poly 0.6g); CARB 2.2g; FIBER 0.8g; CHOL 0mg; IRON 1.3mg; SODIUM 10mg; CALC 28mg

PRIZE-WINNERS

Top Strawberries

When we say these strawberry recipes are winners, we're not kidding. In a Cooking Light contest, they all won top awards.

When *Cooking Light* and the California Strawberry Commission asked readers to share their best strawberry recipes, the mail was deluged with more than 1,000 entries in the categories of Healthy Snacks, Stand-Out Salads, and Dazzling Desserts. The recipes went to the *Cooking Light* Test Kitchens, where they were judged on originality, taste, ease of preparation, visual appeal, and nutritional value. We chose one winning recipe from each category, plus an overall Grand Prize recipe.

STRAWBERRY DESSERT NACHOS

First Prize: Dazzling Desserts,
  —Roz Kelmig,
  Guymon, Oklahoma

3 cups sliced strawberries
⅓ cup sugar
¼ cup amaretto (almond-flavored
  liqueur)
½ cup fat-free sour cream
½ cup frozen reduced-calorie
  whipped topping, thawed
2 tablespoons sugar
⅛ teaspoon ground cinnamon
6 (7-inch) flour tortillas
Butter-flavored vegetable cooking
  spray
2 teaspoons cinnamon-sugar
2 tablespoons sliced almonds,
  toasted
2 teaspoons shaved semi-sweet
  chocolate

Combine first 3 ingredients in a bowl; stir well. Cover and chill 30 minutes. Drain, reserving juice for another use.

Combine sour cream and next 3 ingredients in a bowl; stir well. Cover and chill.

Preheat oven to 400°. Cut each tortilla into 8 wedges. Arrange tortilla wedges on 2 baking sheets; lightly coat with cooking spray. Sprinkle wedges evenly with cinnamon-sugar. Bake at 400° for 7 minutes or until crisp. Cool on a wire rack.

Place 8 tortilla wedges on each of six dessert plates; top each serving with about ⅓ cup strawberry mixture and 2½ tablespoons sour cream mixture. Divide almonds and chocolate evenly between nachos. Yield: 6 servings.

CALORIES 260 (19% from fat); PROTEIN 6g; FAT 5.4g (sat 1.3g, mono 2g, poly 1.8g); CARB 45g; FIBER 3.6g; CHOL 0mg; IRON 2.1mg; SODIUM 214mg; CALC 81mg

STRAWBERRY SOUP WITH STRAWBERRY SORBET AND POUND CAKE CROUTONS

$1,000 Grand Prize Winner:
–Julie deMatteo,
Clementon, New Jersey

2   (10-ounce) packages frozen
    sliced strawberries in syrup,
    thawed
¼   cup sugar
¼   cup lemon juice
1   (8-ounce) carton strawberry
    low-fat yogurt
½   cup sugar
1½ cups sliced strawberries
1   cup peeled, chopped mango
½   cup chopped pineapple
3   (8-ounce) cartons strawberry
    low-fat yogurt
1   cup (½-inch) cubed low-fat
    pound cake
1   cup sliced strawberries
Mint sprigs (optional)

Drain thawed strawberries, reserving 1 cup juice. Combine drained strawberries, ¼ cup sugar, lemon juice, and 1 carton yogurt in a blender; cover and process until smooth. Pour mixture into an 8-inch square baking dish; cover and freeze until firm, stirring occasionally.

Combine reserved strawberry juice and ½ cup sugar in a small saucepan. Cook over medium-high heat 2 minutes or until sugar dissolves, stirring constantly. Let cool slightly.

Combine juice mixture, 1½ cups sliced strawberries, mango, pineapple, and 3 cartons yogurt in blender; cover and process until mixture is smooth. Pour into a bowl; cover and chill.

Place pound cake cubes on a baking sheet; broil 1 minute or until toasted, stirring cubes halfway through cooking time.

Spoon ¾ cup soup in each of 8 small bowls; top each with ¼ cup sorbet, 2 tablespoons cake cubes, and 2 tablespoons sliced strawberries. Garnish with mint, if desired. Yield: 8 servings.

Note 1: For the sorbet, substitute 2 cups sliced fresh strawberries for the 2 (10-ounce) packages of frozen, if desired. Combine strawberries and ½ cup sugar; stir well. Let stand 1 hour; drain, reserving juice. Add drained strawberries, lemon juice, and 1 carton yogurt to blender; cover and process until smooth.

Note 2: The sorbet also can be made in a 1-quart ice cream freezer.

CALORIES 274 (7% from fat); PROTEIN 5.7g; FAT 2.2g (sat 1g, mono 0.4g, poly 0.2g); CARB 60.8g; FIBER 2.5g; CHOL 5mg; IRON 0.9mg; SODIUM 106mg; CALC 178mg

TASTE-OF-SUMMER STRAWBERRY CHUTNEY

First Prize: Healthy Snacks,
–Edwina Gadsby,
Great Falls, Montana

½   cup golden raisins
½   cup firmly packed dark brown
    sugar
½   cup strawberry preserves
½   cup strawberry vinegar
½   cup fresh orange juice
2   teaspoons peeled, minced fresh
    gingerroot
½   teaspoon curry powder
1   medium navel orange, peeled
    and chopped
4   cups whole strawberries,
    hulled and diced
½   cup sliced almonds
Strawberry fans (optional)

Combine first 8 ingredients in a large nonaluminum saucepan; bring to a boil. Cook over medium heat 15 minutes or until slightly thick and syrupy, stirring frequently.

Add diced strawberries, stirring gently; reduce heat, and simmer 10 minutes or until mixture is thick, stirring occasionally. Remove from heat; stir in almonds. Spoon mixture into a bowl; cover and chill.

Serve with fat-free or light cream cheese and gingersnaps. Garnish with strawberry fans, if desired. Yield: 3¼ cups (serving size: 1 tablespoon).

CALORIES 32 (14% from fat); PROTEIN 0.4g; FAT 0.5g (sat 0.1g, mono 0.3g, poly 0.1g); CARB 6.9g; FIBER 0.6g; CHOL 0mg; IRON 0.2mg; SODIUM 3mg; CALC 9mg

STRAWBERRY-AND-STILTON SALAD

First Prize: Stand-Out Salads,
–Patt Brower,
Ben Lomond, California

2   cups sliced strawberries
2   tablespoons chopped fresh
    basil
2   tablespoons raspberry vinegar
½   teaspoon sugar
1   teaspoon olive oil
1   teaspoon water
4   cups gourmet salad greens
¼   cup crumbled Stilton cheese or
    feta cheese
4   (1-ounce) slices French bread

Combine first 4 ingredients in a medium bowl; toss well to coat. Cover and refrigerate 1 hour.

Strain mixture through a sieve into a jar, reserving liquid. Set strawberries aside. Add oil and water to jar. Cover tightly, and shake vigorously. Arrange 1 cup greens on each of 4 salad plates. Top with ½ cup berries, 2 teaspoons dressing, and 1 tablespoon cheese. Serve with French bread. Yield: 4 servings.

CALORIES 158 (23% from fat); PROTEIN 5.3g; FAT 4g (sat 1.5g, mono 1.5g, poly 0.7g); CARB 26.1g; FIBER 3.1g; CHOL 7mg; IRON 1.5mg; SODIUM 275mg; CALC 72mg

Crying for Onions

Vidalias are the sweetest of the sweet, transporting recipes to another taste dimension.

Although there are many different kinds of onions, each with many different uses, there's something special about the sweet onion—and the Vidalia is the sweetest of sweet. They're light golden brown with a white interior, slightly rounded on the bottom, and flat on the stem end. Named after the town in southern Georgia where they thrive, Vidalias—like all sweet onions—have higher natural sugar and water contents than other varieties, which makes them bruise easily and difficult to store. Because of this, Vidalias were once available only during harvest season from April to June, but improved storage methods now make them accessible through the fall.

ASPARAGUS, VIDALIA, AND BEET SALAD

Assemble this salad right before serving it.

- ½ pound small beets
- ½ cup water
- 1 large Vidalia or other sweet onion (about ¾ pound), peeled
- 2 tablespoons water
- 2 cups (2-inch) sliced asparagus (about ¾ pound)
- 2 tablespoons lemon juice
- 1 tablespoon water
- 2 teaspoons olive oil
- 1 teaspoon Dijon mustard
- 1 teaspoon honey
- ½ teaspoon salt
- ¼ teaspoon pepper
- 1 large shallot, peeled and quartered

Preheat oven to 375°.

Leave root and 1 inch stem on beets; scrub with a brush. Place beets in an 11 x 7-inch baking dish; add ½ cup water to dish. Cover; bake at 375° for 45 minutes. Drain and let cool slightly. Peel and cut each beet into 4 wedges; place in a bowl, and set aside.

Place onion in baking dish; add 2 tablespoons water to dish. Cover and bake at 375° for 35 minutes. Add asparagus; cover and bake an additional 10 minutes. Drain and let cool slightly. Cut onion into 8 wedges; place onion and asparagus in a bowl; set aside.

Place lemon juice and next 7 ingredients in a food processor or blender; cover and process until smooth. Pour half of dressing over beets; toss well to coat. Pour remaining half of dressing over onion-asparagus mixture; toss well to coat.

Spoon 1 cup onion-asparagus mixture onto each of 4 salad plates; top each with about ⅓ cup beets. Yield: 4 servings.

CALORIES 93 (26% from fat); PROTEIN 3.3g; FAT 2.7g (sat 0.4g, mono 1.7g, poly 0.3g); CARB 16.3g; FIBER 2.9g; CHOL 0mg; IRON 1.3mg; SODIUM 383mg; CALC 37mg

VIDALIA ONION PIZZA

You can sauté the onions while the pizza crusts rise.

- 1 (16-ounce) box hot roll mix
- 1⅓ cups very warm water (120° to 130° degrees)
- ¼ cup all-purpose flour
- Vegetable cooking spray
- 2½ teaspoons olive oil, divided
- 6 cups vertically sliced Vidalia or other sweet onion (about 1½ pounds)
- 1½ cups (6 ounces) grated Jarlsberg or Swiss cheese
- ½ cup (2 ounces) grated Asiago or Parmesan cheese

Combine contents of roll mix and enclosed yeast packet in a large bowl; stir well. Add very warm water; stir well. Turn dough out onto a lightly floured surface. Knead until smooth and elastic (about 5 minutes); add ¼ cup flour, one tablespoon at a time as needed, to prevent dough from sticking to hands. Cover and let rest 5 minutes.

Divide dough in half. Roll each half of dough into a 12-inch circle on a lightly floured surface. Place each circle of dough on a 12-inch pizza pan coated with cooking spray; pierce several times with a fork. Cover and let rise in a warm place (85°), free from drafts, 15 minutes or until puffy. Brush ½ teaspoon oil over each crust.

Preheat oven to 450°.

Heat remaining 1½ teaspoons oil in a large Dutch oven over medium heat until hot. Add onion, and sauté 20 minutes or until golden brown.

Sprinkle ¾ cup Jarlsberg cheese over each pizza crust. Divide the caramelized onion evenly between pizzas; sprinkle each with ¼ cup Asiago cheese. Bake at 450° for 15 minutes or until lightly browned. Cut each pizza into 8 wedges. Yield: 8 servings (serving size: 2 wedges).

CALORIES 381 (29% from fat); PROTEIN 15.9g; FAT 12.3g (sat 6g, mono 4.8g, poly 0.9g); CARB 49.9g; FIBER 3.6g; CHOL 28mg; IRON 3mg; SODIUM 563mg; CALC 317mg

SWEET-AND-SOUR VIDALIAS WITH CABBAGE

1   tablespoon olive oil
7½ cups vertically sliced Vidalia
    or other sweet onion (about
    1 pound)
8   cups thinly sliced napa
    (Chinese) cabbage
3¼ cups chopped seeded tomato
¼   cup white wine vinegar
1   teaspoon salt
¼   teaspoon pepper
2   tablespoons sugar

Heat oil in a Dutch oven over medium-high heat. Add onion; sauté 5 minutes or until tender. Add cabbage and next 4 ingredients; cook 10 minutes or until cabbage is tender, stirring frequently. Stir in sugar; cook 1 minute. Serve with pot roast or pork. Yield: 7 servings (serving size: 1 cup).

CALORIES 107 (22% from fat); PROTEIN 3.3g; FAT 2.6g (sat 0.4g, mono 1.5g, poly 0.4g); CARB 19.9g; FIBER 4.2g; CHOL 0mg; IRON 1.3mg; SODIUM 399mg; CALC 113mg

ROASTED VIDALIAS

This easy side dish makes a savory accompaniment to grilled fish, poultry, steak, or calf's liver.

4   medium Vidalia or other sweet
    onions, each peeled and cut
    into 8 wedges (about 2
    pounds)
Olive oil-flavored vegetable
    cooking spray
1   teaspoon dried thyme
½   teaspoon salt
¼   teaspoon freshly ground
    pepper
1   tablespoon balsamic vinegar

Preheat oven to 350°.
Arrange onion wedges on a jelly-roll pan coated with cooking spray; lightly coat onions with cooking spray. Sprinkle thyme, salt, and pepper over onions. Bake at 350° for 30 minutes. Turn onion wedges over; bake an additional 25 minutes or until onions are tender. Spoon onions into a serving dish, and drizzle with vinegar. Yield: 4 servings (serving size: ¾ cup).

CALORIES 57 (6% from fat); PROTEIN 1.7g; FAT 0.4g (sat 0.1g, mono 0g, poly 0.1g); CARB 12.6g; FIBER 2.7g; CHOL 0mg; IRON 0.8mg; SODIUM 297mg; CALC 36mg

VEGETABLE SKILLET SUPPER WITH TURKEY MEATBALLS

You can also add the Turkey Meatballs to your favorite spaghetti sauce.

6 to 8 small red potatoes (about 1
    pound), thinly sliced
Turkey Meatballs
2   medium Vidalia or other sweet
    onions (about 1 pound), cut
    into thin wedges
1   medium red bell pepper, cut
    into 1-inch pieces
1   medium green bell pepper, cut
    into 1-inch pieces
2   tablespoons balsamic vinegar
½   teaspoon salt
¼   teaspoon pepper
1   English cucumber, halved
    lengthwise and sliced

Place potatoes in a large skillet; cover with water, and bring to a boil. Cover, reduce heat, and simmer 4 minutes or just until potatoes are tender. Drain; place potatoes in a bowl, and set aside.
Add Turkey Meatballs, onion wedges, and bell peppers to skillet; sauté 3 minutes. Add potatoes; cook 3 minutes, stirring gently.
Remove from heat; stir in vinegar, salt, and pepper. Add cucumber; stir gently. Yield: 6 servings (serving size: 2 cups).

CALORIES 235 (27% from fat); PROTEIN 20.7g; FAT 7g (sat 1.5g, mono 3.4g, poly 1.2g); CARB 22.2g; FIBER 3.3g; CHOL 86mg; IRON 3.1mg; SODIUM 492mg; CALC 55mg

Turkey Meatballs:

1   pound ground turkey or
    chicken
3   tablespoons fine, dry
    breadcrumbs
½   teaspoon salt
¼   teaspoon fennel seeds, crushed
¼   teaspoon dried marjoram
¼   teaspoon dried oregano
¼   teaspoon dried thyme
¼   teaspoon pepper
Dash of ground nutmeg
1   egg
1   garlic clove, crushed
Vegetable cooking spray

Preheat oven to 350°.
Combine first 11 ingredients in a large bowl; stir well. Coat hands with cooking spray, and shape turkey mixture into 24 meatballs (mixture will be sticky). Place meatballs on a baking sheet coated with cooking spray. Bake at 350° for 8 minutes. Turn meatballs over; bake an additional 8 minutes. Yield: 6 servings (serving size: 4 meatballs).

CALORIES 117 (25% from fat); PROTEIN 18g; FAT 3.3g (sat 1g, mono 0.9g, poly 0.8g); CARB 2.7g; FIBER 0.2g; CHOL 85mg; IRON 1.6mg; SODIUM 286mg; CALC 27mg

JULY AUGUST

The Best Ears of Our Lives

This being the corn season, we asked corn expert Betty Fussell to lend us her ears—and her recipes. Nobody knows corn quite like Fussell, America's undisputed queen of the crop. For the last decade, the author of *The Story of Corn* and *Crazy for Corn* has made it her mission to know everything there is to know about this native American grain, from its culinary role in the ancient Maya, Aztec, and Inca cultures to the many innovative ways of serving it today.

Like Fussell, the following recipes are both down-home and joyous, running the gamut from spoon bread to ice cream. Each reflects Fussell's flair for making the ordinary extraordinary, such as putting hazelnuts in a sweet corn spoon bread and roasted kernels in a succotash.

MINI CLAMBAKE

4   ears corn with husks
4   cups water
1   tablespoon salt
8   small red potatoes
2   (1½-pound) live Maine lobsters
16 small clams in shells, scrubbed
¼   cup margarine, cut into small
    pieces
Lemon wedges

Remove husks from corn, and set husks aside. Scrub silks from corn, and set corn aside.

Combine water, salt, and potatoes in a 19-quart stockpot; bring to a boil. Add lobsters; cover and cook 12 minutes. Remove lobsters from pot, and set aside. Add clams to pot; cover and cook 10 minutes or until shells open. Remove clams from pot, and set aside; discard any unopened shells.

Add corn to pot; cover and cook 5 minutes. Remove corn and potatoes from pot, and set aside. Reserve 1 cup cooking liquid.

Combine reserved cooking liquid and margarine in a blender; cover and process until margarine melts.

Arrange cornhusks spokelike on a large serving platter. Arrange lobsters, clams, corn, and potatoes on top of cornhusks. Serve with warm margarine mixture and lemon wedges. Yield: 4 servings (serving size: ½ lobster, 4 clams, 1 ear corn, 2 potatoes, and ¼ cup plus 2 tablespoons sauce).

CALORIES 488 (24% from fat); PROTEIN 25.2g; FAT 13.2g (sat 2.6g, mono 5.4g, poly 4.3g); CARB 73.2g; FIBER 8.3g; CHOL 54mg; IRON 6.1mg; SODIUM 882mg; CALC 110mg

ROASTED SUCCOTASH

Cooking the mixed vegetables over high heat without added fat gives them a robust, smoky taste similar to that of oven-roasted vegetables.

1½ cups fresh corn kernels (about 3
    ears)
1   cup chopped red bell
    pepper
½   cup chopped onion
1   teaspoon ground cumin
1   cup chopped yellow squash
1½ tablespoons olive oil
2   garlic cloves, minced
½   cup low-salt chicken broth
2   tablespoons chopped fresh
    cilantro
½   teaspoon salt
⅛   teaspoon pepper
⅛   teaspoon hot sauce
1   (10-ounce) package frozen baby
    lima beans, thawed

Place a large nonstick skillet over high heat until hot. Add first 4 ingredients; sauté 5 minutes or until vegetables are slightly blackened. Add squash, oil, and garlic; sauté over medium-high heat 1 minute. Add broth, cilantro, salt, pepper, hot sauce, and lima beans; cook 2 minutes or until mixture is thoroughly heated, stirring often. Yield: 5 servings (serving size: 1 cup).

CALORIES 170 (26% from fat); PROTEIN 6.9g; FAT 5.2g (sat 0.7g, mono 3.2g, poly 0.7g); CARB 26.8g; FIBER 3.9g; CHOL 0mg; IRON 2.8mg; SODIUM 337mg; CALC 41mg

SWEET CORN-AND-HAZELNUT SPOON BREAD

Some of the fresh corn for this creamy side dish is puréed and stirred into the batter, enhancing the corn flavor throughout the bread.

¼   cup hazelnuts
1   cup yellow cornmeal
2   cups boiling water
2   cups fresh corn kernels (about
    4 ears), divided
1¼ cups 2% low-fat milk
2   tablespoons margarine,
    melted
1   tablespoon sugar
½   teaspoon salt
2   egg yolks
2   teaspoons baking powder
4   egg whites
Vegetable cooking spray

Preheat oven to 350°.

Place hazelnuts on a baking sheet. Bake at 350° for 15 minutes, stirring once. Turn nuts out onto a towel. Roll up towel; rub off skins. Place nuts in a food processor; process until ground. Spoon into a bowl; set aside.

Place cornmeal in a large bowl. Gradually add boiling water, stirring with a whisk until blended. Let cornmeal mixture stand 10 minutes.

Place 1 cup corn and next 5 ingredients in a food processor; process until mixture is smooth, scraping sides of processor bowl once. Add corn purée mixture to cornmeal mixture. Stir in hazelnuts, remaining 1 cup corn, and baking powder; set mixture aside.

Beat egg whites at high speed of an electric mixer just until stiff peaks form. Gently fold egg whites into cornmeal mixture. Spoon mixture into a 2-quart baking dish coated with cooking spray. Bake at 350° for 30 minutes or until puffy and lightly browned. Yield: 6 servings (serving size: 1 cup).

CALORIES 230 (29% from fat); PROTEIN 9.2g; FAT 7.3g (sat 1.6g, mono 4g, poly 1.1g); CARB 33.8g; FIBER 3g; CHOL 77mg; IRON 1.8mg; SODIUM 267mg; CALC 174mg

SUMMER CORN-AND-ARUGULA SALAD

This salad can be served at room temperature or chilled. It's especially good paired with grilled pork or a simple pasta dish. If you make it ahead of time, be sure to toss it just before serving.

- 3 tablespoons balsamic vinegar
- 1 tablespoon olive oil
- 1 tablespoon water
- ¼ teaspoon pepper
- ⅛ teaspoon salt
- 4 cups fresh corn kernels (about 8 ears)
- 2 cups diced cucumber
- 2 cups halved cherry tomatoes
- 2 cups trimmed, coarsely chopped arugula
- ½ cup diced part-skim mozzarella cheese
- ⅓ cup chopped fresh basil

Combine first 5 ingredients in a large bowl; stir well. Add corn and remaining ingredients; toss gently. Serve at room temperature or chilled. Yield: 8 servings (serving size: 1 cup).

CALORIES 121 (29% from fat); PROTEIN 4.9g; FAT 3.9g (sat 1.1g, mono 1.9g, poly 0.7g); CARB 18.5g; FIBER 3.2g; CHOL 4mg; IRON 0.7mg; SODIUM 121mg; CALC 65mg

MENU SUGGESTION

CREAMY CORN-AND-ZUCCHINI SOUP

Bacon-lettuce-tomato sandwich*

Watermelon wedges

*Use crisp-cooked turkey bacon, light mayonnaise, and whole wheat bread for a healthier version of the BLT.

CREAMY CORN-AND-ZUCCHINI SOUP

Corn purée makes this soup thick and rich without the addition of cream.

- 6 cups low-salt chicken broth
- 2 cups diced zucchini
- ½ cup chopped onion
- 6 cups fresh corn kernels (about 12 ears)
- ½ teaspoon salt
- ¼ teaspoon pepper
- ¾ cup plain fat-free yogurt
- Jalapeño hot sauce (optional)

Bring broth to a simmer in a large saucepan. Add zucchini and onion; cover and simmer 2 minutes. Stir in corn, salt, and pepper; cover and simmer 2 minutes.

Place one-third of corn mixture in a blender; cover and process until mixture is smooth. Repeat procedure with remaining corn mixture. Ladle soup into bowls; top with yogurt. Serve with jalapeño hot sauce, if desired. Yield: 12 servings (serving size: 1 cup soup and 1 tablespoon yogurt).

CALORIES 96 (16% from fat); PROTEIN 4.8g; FAT 1.7g (sat 0.4g, mono 0.6g, poly 0.6g); CARB 18.2g; FIBER 2.7g; CHOL 0mg; IRON 1.1mg; SODIUM 160mg; CALC 35mg

ORANGE-RAISIN CORN MUFFINS

If you can find freshly ground cornmeal (available at mills or farmers' markets), be sure to try it in this corn muffin recipe and in the spoon bread recipe.

- ¾ cup all-purpose flour
- ⅔ cup yellow cornmeal
- 1½ teaspoons baking powder
- ½ teaspoon salt
- ½ teaspoon ground cinnamon
- ½ teaspoon ground nutmeg
- ¼ teaspoon baking soda
- 1 cup fresh corn kernels (about 2 ears)
- 1 cup golden raisins
- ¼ cup chopped pecans, toasted
- 1 tablespoon grated orange rind
- ¼ cup 2% low-fat milk
- ¼ cup fresh orange juice
- 3 tablespoons maple syrup
- 3 tablespoons stick margarine, melted
- 2 egg whites
- 1 egg yolk
- Vegetable cooking spray

Preheat oven to 400°.

Combine first 7 ingredients in a medium bowl; stir well. Stir in corn, raisins, pecans, and orange rind; make a well in center of mixture.

Combine milk and next 5 ingredients; stir well with a whisk. Add to flour mixture, stirring just until moist.

Divide batter evenly among 12 muffin cups coated with cooking spray. Bake at 400° for 18 minutes or until muffins spring back when touched lightly in center. Remove muffins from pan immediately; let cool on a wire rack. Yield: 1 dozen (serving size: 1 muffin).

CALORIES 178 (28% from fat); PROTEIN 3.6g; FAT 5.6g (sat 1g, mono 2.6g, poly 1.6g); CARB 30.4g; FIBER 2g; CHOL 19mg; IRON 1.3mg; SODIUM 174mg; CALC 59mg

SWEET CORN-BOURBON ICE CREAM

Corn for dessert? Why not? This ice cream gets its kick from bourbon—a well-known derivative of corn.

    4   cups 2% low-fat milk
    4   cups fresh corn kernels (about
          8 ears)
    2   eggs
    1   cup sugar
    3   tablespoons bourbon
    2   teaspoons vanilla extract

Combine milk and corn in a large saucepan; bring to a simmer, and cook 1 minute. Place half of corn mixture in a blender; cover and process until smooth. Press puréed corn mixture through a sieve into a large bowl; discard solids. Repeat procedure with remaining corn mixture. Set corn-milk mixture aside.

Place eggs in a medium bowl; stir well with a whisk. Gradually add corn-milk mixture to eggs, stirring constantly with whisk. Return corn-milk mixture to pan. Place over medium heat; cook 1 minute, stirring constantly. Remove from heat; add sugar, bourbon, and vanilla, stirring until sugar dissolves. Pour into a bowl; cover and chill completely.

Pour mixture into the freezer can of an ice cream freezer; freeze according to manufacturer's instructions. Spoon into a freezer-safe container; cover and freeze 2 hours or until firm. Yield: 12 servings (serving size: ½ cup).

CALORIES 172 (16% from fat); PROTEIN 5.4g; FAT 3g (sat 1.3g, mono 1g, poly 0.5g); CARB 30.5g; FIBER 1.6g; CHOL 43mg; IRON 0.4mg; SODIUM 60mg; CALC 105mg

BETTY'S TOP 10 CORN TIPS

Betty Fussell, noted corn expert and author, shares these tips from her latest book *Crazy for Corn*.

◆ Sweet corns are classified by the percentage of sugar in their kernels. **Sweet** corn has 5 to 10 percent, **Sugar-Enhanced** 15 to 18 percent, and **Supersweet** 25 to 30 percent.

◆ Normally the sugar in an ear of corn begins to convert to starch the moment it's picked. That accounts for the "rule" to have your water boiling on the stove before the corn is picked in the field. But today many supersweet varieties are being bred to delay conversion of sugar to starch for two weeks or longer.

◆ Fussell's first suggestion about buying fresh sweet corn is to respect its chastity within the protection that God gave it. It's the tightly closed husk that keeps the seeds within at maximum freshness. You can tell whether a cob is completely filled by feeling the top from the outside of the husk.

◆ Salt toughens the skins of the kernels so don't salt the water you boil for corn. With supersweets, the briefer the dip into boiling water the better. Forget the "3-minute rule." Fussell doesn't dip a corn ear for more than 30 seconds.

◆ Cook corn on the cob with the husks on. The husks not only increase the flavor, they steam the corn rather than boil it. They also retain heat, so that your ears will stay warmer once they've had their hot water bath.

◆ If you prefer to use a steamer to avoid immersing the ears in water, don't steam too long. Length of time depends on how many ears in what size steamer, but it may take as much as 5 to 10 minutes for the ears to heat through.

◆ Fussell has experimented a lot to find the best and easiest ways to get a grilled taste without overcooking the corn. She doesn't like to soak the husks first in cold water as many do, because that steams the corn on the grill. She prefers to either grill the corn in the husks without soaking so that the husks char a bit on the outside and transmit some of that flavor to the kernels, or to husk it and grill the nude ears directly over the heat. This tends to caramelize the sugar in the corn and give it a wonderful color and taste, intensifying sweetness.

◆ For those who can seldom use an outdoor grill, get that same caramelized taste by roasting an ear, husks removed, directly over the flame of a gas stove, the way you would roast a pepper. Hold the ear with a pair of tongs and turn it so that it scorches slightly on all sides, about 3 to 4 minutes.

◆ Roasting corn in a hot oven, 450° to 500°, works better than most oven broilers. If you roast the ears in their husks, you are again steaming the kernels. It takes about 6 to 8 minutes to get the corn hot all the way through.

◆ By all accounts, microwave ovens do well with corn if you are cooking only one or two ears. To keep the corn kernels from drying out, cook the ears with the husk on and at the highest setting.

Sweet Corn-and-Hazelnut
Spoon Bread, page 182

Peaches-and-Cream Ice Cream, page 199

Peach-and-Ginger Custard Tart, page 213

Chicken Caesar Salad, page 210

*Quinoa-Stuffed Poblano
Chiles, page 198*

*Three-Bean Salad with
Balsamic Dressing, page 201*

Chunky Gazpacho, page 214

Raspberry Angel Torte, page 193

Watermelon Margarita Sorbet, page 194

Banana Split Ice Cream,
page 200

Greek Feta Burgers, page 204

Chili Fries, page 207

Red, White, and Blue

With these All-American desserts, you can show your flag-waving colors on the Fourth of July.

Attention Yankee Doodle Dandies: We're celebrating America's birthday with an array of red, white, and blue desserts, all featuring fresh produce from our fruited plains. Because America is about freedom of choice, we offer a variety to choose from, including a Bavarian cream with cherries, a blueberry sorbet, a mixed berry trifle, and a strawberry shake.

As for presentation, our spectacular Raspberry Angel Torte resembles the American flag. Talk about a tasty tribute to Old Glory: Your family and guests will want to stand up and salute it. So on the Fourth of July, celebrate with the red, white, and blue. Just think: You'll not only be serving your friends and family, but your country, too.

RASPBERRY ANGEL TORTE

2 cups raspberries
2 tablespoons sugar
2 tablespoons seedless red raspberry jam, melted
1 (10½-ounce) loaf angel food cake
¼ cup plus 2 tablespoons amaretto, divided
¾ cup vanilla low-fat yogurt
½ cup blueberries
2 tablespoons plus 2 teaspoons sliced almonds, toasted

Place first 3 ingredients in a food processor, and pulse 3 times or until coarsely chopped. Set aside.

Line an 8-inch loaf pan with plastic wrap, allowing plastic wrap to extend over edge of loaf pan. Cut cake horizontally into 6 slices (slices will be very thin). Place 1 cake slice in bottom of loaf pan. Brush cake slice with 1 tablespoon amaretto. Spread 3 tablespoons raspberry mixture over cake slice, and top with another cake slice. Repeat layers, ending with cake slice (do not put amaretto or raspberry mixture on top cake layer). Cover and chill 2 hours.

Place a serving plate upside down on top of pan; invert cake onto plate. Remove plastic wrap. Combine yogurt and remaining 1 tablespoon amaretto in a small bowl; stir well. Cut torte crosswise into 8 slices. Dollop 1½ tablespoons yogurt mixture onto each slice; sprinkle each with 1 tablespoon blueberries and 1 teaspoon almonds. Yield: 8 servings.

CALORIES 207 (7% from fat); PROTEIN 4.1g; FAT 1.7g (sat 0.3g, mono 0.8g, poly 0.4g); CARB 39.7g; FIBER 2.9g; CHOL 1mg; IRON 0.4mg; SODIUM 206mg; CALC 81mg

BERRY-AMARETTO SUMMER TRIFLE

Any combination of berries will work. Even if the dessert isn't red, white, and blue, it will taste revolutionary.

1½ cups sliced strawberries
¾ cup blueberries
2 tablespoons amaretto (almond-flavored liqueur)
1 cup frozen reduced-calorie whipped topping, thawed
1½ cups (1-inch) cubed angel food cake
2 tablespoons frozen reduced-calorie whipped topping, thawed

Combine first 3 ingredients in a medium bowl; stir gently. Let stand 10 minutes.

Spoon ⅓ cup berry mixture into each of 2 (12-ounce) parfait glasses, and top each with ¼ cup whipped topping and about ⅓ cup cake cubes. Repeat layers, ending with berry mixture. Cover and chill 2 hours. Top each parfait with 1 tablespoon whipped topping before serving. Yield: 2 servings.

CALORIES 266 (19% from fat); PROTEIN 3.9g; FAT 5.5g (sat 3.3g, mono 0.1g, poly 2g); CARB 45.2g; FIBER 5.4g; CHOL 1mg; IRON 0.6mg; SODIUM 175mg; CALC 69mg

BERRY PATCH PARFAITS

To round out the texture and flavor of this dessert, serve with a crisp pirouette cookie.

2 cups raspberries or blackberries
¼ cup sugar, divided
1 teaspoon cornstarch
1 (32-ounce) carton vanilla low-fat yogurt
¼ cup frozen reduced-calorie whipped topping, thawed
12 raspberries or blackberries

Place 2 cups raspberries in a food processor or blender; cover and process until puréed. Press puréed berries through a sieve into a microwave-safe bowl, and discard seeds. Add 2 tablespoons sugar and cornstarch to purée; stir with a whisk until blended. Microwave at HIGH 3 minutes or until thick and bubbly, stirring after 1½ minutes. Spoon 1 tablespoon berry mixture into each of 4 (10-ounce) stemmed glasses. Chill, uncovered, 10 minutes.

Spoon yogurt onto several layers of heavy-duty paper towels; spread to ½-inch thickness. Cover with additional paper towels; let stand 5 minutes. Scrape into a bowl using a rubber spatula. Add remaining 2 tablespoons sugar to yogurt; stir well.

Divide yogurt mixture evenly among glasses; top each with 3 tablespoons berry mixture. Cover loosely; chill at least 2 hours. Top each parfait with 1 tablespoon whipped topping and 3 raspberries. Yield: 4 servings.

CALORIES 288 (12% from fat); PROTEIN 11.9g; FAT 3.7g (sat 1.9g, mono 0.8g, poly 0.3g); CARB 53.6g; FIBER 5.2g; CHOL 11mg; IRON 0.6mg; SODIUM 153mg; CALC 407mg

WHITE CHOCOLATE BAVARIAN CREAM WITH FRESH CHERRIES

Here are a few tips for a smooth, creamy texture: Keep a watchful eye while heating the gelatin mixture so that it doesn't come to a boil. Remember to stir it constantly with a whisk. Also, use a light hand while stirring the whipped topping into the white chocolate mixture.

3	cups pitted, halved sweet cherries (about 1¼ pounds)
3	tablespoons kirsch (cherry brandy)
1½	cups skim milk
2	tablespoons sugar
1	large egg yolk, lightly beaten
1	envelope unflavored gelatin
3	ounces premium white chocolate, chopped
1¼	cups frozen reduced-calorie whipped topping, thawed

Combine sweet cherries and kirsch in a bowl, and stir well. Cover and chill 30 minutes.

Combine milk, sugar, and egg yolk in a medium-size heavy saucepan; stir well. Sprinkle gelatin over milk mixture; let stand 1 minute. Cook over medium heat 12 minutes or until gelatin dissolves and mixture is slightly thick, stirring constantly with a whisk. Remove from heat; add white chocolate, stirring until chocolate melts and mixture is smooth.

Pour white chocolate mixture into a medium bowl. Place bowl over a large ice-filled bowl; let stand 15 minutes or just until mixture begins to thicken, stirring every 5 minutes (do not allow gelatin to set). Gently stir in whipped topping.

Spoon ¼ cup cherry mixture into each of 6 (8-ounce) parfait glasses, and top each with ¼ cup white chocolate mixture. Repeat layers with remaining cherry mixture and chocolate mixture. Cover and chill 1 hour. Yield: 6 servings.

CALORIES 230 (30% from fat); PROTEIN 5.7g; FAT 7.8g (sat 3g, mono 1.9g, poly 0.5g); CARB 33.7g; FIBER 1.7g; CHOL 38mg; IRON 0.4mg; SODIUM 57mg; CALC 129mg

STRAWBERRY-MALTED MILK SHAKE

2	cups vanilla low-fat ice cream
1½	cups halved strawberries
¼	cup skim milk
3	tablespoons malted milk powder
1	tablespoon sugar
	Whole strawberries with green caps (optional)

Place first 5 ingredients in a blender; cover and process until smooth. Garnish with whole strawberries, if desired. Serve immediately. Yield: 3 servings (serving size: ¾ cup).

CALORIES 254 (21% from fat); PROTEIN 7.2g; FAT 5.9g (sat 3.4g, mono 1.6g, poly 0.6g); CARB 45.6g; FIBER 1.9g; CHOL 13mg; IRON 0.5mg; SODIUM 182mg; CALC 214mg

WATERMELON MARGARITA SORBET

4	cups seeded, cubed watermelon
¼	cup thawed limeade concentrate, undiluted
¼	cup tequila
3	tablespoons sugar
1	tablespoon triple sec (orange-flavored liqueur)

Place all ingredients in a blender; cover and process until smooth. Pour mixture into a 9-inch square baking pan; cover and freeze until firm.

Remove pan from freezer; cut frozen mixture into desired shapes with a cookie cutter, if desired. Yield: 5 servings (serving size: 1 cup).

Note: To make **Watermelon Margarita Granita**, remove pan from freezer; scrape entire mixture with a fork until fluffy.

CALORIES 134 (4% from fat); PROTEIN 0.8g; FAT 0.6g (sat 0.3g, mono 0.1g, poly 0g); CARB 24.8g; FIBER 0.7g; CHOL 0mg; IRON 0.3mg; SODIUM 3mg; CALC 11mg

BLUEBERRY SORBET

You can also freeze the sorbet in a baking dish, and serve it as a granita.

4	cups lemon-lime soda (such as Sprite), chilled and divided
2	cups blueberries
½	cup sugar
2	teaspoons fresh lemon juice

Place 2 cups soda and remaining 3 ingredients in a blender; cover and process until smooth. Combine blueberry mixture and remaining 2 cups soda in the freezer can of an ice cream freezer; freeze according to manufacturer's instructions. Yield: 6 servings (serving size: 1 cup).

CALORIES 154 (1% from fat); PROTEIN 0.3g; FAT 0.2g (sat 0g, mono 0g, poly 0.1g); CARB 39.2g; FIBER 2.2g; CHOL 0mg; IRON 0.1mg; SODIUM 30mg; CALC 3mg

Note: To make **Blueberry Frozen Yogurt**, stir 2 (8-ounce) cartons vanilla low-fat yogurt into puréed blueberry mixture. Pour into the freezer can of an ice cream freezer; freeze according to manufacturer's instructions. Yield: 8 servings (serving size: 1 cup).

CALORIES 163 (4% from fat); PROTEIN 3g; FAT 0.8g (sat 0.5g, mono 0.2g, poly 0.1g); CARB 37.2g; FIBER 1.6g; CHOL 3mg; IRON 0.1mg; SODIUM 60mg; CALC 99mg

You Can Go Down-Home Again

In the '60s it came to be called soul food: derived, most likely, from the Old South adage that rich folks ate for the body, poor folks for the soul.

The origins of down-home cooking can be traced to the slaves of the Old South, for whom high-fat, hearty food was a solace.

With heart doctors and various public-health organizations working to increase awareness among African-Americans of the dangers of a high-fat diet (high blood pressure, diabetes, heart disease, obesity), these recipes couldn't be more timely.

SHRIMP-AND-GRITS GRATIN

- 3 tablespoons chopped fresh or 1 tablespoon dried basil
- 2 tablespoons fresh lemon juice
- 1 tablespoon olive oil
- 1 tablespoon raspberry vinegar
- 1 teaspoon grated lemon rind
- 1 garlic clove, minced
- 1 pound medium shrimp, peeled and deveined
- 4 cups boiling water
- 3 cups uncooked instant grits
- ¼ cup grated Parmesan cheese, divided
- 2 tablespoons chopped fresh or 2 teaspoons dried parsley
- 1 teaspoon grated lemon rind
- ¼ teaspoon pepper
- Vegetable cooking spray
- ⅛ teaspoon paprika
- Fresh basil sprigs (optional)

Combine chopped basil, lemon juice, olive oil, vinegar, 1 teaspoon grated lemon rind, and minced garlic in a shallow dish; stir well. Add shrimp, stirring to coat. Cover; marinate in refrigerator 2 hours, stirring occasionally. Remove shrimp; set aside. Discard marinade.

Preheat oven to 350°.

Combine 4 cups boiling water and grits in a large bowl; stir well. Add marinated shrimp, 2 tablespoons cheese, parsley, 1 teaspoon lemon rind, and pepper; stir well.

Spoon grits mixture into a 2-quart casserole coated with cooking spray; sprinkle with remaining 2 tablespoons cheese and paprika. Bake at 350° for 30 minutes. Garnish with basil sprigs, if desired. Yield: 6 servings (serving size: 1 cup).

CALORIES 218 (19% from fat); PROTEIN 16.6g; FAT 4.7g (sat 1.1g, mono 2.1g, poly 0.6g); CARB 28.2g; FIBER 1.9g; CHOL 89mg; IRON 16mg; SODIUM 807mg; CALC 91mg

LEAH CHASE'S OVEN-FRIED CHICKEN

For a spicier version, you can substitute red pepper for the white.

- ¼ teaspoon salt
- ¼ teaspoon white pepper
- 1 (3-pound) chicken, skinned and cut into 8 pieces
- 1 cup all-purpose flour
- ½ teaspoon garlic powder
- ½ teaspoon paprika
- ¼ teaspoon ground thyme
- Vegetable cooking spray
- 1 tablespoon margarine, melted

Preheat oven to 400°.

Sprinkle salt and pepper over chicken. Combine chicken, flour, garlic powder, paprika, and thyme in a large heavy-duty, zip-top plastic bag; seal and shake to coat chicken with flour mixture. Remove chicken from bag; discard flour mixture.

Place chicken on a jelly-roll pan coated with cooking spray. Drizzle margarine over chicken. Bake at 400° for 50 minutes or until done. Yield: 6 servings.

CALORIES 194 (28% from fat); PROTEIN 17.3g; FAT 6.1g (sat 1.5g, mono 2.2g, poly 1.6g); CARB 16.3g; FIBER 0.6g; CHOL 46mg; IRON 1.7mg; SODIUM 165mg; CALC 14mg

GULLAH RICE

Gullah is an English-based Creole dialect spoken along the coastal regions of the Carolinas.

- 1 teaspoon butter
- ½ cup chopped celery
- ½ cup chopped carrot
- ¼ cup chopped pistachios
- 3 cups water
- ½ teaspoon salt
- 1 cup uncooked long-grain rice
- 1 tablespoon chopped fresh thyme

Melt butter in a medium saucepan over medium heat. Add celery, carrot, and pistachios; sauté 5 minutes or until tender. Add water and salt; bring to a boil. Add rice and thyme; return to a boil. Cover, reduce heat, and simmer 20 minutes or until most of liquid is absorbed. Let stand, covered, 10 minutes or until liquid is absorbed. Yield: 5 servings (serving size: 1 cup).

CALORIES 186 (20% from fat); PROTEIN 4.2g; FAT 4.2g (sat 1g, mono 2.4g, poly 0.6g); CARB 32.8g; FIBER 1.7g; CHOL 2mg; IRON 2.2mg; SODIUM 259mg; CALC 29mg

GRANDPOP'S MACARONI
AND CHEESE

*This traditional down-home dish has
a twist—fresh vegetables and herbs.*

    2   teaspoons butter
    1   cup sliced mushrooms
    ¾   cup diced red bell pepper
    ½   cup finely chopped celery
    ¼   cup chopped shallots
    ¾   cup part-skim ricotta cheese
  1½   teaspoons minced fresh or
        ½ teaspoon dried tarragon
    1   teaspoon salt
    1   teaspoon granulated tapioca
        (optional)
    ¼   teaspoon white pepper
    ¼   teaspoon ground nutmeg
    1   (12-ounce) can evaporated
        skim milk
    1   large egg, lightly beaten
    4   cups hot cooked elbow
        macaroni (about 7 ounces
        uncooked)
  Vegetable cooking spray
    1   medium tomato, cut into
        ¼-inch-thick slices
    ¼   cup fine, dry breadcrumbs
    ¼   cup grated Parmesan cheese
    1   teaspoon grated lemon rind

  Preheat oven to 350°.
  Melt butter over medium-high heat
in a medium-size nonstick skillet. Add
mushrooms, bell pepper, celery, and
shallots; sauté 4 minutes or until tender. Set aside.
  Combine ricotta cheese and next 7
ingredients in a large bowl; stir until
well-blended. Add mushroom mixture
and macaroni; stir well. Spoon mixture into a 2-quart casserole coated
with cooking spray.
  Press tomato slices gently between
paper towels until barely moist. Arrange
tomatoes in a circular pattern over top
of macaroni mixture. Combine breadcrumbs, Parmesan cheese, and lemon
rind in a small bowl; stir well. Sprinkle
breadcrumb mixture over tomatoes.
Bake at 350° for 35 minutes or until
lightly browned. Yield: 8 servings.

CALORIES 218 (21% from fat); PROTEIN 12g; FAT 5.2g
(sat 2.6g, mono 1.5g, poly 0.5g); CARB 30.9g; FIBER 1.9g;
CHOL 41mg; IRON 2mg; SODIUM 474mg; CALC 247mg

TANGY POTATO SALAD

*Fresh herbs make the difference in this
version of a familiar side dish.*

    ½   cup 1% low-fat cottage cheese
    ¼   cup skim milk
    2   tablespoons white vinegar
    ¼   teaspoon celery salt
    1   teaspoon chopped fresh or
        ¼ teaspoon dried dillweed
    ¼   teaspoon dry mustard
    6   cups peeled, cubed red potato
    ½   cup sliced green onions
    ½   cup diced celery
    2   tablespoons chopped fresh
        parsley
    ¼   teaspoon salt
    ¼   teaspoon white pepper

  Combine first 6 ingredients in a
blender; cover and process until mixture is smooth.
  Place potato in a large saucepan;
cover with water, and bring to a boil.
Reduce heat; simmer 15 minutes or
until tender. Drain well.
  Combine potato, cottage cheese
mixture, green onions, and remaining
ingredients in a bowl; toss well. Cover
and chill at least 1 hour. Yield: 6 servings (serving size: 1 cup).

CALORIES 144 (3% from fat); PROTEIN 6.2g; FAT 0.4g
(sat 0.2g, mono 0.1g, poly 0.1g); CARB 29.6g; FIBER 2.8g;
CHOL 1mg; IRON 1.6mg; SODIUM 288mg; CALC 48mg

SWEET POTATO SPOON
BREAD

    3   small sweet potatoes (about
        1¾ pounds)
    3   cups 1% low-fat milk, divided
    2   cups yellow cornmeal
    ½   teaspoon salt
    3   tablespoons brown sugar
    2   teaspoons baking powder
    1   teaspoon butter, melted
    ½   teaspoon baking soda
    1   large egg
    2   large egg whites
  Vegetable cooking spray

  Preheat oven to 375°.
  Wrap potatoes in aluminum foil;

bake at 375° for 1 hour or until tender.
Let cool. Peel potatoes; mash. Set aside.
  Combine 2 cups milk, cornmeal,
and salt in a large saucepan; stir well
with a whisk. Cook over medium heat
4 minutes or until thick, stirring constantly. Remove from heat; stir in
sweet potato and sugar.
  Combine potato mixture, remaining 1 cup milk, baking powder, butter,
baking soda, and 1 egg in a large bowl;
stir well. Set aside. Beat 2 egg whites in
a bowl at high speed of an electric
mixer until stiff peaks form; gently
fold into potato mixture. Spoon into
an 11 x 7-inch baking dish coated with
cooking spray. Bake at 375° for 50
minutes. Yield: 8 servings (serving
size: ¾ cup).

CALORIES 270 (10% from fat); PROTEIN 8.6g; FAT 2.9g
(sat 1.2g, mono 0.8g, poly 0.5g); CARB 52.1g; FIBER 3.7g;
CHOL 33mg; IRON 2.2mg; SODIUM 309mg; CALC 204mg

MUSTARD GREENS
WITH SMOKED TURKEY

*The flavorful liquid left after cooking
the greens is called pot liquor.*

   18   pounds mustard greens (about
        4 bunches)
    2   quarts water
    1   cup chopped onion
    1   tablespoon seasoned salt
    ½   teaspoon ground red pepper
    5   thyme sprigs
    2   (8-ounce) smoked turkey wing
        drumettes, skinned
    1   bay leaf
  1¼   pounds turnips (about 8
        medium), peeled and
        quartered

  Trim stems from mustard greens.
Coarsely chop leaves. Combine greens,
water, and remaining ingredients in a
large stockpot; bring to a boil. Cover,
reduce heat, and simmer 45 minutes or
until greens are tender. Remove thyme
sprigs, turkey wings, and bay leaf. Yield:
8 servings (serving size: 1 cup).

CALORIES 289 (8% from fat); PROTEIN 28.5g; FAT 2.5g
(sat 0.2g, mono 1g, poly 0.6g); CARB 53.1g; FIBER 7.4g;
CHOL 6mg; IRON 14.3mg; SODIUM 861mg; CALC 1,003mg

COWPEA CHOW CHOW

When served with tortilla chips, this chow chow makes a tasty substitute for salsa.

2   cups seeded, chopped tomato
1   cup chopped onion
1   cup chopped green bell pepper
1   cup chopped red bell pepper
¼   cup chopped fresh cilantro
3   tablespoons fresh lime juice
2   tablespoons white vinegar
2   teaspoons seeded, finely chopped serrano chile
½   teaspoon salt
¼   teaspoon pepper
1   (15-ounce) can black-eyed peas, drained

Combine all ingredients in a large bowl, and stir well. Cover and chill at least 1 hour. Yield: 14 servings (serving size: ½ cup).

CALORIES 39 (9% from fat); PROTEIN 2.2g; FAT 0.4g (sat 0.1g, mono 0g, poly 0.2g); CARB 7.6g; FIBER 1.3g; CHOL 0mg; IRON 0.8mg; SODIUM 148mg; CALC 13mg

INSPIRED VEGETARIAN

These Plates Are Hot

Reliant on beans, grains, and bold flavors, authentic Mexican food can be perfect for meatless meals.

If approached with sensibility and lightness, Mexican cuisine offers a wealth of healthful vegetarian possibilities. This is in strong contrast to the heavy Tex-Mex cuisine that people often think of as traditional Mexican.

Because chiles, cilantro, lime, and other bold flavors are used in Mexican food, any fat is used sparingly. Many dishes are prepared around beans and grains, which makes them even more appealing from a vegetarian perspective. After all, although Mexican food needn't be heavy, it should be comforting. So pass the margaritas—we're vegging in tonight.

MENU SUGGESTION

CHICKPEA-AND-HOMINY STEW

Crackers

*Border salad**

*Combine ¼ cup lime juice, 2 tablespoons each of tequila and orange juice, 2 teaspoons each of oil and honey. Drizzle over watercress, orange sections, and sliced radishes.

CHICKPEA-AND-HOMINY STEW

This dish is really good topped with spicy salsa.

2   teaspoons olive oil
2   cups diced onion
½   cup seeded, minced Anaheim chile
4   garlic cloves, minced
2¾   cups water
1   cup diced tomato
2   (19-ounce) cans chickpeas (garbanzo beans), drained
1   (15.5-ounce) can white hominy, drained
1   (14½-ounce) can vegetable broth
2   cups coarsely chopped spinach
¼   teaspoon pepper
¼   teaspoon ground cumin

Heat oil in a large saucepan over medium-high heat until hot. Add onion, chile, and garlic; sauté 1 minute. Add water and next 4 ingredients; bring to a boil. Cover, reduce heat, and simmer 20 minutes. Remove from heat; stir in spinach, pepper, and cumin. Yield: 6 servings (serving size: 1½ cups).

CALORIES 271 (17% from fat); PROTEIN 12.4g; FAT 5.2g (sat 0.6g, mono 1.9g, poly 1.7g); CARB 46.4g; FIBER 7.5g; CHOL 0mg; IRON 4.4mg; SODIUM 638mg; CALC 98mg

EGGPLANT BURRITO

Because of its unusually moist filling, this dish is easier to eat with a knife and fork.

2   teaspoons olive oil
1   (1½-pound) eggplant, peeled and cut into 3 x 1-inch strips
2   cups red bell pepper strips
1   cup vertically sliced red onion
2   tablespoons seeded, minced jalapeño pepper
1   teaspoon dried oregano
1   teaspoon chili powder
2   garlic cloves, minced
2   cups tomato juice
1   cup water
1   tablespoon lime juice
¼   teaspoon salt
6   (8-inch) flour tortillas
1½   cups (6 ounces) shredded reduced-fat Monterey Jack cheese
¼   cup plus 2 tablespoons plain fat-free yogurt

Preheat oven to 350°.

Heat oil in a large nonstick skillet over high heat until hot. Add eggplant; sauté 3 minutes. Add bell pepper and next 5 ingredients; sauté 1 minute. Add tomato juice and water; cook 12 minutes or until vegetables are tender and liquid is absorbed. Remove from heat; stir in lime juice and salt.

Divide eggplant mixture evenly among tortillas; sprinkle with cheese, and roll up. Place burritos, seam side down, on a jelly-roll pan. Bake at 350° for 5 minutes or until thoroughly heated. Serve with yogurt. Yield: 6 servings (serving size: 1 burrito and 1 tablespoon yogurt).

CALORIES 321 (30% from fat); PROTEIN 15.8g; FAT 10.6g (sat 4g, mono 4.5g, poly 1.8g); CARB 42.7g; FIBER 4.6g; CHOL 19mg; IRON 3.4mg; SODIUM 816mg; CALC 375mg

CHEESY RICE-AND-BEAN STRATA

Because of the store-bought picante sauce, canned beans, and marinara sauce, the sodium content is higher than usual. To lower the sodium, you can use no-salt-added brands or home-made versions.

    2   teaspoons olive oil
    2   cups minced red onion
    1   teaspoon ground cumin
    2   garlic cloves, minced
    1   (10-ounce) bag fresh spinach,
          chopped
    2   (19-ounce) cans kidney beans,
          drained
    1   (16-ounce) jar picante sauce
Vegetable cooking spray
    8   cups cooked basmati rice
          (cooked without salt or fat)
   12   (¼-inch-thick) slices tomato
    1   cup (4 ounces) shredded
          reduced-fat sharp Cheddar
          cheese
    1   cup (4 ounces) shredded
          reduced-fat Monterey Jack
          cheese
    1   cup Quick Mole Marinara
          Sauce
    ½   cup diagonally sliced green
          onions
    ½   cup low-fat sour cream

Preheat oven to 350°.

Heat oil in a large nonstick skillet over medium-high heat until hot. Add red onion, cumin, and garlic; sauté 2 minutes. Add spinach, and sauté 1 minute or until spinach wilts. Remove from heat, and set aside.

Combine beans and picante sauce in a bowl; stir well. Spread 2 cups of bean mixture in the bottom of a 13 x 9-inch baking dish coated with cooking spray. Spread 4 cups rice over bean mixture; top with tomato slices. Layer spinach mixture, remaining 4 cups rice, and 2 cups bean mixture over tomato slices.

Cover and bake strata at 350° for 25 minutes. Sprinkle with cheeses, and bake, uncovered, an additional 10 minutes or until cheese melts. Top each serving with 2 tablespoons Quick

Mole Marinara Sauce, 1 tablespoon green onions, and 1 tablespoon sour cream. Yield: 8 servings.

CALORIES 492 (20% from fat); PROTEIN 20.8g; FAT 10.7g (sat 4.7g, mono 4g, poly 0.9g); CARB 79.4g; FIBER 9.8g; CHOL 25mg; IRON 0.5mg; SODIUM 1,377mg; CALC 377mg

Quick Mole Marinara Sauce:

    2   teaspoons olive oil
    1   cup minced red onion
    3   tablespoons seeded, minced
          Anaheim chile
    1   teaspoon chili powder
    1   teaspoon dried oregano
    1   teaspoon ground cumin
    1   (25-ounce) jar marinara sauce
          (such as Prodotti Villa)
    2   tablespoons unsweetened
          cocoa
    1   tablespoon minced fresh or
          1 teaspoon dried cilantro

Heat oil in a large saucepan over medium-high heat until hot. Add onion and next 4 ingredients; sauté 2 minutes. Add marinara sauce; cook over low heat 30 minutes, stirring occasionally. Remove from heat; stir in cocoa and cilantro. Yield: 3 cups (serving size: 2 tablespoons).

Note: Store the remaining Quick Mole Marinara Sauce in an airtight container in refrigerator up to 1 week or freeze up to 3 months. Serve with any Mexican meal.

CALORIES 29 (47% from fat); PROTEIN 0.7g; FAT 1.5g (sat 0.2g, mono 0.8g, poly 0.3g); CARB 4.1g; FIBER 0.4g; CHOL 0mg; IRON 0.5mg; SODIUM 188mg; CALC 10mg

MEXICAN CORN OFF THE COB

    4   cups torn spinach leaves
    2   cups fresh corn kernels (about
          4 ears)
    1   cup diced red bell pepper
    1   cup peeled, diced jicama
    ½   cup diced red onion
    2   tablespoons minced fresh
          parsley
    2   tablespoons fresh lemon juice
    2   teaspoons vegetable oil
    ¼   teaspoon salt
    ¼   teaspoon ground red pepper
    ¼   cup crumbled goat cheese

Combine first 6 ingredients in a medium bowl. Combine lemon juice, oil, salt, and ground red pepper in a small bowl; stir well with a whisk. Pour over spinach mixture, tossing gently to coat. Sprinkle with goat cheese. Yield: 5 servings (serving size: 1 cup salad and about 1 tablespoon cheese).

CALORIES 119 (31% from fat); PROTEIN 4.8g; FAT 4.1g (sat 1.4g, mono 1g, poly 1.4g); CARB 19.4g; FIBER 4.6g; CHOL 5mg; IRON 2.2mg; SODIUM 228mg; CALC 84mg

QUINOA-STUFFED POBLANO CHILES

    4   (5-inch) poblano chiles
  1½   cups water
    ¾   cup uncooked quinoa
Vegetable cooking spray
    ½   cup chopped green bell pepper
    ½   cup chopped red bell pepper
    ½   cup chopped onion
    2   teaspoons seeded, minced
          jalapeño pepper
    2   garlic cloves, minced
    2   tablespoons unsalted pumpkin
          seed kernels
    ½   cup minced green onions
    1   tablespoon minced fresh or
          1 teaspoon dried cilantro
    1   tablespoon low-sodium soy
          sauce
    1   tablespoon lime juice
    2   cups tomato juice
    1   cup (4 ounces) shredded
          reduced-fat sharp Cheddar
          cheese

Preheat oven to 350°.

Cut chiles in half lengthwise; remove stems and seeds. Set aside.

Combine water and quinoa in a medium saucepan; bring to a boil. Cover, reduce heat, and simmer 13 minutes or until liquid is absorbed. Set aside.

Coat a large nonstick skillet with cooking spray; place over medium-high heat until hot. Add green pepper and next 4 ingredients; sauté 2 minutes. Add pumpkin seed kernels; sauté 2 minutes. Remove from heat; stir in quinoa, green onions, and next 3 ingredients. Spoon ⅓ cup quinoa mixture into each chile half.

Pour tomato juice into a 13 x 9-inch baking dish; place stuffed chiles in dish. Cover and bake at 350° for 20 minutes. Sprinkle cheese over chiles; bake, uncovered, an additional 10 minutes or until cheese melts and chiles are thoroughly heated. Spoon tomato juice over chiles. Yield: 4 servings (serving size: 2 stuffed chile halves).

CALORIES 329 (26% from fat); PROTEIN 20.4g; FAT 9.6g (sat 4.3g, mono 2.5g, poly 2.2g); CARB 47.9g; FIBER 7g; CHOL 19mg; IRON 7.4mg; SODIUM 787mg; CALC 347mg

LIGHTEN UP

A Midsummer Light's Dream

If ever there was a Norman Rockwell image, it's a family eating homemade ice cream on the front porch in the good old summertime. Today, more than ever, the Elysian pleasure of homemade ice cream can be yours—and it's easier on the arms. Electric ice cream makers do all of the cranking, and are not expensive. So why make your own? It's an American tradition that friends and families can enjoy together. If you've been avoiding ice cream because of the fat and calories, then take heart. We've significantly lightened three decadent recipes without losing flavor and creaminess. So now a thing of the past can be a joy forever.

PEACHES-AND-CREAM ICE CREAM

5   cups 1% low-fat milk, divided
4   egg yolks
4   cups peeled, mashed ripe peaches (about 8 medium peaches)
2   tablespoons fresh lemon juice
2   tablespoons vanilla extract
½   teaspoon ground ginger
½   teaspoon almond extract
2   (14-ounce) cans fat-free sweetened condensed skim milk
Mint sprigs (optional)

Combine 2½ cups 1% low-fat milk and egg yolks in a large heavy saucepan, and stir well with a whisk. Cook over medium heat 10 minutes or until mixture thickens and coats a spoon, stirring constantly (do not boil). Combine egg yolk mixture, remaining 2½ cups 1% low-fat milk, peaches, and next 5 ingredients in a large bowl; stir well. Cover and chill completely.

Pour mixture into the freezer can of an ice cream freezer, and freeze according to manufacturer's instructions. Spoon ice cream into a large freezer-safe container; cover and freeze 1 hour or until firm. Garnish with mint sprigs, if desired. Yield: 24 servings (serving size: ½ cup).

CALORIES 140 (9% from fat); PROTEIN 4.9g; FAT 1.4g (sat 0.6g, mono 0.5g, poly 0.2g); CARB 26.2g; FIBER 0.5g; CHOL 40mg; IRON 0.2mg; SODIUM 60mg; CALC 135mg

BEFORE & AFTER	
SERVING SIZE	
½ cup	
CALORIES PER SERVING	
230	140
FAT	
16g	1.4g
PERCENT OF TOTAL CALORIES	
63%	9%
CHOLESTEROL	
80mg	40mg

CRANKING IT UP

Making your own is easier than you may think. Ice cream freezers can be bought for as little as $25 at discount and department stores. Here are some tips to get you started:

◆ Basically, there are two types of ice cream makers: the manual models (such as a Donvier®) and the electric models. Some of the manual models fit on a counter top and don't use salt and ice. The secret is an aluminum tub you store in your freezer before using. All you have to do is turn the crank a few times while the ice cream freezes. Even though the smaller freezers make up to 1½ quarts of ice cream, you can still use our recipes; just cut the recipes in half (or by a fourth).

◆ If you're making ice cream for a crowd, consider buying one of the larger electric models that uses rock salt and ice. They make anywhere from 2 to 4 quarts of ice cream. Simply pour your ice cream mixture into the freezer container, add the appropriate amount of rock salt and ice, and plug in the freezer, periodically adding more salt and ice.

◆ One feature we liked on the electric models was a clear lid. It lets you see how well the mixture is freezing.

◆ After you've processed the ice cream in the freezer, spoon it into a freezer-safe container. Put it into the freezer compartment of your refrigerator for about an hour. This standing time lets the ice cream firm up to just the right consistency for scooping.

◆ When the ice cream is done, don't pour the salt-water mixture down the drain—it can damage pipes.

HOW WE DID IT

We found a way to make home-made ice creams that have smooth, creamy textures without adding heavy cream or artificial stabilizers.

◆ Made a custard using egg yolks and low-fat milk. (Be careful not to overcook the mixture, or you'll get scrambled eggs. Use a candy thermometer to monitor the temperature.)

◆ Used fat-free sweetened condensed skim milk, which adds richness from the milk and concentrated sugar content.

STRAWBERRY CHEESECAKE ICE CREAM

2½   cups 1% low-fat milk, divided
2   egg yolks
4   ounces Neufchâtel cheese, cubed and softened
3   cups finely chopped strawberries
1   tablespoon fresh lime juice
1   tablespoon vanilla extract
1   (14-ounce) can fat-free sweetened condensed skim milk

Combine 1¼ cups 1% low-fat milk and egg yolks in a small heavy saucepan, and stir well with a whisk. Heat milk mixture to 180° or until tiny bubbles form around edge of pan, stirring frequently (do not boil). Remove mixture from heat. Add cheese, stirring until smooth. Combine cheese mixture, remaining 1¼ cups 1% low-fat milk, strawberries, and remaining ingredients in a large bowl, and stir until well-blended. Cover and chill completely.

Pour mixture into the freezer can of an ice cream freezer, and freeze according to manufacturer's instructions. Spoon ice cream into a freezer-safe container; cover and freeze 1 hour or until ice cream is firm. Yield: 8 servings (serving size: ½ cup).

CALORIES 162 (21% from fat); PROTEIN 5.8g; FAT 3.8g (sat 2g, mono 1.2g, poly 0.3g); CARB 25.6g; FIBER 1g; CHOL 47mg; IRON 0.3mg; SODIUM 98mg; CALC 146mg

BEFORE & AFTER	
STRAWBERRY CHEESECAKE ICE CREAM	
SERVING SIZE	
½ cup	
CALORIES PER SERVING	
250	162
FAT	
15g	3.8g
PERCENT OF TOTAL CALORIES	
54%	21%
CHOLESTEROL	
95mg	47mg

BANANA SPLIT ICE CREAM

5   cups 1% low-fat milk, divided
4   egg yolks
2   (14-ounce) cans fat-free sweetened condensed skim milk
2   cups mashed ripe banana
2   tablespoons fresh lime juice
2   tablespoons vanilla extract
¾   cup fat-free double chocolate sundae syrup
½   cup chopped pecans, toasted
⅓   cup maraschino cherries, quartered

Combine 2½ cups 1% low-fat milk and egg yolks in a medium-size heavy saucepan; stir well with a whisk. Cook over medium heat 10 minutes or until mixture thickens and coats a spoon, stirring constantly (do not boil). Combine egg yolk mixture, remaining 2½ cups low-fat milk, and condensed milk in a large bowl. Cover; chill completely.

Add banana, lime juice, and vanilla to milk mixture; stir well. Pour mixture into the freezer can of an ice cream freezer, and freeze according to manufacturer's instructions. Spoon ice cream into a large freezer-safe container; fold in syrup, pecans, and cherries. Cover and freeze 2 hours or until firm. Yield: 24 servings (serving size: ½ cup).

CALORIES 189 (15% from fat); PROTEIN 5.3g; FAT 3.2g (sat 0.8g, mono 1.6g, poly 0.6g); CARB 34.3g; FIBER 0.7g; CHOL 40mg; IRON 0.2mg; SODIUM 67mg; CALC 136mg

BEFORE & AFTER	
BANANA SPLIT ICE CREAM	
SERVING SIZE	
½ cup	
CALORIES PER SERVING	
270	189
FAT	
19g	3.2g
PERCENT OF TOTAL CALORIES	
63%	15%
CHOLESTEROL	
70mg	40mg

FAST FOOD

Side Kicks

To accompany our lightened burgers, we have a picnic table full of classic sides and salads.

It's summertime, and according to Ira Gershwin, the livin' is supposed to be easy. With that in mind, we've recreated some good ol' summer side dishes and fresh salads to go with our delicious burger recipes (see page 204). These American classics are not only lighter than their regular counterparts but just as tasty, if not more so.

During this time of the year, the last thing you want to do is spend hours in the kitchen. These recipes are designed to get you outdoors where the fish are jumpin' and the cotton is high.

STOVETOP "BAKED BEANS"

Preparation time: 15 minutes
Cooking time: 20 minutes

    1   tablespoon margarine
    1¼   cups chopped onion
    ¾   cup chopped green bell pepper
    2   garlic cloves, minced
    1   cup reduced-calorie ketchup
    ¼   cup firmly packed brown sugar
    ¼   cup maple syrup
    2   tablespoons Worcestershire
         sauce
    2   teaspoons barbecue smoke
         seasoning (such as Hickory
         Liquid Smoke)
    2   teaspoons prepared mustard
    1   (16-ounce) can red beans,
         drained
    1   (15.8-ounce) can Great
         Northern beans, drained

Melt margarine in a medium sauce-pan over medium-high heat. Add onion, bell pepper, and garlic; sauté 4 minutes. Stir in ketchup and remaining ingredients; bring to a boil. Reduce heat; simmer 15 minutes, stirring occasionally. Yield: 8 servings (serving size: ½ cup).

CALORIES 179 (10% from fat); PROTEIN 6g; FAT 1.9g (sat 0.4g, mono 0.7g, poly 0.7g); CARB 34.6g; FIBER 3.8g; CHOL 0mg; IRON 2mg; SODIUM 331mg; CALC 53mg

GRILLED CORN SALAD WITH TOMATO AND BASIL

Preparation time: 10 minutes
Cooking time: 20 minutes

    1½   teaspoons olive oil
    4   ears corn
         Vegetable cooking spray
    2   tablespoons fresh lime juice
    1½   teaspoons olive oil
    2   teaspoons sugar
    ½   teaspoon salt
    ¼   teaspoon pepper
    ⅛   teaspoon garlic powder
    1   cup seeded, diced tomato
    1   cup peeled, seeded, and diced
         cucumber
    ½   cup thinly sliced fresh basil

Brush 1½ teaspoons oil over corn. Coat grill rack with cooking spray; place on grill over medium-hot coals (350° to 400°). Place corn on rack; grill 20 minutes or until corn is lightly browned, turning every 5 minutes. Let cool; cut kernels from cobs to measure 2 cups.

Combine lime juice and next 5 ingredients in a medium bowl; stir well. Add corn, tomato, cucumber, and basil; stir well. Yield: 4 servings (serving size: 1 cup).

CALORIES 137 (30% from fat); PROTEIN 3.2g; FAT 4.5g (sat 0.6g, mono 2.8g, poly 0.8g); CARB 25.2g; FIBER 3.6g; CHOL 0mg; IRON 0.8mg; SODIUM 312mg; CALC 19mg

THREE-BEAN SALAD WITH BALSAMIC DRESSING

Preparation time: 30 minutes

    2½   cups (2-inch) sliced green beans
         (about ½ pound)
    ⅓   cup balsamic vinegar
    ¼   cup chopped fresh parsley or
         1 tablespoon plus 1 teaspoon
         dried parsley flakes
    ¼   cup chopped fresh or
         1 tablespoon plus 1 teaspoon
         dried basil
    2   tablespoons grated Parmesan
         cheese
    1   tablespoon fresh or 1 teaspoon
         dried dillweed
    1   tablespoon olive oil
    ½   teaspoon garlic powder
    ¼   teaspoon salt
    ¼   teaspoon pepper
    1½   cups sliced carrot
    ½   cup vertically sliced red onion
    1   (15½-ounce) can chickpeas
         (garbanzo beans), drained
    1   (15-ounce) can kidney beans,
         drained
    1   (14-ounce) can artichoke hearts,
         drained and coarsely chopped
    1   large tomato, cut into 16
         wedges
         Dillweed sprigs (optional)

Arrange green beans in a steamer basket over boiling water. Cover and steam 2 minutes. Rinse under cold water; drain well.

Combine vinegar and next 8 ingredients in a large bowl; stir well. Add green beans, carrot, and next 4 ingredients; toss gently to coat. Serve with tomato wedges; garnish with dillweed sprigs, if desired. Yield: 8 servings (serving size: 1 cup).

CALORIES 162 (18% from fat); PROTEIN 8.6g; FAT 3.3g (sat 0.6g, mono 1.6g, poly 0.8g); CARB 27.1g; FIBER 4.2g; CHOL 1mg; IRON 3mg; SODIUM 269mg; CALC 85mg

GARDEN VEGETABLE PASTA SALAD

Preparation time: 35 minutes

    3   cups cooked rotini (corkscrew
         pasta)
    1   cup broccoli florets
    1   cup quartered cherry tomatoes
    ¾   cup diced lean ham (3 ounces)
    ½   cup sliced carrot
    ½   cup vertically sliced red onion
    ⅓   cup sliced ripe olives
    ¼   cup grated Parmesan cheese
    2   tablespoons chopped fresh or
         2 teaspoons dried basil
    2   tablespoons chopped fresh
         parsley or 2 teaspoons dried
         parsley flakes
    ¼   cup fat-free sour cream
    ¼   cup low-fat buttermilk
    ¼   cup light ranch dressing

Combine first 10 ingredients in a bowl. Combine sour cream, buttermilk, and dressing; stir well. Pour over salad; toss to coat. Yield: 7 servings (serving size: 1 cup).

CALORIES 174 (29% from fat); PROTEIN 8.2g; FAT 5.6g (sat 1.2g, mono 1.9g, poly 1.5g); CARB 22.5g; FIBER 2.5g; CHOL 9mg; IRON 1.6mg; SODIUM 362mg; CALC 87mg

FIREWORKS COLESLAW

Preparation time: 20 minutes
Standing time: 20 minutes

¼ cup reduced-calorie mayonnaise
2 tablespoons cider vinegar
2 tablespoons grated onion
½ teaspoon salt
¼ teaspoon pepper
2 cups thinly sliced green cabbage
2 cups thinly sliced red cabbage
½ cup red bell pepper strips
½ cup yellow bell pepper strips
½ cup coarsely shredded carrot
¼ cup raisins

Combine first 5 ingredients in a medium bowl; stir well. Add green cabbage and remaining ingredients; toss mixture gently to coat. Cover and chill 20 minutes. Yield: 5 servings (serving size: 1 cup).

CALORIES 80 (29% from fat); PROTEIN 1.3g; FAT 2.6g (sat 0.8g, mono 0g, poly 1.7g); CARB 14.2g; FIBER 2.5g; CHOL 0mg; IRON 0.9mg; SODIUM 378mg; CALC 36mg

IN SEASON

The Slice Is Right

In midsummer, watermelons are at their sweetest, juiciest best—as are these recipes.

Watermelons are—with little debate—the quintessential food of summer. There are those who wouldn't trade a slice of it on a hot summer day for anything. Yet this warm-weather delight is actually a vegetable of eight varieties, each with its own distinct shape, size, and color. Watermelons range from small and round to heavy and oval. Their color drifts from pale to deep green, and even the flesh varies from traditional red to pink and yellow. And although watermelons are best known as a picnic headliner, they can play other roles—as shown by our recipes. And better yet, no seeds.

SPINACH-AND-WATERMELON SALAD

You can double the dressing and save it for another salad. Or simply drizzle it over fresh berries and/or melon.

1 tablespoon honey
1 tablespoon balsamic vinegar
1 tablespoon water
1½ teaspoons olive oil
½ teaspoon lemon juice
⅛ teaspoon dried tarragon
Dash of salt
4 cups fresh torn spinach
4 cups thinly sliced romaine lettuce
2 cups (1-inch) watermelon balls
1 cup sliced strawberries
½ cup sliced cucumber
¼ cup thinly sliced onion, separated into rings

Combine first 7 ingredients in a bowl; stir well with a whisk. Set aside.

Combine spinach and remaining 5 ingredients in a large bowl. Drizzle dressing over salad, and toss gently to coat. Serve immediately. Yield: 5 servings (serving size: 2 cups).

CALORIES 72 (13% from fat); PROTEIN 2.8g; FAT 1.8g (sat 0.4g, mono 0.8g, poly 0.4g); CARB 12.2g; FIBER 3.8g; CHOL 0mg; IRON 2mg; SODIUM 46mg; CALC 74mg

GINGERED MELON COMPOTE

1½ cups water
¾ cup sugar
2 tablespoons peeled, coarsely chopped fresh gingerroot
6 whole cloves
6 whole allspice
2 cups seeded, cubed watermelon
1 cup peeled, cubed cantaloupe
1 cup blueberries

Combine water, sugar, gingerroot, cloves, and allspice in a small saucepan; bring to a boil. Reduce heat, and simmer 15 minutes or until sugar dissolves, stirring occasionally. Strain sugar syrup through a sieve into a bowl; discard solids. Cover sugar syrup, and chill.

Divide watermelon, cantaloupe, and blueberries evenly among 6 dessert dishes. Spoon ¼ cup sugar syrup over each serving. Yield: 6 servings.

CALORIES 137 (3% from fat); PROTEIN 0.7g; FAT 0.4g (sat 0.2g, mono 0.1g, poly 0.1g); CARB 34.4g; FIBER 1.7g; CHOL 0mg; IRON 0.2mg; SODIUM 5mg; CALC 9mg

WATERMELON WISDOM

◆ Look for a melon that is firm, symmetrically shaped, and free of dents and cuts. It should feel heavy for its shape and have a nice sheen.
◆ The underside of the melon (the side that grows against the ground) should be pale yellow.
◆ Slap the side of the melon. A resounding, hollow thump is a good indicator that it's ripe, but not a guarantee.
◆ Cut watermelon pieces should have a deep red color and a firm, unbroken flesh.
◆ Store whole watermelons in the refrigerator; cut pieces should be tightly wrapped.

WATERMELON-WINE SORBET

⅔ cup sugar
⅔ cup dry red wine
4 cups seeded, diced watermelon
1 tablespoon fresh lemon juice
⅛ teaspoon ground cinnamon
⅛ teaspoon ground nutmeg

Combine sugar and wine in a small saucepan; stir well. Bring mixture to a boil over medium-high heat; cook 1 minute or until sugar dissolves, stirring constantly. Remove wine mixture from heat; let cool.

Combine wine mixture, diced watermelon, fresh lemon juice, ground cinnamon, and ground nutmeg in a blender; cover and process until smooth. Pour mixture into the freezer can of an ice cream freezer; freeze according to manufacturer's instructions. Yield: 4 servings (serving size: 1 cup).

CALORIES 184 (3% from fat); PROTEIN 1.1g; FAT 0.7g (sat 0.4g, mono 0.1g, poly 0g); CARB 45.7g; FIBER 0.9g; CHOL 0mg; IRON 0.5mg; SODIUM 7mg; CALC 17mg

WATERMELON DAIQUIRI SLUSH

9 cups seeded, cubed watermelon, divided
1 cup white rum
¼ cup fresh lime juice
3 tablespoons sugar
1 (10-ounce) can non-alcoholic frozen strawberry daiquiri mix, thawed and undiluted

Place half of watermelon cubes in a bowl; cover and freeze until firm.

Place remaining watermelon cubes, white rum, and remaining 3 ingredients in a blender; cover and process until smooth. Pour half of puréed mixture into a large pitcher. Add frozen watermelon cubes to remaining puréed mixture in blender; cover and process until smooth. Pour puréed mixture into large pitcher. Serve immediately over ice. Yield: 16 servings (serving size: ½ cup).

CALORIES 126 (3% from fat); PROTEIN 0.6g; FAT 0.4g (sat 0.2g, mono 0.1g, poly 0g); CARB 20.1g; FIBER 0.5g; CHOL 0mg; IRON 0.2mg; SODIUM 2mg; CALC 7mg

WATERMELON MARGARITAS

2 teaspoons sugar
1 lime wedge
3½ cups seeded, cubed watermelon
½ cup tequila
3 tablespoons sugar
3 tablespoons fresh lime juice
1 tablespoon triple sec (orange-flavored liqueur)
Lime wedges (optional)

Place 2 teaspoons sugar in a saucer. Rub rims of 6 glasses with 1 lime wedge; spin rim of each glass in sugar to coat. Set prepared glasses aside.

Combine watermelon and next 4 ingredients in a blender; cover and process until smooth. Fill each prepared glass with ½ cup crushed ice. Add ½ cup margarita to each glass. Garnish each glass with a lime wedge, if desired. Serve immediately. Yield: 6 servings.

Note: Add 2 or 3 drops of red food coloring to blender for a deeper red coloring, if desired.

CALORIES 115 (3% from fat); PROTEIN 0.6g; FAT 0.4g (sat 0.2g, mono 0.1g, poly 0g); CARB 15.8g; FIBER 0.5g; CHOL 0mg; IRON 0.2mg; SODIUM 2mg; CALC 8mg

THE ENLIGHTENED CHEF

Leading the Way in Atlanta

In 1993, "there were no small restaurants in Atlanta when we opened Bacchanalia," says Chef Anne Quatrano. "There were only large, glitzy ones that served huge portions of food."

"Mostly meat and pastas," adds Chef Clifford Harrison, Quatrano's partner in the kitchen and in life.

Bacchanalia was Atlanta's first small prix fixe-menu eatery. In each of the chefs' four imaginative courses, two elements remain constant: building on strong flavors and keeping it light. According to Quatrano, they cook contemporary American fare, using organic and locally grown farm-fresh ingredients (often from their own organic gardens). And no butter or cream is used—except in desserts.

Harrison tends the organic gardens, and with the arrival of the August heat, all of their tomatoes ripen practically on the same day. That's when Chilled Tomato-Miso Soup goes on the menu.

CHILLED TOMATO-MISO SOUP

Miso (MEE-soh) is a basic flavoring in Japanese cooking, and can be found in Oriental markets or in your store's ethnic-food aisle. This fermented soybean paste is rich in B vitamins and protein, and should be refrigerated after opening.

6 large ripe tomatoes, cored and quartered (about 3 pounds)
1 tablespoon peeled, minced fresh gingerroot
½ cup rice vinegar
¼ cup maple syrup
¼ cup miso (soybean paste)
¼ teaspoon salt
1¼ teaspoons basil oil
Basil sprigs (optional)

Combine tomatoes and gingerroot in a food processor; process until smooth. Strain mixture through a sieve into a medium bowl; discard solids.

Combine strained tomato mixture, vinegar, maple syrup, miso, and salt; stir well. Cover and chill. Spoon 1 cup soup into each bowl; drizzle each with ¼ teaspoon oil, and garnish with a basil sprig, if desired. Yield: 5 servings.

CALORIES 130 (19% from fat); PROTEIN 3.5g; FAT 2.7g (sat 0.4g, mono 1.1g, poly 0.9g); CARB 24.9g; FIBER 3.6g; CHOL 0mg; IRON 1.6mg; SODIUM 642mg; CALC 31mg

Summer's Hottest Combo

Because burgers and fries are synonymous with good times and casual living, we lightened—and improved—America's favorite meal.

This summer you can have a hamburger—even a cheeseburger—with fries. We created burgers that are healthier (ours have only half the fat grams of a Quarter Pounder), and tastier—not to mention bigger than most fast-food varieties. We made them flavorful by enhancing them with fresh herbs, spices, seasonings, and even feta cheese. Next, instead of the predictable, high-fat toppings, we came up with healthier, '90s-style alternatives, such as a rich marinara and a cool cucumber-dill sauce. (For healthy side dishes, see Side Kicks on page 200.) Believe us, we know how you feel: A summer without hamburgers and fries is just too much to bear. So when that irresistible urge hits, give in. After all, it's your patty.

TOWARD A LIGHTER BURGER

The key to light burgers is lean ground meats. Most of our burgers rely on ground round: With 7 grams of fat and 146 calories (46% from fat) per 3 ounces, it's about the leanest beef you can get.

	Calories	Fat (grams)	% Calories from Fat
Burger King's Whopper with Cheese	720	46	58
McDonald's Quarter Pounder with Cheese	520	29	50
Wendy's Big Bacon Classic	640	36	51
Wendy's Single (with everything)	440	23	47
Cooking Light's Mexican Chili-Cheese Burger	381	13	31

GREEK FETA BURGERS

Substitute ground round for the ground lamb, if desired.

1 (10-ounce) package frozen chopped spinach, thawed, drained, and squeezed dry
1 tablespoon lemon juice
¼ teaspoon pepper
1 egg white, lightly beaten
¾ pound lean ground lamb
½ cup crumbled feta cheese
¼ cup chopped fresh mint or 4 teaspoons dried mint flakes
Vegetable cooking spray
4 (1½-ounce) hamburger buns with onions
½ cup diced tomato
Cucumber-Dill Sauce

Combine first 4 ingredients in a bowl; stir well. Add lamb, cheese, and mint; stir well. Divide mixture into 4 equal portions, shaping into ½-inch-thick patties.

Coat grill rack with cooking spray; place over medium-hot coals (350° to 400°). Place patties on rack; grill 5 minutes on each side or until done.

Place patties on bottom halves of buns; top each with 2 tablespoons tomato, 2 tablespoons Cucumber-Dill Sauce, and top half of bun. Yield: 4 servings.

CALORIES 336 (31% from fat); PROTEIN 28.9g; FAT 11.4g (sat 4.6g, mono 3.6g, poly 0.9g); CARB 29.2g; FIBER 2.7g; CHOL 74mg; IRON 3.8mg; SODIUM 425mg; CALC 208mg

Cucumber-Dill Sauce:

¼ cup peeled, seeded, and diced cucumber
¼ cup plain low-fat yogurt
½ teaspoon chopped fresh or ⅛ teaspoon dried dillweed
1 small garlic clove, minced

Combine all ingredients in a bowl, and stir well. Yield: ½ cup (serving size: 2 tablespoons).

CALORIES 11 (16% from fat); PROTEIN 0.8g; FAT 0.2g (sat 0.1g, mono 0.1g, poly 0g); CARB 1.4g; FIBER 0.1g; CHOL 1mg; IRON 0.1mg; SODIUM 11mg; CALC 29mg

MUSHROOM PIZZA BURGERS

Jarred sauces work for this recipe, too.

Vegetable cooking spray
½ cup sliced mushrooms
¼ cup chopped onion
½ teaspoon dried oregano
1 garlic clove, minced
1 cup canned crushed tomatoes, undrained
1 pound ground round
1½ cups finely chopped mushrooms
⅓ cup thinly sliced fresh or
    5 teaspoons dried basil
2 tablespoons grated Parmesan cheese
2 tablespoons fine, dry breadcrumbs
½ teaspoon salt
⅛ teaspoon pepper
1 egg white, lightly beaten
4 slices part-skim mozzarella cheese
4 (1½-ounce) hamburger buns, toasted

Coat a small nonstick skillet with cooking spray; place over medium heat until hot. Add sliced mushrooms and onion; sauté 3 minutes. Add oregano and garlic; sauté 1 minute.

Add undrained tomatoes; cook 5 minutes, stirring occasionally. Remove from heat; set tomato sauce aside, and keep warm.

Combine beef and next 7 ingredients in a bowl; stir well. Divide mixture into 4 equal portions, shaping into ½-inch-thick patties.

Coat grill rack with cooking spray; place over medium-hot coals (350° to 400°). Place patties on rack; grill 5 minutes on each side or until done. Top patties with cheese.

Place patties on bottom halves of buns; top each patty with 2 tablespoons tomato sauce and top half of bun. Yield: 4 servings.

Note: Store remaining tomato sauce in an airtight container for up to 1 week. Serve with pasta.

CALORIES 399 (30% from fat); PROTEIN 37g; FAT 13.3g; (sat 5.4g, mono 4.5g, poly 0.8g); CARB 31.5g; FIBER 1.1g; CHOL 84mg; IRON 4.2mg; SODIUM 753mg; CALC 233mg

---

TOPPING TALLY

Here's what the most popular condiments add to your burger. Proportions are per tablespoon unless otherwise noted.

	Calories	Fat (grams)	Sodium (milligrams)
Bacon (2 strips)	59	5	190
Cheese (1 ounce)	80	6	395
Ketchup	18	0	178
Mayonnaise	99	11	78
Mustard	12	0.7	196
Pickle relish	20	0	124
Salsa	4	0	42
Steak sauce	12	0	275
Thousand Island dressing	59	6	109

GARDEN BURGERS

Vegetable cooking spray
1 cup very thinly sliced green cabbage
½ cup chopped green bell pepper
½ cup chopped onion
¼ cup water
1 teaspoon minced fresh or
    ¼ teaspoon dried oregano
½ teaspoon minced fresh or
    ⅛ teaspoon dried rosemary
2 tablespoons fine, dry breadcrumbs
2 tablespoons tomato sauce
¾ teaspoon salt
⅛ teaspoon pepper
1 egg white
¾ pound ground round
2 tablespoons light ranch dressing
4 (1¾-ounce) hamburger buns, toasted
4 curly leaf lettuce leaves
4 (¼-inch-thick) slices tomato
4 (¼-inch-thick) slices onion

Coat a large nonstick skillet with cooking spray; place over medium-high heat until hot. Add cabbage, bell pepper, and chopped onion; sauté 3 minutes. Add water, 1 tablespoon at a time, allowing each tablespoon to evaporate before adding the next; cook 5 minutes or until all liquid evaporates and vegetables are golden. Remove from heat; stir in oregano and rosemary. Let cool slightly.

Combine breadcrumbs and next 4 ingredients in a medium bowl; stir well. Add cabbage mixture and beef; stir well. Divide mixture into 4 equal portions, shaping into ½-inch-thick patties.

Coat grill rack with cooking spray; place over medium-hot coals (350° to 400°). Place patties on rack; grill 5 minutes on each side or until done.

Spread 1½ teaspoons ranch dressing over top half of each bun. Line bottom half of each bun with lettuce leaves, and top each with a patty, tomato slice, onion slice, and top half of bun. Yield: 4 servings.

CALORIES 335 (25% from fat); PROTEIN 25g; FAT 9.4g (sat 2.2g, mono 2.6g, poly 0.7g); CARB 36g; FIBER 2g; CHOL 52mg; IRON 3.5mg; SODIUM 802mg; CALC 54mg

When stuffing burgers like Mexican Chili-Cheese Burgers, it's best to use plum tomatoes inside the burger as they're less watery than other varieties. If you prefer to use fat-free cheese, you'll save about 4 grams of fat per burger.

MEXICAN CHILI-CHEESE BURGERS

1   pound ground round
1   cup seeded, chopped plum
       tomato
¼   cup minced fresh cilantro
1   tablespoon chili powder
2   teaspoons seeded, minced
       jalapeño pepper
½   teaspoon salt
½   teaspoon dried oregano
½   teaspoon ground cumin
¼   teaspoon pepper
Vegetable cooking spray
4   (¾-ounce) slices reduced-fat
       Monterey Jack or Cheddar
       cheese
¼   cup fat-free sour cream
4   (1½-ounce) hamburger buns
4   iceberg lettuce leaves
8   (¼-inch-thick) slices
       tomato
Grilled onions (optional)

Combine first 9 ingredients in a large bowl; stir well. Divide mixture into 4 equal portions; shape into ½-inch-thick patties.

Coat grill rack with cooking spray; place over medium-hot coals (350° to 400°). Place patties on rack; grill 6 minutes on each side or until done. Place 1 cheese slice on top of each patty; cover and grill an additional minute or until cheese melts.

Spread 1 tablespoon of sour cream over top half of each bun; set aside. Place patties on bottom halves of buns; top each with lettuce, tomato, onions (if desired), and top half of bun. Yield: 4 servings.

CALORIES 381 (31% from fat); PROTEIN 36.3g; FAT 13.1g (sat 5g, mono 6.4g, poly 0.7g); CARB 28.1g; FIBER 1.7g; CHOL 84mg; IRON 4.2mg; SODIUM 655mg; CALC 212mg

BLUE CHEESE-STUFFED BURGERS

Vegetable cooking spray
½   cup finely chopped onion
1   pound ground round
3   tablespoons fine, dry
       breadcrumbs
2   tablespoons water
1   egg white, lightly beaten
¼   cup crumbled blue cheese
¼   cup fat-free sour cream
4   (1-ounce) English muffins,
       toasted
4   lettuce leaves
4   (¼-inch-thick) slices tomato

Coat a small nonstick skillet with cooking spray; place over medium heat until hot. Add onion; sauté 5 minutes or until tender. Remove from heat; let cool. Combine onion and next 4 ingredients in a large bowl; stir well. Divide mixture into 8 equal portions, shaping into ½-inch-thick patties. Spoon 1 tablespoon cheese into the center of 4 patties; top with remaining patties. Press edges together to seal.

Coat grill rack with cooking spray; place on grill over medium-hot coals (350° to 400°). Place patties on rack; grill 4 minutes on each side or until patties are done.

Spread 1 tablespoon sour cream over top half of each muffin, and set aside. Line bottom halves of muffins with lettuce leaves; top each with a tomato slice, a patty, and top half of muffin. Yield: 4 servings.

CALORIES 327 (28% from fat); PROTEIN 31.4g; FAT 10.3g (sat 3.9g, mono 3.7g, poly 0.7g); CARB 25.1g; FIBER 1g; CHOL 75mg; IRON 3.8mg; SODIUM 391mg; CALC 116mg

PEPPERED TURKEY-WATERCRESS BURGERS

1   pound ground turkey breast
1½   cups trimmed, chopped
       watercress
¼   cup plain low-fat yogurt
1   teaspoon cracked pepper
½   teaspoon salt
1   teaspoon cracked pepper
Vegetable cooking spray
½   cup plain low-fat yogurt
4   (1½-ounce) hamburger buns,
       toasted
1   cup trimmed watercress
4   (¼-inch-thick) slices tomato

Combine ground turkey, chopped watercress, yogurt, 1 teaspoon cracked pepper, and salt in a large bowl; stir well. Divide mixture into 4 equal portions, shaping into ½-inch-thick patties. Sprinkle 1 teaspoon cracked pepper over both sides of patties, pressing pepper into burgers.

Coat grill rack with cooking spray; place over medium-hot coals (350° to 400°). Place patties on rack; grill 5 minutes on each side or until done.

Spread 2 tablespoons yogurt over cut sides of each bun. Line the bottom half of each bun with ¼ cup watercress; top each with a tomato slice, a patty, and top half of bun. Yield: 4 servings.

CALORIES 295 (16% from fat); PROTEIN 31.9g; FAT 5.2g (sat 1.2g, mono 1g, poly 0.9g); CARB 28.4g; FIBER 1g; CHOL 87mg; IRON 2.6mg; SODIUM 496mg; CALC 139mg

OVEN FRIES

1½   pounds baking potatoes, peeled
       and cut into thin strips
1   tablespoon vegetable oil
½   teaspoon salt

Preheat oven to 450°.

Combine all ingredients in a bowl; toss well. Arrange the potatoes in a single layer on a baking sheet. Bake at 450° for 35 minutes or until golden. Yield: 4 servings.

CALORIES 193 (17% from fat); PROTEIN 3.3g; FAT 3.6g (sat 0.7g, mono 1g, poly 1.7g); CARB 36.6g; FIBER 2.6g; CHOL 0mg; IRON 0.6mg; SODIUM 301mg; CALC 9mg

CHEESE FRIES

1½ pounds baking potatoes, peeled
    and cut into thin strips
1 tablespoon grated Parmesan
    cheese
1 tablespoon vegetable oil
¼ teaspoon salt
¼ teaspoon garlic powder
¼ teaspoon paprika
¼ teaspoon pepper

Preheat oven to 450°.

Combine all ingredients in a bowl, and toss well. Arrange potatoes in a single layer on a baking sheet. Bake at 450° for 35 minutes or until golden. Yield: 4 servings.

CALORIES 200 (18% from fat); PROTEIN 3.9g; FAT 4g (sat 0.9g, mono 1.1g, poly 1.7g); CARB 37g; FIBER 2.6g; CHOL 1mg; IRON 0.7mg; SODIUM 178mg; CALC 27mg

CHILI FRIES

1½ pounds baking potatoes, peeled
    and cut into thin strips
1 tablespoon vegetable oil
2 teaspoons chili powder
½ teaspoon salt
½ teaspoon dried oregano
¼ teaspoon garlic powder
¼ teaspoon ground cumin

Preheat oven to 450°.
Combine all ingredients in a medium bowl, and toss well.
Arrange potatoes in a single layer on a baking sheet. Bake at 450° for 35 minutes or until potatoes are golden. Yield: 4 servings.

CALORIES 199 (17% from fat); PROTEIN 3.6g; FAT 3.8g (sat 0.7g, mono 1.1g, poly 1.8g); CARB 37.6g; FIBER 3g; CHOL 0mg; IRON 0.9mg; SODIUM 314mg; CALC 16mg

---

FRY ME TO THE MOON

By baking our fries instead of deep-frying them, we've practically eliminated the oil. The key to getting crispy fries without the fat is slicing them thin. This also creates more surface area for the seasonings to cover.

	Calories	Fat (grams)	% Calories from Fat
McDonald's small fries	210	10	43
McDonald's large fries	450	22	44
Cooking Light's Oven Fries	193	3.6	17

FOR TWO

Three's Company

By combining vegetables, fresh fruit, and a variety of meats, these salads become light and refreshing dinners. They're what summer eating is all about.

FRESH TUNA SALAD

1½ cups (½-inch) cubed red
    potato
Vegetable cooking spray
1 (8-ounce) tuna steak (about 1
    inch thick)
2 tablespoons chopped fresh
    parsley
1½ tablespoons white vinegar
1½ tablespoons water
1½ teaspoons Dijon mustard
1½ teaspoons olive oil
¼ teaspoon salt
¼ teaspoon pepper
1 cup seedless red grapes,
    halved
Romaine lettuce leaves

Place potato in a saucepan; cover with water, and bring to a boil. Cook 15 minutes or until tender. Drain and set aside.

Coat a small nonstick skillet with cooking spray; place over medium-high heat until hot. Add tuna steak, and cook 3 minutes on each side until medium-rare or to desired degree of doneness. Break the tuna steak into chunks.

Combine parsley, vinegar, 1½ tablespoons water, mustard, olive oil, salt, and pepper in a medium bowl stirring well with a whisk.

Add potato, tuna, and grapes; toss gently to coat. Serve on lettuce-lined plates. Yield: 2 servings (serving size: 1½ cups).

CALORIES 320 (28% from fat); PROTEIN 29g; FAT 9.8g (sat 2.3g, mono 4.3g, poly 2.2g); CARB 29.3g; FIBER 2.4g; CHOL 43mg; IRON 2.5mg; SODIUM 458mg; CALC 21mg

LAYERED CARIBBEAN SALAD

¼ cup low-salt chicken broth
2 tablespoons fresh lime juice
1 tablespoon olive oil
1 tablespoon water
1 teaspoon ground cumin
¼ teaspoon salt
⅛ teaspoon pepper
3 drops hot pepper sauce
2 garlic cloves, minced
1½ cups peeled, cubed mango or
   papaya
½ cup frozen whole-kernel corn,
   thawed
½ cup diced red onion
1 (15-ounce) can black beans,
   rinsed and drained
4 cups thinly sliced romaine
   lettuce
1 cup red bell pepper strips
2 tablespoons chopped fresh
   cilantro

Combine first 9 ingredients in a
medium bowl, and stir well with a
whisk. Reserve 2 tablespoons dressing,
and set aside. Add mango, corn,
onion, and beans to bowl; toss gently
to coat.

Place 2 cups lettuce on each of 2
plates; top each serving with ½ cup
bell pepper strips and 2 cups mango
mixture. Drizzle 1 tablespoon reserved
dressing over each salad; sprinkle each
with 1 tablespoon cilantro. Yield: 2
servings.

CALORIES 418 (20% from fat); PROTEIN 17.6g; FAT 9.1g;
(sat 1.3g, mono 5.4g, poly 1.3g); CARB 74.5g; FIBER 12.6g;
CHOL 0mg; IRON 6.3mg; SODIUM 706mg; CALC 126mg

SHRIMP-AND-MANGO SALAD

*Although large shrimp are called for
(there are fewer to peel), medium-
sized shrimp can also be used.*

¼ cup light mayonnaise
2 tablespoons prepared
   horseradish
1 tablespoon white vinegar
⅛ teaspoon pepper
¾ pound large shrimp, cooked and
   peeled
1 cup peeled, cubed mango
¾ cup cooked rice (cooked
   without salt or fat)
¼ cup chopped red bell pepper
¼ cup chopped green bell pepper

Combine first 4 ingredients in a
medium bowl; stir well with a whisk.
Add shrimp and remaining ingredients; toss gently to coat. Yield: 2 servings (serving size: 1½ cups).

CALORIES 351 (21% from fat); PROTEIN 29.1g; FAT 8g
(sat 2.5g, mono 0.4g, poly 4.8g); CARB 40.2g; FIBER 2.3g;
CHOL 249mg; IRON 5.4mg; SODIUM 629mg; CALC 83mg

ORIENTAL BERRY-BEEF SALAD

*This may sound like an unusual com-
bination of flavors, but the strawberries add a fresh sweetness to the soy
sauce dressing.*

½ teaspoon pepper
½ pound trimmed beef tenderloin
1 large garlic clove, crushed
Vegetable cooking spray
1 cup halved strawberries
2 tablespoons low-sodium soy
   sauce
2 teaspoons sugar
2 teaspoons white vinegar
¼ teaspoon ground ginger
2 cups hot cooked Chinese
   noodles (cooked without salt
   or fat)
1 teaspoon dark sesame oil
⅛ teaspoon salt
⅛ teaspoon pepper
2 cups fresh torn spinach
2 teaspoons sesame seeds, toasted

Sprinkle ½ teaspoon pepper over
beef; rub garlic over beef. Coat a large
nonstick skillet with cooking spray;
place over medium-high heat until
hot. Add beef, and cook 2 minutes or
until browned, turning occasionally.
Cook over medium-low heat 6 minutes or to desired degree of doneness,
turning after 3 minutes. Remove beef
from skillet, and let stand 5 minutes.
Cut beef into ¼-inch-thick slices, and
set aside.

Combine strawberries and next 4
ingredients in a blender; cover and
process until smooth. Set aside.

Combine noodles, oil, salt, and ⅛
teaspoon pepper; toss gently to coat.
Spoon 1 cup noodle mixture onto
each of 2 plates; top each with 1 cup
spinach. Arrange beef slices evenly
over spinach; spoon ⅓ cup strawberry
dressing over each salad. Sprinkle with
sesame seeds. Yield: 2 servings.

CALORIES 429 (28% from fat); PROTEIN 32.6g; FAT 13.5g
(sat 4g, mono 5.5g, poly 3.1g); CARB 48.9g; FIBER 10.6g;
CHOL 71mg; IRON 5.8mg; SODIUM 730mg; CALC 111mg

CHICKEN-AND-FRENCH BEAN SALAD WITH BLUEBERRY RELISH

*You can make the chicken and relish
ahead, then serve them with the salad
greens.*

1 cup (2-inch) sliced green beans
   (about ¼ pound)
¾ cup fresh blueberries
1 tablespoon sugar
2 tablespoons chopped red
   onion
2 tablespoons balsamic vinegar
2 teaspoons fresh lemon juice
3 tablespoons red wine vinegar
1 tablespoon chopped shallots
2 teaspoons honey mustard
1 tablespoon olive oil
¼ teaspoon salt
¼ teaspoon pepper
2 (4-ounce) skinned, boned
   chicken breast halves
1 teaspoon olive oil
2 cups torn romaine lettuce
1 cup plain croutons

Arrange beans in a steamer basket over boiling water. Cover and steam 5 minutes or until crisp-tender. Rinse under cold water; drain and set aside.

Place blueberries and next 4 ingredients in a food processor; pulse until coarsely chopped. Set relish aside.

Combine red wine vinegar, shallots, mustard, and 1 teaspoon oil in a bowl; stir well with a whisk. Set vinaigrette aside.

Sprinkle salt and pepper over chicken. Heat 1 teaspoon oil in a small nonstick skillet over medium heat until hot. Add chicken, and cook 3 minutes on each side or until done. Remove from heat; cut across grain into thin slices, and set aside.

Combine beans, lettuce, and croutons in a bowl. Drizzle vinaigrette over salad; toss gently to coat. Divide salad evenly between 2 plates; top each serving with chicken breast slices. Spoon relish over chicken. Yield: 2 servings.

CALORIES 372 (27% from fat); PROTEIN 25.4g; FAT 11.1g (sat 2.2g, mono 7g, poly 1.6g); CARB 42g; FIBER 4.9g; CHOL 49mg; IRON 2.5mg; SODIUM 426mg; CALC 83mg

QUICK & EASY
WEEKNIGHTS

A European Touch

For an earthy taste of summer, try this fettuccine with clam sauce that's been enlivened with fresh vegetables.

MENU SUGGESTION

FARMERS' MARKET PASTA
WITH CLAM SAUCE

QUICK FOCACCIA

*Tossed
green salad*

*Biscotti with lemon
sorbet*

FARMERS' MARKET PASTA WITH CLAM SAUCE

2   (6½-ounce) cans chopped clams, undrained
1   tablespoon olive oil
½   cup minced fresh onion
½   cup minced carrot
6   garlic cloves, minced
2   cups chopped tomato
½   cup chopped red bell pepper
½   teaspoon salt
½   teaspoon pepper
¼   to ½ teaspoon dried crushed red pepper
½   cup chopped fresh parsley
5   cups hot cooked fettuccine (about 10 ounces uncooked pasta)

Drain clams, reserving 1 cup clam juice. Set clams aside.

Heat olive oil in a large nonstick skillet over medium-high heat until hot. Add minced onion, carrot, and garlic, and sauté 3 minutes. Add reserved clam juice, tomato, bell pepper, salt, and peppers, and bring to a boil. Reduce heat, and simmer 20 minutes or until slightly thick. Remove from heat, and stir in clams and parsley. Serve clam sauce over a bed of fettuccine. Yield: 4 servings (serving size: about ¾ cup sauce and 1¼ cups pasta).

CALORIES 463 (13% from fat); PROTEIN 34g; FAT 6.9g (sat 0.9g, mono 2.8g, poly 1.4g); CARB 65g; FIBER 5.5g; CHOL 61mg; IRON 29.6mg; SODIUM 424mg; CALC 132mg

---

QUICK FOCACCIA

1½   teaspoons olive oil
1   (8-inch) focaccia
¼   cup finely chopped olives
2   tablespoons chopped fresh or 2 teaspoons dried rosemary
2   tablespoons freshly grated Parmesan cheese

Brush olive oil over a purchased focaccia. Sprinkle with remaining ingredients. Broil until cheese melts. Yield: 4 servings.

CALORIES 191 (29% from fat); PROTEIN 6.4g; FAT 6.1g (sat 1.4g, mono 2.9g, poly 1.3g); CARB 29.0g; FIBER 2.4g; CHOL 2mg; IRON 0.5mg; SODIUM 561mg; CALC 56mg

---

SHOPPING LIST

4 carrots

2 tomatoes

1 red bell pepper

1 onion

1 bag mixed salad greens

6 garlic cloves

fresh parsley

fresh rosemary

fettuccine

2 (6½-ounce) cans chopped clams

olive oil

crushed red pepper

olives

Parmesan cheese

focaccia

biscotti

lemon sorbet

Render unto Caesar

Remember the old "diet plate"? Hamburger, cottage cheese, sliced tomato, and lettuce (which, by the way, logged in with roughly the same numbers as a chocolate Dove Bar). Its not-so-novel and certainly not-so-lean replacement is the new star of many modern menus: Grilled Chicken Caesar Salad.

The original chickenless classic was invented as tableside entertainment in the 1920s by chef Caesar Cardini and later performed by the smoothest of maître d's who would take a large wooden bowl and rub it with a large garlic clove. Sometimes they'd crush additional garlic inside the bowl. Or they'd mix anchovy fillets to a paste with "coddled" eggs cooked for one minute only (no longer acceptable given today's concern for salmonella). Then, into this remarkable aromatic base, they'd pour copious quantities of extra-virgin olive oil (6 ounces for four to six portions) to make a clingable mayonnaise-style sauce. Romaine lettuce was the preferred green.

Recently I combined fresh yogurt cheese with Dijon mustard and a drizzle of good balsamic vinegar. I thinned it with a little chicken stock. To this I added crushed garlic and grated Parmesan and discovered a smooth attractive "sauce" for a salad. I didn't add the characteristic anchovy because this would have forced a direct comparison. The chicken breast wasn't grilled but sautéed, sliced, and tossed with the salad at the last moment.

CHICKEN CAESAR SALAD

1 (8-ounce) carton plain low-fat yogurt
1½ tablespoons water
1½ tablespoons Dijon mustard
1½ teaspoons balsamic vinegar
3 garlic cloves, crushed
2 cups (1-inch) cubed whole wheat bread (about 4 slices)
Olive oil-flavored vegetable cooking spray
¼ teaspoon Italian Spice Blend
⅛ teaspoon freshly ground pepper
Dash of salt
1 pound skinned, boned chicken breasts
¼ teaspoon salt
¼ teaspoon Italian Spice Blend
¼ teaspoon freshly ground pepper
6 cups sliced romaine lettuce
3 cups trimmed watercress (about 1 large bunch)
¼ cup freshly grated Parmesan cheese
Freshly ground pepper

Place colander in a 2-quart glass measure or bowl. Line colander with 4 layers of cheesecloth, allowing cheesecloth to extend over outside edges. Spoon yogurt into colander. Cover with plastic wrap; refrigerate 12 hours. Discard liquid. Combine yogurt cheese, water, and next 3 ingredients in a bowl. Set dressing aside.

Preheat oven to 350°. Arrange bread cubes in a single layer on a jelly-roll pan. Lightly coat bread cubes with cooking spray, and sprinkle with ¼ teaspoon Italian Spice Blend, ⅛ teaspoon pepper, and dash of salt; toss well. Bake at 350° for 15 minutes or until lightly browned.

Rub chicken with ¼ teaspoon salt, ¼ teaspoon Italian Spice Blend, and ¼ teaspoon pepper. Coat a large nonstick skillet with cooking spray; place over medium-high heat until hot. Add chicken; cook 4 minutes on each side or until done. Remove from skillet; let cool. Cut chicken across grain into thin slices.

Combine croutons, lettuce, and watercress in a large bowl. Drizzle dressing over lettuce mixture; toss well.

Place 2 cups salad on each of 4 salad plates. Divide sliced chicken evenly among salads, and sprinkle each with 1 tablespoon Parmesan cheese. Serve with additional freshly ground pepper. Yield: 4 servings.

CALORIES 291 (22% from fat); PROTEIN 36.8g; FAT 7.2g (sat 2.7g, mono 2.2g, poly 1.2g); CARB 18.7g; FIBER 3.1g; CHOL 80mg; IRON 2.7mg; SODIUM 682mg; CALC 252mg

Italian Spice Blend:

2 teaspoons dried oregano
1 teaspoon dried basil
1 teaspoon dried mint
1 teaspoon rubbed sage
½ teaspoon fennel seeds
½ teaspoon dried rosemary

Place all ingredients in a clean spice or coffee grinder; process until finely ground. Store in an airtight container. Yield: 1½ tablespoons.

Note: If you don't have a grinder, use a mortar and pestle to grind spices.

Making Ginger a Snap

Until recently, most Americans' experience with ginger was in desserts such as gingersnap cookies and gingerbread persons or in ginger ale. Today, tan-colored, gnarly-looking fresh ginger is a staple of the new American cuisine, available year-round in most supermarkets. Although many herbs and spices can be used either fresh or dried with only minor adjustments for intensity of flavor, that's not the case with ginger. Fresh ginger has a much cleaner, sassier character than its dried counterpart.

The rising popularity of fresh ginger has a lot to do with the influx of Asian cooking, a cuisine that would risk collapse without it. Plus fresh ginger is the perfect partner for many spices. Because it can be paired with robust flavorings such as garlic, ginger can add a lively flair to almost any kind of food. It can be baked in desserts, or used raw in preparations like salad dressings and chutneys.

BRAZILIAN SHELLFISH SOUP

1 pound small clams in shells, scrubbed (about 20 clams)
1 pound small mussels, scrubbed and debearded (about 30 mussels)
1 tablespoon cornmeal
2 cups water
1 tablespoon vegetable oil
2 cups chopped onion
1 cup chopped red bell pepper
1 cup chopped yellow bell pepper
1 tablespoon seeded, minced jalapeño pepper
4 cloves garlic, minced
4 cups peeled, chopped tomato
2 tablespoons peeled, grated fresh gingerroot
2 teaspoons grated orange rind
3 (8-ounce) bottles clam juice
1 (6-ounce) can tomato paste
½ pound medium shrimp, peeled and deveined
2 tablespoons minced green onions
2 tablespoons chopped fresh parsley
2 tablespoons chopped fresh cilantro
½ teaspoon salt
½ teaspoon pepper
1 (12-ounce) can evaporated skim milk
3 tablespoons shredded sweetened coconut, toasted
Cilantro sprigs (optional)

Place clams and mussels in a large bowl; cover with cold water. Sprinkle with cornmeal; let stand 30 minutes. Drain and rinse.

Bring 2 cups water to a boil in a large Dutch oven. Add clams and mussels; cover and cook 6 minutes or until shells open. Discard any unopened shells. Remove clams and mussels from Dutch oven; set aside. Discard cooking liquid.

Heat oil over medium heat until hot. Add onion and next 4 ingredients; sauté 8 minutes. Add tomato and next 4 ingredients; cook 15 minutes, stirring occasionally. Add shrimp;

cook 5 minutes or until done. Remove from heat; stir in clams, mussels, green onions, and next 5 ingredients. Ladle soup into large bowls; sprinkle with coconut. Garnish with cilantro sprigs, if desired. Yield: 6 servings (serving size: 2 cups soup and 1½ teaspoons coconut).

CALORIES 221 (22% from fat); PROTEIN 16.5g; FAT 5.3g (sat 1.7g, mono 1g, poly 1.9g); CARB 29.9g; FIBER 5.2g; CHOL 51mg; IRON 4.9mg; SODIUM 627mg; CALC 242mg

MENU SUGGESTION

GINGER PORK WITH RHUBARB-GINGER CHUTNEY*

Rice

Steamed asparagus

*Fresh rhubarb is highly perishable. Refrigerate, tightly sealed, in a zip-top plastic bag for up to 3 days.

GINGER PORK WITH RHUBARB-GINGER CHUTNEY

Serve slices of this pork on a bed of basmati rice, and top with the chutney.

2 (½-pound) pork tenderloins
4 cups water
2 tablespoons brown sugar
1 tablespoon salt
1 tablespoon peeled, minced fresh gingerroot
1 garlic clove, minced
1 tablespoon olive oil
Vegetable cooking spray
Rhubarb-Ginger Chutney

Trim fat from pork. Combine pork and next 5 ingredients in a large heavy-duty, zip-top plastic bag. Seal bag, and marinate in refrigerator 24 hours, turning bag occasionally.

Remove pork from bag; discard marinade. Pat pork dry with a paper towel.

Preheat oven to 325°.

Heat oil in a large nonstick skillet over medium-high heat until hot. Add pork, and cook 5 minutes or until browned, turning occasionally.

Place pork on a broiler rack coated with cooking spray; insert meat thermometer into thickest portion of tenderloins. Bake at 325° for 35 minutes or until thermometer reaches 160° (slightly pink). Serve with Rhubarb-Ginger Chutney. Yield: 4 servings (serving size: 3 ounces pork and ⅓ cup Rhubarb-Ginger Chutney).

CALORIES 313 (24% from fat); PROTEIN 25.8g; FAT 8.3g (sat 1.9g, mono 4.3g, poly 0.8g); CARB 35.8g; FIBER 0.6g; CHOL 79mg; IRON 2.2mg; SODIUM 508mg; CALC 84mg

Rhubarb-Ginger Chutney:

This can also be served with grilled chicken or spooned over cream cheese and served with crackers.

¼ cup honey
2 tablespoons balsamic vinegar
2 tablespoons orange juice
2 cups diced fresh or frozen rhubarb, thawed
½ cup dried currants
1 tablespoon seeded, minced jalapeño pepper
1 teaspoon peeled, minced fresh gingerroot
¼ cup minced fresh or 1 teaspoon dried mint
¼ teaspoon ground cinnamon

Combine first 3 ingredients in a medium saucepan; stir well. Cook over medium heat 4 minutes. Add rhubarb, currants, jalapeño pepper, and gingerroot; cook over medium-low heat 5 minutes or until rhubarb is tender, stirring occasionally. Remove from heat; stir in mint and cinnamon. Spoon into a bowl; cover and chill. Yield: 1⅓ cups (serving size: ⅓ cup).

CALORIES 134 (4% from fat); PROTEIN 1.3g; FAT 0.6g; CARB 34g; FIBER 0.6g; CHOL 0mg; IRON 0.8mg; SODIUM 10mg; CALC 74mg

BUYING AND STORING GINGER

◆ When buying fresh ginger, look for roots—though they're not really roots, but underground stems called rhizomes—that are very firm to the touch.

◆ Choose unblemished, heavy bulbs with thin, smooth, taut skin.

◆ Because a little goes a long way, you may want to store the unused portion.

◆ To keep it from drying out, wrap the gingerroot in a paper towel, and place it inside a perforated plastic bag.

◆ Then refrigerate, checking every few days for moisture. A plump piece of fresh gingerroot will keep this way for two or more weeks.

1. Peel the outer skin of the gingerroot with a paring knife or vegetable peeler.

2. To grate fresh gingerroot, peel, then cut a piece big enough to hold comfortably while using a fine grater.

3. To chop fresh gingerroot, first crush it under the flat side of a knife.

4. Chop or mince according to recipe instructions.

BLUEBERRY-GINGER CHEESECAKE

Vegetable cooking spray
¼ cup gingersnap cookie crumbs (about 8 cookies)
¾ cup sugar
2 (8-ounce) tubs light cream cheese
2 cups fat-free sour cream
2 tablespoons ginger-flavored liqueur (optional)
2 tablespoons minced crystallized ginger
5 large egg whites
1 large egg yolk
3 cups blueberries
¼ cup sugar
¼ cup water
1 tablespoon cornstarch
2 teaspoons minced crystallized ginger

Preheat oven to 325°.

Coat bottom of a 10-inch springform pan with cooking spray; sprinkle with cookie crumbs. Set aside.

Combine ¾ cup sugar and cream cheese in a food processor; process until smooth. Add sour cream and liqueur, if desired; process until blended. Add 2 tablespoons crystallized ginger, egg whites, and egg yolk; pulse until blended.

Pour batter into prepared pan. Bake at 325° for 45 minutes or until almost set. Remove from oven; let cool 2 hours on a wire rack.

Combine blueberries and remaining 4 ingredients in a medium saucepan; stir well. Bring to a boil; cook 1 minute, stirring constantly. Remove from heat; let cool completely. Spread blueberry mixture evenly over cheesecake. Cover and chill at least 8 hours. Yield: 12 servings (serving size: 1 wedge).

Note: Crystallized ginger can be found in the spice section of most large grocery stores. Canton brand ginger-flavored liqueur is available in liquor stores, and may be omitted.

CALORIES 237 (30% from fat); PROTEIN 8.9g; FAT 7.9g (sat 4.2g, mono 2.9g, poly 0.5g); CARB 32.3g; FIBER 1.7g; CHOL 42mg; IRON 0.7mg; SODIUM 274mg; CALC 68mg

GINGER IS HOT AND COOL

Crystallized ginger, also called candied ginger, is fresh ginger that's been slowly cooked in sugar water and then rolled in coarse sugar. Look for it in crystallized form in the spice section or at an Asian market. Crystallized ginger packs a punch, so use it sparingly.

PEACH-AND-GINGER CUSTARD TART

1 cup graham cracker crumbs
2 tablespoons margarine, melted
1 egg white, lightly beaten
Vegetable cooking spray
1½ cups 1% low-fat milk
¼ cup sugar
3 tablespoons cornstarch
2 tablespoons minced
    crystallized ginger
1 large egg yolk, lightly beaten
1½ teaspoons lemon juice
½ teaspoon vanilla extract
1⅓ cups peeled, thinly sliced
    peaches
¼ cup peach preserves, melted

Preheat oven to 350°.

Combine first 3 ingredients in a medium bowl; toss with a fork until moist. Firmly press into bottom and up sides of a 14 x 4-inch rectangular or 8-inch round removable-bottom tart pan coated with cooking spray. Bake at 350° for 13 minutes; let cool on a wire rack.

Combine milk and next 4 ingredients in a medium-size heavy saucepan; stir well with a whisk. Bring to a boil over medium heat; cook 2 minutes, stirring constantly. Remove from heat; stir in lemon juice and vanilla. Let cool 10 minutes, stirring occasionally. Pour into prepared crust. Cover surface with plastic wrap; chill 1 hour.

Uncover custard, and arrange peaches over custard. Brush melted preserves over peaches. Chill at least 1 hour before serving. Yield: 8 servings (serving size: 1 slice).

CALORIES 185 (26% from fat); PROTEIN 3.3g; FAT 5.3g (sat 1.3g, mono 2.1g, poly 1g); CARB 31.5g; FIBER 0.6g; CHOL 29mg; IRON 1mg; SODIUM 148mg; CALC 72mg

Cool Gazpacho

For the past couple of decades or more, the cold summer soup known as gazpacho has been widely celebrated as a near-perfect example of modern American cuisine at its best. Nothing could be more refreshing, more vitamin-rich, and healthy—or so flavorful and yet so simple. It's been called a modern California classic, and in the highest expression of flattery, it's now imitated everywhere.

But beneath its stylish coat of contemporary fashion, gazpacho is clothed in antiquity. So ancient are its Mediterranean roots that no one can say exactly where it originated or what its name means.

The early Romans and the nomadic Moors of North Africa both figure in the speculations on gazpacho. Raymond Sokolov, a noted food sleuth and author of *Why We Eat What We Eat*, cites the presence of these cultural forces in Spain (unquestionably the motherland of the dish, if not of its name) in building an impressive and persuasive circumstantial file on the now-celebrated salad/soup.

Though it comes to our tables in a variety of forms, the contemporary dish is almost always a soup, a purée, or a coarser blend of garden vegetables—tomatoes and cucumbers foremost—seasoned with garlic, olive oil, vinegar, salt, and peppers. By most

accounts, though, the original dish was made of stale, hard bread soaked to softness in water and then seasoned, much the same as now, with oil, vinegar, garlic, and salt.

John Mariani, in his *Dictionary of American Food and Drink*, says the word gazpacho "comes from the Arabic for 'soaked bread.'" In some Spanish dictionaries it's described as "an Andalusian dish made of bread, oil, vinegar, onions, and garlic." It was in the Andalusian region of southern Spain that the Romans and Moors left their imprint—and it is there that gazpacho remains a familiar and popular dish.

All around the Mediterranean centuries ago, it was common in peasant cultures to revive stale bread by soaking and flavoring it. Then, at the beginning of the 1500s, after Columbus had returned to Spain with tomatoes (among other things), this novelty vegetable/fruit somehow found its way into the gazpacho bowl, where it seemed naturally to belong.

The Romans, Moors, and early Spaniards might not recognize our modern gazpacho as a culinary descendant of theirs, but it's hard to imagine that they—or any lover of fresh, raw garden vegetables, from whatever age—could be unimpressed with a summer soup as flavorful and distinctive as this.

MENU

CHUNKY GAZPACHO

GARLIC-DILL CRACKERS

FRESH FRUIT WITH
TANGY DRESSING

About 374 calories and 12 grams fat
(about 29% calories from fat)

CHUNKY GAZPACHO

This recipe calls for three types of vinegar; but any combination will work.

- 6 cups coarsely chopped tomato (about 3 pounds)
- 1 (32-ounce) bottle low-sodium tomato juice
- 2 cups peeled, coarsely chopped cucumber (about 2 medium)
- 1½ cups chopped green bell pepper
- 1¼ cups finely chopped Vidalia or other sweet onion
- 1 cup finely chopped celery
- 1 tablespoon olive oil
- 1 tablespoon balsamic vinegar
- 1 tablespoon basil-flavored vinegar
- 1 tablespoon rice vinegar
- ¾ teaspoon salt
- ½ teaspoon pepper
- ½ teaspoon hot sauce
- 3 garlic cloves, minced

Combine all ingredients in a large bowl; stir well. Cover and chill. Yield: 8 servings (serving size: 1½ cups).

CALORIES 95 (23% from fat); PROTEIN 3.1g; FAT 2.4g (sat 0.3g, mono 1.3g, poly 0.5g); CARB 17.3g; FIBER 3.7g; CHOL 0mg; IRON 1.3mg; SODIUM 321mg; CALC 29mg

GARLIC-DILL CRACKERS

The calories and fat in this classic snack are a fraction of what's in the original version.

- 1½ tablespoons dry ranch-flavored salad dressing mix
- 2 tablespoons vegetable oil
- 2 teaspoons dried dillweed
- ½ teaspoon garlic powder
- ¼ teaspoon lemon pepper
- 1 (11-ounce) package oyster crackers (about 4½ cups)

Preheat oven to 175°.

Combine first 5 ingredients in a large bowl; stir well. Add crackers; toss well. Spoon mixture into a jelly-roll pan.

Bake at 175° for 30 minutes or until dry, stirring occasionally. Cool completely; store in an airtight container. Yield: 4½ cups (serving size: ¼ cup).

CALORIES 90 (34% from fat); PROTEIN 1.4g; FAT 3.4g (sat 0.3g, mono 0.5g, poly 1.3g); CARB 14g; FIBER 0g; CHOL 0mg; IRON 0.1mg; SODIUM 338mg; CALC 5mg

ENDLESS VARIATIONS

Be creative with gazpacho—it can be modified in countless ways.

- ◆ Add other vegetables such as carrots and radishes.
- ◆ Experiment with different kinds of oils and vinegars.
- ◆ Try adding a splash of Worcestershire or other sauces.
- ◆ Serve spicy croutons along with the gazpacho instead of crackers.
- ◆ Try using V-8 juice instead of plain tomato juice.

FRESH FRUIT WITH TANGY DRESSING

You can make the dressing ahead, but wait to slice the bananas and avocados just before you serve them—they'll turn brown if prepared too far in advance.

- 4 cups sliced banana (about 8 medium)
- 4 cups cubed cantaloupe
- 1 medium avocado, peeled and sliced
- Lettuce leaves
- ⅓ cup sugar
- 1 tablespoon vegetable oil
- ⅓ cup lemon juice
- ¼ cup water
- 1 teaspoon celery seeds
- 1 teaspoon dry mustard
- 1 teaspoon paprika
- ½ teaspoon salt

Arrange ½ cup banana, ½ cup cantaloupe, and one-eighth of avocado on each of 8 lettuce-lined salad plates.

Place sugar and remaining 7 ingredients in a blender; cover and process until well-blended. Drizzle 2 tablespoons dressing over each salad. Yield: 8 servings.

CALORIES 189 (30% from fat); PROTEIN 2.1g; FAT 6.3g (sat 1.1g, mono 3.0g, poly 1.4g); CARB 35.5g; FIBER 3.8g; CHOL 0mg; IRON 0.9mg; SODIUM 158mg; CALC 24mg

SEPTEMBER

The Wheels of Life

When it comes to fresh Parmesan cheese, there's nothing like the real thing: Parmigiano-Reggiano. When you see those words stenciled on the golden rind of a hunk of fresh Parmesan, it means that the cheese was produced in the northern Italian areas of Bologna, Mantua, Modena, or Parma, from which the cheese gets its name. Aged for two years or more, the imported cheese has a sharper, more complex flavor than its American counterparts.

PARMESAN-CRUSTED RACK OF LAMB WITH ROASTED GARLIC POTATOES

1   (1½-pound, 8 rib) lean rack of lamb
Vegetable cooking spray
1   teaspoon water
1   large egg white, lightly beaten
¼   cup fresh breadcrumbs
¼   cup freshly grated Parmesan cheese
2   teaspoons finely chopped fresh rosemary
1   teaspoon minced fresh parsley
⅛   teaspoon ground red pepper
Roasted Garlic Potatoes
Fresh rosemary sprigs (optional)

Preheat oven to 425°.
Trim fat from lamb; place lamb on a broiler pan coated with cooking spray. Insert meat thermometer into thickest portion of lamb, making sure it does not touch bone.
Combine water and egg white; stir well. Brush lamb with egg white mixture. Combine breadcrumbs and next 4 ingredients in a small bowl. Pat breadcrumb mixture into egg white mixture on lamb.
Bake at 425° for 30 minutes or until meat thermometer registers 145° (rare) to 160° (medium-well). Let stand at room temperature 10 minutes before serving. Serve with Roasted Garlic Potatoes, and garnish with rosemary sprigs, if desired. Yield: 4 servings (serving size: 2 lamb chops and ¾ cup potatoes).

CALORIES 416 (27% from fat); PROTEIN 27.2g; FAT 12.7g (sat 4.5g, mono 5g, poly 1.1g); CARB 46.8g; FIBER 3.2g; CHOL 69mg; IRON 2.6mg; SODIUM 486mg; CALC 107mg

Roasted Garlic Potatoes:

1¾   pounds baking potatoes, peeled and cut into 1-inch cubes
3   tablespoons lemon juice
1   teaspoon olive oil
½   teaspoon salt
4   garlic cloves, minced
Vegetable cooking spray

Preheat oven to 425°.
Combine first 5 ingredients in a medium bowl; toss well to coat. Let stand 10 minutes. Spoon potato mixture into an 11 x 7-inch baking dish coated with cooking spray. Bake at 425° for 35 minutes or until potatoes are tender and lightly browned, stirring occasionally. Yield: 4 servings (serving size: ¾ cup).

CALORIES 209 (6% from fat); PROTEIN 4.1g; FAT 1.5g (sat 0.2g, mono 0.8g, poly 0.2g); CARB 44.7g; FIBER 3g; CHOL 0mg; IRON 0.7mg; SODIUM 304mg; CALC 16mg

RISOTTO WITH SUN-DRIED TOMATOES AND BASIL

1   ounce sun-dried tomatoes, packed without oil (about 14)
½   cup boiling water
2   cups water
1   (14½-ounce) can vegetable broth
1   teaspoon olive oil
½   cup finely chopped shallots
1½   cups uncooked Arborio rice or other short-grain rice
1   cup dry white wine
¾   cup freshly grated Parmesan cheese
½   cup thinly sliced fresh basil
⅛   teaspoon pepper

Combine tomatoes and ½ cup boiling water in a bowl; cover and let stand 30 minutes or until soft. Drain and chop tomatoes.
Combine 2 cups water and vegetable broth in a saucepan; bring to a simmer (don't boil). Keep broth mixture warm.
Heat oil in a saucepan over medium heat until hot. Add shallots, and sauté 2 minutes. Stir in rice, and sauté 5 minutes. Add wine, and cook 1 minute or until wine is nearly absorbed, stirring constantly. Add broth mixture, ½ cup at a time, stirring often; cook until each portion of liquid is absorbed before adding next (about 25 minutes). Add tomatoes, and cook 2 minutes, stirring constantly. Remove from heat; stir in cheese, sliced basil, and pepper. Yield: 4 servings (serving size: 1 cup).

CALORIES 271 (17% from fat); PROTEIN 9.6g; FAT 5.1g (sat 2.5g, mono 1.7g, poly 0.3g); CARB 46.2g; FIBER 0.8g; CHOL 10mg; IRON 2.6mg; SODIUM 634mg; CALC 188mg

ROSAMARIA'S STUFFED ZUCCHINI

4   medium zucchini (about 1½ pounds)
2   teaspoons chopped fresh or ½ teaspoon dried rosemary
10 spinach leaves
8   basil leaves
4   garlic cloves, peeled
1   medium onion, peeled and quartered
1   medium carrot, peeled and quartered
1½ teaspoons olive oil
3   large plum tomatoes, chopped
1   teaspoon salt
1   cup fine, dry breadcrumbs
¾   cup freshly grated Parmesan cheese
1   large egg white

Cut each zucchini in half lengthwise; scoop out pulp, leaving a ¼-inch-thick shell. Set pulp aside. Cut each zucchini shell in half crosswise.

Arrange zucchini shells in a steamer basket over boiling water. Cover and steam 3 minutes. Place on paper towels to drain; set aside.

Place zucchini pulp in a food processor; process until pulp is finely chopped. Spoon pulp into a bowl, and set aside.

Place rosemary and next 5 ingredients in food processor, and process until finely chopped.

Heat oil in a Dutch oven over low heat until hot. Add rosemary mixture; cover and cook 5 minutes, stirring occasionally. Add zucchini pulp, tomatoes, and salt; sauté over medium heat 20 minutes. Remove from heat; stir in breadcrumbs. Let mixture cool. Add cheese and egg white; stir well.

Preheat oven to 350°.

Divide mixture evenly among zucchini shells. Place stuffed shells on a baking sheet. Bake at 350° for 25 minutes or until golden brown. Yield: 16 servings (serving size: 1 stuffed zucchini piece).

CALORIES 70 (30% from fat); PROTEIN 3.9g; FAT 2.3g (sat 1g, mono 0.9g, poly 0.3g); CARB 9.1g; FIBER 1.4g; CHOL 4mg; IRON 0.9mg; SODIUM 298mg; CALC 93mg

THE GRATEFUL SHRED

When a recipe calls for cheese to be grated, shredded, or shaved, there is a reason. The success of your dish depends on which method you use.

• GRATED • Rub the cheese against the small, starlike holes on a box-style cheese grater. This gives it a powdery texture like that of canned, processed Parmesan cheese. For the best taste, grate just before using.

• FINELY SHREDDED • Use the next to largest holes on your cheese grater. You can also drop a hunk of cheese into a food processor fitted with a fine-shredding disk. Or you can use a hand-held cheese mill made especially for grating Parmesan; grind it as you would a pepper mill.

• SHREDDED • Use the largest holes on a box-style grater.

• SHAVED • Pull a cheese plane or a swivel-blade peeler across a flat side of the cheese.

STUFFED FIGS WITH MARSALA

1   cup sweet Marsala
¼   cup orange juice
2   tablespoons sugar
12 dried Calimyrna figs
3   ounces Neufchâtel cheese (about ⅓ cup), softened
¼   cup freshly grated Parmesan cheese
1   tablespoon chopped pine nuts
Orange rind curls (optional)
Fresh mint sprigs (optional)
Pine nuts (optional)

Combine first 4 ingredients in a small saucepan; bring to a boil. Remove from heat; cover and let stand 15 minutes. Remove figs from pan with a slotted spoon; set aside, and keep warm. Bring Marsala mixture to a boil; cook 10 minutes or until reduced to ¼ cup.

Combine cheeses and chopped pine nuts in a small bowl; stir until well-blended. Cut each fig to, but not through, stem end. Stuff about 1½ teaspoons cheese mixture into center of each fig. Spoon 1 tablespoon Marsala sauce onto each dessert plate, and arrange stuffed figs evenly on top of sauce. If desired, garnish with orange rind curls, mint sprigs, and pine nuts. Yield: 4 servings.

CALORIES 284 (29% from fat); PROTEIN 6.5g; FAT 9.3g (sat 4.6g, mono 2.8g, poly 1.4g); CARB 48.4g; FIBER 9.7g; CHOL 20mg; IRON 1.6mg; SODIUM 192mg; CALC 172mg

ARUGULA-AND-FENNEL SALAD WITH PARMESAN CURLS

4   (¾-ounce) slices French bread, cut into ¾-inch cubes
5   cups trimmed arugula
2   cups thinly sliced fennel bulb (about 1 small bulb)
1   cup thinly sliced red onion, separated into rings
3   tablespoons water
3   tablespoons lemon juice
¼   teaspoon salt
1   cup shaved fresh Parmesan cheese
Freshly ground pepper

Preheat oven to 350°.

Arrange French bread cubes in a single layer on a baking sheet. Bake at 350° for 15 minutes or until toasted.

Combine croutons, arugula, fennel, and onion in a large bowl. Combine water, lemon juice, and salt; stir well. Drizzle over salad; toss gently to coat.

Spoon salad onto plates; top with Parmesan cheese, and sprinkle with pepper. Yield: 6 servings (serving size: 1 cup salad and about 2 tablespoons cheese).

Note: To shave Parmesan cheese, pull a swivel-blade peeler across the flat side of the cheese.

CALORIES 122 (28% from fat); PROTEIN 7.6g; FAT 3.8g (sat 1.9g, mono 1g, poly 0.3g); CARB 15.5g; FIBER 0.9g; CHOL 8mg; IRON 1.3mg; SODIUM 383mg; CALC 234mg

PARMESAN BREAD

Semolina flour is found next to all-purpose flour in the grocery store. Its texture is similar to that of fine cornmeal. If you can't find it, increase the bread flour to 2¼ cups, and add ½ cup cornmeal.

    1 package dry yeast
    ½ teaspoon sugar
    1 cup warm water (105° to 115°)
    1¾ cups bread flour
    1 cup semolina or pasta flour
    ¾ cup finely shredded Parmesan
       cheese
    1 teaspoon salt
    2 teaspoons olive oil
    Vegetable cooking spray
    1 tablespoon semolina or pasta
       flour

Sprinkle yeast and sugar over warm water in a small bowl; let yeast mixture stand 5 minutes.

Place bread flour, 1 cup semolina flour, cheese, and salt in a food processor; pulse 3 times or until blended. With processor on, slowly add yeast mixture and olive oil through food chute; process until dough forms a ball. Process 40 additional seconds. Turn dough out onto a lightly floured surface, and knead 3 or 4 times.

Place dough in a large bowl coated with cooking spray, turning to coat top. Cover and let rise in a warm place (85°), free from drafts, 1 hour and 15 minutes or until doubled in bulk. Punch dough down, and divide into 2 equal portions. Shape each portion into a 6-inch round loaf.

Place loaves on a large baking sheet coated with cooking spray and sprinkled with 1 tablespoon semolina flour. Make 2 (⅛-inch-deep) diagonal cuts across the top of each loaf. Cover loaves, and let rise 30 minutes or until doubled in bulk.

Preheat oven to 425°.

Lightly spray loaves with water. Bake at 425° for 20 minutes or until loaves sound hollow when tapped, misting loaves every 7 minutes during baking time. Remove loaves from baking sheet; let cool on a wire rack. Yield: 2 loaves, 8 servings per loaf (serving size: 1 slice).

Note: Misting the bread with water gives the crust a chewy texture. Simply fill a clean spray bottle with water, and spritz bread frequently during baking.

CALORIES 81 (18% from fat); PROTEIN 3.5g; FAT 1.6g (sat 0.7g, mono 0.6g, poly 0.2g); CARB 12.9g; FIBER 0.4g; CHOL 1mg; IRON 0.8mg; SODIUM 154mg; CALC 45mg

---

THE VIRTUES OF PARMIGIANO-REGGIANO

This hard, dry, granular cheese from Italy is so flavorful that a little goes a long way, making it an excellent cheese for healthy cooking. Its sharp taste gives dishes a big flavor boost, and the aroma becomes even more inviting as it melts. The texture is crumblier than that of domestic Parmesan, whose creamier consistency is more like that of provolone or Cheddar.

Since Parmigiano-Reggiano is higher in sodium than some other cheeses, it has a saltier taste. Because of this, you shouldn't be tempted to add more salt at the table. Parmigiano-Reggiano is surprisingly high in calcium (336 milligrams in 1 ounce, which is about ¼ cup shredded or crumbled). It will also keep for six months in the refrigerator if tightly wrapped.

Why It's Worth the Cost: In our taste tests, we preferred the complex, sharp flavor of the imported variety to the domestic. (The latter tasted saltier.) If you're not inclined to pay the premium price ($6 to $7 a half pound), domestic Parmesan will work fine.

Bold with No Fold

Finally, an omelet you don't have to walk on eggshells to make.

What's great about frittatas is that there's no intimidating fold at the end, which usually decides the success of your omelet. Instead, the ingredients are mixed with the eggs. And even though they have a breakfast feel to them, frittatas are ideal for lunch or dinner. You can't make an omelet without breaking a few eggs, but at least now you don't need a spatula.

HEARTY O'BRIEN FRITTATA

Serve with a salad of baby greens for an ideal Sunday night dinner.

    1 cup peeled, diced baking potato
    ½ cup (2 ounces) shredded fat-free
       Cheddar cheese, divided
    4 egg whites, lightly beaten
    1 egg yolk, lightly beaten
    2 teaspoons reduced-calorie
       margarine
    ½ cup diced red onion
    ½ cup diced red bell pepper
    ½ cup diced lean Canadian bacon
    2 garlic cloves, minced
    ¼ cup fat-free sour cream

Place potato in a small saucepan; cover with water. Bring to a boil. Cook 10 minutes or until tender; drain.

Preheat oven to 450°.

Combine ¼ cup cheese, egg whites, and egg yolk in a bowl; stir well.

Melt margarine in a 10-inch nonstick skillet over medium heat. Add potato, onion, and next 3 ingredients; sauté 5 minutes. Stir in egg mixture; spread evenly in bottom of skillet. Cook over medium-low heat 5 minutes or until almost set.

Wrap handle of skillet with aluminum foil; place skillet in oven, and bake at 450° for 5 minutes or until set. Sprinkle with remaining ¼ cup cheese; bake an additional minute or until cheese melts. Top each serving with sour cream. Yield: 2 servings.

Note: Substitute ⅔ cup egg substitute for 4 egg whites and 1 egg yolk, if desired.

CALORIES 289 (23% from fat); PROTEIN 26.4g; FAT 7.4g (sat 1.5g, mono 1.9g, poly 0.7g); CARB 27.6g; FIBER 2.6g; CHOL 128mg; IRON 1.3mg; SODIUM 852mg; CALC 240mg

ONION, BACON, AND SPINACH FRITTATA

2   turkey-bacon slices, chopped
⅛   teaspoon pepper
⅛   teaspoon ground nutmeg
6   large egg whites, lightly beaten
1   large egg yolk, lightly beaten
1½ cups thinly sliced sweet onion, separated into rings
2   tablespoons water
¼   teaspoon sugar
4   cups torn fresh spinach
¼   cup (1 ounce) shredded part-skim mozzarella cheese

Preheat oven to 450°.
Cook bacon slices in a 10-inch non-stick skillet over medium heat until crisp. Combine bacon slices and next 4 ingredients in a bowl, and stir well.
Add onion to skillet; cover and cook 5 minutes or until crisp-tender, stirring occasionally. Add water and sugar; sauté 5 minutes or until onion is tender and golden. Add spinach; cover and cook 2 minutes or until spinach wilts. Stir in bacon mixture; spread evenly in bottom of skillet. Cook over medium-low heat 5 minutes or until almost set.
Wrap handle of skillet with aluminum foil; place skillet in oven, and bake at 450° for 5 minutes or until set. Sprinkle with cheese; bake an additional minute or until cheese melts. Yield: 2 servings.
Note: Substitute 1 cup egg substitute for 6 egg whites and 1 egg yolk, if desired.

CALORIES 205 (33% from fat); PROTEIN 21.2g; FAT 7.5g (sat 2.9g, mono 2.7g, poly 1.2g); CARB 13.6g; FIBER 6.1g; CHOL 127mg; IRON 3.6mg; SODIUM 659mg; CALC 238mg

HERBED-SPAGHETTI FRITTATA

Any combination of fresh herbs works well in this frittata.

1   cup cooked spaghetti (about 3 ounces uncooked)
2   tablespoons chopped fresh parsley
1   tablespoon chopped fresh basil
1   teaspoon chopped fresh tarragon
½   teaspoon chopped fresh rosemary
2   ounces chilled fat-free cream cheese (about ¼ cup), cut into small pieces
¼   teaspoon pepper
5   large egg whites, lightly beaten
1   large egg yolk, lightly beaten
Vegetable cooking spray
3   garlic cloves, minced
6   (¼-inch-thick) slices tomato
¼   cup (2 ounces) grated Asiago or Parmesan cheese

Preheat oven to 450°.
Combine first 9 ingredients in a large bowl, and stir well. Set aside.
Coat a 10-inch nonstick skillet with cooking spray; place over medium heat until hot. Add garlic; sauté 3 minutes. Stir in spaghetti mixture; spread evenly in bottom of skillet. Cook over medium-low heat 5 minutes or until almost set. Arrange tomato slices over frittata; sprinkle with Asiago cheese.
Wrap handle of skillet with aluminum foil; place skillet in oven, and bake at 450° for 5 minutes or until set. Yield: 2 servings.
Note: Substitute ¾ cup egg substitute for 5 egg whites and 1 egg yolk, if desired.

CALORIES 328 (30% from fat); PROTEIN 28.3g; FAT 11.1g (sat 5.6g, mono 3.3g, poly 0.8g); CARB 27.2g; FIBER 2.1g; CHOL 133mg; IRON 2.4mg; SODIUM 767mg; CALC 468mg

SUMMER-GARDEN FRITTATA

1   cup chopped tomato
2   tablespoons chopped fresh or 2 teaspoons dried basil
1   tablespoon balsamic vinegar
1   cup cooked small seashell macaroni (about ½ cup uncooked)
¼   teaspoon salt
¼   teaspoon pepper
5   large egg whites, lightly beaten
1   egg yolk, lightly beaten
2   teaspoons reduced-calorie margarine
Vegetable cooking spray
½   cup chopped onion
3   garlic cloves, minced
2   cups diced zucchini
½   cup (2 ounces) shredded part-skim mozzarella cheese

Preheat oven to 450°.
Combine first 3 ingredients in a small bowl; stir well. Set aside. Combine macaroni and next 4 ingredients in a medium bowl; stir well.
Melt margarine over medium heat in a 10-inch nonstick skillet coated with cooking spray. Add onion and garlic; sauté 4 minutes. Add zucchini; sauté 5 minutes. Stir in macaroni mixture; spread evenly in bottom of skillet. Cook over medium-low heat 5 minutes or until almost set.
Wrap handle of skillet with aluminum foil; place skillet in oven, and bake at 450° for 5 minutes or until almost set. Sprinkle with cheese; bake an additional minute or until cheese melts. Top each serving with ½ cup tomato mixture. Yield: 2 servings.
Note: Substitute ¾ cup egg substitute for 5 egg whites and 1 egg yolk, if desired.

CALORIES 329 (30% from fat); PROTEIN 23g; FAT 10.9g (sat 4.3g, mono 3.5g, poly 1.7g); CARB 34.4g; FIBER 3.8g; CHOL 125mg; IRON 2.5mg; SODIUM 656mg; CALC 250mg

TEX-MEX BEAN FRITTATA

⅓ cup thinly sliced green onions
3 tablespoons canned chopped green chiles
1 teaspoon chili powder
½ teaspoon ground cumin
4 large egg whites, lightly beaten
1 large egg yolk, lightly beaten
1 (15-ounce) can no-salt-added black beans, rinsed and drained
Vegetable cooking spray
3 garlic cloves, minced
½ cup (2 ounces) shredded Monterey Jack cheese with jalapeño peppers
2 tablespoons fat-free sour cream
2 tablespoons salsa
1 tablespoon chopped fresh cilantro

Preheat oven to 450°.

Combine first 7 ingredients in a bowl; stir well. Set aside.

Coat a 10-inch nonstick skillet with cooking spray; place over medium heat until hot. Add garlic; sauté 1 minute. Stir in bean mixture; spread evenly in bottom of skillet. Cook over medium-low heat 5 minutes or until almost set.

Wrap handle of skillet with aluminum foil; place skillet in oven, and bake at 450° for 5 minutes or until set. Sprinkle with cheese; bake an additional minute or until cheese melts. Top each serving with sour cream and salsa; sprinkle with cilantro. Yield: 2 servings.

Note: Substitute ⅔ cup egg substitute for 4 egg whites and 1 egg yolk, if desired.

CALORIES 393 (31% from fat); PROTEIN 27.5g; FAT 16.6g (sat 8g, mono 4.8g, poly 2.3g); CARB 36g; FIBER 6.7g; CHOL 137mg; IRON 4.3mg; SODIUM 358mg; CALC 317mg

FRENCH-COUNTRYSIDE FRITTATA

An 8-ounce package of presliced domestic mushrooms can be substituted for the specialty mushroom blend.

1 cup (½-inch) cubed French bread
1 teaspoon dried thyme
2 teaspoons Dijon mustard
¼ teaspoon pepper
6 large egg whites, lightly beaten
1 large egg yolk, lightly beaten
Vegetable cooking spray
½ cup chopped red onion
3 garlic cloves, minced
2 (4-ounce) packages sliced specialty mushroom blend (a blend of sliced crimini, shiitake, and oyster mushrooms)
¼ cup crumbled goat cheese with basil

Preheat oven to 400°.

Place French bread cubes in a single layer on a jelly-roll pan. Bake at 400° for 8 minutes or until bread cubes are toasted. Combine bread cubes, thyme, Dijon mustard, pepper, egg whites, and egg yolk in a bowl; stir well. Set aside.

Increase oven temperature to 450°.

Coat an 8-inch nonstick skillet with cooking spray, and place over medium heat until hot. Add chopped onion and minced garlic, and sauté 3 minutes. Add mushrooms, and sauté 5 minutes. Stir in bread cube mixture, and spread evenly in bottom of skillet. Cook over medium-low heat 5 minutes or until almost set.

Wrap handle of skillet with aluminum foil; place skillet in oven, and bake at 450° for 5 minutes or until set. Sprinkle frittata with cheese; bake an additional minute or until cheese is warm (cheese will not melt). Yield: 2 servings.

Note: Substitute 1 cup egg substitute for 6 egg whites and 1 egg yolk, if desired.

CALORIES 240 (27% from fat); PROTEIN 18.7g; FAT 7.3g (sat 3.2g, mono 1.9g, poly 0.9g); CARB 24.9g; FIBER 3g; CHOL 122mg; IRON 3.4mg; SODIUM 598mg; CALC 133mg

TECHNIQUE

Great Bells of Fire!

When roasted, bell peppers assume a new incarnation, sort of like the phoenix rising from the ashes. When exposed to intense heat, they shed their outer layer, revealing a velvety texture and a sweet, smoky flavor. But don't let their flavor intimidate you—few culinary tricks are as easy to achieve (see our step-by-step photos). And because they keep so well in refrigerated airtight containers, roast extra ones to have on hand. Although our recipes call for red, green, and yellow peppers, they are interchangeable. We've just color-coordinated them.

ROASTED PEPPER RATATOUILLE WITH GRILLED POLENTA

The ratatouille in this recipe can also be used as a sandwich filling or as an appetizer.

1 pound red bell peppers (about 2 large), roasted and peeled
1 pound green bell peppers (about 2 large), roasted and peeled
2 (1-pound) eggplants, peeled and cubed
Vegetable cooking spray
1 tablespoon olive oil
2 cups chopped onion
2 cups (½-inch) cubed zucchini
2 large garlic cloves, minced
2 tablespoons chopped fresh parsley
1½ teaspoons dried basil
1½ teaspoons dried oregano
1½ teaspoons sugar
¼ teaspoon freshly ground pepper
1 (28-ounce) can plum tomatoes, undrained and chopped
1 (8-ounce) can no-salt-added tomato sauce
1 (6-ounce) can tomato paste
Grilled Polenta

Cut bell peppers in half lengthwise; discard seeds and membranes.

Place bell peppers, skin sides up, on an aluminum foil-lined baking sheet; flatten with hand.

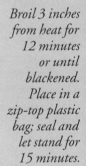

Broil 3 inches from heat for 12 minutes or until blackened. Place in a zip-top plastic bag; seal and let stand for 15 minutes.

Peel and discard skins. Store in an airtight container in the refrigerator.

Preheat oven to 375°.

Chop roasted peppers; set aside. Place eggplant in a 13 x 9-inch baking dish coated with cooking spray; lightly coat eggplant with cooking spray, tossing to coat. Bake at 375° for 40 minutes.

Heat oil in a large Dutch oven over medium-high heat until hot. Add bell pepper, onion, zucchini, and garlic; sauté 15 minutes. Stir in parsley and next 7 ingredients; bring to a boil. Reduce heat; simmer, uncovered, 10 minutes, stirring often. Stir in eggplant; cook an additional 15 minutes. Spoon over Grilled Polenta. Yield: 6 servings (serving size: 1⅓ cups ratatouille and 2 polenta triangles).

CALORIES 392 (22% from fat); PROTEIN 13.2g; FAT 9.6g (sat 2.7g, mono 3.5g, poly 1.6g); CARB 69g; FIBER 9.2g; CHOL 12.6mg; IRON 7.0mg; SODIUM 798mg; CALC 223mg

Grilled Polenta:

1½ cups yellow cornmeal
¾ cup water
3 (10½-ounce) cans low-salt chicken broth
¾ cup crumbled feta cheese
2 teaspoons margarine
¼ teaspoon pepper
⅛ teaspoon salt
Vegetable cooking spray

Place cornmeal in a large saucepan. Gradually add water and broth, stirring constantly with a whisk. Bring to a boil; reduce heat to medium, and cook 15 minutes, stirring often. Remove from heat; stir in cheese, margarine, pepper, and salt.

Spoon polenta into a 13 x 9-inch baking dish coated with cooking spray,

spreading evenly. Press plastic wrap onto surface of polenta, and chill 1 hour or until firm. Remove plastic wrap.

Invert polenta onto a cutting board; cut into 6 squares. Cut each square diagonally into 2 triangles.

Prepare grill. Place polenta triangles on grill rack coated with cooking spray; grill 5 minutes on each side or until lightly browned and thoroughly heated. Yield: 6 servings (serving size: 2 triangles).

CALORIES 196 (27% from fat); PROTEIN 6.5g; FAT 5.9g (sat 2.6g, mono 1.7g, poly 0.9g); CARB 28.9g; FIBER 1.8g; CHOL 12mg; IRON 2.2mg; SODIUM 272mg; CALC 72mg

UPTOWN ROASTED PEPPER GRILLS

This open-faced sandwich is easiest to eat with a knife and fork.

    2   medium zucchini, cut
        lengthwise into ¼-inch-thick
        slices
    2   medium yellow squash, cut
        lengthwise into ¼-inch-thick
        slices
        Vegetable cooking spray
    1   tablespoon chopped fresh or
        1 teaspoon dried oregano
    1   tablespoon chopped fresh or
        1 teaspoon dried basil
    ¼   teaspoon pepper, divided
    ⅛   teaspoon salt
    2   pounds red bell peppers (about
        4 large), roasted and peeled
    2   (2½-ounce) submarine rolls
    1   garlic clove, halved
   12   medium basil leaves
    4   teaspoons red wine vinegar
    1   teaspoon extra-virgin olive oil
    4   (1-ounce) presliced part-skim
        mozzarella cheese slices

Combine zucchini and squash in a large bowl; lightly coat with cooking spray, and toss well. Sprinkle oregano, basil, ⅛ teaspoon pepper, and salt over squash mixture; toss well. Arrange zucchini and squash in a single layer on a baking sheet coated with cooking spray. Broil 3 minutes or until tender and browned.

Cut the roasted bell peppers into 1-inch-thick strips, and set aside.

Cut submarine rolls in half horizontally. Rub cut sides of garlic over cut sides of rolls. Place rolls, cut sides up, on baking sheet. Divide bell pepper strips, zucchini, yellow squash, and basil leaves evenly on roll halves. Drizzle vinegar and oil evenly over sandwiches, and sprinkle with remaining ⅛ teaspoon pepper. Place 1 mozzarella cheese slice over each sandwich, and broil 2 minutes or until cheese melts. Yield: 4 sandwiches (serving size: 1 sandwich).

CALORIES 278 (30% from fat); PROTEIN 14.1g; FAT 9.2g (sat 3.7g, mono 3g, poly 1.6g); CARB 37.7g; FIBER 5.3g; CHOL 16mg; IRON 5.3mg; SODIUM 448mg; CALC 246mg

ROASTED YELLOW PEPPER-AND-BASIL VINAIGRETTE

Serve this colorful vinaigrette over salad greens or sliced tomatoes, or use it as a basting sauce or marinade for grilled chicken.

    1   pound yellow bell peppers
        (about 3 small), roasted and
        peeled
    ⅓   cup white wine vinegar
    2   tablespoons extra-virgin olive
        oil
    1½ teaspoons Dijon mustard
    ½   teaspoon salt
    ¼   teaspoon sugar
    ⅛   teaspoon pepper
    1   garlic clove, minced
    ⅓   cup finely chopped fresh basil

Combine first 8 ingredients in a blender; cover and process until smooth. Stir in basil. Yield: 1½ cups (serving size: 2 tablespoons).

CALORIES 32 (70% from fat); PROTEIN 0.4g; FAT 2.5g (sat 0.3g, mono 1.7g, poly 0.3g); CARB 2.3g; FIBER 0.6g; CHOL 0mg; IRON 0.5mg; SODIUM 118mg; CALC 5mg

ROASTED PEPPER-AND-GOAT CHEESE STRUDELS

    ¾   cup fresh breadcrumbs
    ¼   cup chopped fresh basil
    1   teaspoon chopped fresh
        rosemary
    ¼   teaspoon salt
    ¼   teaspoon pepper
    1   pound red bell peppers
        (about 2 large), roasted
        and peeled
    1   pound green bell peppers
        (about 2 large), roasted and
        peeled
    1   teaspoon olive oil
    1   cup diced carrot
    1   cup finely chopped onion
    1   garlic clove, minced
   12   sheets frozen phyllo dough,
        thawed
        Vegetable cooking spray
    3   ounces goat cheese
    6   tablespoons chopped fresh
        parsley

Preheat oven to 375°.

Combine first 5 ingredients in a small bowl; stir well. Set aside.

Cut bell peppers into 1-inch-thick strips; set aside.

Heat oil in a medium nonstick skillet over medium heat until hot. Add carrot, onion, and garlic, and sauté 8 minutes or until tender and lightly browned. Remove from heat; set aside.

Place 1 phyllo sheet on a large cutting board or work surface (cover remaining phyllo to keep them from drying out); lightly coat with cooking spray. Place another phyllo sheet on top of first sheet; lightly coat with cooking spray. Cut stack in half crosswise; place 1 half on top of the other half. Sprinkle 2 tablespoons breadcrumb mixture along 1 short edge of phyllo stack, leaving a 2-inch border.

Spoon ¼ cup carrot mixture over breadcrumbs; top with 2 red bell pepper strips, 2 green bell pepper strips, ½ ounce cheese, and 1 tablespoon parsley. Fold over the long edges of phyllo to cover 2 inches of filling. Starting at short edge, roll up jelly-roll fashion (do not roll tightly or roll may split).

Place roll, seam side down, on a baking sheet coated with cooking spray; lightly coat the roll with cooking spray. Repeat procedure with remaining phyllo sheets, breadcrumb mixture, carrot mixture, bell pepper strips, cheese, and parsley.

Bake at 375° for 25 minutes or until golden. Serve warm. Yield: 6 servings (serving size: 1 roll).

CALORIES 234 (28% from fat); PROTEIN 7.2g; FAT 7.2g (sat 2.7g, mono 1.8g, poly 1.9g); CARB 36.4g; FIBER 3.9g; CHOL 13mg; IRON 3.8mg; SODIUM 482mg; CALC 109mg

ROASTED PEPPER PESTO CHEESECAKE

There will be some extra pesto left after making the cheesecakes. Toss it with pasta for a quick-and-easy supper.

Vegetable cooking spray
  2 tablespoons fine, dry breadcrumbs
  1 (15-ounce) carton fat-free ricotta cheese
  1 (8-ounce) block light cream cheese, softened
  ⅓ cup freshly grated Parmesan cheese
  ⅛ teaspoon salt
Dash of ground red pepper
  1 egg
1½ cups Roasted Pepper Pesto, divided
  1 teaspoon all-purpose flour
  1 (8-ounce) carton fat-free sour cream
 24 (¾-ounce) slices diagonally cut French bread baguette
 24 roasted red bell pepper strips (optional)

Preheat oven to 325°.

Coat 2 (7-inch) springform pans with cooking spray; sprinkle breadcrumbs evenly over bottoms of pans.

Place ricotta and cream cheese in a large bowl; beat at medium speed of an electric mixer until smooth. Add Parmesan cheese, salt, ground red pepper, and egg; beat until well-blended.

Pour ¾ cup cheese mixture into each prepared pan. Spread ½ cup Roasted Pepper Pesto over each layer; top each pesto layer with ¾ cup cheese mixture. Bake at 325° for 45 minutes or until almost set.

Combine remaining ½ cup Roasted Pepper Pesto, flour, and sour cream in a bowl; stir well. Spread half of mixture over each cheesecake. Bake at 325° for 10 minutes. Remove cheesecakes from oven; let cool to room temperature. Cover and chill. Cut each cheesecake into 12 wedges; serve with baguette slices. Garnish with bell pepper strips, if desired. Yield: 2 cheesecakes, 24 servings (serving size: 1 wedge of cheesecake and 1 baguette slice).

Note 1: Cheesecake can be made in 1 (9-inch) springform pan. Coat pan with cooking spray, and sprinkle 2 tablespoons breadcrumbs over bottom of pan. Spoon 1½ cups cheese mixture into prepared pan. Spread 1 cup Roasted Pepper Pesto over cheese mixture; top with remaining 1½ cups cheese mixture. Bake at 325° for 1 hour. Spread sour cream mixture over cheesecake; bake an additional 10 minutes. Let cool. Cover and chill. Cut cheesecake into 24 wedges, and serve with baguette slices. Yield: 1 cheesecake, 24 servings (serving size: 1 wedge of cheesecake and 1 baguette slice).

Note 2: To freeze cheesecake, wrap tightly and freeze up to 3 months. Thaw, covered, in refrigerator overnight.

CALORIES 124 (24% from fat); PROTEIN 7.4g; FAT 3.3g (sat 1.6g, mono 0.7g, poly 0.4g); CARB 15.8g; FIBER 0.8g; CHOL 19mg; IRON 0.8mg; SODIUM 256mg; CALC 81mg

Roasted Pepper Pesto:

  1 cup fresh basil leaves
  ¼ cup freshly grated Parmesan cheese
  2 tablespoons pine nuts, toasted
  1 tablespoon olive oil
  ¼ teaspoon salt
  ⅛ teaspoon pepper
  2 pounds red bell peppers (about 4 large), roasted and peeled

Place all ingredients in a food processor; process until smooth, scraping sides of processor bowl occasionally. Store in an airtight container in refrigerator up to 1 week. Yield: 3 cups.

Note: Serve remaining 1½ cups pesto with pasta or on grilled chicken or sautéed vegetables.

CALORIES 48 (54% from fat); PROTEIN 2g; FAT 2.9g (sat 0.7g, mono 1.3g, poly 0.7g); CARB 4.5g; FIBER 1.3g; CHOL 2mg; IRON 1.1mg; SODIUM 89mg; CALC 39mg

Pampering Begins at Home

A spa experience doesn't have to cost a fortune. With planning and a little help from your friends, you can create an indulgent one at home. And after all that pampering, you won't want to spend too much time fussing over dinner. This burger's perfect for at-home spa days.

TURKEY BURGERS

  ½ pound ground turkey
  ¼ cup Italian-seasoned breadcrumbs
1½ tablespoons finely chopped onion
  1 tablespoon finely chopped fresh parsley
  ½ teaspoon chili powder
  ¼ teaspoon salt
  ⅛ teaspoon dried oregano
  ⅛ teaspoon pepper
Dash of Worcestershire sauce
  1 garlic clove, minced
  1 egg white, lightly beaten
  2 tablespoons all-purpose flour
Vegetable cooking spray
  2 (1½-ounce) hamburger buns
  2 (⅛-inch-thick) tomato slices
  2 (⅛-inch-thick) red onion slices

Combine first 10 ingredients in a bowl; stir well. Add egg white; stir until blended. Divide mixture into 2 equal portions, shaping into ½-inch-thick patties. Dredge patties in flour.

Coat a medium nonstick skillet with cooking spray; place over medium heat until hot. Add patties; cook 5 minutes on each side. Serve patties on hamburger buns with tomato and onion. Yield: 2 servings.

CALORIES 396 (20% from fat); PROTEIN 33.6g; FAT 8.9g (sat 2.1g, mono 1.6g, poly 2g); CARB 43.5g; FIBER 1.3g; CHOL 79mg; IRON 3.6mg; SODIUM 906mg; CALC 73mg

Hooked on Fish

If fish is so lean, why aren't Americans eating more of it?

This is a question Graham Kerr recently pondered, jotting down some of the obstacles and solutions to deal with them.

- **The—um—aroma.** There are perfectly fresh fish that, when cooked, make their presence known throughout your house. If you want to avoid the problem, there are some virtually odor-free fish in the sea. Among these are halibut, orange roughy, catfish, and sea bass.
- **The serving size.** Lean fish just doesn't seem to satisfy at 4 ounces in the same way as similar-size portions of steak or chicken. So in this recipe, each portion has six ounces of fish, more than two servings of vegetables, and a starch—all totaling 461 calories and less than 10 grams of fat.
- **The dryness factor.** Fish is often overcooked, leaving it dry and stringy. Undercooked white fish isn't very attractive either, but as little as one extra minute to be on the safe side can ruin the natural moisture of the fish.

Here's an efficient way to put this one-dish meal together:

1. Cut up the vegetables, and crush the garlic.
2. Cook the rice while you're preparing the fish and the tomato sauce.
3. Steam the squash and zucchini last (or do it in the microwave).

MEXICAN SEA BASS WITH SUMMER SQUASH

The ingredient list may look lengthy, but included are spices or items that take virtually no time to measure. You can substitute other lean white fish (grouper, orange roughy, or halibut) for sea bass.

- 2 teaspoons olive oil
- 1 cup finely chopped onion
- ¾ cup (2-inch) julienne-cut green bell pepper
- ¾ cup (2-inch) julienne-cut yellow bell pepper
- 1 tablespoon seeded, finely chopped jalapeño pepper
- 3 garlic cloves, crushed
- ½ teaspoon ground cumin
- ¼ teaspoon salt
- ¼ teaspoon pepper
- ¼ teaspoon hot sauce
- 1 (14.5-ounce) can diced tomatoes, undrained
- 4 (6-ounce) sea bass fillets (about 2 inches thick)
- 1 teaspoon fresh lemon juice
- ⅛ teaspoon pepper
- 1 teaspoon cornstarch
- 2 teaspoons water
- 4 medium zucchini (about 1¼ pounds), quartered lengthwise
- 2 medium yellow squash (about 6 ounces), quartered lengthwise
- ¼ teaspoon salt
- ⅛ teaspoon pepper
- 3 cups hot cooked rice (cooked without salt or fat)
- 2 tablespoons chopped cilantro
Lemon wedges

Heat oil in a large skillet over medium heat until hot. Add onion; sauté 1 minute. Add bell peppers, jalapeño, and garlic; sauté 2 minutes. Stir in cumin and next 4 ingredients.

Arrange fish over tomato mixture; sprinkle lemon juice and ⅛ teaspoon pepper over fish. Bring to a boil; cover, reduce heat, and simmer 10 minutes or until fish flakes easily when tested with a fork. Remove fish from skillet; set aside, and keep warm.

Combine cornstarch and water in a small bowl; stir well. Add to skillet; bring to a boil, and cook 1 minute, stirring constantly.

Arrange zucchini and squash in a steamer basket over boiling water. Cover and steam 4 minutes or until crisp-tender. Drain; sprinkle with ¼ teaspoon salt and ⅛ teaspoon pepper.

Spoon rice onto plates; top with tomato mixture and fish. Sprinkle with cilantro. Serve with steamed vegetables and lemon wedges. Yield: 4 servings (serving size: ¾ cup rice, ¾ cup tomato mixture, 1 fish fillet, 4 zucchini pieces, and 2 yellow squash pieces).

CALORIES 461 (19% from fat); PROTEIN 39g; FAT 9.5g (sat 1.8g, mono 4.2g, poly 2.3g); CARB 54.4g; FIBER 4.4g; CHOL 116mg; IRON 6.2mg; SODIUM 590mg; CALC 225mg

Warm Salmon Salad, page 238

Stuffed Figs with Marsala, page 217

Marinated Shrimp with Rémoulade Sauce, page 241

Beef-and-Mushroom Stew, page 234

Mango Upside-Down Orange Cake, page 237

Power Veggies

After examining the latest statistics and studies, broccoli, carrots, spinach, and sweet potatoes have emerged as the souped-up superheroes of the vegetable world. And these power veggies are available year-round in your local supermarket—so available, in fact, that you may be taking them for granted.

Each is loaded with antioxidants—mainly beta carotene and vitamins A, C, and E—which many studies indicate may help prevent heart disease and cancer, bolster the immune system, and even slow aging. Vitamin C also builds body tissue and, along with vitamin E, can help delay the onset of cataracts. Beta carotene and vitamin A also promote good vision as well as maintain healthy skin.

Reap the nutritional benefits of these vegetables in these homey, innovative dishes that in many cases contain, per serving, as much as five times the Recommended Dietary Allowance for vitamin A (5,000 IUs) and at least half the RDA (60 mg) for vitamin C. These dishes are so tasty that everybody will be eating their veggies.

BROCCOLI TABBOULEH

1 cup boiling water
¾ cup uncooked bulgur or cracked wheat
2 cups coarsely chopped broccoli
1 cup shredded carrot
1 cup quartered cherry tomatoes
½ cup finely chopped fresh parsley
3 tablespoons thinly sliced green onions
¼ cup lemon juice
1½ tablespoons olive oil
¼ teaspoon salt
¼ teaspoon pepper
1 small garlic clove, crushed

Combine boiling water and bulgur in a medium bowl; stir well. Let stand 20 minutes or until water is absorbed.

Arrange broccoli in a steamer basket over boiling water; cover and steam 3 minutes. Rinse under cold water; drain well. Add broccoli and next 4 ingredients to bulgur; toss gently.

Combine lemon juice and remaining 4 ingredients in a small bowl; stir

well with a whisk. Pour over bulgur mixture; toss gently to coat. Cover and chill. Yield: 5 servings (serving size: 1 cup).

Note: Besides the nutrients listed below, each serving provides 7,271 IUs vitamin A and 56mg vitamin C.

CALORIES 141 (29% from fat); PROTEIN 4.5g; FAT 4.6g (sat 0.8g, mono 3.0g, poly 0.7g); CARB 23.6g; FIBER 6.5g; CHOL 0mg; IRON 1.6mg; SODIUM 145mg; CALC 45mg

---

THE CUTTING EDGE

To keep vitamins and minerals as intact as possible, cut vegetables just before cooking, and keep the pieces reasonably large (small pieces expose more surface area and therefore increase nutrient loss). Boiling saps nutrients the worst, followed by steaming and microwaving. If you don't overcook the vegetables and you use the liquid that they are cooked in, you retain the nutrients.

BROCCOLI-CHEDDAR SOUP

Vegetable cooking spray
1 cup chopped onion
4 cups chopped fresh broccoli (about ¾ pound), divided
2 cups peeled, diced red potato (about ¾ pound)
½ teaspoon garlic powder
2 (10½-ounce) cans low-salt chicken broth
1 bay leaf
¾ cup (3 ounces) shredded reduced-fat sharp Cheddar cheese
1 (12-ounce) can evaporated skim milk
Dash of pepper

Coat a large Dutch oven with cooking spray; place over medium heat until hot. Add onion; sauté 5 minutes. Add 2 cups broccoli and next 4 ingredients; bring to a boil. Cover, reduce heat, and simmer 20 minutes or until vegetables are tender.

Discard bay leaf. Place half of broccoli mixture in container of a blender; cover and process until smooth. Spoon into a bowl. Repeat procedure with remaining broccoli mixture. Return broccoli purée to pan; add cheese, milk, pepper, and remaining 2 cups broccoli. Cook over medium heat 4 minutes, or until chopped broccoli is just tender, stirring until cheese melts. Yield: 7 servings (serving size: 1 cup).

Note: Besides the nutrients listed below, each serving provides 1,017 IUs vitamin A and 70mg vitamin C.

CALORIES 143 (21% from fat); PROTEIN 10.6g; FAT 3.3g (sat 1.6g, mono 0.9g, poly 0.3g); CARB 19.1g; FIBER 2.5g; CHOL 10mg; IRON 1.4mg; SODIUM 187mg; CALC 278mg

BROCCOLI

- One cup has 1½ times the RDA for vitamin C, or the equivalent of 6 ounces of orange juice.
- High in vitamin A and fiber, it also contains some calcium.
- Contains sulforaphane, indoles, and isothiocyanates—phytochemicals that studies say can protect against cancer.
- The florets have more vitamin C than the stalks; florets that are bluish- or purplish-green have more vitamin C than their paler counterparts.

CARROTS

- The Fort Knox of beta carotene. The deeper the orange, the more beta carotene there is.
- Contains phenolic acids, phytochemicals shown to have reduced the risk of cancer.
- Cooked carrots are better than raw ones because cooking unleashes more of the beta carotene.

SPINACH

- Abundant in beta carotene, vitamin A, and potassium.
- The crisp, dark-green leaves have higher levels of vitamin C.
- High in folacin, a nutrient crucial during early pregnancy to prevent neural-tube defects in children.

SWEET POTATOES

- Rich in beta carotene, vitamin C, and vitamin E.
- One cup has more than six times the recommended amount of beta carotene and 50% of the RDA for vitamin C.
- Cook with the skin on to retain the vitamins, and be sure to eat everything in order to get the most nutrients.

SPINACH, RICE, AND FETA PIE

2 teaspoons margarine
¾ cup chopped onion
2 teaspoons all-purpose flour
½ teaspoon salt
¼ teaspoon pepper
1½ cups 1% low-fat milk
2 cups cooked long-grain rice (cooked without salt or fat)
¾ cup crumbled feta cheese
1 large egg, lightly beaten
2 large egg whites
1 (10-ounce) package frozen chopped spinach, thawed, drained, and squeezed dry
Olive oil-flavored vegetable cooking spray
2 tablespoons grated Parmesan cheese

Preheat oven to 400°.

Melt margarine in a large saucepan over medium heat. Add onion; sauté 3 minutes. Stir in flour, salt, and pepper. Gradually add milk, stirring with a whisk until well-blended. Bring mixture to a simmer, and cook 1 minute or until slightly thick, stirring constantly. Remove saucepan from heat; stir in rice and next 4 ingredients.

Pour mixture into a 9-inch pie plate coated with cooking spray. Sprinkle Parmesan cheese over pie. Bake at 400° for 35 minutes or until set. Broil 2 minutes or until golden. Yield: 6 servings.

Note: Besides the nutrients listed below, each serving provides 3,909 IUs vitamin A and 13mg vitamin C.

CALORIES 198 (30% from fat); PROTEIN 10g; FAT 6.7g (sat 3.4g, mono 1.9g, poly 0.7g); CARB 24.8g; FIBER 2.3g; CHOL 53mg; IRON 1.9mg; SODIUM 494mg; CALC 237mg

SWEET POTATO, CARROT, AND APPLE GRATIN

Flavored with orange juice and ginger, this gratin makes a perfect accompaniment for a main dish of pork or ham.

4 cups water
4 cups (½-inch) peeled, cubed sweet potato
2 cups thinly sliced carrot
1½ cups peeled, diced Granny Smith apple
⅓ cup orange juice
¼ cup dried cranberries
2 tablespoons brown sugar
1 teaspoon peeled, grated fresh gingerroot
¼ teaspoon salt
¼ teaspoon pepper
Vegetable cooking spray
¾ cup (3 ounces) shredded fontina or Cheddar cheese

Preheat oven to 375°.

Combine first 3 ingredients in a large saucepan; bring to a boil. Cover, reduce heat, and simmer 4 minutes or until vegetables are tender. Drain well.

Combine sweet potato mixture, apple, and next 6 ingredients in a bowl; toss gently. Spoon into a 6-cup gratin dish coated with cooking spray; bake at 375° for 25 minutes. Sprinkle with cheese; bake an additional 10 minutes or until cheese is golden. Yield: 6 servings (serving size: 1 cup).

Note: Besides the nutrients listed below, each serving provides 28,295 IUs vitamin A and 31mg vitamin C.

CALORIES 217 (21% from fat); PROTEIN 5.8g; FAT 5g (sat 2.8g, mono 1.3g, poly 0.4g); CARB 39g; FIBER 5.1g; CHOL 16mg; IRON 1mg; SODIUM 124mg; CALC 117mg

---

Yes, No, Maybe

Just how many vegetarians are out there? It depends on how you ask the question. The percentage of American adults who say they never eat any meat, fish, poultry, or dairy products (according to a 1994 Roper survey) is less than 1%. But the percentage of American adults who consider themselves vegetarians (according to a 1992 Yankelovich survey) is 7%; those who never eat red meat, 6%; never eat poultry, 3%; never eat dairy products, 3%; never eat eggs, 4%; never eat fish or seafood, 4%. Meanwhile, the number of college students who call themselves vegetarians has risen to 15%.

PORK STEW WITH SWEET POTATOES AND CORN

1½ pounds lean boned pork loin
1 tablespoon olive oil
2 cups quartered mushrooms
1½ cups thinly sliced leek
2 cups julienne-cut carrot
1 cup low-salt chicken broth
2 teaspoons poultry seasoning
½ teaspoon salt
½ teaspoon coarsely ground pepper
2 (14.5-ounce) cans no-salt-added whole tomatoes, undrained and chopped
2 bay leaves
3½ cups peeled, chopped sweet potato (about 1 pound)
1 (10-ounce) package frozen whole-kernel corn
2 cups coarsely chopped spinach

Trim fat from pork, and cut pork into 1-inch cubes. Heat olive oil in a large Dutch oven over medium-high heat until hot. Add pork cubes, mushrooms, and leek; sauté 10 minutes or until browned.

Stir in carrot and next 6 ingredients; bring to a boil. Cover, reduce heat, and simmer 1 hour or until pork is tender. Add sweet potato and corn; cover and simmer 20 minutes or until sweet potato is tender. Add spinach; cover and simmer 2 minutes. Discard bay leaves. Yield: 6 servings (serving size: 1¾ cups).

Note: Besides the nutrients listed below, each serving provides 27,936 IUs vitamin A and 55mg vitamin C.

CALORIES 394 (27% from fat); PROTEIN 29.4g; FAT 12g (sat 3.4g, mono 5.7g, poly 1.5g); CARB 44.7g; FIBER 6.1g; CHOL 68mg; IRON 4.1mg; SODIUM 344mg; CALC 121mg

SWEET POTATO MINESTRONE WITH TURKEY SAUSAGE

½ pound smoked turkey sausage, cut into ¼-inch-thick slices
1 cup diced onion
1 cup diced carrot
¾ cup thinly sliced celery
3 cups water
2 cups peeled, diced sweet potato (about 9 ounces)
1 teaspoon dried oregano
½ teaspoon coarsely ground pepper
¼ teaspoon salt
2 (14.5-ounce) cans no-salt-added whole tomatoes, undrained and coarsely chopped
1 (15-ounce) can Great Northern beans, rinsed and drained
8 cups coarsely chopped spinach

Combine first 4 ingredients in a Dutch oven; sauté over medium-high heat 7 minutes or until sausage is browned.

Add water and next 6 ingredients. Bring to a boil; cover, reduce heat, and simmer 30 minutes or until vegetables are tender. Stir in spinach; cook an additional 2 minutes. Yield: 7 servings (serving size: 1½ cups).

Note: Besides the nutrients listed below, each serving provides 16,973 IUs vitamin A and 48mg vitamin C.

CALORIES 221 (30% from fat); PROTEIN 12.1g; FAT 7.3g (sat 2.4g, mono 2.7g, poly 2.1g); CARB 29.3g; FIBER 6.3g; CHOL 0mg; IRON 4.2mg; SODIUM 525mg; CALC 189mg

Counting Chickens

There are countless ways to serve chicken. Here are just a few of your favorites.

HERBED CHICKEN PASTA

We eat a lot of pasta because it's fast, and my children like it. That's why a recipe like Herbed Chicken Pasta is a favorite at our house. You get meat and veggies in one dish, and it's easy to put together.

—Julie Mitchell, Helena, Montana

1 teaspoon vegetable oil
1½ cups sliced mushrooms
½ cup chopped onion
1 garlic clove, minced
1 pound skinned, boned chicken breasts, cut into 1-inch pieces
½ teaspoon salt
½ teaspoon dried basil
¼ teaspoon pepper
2 cups coarsely chopped tomato
4 cups hot cooked fettuccine (about 8 ounces uncooked pasta)
¼ cup freshly grated Parmesan cheese

Heat oil in a large nonstick skillet over medium-high heat until hot. Add mushrooms, onion, and garlic; sauté 2 minutes. Add chicken, salt, basil, and pepper; sauté 5 minutes or until chicken is done. Add tomato; sauté 2 minutes. Serve over pasta; sprinkle with cheese. Yield: 4 servings (serving size: 1 cup chicken mixture, 1 cup pasta, and 1 tablespoon cheese).

CALORIES 395 (13% from fat); PROTEIN 37g; FAT 5.7g (sat 1.9g, mono 1.3g, poly 1.4g); CARB 47.5g; FIBER 4.2g; CHOL 71mg; IRON 3.7mg; SODIUM 492mg; CALC 121mg

ROAST CHICKEN WITH GARLIC GRAVY

If company is coming during the week, this recipe is at the top of my list. Preparation is no fuss because all I have to do is put the chicken in the pan and bake it.

—Sue Pontifex,
Surrey, British Columbia, Canada

1   (3-pound) chicken
1   teaspoon dried thyme
¼   teaspoon salt
¼   teaspoon pepper
10 garlic cloves, peeled and divided
½   cup dry white wine
1   (10½-ounce) can low-salt chicken broth, divided
Vegetable cooking spray
1   tablespoon all-purpose flour

Preheat oven to 325°.

Remove and discard giblets and neck from chicken. Rinse chicken under cold water; pat dry. Trim excess fat. Starting at neck cavity, loosen skin from breast and drumsticks by inserting fingers, gently pushing between skin and meat. Rub thyme, salt, and pepper on breast and drumsticks under loosened skin; place 2 garlic cloves in body cavity. Lift wing tips up and over the back; tuck under chicken. Set aside.

Combine remaining 8 garlic cloves, wine, and half of broth in a shallow roasting pan lined with aluminum foil. Place chicken on a rack coated with cooking spray; place rack in pan. Insert meat thermometer into meaty part of thigh, making sure not to touch bone.

Bake at 325° for 1 hour and 45 minutes or until thermometer registers 180°. Discard skin. Place chicken on a platter, reserving pan drippings; set chicken aside. Keep warm.

Place flour in a small saucepan. Gradually add remaining half of broth, stirring with a whisk until blended. Set aside. Place a zip-top plastic bag inside a 2-cup measure. Pour pan drippings into bag; let stand 10 minutes (fat will rise to the top).

Seal bag; carefully snip off 1 bottom corner of bag. Drain drippings into broth mixture in saucepan, stopping before fat layer reaches opening; discard fat. Bring mixture to a boil; cook 1 minute or until thick, stirring constantly with a whisk. Serve gravy with chicken. Yield: 4 servings (serving size: 3 ounces chicken and 3 tablespoons gravy).

CALORIES 116 (31% from fat); PROTEIN 14.2g; FAT 4g (sat 0.9g, mono 1.2g, poly 0.8g); CARB 5.4g; FIBER 0.3g; CHOL 39mg; IRON 1.7mg; SODIUM 213mg; CALC 30mg

---

MENU SUGGESTION

CHICKEN BISCUIT STEW

Red and green apple salad*

Low-fat brownies

*Toss torn curly leaf lettuce, sliced red and green apples, and sliced almonds with a low-fat bottled honey-mustard salad dressing.

CHICKEN BISCUIT STEW

This is one recipe I made sure I copied from Mom when I got married. With this meal, she never had to worry about leftovers.

—Beth Blevins, Alabaster, Alabama

2   tablespoons reduced-calorie stick margarine
½   cup all-purpose flour
¼   teaspoon salt
¼   teaspoon pepper
½   cup skim milk
1   (10½-ounce) can low-salt chicken broth
1½ cups cubed cooked chicken breasts
⅓   cup chopped onion
1   (8½-ounce) can green peas, drained
1   (8¼-ounce) can sliced carrots, drained
1   (4.5-ounce) can refrigerated buttermilk biscuits

Preheat oven to 375°.

Melt margarine in a 9-inch cast-iron skillet over medium-high heat. Stir in flour, salt, and pepper. Gradually add milk and broth, stirring with a whisk until blended. Cook milk mixture 4 minutes or until thick and bubbly, stirring constantly. Add chicken, onion, peas, and carrots; cook 1 minute. Remove from heat.

Carefully split biscuits in half horizontally; place over chicken mixture. Bake at 375° for 20 minutes or until biscuits are golden brown. Yield: 5 servings (serving size: ¾ cup stew and 2 biscuit halves).

CALORIES 251 (30% from fat); PROTEIN 10.2g; FAT 8.4g (sat 1.9g, mono 3.7g, poly 1.7g); CARB 26.4g; FIBER 1g; CHOL 33mg; IRON 2.3mg; SODIUM 612mg; CALC 54mg

---

GINGER CHICKEN

When an Indonesian family came to live with us, I was able to spice up my Oriental cooking and this recipe. I like to serve it as an entrée, but you can also stick the chicken on skewers and serve as an appetizer.

—Kathleen Wynveen,
Sheboygan Falls, Wisconsin

⅓   cup low-sodium soy sauce
¼   cup orange juice
3   tablespoons finely chopped green onions
1   tablespoon peeled, grated fresh gingerroot
1   tablespoon lemon juice
1   tablespoon honey
1   teaspoon dried basil
½   teaspoon pepper
¼   to ½ teaspoon dried crushed red pepper
¼   teaspoon five-spice powder
4   garlic cloves, minced
1   pound skinned, boned chicken breasts, cut into ½-inch-wide strips
2   teaspoons vegetable oil
4   cups hot cooked rice (cooked without salt or fat)

Combine first 12 ingredients in a bowl; stir well. Cover and marinate in refrigerator 30 minutes. Drain chicken, reserving marinade.

Heat oil in a large nonstick skillet over medium heat. Add chicken; sauté 5 minutes. Add reserved marinade; cover, reduce heat, and simmer 5 minutes. Serve over rice. Yield: 4 servings (serving size: 3 ounces chicken and 1 cup rice).

CALORIES 471 (13% from fat); PROTEIN 39.8g; FAT 6.6g (sat 1.6g, mono 2.1g, poly 2g); CARB 58g; FIBER 1.4g; CHOL 96mg; IRON 3.4mg; SODIUM 587mg; CALC 58mg

CHICKEN PITA SANDWICHES WITH YOGURT SAUCE

Although marinating the chicken takes some time, the flavor is worth it, and the dish cooks quickly. In fact, my daughter loves these sandwiches so much she requested them for her birthday dinner. Rice and a fruit dessert are good complements to this recipe.

—Amy Polk, Walled Lake, Michigan

¾ cup fresh lemon juice
1 teaspoon ground turmeric
½ teaspoon ground cumin
½ teaspoon ground allspice
1½ teaspoons olive oil
¼ teaspoon salt
⅛ teaspoon ground cardamom
⅛ teaspoon pepper
3 garlic cloves, minced
2 pounds skinned, boned chicken breasts
1¾ cups thinly sliced cucumber
1 cup thinly sliced onion, separated into rings
1 tablespoon minced fresh mint
1 (8-ounce) carton plain low-fat yogurt
Vegetable cooking spray
8 (6-inch) whole-wheat pita bread rounds, cut in half
1 cup thinly sliced iceberg lettuce
1 cup chopped tomato

Combine first 10 ingredients in a large heavy-duty, zip-top plastic bag; seal and shake well to coat chicken. Marinate in refrigerator 8 hours, turning bag occasionally.

Combine cucumber, onion, mint, and yogurt in a medium bowl; stir well. Cover and chill.

Remove chicken from bag, reserving marinade. Bring marinade to a boil in a small saucepan; remove from heat, and set aside.

Coat grill rack with cooking spray; place rack on grill over medium-hot coals (350° to 400°). Place chicken on rack, and grill 10 minutes on each side or until done, basting occasionally with reserved marinade. Cut chicken diagonally across grain into ¼-inch slices; set aside.

Divide chicken evenly between pita halves; spoon 1 tablespoon lettuce, 1 tablespoon tomato, and 1½ tablespoons yogurt sauce into each pita half. Yield: 8 servings (serving size: 2 pita halves).

CALORIES 295 (18% from fat); PROTEIN 33.2g; FAT 5.9g (sat 1.5g, mono 2.1g, poly 1.3g); CARB 28.4g; FIBER 2.3g; CHOL 75mg; IRON 2.3mg; SODIUM 386mg; CALC 124mg

CHICKEN MARSALA

I couldn't find a chicken Marsala recipe that suited my taste, so I created one of my own.

—Jean M. Converse, Elsinore, California

½ cup dry Marsala wine
1 teaspoon cornstarch
½ teaspoon dried tarragon
⅛ teaspoon salt
¼ cup Italian-seasoned breadcrumbs
2 tablespoons grated Parmesan cheese
⅛ teaspoon garlic powder
4 (4-ounce) skinned, boned chicken breast halves
2 teaspoons olive oil
2 cups hot cooked angel hair (about 4 ounces uncooked pasta)

Combine Marsala wine, cornstarch, tarragon, and salt in a 1-cup glass measure; stir with a whisk until blended. Set aside.

Combine breadcrumbs, cheese, and garlic powder in a shallow dish, and

stir well. Dredge chicken breast halves in breadcrumb mixture.

Heat oil in a large nonstick skillet over medium-high heat until hot. Add chicken; cook 3 minutes on each side or until done.

Microwave wine mixture at HIGH 30 seconds or until slightly thick, stirring once. Arrange chicken over pasta; top with sauce. Yield: 4 servings (serving size: 1 chicken breast, ½ cup pasta, and 1 tablespoon sauce).

CALORIES 306 (20% from fat); PROTEIN 31.9g; FAT 6.7g (sat 1.8g, mono 3g, poly 1g); CARB 27.1g; FIBER 1.2g; CHOL 74mg; IRON 2.2mg; SODIUM 382mg; CALC 63mg

LOW-FAT SALSA CHICKEN

For variety, I add a cup or so of shredded cabbage and mushrooms under the chicken and top it off with the salsa.

—Lisa Phillips, Rutledge, Tennessee

4 (4-ounce) skinned, boned chicken breast halves
Vegetable cooking spray
¾ cup salsa
½ cup sliced green onions
¼ cup grated Parmesan cheese

Preheat oven to 350°.

Place chicken in an 11 x 7-inch baking dish coated with cooking spray. Spoon salsa evenly over chicken; top with green onions. Sprinkle with cheese. Cover and bake at 350° for 30 minutes. Uncover and bake an additional 10 minutes or until chicken is done. Serve with hot cooked rice or baked potatoes. Yield: 4 servings.

CALORIES 164 (18% from fat); PROTEIN 29g; FAT 3.2g (sat 1.4g, mono 0.8g, poly 0.4g); CARB 3.5g; FIBER 1.2g; CHOL 70mg; IRON 1.4mg; SODIUM 295mg; CALC 113mg

Stir Up a Stew

When you're rushed and in need of a hot meal, you can have this hearty beef-and-mushroom stew on the table in no time—with Green-Chile Cornsticks to boot.

BEEF-AND-MUSHROOM STEW

1 pound lean beef stew meat
Vegetable cooking spray
1 cup chopped onion
2 tablespoons all-purpose flour
¼ teaspoon salt
¼ teaspoon pepper
3 cups crimini or button
    mushrooms (about ½ pound),
    halved
1 cup dry vermouth
1 cup low-salt chicken broth
3 tablespoons fresh orange juice
1 teaspoon dried basil
½ teaspoon dried thyme
3 garlic cloves, crushed
1 (14.5-ounce) can diced
    tomatoes, undrained
Fresh flat-leaf parsley sprigs (optional)

Trim fat from beef; cut beef into 1-inch cubes. Coat a large nonstick skillet with cooking spray; place over medium-high heat until hot. Add beef and onion; sauté 5 minutes.

Combine flour, salt, and pepper; sprinkle over beef mixture, and cook 1 minute, stirring constantly. Add mushrooms and next 7 ingredients; bring to a boil. Reduce heat, and simmer, uncovered, 40 minutes or until beef is tender, stirring occasionally. Garnish with parsley, if desired. Yield: 4 servings (serving size: 1½ cups).

Note: Substitute 1 cup chicken broth for the 1 cup vermouth, if desired.

CALORIES 291 (29% from fat); PROTEIN 31.9g; FAT 9.4g (sat 3.3g, mono 3.7g, poly 0.5g); CARB 19.1g; FIBER 1.7g; CHOL 86mg; IRON 5.4mg; SODIUM 608mg; CALC 73mg

GREEN CHILE CORNSTICKS

¾ cup yellow cornmeal
¾ cup all-purpose flour
¼ cup sugar
2 teaspoons baking powder
½ teaspoon salt
⅔ cup skim milk
2 tablespoons vegetable oil
1 egg
¾ cup drained canned whole-
    kernel corn (about 1 [8-ounce]
    can)
1 (4.5-ounce) can chopped green
    chiles, drained
Vegetable cooking spray

Preheat oven to 400°.

Combine first 5 ingredients in a bowl; make a well in center of mixture. Combine milk, oil, and egg; stir well. Add to dry ingredients, stirring just until moist. Fold in corn and green chiles.

Coat cast-iron cornstick pans heavily with cooking spray; place in a 400° oven for 10 minutes. Spoon batter evenly into pans. Bake at 400° for 20 minutes or until lightly browned. Remove cornsticks from pans immediately; serve warm. Yield: 14 cornsticks (serving size: 1 cornstick).

CALORIES 104 (23% from fat); PROTEIN 2.5g; FAT 2.6g (sat 0.5g, mono 0.8g, poly 1.1g); CARB 17.8g; FIBER 0.7g; CHOL 16mg; IRON 0.8mg; SODIUM 126mg; CALC 58mg

SHOPPING LIST

Check the recipes to make sure you have all the staples on hand. We left some of the "basics" off our shopping list.

½ pound crimini mushrooms

packaged salad mix

onions

garlic

light salad dressing

low-salt chicken broth

1 (14.5-ounce) can diced tomatoes

1 (4.5-ounce) can chopped green chiles

canned whole-kernel corn

cornmeal

fresh orange juice

eggs

skim milk

1 pound lean beef stew meat

dry vermouth

Turning the Kitchen Upside Down

Mom's pineapple upside-down cake lives on in these healthy, full-flavored recipes that use all kinds of fruit.

Upside-down cakes using all kinds of toppings and fruits have been around forever. Pineapple upside-down cake, though, was officially invented in 1925, when Dole (then called the Hawaiian Pineapple Co.) sponsored a recipe contest that called for creative dishes using pineapple. Out of 60,000 entries, 2,500 of them were for pineapple upside-down cake.

Much of the upside-down cake's popularity is due to its ease of preparation. Basically, it's made by covering the bottom of a cake pan with butter or margarine (we use margarine) and sugar topped with fruit. Then the cake batter is added. During the baking process, the sugar, margarine, and fruit juices combine to create a gooey, caramelized glaze.

By making them even healthier and using nontraditional, highly flavored ingredients, we may have turned the pineapple upside-down world, well, upside down. We topped our cakes with apricots, cherries, pears, mangoes, and apples. And we didn't stop there—we created innovative cake batters made with ginger, oatmeal, cornmeal, and bananas.

But don't worry—we have a recipe for your basic pineapple upside-down cake, too. Ours has a modern twist, though: It calls for rosemary.

APRICOT UPSIDE-DOWN CORNMEAL CAKE

There should be enough juice left from the canned apricots to yield ¾ cup for the batter. If not, add orange juice to make up the difference.

  1 (16-ounce) can unsweetened apricot halves, undrained
  8 whole almonds, toasted
  1 tablespoon stick margarine, melted
  ¼ cup firmly packed brown sugar
  ¾ cup all-purpose flour
  ½ cup yellow cornmeal
  1 teaspoon baking powder
  ½ teaspoon baking soda
  ⅛ teaspoon salt
  ¼ cup stick margarine, softened
  ½ cup granulated sugar
  1½ teaspoons grated lemon rind
  1 teaspoon vanilla extract
  1 large egg
  2 tablespoons granulated sugar
  2 tablespoons fresh lemon juice

Preheat oven to 350°.

Drain apricots in a colander over a bowl, reserving 8 halves and ¾ cup juice; set juice aside. Reserve remaining apricot halves for another use. Place 1 almond in each of 8 apricot halves.

Coat bottom of a 9-inch round cake pan with melted margarine. Sprinkle the brown sugar over the margarine. Arrange almond-filled apricot halves, cut sides down, over brown sugar; set aside.

Combine flour and next 4 ingredients in a bowl; stir well. Set aside. Beat ¼ cup margarine and ½ cup sugar at medium speed of an electric mixer until well-blended. Add lemon rind, vanilla, and egg; beat well. Add flour mixture to creamed mixture alternately with reserved apricot juice, beginning and ending with flour mixture; beat well after each addition. Pour batter over apricots.

Bake at 350° for 30 minutes or until a wooden pick inserted in center comes out clean. Combine 2 tablespoons sugar and lemon juice; stir well, and drizzle over warm cake. Let cool in pan 5 minutes on a wire rack. Loosen cake from sides of pan, using a narrow metal spatula. Invert onto a cake plate; cut into wedges. Serve warm. Yield: 8 servings (serving size: 1 wedge).

CALORIES 285 (30% from fat); PROTEIN 3.6g; FAT 9.6g (sat 1.8g, mono 4.4g, poly 2.8g); CARB 47.7g; FIBER 1.7g; CHOL 28mg; IRON 1.4mg; SODIUM 232mg; CALC 61mg

MAKING UPSIDE DOWN RIGHT SIDE UP

Remove the cake from the pan while it's warm—if it cools in the pan, the sugar-fruit mixture will harden and stick. When it's first out of the oven, let the cake cool for 5 minutes. Then run a small spatula around the sides to loosen it. Put a serving plate on top; wearing an oven mitt, firmly hold the cake pan, and invert it and the plate. Then remove the pan.

Upside-down cakes are best served within 2 hours or so after baking. To serve later than that, let the cake cool in the pan; then, just before serving, heat it in a 375° oven for about 4 minutes or until the bottom of the pan is hot. Run a spatula around the sides of the cake to loosen it; then invert.

APPLE UPSIDE-DOWN BANANA CAKE

Walnuts or almonds can be substituted for pecans in this tender, fine-grained cake.

    1   tablespoon stick margarine,
         melted
    ¼   cup firmly packed brown sugar
    1½ cups peeled, thinly sliced
         Granny Smith apple
    1¼ cups all-purpose flour
    1   teaspoon baking powder
    ¾   teaspoon ground cinnamon
    ½   teaspoon baking soda
    ¼   teaspoon ground nutmeg
    ⅛   teaspoon salt
    ¼   cup stick margarine, softened
    ⅓   cup granulated sugar
    ⅓   cup firmly packed brown sugar
    ½   cup mashed ripe banana
    1   teaspoon vanilla extract
    1   large egg
    ¼   cup orange juice
    2   tablespoons finely chopped
         pecans, toasted

Preheat oven to 350°.

Coat bottom of a 9-inch round cake pan with melted margarine. Sprinkle ¼ cup brown sugar over margarine. Arrange apple slices spokelike, working from center of pan to edge.

Combine flour and next 5 ingredients in a bowl; stir well. Set aside. Beat ¼ cup margarine, ⅓ cup sugar, and ⅓ cup brown sugar at medium speed of an electric mixer until well-blended. Add banana, vanilla, and egg; beat well. Add flour mixture to creamed mixture alternately with orange juice, beginning and ending with flour mixture; beat well after each addition. Stir in pecans. Pour batter over apple slices.

Bake at 350° for 30 minutes or until a wooden pick inserted in center comes out clean. Let cool in pan 5 minutes on a wire rack. Loosen cake from sides of pan, using a narrow metal spatula. Invert onto a cake plate; cut into wedges. Serve warm. Yield: 8 servings (serving size: 1 wedge).

CALORIES 280 (30% from fat); PROTEIN 3.3g; FAT 9.4g (sat 1.8g, mono 4.2g, poly 2.8g); CARB 47g; FIBER 1.8g; CHOL 28mg; IRON 1.6mg; SODIUM 214mg; CALC 63mg

PINEAPPLE UPSIDE-DOWN CAKE WITH ROSEMARY

Rosemary and pineapple provide an unexpectedly superb flavor combination in this cake. If you prefer a more traditional pineapple upside-down cake, you can just omit the rosemary.

    1   tablespoon stick margarine,
         melted
    ⅓   cup firmly packed dark brown
         sugar
    1   teaspoon chopped rosemary
    6   unsweetened canned pineapple
         slices
    1¼ cups all-purpose flour
    1½ teaspoons baking powder
    ⅛   teaspoon salt
    ¼   cup stick margarine, softened
    ⅔   cup granulated sugar
    1   teaspoon vanilla extract
    1   large egg
    ½   cup skim milk
    Fresh rosemary sprigs (optional)

Preheat oven to 350°.

Coat bottom of a 9-inch round cake pan with melted margarine. Sprinkle brown sugar and chopped rosemary over margarine. Arrange pineapple slices in a single layer over brown sugar-rosemary mixture; set aside.

Combine flour, baking powder, and salt in a bowl; stir well. Set aside. Beat ¼ cup margarine and ⅔ cup sugar at medium speed of an electric mixer until well-blended. Add vanilla and egg; beat well. Add flour mixture to creamed mixture alternately with milk, beginning and ending with flour mixture; beat well after each addition. Pour batter over pineapple slices.

Bake at 350° for 35 minutes or until a wooden pick inserted in center comes out clean. Let cool in pan 5 minutes on a wire rack. Loosen cake from sides of pan, using a narrow metal spatula. Invert onto a cake plate; cut into wedges. Garnish with rosemary sprigs if desired. Serve warm. Yield: 8 servings (serving size: 1 wedge).

CALORIES 257 (28% from fat); PROTEIN 3.4g; FAT 8g (sat 1.6g, mono 3.4g, poly 2.4g); CARB 43.4g; FIBER 0.6g; CHOL 28mg; IRON 1.4mg; SODIUM 141mg; CALC 88mg

APPLE UPSIDE-DOWN DATE-NUT GINGERBREAD CAKE

    1   tablespoon stick margarine,
         melted
    ¼   cup firmly packed brown
         sugar
    2   cups peeled, thinly sliced
         Granny Smith apple
    1¼ cups all-purpose flour
    1   teaspoon ground ginger
    1   teaspoon ground cinnamon
    ¾   teaspoon baking soda
    ¼   teaspoon ground nutmeg
    ⅛   teaspoon salt
    ⅛   teaspoon ground cloves
    ¼   cup stick margarine,
         softened
    ⅓   cup granulated sugar
    ⅓   cup molasses
    1   large egg
    ½   cup plain fat-free yogurt
    ⅓   cup pitted, chopped dates
    3   tablespoons chopped walnuts

Preheat oven to 350°.

Coat bottom of a 9-inch round cake pan with melted margarine. Sprinkle brown sugar over margarine. Arrange apple slices spokelike over brown sugar, working from center of pan to edge; set aside.

Combine flour and next 6 ingredients in a bowl; stir well. Set aside. Beat ¼ cup margarine and ⅓ cup sugar at medium speed of an electric mixer until well-blended. Add molasses and egg; beat well. Add flour mixture to creamed mixture alternately with yogurt, beginning and ending with flour mixture; beat well after each addition. Stir in dates and walnuts. Pour batter over apple slices.

Bake at 350° for 40 minutes or until a wooden pick inserted in center comes out clean. Let cake cool in pan 5 minutes on a wire rack. Loosen cake from sides of pan, using a narrow metal spatula. Invert onto a cake plate; cut cake into wedges. Serve warm. Yield: 8 servings (serving size: 1 wedge).

CALORIES 298 (29% from fat); PROTEIN 4.3g; FAT 9.6g (sat 1.8g, mono 3.8g, poly 3.4g); CARB 50.6g; FIBER 2.1g; CHOL 28mg; IRON 2.1mg; SODIUM 266mg; CALC 80mg

PEAR UPSIDE-DOWN OATMEAL CAKE

This slightly chewy oatmeal cake is even better when served with low-fat vanilla ice cream or frozen yogurt.

2   small Anjou pears (about ¾ pound)
1   tablespoon stick margarine, melted
¼   cup firmly packed brown sugar
2   tablespoons finely chopped walnuts
1¼ cups all-purpose flour
⅓   cup quick-cooking oats
1   teaspoon ground cinnamon
¾   teaspoon baking powder
½   teaspoon baking soda
½   teaspoon ground ginger
⅛   teaspoon salt
¼   cup stick margarine, softened
⅔   cup granulated sugar
1   teaspoon vanilla extract
1   large egg
½   cup 1% low-fat milk

Preheat oven to 350°.

Cut each pear in half lengthwise (do not core). Cut 2 (¼-inch-thick) slices from the cut side of each pear half to get 8 slices; set slices aside. Chop remaining pear to measure ½ cup; set aside.

Coat bottom of a 9-inch round cake pan with melted margarine. Sprinkle brown sugar and walnuts over margarine; set aside. Arrange the pear slices spokelike over the brown sugar-walnut mixture, overlapping slightly; set aside.

Combine flour and next 6 ingredients in a bowl, and stir well. Set aside. Beat ¼ cup margarine and ⅔ cup sugar at medium speed of an electric mixer until well-blended. Add vanilla extract and egg; beat well. Add flour mixture to creamed mixture alternately with milk, beginning and ending with flour mixture; beat well after each addition. Stir in chopped pear. Pour batter over pear slices.

Bake at 350° for 35 minutes or until a wooden pick inserted in center comes out clean. Let cool in pan 5 minutes on a wire rack. Loosen cake from sides of pan, using a narrow metal spatula. Invert onto a cake plate; cut into wedges. Serve warm. Yield: 8 servings (serving size: 1 wedge).

CALORIES 294 (29% from fat); PROTEIN 4.6g; FAT 9.6g (sat 1.9g, mono 3.8g, poly 3.3g); CARB 48.6g; FIBER 2.2g; CHOL 28mg; IRON 1.6mg; SODIUM 218mg; CALC 70mg

CHERRY-ALMOND UPSIDE-DOWN CAKE

1   tablespoon stick margarine, melted
¼   cup firmly packed brown sugar
3   tablespoons sliced almonds, toasted
1   (14.5-ounce) can unsweetened pitted tart or dark sweet cherries, drained
1¼ cups all-purpose flour
1   teaspoon baking powder
½   teaspoon baking soda
½   teaspoon salt
¼   cup stick margarine, softened
⅔   cup granulated sugar
1   teaspoon vanilla extract
½   teaspoon almond extract
1   large egg
½   cup low-fat buttermilk

Preheat oven to 350°.

Coat the bottom of a 9-inch round cake pan with melted margarine. Sprinkle brown sugar and almonds over margarine. Arrange the cherries over the brown sugar-almond mixture; set aside.

Combine flour, baking powder, baking soda, and salt in a bowl; stir well. Set aside. Beat ¼ cup margarine and ⅔ cup sugar at medium speed of an electric mixer until well-blended. Add extracts and egg; beat well. Add flour mixture to creamed mixture alternately with buttermilk, beginning and ending with flour mixture; beat well after each addition. Pour batter over cherries.

Bake at 350° for 30 minutes or until a wooden pick inserted in center comes out clean. Let cool in pan 5 minutes on a wire rack. Loosen cake from sides of pan, using a narrow metal spatula. Invert onto a cake plate; cut into wedges. Serve warm. Yield: 8 servings (serving size: 1 wedge).

CALORIES 277 (30% from fat); PROTEIN 4.2g; FAT 9.3g (sat 1.9g, mono 4.2g, poly 2.7g); CARB 44.8g; FIBER 0.9g; CHOL 28mg; IRON 1.5mg; SODIUM 329mg; CALC 79mg

MANGO UPSIDE-DOWN ORANGE CAKE

1   tablespoon stick margarine, melted
¼   cup firmly packed brown sugar
1½ cups peeled, thinly sliced mango (about 2 medium)
1   cup all-purpose flour
¾   teaspoon baking soda
⅛   teaspoon salt
¼   cup stick margarine, softened
⅔   cup granulated sugar
2   teaspoons grated orange rind
1   teaspoon vanilla extract
1   large egg
½   cup plain fat-free yogurt

Preheat oven to 350°.

Coat bottom of a 9-inch round cake pan with melted margarine. Sprinkle brown sugar over margarine. Arrange mango slices spokelike, working from center of pan to edge; set aside.

Combine flour, baking soda, and salt in a bowl; stir well. Set aside. Beat ¼ cup margarine and ⅔ cup sugar at medium speed of an electric mixer until well-blended. Add orange rind, vanilla, and egg; beat well. Add flour mixture to creamed mixture alternately with yogurt, beginning and ending with flour mixture; beat well after each addition. Pour batter over mango slices.

Bake at 350° for 30 minutes or until a wooden pick inserted in center of cake comes out clean. Let cool in pan 5 minutes on a wire rack. Loosen cake from sides of pan, using a narrow metal spatula. Invert onto a cake plate, and cut into wedges. Serve warm. Yield: 8 servings (serving size: 1 wedge).

CALORIES 250 (29% from fat); PROTEIN 3.5g; FAT 8g (sat 1.7g, mono 3.5g, poly 2.4g); CARB 42g; FIBER 0.9g; CHOL 28mg; IRON 1mg; SODIUM 261mg; CALC 46mg

In the Pink

Because salmon can stand up to bold flavors, we've gone the excitement route, pairing it with ginger, salsa, curry, and other lively ingredients.

Salmon is one of the most exquisite-tasting fish of all, which is one reason that even people who aren't seafood aficionados can get hooked on it. And it's available almost anywhere and quick to prepare.

Something this good must have a catch, right? Yes and no. One reason for salmon's great taste is that it's a high-fat fish. In fact, a plain salmon fillet contains 46% calories from fat. So if you're trying to limit fat in your diet, is salmon a smart choice? Yes, and here's why: A combination of monounsaturated and polyunsaturated fats, those that don't raise blood cholesterol levels, makes up 70% of salmon's total fat content.

Perhaps even more important is that salmon is rich in omega-3 fats, a type of polyunsaturated fat that guards against heart disease. Recent studies show that diets rich in omega-3 fats are adept at lowering levels of artery-damaging fats called triglycerides. Omega-3 fats are also potent anticlotting agents. In addition, salmon delivers a healthy dose of other nutritional pluses: It is high in protein, vitamin E, vitamin B, and the minerals iron, magnesium, and zinc.

Serve our recipes with low-fat sides such as rice, couscous, or potatoes, and you can bring the total meal down to less than 30% calories from fat. So see, you can have your salmon and eat it too.

BRAISED SALMON WITH LEEKS AND DILL

Preparation time: 15 minutes
Cooking time: 20 minutes

   1   teaspoon olive oil
2½   cups chopped leek
   4   garlic cloves, minced
1½   cups coarsely chopped tomato
   ¼   teaspoon salt
   ⅛   teaspoon pepper
   ½   cup dry white wine
   4   (6-ounce) skinned salmon fillets
        (about 1 inch thick)
1½   teaspoons chopped fresh or
        ½ teaspoon dried dillweed

Heat oil in a large nonstick skillet over medium-high heat until hot. Add leek; sauté 3 minutes. Add garlic; sauté 2 minutes. Add tomato, salt, and pepper; sauté 2 minutes. Add wine and salmon; sprinkle with dillweed, and bring to a boil. Cover, reduce heat, and simmer 8 minutes or until fish flakes easily when tested with a fork. Serve with roasted potatoes. Yield: 4 servings (serving size: 1 fillet and ½ cup leek mixture).

CALORIES 259 (35% from fat); PROTEIN 28.1g; FAT 10g (sat 1.5g, mono 3.7g, poly 3.7g); CARB 13.8g; FIBER 1.7g; CHOL 73mg; IRON 2.9mg; SODIUM 227mg; CALC 68mg

BROILED CURRIED SALMON FILLETS

Preparation time: 5 minutes
Marinating time: 20 minutes
Cooking time: 8 minutes

   ¼   cup fresh lemon juice
   1   tablespoon curry powder
   1   tablespoon dark sesame oil
   1   (8-ounce) carton plain low-fat
        yogurt
   4   (6-ounce) salmon fillets (about
        1 inch thick)
Vegetable cooking spray
   ¼   teaspoon salt
   ⅛   teaspoon pepper

Combine first 4 ingredients in a large heavy-duty, zip-top plastic bag.

Add salmon to bag; seal and marinate in refrigerator 20 minutes. Remove salmon from bag; discard marinade.

Arrange salmon on a broiler rack coated with cooking spray; sprinkle with salt and pepper. Broil 8 minutes or until fish flakes easily when tested with a fork. Yield: 4 servings.

CALORIES 316 (46% from fat); PROTEIN 37.8g; FAT 16g (sat 3g, mono 7.5g, poly 3.6g); CARB 2.6g; FIBER 0.1g; CHOL 117mg; IRON 0.9mg; SODIUM 254mg; CALC 64mg

WARM SALMON SALAD

Preparation time: 30 minutes
Cooking time: 23 minutes

   3   cups cubed red potatoes
   4   cups (1-inch) diagonally sliced
        asparagus
   ¼   teaspoon salt
   ¼   teaspoon pepper
1½   pound salmon fillet
   2   teaspoons vegetable oil
   8   cups gourmet salad greens
   4   tablespoons sliced green onions
   8   cherry tomatoes, quartered
   2   tablespoons balsamic vinegar
   2   tablespoons pesto basil sauce
        (such as Pesto Sanremo)

Place potatoes in a large saucepan; cover with water, and bring to a boil. Reduce heat; simmer 12 minutes. Add asparagus; cook 3 minutes or until potatoes are tender. Drain and set aside.

Sprinkle salt and pepper over salmon. Heat oil in a medium nonstick skillet over medium-high heat until hot. Add salmon; cook 4 minutes on each side or until fish flakes easily when tested with a fork. Discard skin from salmon; flake salmon into chunks.

Combine salmon, potato mixture, salad greens, green onions, and tomatoes in a bowl. Combine vinegar and pesto; drizzle over salad, and toss gently. Yield: 4 servings.

CALORIES 506 (39% from fat); PROTEIN 46.1g; FAT 21.8g (sat 3.9g, mono 10.3g, poly 5.3g); CARB 33.9g; FIBER 5.3g; CHOL 117mg; IRON 4.4mg; SODIUM 356mg; CALC 118mg

CHILI-SEARED SALMON WITH SWEET PEPPER SALSA

Preparation time: 10 minutes
Marinating time: 30 minutes
Cooking time: 8 minutes

¾ cup diced red onion
½ cup diced yellow bell pepper
½ cup diced red bell pepper
½ cup diced plum tomato
2 tablespoons chopped fresh cilantro
1 tablespoon seeded, minced jalapeño pepper
1 tablespoon fresh lemon juice
2 teaspoons cider vinegar
¼ teaspoon ground cumin
⅛ teaspoon sugar
⅛ teaspoon salt
⅛ teaspoon ground coriander
⅛ teaspoon ground red pepper
2 tablespoons chili powder
¼ teaspoon salt
⅛ teaspoon black pepper
4 (6-ounce) salmon fillets (about 1 inch thick)
2 teaspoons olive oil

Combine first 13 ingredients in a bowl; stir well. Let stand at least 30 minutes, stirring occasionally.

Combine chili powder, ¼ teaspoon salt, and black pepper; rub evenly over salmon fillets. Heat oil in a large non-stick skillet over medium-high heat until hot. Add fillets; cook 4 minutes on each side or until fish flakes easily when tested with a fork. Serve with salsa. Yield: 4 servings (serving size: 1 fillet and about ⅔ cup salsa).

CALORIES 348 (46% from fat); PROTEIN 37.7g; FAT 17.8g (sat 3g, mono 8.8g, poly 3.8g); CARB 8.9g; FIBER 2.9g; CHOL 115mg; IRON 2.2mg; SODIUM 351mg; CALC 35mg

GRILLED SALMON WITH GINGER-ORANGE MUSTARD GLAZE

Preparation time: 5 minutes
Marinating time: 30 minutes
Cooking time: 12 minutes

¼ cup fresh orange juice
¼ cup tamari or soy sauce
¼ cup cream sherry
¼ cup Dijon mustard
2 tablespoons peeled, grated fresh gingerroot
2 tablespoons honey
4 (6-ounce) salmon fillets (about 1 inch thick)
Vegetable cooking spray
Green onion fans (optional)

Combine first 6 ingredients in a large heavy-duty, zip-top plastic bag. Add salmon to bag; seal and marinate in refrigerator 30 minutes. Remove salmon from bag, reserving marinade.

Prepare grill or broiler. Place salmon on grill rack or broiler pan coated with cooking spray. Cook 6 minutes on each side or until fish flakes easily when tested with a fork, basting frequently with reserved marinade.

Place remaining marinade in a saucepan or microwave-safe bowl; bring to a boil. Serve with salmon; garnish with green onion fans, if desired. Yield: 4 servings (serving size: 1 fillet and 3 tablespoons glaze).

CALORIES 375 (38% from fat); PROTEIN 37.2g; FAT 15.7g (sat 2.6g, mono 7.5g, poly 3.3g); CARB 14.1g; FIBER 0.1g; CHOL 115mg; IRON 1.2mg; SODIUM 1,364mg; CALC 15mg

FISH FACTS

Fresh salmon should be purchased from a reputable store that has quick turnover, regularly replenished stock, and refrigerated storage cases. Fillets should be firm to the touch. They should appear moist and freshly cut with no yellowing or browning around the edges.

Frozen salmon should be wrapped in moisture- and vapor-resistant packaging and should be solidly frozen with no discoloration or freezer burn. There should be little or no air within the wrapping.

THE ENLIGHTENED CHEF

Back to the Basics

Chef Marc Lippman took up in-line skating and hired a personal trainer in an effort to lose weight. But it wasn't until he began indulging in his own light dishes that he dropped 25 pounds.

Actually, eating light is no revelation to the executive chef of Miami Beach's landmark Raleigh Hotel. Lippman recalls his first orientation to the world of healthy food as a kid. "There was no butter in our house because my father had a cholesterol problem; we only had olive oil. My parents, who loved to cook, even grew fresh seasonal herbs in our backyard garden. I was always a little nervous about bringing friends home after school," he adds. "My mother would give us things like grilled vegetables and hummus for a snack."

Lippman has come full circle, returning to his roots and favorite ingredients to create new American specialties. "I'm using only reductions, infusions, and lots of fresh herbs to intensify flavors. And I rely on perfect cooking methods, like searing, to produce the light results I want. Almost no fat is required."

CITRUS TERRINE

2 envelopes unflavored gelatin
1¼ cups orange juice
¼ cup sugar
4 cups pink grapefruit sections
    (about 6 grapefruit)
2 cups orange sections (about
    6 oranges)
1 (12-ounce) package unsweetened
    frozen raspberries, thawed
3 cups orange sorbet
Fresh tarragon sprigs (optional)

Sprinkle gelatin over orange juice in a small saucepan; let stand 1 minute. Add sugar; cook over low heat, stirring until sugar and gelatin dissolve. Remove from heat; let cool slightly.

Line an 8 x 4-inch loaf pan with plastic wrap. Pour ¼ cup gelatin mixture into loaf pan; chill to the consistency of unbeaten egg white. Arrange 1⅓ cups grapefruit sections over gelatin layer, overlapping slightly. Pour ¼ cup gelatin mixture over grapefruit layer; chill 10 minutes. Arrange 1 cup orange sections over gelatin layer. Pour ¼ cup gelatin mixture over orange layer; chill 10 minutes. Repeat layering with remaining grapefruit sections, gelatin mixture, and orange sections, ending with grapefruit sections. Cover terrine with plastic wrap; press down lightly. Chill 8 hours or until set.

Place raspberries in a food processor; process until smooth. Strain through a sieve into a bowl, reserving ¾ cup purée. Discard seeds.

Invert terrine onto a platter; remove plastic wrap. Cut terrine into 12 slices using a serrated knife. Serve the terrine with raspberry purée and sorbet. Garnish terrine with tarragon sprigs, if desired. Yield: 12 servings (serving size: 1 slice citrus terrine, ¼ cup sorbet, and 1 tablespoon raspberry purée).

CALORIES 162 (6% from fat); PROTEIN 2.6g; FAT 1.1g (sat 0.6g, mono 0.3g, poly 0.1g); CARB 37.6g; FIBER 3.6g; CHOL 2mg; IRON 0.4mg; SODIUM 24mg; CALC 52mg

Presenting Their Case for Better Living

After eight years at that high-powered law firm McKenzie, Brackman, Chaney, and Kuzak—attorneys Stuart Markowitz and Ann Kelsey decided a healthy change was definitely in order. So they packed up their belongings and moved to a quaint, artsy town in Northern California. Of course, *L.A. Law* was fiction, but actors Michael Tucker and Jill Eikenberry's decision to reexamine their lives together is anything but. Just as they were an item as Stuart and Ann on TV, they are in real life, too, having been married for 23 years.

To make their years together richer and longer, Michael and Jill adopted a healthier lifestyle. Years ago Michael discovered that cooking is more than just turning groceries into food. "The act of cooking is a way to clear your mind and reacquaint yourself with your senses."

BLUEFISH WITH FRESH TOMATO COULIS

Any white fish, such as red snapper, grouper, or orange roughy, can be easily substituted to pair with the pungent herb cilantro in this fresh tomato topping.

2 cups coarsely chopped tomato
¼ teaspoon salt
3 tablespoons red wine
    vinegar
2 tablespoons chopped fresh
    cilantro
1 tablespoon minced shallot
1 tablespoon olive oil
1 small garlic clove, crushed
6 (6-ounce) bluefish fillets
Vegetable cooking spray
2 teaspoons grated lemon rind
¼ teaspoon salt
¼ teaspoon pepper

Place tomato in a colander; sprinkle with ¼ teaspoon salt, and toss gently. Let drain for 30 minutes.

Combine tomato, vinegar, cilantro, shallot, olive oil, and garlic in a medium bowl, and stir well. Let tomato mixture stand at room temperature 30 minutes.

Place fish on a jelly-roll pan coated with cooking spray, and sprinkle with lemon rind, ¼ teaspoon salt, and pepper. Broil 8 minutes or until fish flakes easily when tested with a fork. Serve with tomato coulis. Yield: 6 servings (serving size: 1 fish fillet and ¼ cup tomato coulis).

CALORIES 207 (21% from fat); PROTEIN 35.5g; FAT 4.9g (sat 0.8g, mono 2.1g, poly 1.1g); CARB 3.6g; FIBER 0.9g; CHOL 63mg; IRON 0.7mg; SODIUM 262mg; CALC 62mg

MUSSELS AND SHALLOT-WINE SAUCE

48 small mussels (about 1¼
    pounds), scrubbed and
    debearded
1 tablespoon cornmeal
4 cups rock salt
½ cup dry red wine
½ cup red wine vinegar
1 tablespoon minced shallots
¼ teaspoon cracked pepper

Place mussels in a large bowl; cover with cold water. Sprinkle with cornmeal; let stand 30 minutes. Drain; rinse mussels.

Preheat oven to 500°.

Place rock salt in bottom of a shallow roasting pan. Arrange mussels in a single layer on rock salt. Bake at 500° for 5 minutes or until shells open. Remove mussels from pan; set aside, and keep warm. Discard rock salt and any unopened shells.

Combine wine, vinegar, shallots, and pepper in a small saucepan. Cook over medium heat 5 minutes or until thoroughly heated. Serve with mussels. Yield: 4 servings (serving size: 12 mussels and ¼ cup wine sauce).

CALORIES 108 (22% from fat); PROTEIN 14g; FAT 2.6g (sat 0.5g, mono 0.6g, poly 0.7g); CARB 6.2g; FIBER 0.1g; CHOL 33mg; IRON 4.1mg; SODIUM 217mg; CALC 23mg

MARINATED SHRIMP WITH RÉMOULADE SAUCE

So the shrimp can absorb the flavors in the marinade, start preparing this elegant first course a day ahead.

    2   cups dry white wine
    2   cups water
    1   cup tarragon vinegar
    ⅛   teaspoon salt
    ⅛   teaspoon black pepper
Dash of ground red pepper
    3   stalks celery, each cut into
          3 pieces
    2   garlic cloves, halved
    2   bay leaves
   24   large shrimp (about 1 pound),
          peeled and deveined
    1   cup finely chopped celery
    ¼   cup spicy brown mustard
    2   tablespoons finely chopped
          fresh parsley
    2   tablespoons finely chopped
          red onion
    2   tablespoons sherry vinegar
    2   teaspoons olive oil
    ¼   teaspoon Hungarian sweet
          paprika
    ⅛   teaspoon black pepper
    2   cups trimmed watercress (about
          1 bunch)

Combine first 9 ingredients in a Dutch oven; bring to a boil. Reduce heat; simmer 30 minutes. Return mixture to a boil; add shrimp. Cook 3 minutes or until done. Drain shrimp in a colander over a medium bowl, reserving cooking liquid. Rinse shrimp under cold water; drain well. Set aside. Discard celery stalks, garlic, and bay leaves from cooking liquid; set cooking liquid aside. Let cool completely.

Add shrimp to cooled cooking liquid; cover and marinate in refrigerator 24 hours.

Combine chopped celery and next 7 ingredients in a small bowl; stir well. Cover rémoulade, and chill 24 hours.

Drain shrimp; discard liquid. Combine shrimp and ½ cup rémoulade in a bowl; stir well. Arrange ½ cup watercress on each of 4 plates; top each with 6 shrimp and 2 tablespoons rémoulade. Yield: 4 appetizers.

CALORIES 142 (29% from fat); PROTEIN 18.9g; FAT 4.8g (sat 0.6g, mono 1.9g, poly 0.8g); CARB 3.9g; FIBER 1.3g; CHOL 129mg; IRON 2.7mg; SODIUM 409mg; CALC 100mg

LIGHTEN UP

Mac Attack

When you've got to have macaroni and cheese, we offer four healthy versions— all more comforting than ever.

In a perfect world there would be no stress, which means you wouldn't need comfort food. Ergo, you would not need macaroni and cheese. But who wants to live in a world without macaroni and cheese? Sadly, many people are trying to do just that. As comforting as macaroni and cheese is, it has an uncomfortable side-effect on waistlines. So we figured out how to cut the fat by almost half, while at the same time making the dish even tastier. Because these mac and cheese recipes are so easy to make, economical, and filling, it seems we've done more than just lighten a classic dish: We've lightened your stress.

ROASTED VEGETABLE MACARONI AND CHEESE

    3   cups peeled, diced eggplant
          (about ¾ pound)
    2   cups sliced mushrooms
    1   cup coarsely chopped red bell
          pepper
    1   cup coarsely chopped yellow
          bell pepper
    1   cup coarsely chopped onion
    1   medium zucchini, quartered
          lengthwise and sliced (about
          1 cup)
    2   teaspoons olive oil
    4   garlic cloves, minced
    ½   cup all-purpose flour
   2¾   cups 1% low-fat milk
    ¾   cup (3 ounces) shredded sharp
          provolone cheese
    ¾   cup freshly grated Parmesan
          cheese, divided
    ¼   teaspoon salt
    ¼   teaspoon freshly ground pepper
    6   cups cooked elbow macaroni
          (about 12 ounces uncooked)
Vegetable cooking spray
Dash of paprika

Preheat oven to 450°. Combine first 8 ingredients in a large shallow roasting pan; toss well. Bake at 450° for 30 minutes or until lightly browned, stirring occasionally. Remove from oven, set aside. Reduce oven temperature to 375°.

Place flour in a large saucepan. Gradually add milk, stirring with a whisk until blended. Cook over medium heat 8 minutes or until thick, stirring constantly. Add provolone cheese, ½ cup Parmesan cheese, salt, and ¼ teaspoon pepper; cook 3 minutes or until cheese melts, stirring often. Remove from heat; stir in roasted vegetables and macaroni.

Spoon mixture into a 3-quart casserole dish coated with cooking spray. Combine remaining ¼ cup Parmesan cheese and paprika; sprinkle over macaroni mixture. Bake at 375° for 20 minutes or until bubbly. Yield: 10 servings (serving size: 1 cup).

CALORIES 268 (25% from fat); PROTEIN 13.6g; FAT 7.3g (sat 3.8g, mono 2.3g, poly 0.6g); CARB 37g; FIBER 2.8g; CHOL 15mg; IRON 2.3mg; SODIUM 329mg; CALC 289mg

HOW WE DID IT

- ◆ Made a low-fat white sauce with 1% milk, minus the butter.
- ◆ Used smaller amounts of cheese.
- ◆ Used a specific blend of cheeses for the most flavor.

CREAMY FOUR-CHEESE MACARONI

The combination of these cheeses packs all the flavor. Fresh Parmesan and a good extra-sharp Cheddar are musts.

⅓ cup all-purpose flour
2⅔ cups 1% low-fat milk
¾ cup (3 ounces) shredded fontina or Swiss cheese
½ cup freshly grated Parmesan cheese
½ cup (2 ounces) shredded extra-sharp Cheddar cheese
3 ounces light processed cheese (such as light Velveeta)
6 cups cooked elbow macaroni (about 3 cups uncooked)
¼ teaspoon salt
Vegetable cooking spray
⅓ cup crushed onion melba toasts (about 12 pieces)
1 tablespoon reduced-calorie margarine, softened

Preheat oven to 375°.
Place flour in a large saucepan.

Gradually add milk, stirring with a whisk until blended. Cook over medium heat 8 minutes or until thick, stirring constantly. Add cheeses; cook 3 minutes or until cheese melts, stirring often. Remove from heat; stir in macaroni and salt.

Spoon mixture into a 2-quart casserole dish coated with cooking spray. Combine crushed toasts and margarine in a small bowl; stir until well-blended. Sprinkle over macaroni mixture. Bake at 375° for 30 minutes or until bubbly. Yield: 8 servings (serving size: 1 cup).

CALORIES 350 (29% from fat); PROTEIN 18g; FAT 11.2g (sat 6.3g, mono 2.9g, poly 0.9g); CARB 42.4g; FIBER 2.1g; CHOL 32mg; IRON 1.9mg; SODIUM 497mg; CALC 306mg

THREE-PEPPER VARIATION

Add these ingredients for a spicier version of our Creamy Four-Cheese Macaroni.

Add 1 cup chopped bottled roasted red bell pepper; 1 tablespoon seeded, chopped pickled jalapeño pepper; and ¼ teaspoon ground red pepper at the same time the macaroni and salt are added to cheeses. Yield: 8 servings (serving size: 1 cup).

THE SECRET'S IN THE WHITE SAUCE

Making a low-fat white sauce without all the butter can be a bit tricky. Lumps are a common occurrence. For a perfectly smooth sauce, measure the flour into a saucepan. Gradually add an equal amount of milk, stirring with a whisk until the mixture is smooth. Then add the remaining milk, and stir with whisk until smooth. Cook over medium heat, stirring constantly with whisk until the sauce thickens—at least 5 to 6 minutes. Do not rush the sauce. If undercooked it will taste "floury."

MENU SUGGESTION

GREEK MACARONI AND CHEESE

Vegetable salad *

Pita bread

*Drizzle an herb vinaigrette over a mixture of sliced red onion, green and red bell pepper rings, sliced radishes, and tomato wedges. Serve with kalamata olives and pepperoncini peppers.

GREEK MACARONI AND CHEESE

⅓ cup all-purpose flour
2¼ cups 1% low-fat milk
¾ cup (3 ounces) shredded fontina or Swiss cheese
⅔ cup crumbled feta cheese
½ cup freshly grated Parmesan cheese
3 ounces light processed cheese (such as light Velveeta)
6 cups cooked medium elbow macaroni (about 3 cups uncooked)
¼ teaspoon salt
1 (10-ounce) package frozen chopped spinach, thawed, drained, and squeezed dry
Vegetable cooking spray
⅓ cup crushed onion melba toasts (about 12 pieces)
1 tablespoon reduced-calorie margarine, softened

Preheat oven to 375°.
Place flour in a large saucepan. Gradually add milk, stirring with a whisk until blended. Cook over medium heat 8 minutes or until thick, stirring constantly. Add cheeses; cook 3 minutes or until cheese melts, stirring often. Remove from heat; stir in macaroni, salt, and spinach.

Spoon mixture into a 2-quart casserole dish coated with cooking spray. Combine crushed toasts and margarine in a small bowl; stir until well-blended. Sprinkle over macaroni mixture. Bake at 375° for 30 minutes or until bubbly. Yield: 8 servings (serving size: 1 cup).

CALORIES 349 (28% from fat); PROTEIN 18.2g; FAT 10.8g (sat 5.4, mono 2.6g, poly 0.9g): CARB 43.5g; FIBER 3.3g; CHOL 32mg; IRON 2.7mg; SODIUM 579mg; CALC 325mg

INSPIRED VEGETARIAN

Spuds with Spunk

Stuffed potatoes are a versatile food—they mostly serve as a side or appetizer but can also be a substantial main dish. And to top it off, potatoes are a strong nutritional package, full of vitamin C, potassium, fiber, and complex carbohydrates. The sweet potato is also rich in beta carotene. So no matter how they're stuffed, these potatoes give new meaning to the word "loaded."

CHEESE-AND-CORN STUFFED POTATOES

4   (8-ounce) baking potatoes
2   teaspoons olive oil
1   cup chopped leek
1   cup chopped onion
2   garlic cloves, minced
¾   cup frozen whole-kernel corn, thawed and drained
½   cup 1% low-fat cottage cheese
½   cup plain nonfat yogurt
½   teaspoon salt
¼   teaspoon ground red pepper

Preheat oven to 375°.
Wrap potatoes in aluminum foil, and bake at 375° for 1 hour or until tender.
Heat oil in a medium nonstick skillet over medium-high heat until hot. Add leek, onion, and garlic; sauté 4 minutes or until tender. Set aside.
Unwrap potatoes. Split open each potato; scoop pulp from potatoes,

leaving a ¼-inch-thick shell. Combine potato pulp, onion mixture, corn, cottage cheese, yogurt, salt, and red pepper in a bowl; stir well.
Stuff shells with potato mixture; place on a baking sheet. Bake at 375° for 10 minutes or until thoroughly heated. Yield: 4 servings.

CALORIES 301 (9% from fat); PROTEIN 12.5g; FAT 3g (sat 0.6g, mono 1.8g, poly 0.4g); CARB 58.7g; FIBER 5.9g; CHOL 2mg; IRON 3.8mg; SODIUM 455mg; CALC 134mg

BROCCOLI, BUTTERMILK, AND DILL POTATOES

4   (8-ounce) baking potatoes
2   teaspoons olive oil
1½   cups coarsely chopped broccoli florets
1   cup diced onion
⅓   cup low-fat sour cream
½   cup low-fat buttermilk
2   tablespoons minced fresh or 2 teaspoons dried dillweed
1   tablespoon grated Parmesan cheese
½   teaspoon salt
¼   teaspoon pepper
½   cup (2 ounces) shredded reduced-fat Cheddar cheese

Preheat oven to 375°.
Wrap potatoes in aluminum foil; bake at 375° for 1 hour or until potatoes are tender.
Heat oil in a medium nonstick skillet over medium heat until hot. Add broccoli and onion; sauté 4 minutes or until tender. Set aside.
Unwrap potatoes. Split open each potato; scoop out pulp, leaving a ¼-inch-thick shell. Combine potato pulp, broccoli mixture, sour cream, buttermilk, dillweed, Parmesan cheese, salt, and pepper in a medium bowl; mash.
Stuff shells with potato mixture, and sprinkle with Cheddar cheese. Place on a baking sheet, and bake at 375° for 10 minutes or until thoroughly heated. Yield: 4 servings.

CALORIES 323 (24% from fat); PROTEIN 13.7g; FAT 8.7g (sat 4.1g, mono 2.5g, poly 0.6g); CARB 50g; FIBER 5.9g; CHOL 18mg; IRON 3.8mg; SODIUM 478mg; CALC 258mg

MOROCCAN STUFFED POTATOES

¼   cup tahini (sesame-seed paste)
2   tablespoons minced fresh parsley
½   teaspoon salt
1   small garlic clove, minced
1   (8-ounce) carton plain low-fat yogurt
6   (8-ounce) baking potatoes
2   tablespoons lemon juice
1   teaspoon ground cumin
2   teaspoons olive oil
¼   teaspoon ground red pepper
4   cups peeled, diced eggplant
1   cup diced onion
1   cup diced red bell pepper
Vegetable cooking spray

Preheat oven to 375°.
Combine first 5 ingredients in a small bowl; stir well. Cover and chill.
Wrap potatoes in aluminum foil; bake at 375° for 1 hour or until tender.
Combine lemon juice and next 3 ingredients in a large bowl. Add eggplant, onion, and bell pepper; toss well to coat. Place on a jelly-roll pan coated with cooking spray. Bake at 375° for 40 minutes, stirring after 20 minutes.
Unwrap potatoes; split open each potato. Spoon 2 tablespoons yogurt mixture into each potato; fluff pulp with a fork. Spoon about ⅔ cup eggplant mixture into center of each potato; top each with 1 tablespoon yogurt mixture. Yield: 6 servings.

CALORIES 317 (23% from fat); PROTEIN 10.5g; FAT 8.1g (sat 1.4g, mono 3.3g, poly 2.6g); CARB 54.3g; FIBER 6.8g; CHOL 2mg; IRON 4.9mg; SODIUM 256mg; CALC 177mg

MUSHROOM-SWISS STUFFED POTATOES

6 (8-ounce) baking potatoes
2 teaspoons olive oil
2 cups quartered mushrooms
2 cups (½-inch) diced portobello
    mushrooms
1 cup sliced shiitake mushroom
    caps
¼ cup finely chopped onion
2 garlic cloves, minced
2 tablespoons all-purpose flour
½ teaspoon salt
⅛ teaspoon white pepper
1 cup skim milk
1 tablespoon dry sherry
1 cup (4 ounces) shredded Swiss
    cheese

Preheat oven to 375°.

Wrap potatoes in aluminum foil; bake at 375° for 1 hour or until tender.

Heat oil in a large nonstick skillet over medium heat until hot. Add mushrooms, onion, and garlic; sauté 2 minutes. Stir in flour, salt, and white pepper. Gradually add milk and sherry, stirring with a whisk until blended. Cook 2 minutes or until thick and bubbly. Add cheese; cook 1 minute or until cheese melts, stirring constantly.

Unwrap potatoes. Split open each potato; fluff pulp with a fork. Spoon ⅓ cup mushroom sauce into center of each potato. Place potatoes on a baking sheet; broil 4 minutes or until sauce begins to brown. Yield: 6 servings.

Note: Substitute any combination of exotic and domestic fresh mushrooms to measure 5 cups, if desired.

CALORIES 312 (21% from fat); PROTEIN 13.9g; FAT 7.3g (sat 3.7g, mono 2.5g, poly 0.5g); CARB 49.9g; FIBER 5g; CHOL 18mg; IRON 3.9mg; SODIUM 286mg; CALC 271mg

ATHENIAN STUFFED POTATOES

6 (8-ounce) baking potatoes
1 (6-ounce) jar marinated
    artichoke hearts, undrained
2 teaspoons olive oil
1 cup diced onion
1 cup diced green bell pepper
1 cup diced red bell pepper
1 cup diced tomato
2 garlic cloves, minced
1 cup crumbled feta cheese
2 tablespoons minced kalamata
    olives
1 teaspoon dried oregano

Preheat oven to 375°.

Wrap potatoes in aluminum foil; bake at 375° for 1 hour or until tender.

Drain artichokes in a colander over a bowl, reserving 1 tablespoon marinade. Chop artichokes, and set aside.

Heat olive oil in a large nonstick skillet over medium-high heat until hot. Add onion and next 4 ingredients; sauté 8 minutes. Add artichokes, reserved marinade, cheese, olives, and oregano; sauté 1 minute or until thoroughly heated.

Unwrap potatoes. Split open each potato; fluff pulp with a fork. Spoon ¾ cup vegetable mixture into center of each potato. Yield: 6 servings.

CALORIES 306 (22% from fat); PROTEIN 10.3g; FAT 7.5g (sat 3.3g, mono 2.4g, poly 0.7g); CARB 52.7g; FIBER 5.9g; CHOL 17mg; IRON 4.6mg; SODIUM 306mg; CALC 159mg

NEW ENGLAND STUFFED SWEET POTATOES

6 (8-ounce) sweet potatoes
⅓ cup chopped pecans, toasted
¼ cup dried cranberries
¼ cup maple syrup
1 tablespoon peeled, grated fresh
    gingerroot
½ teaspoon salt
¼ teaspoon ground red pepper

Preheat oven to 375°.

Wrap potatoes in aluminum foil; bake at 375° for 1 hour or until tender.

Unwrap potatoes. Split open each potato, and scoop out pulp, leaving a ¼-inch-thick shell. Combine pulp, pecans, and remaining 5 ingredients. Stuff each shell with ¾ cup potato mixture; place on a baking sheet. Bake at 375° for 10 minutes or until thoroughly heated. Yield: 6 servings.

CALORIES 276 (17% from fat); PROTEIN 3.5g; FAT 5.1g (sat 0.5g, mono 2.8g, poly 1.4g); CARB 56.3g; FIBER 5.9g; CHOL 0mg; IRON 1.4mg; SODIUM 221mg; CALC 52mg

Molasses-Spice Crackles, page 260

Three-Greens Salad with
Garbanzos, page 263

Caramelized Onion, Fig, and Blue Cheese Strudel, page 270

Hearty Vegetable Stew Seasoned with Beef, page 256

Spicy Hash Browns, page 267

Brownie Snack Cake, page 260

OCTOBER

Perfection on a Platter

From Paris to San Francisco, bistros are famous for their perfectly roasted chicken. With our easy recipes, you can enjoy these classic dishes, plus some creative variations, in your own home.

From the most upscale of eateries to fast-food chains, roasted chicken is the latest culinary crossover success. Although people have been roasting chickens since chickens first crossed the road, the modest European bistro is the inspiration for today's healthy casual-eating trend.

Bistro-style, herb-infused roasted chicken—golden brown, with meat so tender and juicy that it practically falls off the bone—is the standard by which all other roasted chicken is judged, or should be. Amazing as it may seem, there is no great secret to making such perfection on a platter. Virtually all you do is tuck seasonings under the chicken's skin, then start it in the oven at a high temperature. So get ready to let the intoxicating aroma of roasted chicken fill your kitchen.

ROASTING TIPS

♦ To seal in the juices and keep the chicken moist and tender, roast it at a high temperature (450°) for a short time, then lower it to a moderate temperature (350°) for the remaining cooking time.

♦ We recommend using a roasting chicken. While you can roast a broiler/fryer with good results, chickens specifically for roasting are labeled "roasting broilers." These birds generally weigh more, are meatier, moister, and more succulent (due in part to an added salt solution, which increased our sodium figures only negligibly). However, if you are roasting a broiler/fryer (which normally weighs about 3 pounds), decrease the baking time by about 45 minutes.

♦ Always roast the chicken on a rack so the fat can drip off and away from the bird.

♦ Don't fret that all of the flavorings are lost when the skin is removed. The seasonings that are tucked under the skin will permeate not only the meat, but the pan drippings as well, creating flavorful juices for the gravy and sauce.

♦ Let the roasted chicken stand for about 10 minutes after removing it from the oven. This standing time "sets" the juices and makes for a moister, more flavorful bird.

CHINESE TANGERINE CHICKEN

- 2 tablespoons fine, dry breadcrumbs
- 1 teaspoon grated tangerine or orange rind
- 2 tablespoons fresh tangerine or orange juice
- 2 tablespoons peeled, grated fresh gingerroot
- 1 tablespoon low-sodium soy sauce
- 1 tablespoon honey
- 1 teaspoon dark sesame oil
- 1 (5- to 6-pound) roasting chicken
- 8 pieces peeled, sliced fresh gingerroot
- 6 tangerines or oranges, halved crosswise
- 1 tablespoon all-purpose flour
- 1 cup low-salt chicken broth
- ¼ cup dry sherry
- ⅓ cup tangerine or orange juice

Preheat oven to 450°.

Combine first 7 ingredients in a small bowl; stir well. Set aside.

Remove giblets and neck from chicken; discard. Rinse chicken under cold water; pat dry. Trim excess fat. Starting at neck cavity, loosen skin from breast and drumsticks by inserting fingers and gently pushing between skin and meat. Spread breadcrumb mixture beneath skin on breast and drumsticks. Place 8 ginger slices and 4 tangerine halves into cavity. Lift wing tips up and over back; tuck under chicken.

Place chicken, breast side up, on a broiler pan. Arrange 8 tangerine halves, cut side up, around chicken. Insert meat thermometer into meaty part of thigh, making sure not to touch bone. Bake at 450° for 20 minutes. Reduce oven temperature to 350°; bake an additional 1 hour and 30 minutes or until thermometer registers 180°. Discard the skin.

Place chicken on a platter. Set aside; keep warm. Pour pan drippings into a heavy-duty, zip-top plastic bag. Snip off 1 corner of bag. Drain liquid into a saucepan, stopping before fat layer reaches the opening. Discard fat.

Combine flour and broth in a small bowl; stir with a whisk. Add to pan drippings. Stir in sherry and ⅓ cup juice. Bring to a boil; cook 1 minute or until thick, stirring constantly with a whisk. Serve with chicken. Yield: 8 servings (serving size: 3 ounces chicken, 3 tablespoons gravy, and 1 tangerine half).

CALORIES 215 (30% from fat); PROTEIN 25.5g; FAT 7.2g (sat 1.8g, mono 2.5g, poly 1.7g); CARB 8.7g; FIBER 0.5g; CHOL 76mg; IRON 1.4mg; SODIUM 202mg; CALC 24mg

JAMAICAN JERK ROASTED CHICKEN AND BANANAS

¼ cup plain nonfat yogurt
1 teaspoon sugar
1 teaspoon ground allspice
½ teaspoon salt
½ teaspoon dried thyme
½ teaspoon ground red pepper
¼ teaspoon ground mace
¼ teaspoon ground nutmeg
¼ teaspoon black pepper
1 (5- to 6-pound) roasting chicken
4 medium-size unripe bananas, peeled and cut in half lengthwise
1 tablespoon all-purpose flour
1 cup low-salt chicken broth
½ cup orange juice
2 tablespoons dark rum

Preheat oven to 450°.
Combine first 9 ingredients in a small bowl; stir well. Set aside.
Remove the giblets and neck from chicken; discard. Rinse chicken under cold water; pat dry. Trim excess fat. Starting at neck cavity, loosen skin from breast and drumsticks by inserting fingers and gently pushing between the skin and meat. Spread yogurt mixture beneath skin on breast and drumsticks. Lift wing tips up and over back; tuck under chicken.
Place chicken, breast side up, on a broiler pan. Insert meat thermometer into meaty part of thigh, making sure not to touch bone. Bake at 450° for 20 minutes. Reduce oven temperature to 350°. Arrange bananas around chicken,

and bake an additional 1 hour and 30 minutes or until thermometer registers 180°. Discard skin.
Place chicken and bananas on a platter. Set aside; keep warm. Pour pan drippings into a heavy-duty, zip-top plastic bag. Snip off 1 corner of bag; drain liquid into a small saucepan, stopping before fat layer reaches the opening. Discard fat.
Combine flour and broth in a small bowl, and stir with a whisk; add to pan drippings in saucepan. Stir in orange juice and rum. Bring to a boil; cook 1 minute or until thick, stirring constantly with whisk. Serve with chicken and bananas. Yield: 8 servings (serving size: 3 ounces chicken, 1 banana half, and 3 tablespoons gravy).

CALORIES 249 (25% from fat); PROTEIN 26.1g; FAT 6.9g (sat 1.9g, mono 2.3g, poly 1.5g); CARB 18g; FIBER 1.9g; CHOL 76mg; IRON 1.6mg; SODIUM 290mg; CALC 36mg

GARLIC-ROSEMARY ROASTED CHICKEN

1 (5- to 6-pound) roasting chicken
1 tablespoon chopped fresh rosemary
8 garlic cloves, crushed
8 medium red onions, peeled
2 whole garlic heads
2 teaspoons olive oil
Fresh rosemary sprigs (optional)

Preheat oven to 450°.
Remove the giblets and neck from chicken; discard. Rinse chicken under cold water; pat dry. Trim excess fat. Starting at neck cavity, loosen skin from breast and drumsticks by inserting fingers and gently pushing between the skin and meat. Place chopped rosemary and crushed garlic cloves beneath skin on breasts and drumsticks. Lift the wing tips up and over back; tuck under chicken.
Place chicken, breast side up, on a broiler pan. Remove white papery skins from garlic heads (do not peel or separate cloves). Cut tops off garlic heads, leaving root end intact.

Brush onions and garlic heads with olive oil. Arrange onions and garlic heads around chicken. Insert meat thermometer into meaty part of thigh, making sure not to touch bone. Bake at 450° for 30 minutes. Reduce oven temperature to 350°, and bake an additional 1 hour and 15 minutes or until meat thermometer registers 180°. Discard skin. Transfer to a serving platter, and garnish with rosemary sprigs, if desired. Yield: 8 servings (serving size: 3 ounces chicken and 1 onion).
Note: Squeeze pulp from the roasted garlic heads; spread on French bread, if desired.

CALORIES 231 (30% from fat); PROTEIN 26.5g; FAT 7.7g (sat 1.9g, mono 3.1g, poly 1.6g); CARB 13.5g; FIBER 2.7g; CHOL 76mg; IRON 1.4mg; SODIUM 133mg; CALC 50mg

SIMPLE ROASTED CHICKEN

1 (5- to 6-pound) roasting chicken
Vegetable cooking spray
1 teaspoon dried herbs (such as basil, oregano, or thyme)
¼ teaspoon salt
⅛ teaspoon pepper

Preheat oven to 450°.
Remove the giblets and neck from chicken; discard. Rinse chicken under cold water; pat dry. Trim excess fat.
Place chicken, breast side up, on a broiler pan. Insert meat thermometer into meaty part of thigh, making sure not to touch bone. Coat chicken with cooking spray; sprinkle with herbs, salt, and pepper.
Bake at 450° for 30 minutes. Reduce oven temperature to 400°; bake an additional 45 minutes or until thermometer registers 180°. Discard skin. Yield: 8 servings (serving size: 3 ounces chicken).

CALORIES 163 (36% from fat); PROTEIN 24.6g; FAT 6.4g (sat 1.7g, mono 2.3g, poly 1.4g); CARB 0.1g; FIBER 0g; CHOL 76mg; IRON 1.1mg; SODIUM 146mg; CALC 19mg

ROASTED CHUTNEY CHICKEN AND PINEAPPLE

½ cup mango chutney
1 teaspoon curry powder
1 medium pineapple, peeled and cored
1 (5- to 6-pound) roasting chicken
1 tablespoon all-purpose flour
½ cup low-sodium chicken broth
¼ cup apple cider
¼ cup orange juice
¼ teaspoon salt
¼ teaspoon pepper

Preheat oven to 450°.

Combine chutney and curry powder. Cut pineapple lengthwise into 8 wedges; set aside.

Remove giblets and neck from chicken; discard. Rinse chicken under cold water; pat dry. Trim excess fat. Starting at neck cavity, loosen skin from breast and drumsticks by inserting fingers and gently pushing between the skin and meat.

Reserve 2 tablespoons chutney mixture. Place remaining chutney mixture beneath skin on breasts and drumsticks. Lift wing tips up and over back; tuck under chicken.

Place chicken, breast side up, on a broiler pan. Arrange pineapple around chicken. Insert meat thermometer into meaty part of thigh, making sure not to touch bone. Bake at 450° for 20 minutes. Brush reserved chutney mixture over chicken. Reduce oven temperature to 350°; bake an additional 1 hour and 20 minutes or until thermometer registers 180°. Discard skin.

Place the chicken and pineapple on a serving platter; set aside, and keep warm. Pour the pan drippings into a heavy-duty, zip-top plastic bag. Snip off 1 corner of bag, and drain into a medium saucepan, stopping before the fat layer reaches the opening. Discard fat.

Combine flour and broth in a small bowl, stirring with a whisk; add to pan drippings in saucepan. Stir in cider and remaining 3 ingredients. Bring to a boil; cook 1 minute or until thick, stirring constantly with a whisk. Serve with chicken and roasted pineapple. Yield: 8 servings (serving size: 3 ounces chicken, 1 pineapple wedge, and ¼ cup sauce).

CALORIES 255 (24% from fat); PROTEIN 25.4g; FAT 6.9g (sat 1.8g, mono 2.3g, poly 1.6g); CARB 23g; FIBER 1.3g; CHOL 76mg; IRON 1.8mg; SODIUM 241mg; CALC 26mg

PORCINI ROASTED CHICKEN

Dried porcinis are dehydrated mushrooms that come in small bags. They can be found in the produce section or next to the canned vegetables.

1½ cups hot water
½ cup dried porcini mushrooms (about ½ ounce)
½ cup freshly grated Parmesan cheese
½ teaspoon rubbed sage
3 tablespoons dry white wine
1 (5- to 6-pound) roasting chicken
6 medium-size red potatoes, quartered (about 2¼ pounds)
Vegetable cooking spray
⅛ teaspoon salt
⅛ teaspoon pepper
2 tablespoons all-purpose flour
¼ cup dry white wine
¼ teaspoon salt

Combine water and mushrooms in a medium bowl; cover and let stand 30 minutes. Drain mushrooms into a sieve over a bowl, reserving 1 cup liquid. Rinse and finely chop mushrooms. Combine mushrooms, cheese, sage, and 3 tablespoons wine; stir well.

Preheat oven to 450°.

Remove the giblets and neck from chicken; discard. Rinse chicken under cold water, and pat dry. Trim excess fat. Starting at neck cavity, loosen skin from breast and drumsticks by inserting fingers and gently pushing between the skin and meat. Spread mushroom mixture beneath skin on breast and drumsticks. Lift the wing tips up and over back; tuck under chicken.

Place chicken, breast side up, on a broiler pan. Place potatoes in a bowl; coat with cooking spray. Sprinkle with ⅛ teaspoon salt and pepper; toss well. Arrange potatoes around chicken. Insert meat thermometer into meaty part of thigh, making sure not to touch bone. Bake at 450° for 30 minutes. Reduce oven temperature to 350°, and bake an additional 1 hour and 15 minutes or until thermometer registers 180°. Discard skin.

Place chicken and potatoes on a serving platter. Set aside; keep warm. Pour pan drippings into a heavy-duty, zip-top plastic bag. Snip off 1 corner of bag; drain into a medium saucepan, stopping before the fat layer reaches the opening. Discard fat.

Combine flour and reserved mushroom liquid in a small bowl, stirring with a whisk; add mixture to pan drippings in saucepan. Stir in ¼ cup wine and ¼ teaspoon salt. Bring mixture to a boil; cook 1 minute or until thick, stirring constantly with a whisk. Serve gravy with chicken and potatoes. Yield: 8 servings (serving size: 3 ounces chicken, 3 potato quarters, and 3 tablespoons gravy).

CALORIES 302 (26% from fat); PROTEIN 30.4g; FAT 8.7g (sat 3.1g, mono 2.9g, poly 1.5g); CARB 22.1g; FIBER 2.3g; CHOL 81mg; IRON 2.8mg; SODIUM 378mg; CALC 128mg

CRUSTLESS CHICKEN-AND-BROCCOLI QUICHE

2 cups coarsely chopped broccoli florets
Vegetable cooking spray
2 tablespoons fine, dry breadcrumbs
3 tablespoons all-purpose flour
1 teaspoon dried basil
¼ teaspoon salt
⅛ teaspoon pepper
1 cup 1% low-fat milk
1 tablespoon Dijon mustard
1 (4-ounce) carton egg substitute
1½ cups chopped roasted chicken
½ cup (2 ounces) shredded reduced-fat extra-sharp Cheddar cheese, divided
¼ teaspoon paprika

Preheat oven to 350°.

Cook chopped broccoli in boiling water 3 minutes or until crisp-tender; drain.

Coat a 9-inch pie plate with cooking spray; sprinkle with breadcrumbs. (Do not remove excess breadcrumbs.) Set aside.

Combine flour, basil, salt, and pepper in a large bowl; add milk and mustard, stirring with a whisk. Stir in broccoli and egg substitute. Add chicken and ¼ cup cheese; stir well. Pour mixture into prepared pan. Sprinkle with remaining cheese and paprika. Bake at 350° for 45 minutes or until set. Let cool on a wire rack 15 minutes. Yield: 6 servings.

CALORIES 167 (29% from fat); PROTEIN 18.7g; FAT 5.3g (sat 2.1g, mono 1.6g, poly 0.8g); CARB 10.9g; FIBER 1.9g; CHOL 39mg; IRON 1.6mg; SODIUM 353mg; CALC 186mg

ROASTED-CHICKEN NOODLE SOUP

For the sake of convenience, we call for canned low-salt chicken broth.

2   teaspoons olive oil
1   cup chopped onion
1   cup diced carrots
1   cup sliced celery
1   garlic clove, minced
¼   cup all-purpose flour
½   teaspoon dried oregano
¼   teaspoon dried thyme
¼   teaspoon poultry seasoning
6   cups low-salt chicken broth
4   cups peeled, diced baking
    potato
1   teaspoon salt
2   cups diced roasted
    chicken
1   cup evaporated skim milk
4   ounces (2 cups) uncooked wide
    egg noodles
Fresh thyme sprigs (optional)

Heat olive oil in a Dutch oven over medium heat. Add onion and next 3 ingredients; sauté 5 minutes.

Sprinkle flour and next 3 ingredients over vegetables, and cook 1 minute. Stir in broth, potato, and salt. Bring to a boil; reduce heat, and simmer, partially covered, 25 minutes or until potato is tender.

Add roasted chicken, milk, and noodles, and cook 10 minutes or until noodles are tender. Garnish with fresh thyme, if desired. Yield: 2½ quarts (serving size: 1 cup).

CALORIES 215 (19% from fat); PROTEIN 14.9g; FAT 4.6g (sat 0.9g, mono 1.6g, poly 0.8g); CARB 28.6g; FIBER 2.6g; CHOL 37mg; IRON 2.4mg; SODIUM 355mg; CALC 101mg

BISTRO SHOESTRING POTATOES

1½ pounds baking potatoes, cut
    lengthwise into thin strips
1   tablespoon olive oil
¼   teaspoon salt
¼   teaspoon pepper

Preheat oven to 450°.

Combine all ingredients in a large heavy-duty, zip-top plastic bag. Seal; shake to coat potatoes. Arrange potatoes in a single layer on a baking sheet. Bake at 450° for 30 minutes or until crisp and golden. Yield: 4 servings.

CALORIES 156 (20% from fat); PROTEIN 3.7g; FAT 3.5g (sat 0.5g, mono 2.5g, poly 0.4g); CARB 28.2g; FIBER 2.7g; CHOL 0mg; IRON 2.1mg; SODIUM 158mg; CALC 22mg

FAST FOOD

Another Opening

What you see is what you get with open-face sandwiches, and what you get is absolutely fabulous.

We've taken six classic American sandwiches—including a tuna melt, Sloppy Joe, and Hot Brown—and opened them up. For these sandwiches to be truly quick and easy, we relied on convenience products such as deli meats, condiments, and salad dressings. So the next time you want a filling lunch or dinner that requires little effort, try one of these open-face sandwiches. You'll love it—it's an open-and-shut case.

HOT BROWN SANDWICH

The Hot Brown began at the Brown Hotel in Louisville, Kentucky.
Preparation time: 18 minutes
Cooking time: 19 minutes

¼   cup plus 2 tablespoons
     all-purpose flour
⅓   cup 2% low-fat milk
2   (10½-ounce) cans low-salt
     chicken broth
1   tablespoon reduced-calorie
     stick margarine
½   cup preshredded fresh
     Parmesan cheese, divided
1½   tablespoons sherry
8   (¾-ounce) slices wheat bread,
     toasted
¾   pound shaved oven-roasted
     fat-free deli turkey breast
8   (¼-inch-thick) slices tomato
2   tablespoons plus 2 teaspoons
     crumbled real bacon bits
Freshly ground pepper

Preheat oven to 450°.

Place flour in a medium bowl. Gradually add milk and broth, stirring with a whisk until blended.

Melt margarine in a medium saucepan over medium heat; stir in chicken broth mixture. Cook 8 minutes or until thick and bubbly, stirring constantly with a whisk. Add ¼ cup cheese; cook 1 minute. (Cheese will not completely melt.) Remove from heat; stir in sherry.

Slice each toasted bread slice in half diagonally. Arrange 4 toast triangles on a baking sheet, overlapping triangles. Top each with 3 ounces turkey, about ¾ cup cheese sauce, 2 tomato slices, 2 teaspoons bacon bits, and 1 tablespoon remaining cheese. Repeat procedure with remaining ingredients to make 4 sandwiches. Bake at 450° in the upper third of the oven for 8 minutes or until thoroughly heated. Sprinkle with pepper. Yield: 4 servings.

CALORIES 355 (30% from fat); PROTEIN 27.1g; FAT 12g (sat 4.8g, mono 4.3g, poly 2g); CARB 36.8g; FIBER 2.2g; CHOL 40mg; IRON 3mg; SODIUM 1,554mg; CALC 239mg

CAROLINA BLOND-
BARBECUE SANDWICH

Preparation time: 15 minutes
Cooking time: 12 minutes

- 1 (12-ounce) bag coleslaw
- ⅓ cup light coleslaw dressing (such as Marzetti)
- ¼ teaspoon celery seeds
- 1 cup no-salt-added ketchup
- ½ cup water
- ¼ cup cider vinegar
- 2 tablespoons instant minced onion
- 2 tablespoons dark brown sugar
- 1 tablespoon prepared mustard
- 1 teaspoon pepper
- 1 teaspoon hot sauce
- ½ teaspoon garlic powder
- 1½ cups (¾ pound) skinned, shredded roasted chicken breast (such as Tyson)
- 4 (2-ounce) slices Texas toast, lightly toasted

Combine first 3 ingredients in a bowl; toss well to coat.

Combine ketchup and next 8 ingredients in a medium saucepan; bring to a boil. Reduce heat; simmer 5 minutes or until mixture begins to thicken. Stir in chicken, and cook 4 minutes or until chicken is thoroughly heated.

Top each bread slice with ½ cup chicken mixture and ½ cup coleslaw mixture. Yield: 4 servings.

CALORIES 421 (19% from fat); PROTEIN 26.5g; FAT 8.9g (sat 1.9g, mono 2.3g, poly 3.3g); CARB 64.4g; FIBER 3.5g; CHOL 76mg; IRON 4mg; SODIUM 1,075mg; CALC 115mg

SODIUM SENSE

Because we used convenience products in our open-face sandwich recipes, the sodium counts are higher than those of most other main dishes in the magazine. This shouldn't be a problem for most people. Unless your salt intake is restricted, you can enjoy these recipes as part of a healthy diet.

MENU SUGGESTION
TUNA MELT
Creamy tomato soup*
Grapes

*Sauté ½ cup each of chopped onion and chopped green bell pepper until tender. Purée sautéed vegetables, ½ teaspoon dried basil, 2 cups tomato juice, and 1 cup buttermilk. Heat until warm.

TUNA MELT

Preparation time: 20 minutes
Cooking time: 14 minutes

- 2 medium zucchini (about 7 ounces each)
- Olive oil-flavored vegetable cooking spray
- 2 teaspoons dried basil
- 1 teaspoon dried thyme
- ⅛ teaspoon pepper
- 4 (1-ounce) slices multigrain bread, toasted
- 1 (9-ounce) can solid white tuna in water, drained
- ¼ cup light mayonnaise
- 2 tablespoons finely chopped red onion
- 16 (¼-inch-thick) slices plum tomato
- 4 (¾-ounce) slices ⅓-less-fat Swiss or fat-free American cheese

Slice zucchini in half crosswise; then slice into ¼-inch lengthwise slices.

Coat a large nonstick skillet with cooking spray; place over medium-high heat until hot. Add half of the zucchini; cook 5 minutes. Turn slices over, and sprinkle with half of basil, thyme, and pepper; cook 5 minutes or until tender. Repeat with remaining zucchini, herbs, and pepper. Divide zucchini slices evenly among toast slices.

Combine tuna, mayonnaise, and onion in a small bowl, stirring well. Spread ½ cup tuna mixture over each zucchini-topped bread slice; top each with 4 tomato slices and 1 cheese slice.

Place sandwiches on a baking sheet; broil 2 minutes or until cheese melts. Yield: 4 servings.

CALORIES 255 (24% from fat); PROTEIN 21.3g; FAT 6.9g (sat 1.2g, mono 1.6g, poly 3g); CARB 24.7g; FIBER 3.5g; CHOL 31mg; IRON 2.7mg; SODIUM 882mg; CALC 314mg

TURKEY-VEGETABLE
SLOPPY JOES

Preparation time: 9 minutes
Cooking time: 15 minutes

- 1 pound ground turkey
- 1 cup chopped onion
- 1 garlic clove, minced
- ½ cup chopped green bell pepper
- 1 (14½-ounce) can diced tomatoes
- ¼ cup tomato paste
- 1 tablespoon prepared mustard
- 1 teaspoon chili powder
- ¾ teaspoon ground cumin
- ½ teaspoon salt
- ½ teaspoon black pepper
- 4 (2-ounce) kaiser rolls or hamburger buns, split
- 1 cup (4 ounces) shredded reduced-fat sharp Cheddar cheese

Cook turkey, onion, and garlic in a large nonstick skillet over medium-high heat until turkey is browned, stirring to crumble. Stir in bell pepper and next 7 ingredients. Bring to a boil; cover, reduce heat, and simmer 10 minutes.

Spoon ½ cup turkey mixture onto each roll half; top each with 2 tablespoons cheese. Yield: 8 servings.

CALORIES 232 (25% from fat); PROTEIN 20.8g; FAT 6.4g (sat 2.5g, mono 1.9g, poly 1.1g); CARB 22.8g; FIBER 1.4g; CHOL 46mg; IRON 3mg; SODIUM 576mg; CALC 170mg

PHILLY CHEESE SANDWICH

Preparation time: 5 minutes
Cooking time: 17 minutes

- 1 teaspoon olive oil
- 1½ cups sliced onion
- 1½ cups sliced green bell pepper
- ¼ teaspoon black pepper
- 4 (1-ounce) slices French bread
- Olive oil-flavored vegetable cooking spray
- 8 ounces thinly sliced deli roast beef
- 4 (1-ounce) slices reduced-fat Swiss cheese

Heat oil in a nonstick skillet over medium heat until hot. Add onion; cook 10 minutes, stirring frequently. Add bell pepper and black pepper; cook 3 minutes or until bell pepper is crisp-tender.

Coat top sides of bread with cooking spray. Top each slice with 2 ounces beef, ¼ cup onion mixture, and 1 cheese slice.

Place sandwiches on a baking sheet coated with cooking spray; broil 2 minutes or until cheese melts. Yield: 4 servings.

CALORIES 291 (27% from fat); PROTEIN 24.8g; FAT 8.6g (sat 3.7g, mono 3.2g, poly 0.8g); CARB 28.4g; FIBER 2.6g; CHOL 39mg; IRON 3.2mg; SODIUM 819mg; CALC 365mg

VEGGIE-LOVER'S SPECIAL

Preparation time: 40 minutes

- 4 (1½-ounce) slices multigrain bread, toasted
- Hummus Spread
- 1 cup alfalfa sprouts
- 1 cup sliced cucumber
- 8 (¼-inch-thick) slices tomato
- 8 (¼-inch-thick) slices avocado
- 2 (¼-inch-thick) slices red onion, separated into rings
- Feta-Dill Dressing

Spread each bread slice with 3 tablespoons Hummus Spread. Top each with ¼ cup sprouts, ¼ cup cucumber slices, 2 tomato slices, and 2 avocado slices. Top with onion rings. Drizzle each sandwich with 3 tablespoons Feta-Dill Dressing. Yield: 4 servings.

CALORIES 287 (23% from fat); PROTEIN 12.5g; FAT 7.4g (sat 1.7g, mono 2.9g, poly 2.5g); CARB 43.6g; FIBER 4.1g; CHOL 7mg; IRON 4mg; SODIUM 289mg; CALC 192mg

Hummus Spread:

- 4 garlic cloves
- ¼ cup coarsely chopped fresh parsley
- 1 (15-ounce) can no-salt-added chickpeas (garbanzo beans), undrained
- 2 tablespoons lemon juice
- 2 tablespoons tahini (sesame-seed paste)

Drop garlic and parsley through food chute with food processor on, and process until minced. Add chickpeas, juice, and tahini; process until smooth. Yield: 1½ cups (serving size: 3 tablespoons).

Note: Serve remaining Hummus Spread as a tasty snack with baked pita bread wedges.

CALORIES 112 (27% from fat); PROTEIN 5.5g; FAT 3.4g (sat 0.4g, mono 0.1g, poly 1.5g); CARB 11.6g; FIBER 2.3g; CHOL 0mg; IRON 2mg; SODIUM 8mg; CALC 48mg

Feta-Dill Dressing:

- ⅔ cup plain nonfat yogurt
- 2 tablespoons crumbled feta cheese
- 1 tablespoon lemon juice
- ¼ teaspoon dried dillweed

Combine all ingredients in a small bowl; stir well. Cover and chill. Yield: ¾ cup (serving size: 3 tablespoons).

Note: This is also good with lamb or as a topping for sliced tomatoes.

CALORIES 32 (23% from fat); PROTEIN 2.7g; FAT 0.8g (sat 0.6g, mono 0.2g, poly 0g); CARB 3.4g; FIBER 0g; CHOL 7mg; IRON 0.1mg; SODIUM 69mg; CALC 95mg

COOKING WITH KERR

The Meat of the Matter

A simple cooking technique has this low-fat beef stew tasting as meaty as heavier versions.

In days gone by, I used to make hearty beef stews with two pounds of well-marbled blade steak. But now 8 ounces of beef per serving (with 33 grams of fat) is just too much.

In the end, I settled on a recipe with 8 ounces of meat for four people. After experimenting with top and bottom round, I selected a chuck roast with the fat trimmed off; the cut is well worth it because of its quality and tenderness.

As with any red-meat stew, I seared the beef cubes in a hot pan on one side only. This keeps juices from boiling out of the meat and leaves three "naked" sides that more readily absorb flavors of the cooking liquids.

With a dark stew, I always use the trick of letting the tomato paste cook down so the sugars caramelize and become more flavor-complex. When this reduction combines with the wine (remember: never cook with a wine you wouldn't drink), it provides a depth of flavor usually associated with the presence of more meat.

This stew has turned out to be a hands-down winner, especially for meat-and-potatoes people who normally would never be happy with only a 2-ounce piece of meat. See what you think.

HEARTY VEGETABLE STEW SEASONED WITH BEEF

2 (14¼-ounce) cans fat-free beef
    broth
½ pound lean, boned chuck roast
1 teaspoon olive oil, divided
4 cups vertically sliced onion
⅓ cup tomato paste
3 garlic cloves, minced
3 cups cubed carrots
3 cups cubed red potatoes
2½ cups quartered mushrooms
½ cup dry red wine
¼ teaspoon salt
¼ teaspoon pepper
1 (10-ounce) package frozen
    green peas, thawed
2 tablespoons water
1 tablespoon cornstarch
Chopped fresh parsley (optional)

Bring beef broth to a boil in a small saucepan; cook 15 minutes or until reduced to 2 cups. Set aside.

Trim fat from roast; cut roast into ½-inch cubes. Heat ½ teaspoon oil in a large Dutch oven over medium-high heat until hot. Add beef; brown on one side. Remove from pan, and set aside.

Heat remaining ½ teaspoon oil in pan over medium-high heat until hot. Add onion, tomato paste, and garlic; cook 5 minutes, stirring constantly. Return beef to pan. Add reduced broth, carrots, potatoes, mushrooms, red wine, salt, pepper, and green peas; bring to a boil. Cover, reduce heat, and simmer 45 minutes or until vegetables are tender.

Combine water and cornstarch in a small bowl; stir well. Add cornstarch mixture to stew. Bring to a boil; cook 1 minute, stirring constantly. Ladle into soup bowls; garnish with parsley, if desired. Yield: 4 servings (serving size: 2 cups).

Note: If you don't want to use alcohol in your stew, you can substitute a dealcoholized wine (Graham used Ariel Cabernet Sauvignon Barrel Select).

CALORIES 371 (12% from fat); PROTEIN 22.6g; FAT 5g (sat 1.4g, mono 2g, poly 0.7g); CARB 59.5g; FIBER 11.4g; CHOL 34mg; IRON 5.6mg; SODIUM 458mg; CALC 93mg

Orchards in the Sky

Warmed by the southwest winds,
a remote Rocky Mountain valley produces
some amazing apples.

Standing among the rows of Jonathan, Red and Golden Delicious, Rome, and Winesap apple trees that grow on a mountainside farm, it's hard to keep your eyes from wandering to the horizon. With miles of parched, rugged terrain to its west and the soaring peaks of Colorado's Rocky Mountains to its east, you have to wonder how any substantial fruit crop can grow in this valley. But fed by snowmelt tumbling from nearby 14,000-foot peaks and warmed by temperate southwest winds, this land holds a six-month growing season that defies expectations.

Colorado's apple crop isn't a threat to that of the nation's better-known growing regions, yet its annual 2.5 million-bushel harvest has charmed those searching for distinctly regional qualities in their fruit.

APPLE-FILLED PORK ROAST

Vegetable cooking spray
⅓ cup chopped onion
1 cup sliced mushrooms
½ teaspoon dried thyme
⅛ teaspoon dried rosemary,
    crushed
1 cup peeled, diced Rome
    apple (about ½ pound)
¼ teaspoon grated lemon
    rind
1 teaspoon fresh lemon
    juice
⅛ teaspoon salt
⅛ teaspoon pepper
8 large pitted prunes,
    diced
1 (2-pound) lean, boned
    pork loin roast
½ teaspoon dried thyme
¼ teaspoon dried rosemary,
    crushed
⅛ teaspoon salt
¼ cup apple juice
Fresh rosemary sprigs
    (optional)

Preheat oven to 325°.

Coat a large nonstick skillet with cooking spray, and place over medium heat until hot. Add onion, and sauté 2 minutes. Add mushrooms, ½ teaspoon thyme, and ⅛ teaspoon rosemary; sauté 3 minutes. Add apple, lemon rind, lemon juice, ⅛ teaspoon salt, pepper, and prunes; sauté 2 minutes or until apple is crisp-tender. Set aside.

Trim fat from pork roast. Cut a wide, deep pocket in side of roast. Stuff the apple mixture into pocket. Tie roast at 1-inch intervals with heavy string. Sprinkle roast with ½ teaspoon thyme, ¼ teaspoon rosemary, and ⅛ teaspoon salt.

Place roast on a broiler pan coated with cooking spray. Insert meat thermometer into roast. Bake at 325° for 1 hour and 20 minutes or until meat thermometer registers 160°, basting frequently with apple juice. Garnish roast with rosemary sprigs, if desired. Yield: 6 servings.

CALORIES 266 (44% from fat); PROTEIN 24.6g; FAT 13g (sat 4.3g, mono 5.6g, poly 1.6g); CARB 11.8g; FIBER 1.1g; CHOL 81mg; IRON 1.8mg; SODIUM 166mg; CALC 23mg

WHIPPED RUTABAGA AND APPLE

Serve this side dish with ham, pork chops, or roast chicken. The consistency is similar to that of applesauce.

1   small rutabaga (about 1½ pounds), peeled and thinly sliced
2   large Rome apples, peeled and quartered
½   cup apple juice
2   tablespoons thawed orange juice concentrate, undiluted
1   tablespoon honey
⅛   teaspoon salt
Dash of ground nutmeg

Place the rutabaga and apple in a saucepan; add water to pan to a depth of 1 inch. Bring to a boil; cover, reduce heat, and simmer 1 hour or until tender. Drain.

Place rutabaga mixture, apple juice, and remaining ingredients in a food processor; process until smooth. Yield: 8 servings (serving size: ½ cup).

CALORIES 81 (4% from fat); PROTEIN 1.2g; FAT 0.4g (sat 0.1g, mono 0g, poly 0.2g); CARB 19.7g; FIBER 2.3g; CHOL 0mg; IRON 0.6mg; SODIUM 53mg; CALC 45mg

MICROWAVE APPLESAUCE

4½   cups peeled, thinly sliced Golden Delicious apples (about 1 pound)
4½   cups peeled, thinly sliced Winesap apples (about 1 pound)
¾   cup apple cider
2   tablespoons dark brown sugar
½   teaspoon ground cinnamon
⅛   teaspoon ground cloves

Combine all ingredients in a 3-quart casserole; toss well. Cover surface with plastic wrap; vent. Microwave at HIGH 12 minutes or until tender, stirring every 3 minutes; let cool.

Place apple mixture in a food processor; process until smooth. Return apple mixture to casserole. Cover with wax paper; microwave at HIGH 6 to 8 minutes, stirring every 3 minutes. Cover and chill. Yield: 6 servings (serving size: ½ cup).

CALORIES 121 (4% from fat); PROTEIN 0.3g; FAT 0.6g (sat 0.1g, mono 0g, poly 0.2g); CARB 31.2g; FIBER 4.5g; CHOL 0mg; IRON 0.4mg; SODIUM 2mg; CALC 14mg

BRANDIED APPLES AND PEARS

Spoon this rich, chunky sauce into a balloon wine glass over a dollop of low-fat ice cream.

2   peeled Bosc pears, cored and quartered
2   peeled Golden Delicious apples, cored and quartered
2   peeled Rome apples, cored and quartered
¼   cup golden raisins
1   teaspoon ground cinnamon
¼   cup apricot preserves
¼   cup apple juice
3   tablespoons Calvados (apple brandy)

Combine all ingredients in a heavy saucepan, and cook over low heat 30 minutes or until fruit is soft, stirring occasionally. Yield: 8 servings (serving size: ½ cup).

CALORIES 93 (4% from fat); PROTEIN 0.4g; FAT 0.4g (sat 0.1g, mono 0g, poly 0.1g); CARB 24.4g; FIBER 2.7g; CHOL 0mg; IRON 0.4mg; SODIUM 5mg; CALC 14mg

APPLE-AND-PARSNIP SLAW

¼   cup low-fat buttermilk
¼   cup fat-free sour cream
½   teaspoon sugar
¼   teaspoon salt
Dash of ground red pepper
2   cups peeled, coarsely shredded parsnips
1½   cups coarsely shredded Red Delicious apple
2   tablespoons sliced green onions

Combine first 5 ingredients in a bowl. Stir well; set aside.

Combine parsnips, apple, and green onions in a bowl; toss well. Add buttermilk mixture; toss gently. Serve chilled or at room temperature. Yield: 3 servings (serving size: 1 cup).

CALORIES 113 (3% from fat); PROTEIN 3.2g; FAT 0.5g (sat 0.1g, mono 0.1g, poly 0.1g); CARB 25g; FIBER 3.3g; CHOL 1mg; IRON 0.6mg; SODIUM 239mg; CALC 60mg

APPLE SLAW WITH BLUE CHEESE

2   large Red Delicious apples, cored and cut into ¼-inch wedges
2   tablespoons lemon juice
6   cups thinly sliced red cabbage (about 1¼ pounds)
6   cups thinly sliced napa (Chinese) cabbage (about 1¼ pounds)
1   tablespoon sugar
2   tablespoons water
2   tablespoons cider vinegar
2   tablespoons red wine vinegar
1   teaspoon olive oil
½   teaspoon salt
½   teaspoon celery seeds
½   teaspoon ground coriander
½   teaspoon pepper
½   cup crumbled blue cheese

Combine apple and juice in a large bowl; toss well. Add cabbages; toss gently.

Combine sugar and next 8 ingredients in a bowl; stir well. Pour over cabbage mixture; toss gently. Add cheese; toss gently. Yield: 6 servings (serving size: 2 cups).

CALORIES 62 (29% from fat); PROTEIN 2.1g; FAT 2g (sat 1g, mono 0.7g, poly 0.2g); CARB 10.3g; FIBER 2.3g; CHOL 4mg; IRON 0.6mg; SODIUM 190mg; CALC 85mg

APPLE 'N SPICE MUFFINS

1¼   cups all-purpose flour
½   cup cornmeal
⅓   cup sugar
1   teaspoon baking powder
1   teaspoon ground cinnamon
½   teaspoon baking soda
¼   teaspoon salt
¼   teaspoon ground ginger
1¾   cups shredded Golden
      Delicious apple
¾   cup low-fat buttermilk
2   tablespoons vegetable oil
1   large egg, lightly beaten
   Vegetable cooking spray
2   teaspoons sugar
¼   teaspoon ground cinnamon

Preheat oven to 400°.

Combine first 8 ingredients in a large bowl; make a well in center of mixture. Combine apple, buttermilk, oil, and egg; stir well. Add to dry ingredients, stirring just until moist.

Divide batter evenly among 12 muffin cups coated with cooking spray. Combine 2 teaspoons sugar and ¼ teaspoon cinnamon; sprinkle over muffins. Bake at 400° for 20 minutes or until golden. Remove from pans immediately. Serve warm. Yield: 1 dozen.

CALORIES 139 (23% from fat); PROTEIN 3g; FAT 3.5g (sat 0.8g, mono 0.9g, poly 1.3g); CARB 24.2g; FIBER 1.2g; CHOL 18mg; IRON 1.1mg; SODIUM 115mg; CALC 50mg

GINGERED PEAR-APPLE BETTY

Coat your knife with cooking spray to mince the crystallized ginger.

5   (1-ounce) slices cinnamon-
      raisin bread, cubed
2½   cups peeled, sliced firm pear
2   cups peeled, sliced Jonathan
      apple
⅓   cup firmly packed brown sugar
2   tablespoons minced crystallized
      ginger
   Vegetable cooking spray
¼   cup water
2   tablespoons lemon juice
2   tablespoons margarine, melted

Preheat oven to 350°.

Place bread cubes in a food processor; process until finely ground.

Combine 1 cup breadcrumbs, pear, apple, sugar, and ginger in a bowl; stir well. Spoon mixture into an 11 x 7-inch baking dish coated with cooking spray. Add water and lemon juice.

Combine remaining breadcrumbs and margarine; sprinkle over pear mixture. Bake at 350° for 40 minutes or until bubbly. Yield: 6 servings (serving size: ½ cup).

CALORIES 221 (20% from fat); PROTEIN 1.9g; FAT 4.9g (sat 0.9g, mono 2g, poly 1.5g); CARB 44.8g; FIBER 3.7g; CHOL 1mg; IRON 1.7mg; SODIUM 138mg; CALC 49mg

APPLE-CURRANT BARS

If you don't have currants, you can substitute chopped raisins.

1   cup all-purpose flour
1   teaspoon ground cinnamon
¾   teaspoon baking powder
¼   teaspoon baking soda
¼   teaspoon salt
¼   teaspoon ground nutmeg
⅓   cup margarine
¾   cup firmly packed dark
      brown sugar
1   large egg
1   teaspoon vanilla extract
1   cup peeled, diced Rome apple
¾   cup regular oats, uncooked
½   cup dried currants
   Vegetable cooking spray
1   tablespoon powdered sugar

Preheat oven to 350°.

Combine first 6 ingredients. Stir well; set aside.

Cream margarine in a large bowl; gradually add brown sugar, beating at medium speed of an electric mixer until light and fluffy. Add egg; beat well. Add flour mixture to creamed mixture; beat just until dry ingredients are moist. Stir in vanilla, apple, oats, and currants.

Spoon batter into a 9-inch square baking pan coated with cooking spray.

Bake at 350° for 40 minutes or until a wooden pick inserted in center comes out clean. Cool completely in pan on a wire rack. Sprinkle powdered sugar over top. Yield: 16 squares.

CALORIES 141 (29% from fat); PROTEIN 2g; FAT 4.6g (sat 0.9g, mono 1.9g, poly 1.4g); CARB 23.4g; FIBER 0.9g; CHOL 14mg; IRON 1mg; SODIUM 111mg; CALC 34mg

THE ENLIGHTENED CHEF

The Best of the West

For Marion Gillcrist, creating a contemporary Western menu was like coming home again.

When Marion Gillcrist signed on as executive chef at the Double A restaurant in Santa Fe, New Mexico, she was saddled with a Western theme for her new menu. For Texas-born Gillcrist, a graduate of the California Culinary Academy in San Francisco, that was no problem.

Coming up with a contemporary Western menu was a natural for Gillcrist. But her new dishes have been redefined and modernized. Everything is cooked with a lighter approach. And her slow-cooked Fall Stew, made with either beef or lamb, is no exception. "I just think back to being a kid at home in Austin—my parents used to have big parties, especially barbecues, and we'd all be in the kitchen cooking. By the time I was 12 years old, I'd already cooked dinner for 30 with ingredients like wild boar."

Gillcrist has since left the Double A to open her own restaurant in Dallas.

FALL STEW

Despite the number of ingredients, the preparation time is relatively quick.

2 teaspoons olive oil
¾ pound lean boned leg of lamb or lean, boned chuck roast, cut into 1-inch cubes
1 cup chopped Vidalia or other sweet onion
1 cup chopped celery
¾ cup chopped carrot
3 garlic cloves, minced
½ cup dry red wine
1½ cups cubed baking potato
1 cup peeled, chopped rutabaga
1 cup peeled, chopped turnip
½ teaspoon salt
7 (10½-ounce) cans low-salt chicken broth or 8 cups homemade chicken stock
2 bay leaves
½ cup chopped plum tomato
½ cup chopped zucchini
¼ cup chopped fresh cilantro
1 teaspoon dried oregano
1 teaspoon ground cumin
¼ teaspoon ground red pepper
¼ teaspoon black pepper

Heat oil in a large Dutch oven until hot; add lamb, browning on all sides. Add onion, celery, carrot, and garlic; sauté 5 minutes. Add wine, and cook 3 minutes, stirring frequently.

Add potato and next 5 ingredients; bring to a boil. Reduce heat to medium; cook 1 hour and 20 minutes or until vegetables are tender. Add tomato and remaining ingredients; cook an additional 10 minutes. Discard bay leaves. Yield: 4 servings (serving size: 2 cups).

CALORIES 312 (29% from fat); PROTEIN 26.3g; FAT 10.2g (sat 2.6g, mono 5.4g, poly 1.4g); CARB 30.7g; FIBER 4.6g; CHOL 54mg; IRON 6.2mg; SODIUM 595mg; CALC 88mg

Tricks & Treats

When it comes to making perfect desserts, don't scream! With these tricks of the trade, you can easily conquer your fears.

We're going to help put an end to your culinary nightmares with these dessert recipes. We asked our Test Kitchens staff to give us their tricks for making perfect treats. So now you can spook your friends and family with your professional, cheflike skills. Think how everyone will be awed when you serve a cake with a spider-web frosting or when they cut into that chocolate Bundt cake and discover a ring of coconut inside. When they ask, *How'd you do that?* just smile slyly and say nothing. They'll think it's witchcraft.

CHOCOLATE MACAROON TUNNEL CAKE

1¼ cups sugar
¼ cup plus 2 tablespoons vegetable oil
2 large eggs
3 cups all-purpose flour
1¼ teaspoons baking soda
¼ teaspoon salt
1½ cups low-fat buttermilk
2 teaspoons vanilla extract
½ cup flaked sweetened coconut
1½ teaspoons coconut flavoring, divided
⅓ cup unsweetened cocoa
Vegetable cooking spray
¾ cup sifted powdered sugar
1 tablespoon skim milk

Preheat oven to 350°.

Combine 1¼ cups sugar and oil in a large bowl, beating well at medium speed of an electric mixer. Add eggs, one at a time, beating well after each addition.

Combine flour, baking soda, and salt; add flour mixture to sugar mixture alternately with buttermilk, beginning and ending with flour mixture. Mix after each addition. Stir in vanilla.

Combine 1 cup batter, coconut, and 1 teaspoon coconut flavoring in a small bowl; stir well. Set aside. Add cocoa to remaining batter in large bowl; stir well. Reserve 1 cup chocolate batter, and set aside. Pour remaining chocolate batter into a 12-cup Bundt pan coated with cooking spray. Spoon coconut batter over center of batter to form a ring, making sure not to touch sides of pan. Top with reserved chocolate batter, spreading evenly to cover.

Bake at 350° for 40 minutes or until a wooden pick inserted in center comes out clean. Cool in pan 10 minutes; remove from pan. Cool on a wire rack. Combine remaining ½ teaspoon coconut flavoring, powdered sugar, and skim milk; stir well. Drizzle over cake. Yield: 16 servings.

CALORIES 258 (27% from fat); PROTEIN 4.7g; FAT 7.7g (sat 2.2g, mono 1.8g, poly 2.7g); CARB 42.6g; FIBER 0.8g; CHOL 28mg; IRON 1.6mg; SODIUM 164mg; CALC 38mg

CAPPUCCINO PUDDING
CAKE

Trick: To ensure ending up with two perfect cake layers, be certain not to stir the coffee mixture after it's poured over the cake batter.

CAPPUCCINO PUDDING CAKE

1 cup all-purpose flour
⅔ cup sugar
2 tablespoons unsweetened cocoa
2 teaspoons baking powder
¼ teaspoon salt
½ cup evaporated skim milk
1 teaspoon vegetable oil
1 teaspoon vanilla extract
¼ cup semisweet chocolate morsels
1 cup firmly packed dark brown sugar
¼ cup unsweetened cocoa
1¾ cups hot water
2 (.77-ounce) envelopes instant cappuccino coffee mix or ¼ cup other instant flavored coffee mix
½ cup plus 1 tablespoon frozen vanilla yogurt

Preheat oven to 350°.
Combine first 5 ingredients in a 9-inch square baking pan, and stir well. Add milk, oil, and vanilla, stirring until smooth. Stir in chocolate morsels.
Combine brown sugar and ¼ cup cocoa; sprinkle over batter. Combine water and coffee mix, stirring to dissolve. Pour coffee mixture over batter; do not stir. Bake at 350° for 40 minutes or until cake springs back when

touched lightly in center. Serve warm with frozen yogurt. Yield: 9 servings.

CALORIES 247 (11% from fat); PROTEIN 4.2g; FAT 3.0g (sat 1.5g, mono 0.5g, poly 0.4g); CARB 52.4g; FIBER 0.3g; CHOL 1mg; IRON 2mg; SODIUM 123mg; CALC 175mg

BROWNIE SNACK CAKE

Trick: To create the "web," start at the center of the cake, and pull a wooden pick or tip of a knife through circles to edge of cake at regular intervals.

BROWNIE SNACK CAKE

¾ cup sugar
¼ cup vegetable oil
¼ cup plain nonfat yogurt
1 teaspoon vanilla extract
3 large egg whites or ⅔ cup egg substitute
½ cup all-purpose flour
⅓ cup unsweetened cocoa
¼ teaspoon salt
¼ teaspoon baking powder
Vegetable cooking spray
1½ cups powdered sugar
2½ tablespoons skim milk
1 teaspoon unsweetened cocoa

Preheat oven to 375°.
Combine first 5 ingredients in a bowl; beat at medium speed of an electric mixer until well-blended. Combine flour and next 3 ingredients; stir well. Add flour mixture to sugar mixture, beating just until blended.
Pour batter into a 9-inch round cake pan coated with cooking spray. Bake at 375° for 25 minutes or until a wooden pick inserted in center comes

out clean. Cool in pan 10 minutes; remove from pan, and let cool completely on a wire rack.
Combine powdered sugar and milk; beat at low speed until glaze is smooth. Spread ½ cup glaze over cake. Add 1 teaspoon cocoa to remaining glaze, stirring with a whisk until blended. Spoon into a small zip-top plastic bag. Snip off 1 corner of bag, making a small hole. Starting in center of cake, pipe glaze in 5 concentric circles. Starting at center circle, pull a wooden pick or the tip of a knife through circles at regular intervals to edge of cake to form a "web" design. Yield: 12 servings (serving size: 1 wedge).

CALORIES 186 (24% from fat); PROTEIN 2.5g; FAT 5g (sat 1g, mono 1.4g, poly 2.2g); CARB 33.3g; FIBER 0.1g; CHOL 0mg; IRON 0.7mg; SODIUM 69mg; CALC 25mg

MOLASSES-SPICE
CRACKLES

Trick: To get a crackled texture and appearance, dip balls of cookie dough in cold water; then roll balls in sugar. (The balls spread out during baking.)

MOLASSES-SPICE CRACKLES

1⅓ cups all-purpose flour
1 teaspoon baking soda
½ teaspoon ground cinnamon
½ teaspoon ground ginger
¼ teaspoon ground cloves
¼ teaspoon salt
½ cup firmly packed brown sugar
¼ cup stick margarine, softened
2 tablespoons molasses
1 large egg white
¼ cup granulated sugar

Combine first 6 ingredients in a bowl, and stir well. Set aside.

Place brown sugar and next 3 ingredients in a food processor bowl, and process until blended. Add dry ingredients to processor bowl, and process until blended, scraping sides of processor bowl once. Gently press mixture into a ball; wrap in plastic wrap. Chill 2 hours.

Preheat oven to 375°. Shape dough into 40 (¾-inch) balls. Place granulated sugar in a bowl. Dip balls in cold water; shake to remove excess moisture. Roll wet balls in sugar. Place 3 inches apart on a baking sheet. Bake at 375° for 10 minutes. Remove from pan; let cool on a wire rack. Yield: 40 cookies (serving size: 1 cookie).

CALORIES 40 (27% from fat); PROTEIN 0.5g; FAT 1.2g (sat 0.2g, mono 0.5g, poly 0.4g); CARB 6.9g; FIBER 0.1g; CHOL 0mg; IRON 0.3mg; SODIUM 62mg; CALC 5mg

ALMOND CRÈME CARAMEL

Trick: To caramelize sugar, place the pan over medium heat, and cook six minutes or until the sugar is golden. Be sure to shake the pan occasionally.

ALMOND CRÈME CARAMEL

½ cup sugar
4 large eggs
1 teaspoon vanilla extract
½ teaspoon almond extract
1 (14-ounce) can fat-free sweetened condensed milk
1 (12-ounce) can evaporated skim milk
¼ cup coarsely chopped almonds

Preheat oven to 350°.

Pour sugar into a 9-inch round cake pan. Place cake pan over medium heat. Cook 6 minutes or until sugar is dissolved and golden, shaking cake pan occasionally with tongs. Immediately remove from heat; set aside.

Place eggs in a medium bowl; stir with a whisk until foamy. Add extracts and milks; stir with a whisk. Stir in ¼ cup almonds. Pour mixture into prepared cake pan; cover with aluminum foil, and place in a large shallow roasting pan. Place roasting pan in oven; add water to roasting pan to a depth of 1 inch. Bake at 350° for 55 minutes or until a knife inserted in center comes out clean.

Remove cake pan from water; place on a wire rack. Remove aluminum foil. Let custard cool in cake pan 30 minutes. Loosen edges with a knife or rubber spatula. Place a serving plate upside down on top of cake pan; invert custard onto plate, allowing syrup to drizzle over custard. Sprinkle with additional chopped almonds, if desired. Yield: 9 servings.

CALORIES 253 (15% from fat); PROTEIN 9.8g; FAT 4.3g (sat 0.9g, mono 2.1g, poly 0.7g); CARB 43.1g; FIBER 0.4g; CHOL 100mg; IRON 0.6mg; SODIUM 118mg; CALC 131mg

ORANGE SOUFFLÉ

Vegetable cooking spray
1 tablespoon sugar
3 tablespoons all-purpose flour
¾ cup 2% low-fat milk
¼ cup sugar
1 teaspoon grated orange rind
¼ cup fresh orange juice
5 large egg whites
¼ teaspoon cream of tartar
Dash of salt
2 tablespoons sugar
1 teaspoon powdered sugar

Preheat oven to 375°.

Coat a 1½-quart soufflé dish with cooking spray; sprinkle with 1 tablespoon sugar. Set aside.

Place flour in a small saucepan. Gradually add milk, stirring with a whisk until blended. Add ¼ cup sugar and rind; stir well. Bring to a boil over medium heat; cook 1 minute or until thickened, stirring constantly. Stir in juice; set aside.

Beat egg whites, cream of tartar, and salt at high speed of an electric mixer until soft peaks form. Gradually add 2 tablespoons sugar, 1 tablespoon at a time, beating until stiff peaks form. Gently fold one-fourth egg white mixture into orange mixture; gently fold in remaining egg white mixture. Spoon mixture into prepared soufflé dish.

Bake soufflé at 375° for 40 minutes or until puffy and set. Sprinkle with powdered sugar. Serve immediately. Yield: 4 servings.

CALORIES 160 (6% from fat); PROTEIN 6.4g; FAT 1.1g (sat 0.6g, mono 0.3g, poly 0.1g); CARB 31.5g; FIBER 0.2g; CHOL 4mg; IRON 0.3mg; SODIUM 96mg; CALC 62mg

ORANGE SOUFFLÉ

Trick: To make your soufflé rise higher, beat egg whites at room temperature (do not overbeat). Lift beaters from bowl to see if the peaks hold their shape.

For Goodness Steak

When you need something special that requires little fuss (like when your spouse invites the boss to dinner), filet mignon is the answer.

SHOPPING LIST

2 pounds Yukon gold or Finnish potatoes

1 pound green beans

5 garlic cloves

1 lemon

4 pears

dried green peppercorns

black peppercorns

cinnamon sticks

1 can beef broth

brown sugar

honey

4 tenderloin steaks

skim milk

½ cup fat-free sour cream

brandy

vermouth

1½ cups dry red wine

vanilla extract

MENU

PAN-BROILED FILET MIGNONS

GARLIC-POTATO MASH

Steamed green beans

POACHED PEARS WITH SPICED-WINE SYRUP

PAN-BROILED FILET MIGNONS

4 (4-ounce) beef tenderloin steaks (1 inch thick)
3 tablespoons dried green peppercorns
3 tablespoons black peppercorns
½ cup dry vermouth
½ cup beef broth
½ cup brandy

Trim fat from steaks. Firmly press peppercorns into steaks. Place a medium nonstick skillet over medium-high heat until hot. Add steaks; cook 1 minute on each side or until browned. Cook over medium-low heat 4 minutes on each side or to desired degree of doneness. Place steaks on a serving platter. Set aside; keep warm.

Add vermouth and broth to skillet; bring to a boil. Cook 4 minutes or until reduced by half, scraping up brown bits in bottom of skillet. Add brandy. Bring to a boil, and cook 4 minutes or until reduced by half. Serve steaks with sauce. Yield: 4 servings (serving size: 1 steak and ¼ cup sauce).

CALORIES 182 (37% from fat); PROTEIN 24.9g; FAT 7.4g (sat 3g, mono 2.8g, poly 0.4g); CARB 1.9g; FIBER 0g; CHOL 76mg; IRON 3.3mg; SODIUM 264mg; CALC 9mg

GARLIC-POTATO MASH

Yukon gold and Finnish potatoes have such a rich, creamy texture, you'll think they've already been buttered.

2 pounds peeled Yukon gold or Finnish potatoes, cut into 1-inch pieces
5 garlic cloves
¼ cup skim milk
½ cup fat-free sour cream
½ teaspoon salt
⅛ teaspoon white pepper

Place potato and garlic in a saucepan. Cover with water; bring to a boil. Reduce heat, and simmer 15 minutes or until tender; drain. Return potato and garlic to pan. Mash to desired consistency.

Heat milk and sour cream in a small saucepan over low heat until warm, stirring constantly. Add milk mixture, salt, and pepper to potato mixture, stirring until well-blended. Yield: 4 servings (serving size: 1 cup).

CALORIES 163 (2% from fat); PROTEIN 8.6g; FAT 0.3g (sat 0g, mono 0g, poly 0g); CARB 32.2g; FIBER 4.1g; CHOL 0mg; IRON 7.4mg; SODIUM 344mg; CALC 94mg

POACHED PEARS WITH SPICED-WINE SYRUP

1½ cups dry red wine
1 cup water
½ cup firmly packed dark brown sugar
1 (3-inch) cinnamon stick
10 black peppercorns
3 tablespoons honey
1 teaspoon vanilla extract
1 tablespoon fresh lemon juice
4 firm, ripe Bartlett or Bosc pears

Combine first 8 ingredients in a 3-quart microwave-safe dish; microwave at HIGH 5 minutes or until mixture boils.

Peel and core pears, leaving stems intact. Slice about ¼ inch from base of each pear so it will sit flat. Add pears to poaching liquid; cover and microwave at HIGH 10 minutes or until tender. Let cool in dish 5 minutes. Remove pears with a slotted spoon; set aside.

Microwave liquid at HIGH 5 minutes or until reduced to 1 cup. Place each pear in a shallow bowl. Spoon ¼ cup sauce over each pear. Yield: 4 servings.

Note: Look for pears that have long stems for a dramatic presentation. To core a pear, hold it in your left hand. Using a melon baller, make three or four cuts into pear from the bottom.

CALORIES 257 (3% from fat); PROTEIN 0.9g; FAT 0.8g (sat 0.1g, mono 0.1g, poly 0.2g); CARB 66g; FIBER 2.7g; CHOL 0mg; IRON 1.4mg; SODIUM 18mg;CALC50mg

---

PUTTING IT TOGETHER

1. Prepare Poached Pears with Spiced-Wine Syrup.
2. Start Garlic-Potato Mash, cooking potatoes until tender.
3. While potatoes cook, prepare Pan-Broiled Filet Mignons.
4. Steam green beans in a steamer basket until crisp-tender.
5. Mash potatoes, and stir in milk.

The Beans, Greens, and Pasta Scene

These Mediterranean-inspired one-dish meals are more than just tasty: Studies show that they more than satisfy the latest nutritional requirements.

Once upon a time, people ate for sustenance and pleasure. No one worried about how much fat and cholesterol food might contain. Although that may sound like a fairy tale in these health-conscious times, that's the way it was—and still is in countries like Italy, where recipes are handed down from generation to generation.

Before scientific studies identified disease-fighting chemicals and other beneficial ingredients in food, Mediterranean families routinely dished up entrées, soups, and salads based on a simple, flavorful, and filling trio of basic ingredients: beans, greens, and pasta—sometimes called the "Mediterranean trinity."

Today, this meatless, peasant-style cuisine is touted by many nutrition experts. Reliant on greens, vegetables, beans, and olive oil, the recipes we've created for you are low in fat, high in fiber, and rich in nutrients. In addition, they're economical, extremely simple to make, and well-suited to one-dish preparation.

Research shows that greens and beans contain substances that may help protect against all kinds of chronic diseases ranging from heart disease to cancer. For instance, we've included a recipe that calls for arugula, a cruciferous vegetable that contains cancer-blocking compounds called indoles. And the recipes call for canned dried beans, which are rich in the B vitamin folic acid, a nutrient heralded for its potential role in warding off heart disease.

THREE-GREENS SALAD WITH GARBANZOS

4 cups cooked farfalle (about 3½ cups uncooked bow tie pasta)
4 cups trimmed arugula
2 cups thinly sliced radicchio
2 medium heads Belgian endive, quartered and thinly sliced lengthwise
1 (19-ounce) can chickpeas (garbanzo beans), drained
¼ cup plus 2 tablespoons balsamic vinegar
¼ cup low-salt chicken broth
2 tablespoons extra-virgin olive oil
¼ cup finely chopped fresh flat-leaf parsley
2 ounces shaved fresh Parmesan cheese

Combine first 5 ingredients in a large bowl; toss well. Combine vinegar, broth, and oil; stir well with a whisk. Pour over pasta mixture; toss gently to coat. Sprinkle with parsley and cheese. Yield: 6 servings (serving size: 2 cups).

CALORIES 290 (27% from fat); PROTEIN 12g; FAT 8.6g (sat 2.3g, mono 4.3g, poly 1g); CARB 41.7g; FIBER 5.1g; CHOL 6mg; IRON 2.4mg; SODIUM 339mg; CALC 203mg

Cavatappi with Spinach, Beans, and Asiago Cheese

Warm pasta slightly wilts the spinach and softens the cheese during tossing.

8 cups chopped spinach leaves
4 cups hot cooked cavatappi (about 6 ounces uncooked spiral-shaped pasta)
2 tablespoons olive oil
¼ teaspoon salt
¼ teaspoon pepper
1 (19-ounce) can cannellini beans or other white beans, drained
2 garlic cloves, crushed
½ cup (2 ounces) shredded Asiago or Parmesan cheese
Freshly ground black pepper (optional)

Combine all ingredients in a large bowl, and toss well. Sprinkle with freshly ground black pepper, if desired. Yield: 4 servings (serving size: 2 cups).

CALORIES 401 (27% from fat); PROTEIN 18.8g; FAT 12g (sat 3.4g, mono 6.2g, poly 1.2g); CARB 54.7g; FIBER 6.7g; CHOL 10mg; IRON 6.4mg; SODIUM 464mg; CALC 306mg

Penne with Garbanzos, Escarole, and Plum Tomatoes

1 tablespoon olive oil
3 garlic cloves, crushed
8 cups coarsely chopped escarole
2 cups seeded, diced plum tomatoes
½ cup chopped fresh basil
2 tablespoons chopped fresh sage
¼ teaspoon salt
¼ teaspoon pepper
1 (15-ounce) can chickpeas (garbanzo beans), drained
4 cups cooked penne (about 2½ cups uncooked tubular-shaped pasta)
¼ cup red wine vinegar

Heat oil in a skillet over medium heat. Add garlic; sauté 1 minute. Add escarole; sauté 4 minutes. Add tomatoes and next 5 ingredients; cook 2 minutes, stirring occasionally. Stir in pasta and vinegar; cook 2 minutes or until heated. Yield: 4 servings (serving size: 2 cups).

CALORIES 349 (15% from fat); PROTEIN 12.3g; FAT 5.7g (sat 0.8g, mono 2.9g, poly 1.3g); CARB 63.7g; FIBER 8.9g; CHOL 0mg; IRON 4.4mg; SODIUM 391mg; CALC 118mg

---

MENU SUGGESTION
RAVIOLI WITH HERB-TOMATO SAUCE
Garden salad
*Amaretti-stuffed peaches**
*Boil ½ cup each of sugar and Chardonnay 5 minutes. Fill 10 canned unsweetened peach halves with an amaretti cookie; drizzle with wine syrup.

Ravioli with Herb-Tomato Sauce

A purée of beans and escarole forms the basis for a lively filling for the ravioli.

4 cups torn escarole
¼ cup finely grated fresh Parmesan cheese
1½ teaspoons minced fresh rosemary
⅛ teaspoon salt
⅛ teaspoon pepper
1 garlic clove, chopped
1 (15-ounce) can cannellini beans or other white beans, drained
40 won ton wrappers
Herb-Tomato Sauce
Fresh rosemary sprigs (optional)

Place first 7 ingredients in a food processor, and process until smooth, scraping sides of processor bowl occasionally.

Working with 1 won ton wrapper at a time (cover remaining wrappers with a damp towel to keep them from drying out), spoon about 1 tablespoon bean mixture into center of wrapper. Moisten edges of wrapper with water; place another wrapper over filling. Pinch 4 edges together to seal. Repeat with remaining won ton wrappers and bean mixture. Place ravioli on a baking sheet; let stand 30 minutes.

Cook ravioli in boiling water 2 minutes or until tender; drain well. Spoon Herb-Tomato Sauce over ravioli. Garnish with rosemary sprigs, if

---

Mediterranean Medicine

A big advantage to these recipes is that virtually every ingredient, no matter how minor, is good for you. Here are just some of the reasons why.

• **GREENS** • Dark leafy greens (the darker the better) such as spinach, kale, and escarole contain rich amounts of carotenoids like beta carotene, lutein, and zeaxanthin. Powerful antioxidants, these compounds may help protect against various forms of cancer and heart disease, and they may even prevent damage to the eyes. Most greens are also rich in calcium, iron, and the B vitamin folic acid, which can reduce the risk of neural-tube birth defects and may help cut the risks of heart disease and stroke.

• **BEANS** • Beans such as red kidney beans, garbanzos, and cannellini beans are rich in folic acid and iron. They are also high in protein, making them good low-fat, low-cholesterol alternatives to meat. More important, they're high in fiber—most of which is water-soluble and adept at lowering blood cholesterol levels.

• **GARLIC** • After pooling the results of five studies, researchers at New York Medical College discovered that as little as one-half to one clove of garlic per day could be enough to lower blood cholesterol levels an average of 9%.

• **OLIVE OIL** • For thousands of years, olive oil has been the primary fat used in Mediterranean cooking. It's high in monounsaturated fats, the kind of fats some studies suggest may help reduce the risk of atherosclerosis.

desired. Yield: 5 servings (serving size: 4 ravioli and 6 tablespoons Herb-Tomato Sauce).

CALORIES 326 (16% from fat); PROTEIN 13.3g; FAT 5.9g (sat 1.6g, mono 2.6g, poly 0.9g); CARB 54.9g; FIBER 1.8g; CHOL 10mg; IRON 5.1mg; SODIUM 784mg; CALC 194mg

Herb-Tomato Sauce:

-   1   tablespoon olive oil
-   1   large garlic clove, minced
-   2   tablespoons finely chopped fresh oregano
-   2   tablespoons finely chopped fresh thyme
-   2   tablespoons finely chopped fresh flat-leaf parsley
-   2   tablespoons finely chopped fresh basil
-   ¼   teaspoon pepper
-   1   (28-ounce) can Italian-style tomatoes, undrained and chopped

Heat oil in a large saucepan over medium heat until hot. Add garlic, and sauté 1 minute. Add oregano and remaining ingredients. Bring to a simmer over medium-high heat; cook 25 minutes or until reduced to 2 cups. Yield: 2 cups.

Note: Sauce can be made ahead and kept covered in refrigerator up to 4 days.

CALORIES 61 (46% from fat); PROTEIN 1.7g; FAT 3.1g (sat 0.5g, mono 2.1g, poly 0.4g); CARB 7.9g; FIBER 1.4g; CHOL 0mg; IRON 1.6mg; SODIUM 260mg; CALC 61mg

PASTA-AND-BEAN SOUP WITH SPINACH

A loaf of crusty peasant bread is the only accompaniment needed for this classic soup.

-   1   tablespoon olive oil
-   ½   cup chopped onion
-   3   garlic cloves, crushed
-   2   cups water
-   1½   cups cooked tubetti (about ¾ cup uncooked small tubular-shaped pasta)
-   1   teaspoon dried oregano
-   ¼   teaspoon salt
-   ¼   teaspoon pepper
-   1   (16-ounce) can tomato purée
-   1   (10½-ounce) can low-salt chicken broth
-   8   cups chopped spinach leaves
-   1   (19-ounce) can cannellini beans or other white beans, drained
-   2   tablespoons hot pepper sauce
-   2   tablespoons plus 2 teaspoons grated Parmesan cheese
-   5   lemon wedges
    Fresh oregano sprigs (optional)

Heat oil in a large Dutch oven over medium heat until hot. Add onion, and sauté 3 minutes. Add garlic, and sauté 1 minute. Add water and next 6 ingredients. Bring to a boil; reduce heat, and simmer 20 minutes. Add spinach and beans; cook 3 minutes. Stir in pepper sauce. Sprinkle with cheese. Serve with lemon wedges, and garnish with fresh oregano sprigs, if desired. Yield: 5 servings (serving size: about 1½ cups).

CALORIES 223 (20% from fat); PROTEIN 11.3g; FAT 4.9g (sat 1.1g, mono 2.4g, poly 0.6g); CARB 36.1g; FIBER 6.8g; CHOL 2mg; IRON 5.5mg; SODIUM 657mg; CALC 166mg

Sidelights

From breakfast potatoes to ratatouille, bold flavors define these vegetable sides.

HERB-ROASTED VEGETABLES

I love this dish because it's so versatile. You can work with whatever vegetables or spices you have on hand. I serve it with fish or as a main dish over rice or pasta.

—Susan Hoffman, Altamonte Springs, Florida

-   2½   cups (½-inch-thick) sliced zucchini
-   1½   cups (1-inch-square) cut red bell pepper
-   1½   cups (½-inch-thick) sliced yellow squash
-   1   cup (1-inch) cut green beans (about ¼ pound)
-   1   cup (½-inch-thick) sliced carrot
-   3   tablespoons balsamic vinegar
-   1½   tablespoons olive oil
-   ½   teaspoon dried basil
-   ½   teaspoon dried oregano
-   ½   teaspoon dried tarragon
-   ½   teaspoon dried thyme
-   ½   teaspoon dried parsley
-   ½   teaspoon dried rosemary
-   ¼   teaspoon salt
-   ¼   teaspoon pepper
-   4   garlic cloves, thinly sliced
-   2   medium onions, peeled and quartered

Preheat oven to 425°.

Place all ingredients in a 13 x 9-inch baking dish; stir well to coat.

Cover and bake at 425° for 40 minutes or until vegetables are tender. Yield: 9 servings (serving size: about ¾ cup).

CALORIES 53 (31% from fat); PROTEIN 1.7g; FAT 1.8g (sat 0.5g, mono 1.1g, poly 0.3g); CARB 8.9g; FIBER 2.3g; CHOL 0mg; IRON 1.1mg; SODIUM 74mg; CALC 33mg

RAPID RATATOUILLE

I took this recipe from my mom's collection and lightened it for my family. Although it's tasty as a side dish, I often add kielbasa to make it a meal in itself.

—Amber Barger, Sacramento, California

    5   cups sliced zucchini
 1½   cups vertically sliced onion
    1   cup green bell pepper strips
    1   teaspoon dried Italian
          seasoning
    1   (28-ounce) can whole
          tomatoes, drained and
          coarsely chopped

Combine all ingredients in a shallow 2-quart baking dish; cover and microwave at HIGH 14 minutes, stirring after 7 minutes. Yield: 6 cups (serving size: 1 cup).

CALORIES 48 (6% from fat); PROTEIN 2.5g; FAT 0.3g (sat 0.1g, mono 0g, poly 0.1g); CARB 10.7g; FIBER 1.4g; CHOL 0mg; IRON 1.4mg; SODIUM 329mg; CALC 59mg

VEGETABLE BAKE

After my daughter, Rachel, was born, I couldn't jump back into exercise immediately. So I decided to start with my diet first. This recipe provided a delicious way to eat my vegetables. My vegetarian brother-in-law loves it with vegetable pizza, but it also goes well with beef roast or chicken breasts.

—Kris D. Rial, Moyock, North Carolina

    8   small red potatoes, quartered
          (about 1 pound)
    1   medium yellow squash, cut
          into 1-inch pieces (about
          ½ pound)
    1   large sweet onion, cut into
          1-inch pieces (about 1 pound)
    2   teaspoons vegetable oil
 ¼   teaspoon garlic salt
 ¼   teaspoon pepper
 ¼   teaspoon dried parsley flakes

Preheat oven to 350°.
Pierce potato quarters with a fork; place in a 9-inch pie plate. Microwave at HIGH 8 minutes or until crisp-tender, stirring every 2 minutes.

Combine potato, squash, and remaining ingredients in a 13 x 9-inch baking dish; toss well. Bake at 350° for 35 minutes or until tender. Yield: 4 servings (serving size: 1 cup).

CALORIES 265 (9% from fat); PROTEIN 6.9g; FAT 2.7g (sat 0.4g, mono 1.7g, poly 0.4g); CARB 55.7g; FIBER 6.3g; CHOL 0mg; IRON 2.5mg; SODIUM 150mg; CALC 42mg

ZESTY ZUCCHINI CUBES

By itself, zucchini is bland but this recipe proves that it is a good flavor-carrier. I serve this dish with something plain-tasting, such as roast chicken or broiled fish.

—Roxanne Chan, Albany, California

 ¼   cup red wine vinegar
 ¼   cup dry red wine
 ¼   cup honey
    1   tablespoon chopped red onion
    1   tablespoon Worcestershire
          sauce
    1   tablespoon olive oil
 ½   teaspoon chili powder
 ½   teaspoon ground cumin
 ¼   teaspoon ground red pepper
    1   clove garlic, minced
    4   cups diced zucchini

Combine first 10 ingredients in a microwave-safe bowl, and stir well. Microwave at HIGH 2 minutes or until mixture is hot; stir in zucchini. Cover; marinate in refrigerator at least 1 hour. Drain and serve. Yield: 8 servings (serving size: ½ cup).

CALORIES 61 (27% from fat); PROTEIN 0.9g; FAT 1.8g (sat 0.3g, mono 1.3g, poly 0.2g); CARB 11.7g; FIBER 0.4g; CHOL 0mg; IRON 0.5mg; SODIUM 23mg; CALC 15mg

INDIAN CAULIFLOWER

Working at the National Cancer Institute, I am inundated with info about a healthy diet's impact on preventing cancer. So I try lots of recipes like this one: light but flavorful.

—Susan L. Schwarz, Kensington, Maryland

    1   tablespoon light butter
    1   teaspoon ground coriander
 ½   teaspoon curry powder
 ¼   teaspoon ground ginger
 ½   cup finely chopped onion
 ¼   cup ketchup
    8   cups cauliflower florets
Vegetable cooking spray

Combine first 4 ingredients in a microwave-safe dish; microwave butter mixture at HIGH 30 seconds. Stir in onion and ketchup; microwave onion mixture at HIGH 1 minute.

Place cauliflower florets in a 2-quart casserole coated with cooking spray. Spoon onion mixture over cauliflower; toss well. Cover and microwave at HIGH 9 minutes, turning after 4 minutes. Yield: 6 servings (serving size: 1 cup).

CALORIES 61 (22% from fat); PROTEIN 3.1g; FAT 1.5g (sat 1.1g, mono 0.1g, poly 0.2g); CARB 11.2g; FIBER 3.7g; CHOL 3mg; IRON 0.8mg; SODIUM 171mg; CALC 37mg

CHEDDAR POTATOES AND ONIONS

Vidalia onions add the best flavor in this recipe, but Walla Wallas also work nicely. I serve this easy-to-make dish with beef, poultry, or fish.

—Jane Kay, Milwaukee, Wisconsin

    8   small red potatoes (about 1
          pound)
    1   medium Vidalia or other sweet
          onion, cut into ¼-inch-thick
          wedges
Vegetable cooking spray
 ¾   teaspoon lemon pepper
 ½   teaspoon salt
 ½   cup (2 ounces) shredded
          Cheddar cheese

Preheat oven to 350°.

Pierce potatoes with a fork; arrange on paper towels in microwave oven. Microwave at HIGH for 5 to 6 minutes, turning once. Let stand 1 minute. Cut potatoes lengthwise into quarters.

Place potatoes and onion wedges in an 8-inch square baking pan coated with cooking spray. Lightly coat tops of vegetables with cooking spray, and sprinkle evenly with lemon pepper and salt. Bake at 350° for 30 minutes. Sprinkle with cheese; cook an additional 3 minutes or until cheese melts. Yield: 4 servings (serving size: 1 cup).

CALORIES 157 (29% from fat); PROTEIN 6.5g; FAT 5g (sat 3g, mono 1.3g, poly 0.2g); CARB 22.3g; FIBER 2.8g; CHOL 15mg; IRON 1.8mg; SODIUM 390mg; CALC 126mg

SPICY HASH BROWNS

Our favorite meal is Sunday breakfast. For five years, I've made pancakes and my hash browns every Sunday morning. The hash browns are so tasty, they're good with almost anything from meatballs to steak. But they're best with my Sunday-morning pancakes.

—Galit Stevens, Raleigh, North Carolina

2 tablespoons olive oil
1 teaspoon paprika
¾ teaspoon chili powder
½ teaspoon salt
¼ teaspoon ground red pepper
⅛ teaspoon black pepper
6½ cups diced baking potato (about 2½ pounds)
Vegetable cooking spray

Preheat oven to 400°.

Combine first 6 ingredients in a large bowl, and stir well. Add potatoes, and stir well to coat. Place potatoes in a single layer on a baking sheet coated with cooking spray. Bake at 400° for 30 minutes or until potatoes are browned. Yield: 5 servings (serving size: about 1 cup).

CALORIES 299 (18% from fat); PROTEIN 5.1g; FAT 5.9g (sat 0.8g, mono 4g, poly 0.6g); CARB 57.7g; FIBER 4.4g; CHOL 0mg; IRON 3.3mg; SODIUM 257mg; CALC 25mg

MIXED GREENS WITH VINEGAR SALAD DRESSING

I love homemade salad dressings but they all require oil, so I decided to create a healthier dressing. The tartness of the vinegar blends well with salad greens, but I've also found it tastes great on a fruit salad.

—Patricia Hobbs Hendry, San Clemente, California

¼ cup white vinegar
2 tablespoons sugar
1 tablespoon ketchup
¼ teaspoon garlic salt
¼ teaspoon pepper
¼ teaspoon Worcestershire sauce
8 cups torn salad greens

Combine first 6 ingredients in a bowl; stir well. Serve over salad greens. Yield: 8 servings (serving size: 1 cup greens and 1 tablespoon dressing).

CALORIES 23 (4% from fat); PROTEIN 0.8g; FAT 0.1g (sat 0g, mono 0g, poly 0.1g); CARB 5.4g; FIBER 0.4g; CHOL 0mg; IRON 0.2mg; SODIUM 92mg; CALC 1mg

TECHNIQUE

Stressless Strudels

With a few simple pointers and some phyllo dough, you ,too, can make strudels like the masters.

You really can make stressless strudels in a relatively short amount of time. How? First, begin with the dough. We switched the traditional butter-rich dough with phyllo dough that comes ready-made in the supermarket and has the delicate texture necessary for crisp, flaky strudels.

Strudels are usually brushed with butter between layers, but these were coated with a butter-flavored vegetable cooking spray that drastically cuts the fat and calories. And most important: We kept the filling, folding, and procedures simple and consistent, so once you have them down, putting the recipes together is a breeze.

APPLE STRUDEL

This classic dessert tastes best served warm from the oven.

⅓ cup raisins
3 tablespoons amaretto (almond-flavored liqueur)
3 cups peeled, coarsely chopped Granny Smith apple (about 1 pound)
⅓ cup sugar
3 tablespoons all-purpose flour
¼ teaspoon ground cinnamon
8 sheets frozen phyllo dough, thawed
Butter-flavored vegetable cooking spray
2 cups vanilla low-fat ice cream

Combine raisins and amaretto in a bowl. Microwave at HIGH 1½ minutes; drain well.

Combine raisins, apple, sugar, flour, and cinnamon in a bowl. Toss well, and set aside.

Place 1 phyllo sheet on work surface (cover remaining dough to keep from drying); lightly coat with cooking spray. Working with 1 phyllo sheet at a time, coat remaining 7 phyllo sheets with cooking spray, placing one on top of the other. Place a sheet of plastic wrap over phyllo, pressing gently to seal sheets together; discard plastic wrap.

Spoon apple mixture along 1 long edge of phyllo, leaving a 2-inch border. Fold over the short edges of phyllo to cover 2 inches of apple mixture on each end. Starting at long edge with 2-inch border, roll up phyllo jelly-roll fashion. (Do not roll tightly, or strudel may split.) Place strudel, seam side down, on a jelly-roll pan coated with cooking spray. Score diagonal slits into top of strudel using a sharp knife. Lightly coat strudel with cooking spray.

Bake strudel at 350° for 35 minutes or until golden. Serve warm with ice cream. Yield: 8 servings (serving size: 1 slice and ¼ cup ice cream).

CALORIES 211 (15% from fat); PROTEIN 3.1g; FAT 3.6g (sat 1.2g, mono 0.9g, poly 1.2g); CARB 40.3g; FIBER 1.5g; CHOL 5mg; IRON 0.9mg; SODIUM 121mg; CALC 53mg

1. Working with one phyllo sheet at a time, coat each sheet with cooking spray, and place one on top of the other.

2. Place a sheet of plastic wrap over phyllo, pressing gently to seal sheets together. Discard plastic wrap.

3. Spoon filling mixture along one long edge of phyllo sheet, leaving a two-inch border. Fold over short edges of phyllo to cover 2 inches of filling on each end.

4. Roll phyllo in a jelly-roll fashion. Do not roll too tightly, or the strudel may split.

5. Using a knife, cut several diagonal slits into top.

ROAST CHICKEN-AND-SHIITAKE STRUDEL

If you can't find shiitake mushrooms, substitute sliced button mushrooms.

- 1 slice bacon
- 4 cups thinly sliced shiitake mushroom caps (about ½ pound mushrooms)
- 1 tablespoon all-purpose flour
- ½ cup dry sherry
- 2 tablespoons low-sodium Worcestershire sauce
- 3 cups skinned, boned, shredded roasted chicken breast
- ¼ teaspoon pepper
- ¼ cup thinly sliced green onions
- 8 sheets frozen phyllo dough, thawed
- Butter-flavored vegetable cooking spray

Preheat oven to 350°.

Cook bacon in a large nonstick skillet over medium-high heat until crisp. Remove bacon from skillet. Crumble; set aside. Add mushrooms to bacon fat in skillet; sauté 2 minutes. Stir in flour; cook 1 minute. Add sherry and Worcestershire sauce; bring to a boil, and cook 1 minute or until thick and bubbly. Stir in crumbled bacon, chicken, and pepper; cook until thoroughly heated. Stir in onions, and set aside.

Place 1 phyllo sheet on work surface (cover remaining dough to keep from drying); lightly coat with cooking spray. Working with 1 phyllo sheet at a time, coat remaining 7 phyllo sheets with cooking spray, placing one on top of the other. Place a sheet of plastic wrap over phyllo, pressing gently to seal sheets together; discard plastic wrap.

Spoon chicken mixture along 1 long edge of phyllo, leaving a 2-inch border. Fold over the short edges of phyllo to cover 2 inches of chicken mixture on each end.

Starting at long edge with 2-inch border, roll up jelly-roll fashion. (Do not roll tightly, or strudel may split.) Place strudel, seam side down, on a jelly-roll pan coated with cooking spray. Score diagonal slits into top of strudel using a sharp knife. Lightly coat strudel with cooking spray.

Bake at 350° for 30 minutes or until golden. Yield: 8 servings.

CALORIES 172 (25% from fat); PROTEIN 17.3g; FAT 4.7g (sat 1.1g, mono 1.4g, poly 1.7g); CARB 14g; FIBER 0.6g; CHOL 42mg; IRON 1.7mg; SODIUM 167mg; CALC 15mg

---

MENU SUGGESTION

MEDITERRANEAN LAMB STRUDEL

*Pan-sautéed squash**

Garlic-sautéed Swiss chard with pine nuts

*Sauté ⅓ cup diced celery, ¼ cup diced onion, and 1 minced garlic clove in olive oil. Add 1 peeled, sliced, and steamed butternut squash. Toss with capers, olives, chopped parsley, and grated Parmesan cheese.

MEDITERRANEAN LAMB STRUDEL

- ¾ **pound ground lean lamb**
- ½ **cup chopped onion**
- ⅔ **cup water**
- ½ **cup golden raisins**
- ¾ **teaspoon beef-flavored bouillon granules**
- ⅛ **teaspoon salt**
- ⅛ **teaspoon ground cinnamon**
- ⅛ **teaspoon ground nutmeg**
- ⅛ **teaspoon ground cumin**
- ⅛ **teaspoon ground red pepper**
- ⅛ **teaspoon black pepper**
- ½ **cup uncooked couscous**
- 8 **sheets frozen phyllo dough, thawed**
- **Butter-flavored vegetable cooking spray**
- ½ **cup mango chutney**

Preheat oven to 350°.

Combine lamb and onion in a large nonstick skillet; cook over medium-high heat 5 minutes or until lamb is browned and onion is tender. Drain well. Wipe skillet clean with a paper towel; return lamb to skillet. Add water and next 8 ingredients; bring to a boil. Cover, reduce heat, and simmer 5 minutes. Stir in couscous; cover, remove from heat, and let stand 5 minutes. Cool to room temperature.

Place 1 phyllo sheet on work surface (cover remaining dough to keep from drying); lightly coat with cooking spray. Working with 1 phyllo sheet at a time, coat remaining 7 phyllo sheets with cooking spray, placing one on top of the other. Place a sheet of plastic wrap over phyllo, pressing gently to seal sheets together; discard plastic wrap.

Spoon lamb mixture along 1 long edge of phyllo, leaving a 2-inch border. Carefully indent the lamb mixture with the back of a small spoon; fill evenly with chutney. Fold over the short edges of phyllo to cover 2 inches of lamb mixture on each end.

Starting at long edge with 2-inch border, roll up jelly-roll fashion. (Do not roll tightly, or strudel may split.) Place strudel, seam side down, on a jelly-roll pan coated with cooking spray. Score diagonal slits into top of strudel using a sharp knife. Lightly coat strudel with cooking spray. Bake at 350° for 30 minutes or until golden. Let cool to room temperature. Yield: 8 servings.

CALORIES 243 (20% from fat); PROTEIN 12.8g; FAT 5.3g (sat 1.4g, mono 1.8g, poly 1.4g); CARB 36.4g; FIBER 1.1g; CHOL 30mg; IRON 1.9mg; SODIUM 282mg; CALC 22mg

---

HEARTY SALMON STRUDEL WITH DILL

- 1 **(1-pound) salmon fillet (about 1 inch thick), skinned**
- **Butter-flavored vegetable cooking spray**
- ¼ **teaspoon salt**
- ¼ **teaspoon garlic powder**
- ¼ **teaspoon freshly ground pepper**
- 1½ **cups peeled, (½-inch) cubed red potato**
- ¾ **cup evaporated skim milk**
- ½ **cup thinly sliced leek**
- 2 **teaspoons water**
- ½ **teaspoon cornstarch**
- 1 **teaspoon dried dillweed**
- 3 **tablespoons grated Parmesan cheese**
- 8 **sheets frozen phyllo dough, thawed**

Place salmon fillet on a broiler pan coated with cooking spray. Sprinkle salt, garlic powder, and pepper evenly over fillet. Broil 10 minutes or until fish flakes easily when tested with a fork. Cut fillet into small chunks; set aside.

Preheat oven to 350°.

Combine potato, milk, and leek in a small saucepan; bring to a boil. Cover, reduce heat, and simmer 10 minutes or until potato is tender. Combine water and cornstarch in a small bowl. Stir well; add to pan. Bring to a boil; cook 1 minute, stirring constantly. Gently stir in fish chunks, dillweed, and cheese. Set aside.

Place 1 phyllo sheet on work surface (cover remaining dough to keep from drying); lightly coat with cooking spray. Working with 1 phyllo sheet at a time, coat remaining 7 phyllo sheets with cooking spray, placing one on top of the other. Place a sheet of plastic wrap over phyllo, pressing gently to seal sheets together; discard plastic wrap.

Spoon potato mixture along 1 long edge of phyllo, leaving a 2-inch border. Fold over the short edges of phyllo to cover 2 inches of potato mixture on each end.

Starting at long edge with 2-inch border, roll up jelly-roll fashion. (Do not roll tightly, or strudel may split.) Place strudel, seam side down, on a jelly-roll pan coated with cooking spray. Score diagonal slits into top of strudel using a sharp knife. Lightly coat strudel with cooking spray.

Bake strudel at 350° for 30 minutes or until golden. Serve warm. Yield: 8 servings.

CALORIES 215 (31% from fat); PROTEIN 16.8g; FAT 7.5g (sat 1.5g, mono 3g, poly 2.2g); CARB 19.1g; FIBER 0.6g; CHOL 41mg; IRON 1.4mg; SODIUM 260mg; CALC 109mg

CARAMELIZED ONION, FIG, AND BLUE CHEESE STRUDEL

This strudel got the highest possible rating for taste in our Test Kitchens. You can serve it with roasted pork or lamb.

    1   cup diced dried figs (about 10
        figs)
    ½   cup raisins
    ½   cup apricot or peach nectar
    ⅓   cup honey
        Butter-flavored vegetable cooking
        spray
    2   cups coarsely chopped
        sweet onion
    2   tablespoons balsamic vinegar
    4   ounces crumbled blue cheese
    8   sheets frozen phyllo dough,
        thawed
    2   teaspoons powdered sugar

Preheat oven to 350°.

Combine first 4 ingredients in a small saucepan. Bring to a boil, and cook 5 minutes. Remove from heat; cover and let stand 30 minutes.

Coat a medium nonstick skillet with cooking spray; place over medium-high heat until hot. Add onion and vinegar; cook 20 minutes or until deep golden, stirring frequently. Remove from heat; stir in fig mixture and cheese. Set aside.

Place 1 phyllo sheet on work surface (cover remaining dough to keep from drying); lightly coat with cooking spray. Working with 1 phyllo sheet at a time, coat remaining 7 phyllo sheets with cooking spray, placing one on top of the other. Place a sheet of plastic wrap over phyllo, pressing gently to seal sheets together; discard plastic wrap.

Spoon onion mixture along 1 long edge of phyllo, leaving a 2-inch border. Fold over the short edges of phyllo to cover 2 inches of onion mixture on each end.

Starting at long edge with 2-inch border, roll up jelly-roll fashion. (Do not roll tightly, or strudel may split.) Place strudel, seam side down, on a jelly-roll pan coated with cooking spray. Score diagonal slits into top of strudel using a sharp knife. Lightly coat strudel with cooking spray.

Bake at 350° for 30 minutes or until golden. Sprinkle with powdered sugar. Serve warm. Yield: 8 servings.

CALORIES 272 (21% from fat); PROTEIN 6g; FAT 6.4g (sat 3g, mono 1.6g, poly 1.4g); CARB 51g; FIBER 5.3g; CHOL 11mg; IRON 1.6mg; SODIUM 296mg; CALC 125mg

SPANAKOPITA

    ¼   cup water
    1   (10-ounce) package frozen
        chopped spinach
    1   ounce chopped sun-dried
        tomatoes, packed without
        oil (about 12)
    2   teaspoons olive oil
    ½   cup chopped onion
    2   garlic cloves, minced
    2   cups cooked basmati or long-
        grain rice (cooked without
        salt or fat)
    1   tablespoon minced fresh
        oregano or 1 teaspoon dried
        oregano
    ¼   teaspoon freshly ground
        pepper
    ⅛   teaspoon salt
    4   ounces feta cheese, crumbled
    8   sheets frozen phyllo dough,
        thawed
        Butter-flavored vegetable cooking
        spray

Preheat oven to 350°.

Combine first 3 ingredients in a medium saucepan; bring to a boil. Cover, reduce heat to medium, and cook 10 minutes. Place spinach mixture in a colander, pressing with the back of a spoon until barely moist. Set aside.

Heat oil in pan over medium-high heat until hot. Add onion and garlic; sauté 3 minutes. Remove from heat. Add spinach mixture, rice, and next 4 ingredients, stirring until well-blended. Set aside.

Place 1 phyllo sheet on work surface (cover remaining dough to keep from drying); lightly coat with cooking spray. Working with 1 phyllo sheet at a time, coat the remaining 7 phyllo sheets with cooking spray, placing one on top of the other. Place a sheet of plastic wrap over phyllo, pressing gently to seal sheets together; discard plastic wrap.

Spoon spinach mixture along 1 long edge of phyllo, leaving a 2-inch border. Fold over the short edges of phyllo to cover 2 inches of spinach mixture on each end.

Starting at long edge with 2-inch border, roll up jelly-roll fashion. (Do not roll tightly, or strudel may split.) Place strudel, seam side down, on a jelly-roll pan coated with cooking spray. Score diagonal slits into top of strudel using a sharp knife. Lightly coat strudel with cooking spray.

Bake strudel at 350° for 35 minutes or until golden. Serve warm. Yield: 8 servings.

CALORIES 192 (30% from fat); PROTEIN 6.2g; FAT 6.5g (sat 2.6g, mono 1.9g, poly 1.4g); CARB 27.9g; FIBER 1.7g; CHOL 13mg; IRON 2.2mg; SODIUM 387mg; CALC 133mg

---

SECRETS FOR STRUDEL SUCCESS

Phyllo dough is typically found with the frozen foods in the grocery store, though a specialty market may carry it unfrozen. If the phyllo has been frozen, thaw it in the refrigerator for two days before you plan to use it.

Set up an assembly line as you prepare to coat, layer, fill, and fold the strudel. A little organization goes a long way with phyllo recipes.

Don't be in a hurry. Handle phyllo sheets slowly and gently. The pastry is thin and delicate; rough handling will cause breaks or tears.

Phyllo dries out easily. Always keep it covered with a damp cloth and plastic wrap when you're not working with it.

The Big Enchilada

Big in flavor, yet low in fat and calories, this Chicken Enchilada Casserole is a simple, warming entrée.

Because enchiladas are among the most popular Mexican dishes, it's no surprise they have come to mean importance, as in "the Big Enchilada." With their rich fillings of gooey cheese and meat, though, enchiladas can be "big" in other ways, too—like around the waist. Here, we turn enchiladas into an easy-to-make Chicken Enchilada Casserole and take out the "big." We eliminate the messy rolling by layering the ingredients and a rich white sauce in a casserole dish. We've cut the fat by an astonishing two-thirds and the cholesterol by more than half with a few simple reductions, such as decreasing the olives and cheese and lightening the sauce—all this while keeping its spicy flavor and creamy texture. This casserole also can be made ahead then frozen, and because it's basically a one-dish meal, just serve it with a salad.

BEFORE & AFTER	
SERVING SIZE	
1 wedge	
CALORIES	
535	309
FAT	
30.1g	9.7g
PERCENT OF TOTAL CALORIES	
51%	28%
CHOLESTEROL	
145mg	63mg
SODIUM	
1,235mg	753mg

CHICKEN ENCHILADA CASSEROLE

Vegetable cooking spray
1¼ pounds skinned, boned chicken breast
1½ cups chopped onion
4 garlic cloves, minced
½ cup beer
¼ to ½ teaspoon ground red pepper
1 (28-ounce) can whole tomatoes, drained and chopped
½ cup thinly sliced green onions
1 (2¼-ounce) can sliced ripe olives, drained
2 (4.5-ounce) cans chopped green chiles, drained
¼ cup plus 1 tablespoon all-purpose flour
½ teaspoon salt
½ teaspoon ground cumin
¼ teaspoon ground coriander
2 cups 1% low-fat milk
2 large egg whites, lightly beaten or ¼ cup plus 2 tablespoons egg substitute
¾ cup (3 ounces) shredded sharp Cheddar cheese
¾ cup (3 ounces) shredded Monterey Jack cheese
6 (6-inch) corn tortillas, cut in half
½ cup fat-free sour cream
½ cup salsa

Preheat oven to 350°.

Coat a nonstick skillet with cooking spray; place over medium heat until hot. Add chicken; cook 6 minutes on each side or until done. Remove from skillet; let cool. Shred with 2 forks; set aside.

Coat skillet with cooking spray; place over medium heat until hot. Add onion and garlic; sauté 5 minutes or until tender. Add chicken, beer, red pepper, and tomatoes; cook 10 minutes or until most of liquid evaporates. Remove from heat. Reserve 1 tablespoon green onions and 1 tablespoon olives for garnish. Stir remaining green onions, remaining olives, and chiles into chicken mixture; set aside.

Combine flour, salt, cumin, and coriander in a saucepan. Gradually add

milk, stirring with a whisk until blended. Place over medium heat; cook 7 minutes or until thick, stirring constantly. Gradually add hot milk mixture to egg whites, stirring constantly with whisk. Set aside.

Place cheeses in a bowl; toss well. Set aside.

Spread ½ cup white sauce in bottom of a 2½-quart round casserole or soufflé dish coated with cooking spray. Arrange 4 tortilla halves over sauce; top with 2 cups chicken mixture, ½ cup white sauce, and ½ cup cheese mixture. Repeat layers twice, ending with sauce. Set remaining ½ cup cheese mixture aside.

Bake, uncovered, at 350° for 40 minutes or until hot. Sprinkle with remaining ½ cup cheese mixture, reserved green onions, and reserved olives; bake an additional 5 minutes. Let stand 10 minutes before serving. Serve with sour cream and salsa. Yield: 8 servings (serving size: 1 wedge, 1 tablespoon sour cream, and 1 tablespoon salsa).

Note: You can assemble the casserole ahead of time; cover and chill in the refrigerator overnight, then bake at 350° for 1 hour or until bubbly. Or freeze casserole, thaw in refrigerator 24 hours, then bake for 1 hour or until thoroughly heated.

CALORIES 309 (28% from fat); PROTEIN 28.7g; FAT 9.7g (sat 5.1g, mono 2.9g, poly 0.9g); CARB 26.6g; FIBER 2.6g; CHOL 63mg; IRON 2.1mg; SODIUM 753mg; CALC 324mg

HOW WE DID IT

◆ Decreased amount of olives
◆ Used egg whites instead of whole eggs
◆ Switched to low-fat milk
◆ Omitted butter in white sauce
◆ Reduced amount of cheese
◆ Used fat-free sour cream

The Monarchs' Migratory Waltz

The annual flight of millions of butterflies to their winter home in Mexico is an as-yet-undiscovered ecotourism phenomenon. As you hike through dense forests turned iridescent from millions of butterfly wings, it's easy to believe in the power of nature to overcome.

Butterflies have mythology on their side, too. Mexico, ever the place of legends, has one for the butterflies. The first day of each November not only marks the beginning of the butterflies' arrival, it's also a holiday which honors family members who have died. As the butterflies wing their way across the sky, parents point to the monarchs and tell their children that the monarchs are souls of long-lost relatives who have returned home to be with their families.

CHICKEN WITH MOLE SAUCE

The butterflies may not be able to go home with you, but this Mexican delicacy can. Mole (MOH-lay) comes from molli, *the Nahuatl word for "concoction." It refers to a dark, rich sauce of nuts, seeds, chile peppers, spices, and chocolate. Serve this dish with Spanish rice.*

- 6 (4-ounce) skinned, boned chicken breast halves
- ½ teaspoon salt, divided
- Vegetable cooking spray
- ¼ cup chopped onion
- 1 tablespoon minced jalapeño pepper
- 2 garlic cloves, minced
- 1 teaspoon ground cinnamon
- ¾ teaspoon chili powder
- ¼ teaspoon ground cumin
- ⅛ teaspoon ground allspice
- ⅛ teaspoon ground cloves
- 3 tablespoons blanched almonds, toasted
- 1 (6-inch) day-old corn tortilla, broken into pieces
- 1 (8½-ounce) can whole tomatoes, undrained
- Dash of barbecue smoked seasoning (such as Hickory Liquid Smoke)
- ¾ ounce sweet baking chocolate
- ¼ cup water
- 1 tablespoon sesame seeds, toasted

Sprinkle chicken with ¼ teaspoon salt. Coat a large nonstick skillet with cooking spray; place over medium-high heat until hot. Add chicken; cook 4 minutes on each side or until done. Remove chicken from pan. Set aside; keep warm.

Add onion, jalapeño pepper, and garlic to skillet; cook 3 minutes or until tender. Add cinnamon and next 4 ingredients. Cook 1 minute; set aside.

Place almonds and tortilla pieces in a food processor. Process until finely ground. Add onion mixture, remaining ¼ teaspoon salt, tomatoes, and smoked seasoning; process until smooth.

Return mixture to skillet. Add chocolate; cook over low heat until chocolate melts. Add water; cook until thoroughly heated, stirring frequently.

Spoon sauce over chicken; sprinkle with sesame seeds. Yield: 6 servings (serving size: 1 chicken breast half, ¼ cup sauce, and ½ teaspoon sesame seeds).

CALORIES 206 (27% from fat); PROTEIN 28.5g; FAT 6.2g (sat 1.5g, mono 2.7g, poly 1.4g); CARB 9g; FIBER 1.6g; CHOL 66mg; IRON 1.9mg; SODIUM 347mg; CALC 70mg

SHOPTALK

Who's the super food-shopper in most households? (As if you didn't already know.) According to a Progressive Grocer survey, 72% of the female heads of households fill up the shopping cart, compared with just 13% of the males; 15% said they shared the duty.

But men deserve a few brownie points, too: A 1995 study by the Point-of-Purchase Advertising Institute in Washington, D.C., found that women spend nearly 15% more money than men at supermarkets. Men are also faster, spending 9% less time shopping (49.9 minutes versus 54.6 minutes). And in the checkout line, men are more likely to pay with cash than women, who tend to write a check instead.

NOVEMBER DECEMBER

When Tradition Is Everything

Of all the meals that you'll serve during the holidays, Thanksgiving and Christmas dinners present the biggest challenges—they need to be this, and they need to be that. For example: On Thanksgiving and Christmas, people cherish traditions, so these dinners need to feature familiar, comfy fare such as turkey with all the trimmings. At the same time, these dinners need to be elegant and creative to underscore the festiveness of the season. But can these dinners be plentiful and still be light? Absolutely, as the following menu proves. We created it to satisfy all of the above requirements. So when you announce that dinner is served—be it on Thanksgiving, Christmas, or both—you'll be the picture of graciousness.

ROAST TURKEY WITH APPLE-CIDER GLAZE

1   (12-pound) fresh or frozen
    whole turkey, thawed
⅔   cup apple butter
2   tablespoons brown sugar
2   tablespoons Dijon mustard
¼   teaspoon ground nutmeg
1   medium Granny Smith apple,
    quartered
1   medium onion, quartered
1   (1-ounce) bunch fresh parsley
    sprigs
1¼ teaspoons salt, divided
1¼ teaspoons black pepper, divided
⅛   teaspoon ground red pepper
2   (10½-ounce) cans low-salt
    chicken broth
Vegetable cooking spray
3   tablespoons all-purpose flour
¾   cup apple cider
¼   cup 1% low-fat milk

Preheat oven to 325°.
Remove giblets and neck from turkey; discard, if desired. Rinse turkey thoroughly with cold water; pat dry. Tie ends of legs to tail with cord, or tuck ends of legs into flap of skin around tail. Lift wing tips up and over back, and tuck under turkey. Starting at neck cavity, loosen skin from breast and drumsticks by inserting fingers, gently pushing between skin and meat.

Combine apple butter, sugar, mustard, and nutmeg in a small bowl; stir well. Spread apple butter mixture under loosened skin, and rub the body cavity. Stuff turkey cavity with quartered apple, onion, and parsley sprigs. Sprinkle turkey with 1 teaspoon salt, 1 teaspoon black pepper, and red pepper.

Pour broth and enough water to equal 3 cups liquid into pan. Place turkey on a rack coated with cooking spray; place rack in a shallow roasting pan. Insert meat thermometer into meaty part of thigh, making sure not to touch bone. Bake at 325° for 3 hours or until thermometer registers 160°. Cover turkey loosely with aluminum foil; let stand 10 minutes. Discard skin.

Remove turkey from pan, reserving 1½ cups cooking liquid; reserve remaining cooking liquid for another use. Place turkey on a platter. Set aside; keep warm. Pour reserved 1½ cups cooking liquid into a heavy-duty, zip-top plastic bag. Snip off 1 corner of bag; drain liquid into a measuring cup, reserving 1 cup broth, and stopping before the fat layer reaches the opening. Drain fat layer into bowl, reserving 2 tablespoons. Discard remaining fat.

Combine reserved fat and flour in a medium saucepan over medium heat; stir until smooth. Stir in reserved 1 cup broth, cider, and milk. Bring to a boil; reduce heat, and simmer 3 minutes, stirring constantly until thick and bubbly. Stir in remaining ¼ teaspoon salt and ¼ teaspoon black pepper. Serve gravy with skinned turkey. Yield: 12 servings (serving size: 6 ounces turkey and 2 tablespoons gravy).

CALORIES 372 (24% from fat); PROTEIN 53.4g; FAT 10g (sat 3.2g, mono 2.2g, poly 0.8g); CARB 13.4g; FIBER 0.2g; CHOL 130mg; IRON 3.4mg; SODIUM 524mg; CALC 52mg

MAPLE-CRANBERRY SAUCE

3   cups fresh cranberries
⅔   cup golden raisins
½   cup maple syrup
½   cup honey
¼   cup cider vinegar
½   teaspoon ground allspice

Combine all ingredients in a large saucepan. Bring to a boil; reduce heat, and simmer 10 minutes. Serve warm. Yield: 2 cups (serving size: ¼ cup).

CALORIES 171 (1% from fat); PROTEIN 0.6g; FAT 0.2g (sat 0g, mono 0g, poly 0.1g); CARB 45.3g; FIBER 1.1g; CHOL 0mg; IRON 0.7mg; SODIUM 5mg; CALC 24mg

SOUTHERN CORN BREAD DRESSING

Speckled Corn Bread
1 (12-ounce) can refrigerated buttermilk biscuits
2 tablespoons rubbed sage
1 teaspoon poultry seasoning
¼ to ½ teaspoon pepper
1 teaspoon margarine
Vegetable cooking spray
1 cup chopped celery
1 cup chopped onion
4 (10½-ounce) cans low-salt chicken broth
2 large egg whites, lightly beaten

Crumble Speckled Corn Bread; set aside.

Bake biscuits according to package directions; let cool. Tear 8 biscuits into small pieces; reserve remaining 2 biscuits for another use. Combine crumbled corn bread, torn biscuits, sage, poultry seasoning, and pepper in a large bowl; set aside.

Preheat oven to 350°.

Melt margarine over medium-high heat in a medium nonstick skillet coated with cooking spray. Add celery and onion; sauté 8 minutes or until tender. Let cool slightly. Add vegetable mixture to bread mixture, and gently stir in broth and egg whites. Spoon into a 13 x 9-inch baking dish coated with cooking spray. Bake at 350° for 55 minutes. Yield: 10 servings.

CALORIES 262 (25% from fat); PROTEIN 8.8g; FAT 7.2g (sat 1.6g, mono 3.2g, poly 1.3g); CARB 9.3g; FIBER 1.3g; CHOL 1mg; IRON 3.2mg; SODIUM 782mg; CALC 150mg

Speckled Corn Bread:

1 teaspoon margarine
Vegetable cooking spray
1 cup frozen whole-kernel corn, thawed
1 cup chopped red bell pepper
1⅓ cups self-rising yellow cornmeal mix
⅔ cup self-rising flour
1 teaspoon sugar
⅛ teaspoon ground red pepper
1¼ cups skim milk
2 large egg whites, lightly beaten

Preheat oven to 400°.

Melt margarine over medium-high heat in a nonstick skillet coated with cooking spray. Add corn and bell pepper; sauté 8 minutes or until corn is lightly browned and pepper is tender; stir often. Let cool.

Combine vegetable mixture, cornmeal mix, and next 3 ingredients in a large bowl; add milk and egg whites, stirring until moist. Pour batter into a 9-inch round cake pan coated with cooking spray. Bake at 400° for 30 minutes or until a wooden pick inserted in center comes out clean. Remove from pan; let cool completely on a wire rack. Yield: 12 servings (serving size: 1 wedge).

CALORIES 100 (9% from fat); PROTEIN 3.8g; FAT 1g (sat 0.2g, mono 0.3g, poly 0.4g); CARB 19.8g; FIBER 0.5g; CHOL 1mg; IRON 1.3mg; SODIUM 381mg; CALC 105mg

GREEN BEANS WITH BACON-BALSAMIC VINAIGRETTE

2 pounds green beans
2 bacon slices
¼ cup minced shallots
3 tablespoons coarsely chopped almonds
2 tablespoons brown sugar
¼ cup white balsamic vinegar

Cook green beans in boiling water for 2 minutes. Drain and rinse under cold water. Drain green beans well, and set aside.

Cook bacon in a small skillet over medium-high heat until crisp. Remove bacon from skillet. Crumble and set aside. Add shallots to bacon fat in skillet, and sauté 1 minute. Add almonds, and sauté 1 minute. Remove and let cool. Add sugar and vinegar; stir until sugar dissolves. Add crumbled bacon to green bean mixture.

Pour vinaigrette over beans, tossing gently to coat. Yield: 8 servings (serving size: ¾ cup).

CALORIES 75 (31% from fat); PROTEIN 3.4g; FAT 2.6g (sat 0.5g, mono 1.4g, poly 0.5g); CARB 11.8g; FIBER 2.8g; CHOL 0mg; IRON 1.4mg; SODIUM 50mg; CALC 54mg

PUTTING IT TOGETHER

ONE TO TWO WEEKS AHEAD

1. Make Southern Corn Bread Dressing. Bake and cool completely. Wrap tightly in aluminum foil; freeze.
2. Make Maple-Cranberry Sauce. Cover and chill.
3. Bake Maple-Pecan Cheesecake. Wrap tightly in aluminum foil; freeze.

ONE TO TWO DAYS AHEAD

1. Cook the green beans for Green Beans with Bacon-Balsamic Vinaigrette; chill.
2. Grate tangerine rind, and squeeze tangerine juice for Tangerine Sweet Potatoes.
3. If turkey is frozen, thaw in the refrigerator or in cold water.
4. Make Garlic Mashed Potatoes. Spoon into a casserole dish; chill.

DAY OF DINNER

1. Bake Roast Turkey with Apple-Cider Glaze.
2. Assemble Green Beans with Bacon-Balsamic Vinaigrette.
3. Thaw Maple-Pecan Cheesecake 3 hours at room temperature; refrigerate.
4. Thaw Southern Corn Bread Dressing 4 hours. Bake at 375° for 30 minutes or until thoroughly heated.
5. Bake Garlic Mashed Potatoes, covered, at 350° for 20 minutes or until thoroughly heated.
6. Assemble Tangerine Sweet Potatoes.

TANGERINE SWEET POTATOES

 9 cups peeled, thinly sliced sweet
     potato (about 2½ pounds)
 8 lemon slices
Vegetable cooking spray
 ⅔ cup firmly packed brown sugar
 1 tablespoon grated tangerine or
     orange rind
 ½ cup fresh tangerine or orange
     juice
 2 tablespoons margarine, melted

Preheat oven to 400°.

Arrange sweet potato and lemon slices in a 13 x 9-inch baking dish coated with cooking spray. Combine brown sugar and remaining 3 ingredients. Drizzle sugar mixture over potatoes; cover with aluminum foil. Bake at 400° for 35 minutes. Uncover potatoes and stir well; bake an additional 30 minutes. Yield: 12 servings (serving size: ½ cup).

CALORIES 168 (13% from fat); PROTEIN 2.1g; FAT 2.4g (sat 0.5g, mono 0.9g, poly 0.8g); CARB 36.7g; FIBER 3.2g; CHOL 0mg; IRON 1mg; SODIUM 39mg; CALC 42mg

GARLIC MASHED POTATOES

 7 cups peeled, cubed baking
     potato
 6 garlic cloves, peeled
 ½ cup 2% low-fat milk
 ¼ cup grated Parmesan
     cheese
 2 tablespoons margarine
 ½ teaspoon salt
 ⅛ teaspoon pepper

Place potato and garlic in a medium saucepan. Cover with water, and bring to a boil. Reduce heat. Simmer 20 minutes, and drain. Return potato and garlic to pan. Add milk, Parmesan cheese, margarine, salt and pepper; beat at medium speed of an electric mixer until smooth. Yield: 8 servings (serving size: ¾ cup).

CALORIES 251 (17% from fat); PROTEIN 9.7g; FAT 4.8g (sat 1.6g, mono 1.7g, poly 1.1g); CARB 46.8g; FIBER 11g; CHOL 4mg; IRON 3.9mg; SODIUM 451mg; CALC 168mg

MAPLE-PECAN CHEESECAKE

Mix crust ingredients in springform pan, then press to form crust. This cheesecake can be made in advance, frozen, then thawed before serving.

 ⅔ cup graham cracker crumbs
     (about 8 cookie squares)
 2 tablespoons sugar
 1 tablespoon margarine,
     melted
 ½ teaspoon ground cinnamon
Vegetable cooking spray
 2 (8-ounce) blocks Neufchâtel
     cheese, softened
 2 (8-ounce) blocks fat-free cream
     cheese, softened
 2 tablespoons cornstarch
 ¼ teaspoon salt
 1¼ cups maple syrup
 3 large egg whites
 ¼ cup chopped pecans, toasted
 1 pecan half (optional)
Flowering mint sprig (optional)

Preheat oven to 400°.

Combine first 4 ingredients in an 8-inch springform pan coated with cooking spray; toss with a fork until blended. Press crumb mixture into bottom of pan. Bake at 400° for 8 minutes. Let cool on a wire rack.

Increase oven temperature to 525°.

Combine cheeses, cornstarch, and salt in a large bowl; beat at high speed of an electric mixer until smooth. Gradually add maple syrup; beat well. Add egg whites, and beat just until combined.

Pour half of cheese mixture into prepared pan, and sprinkle with chopped pecans. Top with remaining cheese mixture. Bake at 525° for 7 minutes. Reduce oven temperature to 200°, and bake 45 minutes or until almost set. Remove from oven, and let cool to room temperature. Cover and chill at least 8 hours. Garnish with pecan half and mint sprig, if desired. Yield: 12 servings (serving size: 1 wedge).

CALORIES 282 (39% from fat); PROTEIN 10.5g; FAT 12.2g (sat 5.9g, mono 4g, poly 1g); CARB 32.6g; FIBER 0.2g; CHOL 35mg; IRON 0.8mg; SODIUM 489mg; CALC 162mg

FOR TWO

Romantic Ticket

A dinner that features fresh sea scallops, pesto, and figs in wine sauce deserves an "R" rating—for romance, that is.

If this elegant menu seems a bit on the gourmet-price side, remember: It's for two and in honor of romance. As we indicated by our rating, this is not the kiddie matinée.

ROASTED ORANGE-AND-BELL PEPPER SOUP

Make up to two days ahead; cover and chill. Reheat over low heat.

 1 large navel orange
 1 large yellow bell pepper
 2 teaspoons margarine
 ½ cup chopped onion
 ⅓ cup grated carrot
 1½ teaspoons all-purpose flour
 1 cup fat-free chicken broth
 ½ cup 1% low-fat milk
 ⅛ teaspoon salt
 ⅛ teaspoon pepper
 ⅛ teaspoon paprika
Quartered orange slices (optional)

Cut navel orange in half crosswise; slice about ¼ inch from bottom of each half so they will sit flat. Cut bell pepper in half lengthwise; discard seeds and membranes. Place orange halves, cut sides up, and pepper halves, skin sides up, on an aluminum foil-lined baking sheet; flatten peppers with hand. Broil 15 minutes or until blackened.

Place pepper halves in a zip-top plastic bag; seal. Let stand 20 minutes; peel. Squeeze juice from orange over a bowl to equal ¼ cup; discard oranges. Place peppers and orange juice in a food processor or blender; set aside.

Heat margarine in a small saucepan over medium heat. Add onion and carrot; sauté 12 minutes or until carrot is tender. Add onion mixture to food processor; cover and process until smooth.

Combine flour, broth, and milk in saucepan; stir with a whisk until blended. Place over medium heat; bring to a boil. Reduce heat. Add pepper mixture, salt, ⅛ teaspoon pepper, and paprika; simmer 10 minutes, stirring occasionally. Garnish with orange slices, if desired. Yield: 2 servings (serving size: 1¼ cups).

CALORIES 118 (30% from fat); PROTEIN 3.9g; FAT 3.9g (sat 0.8g, mono 1.1g, poly 0.8g); CARB 16.4g; FIBER 2.4g; CHOL 2mg; IRON 1.1mg; SODIUM 270mg; CALC 96mg

SCALLOPS AND PASTA WITH PISTACHIO-PARSLEY PESTO

Make pesto up to two days ahead; cover and chill. • Buy sea scallops, not bay scallops. Sea scallops are bigger than bay scallops (about 1½ inches in diameter compared with about ½ inch in diameter).

  1 cup chopped fresh parsley
  3 tablespoons coarsely chopped
       pistachios
  1 teaspoon grated lemon rind
  ¼ teaspoon ground cumin
  ¼ teaspoon pepper
  ⅛ teaspoon salt
  ⅛ teaspoon paprika
  2 tablespoons fresh lemon juice
1¼ teaspoons olive oil
  ¾ pound sea scallops
  ¼ cup all-purpose flour
  ⅛ teaspoon salt
  2 teaspoons margarine
  2 cups hot cooked angel hair
       (about 4 ounces uncooked
       pasta)
Freshly ground pepper

Place first 9 ingredients in a food processor; cover and process until smooth, scraping sides of processor bowl occasionally.

Combine scallops, flour, and ⅛ teaspoon salt in a large heavy-duty, zip-top plastic bag; seal and shake to coat.

Heat margarine in a nonstick skillet over medium-high heat. Add scallops; cook 3½ minutes on each side or until scallops are done.

Combine parsley mixture and pasta in a large bowl; toss well. Arrange 1 cup pasta mixture on each plate, and divide scallops evenly between plates. Sprinkle with freshly ground pepper. Yield: 2 servings.

CALORIES 572 (29% from fat); PROTEIN 41.3g; FAT 17.7g (sat 2.5g, mono 9.7g, poly 3.6g); CARB 62.2g; FIBER 5.9g; CHOL 56mg; IRON 6.4mg; SODIUM 620mg; CALC 125mg

SPICED FIGS IN RED WINE

Poach figs and make syrup up to two days ahead; cover and chill. • If you want just a hint of flavor, take the rosemary sprig out of the wine mixture after 10 minutes. • Serve the remaining wine sauce over pound cake. • Present this dessert on one plate; it's meant to be shared.

  ⅓ cup sugar
  1 cup dry red wine
  2 tablespoons fresh lemon juice
  1 tablespoon honey
  ½ teaspoon vanilla
  3 dried figs, halved
  3 black peppercorns
  1 (4-inch) rosemary sprig
  1 (3-inch) thyme sprig
  ½ cup vanilla fat-free frozen
       yogurt
Fresh rosemary sprig (optional)

Combine first 9 ingredients in a small heavy saucepan. Bring to a boil; cook 25 minutes or until reduced to ½ cup. Discard peppercorns, rosemary sprig, and thyme sprig.

Spoon ¼ cup sauce onto a dessert plate, and reserve remaining sauce for another use. Arrange figs and yogurt on top of sauce. Garnish with a fresh rosemary sprig, if desired. Yield: 2 servings.

CALORIES 201 (1% from fat); PROTEIN 2.5g; FAT 0.3g (sat 0g, mono 0.1g, poly 0.2g); CARB 50.6g; FIBER 4.8g; CHOL 0mg; IRON 0.9mg; SODIUM 34mg; CALC 34mg

SIMPLIFY YOUR HOLIDAYS

To make this holiday season as stress-free as possible, we've created menus for every occasion, from Thanksgiving clear through to New Year's Eve. Along with each menu, we've explained the easiest way to put together each meal. You see, it's our goal for you to serve fabulous food and still have time to enjoy the company of your guests and family.

Home Sweet Home

When you tell friends to drop by for coffee and dessert, imagine how delighted they'll be to discover a bountiful spread that includes an eggnog bread pudding, coconut cream puffs, and fruit-filled cake. And because it serves 10, there's plenty to go around.

MENU

OVERNIGHT EGGNOG
BREAD PUDDING WITH
APRICOT-WHISKEY SAUCE

GREAT BIG CAKE WITH
FIVE DRIED FRUITS

THIN FUDGY CHOCOLATE
STRIPPERS

COCONUT CREAM PUFFS

(Serves 10)

OVERNIGHT EGGNOG BREAD PUDDING WITH APRICOT-WHISKEY SAUCE

20 to 22 (½-ounce) slices day-old
    French bread (about ½ inch
    thick), crusts removed
Butter-flavored vegetable cooking
    spray
 1 cup sugar, divided
½ cup golden raisins
 3 large eggs
 4 large egg whites
½ teaspoon ground nutmeg
¼ teaspoon salt
 4 cups 2% low-fat milk
 1 cup evaporated skim milk
⅓ cup whiskey
 2 teaspoons vanilla extract
½ teaspoon ground cinnamon
Apricot-Whiskey Sauce

Arrange one-third of bread slices in a single layer in a 13 x 9-inch baking dish coated with cooking spray. Coat bread lightly with cooking spray; sprinkle with 2 tablespoons sugar and ¼ cup raisins. Repeat procedure; top with remaining bread slices. Sprinkle top layer with 2 tablespoons sugar; coat with cooking spray.

Combine ½ cup sugar, 3 eggs, and next 7 ingredients; stir with a whisk until well-blended. Pour milk mixture over bread. Cover and refrigerate overnight.

Preheat oven to 350°

Combine remaining 2 tablespoons sugar and cinnamon; sprinkle over pudding. Bake at 350° for 1 hour and 10 minutes or until set. Serve warm with Apricot-Whiskey Sauce. Yield: 16 servings (serving size: ½ cup pudding and 2 tablespoons Apricot-Whiskey Sauce).

CALORIES 268 (9% from fat); PROTEIN 7.3g; FAT 2.7g (sat 1.2g, mono 0.9g, poly 0.4g); CARB 55.2g; FIBER 1g; CHOL 47mg; IRON 0.9mg; SODIUM 230mg; CALC 144mg

Apricot-Whiskey Sauce:

 2 cups apricot preserves (about
    2 [12-ounce] jars)
½ cup water
⅓ cup whiskey

Combine preserves and water in a medium-heavy saucepan. Bring to a boil; cook 1 minute. Strain mixture through a sieve into a medium bowl; stir in whiskey. Yield: 2 cups.

This light fruitcake is ideal for those who usually shy away from the traditional heavy version. • Chop the dried fruit with scissors or a knife coated with cooking spray. • Substitute two 8-ounce bags dried mixed fruit for peaches, dates, pears, cranberries, and cherries, if desired.

Vegetable cooking spray
 3 cups all-purpose flour
½ cup cornstarch
¼ teaspoon salt
½ cup chopped dried peaches
½ cup chopped dried dates
½ cup chopped dried pears
½ cup dried cranberries
½ cup dried sour cherries
 2 cups sugar
½ cup stick margarine, softened
 1 (8-ounce) block Neufchâtel
    cheese
 1 tablespoon grated lemon rind
 1 tablespoon vanilla extract
 4 large eggs
 2 large egg whites
 1 cup fat-free sour cream
 1 teaspoon baking soda
 1 tablespoon powdered sugar

Preheat oven to 350°.

Coat a 12-cup Bundt pan with cooking spray; set aside.

Sift together flour, cornstarch, and salt twice; set aside. Combine dried fruits with ¼ cup flour mixture, tossing to coat.

Combine 2 cups sugar and next 4 ingredients in a large bowl, and beat at medium speed of an electric mixer until well-blended (about 5 minutes). Add eggs and egg whites, one at a time, beating well after each addition. Combine sour cream and baking soda; stir well. Add flour mixture (without fruit) to sugar mixture alternately with sour cream mixture, beginning and ending with flour mixture. Mix well after each addition. Gently fold in dried fruit mixture.

Pour batter into prepared pan. Bake at 350° for 1 hour or until a wooden pick inserted in center comes out clean. Cool in pan 10 minutes on a wire rack; remove from pan. Let cool completely on wire rack. Dust with powdered sugar. Yield: 24 servings (serving size: 1 slice).

CALORIES 259 (25% from fat); PROTEIN 5.1g; FAT 7.1g (sat 2.5g, mono 2.7g, poly 1.5g); CARB 44.4g; FIBER 1.6g; CHOL 44mg; IRON 1.3mg; SODIUM 183mg; CALC 22mg

THIN FUDGY CHOCOLATE STRIPPERS

Make a day in advance, and store in an airtight container. • Drizzle melted chocolates onto the bars the day of the party.

- 1½ cups all-purpose flour
- ⅓ cup unsweetened cocoa
- ½ teaspoon baking soda
- ¼ teaspoon salt
- 1 cup sugar
- 3 tablespoons stick margarine, softened
- 1 teaspoon instant espresso granules or 2 teaspoons instant coffee granules
- 1 teaspoon vanilla extract
- 1 (2½-ounce) jar prune baby food
- 1 large egg
- Vegetable cooking spray
- 1 (1-ounce) square semisweet chocolate, chopped
- 1 (1-ounce) square white baking chocolate (such as Baker's white baking chocolate), chopped

Preheat oven to 350°.

Combine first 4 ingredients in a bowl; stir well. Combine sugar and next 5 ingredients in a large bowl; beat at high speed of an electric mixer for 2 minutes. Stir in dry ingredients (dough will be thick). Spoon dough into a 15 x 10-inch jelly-roll pan coated with cooking spray (dough will be spread thin). Bake at 350° for 13 minutes. (Do not overcook.) Let cool completely in pan. Cut into 36 bars. Place bars on wax paper.

Place semisweet chocolate in a heavy-duty, zip-top plastic bag; place white chocolate in a heavy-duty, zip-top

plastic bag. Microwave both bags at MEDIUM-LOW (30% power) for 1 minute or until chocolate is melted. Knead bags until smooth. Snip a tiny hole in corner of each bag; drizzle chocolates over bars. Let bars stand until drizzle hardens. Yield: 3 dozen (serving size: 1 bar).

CALORIES 65 (25% from fat); PROTEIN 1.1g; FAT 1.8g (sat 0.6g, mono 0.6g, poly 0.4g); CARB 11.3g; FIBER 0.2g; CHOL 6mg; IRON 0.4mg; SODIUM 48mg; CALC 5mg

COCONUT CREAM PUFFS

You can make and freeze the puffs ahead. Make the filling ahead, and refrigerate. When the puffs are needed, just reheat and fill.

- 1 cup all-purpose flour
- 2 teaspoons sugar
- ¼ teaspoon salt
- 1 cup skim milk
- 2 tablespoons margarine
- 3 large egg whites
- 1 large egg yolk
- Vegetable cooking spray
- ½ teaspoon unflavored gelatin
- 1 tablespoon water
- 2 tablespoons sugar
- 1½ tablespoons cornstarch
- 1 large egg
- ¾ cup skim milk
- 1½ teaspoons margarine
- 3 tablespoons cream of coconut
- ½ teaspoon coconut extract
- ½ teaspoon vanilla extract
- ¾ cup frozen reduced-calorie whipped topping, thawed
- 2 tablespoons powdered sugar
- Fresh mint sprigs (optional)

Preheat oven to 425°.

Combine first 3 ingredients; set aside. Combine 1 cup milk and 2 tablespoons margarine in a large saucepan; bring to a boil. Reduce heat to low; add flour mixture, stirring well until mixture is smooth and pulls away from sides of pan. Remove from heat; let cool 5 minutes.

Add egg whites and egg yolk, one at a time, beating at low speed of an electric mixer until smooth. Drop dough

by level tablespoons, 2 inches apart, onto baking sheets coated with cooking spray. Bake at 425° for 10 minutes. Reduce oven temperature to 350°; bake an additional 10 minutes or until browned and crisp. Remove from oven; pierce the side of each cream puff with the tip of a sharp knife. Turn off oven; let cream puffs stand in partially closed oven for 5 minutes. Remove from baking sheet to a wire rack; let cool.

Sprinkle gelatin over water in a small bowl; set aside. Combine 2 tablespoons sugar, cornstarch, and egg in a medium bowl. Stir with a whisk; set aside.

Heat ¾ cup milk over medium-high heat in a heavy saucepan to 180° or until tiny bubbles form around edge (do not boil). Gradually add hot milk to egg mixture; stirring constantly with a whisk. Return milk mixture to pan; add 1½ teaspoons margarine. Bring to a boil over medium heat; cook 1 minute or until thick, stirring constantly with a whisk.

Add soft gelatin to milk mixture; cook over low heat 1 minute, stirring until gelatin dissolves. Remove pan from heat; stir in cream of coconut, coconut extract, and vanilla. Place pan in a large ice-filled bowl; let stand 15 minutes or until room temperature (do not allow gelatin mixture to set). Remove pan from ice. Gently whisk in whipped topping. Cover and chill 4 hours or until thick.

Cut tops off cream puffs; fill each cream puff with 1 tablespoon filling, and replace top. Sprinkle powdered sugar over cream puffs. Garnish with mint sprigs, if desired. Serve immediately. Yield: 2 dozen (serving size: 1 cream puff).

Note: To make ahead, place baked and cooled cream puffs in a large heavy-duty, zip-top plastic bag; seal. Freeze cream puffs. Cover and chill cooked filling. To reheat, remove from bag, and place on a large baking sheet. Bake at 325° for 10 minutes or until crisp. Remove from baking sheet to a wire rack; let cool completely. Fill according to recipe directions.

CALORIES 65 (36% from fat); PROTEIN 2.2g; FAT 2.6g (sat 1.1g, mono 0.7g, poly 0.5g); CARB 8g; FIBER 0.1g; CHOL 19mg; IRON 0.4mg; SODIUM 59mg; CALC 27mg

Low-Fat Sweet Results

When successful fashion retailer Elena Castaneda casually announced she was opening a bakery featuring low-fat, all-natural products, she says her friends were "shocked." Most had never seen her in the kitchen before. Her family, however, was very supportive, knowing firsthand her childhood secret—a passion for baking.

Yet the New York City-based founder of Madison Avenue's Better Baker never realized the challenge she would face in making low-fat goodies. "Naive thinking got me into this business," she says. "I planned six months for testing and six months to build a bakery." Actually, it took Castaneda two years to create the taste and texture she—and her critical testers—considered satisfying. "Hundreds of baking experiments ended up in the trash. You can't simply take out the butter with reduced-fat baking. At that point, the recipes become very unforgiving—they don't work."

All trials and tribulations aside, some of her most delicious low- and reduced-fat accomplishments to date include cheesecakes with only 6 grams of fat per slice, reduced from an average of 33 grams; muffins with only 4.5 fat grams instead of the average 14; and chocolate-chip cookies with 3.5 grams of fat—about two-thirds less than the heavy recipe. Her sin-free signature cakes include Chocolate Decadence and Cocoa Berry Cake, each with a minuscule 7 grams of fat per serving and calories shaved to about half those of a typical slice. To satisfy your sweet tooth, we've given you the recipe for Cocoa Berry Cake.

COCOA BERRY CAKE

Vegetable cooking spray
⅔ cup water
1 cup dried cranberries
⅓ cup orange juice
1 tablespoon margarine
1½ cups sugar
1 cup unsweetened cocoa
½ cup all-purpose flour
¼ cup boiling water
1 tablespoon Grand Marnier (orange-flavored liqueur)
1 teaspoon vanilla extract
5 ounces unsweetened chocolate, melted
2 large egg yolks
1 teaspoon cream of tartar
10 large egg whites
¼ cup sugar
Chocolate Glaze

Preheat oven to 350°.

Coat bottoms of 2 (9-inch) round cake pans with cooking spray; line bottoms of pans with wax paper. Coat wax paper with cooking spray, and set pans aside.

Combine ⅔ cup water, cranberries, orange juice, and margarine in a small saucepan. Bring mixture to a boil, and cook 5 minutes.

Combine 1½ cups sugar, cocoa, and flour in a large bowl. Add cranberry mixture and boiling water; stir until well-blended. Add Grand Marnier, vanilla, chocolate, and egg yolks to cranberry mixture; stir until well-blended. Set batter aside.

Beat cream of tartar and egg whites at high speed of an electric mixer until foamy. Gradually add ¼ cup sugar, 1 tablespoon at a time, beating until stiff peaks form. Gently stir one-fourth of egg white mixture into batter; gently fold in remaining egg white mixture.

Pour batter into prepared pans. Bake at 350° for 35 minutes or until cake springs back when touched lightly in center. Let cool in pans 10 minutes on a wire rack; remove from pans. Peel off wax paper; let cool completely.

Place 1 cake layer on a plate; spread with half of Chocolate Glaze, and top with other cake layer. Spread remaining glaze over top of cake. Yield: 16 servings (serving size: 1 slice).

CALORIES 249 (27% from fat); PROTEIN 6.3g; FAT 7.1g (sat 3.7g, mono 2.1g, poly 0.5g); CARB 43.6g; FIBER 0.8g; CHOL 28mg; IRON 2.4mg; SODIUM 47mg; CALC 29mg

Chocolate Glaze:

⅓ cup sugar
⅓ cup unsweetened cocoa
3 tablespoons hot water
1 teaspoon instant espresso or 2 teaspoons instant coffee granules

Combine all ingredients; stir well. Yield: ½ cup.

Spiced Winter Fruit, page 303

Cinnamon Streusel Coffeecake, page 304

Minty Hot Mocha, page 302

Maple-Pecan Cheesecake, page 276

French Chicken in Vinegar Sauce with Pepper-Spiked Polenta, page 299

Roast Turkey with Apple-Cider Glaze, page 274

Southern Corn Bread Dressing, page 275

Star of David Mandelbrot, page 292

Vegetable-and-Cheese Strata, page 292

Green Onion Drop Biscuits, page 290

Cheddar Chicken Chowder, page 290

Cranberry Chutney, page 293

Peppered Flank Steak, page 300

Christmas Pudding with Brandy Sauce, page 308

Citrus-Shrimp Salad, page 307

In from the Cold

This may be a cold time of year, but there are plenty of reasons to be outdoors: caroling, buying a tree, sledding, shoveling the driveway, and putting up the Christmas lights. We created this menu to take the chill off friends and family members who've just come in the door. As they take off their scarves, overcoats, and boots, you can greet them with a mug of our Pineapple Wassail or Hot Mocha. (Now that's a warm welcome!) Even though being outside this time of year can give you the appetite of a grizzly bear, our hearty menu will satisfy your hunger.

HOT MOCHA

6 cups brewed coffee
½ cup sugar
½ cup unsweetened cocoa
¼ cup plus 2 tablespoons Kahlúa
   (coffee-flavored liqueur)

Combine brewed coffee, sugar, and cocoa in a medium saucepan; stir well. Cook coffee mixture over medium heat until hot. (Do not boil.) Remove coffee mixture from heat, and stir in Kahlúa. Yield: 13 servings (serving size: ½ cup).

CALORIES 69 (6% from fat); PROTEIN 1.1g; FAT 0.5g (sat 0.3g, mono 0.2g, poly 0g); CARB 11.8g; FIBER 0g; CHOL 0mg; IRON 1mg; SODIUM 4mg; CALC 7mg

PINEAPPLE WASSAIL

2½ cups water
2 regular-size orange pekoe tea
   bags
¾ cup unsweetened pineapple
   juice
½ cup frozen orange juice
   concentrate, thawed
2 tablespoons honey
½ teaspoon lemon juice
3 whole cloves
1 (3-inch) cinnamon stick

Bring water to a boil; pour over tea bags. Cover; let stand 10 minutes. Discard bags.

Combine tea, pineapple juice, and remaining ingredients in a saucepan; cook over medium-low heat 15 minutes or until heated. Discard whole spices. Pour into mugs. Yield: 7 servings (serving size: ½ cup).

CALORIES 66 (1% from fat); PROTEIN 0.6g; FAT 0.1g; CARB 16.5g; FIBER 0.2g; CHOL 0mg; IRON 0.2mg; SODIUM 1mg; CALC 11mg

PUTTING IT TOGETHER

ONE TO TWO WEEKS AHEAD

1. Make dough for Almond Sugar Cookies; roll into logs. Wrap tightly in plastic wrap; freeze.
2. Make Peanut Butter Swirl Cake. Wrap tightly; freeze.
3. Make Fudgy Cream Cheese Brownies: Line pan with aluminum foil coated with cooking spray. Pour batter into pan; bake. Wrap brownies tightly in aluminum foil; freeze.

TWO TO THREE DAYS AHEAD

1. Make Pineapple Wassail; chill.
2. Make Cheddar Chicken Chowder. Refrigerate in airtight container.

ONE DAY AHEAD

1. Thaw Peanut Butter Swirl Cake and Fudgy Cream Cheese Brownies.

DAY OF GET-TOGETHER

1. Make Green Onion Drop Biscuits and Honeyed Apple Slaw.
2. Thaw Almond Sugar Cookies in the refrigerator for 30 minutes that afternoon; slice, sprinkle with sugar, and bake.
3. Make Hot Mocha an hour before guests arrive.
4. Reheat Cheddar Chicken Chowder gently over low heat for 15 minutes or until warm.
5. Reheat the Pineapple Wassail just before serving.

CHEDDAR CHICKEN CHOWDER

2 slices bacon
Vegetable cooking spray
1 pound skinned, boned chicken breast, cut into bite-size pieces
1 cup chopped onion
1 cup diced red bell pepper
2 garlic cloves, minced
4½ cups fat-free chicken broth
1¾ cups peeled, diced red potatoes
2¼ cups frozen whole-kernel corn
½ cup all-purpose flour
2 cups 2% low-fat milk
¾ cup (3 ounces) shredded Cheddar cheese
½ teaspoon salt
¼ teaspoon pepper

Cook bacon in a Dutch oven coated with cooking spray over medium-high heat until crisp. Remove bacon from Dutch oven. Crumble; set aside.

Add chicken and next 3 ingredients to bacon fat in Dutch oven; sauté 5 minutes. Add broth and potatoes; bring to boil. Cover, reduce heat, and simmer 20 minutes or until potatoes are tender. Stir in corn. Place flour in a bowl. Gradually add milk, stirring with a whisk until blended; add to soup. Cook over medium heat 15 minutes or until thick, stirring often. Stir in cheese, salt, and ¼ teaspoon pepper. Top with bacon. Yield: 7 servings (serving size: 1½ cups).

CALORIES 306 (22% from fat); PROTEIN 25g; FAT 7.5g (sat 4g, mono 2.2g, poly 0.6g); CARB 33.7g; FIBER 2.9g; CHOL 58mg; IRON 1.6mg; SODIUM 376mg; CALC 193mg

GREEN ONION DROP BISCUITS

This dough can also be rolled out and cut into biscuits.

2 cups all-purpose flour
2 teaspoons baking powder
½ teaspoon salt
¼ teaspoon baking soda
3 tablespoons vegetable shortening
¼ cup finely chopped green onions
1 cup low-fat buttermilk
Vegetable cooking spray

Preheat oven to 400°.

Combine first 4 ingredients in a bowl; cut in shortening with a pastry blender until mixture resembles coarse meal. Stir in onions. Add buttermilk, stirring just until flour mixture is moist.

Drop dough by heaping tablespoons onto a baking sheet coated with cooking spray. Bake at 400° for 15 minutes or until lightly browned. Yield: 16 servings (serving size: 1 biscuit).

CALORIES 111 (26% from fat); PROTEIN 2.9g; FAT 3.2g (sat 1g, mono 1g, poly 0.9g); CARB 17.2g; FIBER 0.6g; CHOL 0mg; IRON 1.1mg; SODIUM 135mg; CALC 74mg

HONEYED APPLE SLAW

3 cups thinly sliced green cabbage
2 cups thinly sliced red cabbage
2 cups chopped Granny Smith apple
½ cup plain low-fat yogurt
3 tablespoons honey
1 tablespoon coarse-grained mustard
⅛ teaspoon salt

Combine first 3 ingredients in a bowl. Combine yogurt and remaining 3 ingredients in a bowl; stir well. Add to cabbage mixture; toss. Cover and chill. Yield: 6 servings (serving size: 1 cup).

CALORIES 81 (4% from fat); PROTEIN 2.1g; FAT 0.4g (sat 0.1g, mono 0g, poly 0.1g); CARB 19g; FIBER 2.3g; CHOL 0mg; IRON 0.4mg; SODIUM 107mg; CALC 72mg

FUDGY CREAM CHEESE BROWNIES

¾ cup sugar
¼ cup plus 2 tablespoons reduced-calorie stick margarine, softened
1 large egg
1 large egg white
½ cup all-purpose flour
¼ cup unsweetened cocoa
1 tablespoon vanilla extract
Vegetable cooking spray
1 (8-ounce) block fat-free cream cheese, softened
¼ cup sugar
1 large egg white

Preheat oven to 350°.

Cream ¾ cup sugar and margarine at medium speed of an electric mixer until light and fluffy. Add egg and 1 egg white; beat well.

Add flour and cocoa to creamed mixture; beat well. Add vanilla; beat well. Pour into a 9-inch square baking pan coated with cooking spray; set aside.

Beat cream cheese and ¼ cup sugar at high speed of mixer until smooth. Add 1 egg white; beat well. Pour cream cheese mixture over chocolate mixture; swirl together using the tip of a knife to marble.

Bake at 350° for 30 minutes or until done. Cool completely on a wire rack. Yield: 16 servings (serving size: 1 brownie).

CALORIES 113 (26% from fat); PROTEIN 3.6g; FAT 3.3g (sat 0.8g, mono 1.3g, poly 0.9g); CARB 16.8g; FIBER 0.1g; CHOL 16mg; IRON 0.5mg; SODIUM 138mg; CALC 45mg

PEANUT BUTTER SWIRL CAKE

Vegetable cooking spray
1 tablespoon all-purpose flour
½ cup reduced-calorie stick margarine, softened
1¼ cups firmly packed brown sugar
1 teaspoon vanilla extract
3 large egg whites
1 large egg
1½ cups all-purpose flour
½ teaspoon baking powder
¼ cup unsweetened cocoa
¼ cup reduced-fat creamy peanut butter

Preheat oven to 350°.

Coat a 9-inch square baking pan with cooking spray; dust with 1 tablespoon flour. Set aside.

Beat margarine at medium speed of an electric mixer until creamy. Gradually add sugar; beat until well-blended. Add vanilla, egg whites, and egg; mix until blended.

Combine 1½ cups flour and baking powder; with mixer at low speed, add flour mixture to creamed mixture.

Reserve 1½ cups batter; pour remaining batter into a bowl.

Stir cocoa into reserved batter; stir peanut butter into remaining batter. Spoon cocoa batter alternately with peanut butter batter into prepared pan. Swirl together using the tip of a knife. Bake at 350° for 30 minutes or until a wooden pick inserted in center comes out clean. Yield: 16 servings.

CALORIES 156 (33% from fat); PROTEIN 3.7g; FAT 5.8g (sat 1.2g, mono 2.5g, poly 1.7g); CARB 23.1g; FIBER 0.3g; CHOL 14mg; IRON 1.1mg; SODIUM 93mg; CALC 24mg

ALMOND SUGAR COOKIES

    3   tablespoons sugar
    ⅛   teaspoon ground cinnamon
    1   cup sugar
    ¼   cup plus 3 tablespoons stick
        margarine, softened
    ¼   cup skim milk
    ½   teaspoon almond extract
    ½   teaspoon vanilla extract
    1   large egg white
  2½   cups all-purpose flour
    ¼   cup ground almonds
    ⅛   teaspoon salt
Vegetable cooking spray

Preheat oven to 325°.
Combine 3 tablespoons sugar and cinnamon in a bowl; stir well. Set aside.
Cream 1 cup sugar and margarine at medium speed of an electric mixer until light and fluffy. Add milk, extracts, and egg white; beat well. Combine flour, almonds, and salt; add to creamed mixture, beating well.
Divide dough in half; cover and refrigerate half of dough. Shape remaining half of dough into 30 (1-inch) balls; roll balls in sugar mixture, coating well. Place balls 2 inches apart on baking sheets coated with cooking spray. Flatten each ball with the bottom of a glass. Bake at 325° for 14 minutes. Cool on wire racks. Repeat procedure with remaining dough and sugar mixture. Yield: 5 dozen (serving size: 1 cookie).

CALORIES 50 (31% from fat); PROTEIN 0.8g; FAT 1.7g (sat 0.3g, mono 0.8g, poly 0.5g); CARB 8.1g; FIBER 0.2g; CHOL 0mg; IRON 0.3mg; SODIUM 22mg; CALC 4mg

HANUKKAH

A Celebration of Light

After lighting the menorah, sit down to a cozy dinner that begins with Grandma's Simple Roast Chicken and ends with Mandelbrot.

GRANDMA'S SIMPLE ROAST CHICKEN

    1   (4- to 5-pound) roasting
        chicken
    ½   teaspoon salt
    ½   teaspoon pepper
    ½   teaspoon paprika
    1   medium onion, trimmed and
        quartered
    1   celery stalk, cut into 3-inch
        pieces
    1   medium carrot, cut into 3-inch
        pieces
    1   garlic clove
    1   bay leaf
Vegetable cooking spray

Preheat oven to 400°.
Remove and discard giblets and neck from chicken. Rinse chicken under cold water; pat dry. Trim fat from chicken.
Combine salt, pepper, and paprika; sprinkle over breast, drumsticks, and into the body cavity of chicken. Place onion, celery, carrot, garlic, and bay leaf in body cavity. Tie ends of legs together with cord. Lift wing tips up and over back; tuck under chicken.
Place chicken, breast side up, on a broiler pan coated with cooking spray. Insert meat thermometer into meaty part of thigh, making sure not to touch bone. Bake at 400° for 1 hour or until thermometer registers 180°. Cover chicken loosely with aluminum foil; let stand 10 minutes. Discard skin, vegetables, and bay leaf. Yield: 8 servings (serving size: 3 ounces chicken).

CALORIES 163 (35% from fat); PROTEIN 24.6g; FAT 6.4g (sat 1.7g, mono 2.3g, poly 1.5g); CARB 0.2g; FIBER 0.1g; CHOL 76mg; IRON 1.1mg; SODIUM 220mg; CALC 14mg

SWEET POTATO CAKES

Serve with our Homemade Applesauce.

    4   cups peeled, shredded sweet
        potato (about 1 pound)
    ¼   cup all-purpose flour
    1   teaspoon instant minced onion
    ⅛   teaspoon salt
    ⅛   teaspoon pepper
Dash of ground nutmeg
    1   large egg, lightly beaten
Vegetable cooking spray

Combine first 7 ingredients in a bowl; stir well.
Coat a nonstick griddle or large nonstick skillet with cooking spray. For each cake, spoon about ¼ cup potato mixture onto hot griddle or skillet; flatten slightly with a spatula. Cook 4 minutes on each side or until golden. Yield: 6 servings (serving size: 2 cakes).

CALORIES 127 (9% from fat); PROTEIN 3.1g; FAT 1.3g (sat 0.3g, mono 0.3g, poly 0.3g); CARB 25.9g; FIBER 2.8g; CHOL 37mg; IRON 0.9mg; SODIUM 72mg; CALC 26mg

HOMEMADE APPLESAUCE

  10   cups coarsely chopped red
        cooking apple (about 3
        pounds)
    1   cup apple cider
    ½   cup firmly packed brown sugar

Combine all ingredients in a large saucepan. Bring to a boil. Reduce heat; simmer 1 hour or until apples are tender, stirring occasionally. Yield: 10 servings (serving size: ½ cup).

CALORIES 118 (3% from fat); PROTEIN 0.2g; FAT 0.4g (sat 0.1g, mono 0g, poly 0.1g); CARB 30.4g; FIBER 3.5g; CHOL 0mg; IRON 0.5mg; SODIUM 5mg; CALC 19mg

MANDELBROT (JEWISH BISCOTTI)

This recipe makes standard biscotti that are all the same size. To make the Star of David, you'll need biscotti of varying lengths.

    1   cup sugar
    ⅔   cup vegetable oil
    1   (8-ounce) carton egg substitute
    1   tablespoon grated orange rind
    1   teaspoon vanilla extract
    4½ cups all-purpose flour
    ½   cup finely ground toasted
        almonds (about 3 ounces)
    1½ tablespoons baking powder
    1   teaspoon ground cinnamon
    ½   teaspoon salt
    ¼   teaspoon ground cloves
    ¼   teaspoon ground coriander
    ¼   teaspoon ground nutmeg
    Vegetable cooking spray
    Orange Marmalade Frosting

Preheat oven to 350°.

Combine first 5 ingredients in a large bowl; beat at medium speed of an electric mixer until well-blended. Combine flour and next 7 ingredients; gradually add to sugar mixture, beating until well-blended.

Turn dough out onto a lightly floured surface; knead lightly. Shape dough into 2 (12-inch-long) rolls. Place rolls on a baking sheet coated with cooking spray; flatten to 1-inch thickness.

Bake at 350° for 20 minutes. Remove rolls from baking sheet, and let cool 10 minutes on a wire rack.

Cut each roll into 24 (½-inch-thick) slices. Place slices, cut sides down, on baking sheet. Bake at 350° for 10 minutes. Turn cookies over, and bake an additional 10 minutes (cookies will be slightly soft in center but will harden as they cool). Remove cookies from baking sheet, and let cool completely on wire rack. Drizzle each cookie with Orange Marmalade Frosting. Yield: 4 dozen cookies (serving size: 1 cookie).

Star of David Mandelbrot: To construct the Star of David, you'll need varying lengths of biscotti. For this,

divide dough into 3 equal portions, then shape each portion into a quadrilateral that is 9 inches at the bottom, 4 inches at the top, and 12 inches on each side. Bake as directed in paragraph 4. Beginning at the 9-inch bottom, cut each portion into ½-inch-thick slices, then bake as directed in paragraph 5. Frost and let stand 10 minutes. To assemble the star, begin with the 3 longest pieces of biscotti, and form a triangle, which is the base of the star. Continue to stack biscotti, using the longest pieces first. You will have enough biscotti to make 1 large star with 6 layers. Serve remaining biscotti on a tray.

Note: Make biscotti up to three weeks ahead, and freeze.

CALORIES 121 (30% from fat); PROTEIN 2.1g; FAT 4.1g (sat 0.7g, mono 1.5g, poly 1.7g); CARB 19.2g; FIBER 0.6g; CHOL 0mg; IRON 0.8mg; SODIUM 32mg; CALC 34mg

Orange Marmalade Frosting:

    2   cups sifted powdered sugar
    2   tablespoons orange marmalade
    1   teaspoon orange juice

Place all ingredients in a food processor; cover and process until smooth. Place frosting in a heavy-duty, zip-top plastic bag. Snip a tiny hole in one corner of bag; drizzle frosting over biscotti. Yield: 1 cup.

'ROUND MIDNIGHT

The Late, Late Show

Late-night holiday activities can really work up an appetite, whether it's attending plays, concerts, or church services. These brunchlike, make-ahead dishes are ideal for serving people afterward, when you and the moon are still shining.

MENU

VEGETABLE-AND-CHEESE
STRATA

CRANBERRY-WALDORF
GELATIN SALAD

LEMON-POPPY SEED
MUFFINS

(Serves 8)

VEGETABLE-AND-CHEESE STRATA

Buy canned, quartered artichoke hearts because they're less expensive than whole artichoke hearts. • Buy presliced mushrooms.

    1   teaspoon olive oil
    2   cups diced zucchini
    2   cups sliced mushrooms
    1   cup diced red bell pepper
    1   cup diced onion
    2   garlic cloves, crushed
    ¾   cup drained and chopped
        canned artichoke hearts
    8   cups (1-inch) cubed Italian
        bread (about 8 ounces)
    Vegetable cooking spray
    1   cup (4 ounces) shredded
        reduced-fat extra-sharp
        Cheddar cheese
    ¼   cup freshly grated Parmesan
        cheese
    1½ cups egg substitute
    1   teaspoon dried Italian seasoning
    ½   teaspoon dry mustard
    ¼   teaspoon salt
    ¼   teaspoon pepper
    1   (12-ounce) can evaporated skim
        milk
    Fresh oregano sprigs (optional)

Heat oil in a nonstick skillet over medium-high heat until hot. Add zucchini, mushrooms, bell pepper, onion, and garlic; sauté vegetable mixture 6 minutes or until tender. Remove from heat. Stir in artichokes, and set aside.

Arrange Italian bread cubes in a 13 x 9-inch baking dish coated with cooking spray. Spoon zucchini mixture evenly over bread cubes, and sprinkle mixture with cheeses.

Combine egg substitute and next 5 ingredients in a large bowl; stir with a whisk. Pour egg mixture over zucchini mixture. Cover mixture with aluminum foil; chill in refrigerator 8 hours.

Preheat oven to 325°. Bake strata, covered, 1 hour or until bubbly. Garnish with oregano sprigs, if desired. Yield: 8 servings.

CALORIES 229 (19% from fat); PROTEIN 17.5g; FAT 4.9g (sat 2.3g, mono 1.5g, poly 0.3g); CARB 29.1g; FIBER 1.9g; CHOL 14mg; IRON 2.7mg; SODIUM 570mg; CALC 336mg

CRANBERRY-WALDORF GELATIN SALAD

Do not substitute sugar-free gelatin for regular gelatin. • Make the salad and the cream cheese mixture a day ahead; chill.

- 2 (3-ounce) packages cranberry-flavored gelatin
- 1¾ cups boiling water
- ¾ cup cold water
- ¾ cup diced Red Delicious apple
- ¾ cup diced Golden Delicious apple
- ½ cup seedless green grapes, quartered
- ¼ cup finely chopped pecans
- Vegetable cooking spray
- ½ (8-ounce) block fat-free cream cheese, softened
- ¾ cup low-fat sour cream
- 2 tablespoons sugar
- ¼ teaspoon vanilla extract
- Lettuce leaves
- Apple slices (optional)
- Chopped pecans (optional)

Combine gelatin and boiling water in a bowl; stir until gelatin dissolves. Stir in cold water. Cover and chill 1½ hours or until the consistency of unbeaten egg white. Fold in diced apples, grapes, and ¼ cup pecans.

Spoon mixture into a 5-cup gelatin mold coated with cooking spray. Chill until firm.

Beat cream cheese at medium speed of an electric mixer until smooth. Add sour cream, sugar, and vanilla; beat well. Invert mold onto a serving plate; cut into 8 pieces. Serve on lettuce-lined plates; top with 2 tablespoons cream cheese mixture. Garnish with apple slices and chopped pecans, if desired. Yield: 8 servings.

CALORIES 180 (27% from fat); PROTEIN 4.5g; FAT 5.4g (sat 1.9g, mono 2.4g, poly 0.8g); CARB 28.9g; FIBER 1g; CHOL 11mg; IRON 0.2mg; SODIUM 153mg; CALC 67mg

LEMON-POPPY SEED MUFFINS

Grate only the yellow-colored part of lemon rind. • Grate rind before extracting juice. • Make muffins ahead, and freeze.

- 2 cups all-purpose flour
- ½ cup sugar
- 2 tablespoons poppy seeds
- 1 teaspoon baking powder
- 1 teaspoon baking soda
- ¼ teaspoon salt
- 3 tablespoons vegetable oil
- 1 teaspoon grated lemon rind
- 2 tablespoons fresh lemon juice
- 1 (8-ounce) carton lemon low-fat yogurt
- 1 large egg, lightly beaten
- Vegetable cooking spray

Preheat oven to 400°.

Combine first 6 ingredients in a medium bowl; make a well in center of mixture. Combine oil, rind, juice, yogurt, and egg; stir well. Add to dry ingredients, stirring just until moist.

Spoon batter evenly into 12 muffin cups coated with cooking spray.

Bake at 400° for 14 minutes or until golden. Remove muffins from pan immediately; place on a wire rack. Yield: 1 dozen.

CALORIES 179 (25% from fat); PROTEIN 3.7g; FAT 4.9g (sat 0.9g, mono 1.3g, poly 2.2g); CARB 30.5g; FIBER 0.7g; CHOL 18mg; IRON 1.2mg; SODIUM 172mg; CALC 73mg

Gifted Cooks

Often the best present doesn't come from a store. It's something homemade and from the kitchen.

CRANBERRY CHUTNEY

For Christmas dinner we always have the traditional turkey, mashed rutabaga and carrots, and, of course, my Cranberry Chutney. We love it with turkey, but it's good with pork or chicken. It wouldn't be Christmas without our chutney on the table.

*Corinne Journeau,
Queenston, Ontario, Canada*

- 1 cup chopped Granny Smith apple
- 1 cup raisins
- 1 cup chopped onion
- 1 cup sugar
- 1 cup white vinegar
- ¾ cup chopped celery
- ¾ cup water
- 2 teaspoons ground cinnamon
- 1½ teaspoons ground ginger
- ¼ teaspoon ground cloves
- 1 (12-ounce) bag fresh or frozen cranberries

Combine all ingredients in a large saucepan; bring to a boil. Reduce heat, and simmer, uncovered, 30 minutes or until slightly thick, stirring occasionally. Serve with turkey, chicken, roast pork, or ham. Yield: 4 cups (serving size: ¼ cup).

Note: Store chutney in an airtight container in refrigerator.

CALORIES 98 (2% from fat); PROTEIN 0.6g; FAT 0.2g (sat 0g, mono 0g, poly 0.1g); CARB 25.6g; FIBER 1.3g; CHOL 0mg; IRON 0.4mg; SODIUM 7mg; CALC 15mg

CRANBERRY-SWEET POTATO QUICK BREAD

I make this bread year-round, but it's best at Christmas because of the cranberries. This makes a lovely gift wrapped in colorful cellophane and decorated with ribbon.

—Janet Riley, Lodi, California

2½ cups all-purpose flour
1 cup firmly packed brown sugar
1½ teaspoons baking powder
½ teaspoon baking soda
½ teaspoon salt
¼ teaspoon ground cinnamon
¼ teaspoon ground nutmeg
¾ cup no-sugar-added canned mashed sweet potato
¾ cup egg substitute
⅓ cup orange juice
¼ cup margarine, melted
1 cup chopped cranberries
Vegetable cooking spray
2 tablespoons sliced almonds

Preheat oven to 350°.

Combine first 7 ingredients in a large bowl; make a well in center of mixture. Combine sweet potato, egg substitute, orange juice, and margarine in a bowl; add to dry ingredients. Stir just until moist. Fold in cranberries.

Spoon batter into a 9 x 5-inch loaf pan coated with cooking spray; sprinkle almonds over batter. Bake at 350° for 1 hour and 10 minutes or until a wooden pick inserted in center comes out clean. Let cool in pan 10 minutes on a wire rack; remove from pan. Let cool completely on wire rack. Yield: 16 servings (serving size: 1 slice).

CALORIES 163 (20% from fat); PROTEIN 3.6g; FAT 3.6g (sat 0.7g, mono 1.6g, poly 1.1g); CARB 29.3g; FIBER 1.2g; CHOL 0mg; IRON 1.5mg; SODIUM 169mg; CALC 47mg

MOM'S BANANA BREAD

My mom's recipe was the model for this banana bread. My husband likes the new version so much we make it all the time—at least every two weeks. I think the miniloaves would be a perfect holiday gift.

—Stacey A. Johnson, Arlington, Washington

1 cup sugar
¼ cup light butter, softened
1⅔ cups mashed ripe banana (about 3 bananas)
¼ cup skim milk
¼ cup low-fat sour cream
2 large egg whites
2 cups all-purpose flour
1 teaspoon baking soda
½ teaspoon salt
Vegetable cooking spray

Preheat oven to 350°.

Combine sugar and butter in a bowl; beat at medium speed of an electric mixer until well-blended. Add banana, milk, sour cream, and egg whites; beat well, and set aside.

Combine flour, baking soda, and salt; stir well. Add dry ingredients to creamed mixture, beating until mixture is blended.

Spoon batter into 4 (5 x 2½-inch) miniature loaf pans coated with cooking spray. Bake at 350° for 45 minutes or until a wooden pick inserted in center comes out clean. Let cool in pans 10 minutes on a wire rack; remove from pans. Let cool completely on wire rack. Yield: 4 loaves, 4 servings per loaf (serving size: 1 slice).

Note: To make one 9-inch loaf, spoon batter into a 9 x 5-inch loaf pan coated with cooking spray; bake at 350° for 1 hour and 10 minutes. Yield: 1 loaf, 16 servings (serving size: 1 slice).

CALORIES 147 (14% from fat); PROTEIN 2.5g; FAT 2.2g (sat 1.4g, mono 0.2g, poly 0.1g); CARB 30.2g; FIBER 1.1g; CHOL 7mg; IRON 0.8mg; SODIUM 180mg; CALC 13mg

ORANGE-SESAME BISCOTTI

Biscotti makes a great holiday gift. I've found that the best way to package it is in a clear plastic airtight container. It stores longer, and I use paint markers and ribbon to decorate the bags and make the gift more personal.

—Becky Anderson, Ames, Iowa

2¾ cups all-purpose flour
1 cup sugar
¼ cup sesame seeds
1 teaspoon ground ginger
1 teaspoon baking powder
½ teaspoon baking soda
¼ teaspoon salt
2 large eggs
1 large egg white
1 teaspoon vanilla extract
3 tablespoons grated orange rind
1 tablespoon thawed orange juice concentrate, undiluted
Vegetable cooking spray

Preheat oven to 325°.

Combine first 7 ingredients in a bowl. Stir well; set aside.

Combine 2 eggs and next 4 ingredients in a large bowl; stir with a whisk. Add flour mixture; stir until well-blended.

Turn dough out onto a baking sheet coated with cooking spray. Shape dough into two 13-inch-long rolls; flatten to 1-inch thickness. Bake at 325° for 25 minutes or until firm to the touch. Remove from baking sheet; let cool 10 minutes on a wire rack.

Reduce oven temperature to 275°.

Cut each roll diagonally into 18 (½-inch-thick) slices. Place slices, cut sides down, on baking sheet. Bake at 275° for 40 minutes (cookies will be slightly soft in center but will harden as they cool). Remove from baking sheet; let cool completely on wire racks. Yield: 3 dozen (serving size: 1 cookie).

CALORIES 70 (12% from fat); PROTEIN 1.7g; FAT 0.9g (sat 0.2g, mono 0.3g, poly 0.3g); CARB 13.9g; FIBER 0.3g; CHOL 13mg; IRON 0.7mg; SODIUM 40mg; CALC 22mg

GOOD-FOR-YOU CHOCOLATE CHIP COOKIES

As a tour operator, I'm on the road a lot. I'm always eating someone else's food, so when I come home it's a treat to cook in my own kitchen. And because baking is my real passion, I had fun trying out chocolate chip cookie recipes and coming up with this combination.

—Dyan McCammon,
Aurora, Colorado

1¼ cups all-purpose flour
1¼ cups whole-wheat flour
1 teaspoon baking soda
½ teaspoon salt
¾ cup reduced-calorie stick margarine, softened
⅔ cup sugar
⅔ cup firmly packed brown sugar
¼ cup applesauce
1 teaspoon vanilla extract
1 large egg
1 large egg white
½ cup reduced-fat semisweet chocolate chips
Vegetable cooking spray

Preheat oven to 350°.

Combine first 4 ingredients in a bowl, and stir well. Set aside. Combine margarine and sugars in a large bowl; beat at medium speed of an electric mixer until light and fluffy. Add applesauce and next 3 ingredients; beat well. Add flour mixture; beat at low speed until well-blended. Stir in chips.

Drop dough by level teaspoons 1 inch apart onto baking sheets coated with cooking spray. Bake at 350° for 12 minutes or until almost set. Remove from oven; let stand 2 to 3 minutes or until firm. Remove cookies from pan; let cool on wire racks. Yield: 5 dozen (serving size: 1 cookie).

CALORIES 52 (35% from fat); PROTEIN 0.8g; FAT 2.0g (sat 0.8g, mono 1g, poly 0.5g); CARB 8.7g; FIBER 0.4g; CHOL 4mg; IRON 0.2mg; SODIUM 65mg; CALC 3mg

CRUNCHY SPICE GRANOLA

I've searched a long time for a tasty granola without added fat. After years of experimenting I came up with my own. One batch should last a while if you store it in an airtight container.

—Diane Lenicheck,
Mesquite, Texas

3 cups regular oats
½ cup wheat germ
½ cup wheat bran
½ cup honey
1 tablespoon ground cinnamon
½ teaspoon pumpkin pie spice
½ teaspoon ground nutmeg
¼ teaspoon ground allspice
1 (6-ounce) jar pear baby food
1 cup wheat bran flakes cereal with raisins
1 cup crispy corn and rice cereal
⅓ cup golden raisins
¼ cup sunflower seeds
¼ cup flaked coconut
¼ cup chopped dates
Vegetable cooking spray

Preheat oven to 350°.

Spread regular oats, wheat germ, and wheat bran on a jelly-roll pan. Bake at 350° for 20 minutes, stirring occasionally. Remove from oven.

Reduce oven temperature to 250°.

Combine honey and next 5 ingredients in a small saucepan. Bring to a boil; cook 1 minute.

Combine oat mixture, honey mixture, bran flakes, and next 5 ingredients; stir well. Spread mixture on a jelly-roll pan coated with cooking spray. Bake at 250° for 1 hour, stirring every 20 minutes. Let cool to room temperature. Store in an airtight container. Yield: 8 cups (serving size: 2 tablespoons).

Note: Sprinkle over yogurt, fresh fruit slices, or frozen yogurt as a quick topping.

CALORIES 43 (19% from fat); PROTEIN 1.2g; FAT 0.9g (sat 0.3g, mono 0.2g, poly 0.3g); CARB 8.3g; FIBER 1g; CHOL 0mg; IRON 0.5mg; SODIUM 8mg; CALC 6mg

FAST FOOD

Micro-Managing

Avoid the cooktop rush during the holidays by taking advantage of your microwave. Let this culinary ally handle sweet potatoes and our innovative recipes (which aren't all just side dishes, either). If you need a quick, after-work meal, we have two hearty entrées, a warming soup, and a couple of side dishes. So don't let the microwave sit like an unopened present. Give it sweet potatoes, and let your stove catch its breath.

HONEY-GLAZED SWEET POTATOES AND CHICKEN

Preparation time: 3 minutes
Cooking time: 16 minutes

⅔ cup evaporated skim milk
2 tablespoons honey
1 tablespoon cornstarch
½ teaspoon poultry seasoning
½ teaspoon salt
2 medium sweet potatoes, peeled and cut into 1-inch pieces (about 3 cups)
4 (4-ounce) skinned, boned chicken breast halves
¼ cup sliced green onions
⅓ cup dried tart cherries

Combine first 5 ingredients in an 8-inch square baking dish, and stir well. Add potato to milk mixture, and toss gently to coat. Cover dish with plastic wrap, and vent. Microwave at HIGH 9 minutes, stirring after 4 minutes.

Arrange chicken in bottom of dish, nestling into potatoes; top with green onions and cherries. Microwave at HIGH 7 minutes or until chicken is tender. Yield: 4 servings (serving size: 1 chicken breast half and ¾ cup potatoes).

CALORIES 341 (5% from fat); PROTEIN 31.6g; FAT 1.9g (sat 0.5g, mono 0.4g, poly 0.5g); CARB 49.7g; FIBER 3.8g; CHOL 67mg; IRON 1.9mg; SODIUM 432mg; CALC 171mg

RAGOÛT OF PORK WITH SWEET POTATOES

Preparation time: 10 minutes
Cooking time: 24 minutes

- ¾ cup chopped onion
- 3 cups peeled, cubed (½-inch) sweet potato (about 1 pound)
- 2 tablespoons tomato paste
- 1½ teaspoons curry powder
- ½ teaspoon salt
- ½ teaspoon ground cumin
- ¼ teaspoon pepper
- 2 garlic cloves, minced
- 1 (10½-ounce) can low-salt chicken broth, undiluted
- 1 pound lean, boned pork loin, cut into ½-inch pieces
- 1 cup frozen green peas

Place onion in a 2-quart casserole. Cover and microwave at HIGH 2 minutes. Add potato and next 7 ingredients, stirring well. Cover and microwave at HIGH 10 minutes.

Add pork; cover and microwave at HIGH 10 minutes or until potato is tender. Add peas; cover and microwave at HIGH 2 minutes. Yield: 5 servings (serving size: 1 cup).

CALORIES 277 (25% from fat); PROTEIN 22.9g; FAT 7.7g (sat 2.5g, mono 3.3g, poly 0.9g); CARB 28.2g; FIBER 3.4g; CHOL 54mg; IRON 2.6mg; SODIUM 362mg; CALC 45mg

SWEET POTATO-APPLE BAKE

Preparation time: 10 minutes
Cooking time: 10 minutes

- Vegetable cooking spray
- 6 cups peeled, thinly sliced sweet potato (about 2 pounds)
- 3 cups peeled, sliced Granny Smith apple
- ½ teaspoon salt
- 3 tablespoons maple syrup
- 2 tablespoons margarine, melted

Coat a 10-inch square casserole with cooking spray. Arrange 3 cups sweet potato and 1½ cups apple in casserole; sprinkle with ¼ teaspoon salt. Combine syrup and margarine; stir well. Drizzle half of syrup mixture over potatoes. Repeat procedure with remaining ingredients. Cover with plastic wrap; microwave at HIGH 10 minutes, rotating a half-turn after 5 minutes. Let stand, covered, 5 minutes. Yield: 8 servings (serving size: ½ cup).

CALORIES 174 (18% from fat); PROTEIN 1.7g; FAT 3.4g (sat 0.6g, mono 1.3g, poly 1.1g); CARB 35.3g; FIBER 4.1g; CHOL 0mg; IRON 0.7mg; SODIUM 193mg; CALC 30mg

CRANBERRY-GLAZED SWEET POTATOES

Preparation time: 5 minutes
Cooking time: 23 minutes

- 6 medium sweet potatoes, peeled and cut into 1-inch pieces (about 3 pounds)
- ½ cup firmly packed brown sugar
- 2 tablespoons margarine
- 2 tablespoons orange juice
- ½ teaspoon salt
- 1 cup whole-berry cranberry sauce
- Orange rind (optional)

Place potato, covered, in a 2-quart casserole dish; microwave at HIGH 10 minutes or until potato is tender.

Combine sugar, margarine, orange juice, and salt in a 2-cup glass measure. Microwave at HIGH 3 minutes, stirring every minute. Add sugar mixture and cranberry sauce to potato; toss gently. Microwave at HIGH 10 minutes or until heated through, basting with sauce twice during cooking. Garnish with orange rind, if desired. Yield: 8 servings (serving size: ¾ cup).

CALORIES 292 (10% from fat); PROTEIN 2.9g; FAT 3.4g (sat 0.7g, mono 1.3g, poly 1.1g); CARB 64g; FIBER 5.2g; CHOL 0mg; IRON 1.2mg; SODIUM 215mg; CALC 48mg

CREAMY SWEET POTATO SOUP

Preparation time: 15 minutes
Cooking time: 10 minutes

- 2 cups peeled, cubed (¼-inch) sweet potato
- 1½ cups thinly sliced leek (about 1 medium)
- 1¼ cups fat-free chicken broth, divided
- ⅔ cup evaporated skim milk
- 1½ teaspoons Dijon mustard
- ½ teaspoon salt
- Dash of white pepper
- Dash of ground nutmeg
- Chopped leek (optional)

Combine sweet potato, sliced leek, and ¼ cup broth in a 1½-quart casserole; stir well. Cover and microwave at HIGH 10 minutes, stirring after 5 minutes.

Place sweet potato mixture in a blender or food processor; cover and process until smooth. Add 1 cup broth, milk, and next 4 ingredients; process 30 seconds or until blended. Garnish with chopped leek, if desired. Serve warm. Yield: 4 servings (serving size: ¾ cup).

CALORIES 136 (3% from fat); PROTEIN 5g; FAT 0.5g (sat 0.1g, mono 0.1g, poly 0.2g); CARB 27.2g; FIBER 2.5g; CHOL 2mg; IRON 1.3mg; SODIUM 416mg; CALC 162mg

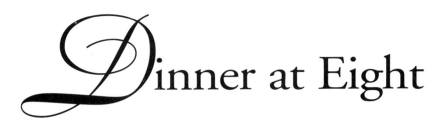

Dinner at Eight

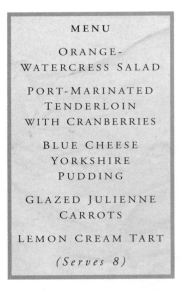
How about an elegant dinner party, one where the guests can play grownup: candles, champagne, fancy clothes, and Cole Porter on the stereo? More important, you can prepare food that is sophisticated and complex in flavor—in other words, our New Year's Eve menu.

As easy as the entrée is to prepare, timing is all-important. You'll want to make sure that the beef and Yorkshire pudding go quickly from the oven to the table. For dessert, we have a super-rich lemon cream tart that is just that—tart, not cloyingly sweet. So this New Year's Eve, go the celebratory, dignified route: Get out the good china, silverware, and glasses. With the following menu, you can start a new year in the light direction.

occasionally. Remove tenderloin from bag, reserving marinade.

Preheat oven to 500°. Place tenderloin on a broiler pan coated with cooking spray. Insert meat thermometer into thickest portion of tenderloin. Place in oven; immediately reduce oven temperature to 350°. Bake 1 hour and 10 minutes or until thermometer registers 145° (medium-rare) to 160° (medium). Let stand 10 minutes.

Combine flour and 2 tablespoons reserved marinade in a large skillet; stir with a whisk. Add remaining marinade to skillet, stirring with whisk until blended. Bring to a boil; cook 8 minutes or until thick, stirring constantly. Serve with tenderloin. Yield: 12 servings (serving size: 3 ounces beef and about 2 tablespoons sauce).

CALORIES 201 (21% from fat); PROTEIN 14.8g; FAT 4.8g (sat 1.8g, mono 1.8g, poly 0.2g); CARB 19.6g; FIBER 0.7g; CHOL 42mg; IRON 2.4mg; SODIUM 166mg; CALC 16mg

ORANGE-WATERCRESS SALAD

- 7 cups torn Bibb lettuce
- 2 cups trimmed watercress
- ¼ cup sliced green onions
- ¼ cup plus 2 tablespoons fresh orange juice
- 2 tablespoons tarragon vinegar
- 2 teaspoons extra-virgin olive oil
- 2 teaspoons honey
- ½ teaspoon dry mustard
- 2 cups orange sections (about 4 oranges)
- 2 tablespoons chopped pistachios

Combine first 3 ingredients in a large bowl; toss gently. Combine juice and next 4 ingredients in a small bowl, stirring with a whisk; drizzle over lettuce. Toss gently. Place 1 cup lettuce mixture on each of 8 salad plates; top with orange sections and pistachios. Serve immediately. Yield: 8 servings (serving size: 1 cup).

CALORIES 67 (36% from fat); PROTEIN 2g; FAT 2.7g (sat 0.4g, mono 1.8g, poly 0.4g); CARB 10.2g; FIBER 2.9g; CHOL 0mg; IRON 0.5mg; SODIUM 7mg; CALC 36mg

PORT-MARINATED TENDERLOIN WITH CRANBERRIES

Squeeze the air out of the zip-top plastic bag before sealing so the marinade surrounds entire piece of meat. • For easy cleanup, line broiler pan with aluminum foil.

- 1 (3-pound) beef tenderloin
- 1 cup dried cranberries
- 1 cup cranberry juice cocktail
- 1 cup tawny port
- 3 tablespoons brown sugar
- 2 tablespoons low-sodium soy sauce
- 1 teaspoon coarsely ground pepper
- ¼ teaspoon salt
- 3 garlic cloves, minced
- Vegetable cooking spray
- 1 tablespoon all-purpose flour

Trim fat from tenderloin. Combine tenderloin, cranberries, and next 7 ingredients in a large heavy-duty, zip-top plastic bag; seal bag. Marinate in refrigerator 24 hours, turning bag

BLUE CHEESE YORKSHIRE PUDDING

- 2 cups all-purpose flour
- ¾ cup 2% low-fat milk
- ⅓ cup crumbled blue cheese
- 1½ teaspoons sugar
- ⅛ teaspoon salt
- 1 large egg
- 1 large egg white
- 1 tablespoon vegetable oil
- Vegetable cooking spray

Preheat oven to 450°.

Combine first 7 ingredients in a bowl; beat at medium speed of an electric mixer until smooth. Beat at high speed 15 seconds; set aside.

Divide oil evenly among 8 muffin cups; coat sides of cups with cooking spray. Place muffin cups in a 450° oven for 3 minutes. Divide batter evenly among prepared cups; bake at 450° for 10 minutes. Reduce oven temperature to 350°; bake an additional 15 minutes or until golden. Serve immediately. Yield: 8 servings.

CALORIES 189 (28% from fat); PROTEIN 7.2g; FAT 5.9g (sat 2.6g, mono 1.6g, poly 1.1g); CARB 26.1g; FIBER 0.8g; CHOL 37mg; IRON 1.6mg; SODIUM 195mg; CALC 86mg

GLAZED JULIENNE CARROTS

2 tablespoons reduced-calorie margarine
¼ cup firmly packed brown sugar
4 cups (2-inch) julienne-cut carrot
¼ teaspoon salt
¼ teaspoon pepper
¼ cup chopped fresh parsley

Melt margarine in a large nonstick skillet over medium heat; add sugar, stirring until melted.

Add carrot, salt, and pepper; cook 10 minutes or until carrots are crisp-tender, stirring occasionally. Remove from heat. Stir in parsley. Yield: 8 servings (serving size: ½ cup).

CALORIES 57 (30% from fat); PROTEIN 0.6g; FAT 1.9g (sat 0.4g, mono 0.8g, poly 0.6g); CARB 10.1g; FIBER 1.9g; CHOL 0mg; IRON 0.5mg; SODIUM 123mg; CALC 22mg

LEMON CREAM TART

1 large egg white
2 tablespoons stick margarine
3 tablespoons sugar
3 cups reduced-fat vanilla wafer crumbs (about 36 cookies)
Vegetable cooking spray
3 large eggs
1 (14-ounce) can low-fat sweetened condensed milk (not evaporated skim milk)
1 tablespoon grated lemon rind
½ cup fresh lemon juice
1 cup frozen reduced-calorie whipped topping, thawed
10 lemon rind strips (optional)
Fresh mint leaves (optional)

Preheat oven to 325°.

Combine first 3 ingredients; beat at high speed of an electric mixer until blended. Add crumbs; toss with a fork until moist.

Press crumb mixture into bottom and up sides of a 9-inch round tart pan coated with cooking spray. Bake at 325° for 15 minutes or until crust is lightly browned. Let cool on a wire rack.

Combine eggs, milk, grated lemon rind, and juice in a bowl, stirring with a whisk until blended. Pour mixture into prepared crust. Bake at 325° for 30 minutes or until filling is set. Let cool completely. Top with whipped topping. Garnish with lemon rind strips and mint, if desired. Yield: 10 servings (serving size: 1 wedge and 1½ tablespoons whipped topping).

CALORIES 256 (27% from fat); PROTEIN 6.5g; FAT 7.8g (sat 2.7g, mono 2.1g, poly 1.2g); CARB 41g; FIBER 0g; CHOL 71mg; IRON 0.2mg; SODIUM 159mg; CALC 33mg

LIGHTEN UP

Life Begins at 40

Made famous by the late James Beard, Chicken with 40 Cloves of Garlic is a classic Provençal-style dish in which thighs and drumsticks are baked in the oven for an hour and a half. And, yes, it calls for garlic—lots of garlic. Fear not, though: "The slow braising softens the garlic to a lovely buttery consistency and delicate flavor," Beard wrote in his cookbook, *The New James Beard*.

Lightening this dish does not affect its rich, aromatic flavor. By using skinned chicken pieces and omitting the oil, we reduced the fat to one-fifth of the original and cut the calories in half. And for a bonus: Try spreading pieces of French bread with the softened garlic, then dipping them into the juices from the chicken.

Because Chicken with 40 Cloves of Garlic is so hearty and easy to assemble—all of the ingredients bake together in a casserole dish—it's perfect for the holidays. Just make sure that you have plenty of fresh garlic on hand. Chicken with 37 Cloves might not be the same.

CHICKEN WITH 40 CLOVES OF GARLIC

2½ cups chopped onion
1 teaspoon dried tarragon
6 fresh parsley sprigs
4 celery stalks, each cut into 3 pieces
8 chicken thighs, skinned (about 2¾ pounds)
8 chicken drumsticks, skinned (about 1¾ pounds)
½ cup dry vermouth
1½ teaspoons salt
¼ teaspoon pepper
Dash of ground nutmeg
40 unpeeled garlic cloves (about 4 heads)
Fresh tarragon sprigs (optional)
French bread (optional)

Preheat oven to 375°.

Combine first 4 ingredients in a 4-quart casserole. Arrange chicken over vegetables. Drizzle with vermouth; sprinkle with salt, pepper, and nutmeg. Nestle garlic around chicken. Cover casserole with aluminum foil and casserole lid. Bake at 375° for 1½ hours. Garnish with tarragon sprigs, and serve with French bread, if desired. Yield: 8 servings (serving size: 1 thigh, 1 drumstick, ¼ cup vegetable mixture, and 5 garlic cloves).

CALORIES 294 (24% from fat); PROTEIN 43.1g; FAT 7.8g (sat 2g, mono 2.4g, poly 2g); CARB 11g; FIBER 1.6g; CHOL 165mg; IRON 2.7mg; SODIUM 641mg; CALC 73mg

BEFORE & AFTER	
SERVING SIZE	
1 serving	
CALORIES	
590	294
FAT	
43.4g	7.8g
PERCENT OF TOTAL CALORIES	
66%	24%
CHOLESTEROL	
170mg	165mg
SODIUM	
624mg	641mg

Family Affair

Amid all the hustle and bustle, take time for a peaceful evening with just the family. Celebrate this special occasion with an extra-special, French-inspired menu for four, which has all the warmth and sparkle of an intimate fire.

FRENCH CHICKEN IN VINEGAR SAUCE WITH PEPPER-SPIKED POLENTA

Buy boneless, skinless chicken thighs, or ask your butcher to bone and skin them for you.

Olive oil-flavored vegetable cooking
   spray
2½ cups coarsely chopped onion
8 (3-ounce) skinned, boned
   chicken thighs
½ cup dry white wine
½ cup fat-free chicken broth
3 tablespoons tomato paste
2 tablespoons balsamic vinegar
1 teaspoon minced fresh or
   ½ teaspoon dried tarragon
½ teaspoon brown sugar
½ teaspoon salt
¼ teaspoon ground red pepper
Dash of black pepper
Pepper-Spiked Polenta
Fresh tarragon sprigs (optional)

Coat a large nonstick skillet with cooking spray, and place skillet over medium-high heat until hot. Add onion, and cook 5 minutes or until lightly browned. Add chicken, and sauté on each side 3 minutes or until browned.

Combine wine and next 8 ingredients in a medium bowl; stir well. Add wine mixture to chicken mixture; cover, reduce heat, and simmer 20 minutes. Serve with Pepper-Spiked Polenta. Garnish with tarragon sprigs, if desired. Yield: 4 servings (serving size: 2 thighs, ½ cup sauce, and 1 cup polenta).

CALORIES 372 (20% from fat); PROTEIN 33.5g; FAT 8.2g (sat 2.4g, mono 2.3g, poly 1.7g); CARB 39.7g; FIBER 4.4g; CHOL 116mg; IRON 3.8mg; SODIUM 827mg; CALC 118mg

Pepper-Spiked Polenta:

Vegetable cooking spray
4 cups water
1 cup yellow cornmeal
½ teaspoon salt
¼ teaspoon dried crushed red
   pepper
¼ cup grated Parmesan
   cheese

Coat a 2-quart casserole with cooking spray. Combine water, cornmeal, salt, and pepper, stirring well. Cover with casserole lid; microwave at HIGH 12 minutes or until mixture is thick, stirring after 6 minutes. Stir in cheese. Serve immediately. Yield: 4 servings (serving size: 1 cup).

CALORIES 151 (13% from fat); PROTEIN 5g; FAT 2.2g (sat 1g, mono 0.6g, poly 0.3g); CARB 27.1g; FIBER 1.8g; CHOL 4mg; IRON 1.5mg; SODIUM 388mg; CALC 71mg

SAUTÉED BRUSSELS SPROUTS WITH THYME

Wash and trim Brussels sprouts up to two days ahead. Buy small, bright-green sprouts with compact heads.
• *Mince or chop fresh herbs in a cup with scissors.*

4 cups trimmed Brussels sprouts
1 teaspoon olive oil
2 teaspoons minced fresh or
   ½ teaspoon dried thyme
¼ cup water
¼ teaspoon salt
⅛ teaspoon pepper
¼ cup chopped fresh flat-leaf
   parsley

Wash Brussels sprouts thoroughly under cold water; remove discolored leaves. Cut off stem ends; cut sprouts in half.

Heat oil in a large nonstick skillet over medium heat until hot. Add sprouts and thyme; sauté 10 minutes. Add water, salt, and pepper; cover and cook 3 minutes or until sprouts are tender, stirring occasionally. Remove from heat; stir in parsley. Yield: 4 servings (serving size: ¾ cup).

CALORIES 50 (25% from fat); PROTEIN 3.1g; FAT 1.4g (sat 0.2g, mono 0.9g, poly 0.2g); CARB 8.3g; FIBER 4g; CHOL 0mg; IRON 1.6mg; SODIUM 171mg; CALC 44mg

VANILLA-CARAMEL FLAN

Make up to two days ahead and refrigerate; invert onto serving plates just before serving.

- ⅓ cup sugar
- 1 tablespoon water
- Vegetable cooking spray
- ½ cup sugar
- 2 large eggs
- 2 large egg whites
- 1½ cups 2% low-fat milk
- 1 cup evaporated skim milk
- 1 (6-inch) vanilla bean, split lengthwise or 1 tablespoon vanilla extract
- Fresh mint sprigs (optional)

Preheat oven to 325°.

Combine ⅓ cup sugar and water in a small heavy saucepan over medium-high heat; cook 5 minutes or until golden, stirring occasionally. Immediately pour into 6 (6-ounce) custard cups coated with cooking spray, tipping quickly until sugar coats bottoms of cups; set aside.

Combine ½ cup sugar, eggs, and egg whites in a large bowl; stir well with a whisk. Add milks; stir until smooth. Scrape seeds from vanilla bean; stir seeds into milk mixture, reserving bean for another use. Divide mixture evenly among prepared cups. Place cups in a 13 x 9-inch baking dish; add hot water to a depth of 1 inch. Bake at 325° for 1 hour or until a knife inserted in center comes out clean. Remove cups from dish; let cool completely on a wire rack. Cover and chill at least 3 hours.

Loosen edges of custards with a knife or rubber spatula. Place a dessert plate, upside down, on top of each cup; invert custards onto plates. Drizzle any remaining syrup over custards. Garnish with mint sprigs, if desired. Yield: 6 servings.

CALORIES 209 (13% from fat); PROTEIN 8.5g; FAT 3.1g (sat 1.3g, mono 1g, poly 0.3g); CARB 36g; FIBER 0g; CHOL 80mg; IRON 0.4mg; SODIUM 119mg; CALC 208mg

---

QUICK & EASY
WEEKNIGHTS

Italian Light

Balsamic vinegar adds tang to flank steak and awakens winter tomatoes. Add Parmesan-basil pilaf and sautéed zucchini, and you have an Italian meal.

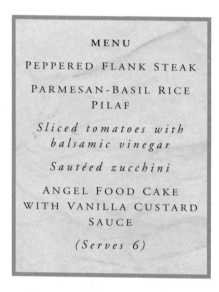

MENU

PEPPERED FLANK STEAK

PARMESAN-BASIL RICE PILAF

Sliced tomatoes with balsamic vinegar

Sautéed zucchini

ANGEL FOOD CAKE WITH VANILLA CUSTARD SAUCE

(Serves 6)

PEPPERED FLANK STEAK

- 1 (1½-pound) lean flank steak
- 1 teaspoon cracked or freshly ground pepper
- 1 teaspoon bottled minced garlic
- ¼ teaspoon salt
- 1 teaspoon olive oil
- 1 tablespoon balsamic vinegar
- 2 tablespoons fresh lemon juice

Trim fat from steak. Rub steak with pepper, garlic, and salt.

Heat oil in a large skillet over medium-high heat until hot. Add steak; cook 6 minutes on each side or until steak is desired degree of doneness, basting with vinegar.

Cut steak across grain into thin slices. Drizzle lemon juice over steak. Yield: 6 servings (serving size: 3 ounces steak).

CALORIES 202 (51% from fat); PROTEIN 22.7g; FAT 11.4g (sat 4.9g, mono 4.8g, poly 0.5g); CARB 1.1g; FIBER 0.1g; CHOL 57mg; IRON 2.4mg; SODIUM 181mg; CALC 9mg

---

PARMESAN-BASIL RICE PILAF

- 1 teaspoon olive oil
- 1 teaspoon bottled minced garlic
- 2 cups uncooked long-grain rice
- ½ cup water
- 2 (14¼-ounce) cans fat-free chicken broth
- 1 cup frozen green peas, thawed
- ½ cup preshredded fresh Parmesan cheese
- ¼ cup chopped green onions
- ½ teaspoon dried basil
- ¼ teaspoon pepper

Heat oil in a saucepan over medium-high heat until hot. Add garlic; sauté 30 seconds or until lightly browned. Add rice; cook 2 minutes, stirring constantly. Stir in water and broth; bring to a boil.

Cover and reduce heat to medium-low. Cook 20 minutes or until liquid is almost absorbed. Remove from heat; fluff with a fork. Add peas and remaining ingredients, tossing well. Yield: 6 servings (serving size: 1 cup).

CALORIES 305 (10% from fat); PROTEIN 12.7g; FAT 3.5g (sat 1.7g, mono 1.3g, poly 0.2g); CARB 53.9g; FIBER 2.2g; CHOL 6mg; IRON 2.3mg; SODIUM 179mg; CALC 144mg

---

ANGEL FOOD CAKE WITH VANILLA CUSTARD SAUCE

- 1½ cups 2% low-fat milk
- ¼ cup sugar
- 4 large egg yolks
- 1 tablespoon vanilla extract
- 8 (2-ounce) slices angel food cake

Place milk in a 1-quart glass measure. Microwave at HIGH 3 minutes.

Combine sugar and egg yolks in a medium bowl; stir with a whisk. Gradually add hot milk to egg mixture, stirring constantly with a whisk. Return milk mixture to glass measure. Microwave at HIGH 2½ minutes, stirring after 1½ minutes. Stir in vanilla. Cover and cool to room temperature. Serve over angel food cake. Yield: 8 servings (serving size: 1 slice cake and ¼ cup sauce).

CALORIES 228 (15% from fat); PROTEIN 6.4g; FAT 3.7g (sat 1.4g, mono 1.3g, poly 0.5g); CARB 42.1g; FIBER 0g; CHOL 113mg; IRON 0.5mg; SODIUM 315mg; CALC 115mg

COOKING WITH KERR

Give Turkey a Rest

On Thanksgiving, we feast in common, and struggle to balance television and table. And for this struggle, try a fresh approach to your holiday feast.

Turkey breast is naturally low in fat, and Cornish game hens are, too. But to my taste, the game hen has slightly more flavor. The Rock Cornish game hens were developed in the United States in the 1800s, a cross between a Cornish hen and a White Rock chicken. They generally come to market at five or six weeks of age and weigh between ¾ and 2 pounds; larger ones easily serve two people.

GAME HENS WITH FRUIT AND SAUSAGE STUFFING

Don't be intimidated by the length of this recipe; it's really four recipes in one.

- 2 (1½-pound) Rock Cornish game hens
- ½ teaspoon Southern France Spice Mix
- 1 teaspoon olive oil
- ¼ cup chopped shallot
- 2 cups (1-inch) French bread cubes (about 2 [1-ounce] slices)
- 1 cup peeled, chopped Rome apple
- ¼ pound diced smoked turkey sausage
- ¼ cup dried cranberries
- ¼ cup pitted coarsely chopped prunes
- 1 teaspoon Southern France Spice Mix
- ¼ teaspoon pepper
- ⅛ teaspoon salt
- 4 (½-inch-thick) slices French bread
- ¼ cup boiling water
- 2 tablespoons dried cranberries
- 2 tablespoons chopped shallot
- 6 black peppercorns
- 1 cup apple juice
- 1 cup cranberry juice cocktail
- 2 tablespoons dry red wine
- 2 teaspoons cornstarch
- ½ teaspoon fresh lemon juice
- ⅛ teaspoon Southern France Spice Mix

Chopped fresh parsley (optional)
Fresh sage sprigs (optional)

Preheat oven to 350°.

For the hens: Remove and reserve giblets and necks from hens. Rinse hens under cold water; pat dry. Split hens in half lengthwise; trim excess fat. Loosen skin from breasts and drumsticks by inserting fingers and gently pushing between skin and meat. Rub ⅛ teaspoon Southern France Spice Mix beneath skin on each breast and drumstick. Set aside.

For the stuffing: Heat oil in a large nonstick skillet over medium-high heat until hot. Add ¼ cup shallot;

sauté 2 minutes. Add bread cubes and next 7 ingredients; cook 1 minute, stirring until well-blended. Remove from heat.

Arrange bread slices in a 13 x 9-inch baking dish. Spoon ¾ cup stuffing mixture onto each bread slice. Place 1 hen half, skin side up, over each mound of stuffing mixture. Bake at 350° for 45 minutes.

For the sauce: Combine ¼ cup boiling water and 2 tablespoons cranberries in a small bowl. Let stand 30 minutes. Drain.

Cook reserved giblets, necks, 2 tablespoons shallot, and peppercorns in large nonstick skillet over medium-high heat until browned.

Add apple juice and cranberry juice; bring to a boil. Reduce heat; simmer, uncovered, 20 minutes or until reduced to 1 cup. Strain mixture through a sieve over a bowl; discard solids. Return liquid to skillet.

Combine wine and cornstarch in a small bowl; stir well. Add cornstarch mixture, rehydrated cranberries, lemon juice, and ⅛ teaspoon Southern France Spice Mix to skillet. Bring to a boil; cook 1 minute or until thick, stirring constantly. Serve sauce with hens and stuffing. Garnish with parsley and sage sprigs, if desired. Yield: 4 servings (serving size: 1 hen half, ¾ cup stuffing, and ¼ cup sauce).

CALORIES 638 (31% from fat); PROTEIN 42.5g; FAT 22g (sat 5.9g, mono 7.9g, poly 5.5g);CARB 67.3g; FIBER 3.8g; CHOL 83mg; IRON 5mg; SODIUM 604mg; CALC 76mg

Southern France Spice Mix:

- 1 teaspoon dried oregano, crushed
- 1 teaspoon dried marjoram, crushed
- 1 teaspoon rubbed sage
- ½ teaspoon dried rosemary, crushed
- ½ teaspoon dried basil, crushed
- ¼ teaspoon ground bay leaf

Combine all ingredients; stir well. Yield: 1 tablespoon plus 1 teaspoon.

Note: Store remaining Southern France Spice Mix in an airtight container.

*M*orning Glory

As everyone knows, the holidays are sofa-bed season, when friends and relatives come to stay. How much simpler life would be if everyone ate only dinner this time of year, but that's not the way it works. People still want breakfast and lunch, too; after all, unwrapping presents can really build up an appetite.

So what's a good host to do? We have a solution: brunch. Even though we created the following menu for Thanksgiving or Christmas morning, it's appropriate any day of the week. With this kind of a meal so early in the day, your friends and in-laws may decide to extend their stays.

MENU

CRANBERRY-RASPBERRY
SPRITZER
OR
MINTY HOT MOCHA

CRAB QUICHE
FLORENTINE
OR
HAM-AND-CHEESE
QUICHE

SPICED WINTER FRUIT

FRESH GINGER-AND-
LEMON MUFFINS
OR
DATE-AND-MAPLE
SCONES
OR
CINNAMON STREUSEL
COFFEECAKE,

(Serves 6)

PUTTING IT TOGETHER

ONE TO TWO WEEKS AHEAD

1. Make the coffeecake, scones, or muffins; bake and cool completely. Wrap tightly, and freeze.

ONE TO TWO DAYS AHEAD

1. Make Spiced Winter Fruit; chill.
2. Make spinach mixture for Crab Quiche Florentine; remove shell pieces from crab, shred cheese, and combine milk with egg substitute. Cover and chill mixtures in 4 separate airtight containers.
3. Make ham mixture for Ham-and-Cheese Quiche; shred cheese, and combine milk with egg substitute. Cover; chill mixtures in 3 separate airtight containers.

THE NIGHT BEFORE

1. Thaw cake, scones, or muffins.

DAY OF BRUNCH

1. Assemble and bake quiche.

15 MINUTES AHEAD

1. Prepare Cranberry-Raspberry Spritzer and/or Minty Hot Mocha.

CRANBERRY-RASPBERRY SPRITZER

To garnish this drink, thread fresh cranberries and fresh lemon slices onto wooden skewers.

    3   cups unsweetened raspberry-
        flavored sparkling water,
        chilled
    3   cups cranberry-raspberry drink,
        chilled
    ¼   cup plus 2 tablespoons crème de
        cassis (black currant-flavored
        liqueur)

Combine sparkling water and cranberry-raspberry drink in a pitcher; stir well.

Spoon 1 tablespoon crème de cassis into each of 6 glasses, and add 1 cup juice mixture to each. Yield: 6 servings.

Note: For a nonalcoholic version, omit the crème de cassis—the recipe works fine without it.

CALORIES 82 (0% from fat); PROTEIN 0.4g; FAT 0g; CARB 16.5g; FIBER 0g; CHOL 0mg; IRON 0.2mg; SODIUM 3mg; CALC 3mg

MINTY HOT MOCHA

    ¼   cup sugar
    ¼   cup unsweetened cocoa
    1   cup water
    2   tablespoons instant coffee
        granules
    4¾ cups skim milk
    ½   teaspoon peppermint extract

Combine sugar and cocoa in a medium saucepan; stir well. Add water; bring to a boil, stirring constantly. Stir in coffee granules. Gradually add milk, stirring well. Cook over medium heat 5 minutes or until mixture is thoroughly heated, stirring often. Remove from heat, and stir in peppermint. Beat with a whisk until foamy. Serve warm. Yield: 6 servings (serving size: 1 cup).

CALORIES 122 (6% from fat); PROTEIN 7.9g; FAT 0.8g (sat 0.5g, mono 0.1g, poly 0g); CARB 20.2g; FIBER 0g; CHOL 4mg; IRON 0.8mg; SODIUM 103mg; CALC 247mg

CRAB QUICHE FLORENTINE

Place the pie plate on a baking sheet in case the filling bubbles over.

1   (7-ounce) can refrigerated
     breadstick dough
Vegetable cooking spray
¾   cup (3 ounces) grated Gruyère
     cheese
8   ounces lump crabmeat, drained
     and shell pieces removed
½   cup chopped onion
4   cups coarsely chopped spinach
⅛   teaspoon dried tarragon
⅛   teaspoon Old Bay seasoning
⅛   teaspoon ground nutmeg
⅛   teaspoon pepper
1   cup evaporated skim milk
½   cup egg substitute

Unroll dough, separating into strips. Working on a flat surface, coil one strip of dough around itself in a spiral pattern. Add second strip of dough to the end of the first strip, pinching ends together to seal; continue coiling dough. Repeat procedure with remaining dough strips. Cover dough with a towel; let rest 20 minutes. Roll dough into a 13-inch circle; fit into a 9-inch pie plate coated with cooking spray. Fold edges under; flute. Sprinkle cheese over bottom of crust. Top with crabmeat; set aside.

Preheat oven to 375°.

Coat a large nonstick skillet with cooking spray; place over medium-high heat until hot. Add onion; sauté 4 minutes. Add spinach and next 4 ingredients; cook 2 minutes or until spinach wilts. Arrange spinach mixture over crabmeat.

Combine milk and egg substitute; stir well with a whisk. Pour over spinach mixture. Bake at 375° for 45 minutes or until a knife inserted in center comes out clean; let stand 10 minutes. Yield: 6 servings.

CALORIES 248 (29% from fat); PROTEIN 20.8g; FAT 7.7g (sat 3.7g, mono 2.1g, poly 1.4g); CARB 23.2g; FIBER 2.6g; CHOL 55mg; IRON 1.9mg; SODIUM 556mg; CALC 354mg

Ham-and-Cheese Quiche:

Substitute Swiss cheese for Gruyère cheese and ¾ cup chopped reduced-fat, low-salt ham (about ¼ pound) for crabmeat. Omit spinach, tarragon, Old Bay seasoning, and nutmeg; add ⅛ teaspoon salt.

Prepare crust as directed at left, and sprinkle with cheese. Cook ham, onion, salt, and pepper 4 minutes in a skillet coated with cooking spray. Arrange ham mixture over cheese. Proceed with directions at left. Yield: 6 servings.

CALORIES 220 (30% from fat); PROTEIN 15.3g; FAT 7.2g (sat 3.4g, mono 1.6g, poly 1g); CARB 22.6g; FIBER 1.1g; CHOL 24mg; IRON 1.2mg; SODIUM 557mg; CALC 270mg

SPICED WINTER FRUIT

To section grapefruit, hold peeled fruit in one hand. Starting at the top of the fruit, slip a paring knife into the section, keeping close to the membrane. Cut section out by running knife down the length of section and into the fruit, cutting as close to membrane as possible.

2   large pink grapefruit
⅓   cup small pitted prunes
⅓   cup dried figs, cut into quarters
3   tablespoons light brown sugar
7   whole cloves
1   (3-inch) cinnamon stick
1   cup seedless red grapes, halved

Peel and section grapefruit over a bowl; squeeze membranes to extract juice. Set sections aside; reserve juice, and add water to equal 1¼ cups.

Combine juice mixture, prunes, figs, sugar, cloves, and cinnamon in a medium saucepan; bring to a boil. Reduce heat; simmer 15 minutes, stirring occasionally. Remove from heat; let cool. Discard cloves and cinnamon stick. Stir in grapefruit sections and grapes. Yield: 8 servings (serving size: ½ cup).

CALORIES 97 (3% from fat); PROTEIN 1.1g; FAT 0.3g (sat 0g, mono 0.1g, poly 0.1g); CARB 25g; FIBER 2.6g; CHOL 0mg; IRON 0.6mg; SODIUM 3mg; CALC 32mg

FRESH GINGER-AND-LEMON MUFFINS

Fruit purées such as prune butter help replace some of the fat in baked recipes. Look for Lekvar or Sunsweet Lighter Bake prune butter in your grocery store.

1   cup sugar, divided
¼   teaspoon ground ginger
¼   teaspoon ground cinnamon
¼   cup peeled, chopped fresh
     gingerroot
1   tablespoon grated lemon rind
2   cups plus 2 tablespoons
     all-purpose flour
¾   teaspoon baking soda
¼   teaspoon salt
¾   cup low-fat buttermilk
⅓   cup prune butter
1   tablespoon vegetable oil
1   large egg
1   large egg white
Vegetable cooking spray

Preheat oven to 375°.

Combine 1 tablespoon sugar, ground ginger, and cinnamon in a bowl; stir well. Set cinnamon mixture aside.

Place ½ cup sugar, gingerroot, and lemon rind in a food processor; process until finely chopped. Set aside.

Combine remaining ¼ cup plus 3 tablespoons sugar, flour, baking soda, and salt in a large bowl; make a well in center of mixture. Combine gingerroot mixture, buttermilk, and next 4 ingredients; stir with a whisk. Add to flour mixture, stirring just until moist.

Divide batter evenly among 12 muffin cups coated with cooking spray; sprinkle ¼ teaspoon cinnamon mixture over each muffin. Bake at 375° for 20 minutes or until golden. Remove from pans immediately; let cool on a wire rack. Yield: 1 dozen (serving size: 1 muffin).

CALORIES 181 (10% from fat); PROTEIN 3.6g; FAT 2.1g (sat 0.4g, mono 0.6g, poly 0.8g); CARB 37.6g; FIBER 0.9g; CHOL 18mg; IRON 1.2mg; SODIUM 128mg; CALC 28mg

DATE-AND-MAPLE SCONES

Cut dates with scissors or a knife coated with cooking spray.

2 cups all-purpose flour
¼ cup firmly packed brown sugar
1½ teaspoons baking powder
½ teaspoon baking soda
¼ teaspoon salt
⅓ cup chilled stick margarine, cut into small pieces
½ cup pitted, chopped dates
½ cup 1% low-fat milk
3 tablespoons maple syrup
Vegetable cooking spray

Preheat oven to 400°.
Combine first 5 ingredients in a bowl; cut in margarine with a pastry blender or 2 knives until mixture resembles coarse meal. Add dates; toss well. Combine milk and syrup. Add to flour mixture, stirring just until moist.
Turn dough out onto a lightly floured surface; knead 4 or 5 times. Pat dough into an 8-inch circle on a baking sheet coated with cooking spray. Cut dough into 12 wedges, cutting into, but not through, dough. Do not separate wedges.
Bake at 400° for 15 minutes or until golden. Serve warm. Yield: 1 dozen.

CALORIES 176 (28% from fat); PROTEIN 2.7g; FAT 5.5g (sat 1.1g, mono 2.3g, poly 1.7g); CARB 29.8g; FIBER 1.2g; CHOL 0mg; IRON 1.3mg; SODIUM 168mg; CALC 61mg

CINNAMON STREUSEL COFFEECAKE

⅓ cup chopped walnuts
⅓ cup firmly packed brown sugar
3 tablespoons all-purpose flour
1 tablespoon ground cinnamon
Vegetable cooking spray
1¼ cups sugar
⅓ cup vegetable oil
2 large eggs
3 cups all-purpose flour
1 teaspoon baking powder
1 teaspoon baking soda
½ teaspoon salt
1½ cups low-fat buttermilk
1 tablespoon vanilla extract

Preheat oven to 350°.
Combine first 4 ingredients in a small bowl, and stir well. Coat a 12-cup Bundt pan with cooking spray; sprinkle ⅓ cup walnut mixture into pan. Set remaining walnut mixture aside.
Combine 1¼ cups sugar and vegetable oil in a large bowl; beat at medium speed of an electric mixer until well-blended. Add eggs, one at a time, beating well after each addition.
Combine flour, baking powder, baking soda, and salt; stir well. Add flour mixture to creamed mixture alternately with buttermilk, beginning and ending with flour mixture; mix after each addition. Stir in vanilla.
Measure 2 cups batter; set aside. Pour remaining batter into prepared pan; sprinkle remaining walnut mixture over batter. Pour reserved 2 cups batter over walnut mixture. Bake at 350° for 45 minutes or until a wooden pick inserted in center comes out clean. Let cool in pan 10 minutes on a wire rack; remove from pan. Let cool completely on wire rack. Yield: 16 servings.

CALORIES 249 (26% from fat); PROTEIN 4.9g; FAT 7.3g (sat 1.4g, mono 1.9g, poly 3.3g); CARB 41.1g; FIBER 0.9g; CHOL 28mg; IRON 1.6mg; SODIUM 175mg; CALC 63mg

INSPIRED VEGETARIAN

Comfort and Joy

If you're not a meat-eater, the holidays can be an uneasy time of year, since turkey and ham are the traditional entrées. Here's a vegetarian holiday menu that should appeal to every taste bud—and schedule, too, because all the dishes can be prepared ahead and served either warm or at room temperature. (You can choose between two entrées.) Because the holidays are supposed to be about celebration, it's nice to know you can spend more time with guests and less time in the kitchen. With food this good, maybe Christmas should come twice a year?

MENU

GARLICKY BEAN SPREAD

LASAGNA RUSTICA
OR
ARTICHOKE PASTA PICCATA

FIELD SALAD WITH WARM
SOY DRESSING

MAPLE-CRANBERRY
BAKED APPLES

(*Serves 8*)

GARLICKY BEAN SPREAD

This bean dip is ideal on toasted French bread or as a sandwich filler. It makes enough for the Lasagna Rustica and an appetizer. The spread can be made up to one week ahead and then refrigerated in an airtight container. Note: If you don't have tahini, it can be omitted.

1 whole garlic head
2 tablespoons lemon juice
1 tablespoon olive oil
1 tablespoon tahini (sesame-seed paste)
2 teaspoons minced fresh or ½ teaspoon dried rosemary
2 teaspoons hot sauce
4 (15.8-ounce) cans Great Northern beans, drained

Preheat oven to 375°.
Remove white papery skin from garlic head (do not peel or separate the cloves). Wrap garlic head in aluminum foil. Bake at 375° for 45 minutes or until tender; let cool 10 minutes. Separate cloves; squeeze to extract garlic pulp. Discard skins.
Combine garlic pulp, lemon juice, and remaining ingredients in a food processor; process until smooth, scraping sides of processor bowl occasionally. Serve with French bread. Yield: 5¼ cups (serving size: 1 tablespoon).

CALORIES 16 (17% from fat); PROTEIN 0.9g; FAT 0.3g (sat 0g, mono 0.2g, poly 0.1g); CARB 2.6g; FIBER 0.6g; CHOL 0mg; IRON 0.2mg; SODIUM 53mg; CALC 8mg

LASAGNA RUSTICA

To prepare ahead, assemble the lasagna, cover it tightly, and freeze it.

2½ cups Garlicky Bean Spread
1½ cups (6 ounces) shredded part-skim mozzarella cheese, divided
2 teaspoons dried Italian seasoning
1 teaspoon dried crushed red pepper
1 pound firm light tofu, drained and crumbled
1 (10-ounce) package frozen chopped spinach, thawed and drained
1 (15-ounce) carton part-skim ricotta cheese
1 (27.5-ounce) jar light garden harvest pasta sauce
Vegetable cooking spray
9 cooked lasagna noodles

Preheat oven to 375°.
Combine Garlicky Bean Spread, 1 cup mozzarella cheese, Italian seasoning, red pepper, tofu, spinach, and ricotta cheese in a large bowl. Stir well; set aside.
Spread ½ cup pasta sauce in bottom of a 13 x 9-inch baking dish coated with cooking spray. Arrange 3 noodles over pasta sauce; top with one-third of spinach mixture and about 1 cup pasta sauce. Repeat layers, ending with noodles, spinach mixture, and remaining sauce. Sprinkle with remaining ½ cup mozzarella cheese. Cover and bake at 375° for 50 minutes or until thoroughly heated. Uncover and bake an additional 10 minutes. Let lasagna stand 10 minutes before cutting. Yield: 9 servings.

CALORIES 325 (25% from fat); PROTEIN 22.2g; FAT 9.2g (sat 4.8g, mono 2.9g, poly 0.8g); CARB 38.9g; FIBER 5.1g; CHOL 26mg; IRON 3.2mg; SODIUM 584mg; CALC 339mg

ARTICHOKE PASTA PICCATA

Most of this recipe's sodium comes from the marinara sauce. If you're watching your sodium intake, choose a low-sodium sauce. • Check the label for a six- to eight-count to ensure large canned artichoke hearts.

4 (14-ounce) cans artichoke hearts (6- to 8-count), drained
8 large egg whites
4 large eggs
⅔ cup grated Parmesan cheese
½ cup fine, dry breadcrumbs
1 tablespoon plus 1 teaspoon dried Italian seasoning
1 teaspoon pepper
Vegetable cooking spray
1 cup all-purpose flour
8 cups hot cooked angel hair (about 16 ounces uncooked pasta)
4 cups bottled marinara sauce
½ cup chopped fresh flat-leaf parsley

Preheat oven to 400°.
Place 24 artichokes in a colander, pressing with the back of a spoon to remove juice from artichokes; set aside. (Reserve any remaining artichokes for another use.)
Combine egg whites and next 5 ingredients; stir with a whisk. Coat a large nonstick skillet with cooking spray; place over medium-high heat until hot. Working with 1 artichoke at a time, dredge 12 artichokes in flour, and dip in egg white mixture. Place artichokes in skillet; cook 3 minutes, turning to brown on all sides. Remove artichokes from skillet; place on a baking sheet coated with cooking spray. Repeat procedure with remaining 12 artichokes, flour, and egg white mixture.
Bake artichokes at 400° for 15 minutes or until hot. Serve over hot pasta and heated marinara sauce. Sprinkle with parsley. Yield: 8 servings (serving size: 3 artichokes, 1 cup pasta, and ½ cup marinara sauce).

CALORIES 526 (19% from fat); PROTEIN 25.2g; FAT 11g (sat 3.1g, mono 4.2g, poly 2.3g); CARB 85.9g; FIBER 4.3g; CHOL 116mg; IRON 7.3mg; SODIUM 1,247mg; CALC 241mg

FIELD SALAD WITH WARM SOY DRESSING

Any combination of salad greens will work, but we used prepackaged greens labeled "spring mix." • Toast pine nuts on a baking sheet at 350° for 5 minutes. They burn quickly, so watch them. • Look for mirin in the Oriental section of your grocery store.

2 (5-ounce) bags gourmet salad greens (about 16 cups)
1 cup red bell pepper strips
1 cup diagonally sliced snow pea pods
⅓ cup diagonally sliced green onions
2 tablespoons pine nuts, toasted
¼ cup low-sodium soy sauce
3 tablespoons apple juice
2 tablespoons rice vinegar
1 tablespoon mirin (sweet rice wine)
1 tablespoon dark sesame oil
1 teaspoon peeled, minced fresh gingerroot
1 garlic clove, minced

Combine first 5 ingredients in a large bowl. Combine soy sauce and remaining 6 ingredients in a microwave-safe bowl. Microwave at HIGH 90 seconds, and stir mixture well. Pour dressing over salad, tossing gently to coat. Yield: 8 servings (serving size: about 2 cups).

CALORIES 52 (55% from fat); PROTEIN 1.8g; FAT 3.2g (sat 0.5g, mono 1.2g, poly 1.3g); CARB 4.3g; FIBER 1.1g; CHOL 0mg; IRON 1mg; SODIUM 199mg; CALC 13mg

MAPLE-CRANBERRY BAKED APPLES

Use real maple syrup instead of pan-cake syrup. The flavor is worth the ex-tra cost. • Peel the top half of the apples, or they may explode in the oven. • Use raisins in place of dried cranberries, if desired. • Shave white chocolate with a vegetable peeler. Also, be sure to store the chocolate at room temperature because cold temperatures can make it crumble.

2½ cups cranberry juice cocktail
½ cup maple syrup
¼ cup firmly packed light brown
     sugar
1 tablespoon lemon juice
2 teaspoons peeled, grated fresh
     gingerroot
1 teaspoon ground cinnamon
1 teaspoon cornstarch
1 teaspoon vanilla extract
8 medium Rome apples, cored
¾ cup dried cranberries
¼ cup chopped pecans
¼ cup shaved white chocolate

Preheat oven to 350°.
Combine first 8 ingredients. Stir well; set aside.
Peel top half of each apple; place in a shallow roasting pan. Fill centers of apples evenly with cranberries and pecans. Pour cranberry-maple mixture over apples. Bake at 350° for 1 hour or until tender, basting apples twice with syrup from pan. To serve, drizzle apples with remaining syrup. Sprinkle with shaved white chocolate. Yield: 8 servings (serving size: 1 apple, 2 tablespoons syrup, and ½ tablespoon white chocolate).

CALORIES 286 (14% from fat); PROTEIN 1.2g; FAT 4.6g (sat 1.2g, mono 2.6g, poly 0.8g); CARB 64g; FIBER 4.4g; CHOL 0mg; IRON 1mg; SODIUM 13mg; CALC 47mg

---

MENU

SMOKY RED
PEPPER DIP

CURRIED
ARTICHOKE DIP

PORK-FILLED
DIJON-PEPPER
BISCUITS

CITRUS-SHRIMP
SALAD

CHRISTMAS
PUDDING WITH
BRANDY SAUCE

CRANBERRY
UPSIDE-DOWN
CAKE

RUBY-RED
GRAPEFRUIT
PUNCH

Opening Night

The holidays give you a great excuse to have people over. You can just say, "Drop by." Of course, once you've said it and half the office replies, "Cool, what time?" you have to think about what to feed everyone. Take our easy-to-do open house menu: Guaranteed to take the frost off any social situation, it features two sassy dips, a refreshing shrimp salad, flaky biscuit sandwiches filled with spicy pork, two holiday-themed desserts, and a cooling wine punch. Almost all of this plentiful, but light, menu can be made ahead and set out before guests arrive. You don't even have to serve them: Just make sure they have a fork and plate, and they're on their own. With this menu, you'll be free to mingle.

SMOKY RED PEPPER DIP

2 medium red bell peppers
2 cups sliced red onion
2 garlic cloves
¼ cup dry breadcrumbs
¼ cup plain fat-free yogurt
1 tablespoon red wine vinegar
2 teaspoons olive oil
⅛ teaspoon salt
⅛ teaspoon hot sauce

Cut peppers in half lengthwise; discard seeds and membranes. Place, skin sides up, on a aluminum foil-lined baking sheet; flatten with hand. Arrange onion and garlic around peppers. Broil 10 minutes or until blackened. Place in a zip-top plastic bag; seal. Let stand 15 minutes; peel. Place in a food processor; process until finely chopped. Add breadcrumbs and remaining ingredients; process until smooth. Serve with toasted pita triangles. Yield: 1¾ cups (serving size: 1 tablespoon).

CALORIES 13 (28% from fat); PROTEIN 0.4g; FAT 0.4g (sat 0.1g, mono 0.3g, poly 0.1g); CARB 1.9g; FIBER 0.3g; CHOL 0mg; IRON 0.1mg; SODIUM 21mg; CALC 9mg

---

CURRIED ARTICHOKE DIP

½ cup 1% low-fat cottage cheese
¼ cup low-fat sour cream
2 teaspoons lemon juice
½ teaspoon curry powder
1 (14-ounce) can artichoke hearts,
     drained
1 tablespoon chopped fresh
     parsley
1 tablespoon sliced green onions

Place first 4 ingredients in a food processor; process until smooth. Add artichokes, parsley, and green onions; pulse 10 times or until coarsely chopped. Serve with breadsticks, unsalted crackers, or raw vegetables. Yield: 1¾ cups (serving size: 1 tablespoon).

CALORIES 10 (27% from fat); PROTEIN 0.8g; FAT 0.3g (sat 0.2g, mono 0.1g, poly 0g); CARB 1.1g; FIBER 0.1g; CHOL 1mg; IRON 0.1mg; SODIUM 32mg; CALC 7mg

---

PORK-FILLED
DIJON-PEPPER BISCUITS

For an easy cleanup, line the broiler pan with aluminum foil before roasting.

1   (1-pound) pork tenderloin
4   cups water
2   tablespoons sugar
1   tablespoon salt
1½ teaspoons dried thyme
1   teaspoon whole allspice
1   bay leaf
1   teaspoon dried rosemary, crushed
1   tablespoon plus 1 teaspoon olive oil, divided
Vegetable cooking spray
Dijon-Pepper Biscuits
¾   cup purchased cranberry-orange relish

Trim fat from pork. Combine pork, water, and next 5 ingredients in a large heavy-duty, zip-top plastic bag. Seal and marinate in refrigerator 2½ hours.

Preheat oven to 350°.

Remove pork from bag; discard marinade. Pat pork dry with a paper towel. Combine rosemary and 1 teaspoon oil; rub over pork.

Heat remaining 1 tablespoon oil in a nonstick skillet over medium-high heat until hot. Add pork; cook 5 minutes, browning on all sides. Place pork on broiler pan coated with cooking spray. Insert meat thermometer into thickest portion of pork, making sure it does not touch bone. Bake at 350° for 35 minutes or until thermometer registers 160° (slightly pink). Wrap in aluminum foil; chill 3 hours or overnight.

Cut pork diagonally across grain into 24 slices. Split Dijon-Pepper Biscuits. Place 1 slice pork on bottom half of each biscuit. Top each slice with 1½ teaspoons relish; cover with top halves. Yield: 24 appetizers (serving size: 1 appetizer).

CALORIES 120 (27% from fat); PROTEIN 5.7g; FAT 3.6g (sat 0.7g, mono 1.7g, poly 0.8g); CARB 15.7g; FIBER 0.5g; CHOL 13mg; IRON 0.9mg; SODIUM 215mg; CALC 41mg

Dijon-Pepper Biscuits:

2   cups all-purpose flour
2   teaspoons baking powder
¾   teaspoon coarsely ground pepper
½   teaspoon salt
⅛   teaspoon garlic powder
3   tablespoons stick margarine, cut into small pieces and chilled
½   cup 1% low-fat milk
2   tablespoons Dijon mustard
Vegetable cooking spray

Preheat oven to 425°.

Combine first 5 ingredients in a bowl; cut in margarine with a pastry blender or 2 knives until mixture resembles coarse meal. Combine milk and mustard; add to flour mixture. Stir until flour mixture is moist.

Turn dough out onto a lightly floured surface. Knead 5 or 6 times. Roll dough to about ½-inch thickness, and cut with a 1¾-inch biscuit cutter. Place on a baking sheet coated with cooking spray. Bake at 425° for 12 to 15 minutes or until lightly browned. Yield: 2 dozen (serving size: 1 biscuit).

CALORIES 55 (28% from fat); PROTEIN 1.3g; FAT 1.7g (sat 0.3g, mono 0.7g, poly 0.5g); CARB 8.4g; FIBER 0.3g; CHOL 0mg; IRON 0.5mg; SODIUM 105mg; CALC 31mg

CITRUS-SHRIMP SALAD

2½ quarts water
2   pounds medium shrimp
¼   cup reduced-calorie Italian salad dressing
3   tablespoons finely chopped shallots
2   tablespoons red wine vinegar
2   tablespoons plain fat-free yogurt
2   tablespoons orange juice
1½ tablespoons Dijon mustard
1   tablespoon honey
⅛   teaspoon pepper
4   cups sliced romaine lettuce
2   cups pink grapefruit sections (about 4 large grapefruit)
2   cups orange sections (about 5 oranges)
¼   cup chopped fresh chives

Bring water to a boil, and add shrimp. Cook shrimp 3 to 5 minutes. Drain and rinse with cold water. Peel and devein shrimp; chill.

Combine salad dressing and next 7 ingredients in a large bowl, and stir well. Stir in shrimp.

Line a large platter with lettuce. Spoon shrimp mixture into center of platter; arrange grapefruit sections and orange sections around salad. Sprinkle with chives. Yield: 8 servings.

CALORIES 163 (18% from fat); PROTEIN 19.1g; FAT 3.2g (sat 0.6g, mono 0.8g, poly 1.5g); CARB 14.1g; FIBER 2.6g; CHOL 168mg; IRON 2.9mg; SODIUM 321mg; CALC 71mg

PUTTING IT TOGETHER

ONE WEEK AHEAD

1. Chill all ingredients for Ruby-Red Grapefruit Punch.
2. Bake Dijon-Pepper Biscuits. Store in a heavy-duty, zip-top bag; freeze.
3. Make pudding for Christmas Pudding with Brandy Sauce. Cover tightly; store in refrigerator. (Steamed pudding gets better with age.)

ONE TO TWO DAYS AHEAD

1. Make pork tenderloin. Wrap tightly, and chill.
2. Make Smoky Red Pepper Dip and Curried Artichoke Dip. Refrigerate in airtight containers.
3. Cook, peel, and chill shrimp for Citrus-Shrimp Salad. Peel and section fruit. Store in separate airtight containers in refrigerator.
4. Make salad dressing for Citrus-Shrimp Salad.
5. Make Cranberry Upside-Down Cake.

DAY OF OPEN HOUSE

1. Thaw Dijon-Pepper Biscuits.
2. Assemble Pork-Filled Dijon-Pepper Biscuits on a tray.
3. Make Ruby-Red Grapefruit Punch just before serving.
4. Assemble Citrus-Shrimp Salad.
5. Bring Christmas Pudding to room temperature; make Brandy Sauce just before serving.

CHRISTMAS PUDDING WITH BRANDY SAUCE

Use a round cake-cooling rack inside the stockpot.

    2   cups peeled, shredded sweet
            potato
    1   cup whole-wheat flour
    ¾   cup raisins
    ½   cup chopped dried apricots
    ⅓   cup firmly packed brown sugar
    ¼   cup stick margarine, softened
    ½   teaspoon ground cinnamon
    ½   teaspoon ground nutmeg
    ¼   teaspoon salt
    ¼   teaspoon ground cloves
    1   large egg white
    2   tablespoons skim milk
    ½   teaspoon baking soda
    ½   teaspoon white vinegar
        Vegetable cooking spray
    1¼ cups vanilla low-fat ice cream,
            softened
    2   tablespoons brandy

Combine first 11 ingredients in a bowl; stir well. Combine milk, baking soda, and vinegar; add to sweet potato mixture, stirring until dry ingredients are moist.

Press sweet potato mixture into a 6-cup steamed-pudding mold coated with cooking spray. Cover tightly with aluminum foil or lid coated with cooking spray.

Place mold on a shallow rack in a stockpot; add boiling water to halfway up sides of mold. Cover and cook in simmering water 3 hours or until a knife inserted in center comes out clean, adding water to stockpot as needed. Invert pudding onto a plate; cut into 10 slices. Combine softened ice cream and brandy, stirring with a whisk until blended. Serve with pudding. Yield: 10 servings (serving size: 1 wedge and 2 tablespoons sauce).

CALORIES 219 (24% from fat); PROTEIN 3.5g; FAT 5.8g (sat 1.4g, mono 2.3g, poly 1.6g); CARB 39.5g; FIBER 3.1g; CHOL 2mg; IRON 1.4mg; SODIUM 204mg; CALC 56mg

CRANBERRY UPSIDE-DOWN CAKE

    1   tablespoon margarine, melted
    ½   cup firmly packed brown sugar
    2   cups cranberries
    ¼   cup stick margarine, softened
    1   cup sugar
    2   large eggs
    1½ teaspoons vanilla extract
    1½ cups sifted cake flour
    1½ teaspoons baking powder
    1   teaspoon ground cinnamon
    ¾   cup low-fat buttermilk

Preheat oven to 350°.

Pour melted margarine in bottom of a 9-inch springform pan. Combine brown sugar and cranberries; arrange in a single layer over margarine.

Cream ¼ cup margarine and 1 cup sugar, beating at medium speed of an electric mixer until well-blended. Add eggs, one at time, beating well after each addition; add vanilla. Combine flour, baking powder, and cinnamon; stir well. Add dry ingredients to creamed mixture alternately with buttermilk, beginning and ending with dry ingredients.

Spoon batter evenly over cranberries. Bake at 350° for 45 minutes or until a wooden pick inserted in center comes out clean. Invert cake onto a serving platter. Yield: 8 servings (serving size: 1 wedge).

CALORIES 314 (26% from fat); PROTEIN 4.3g; FAT 9g (sat 2.1g, mono 3.7g, poly 2.5g); CARB 54.7g; FIBER 0.4g; CHOL 55mg; IRON 2.1mg; SODIUM 116mg; CALC 104mg

RUBY-RED GRAPEFRUIT PUNCH

    1   (48-ounce) bottle ruby-red
            grapefruit juice drink, chilled
    1   (33.8-ounce) bottle club soda,
            chilled
    1   (25.4-ounce) bottle dry white
            wine, chilled

Combine all ingredients in a large punch bowl; stir well. Yield: 17 servings (serving size: ¾ cup).

CALORIES 60 (2% from fat); PROTEIN 0.5g; FAT 0.1g; CARB 7.8g; FIBER 0g; CHOL 0mg; IRON 1.8mg; SODIUM 16mg; CALC 12mg

TECHNIQUE

Chestnuts Roasting

Chestnuts are surprisingly low in fat. Enjoy them roasted or in main and side dishes.

Although a longtime staple of European cooking, chestnuts are almost a novelty food in America. That's a shame when you consider their sweet-nutty flavor, versatility, and health factors—low in fat and high in carbohydrates. In France, where they're called *marrons*, chestnuts are commonly served as side dishes and in desserts. So treasured are they in Italy that in October, when they're harvested, chestnut festivals are held throughout the countryside. Had it not been for a chestnut blight in the first half of this century that decimated America's chestnut trees—some nine million acres of forest—chestnuts might be a staple here, too. Most chestnuts today are imported, usually from Italy, France, and Japan.

Because the chestnut's rich flavor blends so harmoniously with other foods, the following recipes use it in some unexpected ways: in a main-course stew, in vegetable and fruit side dishes, in biscotti, and as the star ingredient of a hearty soup. And because chestnuts roasting on an open fire have become so associated with the holidays, we give you instructions (page 310) on how to roast them in your very own fireplace, oven, or microwave. As for Jack Frost nipping at your nose, try dressing warmly.

CHESTNUT BEEF STEW

1 pound lean beef stew meat
3 tablespoons all-purpose flour
1 tablespoon vegetable oil
1½ cups water
½ teaspoon dried thyme
½ teaspoon pepper
¼ teaspoon dried marjoram
⅛ teaspoon dried sage
6 garlic cloves, peeled
2 (10½-ounce) cans beef broth
2 tablespoons cold water
1 tablespoon all-purpose flour
3 cups (1-inch) peeled, cubed
   eggplant
2 cups quartered small red
   potatoes
1½ cups cooked, shelled, and
   halved chestnuts (about 1½
   pounds in shells)
1 (14.5-ounce) can no-salt-added
   stewed tomatoes
Fresh thyme sprigs (optional)

Trim fat from beef. Cut beef into 1-inch cubes. Combine beef and 3 tablespoons flour in a large heavy-duty, zip-top plastic bag. Seal bag; shake well to coat. Heat oil in a large Dutch oven over medium heat until hot. Add beef; cook 5 minutes, browning on all sides. Add 1½ cups water and next 6 ingredients; bring to a boil. Cover, reduce heat to low, and simmer 1 hour.

Combine cold water and 1 tablespoon flour in a small bowl; stir well. Add flour mixture, eggplant, potatoes, chestnuts, and tomatoes to stew; bring to a boil. Cover; reduce heat to medium-low. Simmer 30 minutes or until vegetables are tender and stew is thick. Garnish with thyme sprigs, if desired. Yield: 6 servings (serving size: 1½ cups).

CALORIES 328 (17% from fat); PROTEIN 25.4g; FAT 6.3g (sat 1.7g, mono 2.2g, poly 1.6g); CARB 42.4g; FIBER 5.9g; CHOL 62mg; IRON 3.8mg; SODIUM 704mg; CALC 61mg

SAUTÉED BRUSSELS SPROUTS WITH CHESTNUTS

1 teaspoon margarine
2 tablespoons minced shallots
1 garlic clove, minced
1 pound Brussels sprouts,
   trimmed and quartered
⅓ cup dry white wine
⅓ cup water
¾ cup cooked, shelled, and
   halved chestnuts (about
   ¾ pound in shells)
2 tablespoons chopped pecans
¼ teaspoon salt
¼ teaspoon pepper

Melt margarine in a nonstick skillet over medium heat. Add shallots and garlic; sauté 2 minutes. Add sprouts; sauté 3 minutes. Add wine and water; bring to a boil. Cover; reduce heat. Simmer 10 minutes. Uncover; cook over medium heat 1 minute or until most of liquid is evaporated. Stir in chestnuts and remaining ingredients. Yield: 5 servings (serving size: 1 cup).

CALORIES 117 (27% from fat); PROTEIN 4g; FAT 3.5g (sat 0.5g, mono 1.8g, poly 1.1g); CARB 19.7g; FIBER 6.6g; CHOL 0mg; IRON 1.7mg; SODIUM 151mg; CALC 50mg

TANGY BEET-AND-CHESTNUT COMBO

2 (10½-ounce) cans low-salt
   chicken broth
¼ teaspoon salt
4 cups peeled, chopped
   beets
¼ cup balsamic vinegar
2 tablespoons brown sugar
1 cup cooked, shelled, and
   quartered chestnuts (about
   1 pound in shells)

Bring chicken broth and salt to a boil in a large nonstick skillet; add beets, vinegar, and brown sugar, stirring well. Cover, reduce heat, and simmer 30 minutes. Uncover; cook 10 minutes or until beets are tender. Stir in chestnuts, and cook until

thoroughly heated. Yield: 3 servings (serving size: 1 cup).

CALORIES 259 (9% from fat); PROTEIN 6.4g; FAT 2.7g (sat 0.6g, mono 0.9g, poly 0.7g); CARB 54.2g; FIBER 7g; CHOL 0mg; IRON 3mg; SODIUM 408mg; CALC 51mg

SWEET APPLE-AND-CHESTNUT SAUTÉ

1 tablespoon margarine
1½ cups diced onion
¾ cup thinly sliced celery
1 cup cooked, shelled, and
   coarsely chopped chestnuts
   (about 1 pound in shells)
1 large Granny Smith apple,
   peeled and cut into 16
   wedges
¼ cup maple syrup
Fresh thyme sprigs (optional)

Melt margarine in a large nonstick skillet over medium heat. Add diced onion and sliced celery; sauté 4 minutes. Add chopped chestnuts and apple wedges; sauté 8 minutes. Add maple syrup, and sauté 1 minute. Garnish with fresh thyme sprigs, if desired. Yield: 3 servings (serving size: 1 cup).

CALORIES 293 (25% from fat); PROTEIN 2.9g; FAT 5g (sat 1g, mono 2.1g, poly 1.8g); CARB 60.9g; FIBER 9.3g; CHOL 0mg; IRON 1.1mg; SODIUM 121mg; CALC 66mg

...ON AN OPEN FIRE

If you prefer to roast your chestnuts in an authentic European chestnut-roasting pan, you can order the real thing from The Gourmet Trading Co. Ltd. Call the company toll-free at 888/275-8070, or write to The Gourmet Trading Co., 93 The Great Road, Bedford, MA 01730. Cost is $24.95 (includes shipping and handling). Each 12-inch steel pan comes with a pound of fresh chestnuts.

A DIFFERENT NUT TO CRACK

1. Soak chestnuts in a bowl of water for about 30 minutes; drain well. Cut a slit in the shell in the rounded side of the chestnut. Make sure the cut goes all the way through the shell; otherwise, it can explode.

2. To roast over an open flame: Arrange nuts in a single layer in a chestnut pan. Place over flame; roast 25 minutes, shaking frequently.
To roast in oven: *Arrange nuts on baking sheet; bake at 400° for 25 minutes.*
To microwave: *Arrange nuts in a single layer in a microwave-safe dish. Microwave at HIGH 2 minutes. Microwave a maximum of 12 nuts at a time so that they cook evenly.*

3. Let the chestnuts cool about 5 minutes. Peel.

CHESTNUT SOUP

 1 tablespoon margarine
 1 cup chopped onion
 ½ cup chopped celery
 ½ cup chopped carrot
 1 cup peeled, cubed baking potato
 1 cup cooked, shelled chestnuts
      (about 1 pound in shells)
 ¼ teaspoon dried thyme
 ⅛ teaspoon salt
 ⅛ to ¼ teaspoon pepper
 5 (10½-ounce) cans low-salt
      chicken broth
 ½ cup 2% low-fat milk
 1¼ cups plain croutons
 Paprika

Melt margarine in a large saucepan over medium heat. Add onion; sauté 4 minutes. Add celery and carrot; sauté 6 minutes. Add potato and next 5 ingredients. Bring to a boil; reduce heat, and simmer 40 minutes.

Place chestnut mixture in a blender; cover and process until smooth. Return to pan; stir in milk. Cook until thoroughly heated. Ladle soup into individual bowls; top with croutons, and sprinkle with paprika. Yield: 5 servings (serving size: 1 cup soup and ¼ cup croutons).

CALORIES 247 (29% from fat); PROTEIN 7.2g; FAT 8g (sat 2.1g, mono 3.6g, poly 1.8g); CARB 36.8g; FIBER 4.9g; CHOL 2mg; IRON 2.4mg; SODIUM 213mg; CALC 67mg

CHESTNUT BISCOTTI

 ½ cup sugar
 2 tablespoons stick margarine,
      softened
 1 large egg
 1½ teaspoons vanilla extract
 1¼ cups all-purpose flour
 1 teaspoon baking powder
 ¼ teaspoon ground nutmeg
 Dash of salt
 ½ cup cooked, shelled, and finely
      chopped chestnuts (about
      ½ pound in shells)
 Vegetable cooking spray

Preheat oven to 350°.
Combine sugar and margarine in a large bowl; beat at medium speed of an electric mixer until well-blended. Add egg and vanilla; beat well. Combine flour, baking powder, nutmeg, and salt; gradually add to sugar mixture, beating until well-blended. Add chestnuts; beat well.

Turn dough out onto a lightly floured surface; knead lightly 7 times. Shape dough into a 12-inch-long roll. Place roll on a baking sheet coated with cooking spray, and flatten to a 1-inch thickness.

Bake roll at 350° for 30 minutes. Remove roll from baking sheet; let cool 10 minutes on a wire rack.

Cut roll diagonally into 16 (½-inch-thick) slices. Place slices, cut sides down, on baking sheet. Bake at 350° for 5 minutes. Turn cookies over, and bake an additional 5 minutes (biscotti will be slightly soft in center but will harden as they cool). Remove from baking sheet; let cool completely on wire rack. Yield: 16 biscotti (serving size: 1 biscotto).

Note: Store the biscotti in an airtight container.

CALORIES 90 (20% from fat); PROTEIN 1.6g; FAT 2g (sat 0.4g, mono 0.8g, poly 0.6g); CARB 16.3g; FIBER 0.8g; CHOL 14mg; IRON 0.6mg; SODIUM 23mg; CALC 22mg

Holiday Bonus

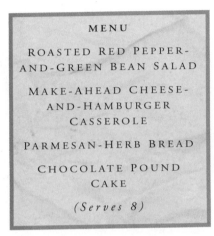

For this year's office party, leave behind the store-bought cookies, dips, and chips in favor of these healthy, easy-to-make dishes that travel well from home to office.

ROASTED RED PEPPER-AND-GREEN BEAN SALAD

Almost any kind of vegetable can be used. We recommend cauliflower, artichokes, or carrots. • Steaming fresh vegetables over boiling water preserves more vitamins than cooking the vegetables directly in boiling water.

½   cup chopped fresh cilantro
½   cup red wine vinegar
1   tablespoon olive oil
1   teaspoon ground cumin
1   teaspoon pepper
¼   teaspoon salt
1   pound fresh green beans, trimmed
4   cups sliced mushrooms
2   (12-ounce) bottles roasted red bell peppers, drained and cut into 3-inch strips

Combine first 6 ingredients in a large bowl. Stir well; set aside.

Arrange green beans in a steamer basket over boiling water. Cover and steam 3 minutes or until tender. Drain and rinse under cold water; drain well. Add beans, mushrooms, and peppers to bowl; toss gently to coat. Cover and marinate in refrigerator up to 24 hours. Serve with a slotted spoon. Yield: 8 servings (serving size: 1 cup).

CALORIES 69 (30% from fat); PROTEIN 2.5g; FAT 2.3g (sat 0.3g, mono 1.2g, poly 0.3g); CARB 10.1g; FIBER 2.5g; CHOL 0mg; IRON 1.8mg; SODIUM 85mg; CALC 40mg

MAKE-AHEAD CHEESE-AND-HAMBURGER CASSEROLE

The penne doesn't have to be cooked beforehand because it absorbs the liquid when refrigerated overnight. If you want to make it the same day, cook the pasta before combining with other ingredients. • For convenience, use precrumbled feta and preshredded mozzarella cheese.

1   pound ground round
1   cup chopped onion
3   garlic cloves, crushed
1   (8-ounce) package presliced mushrooms
¼   cup plus 2 tablespoons tomato paste
1   teaspoon sugar
1   teaspoon dried thyme
1   teaspoon dried oregano
¼   teaspoon pepper
1   (28-ounce) can whole tomatoes, undrained and chopped
⅓   cup all-purpose flour
2½   cups 2% low-fat milk
1   cup crumbled feta cheese
¾   cup (3 ounces) shredded part-skim mozzarella cheese
4   cups uncooked penne (tubular-shaped pasta)
1   tablespoon chopped fresh parsley (optional)

Combine first 3 ingredients in a large nonstick skillet; cook over medium-high heat until meat is browned, stirring to crumble. Add mushrooms; cook 5 minutes or until tender. Add tomato paste and next 5 ingredients; stir well. Bring to a boil; reduce heat, and simmer, uncovered, 20 minutes. Set aside.

Place flour in a medium saucepan. Gradually add milk, stirring with a whisk until blended. Place over medium heat; cook 10 minutes or until thick, stirring constantly.

Stir in cheeses; cook 3 minutes or until cheeses melt, stirring constantly. Reserve ½ cup cheese sauce. Pour remaining cheese sauce, beef mixture, and pasta into a 13 x 9-inch baking dish, and stir gently. Drizzle reserved cheese sauce over pasta mixture. Cover and refrigerate 24 hours.

Preheat oven to 350°.

Bake at 350°, covered, for 1 hour and 10 minutes or until mixture is thoroughly heated and pasta is tender; sprinkle with parsley, if desired. Yield: 8 servings.

CALORIES 412 (23% from fat); PROTEIN 27.5g; FAT 10.8g (sat 5.5g, mono 3.2g, poly 0.9g); CARB 51.1g; FIBER 3.2g; CHOL 60mg; IRON 4.9mg; SODIUM 448mg; CALC 286mg

TIME-SAVING TIPS

◆ Take advantage of the products in the pre-prepared/packaged section of the grocery store. Packages of salad greens, slaw mix, and stir-fry vegetables make quick dishes even easier to prepare.

◆ Make a huge pot of spaghetti sauce or chili for dinner one night. The following nights use the same sauce to make manicotti, lasagna, enchiladas, and casseroles until the sauce is gone.

◆ Prepare complicated recipes in steps—chop and bag vegetables after dinner one night; the next evening, brown the meat, and add the broth and other ingredients; the third night enjoy an "almost instant" dish.

PARMESAN-HERB BREAD

These loaves tend to spread while baking. For taller loaves, use a baguette pan. • You can vary the flavor by using provolone, Asiago, Romano, or sharp Cheddar cheeses. •To save time, make the dough in a food processor or bread machine. After baking, let the bread completely cool, then wrap tightly in aluminum foil, and freeze. Thaw at room temperature, and reheat at 300° for 20 minutes.

  2 packages dry yeast
  1 teaspoon sugar
  1 cup warm water (105° to 115°)
  5 cups all-purpose flour, divided
  1 cup plain low-fat yogurt
 ⅓ cup grated Parmesan cheese
  2 tablespoons vegetable oil
  2 teaspoons salt
 ¾ teaspoon dried basil
 ½ teaspoon garlic powder
 ½ teaspoon dried oregano
 ¼ teaspoon fennel seeds, crushed
Vegetable cooking spray

Combine yeast and sugar in warm water in a large bowl; let stand 5 minutes. Add 2 cups flour and next 8 ingredients; stir well. Stir in 2¼ cups remaining flour to form a soft dough.

Turn dough out onto a lightly floured surface. Knead until smooth and elastic (about 15 minutes); add enough of remaining ¾ cup flour, one tablespoon at a time, to keep dough from sticking to hands.

Place dough in a large bowl coated with cooking spray, turning to coat top. Cover and let rise in a warm place (85°), free from drafts, 45 minutes or until doubled in bulk. Punch dough down; cover and let rest 5 minutes. Divide dough in half. Working with one portion at a time (cover remaining dough to keep from drying), shape each portion into a 15-inch-long rope. Place ropes diagonally on a large baking sheet coated with cooking spray. Cover and let rise 30 minutes or until doubled in bulk.

Preheat oven to 375°.

Uncover dough. Bake at 375° for 25 minutes or until loaves sound hollow when tapped. Remove from pan, and let cool on wire racks. Yield: 2 loaves, 18 servings per loaf (serving size: 1 slice).

CALORIES 76 (15% from fat); PROTEIN 2.5g; FAT 1.3g (sat 0.4g, mono 0.3g, poly 0.4g); CARB 13.4g; FIBER 0.6g; CHOL 1mg; IRON 0.9mg; SODIUM 149mg; CALC 26mg

CHOCOLATE POUND CAKE

You can use cooking spray and 1 teaspoon of flour to dust the pan if baking spray with flour isn't available.

 ¾ cup stick margarine, softened
1½ cups sugar
  2 large eggs
  2 large egg whites
1½ cups low-fat buttermilk
  1 teaspoon baking soda
3½ cups all-purpose flour
 ¾ cup unsweetened cocoa
  1 teaspoon baking powder
 ¼ teaspoon salt
  2 teaspoons vanilla extract
Baking spray with flour
  1 teaspoon powdered sugar

Preheat oven to 350°.

Beat margarine at medium speed of an electric mixer until creamy. Gradually add 1½ cups sugar, and beat well. Add eggs and egg whites, one at a time, beating well after each addition.

Combine buttermilk and baking soda; stir well. Combine flour, cocoa, baking powder, and salt; stir well. Add flour mixture to margarine mixture alternately with buttermilk mixture, beginning and ending with flour mixture. Stir in vanilla.

Pour batter into a 12-cup Bundt pan coated with baking spray. Bake at 350° for 45 minutes or until a wooden pick inserted in center of cake comes out clean. Let cake cool in pan 10 minutes on a wire rack; remove cake from pan. Let cake cool completely on wire rack. Sift powdered sugar over top of cake. Yield: 18 servings (serving size: 1 slice).

CALORIES 259 (32% from fat); PROTEIN 5.4g; FAT 9.2g (sat 2.2g, mono 3.7g, poly 2.5g); CARB 38.4g; FIBER 0.6g; CHOL 25mg; IRON 1.8mg; SODIUM 217mg; CALC 55mg

TV BUFFET

Great Reception

> **MENU**
>
> **MARINATED CUCUMBER, MUSHROOM, AND ONION SALAD**
>
> **BLACK BEAN-AND-SMOKED TURKEY SOUP**
>
> **HERB-CHEESE BREAD**
>
> **EASY CHOCOLATE-CARAMEL BROWNIES**
>
> *(Serves 6)*

Here's a casual, warming buffet that can be eaten away from the table—namely in front of the TV. Because all of the dishes can be made ahead, you don't have to be in the kitchen missing out on all the fun (touchdowns, parades, and angels getting their wings).

MARINATED CUCUMBER, MUSHROOM, AND ONION SALAD

Peel cucumber, and cut in half lengthwise. Scoop seeds out of each half with a spoon, and cut into slices.

 ⅓ cup sherry vinegar
  2 teaspoons olive oil
  2 teaspoons Dijon mustard
 ½ teaspoon salt
 ¼ teaspoon dried oregano
 ⅛ teaspoon pepper
  6 cups peeled, seeded, and sliced cucumber
  3 cups sliced mushrooms
  1 cup vertically sliced red onion

Combine first 6 ingredients in a large bowl, and stir well. Add cucumber, mushrooms, and onion; toss gently.

Cover and chill 2 hours. Serve with a slotted spoon. Yield: 8 servings (serving size: 1 cup).

CALORIES 49 (26% from fat); PROTEIN 1.4g; FAT 1.4g (sat 0.2g, mono 0.8g, poly 0.2g); CARB 6.4g; FIBER 1.1g; CHOL 0mg; IRON 0.7mg; SODIUM 250mg; CALC 23mg

BLACK BEAN-AND-SMOKED TURKEY SOUP

Crush cumin seeds with a mortar and pestle. Or place seeds in a heavy-duty, zip-top plastic bag, and crush with a mallet or rolling pin. • Make soup ahead, and freeze in an airtight container for up to three months. Or store in the refrigerator for up to four days in a nonaluminum container. Thaw if frozen, then reheat over low heat.

1 tablespoon vegetable oil
1 cup chopped red onion
1 cup chopped celery
1 cup chopped carrot
1 tablespoon cumin seeds, crushed
1 teaspoon dried oregano
3 garlic cloves, minced
2 cups water
¾ teaspoon salt
3 (10½-ounce) cans low-salt chicken broth
2 (15-ounce) cans no-salt-added black beans, drained
½ pound smoked fat-free turkey breast, chopped
½ cup chopped red bell pepper
¼ cup chopped fresh or 1 tablespoon dried parsley
2 tablespoons sherry
½ teaspoon hot sauce
¼ cup plus 2 tablespoons low-fat sour cream
Fresh cilantro sprigs (optional)

Heat vegetable oil in a Dutch oven over medium heat until hot. Add onion, celery, carrot, cumin seeds, oregano, and garlic; sauté 5 minutes. Stir in water, salt, broth, and beans. Bring mixture to a boil; cover, reduce heat, and simmer 45 minutes or until tender.

Place half of bean mixture in a blender or food processor; cover and process until smooth. Return puréed bean mixture to Dutch oven. Stir in turkey and next 4 ingredients; cook an additional 5 minutes or until thoroughly heated. Ladle soup into bowls, and top with sour cream. Garnish with cilantro sprigs, if desired. Yield: 6 servings (serving size: 1½ cups soup and 1 tablespoon sour cream).

CALORIES 223 (24% from fat); PROTEIN 14.9g; FAT 5.9g (sat 2g, mono 1.8g, poly 1.6g); CARB 29.5g; FIBER 5.3g; CHOL 14mg; IRON 3.8mg; SODIUM 737mg; CALC 77mg

HERB-CHEESE BREAD

To make ahead, assemble loaf, wrap in aluminum foil, and store in refrigerator. Bring to room temperature, and bake as directed.

¼ cup reduced-calorie margarine
¼ cup minced green onions
2 garlic cloves, crushed
¼ teaspoon dried oregano
¼ teaspoon ground cumin
⅛ teaspoon dried crushed red pepper
⅛ teaspoon salt
1 (1-pound) loaf Italian bread, split
½ cup (2 ounces) shredded reduced-fat Monterey Jack cheese

Preheat oven to 400°.
Melt margarine in a small skillet over medium-high heat. Add minced green onions and garlic; sauté 2 minutes. Stir in oregano, cumin, red pepper, and salt.
Brush margarine mixture evenly on cut sides of bread. Sprinkle cheese over bottom half of loaf; top with top half of loaf. Wrap in aluminum foil; bake at 400° for 20 minutes. Serve warm. Yield: 12 servings.

CALORIES 140 (23% from fat); PROTEIN 4.9g; FAT 3.6g (sat 1g, mono 1.4g, poly 0.8g); CARB 21.8g; FIBER 1.1g; CHOL 3mg; IRON 0.9mg; SODIUM 313mg; CALC 48mg

EASY CHOCOLATE-CARAMEL BROWNIES

Use a cake mix that contains pudding; otherwise, the recipe won't work.
• Cut brownies after they've cooled.
• To make ahead: Cool completely, wrap tightly in heavy-duty plastic wrap, and freeze.

2 tablespoons skim milk
27 small soft caramel candies (about 8 ounces)
½ cup fat-free sweetened condensed milk (not evaporated skim milk)
1 (18.25-ounce) package devil's food cake mix with pudding (such as Pillsbury)
¼ cup plus 3 tablespoons reduced-calorie stick margarine, melted
1 large egg white, lightly beaten
Vegetable cooking spray
1 teaspoon all-purpose flour
½ cup reduced-fat chocolate baking chips

Preheat oven to 350°.
Combine skim milk and candies in a bowl. Microwave at HIGH 1½ to 2 minutes or until caramels melt and mixture is smooth, stirring with a whisk after every minute. Set aside.
Combine sweetened condensed milk, cake mix, margarine, and egg white in a bowl; stir well (batter will be very stiff). Coat bottom only of a 13 x 9-inch baking pan with cooking spray; dust lightly with flour. Press two-thirds of batter into prepared pan using floured hands; pat evenly (layer will be thin).
Bake at 350° for 10 minutes. Remove from oven; sprinkle with chocolate chips. Drizzle caramel mixture over chips; carefully drop remaining batter by spoonfuls over caramel mixture. Bake at 350° for 30 minutes. Let cool completely in pan on a wire rack. Yield: 3 dozen (serving size: 1 brownie).

CALORIES 122 (30% from fat); PROTEIN 1.6g; FAT 4g (sat 1.6g, mono 1.3g, poly 0.6g); CARB 20.4g; FIBER 0.4g; CHOL 1mg; IRON 0.5mg; SODIUM 224mg; CALC 34mg

Menu Index

Each menu includes recipes from the magazine and appropriate generic items to round out the meal.
Refer to the page number with each menu to locate the recipe.

Month-by-Month Index

General Recipe Index

METRIC EQUIVALENTS

The recipes that appear in this cookbook use the standard United States method
for measuring liquid and dry or solid ingredients (teaspoons, tablespoons, and cups).
The information in the following charts is provided to help cooks outside the U.S.
successfully use these recipes. All equivalents are approximate.

METRIC EQUIVALENTS FOR DIFFERENT TYPES OF INGREDIENTS

A standard cup measure of a dry or solid ingredient will
vary in weight depending on the type of ingredient.
A standard cup of liquid is the same volume for any type of
liquid. Use the following chart when converting standard
cup measures to grams (weight) or milliliters (volume).

Standard Cup	Fine Powder (ex. flour)	Grain (ex. rice)	Granular (ex. sugar)	Liquid Solids (ex. butter)	Liquid (ex. milk)
1	140 g	150 g	190 g	200 g	240 ml
¾	105 g	113 g	143 g	150 g	180 ml
⅔	93 g	100 g	125 g	133 g	160 ml
½	70 g	75 g	95 g	100 g	120 ml
⅓	47 g	50 g	63 g	67 g	80 ml
¼	35 g	38 g	48 g	50 g	60 ml
⅛	18 g	19 g	24 g	25 g	30 ml

USEFUL EQUIVALENTS FOR LIQUID INGREDIENTS BY VOLUME

¼ tsp					=	1 ml	
½ tsp					=	2 ml	
1 tsp					=	5 ml	
3 tsp	=	1 tbls		=	½ fl oz	=	15 ml	
		2 tbls	=	⅛ cup	=	1 fl oz	=	30 ml
		4 tbls	=	¼ cup	=	2 fl oz	=	60 ml
		5⅓ tbls	=	⅓ cup	=	3 fl oz	=	80 ml
		8 tbls	=	½ cup	=	4 fl oz	=	120 ml
		10⅔ tbls	=	⅔ cup	=	5 fl oz	=	160 ml
		12 tbls	=	¾ cup	=	6 fl oz	=	180 ml
		16 tbls	=	1 cup	=	8 fl oz	=	240 ml
		1 pt	=	2 cups	=	16 fl oz	=	480 ml
		1 qt	=	4 cups	=	32 fl oz	=	960 ml
						33 fl oz	=	1000 ml	=	1 l

USEFUL EQUIVALENTS FOR DRY INGREDIENTS BY WEIGHT
(To convert ounces to grams,
multiply the number of ounces by 30.)

1 oz	=	¹⁄₁₆ lb	=	30 g
4 oz	=	¼ lb	=	120 g
8 oz	=	½ lb	=	240 g
12 oz	=	¾ lb	=	360 g
16 oz	=	1 lb	=	480 g

USEFUL EQUIVALENTS FOR LENGTH
(To convert inches to centimeters,
multiply the number of inches by 2.5.)

1 in			=	2.5 cm		
6 in	=	½ ft	=	15 cm		
12 in	=	1 ft	=	30 cm		
36 in	=	3 ft	= 1 yd	=	90 cm		
40 in			=	100 cm	=	1 m

USEFUL EQUIVALENTS FOR COOKING/OVEN TEMPERATURES

	Fahrenheit	Celcius	Gas Mark
Freeze Water	32° F	0° C	
Room Temperature	68° F	20° C	
Boil Water	212° F	100° C	
Bake	325° F	160° C	3
	350° F	180° C	4
	375° F	190° C	5
	400° F	200° C	6
	425° F	220° C	7
	450° F	230° C	8
Broil			Grill

Acknowledgments and Credits

ADDITIONAL PHOTOGRAPHY:

Paul Boisvert: page 285

Grey Crawford: page 227

Randy Mayor: pages 151, 188, 284

Karl Petzke: page 226

Tim Turner: page 74

ADDITIONAL PHOTO STYLING:

Dan Becker: pages 226, 227

Donna Creel: cover (food styling)

Connie Formby: page 76

Maya Metz Logue: page 74

Donna Shields: page 152

Ashley Johnson Wyatt: pages 37, 38, 39, 40, 73, 75, 149, 150, 152

RECIPE DEVELOPERS:

Nancy Baggett

Leslye Michlin Borden

Susan S. Bradley

Pasquale Bruno

Danella Carter

Leah Chase

Barbara Chernetz

Esther J. Danielson

Abby Duchin Dinces

Dave DiResta

Linda W. Eckhardt

John Egerton

Florence Fabricant

Jim Fobel

Stella Fong

Betty Fussell

Linda Gassenheimer

Barbara Gill

Luli Gray

Sam Gugino

Jay Harlow

Mary Holloway

Nancy S. Hughes

Vanessa Taylor Johnson

Jeanne Jones

Jean Kressy

Linda Romanelli Leahy

Karen Levin

Lily Loh

Karen Mangum

Marcy Marceau

Greg Patent

Leslie Glover Pendleton

Steven Petusevsky

Steven Raichlen

Jane Reinsel

Norma Schonwetter

Angie Sinclair

Sue Spitler

Elizabeth J. Taliaferro

Robin Vitetta

Kenneth Wapner

Jan Weimer